THE AMERICAN

AN AUTHORITATIVE TEXT
BACKGROUNDS AND SOURCES
CRITICISM

W.W. NORTON & COMPANY, INC.
also publishes

THE NORTON ANTHOLOGY OF AMERICAN LITERATURE
edited by Nina Baym et al.

THE NORTON ANTHOLOGY OF ENGLISH LITERATURE
edited by M. H. Abrams et al.

THE NORTON ANTHOLOGY OF LITERATURE BY WOMEN
edited by Sandra M. Gilbert and Susan Gubar

THE NORTON ANTHOLOGY OF MODERN POETRY
edited by Richard Ellmann and Robert O'Clair

THE NORTON ANTHOLOGY OF POETRY
edited by Alexander W. Allison et al.

THE NORTON ANTHOLOGY OF SHORT FICTION
edited by R. V. Cassill

THE NORTON ANTHOLOGY OF WORLD MASTERPIECES
edited by Maynard Mack et al.

THE NORTON FACSIMILE OF
THE FIRST FOLIO OF SHAKESPEARE
prepared by Charlton Hinman

THE NORTON INTRODUCTION TO LITERATURE
edited by Carl E. Bain, Jerome Beaty, and J. Paul Hunter

THE NORTON INTRODUCTION TO THE SHORT NOVEL
edited by Jerome Beaty

THE NORTON READER
edited by Arthur M. Eastman et al.

THE NORTON SAMPLER
edited by Thomas Cooley

A NORTON CRITICAL EDITION

HENRY JAMES

THE AMERICAN

AN AUTHORITATIVE TEXT
BACKGROUNDS AND SOURCES
CRITICISM

Edited by

JAMES W. TUTTLETON
NEW YORK UNIVERSITY

W · W · NORTON & COMPANY
New York · London

Library of Congress Cataloging in Publication Data
James, Henry, 1843–1916.
The American.
(A Norton critical edition)
Bibliography: p.
1. James, Henry, 1843–1916. The American.
I. Tuttleton, James W II. Title.
PZ3.J234Ame 1978 [PS2116] 813'.4 77-27622

ISBN 0-393-04476-9
ISBN 0-393-09091-4 pbk.

Printed in the United States of America.

W. W. Norton & Company, Inc., 500 Fifth Avenue, New York, N.Y. 10110

7 8 9 0

Contents

Criticism

Contemporary Reception

Preface

The American, first published in 1877, is the earliest novel by Henry James in which the artist's command of his developing technique begins to be apparent. James's first novel, *Watch and Ward,* was a minor affair which the author saw fit to suppress. Never republished in his lifetime, the novel was virtually disowned by James, who pointedly excluded it from the collected "New York Edition" published between 1907 and 1917. His second novel, *Roderick Hudson,* was a considerably better work, although it was marred by excesses in characterization, structural weaknesses, and infelicities of style. Even *The American,* his third novel, is not a perfect book in its structure; but in this work of fiction, the acute social witness, the novelist of manners with brilliant comic gifts, made his first appearance.

As indicated by contemporary reviews, James's provocative novel made a lively impression on his contemporaries, who were quick to lament its lack of wedding bells for the hero and to argue the cultural implications of the "national type" James had created in Christopher Newman. The very idea of writing a novel about the American character and identity was in itself distinctively American. What European novelist, Constance Rourke asked long ago, could have conceived of writing a novel entitled *The Englishman* or *Le Français*? Aside from its interest as a love story, or as a romance of gothic suspense, the work brilliantly satirized the formlessness of our American manners in The Gilded Age, even while it defended an American innocence traduced by sophisticated European guile. Its superb central character, the flow of its narrative line, and its wit and social comedy—which darken toward the end into doubtful melodrama—have nevertheless kept *The American* alive, as one of the more significant achievements of James's early career.

This edition has two purposes. First, I have sought to present a reliable text of *The American,* based upon an examination of the five printed forms of the work which have a claim to textual significance. (The text selected for this Norton Critical Edition is the London Macmillan edition of 1879, emended and corrected, as necessary, by the editor. To this text has been prefixed Henry James's Preface to *The American,* first printed in 1907 in the New York Edition published by Scribner's.) And, second, I have wished to present a selection of related materials that serve to establish the context for a critical discussion of the novel. Included are excerpts from James's correspondence touching the composition and publication of the novel, early periodical reviews, background materials that throw a significant light on James's subjects and methods, and selections of twentieth-century criticism which disclose the aesthetic and social character of the novel as a work of art. A bibliography is also appended for the benefit of those who wish to do additional reading about James or about this novel.

Although the selections contained herein reflect the editor's judgment, this volume has been enriched by the labor of many other scholars whose thinking has irresistibly shaped my own. Foremost among them is of course my colleague Leon Edel, who held for many years the Henry James Professorship of English and American Letters at New York University. Here I must also name the late Oscar Cargill, my predecessor as chairman of the English department at New York University, who also set a commendably high standard of Henry James criticism. And finally I must mention Louis Auchincloss, whose acute perception of how Henry James engaged and resolved his technical problems has proved invariably helpful. To these critics and scholars, among many other Jameseans who must perforce go unnamed, I gratefully acknowledge my indebtedness. Also, to Carole Rowe, Mary Tedeschi, and Janet Rasmussen I owe a special debt for their assistance in the preparation of this edition. Finally, I should like to thank the staffs of the New York Public Library and the Elmer H. Bobst Library of New York University for their unfailing courtesy and assistance in the preparation of this volume.

JAMES W. TUTTLETON

The Text of
The American

Preface to the New York Edition (1907)†

"The American," which I had begun in Paris early in the winter of 1875–76, made its first appearance in "The Atlantic Monthly" in June of the latter year and continued there, from month to month, till May of the next. It started on its course while much was still unwritten, and there again come back to me, with this remembrance, the frequent hauntings and alarms of that comparatively early time; the habit of wondering what would happen if anything *should* "happen," if one should break one's arm by an accident or make a long illness or suffer, in body, mind, fortune, any other visitation involving a loss of time. The habit of apprehension became of course in some degree the habit of confidence that one would pull through, that, with opportunity enough, grave interruption never yet *had* descended, and that a special Providence, in short, despite the sad warning of Thackeray's "Denis Duval" and of Mrs. Gaskell's "Wives and Daughters" (that of Stevenson's "Weir of Hermiston" was yet to come) watches over anxious novelists condemned to the economy of serialisation. I make myself out in memory as having at least for many months and in many places given my Providence much to do: so great a variety of scenes of labour, implying all so much renewal of application, glimmer out of the book as I now read it over. And yet as the faded interest of the whole episode becomes again mildly vivid what I seem most to recover is, in its pale spectrality, a degree of joy, an eagerness on behalf of my recital, that must recklessly enough have overridden anxieties of every sort, including any view of inherent difficulties.

I seem to recall no other like connexion in which the case was met, to my measure, by so fond a complacency, in which my subject can have appeared so apt to take care of itself. I see now that I might all the while have taken much better care of it; yet, as I had at the time no sense of neglecting it, neither acute nor rueful solicitude, I can but speculate all vainly to-day on the oddity of my composure. I ask myself indeed if, possibly, recognising after I was launched the danger of an inordinate leak—since the ship has truly a hole in its side more than sufficient to have sunk it—I may not have managed, as a counsel of mere despair, to stop my ears against the noise of waters and *pretend* to myself I was afloat; being

† This Preface was written for the Scribner's New York Edition of 1907. It is here reprinted from *The Art of the Novel: Critical Prefaces by Henry James, with an Introduction by Richard P. Blackmur*. New York: Charles Scribner's Sons, 1934), pp. 20–39.

indubitably, in any case, at sea, with no harbour of refuge till the end of my serial voyage. If I succeeded at all in that emulation (in another sphere) of the pursued ostrich I must have succeeded altogether; must have buried my head in the sand and there found beatitude. The explanation of my enjoyment of it, no doubt, is that I was more than commonly enamoured of my idea, and that I believed it, so trusted, so imaginatively fostered, not less capable of limping to its goal on three feet than on one. The lameness might be what it would: I clearly, for myself, felt the thing *go*—which is the most a dramatist can ever ask of his drama; and I shall here accordingly indulge myself in speaking first of how, superficially, it did so proceed; explaining then what I mean by its practical dependence on a miracle.

It had come to me, this happy, halting view of an interesting case, abruptly enough, some years before: I recall sharply the felicity of the first glimpse, though I forget the accident of thought that produced it. I recall that I was seated in an American "horse-car" when I found myself, of a sudden, considering with enthusiasm, as the theme of a "story," the situation, in another country and an aristocratic society, of some robust but insidiously beguiled and betrayed, some cruelly wronged, compatriot: the point being in especial that he should suffer at the hands of persons pretending to represent the highest possible civilisation and to be of an order in every way superior to his own. What would he "do" in that predicament, how would he right himself, or how, failing a remedy, would he conduct himself under his wrong? This would be the question involved, and I remember well how, having entered the horse-car without a dream of it, I was presently to leave that vehicle in full possession of my answer. He would behave in the most interesting manner—it would all depend on that: stricken, smarting, sore, he would arrive at his just vindication and then would fail of all triumphantly and all vulgarly enjoying it. He would hold his revenge and cherish it and feel its sweetness, and then in the very act of forcing it home would sacrifice it in disgust. He would let them go, in short, his haughty contemners, even while feeling them, with joy, in his power, and he would obey, in so doing, one of the large and easy impulses *generally* characteristic of his type. He wouldn't "forgive"—that would have, in the case, no application; he would simply turn, at the supreme moment, away, the bitterness of his personal loss yielding to the very force of his aversion. All he would have at the end would be therefore just the moral convenience, indeed the moral necessity, of his practical, but quite unappreciated, magnanimity; and one's last view of him would be that of a strong man indifferent to his strength and too one of the Ministères that front on the Place Vendôme; an panse marked, along a considerable stretch of the street, by one those high painted and administratively-placarded garden walls at form deep, vague, recurrent notes in the organic vastness of e city. I have but to re-read ten lines to recall my daily effort not waste time in hanging over the window-bar for a sight of the valry the hard music of whose hoofs so directly and thrillingly pealed; an effort that inveterately failed—and a trivial circum-ance now dignified, to my imagination, I may add, by the fact at the fruits of this weakness, the various items of the vivid cture, so constantly recaptured, must have been in themselves ggestive and inspiring, must have been rich strains, in their way, the great Paris harmony. I have ever, in general, found it diffi-ılt to write of places under too immediate an impression—the npression that prevents standing off and allows neither space nor me for perspective. The image has had for the most part to be dim the reflexion was to be, as is proper for a reflexion, both sharp ıd quiet: one has a horror, I think, artistically, of agitated re-exions.

Perhaps that is why the novel, after all, was to achieve, as it went n, no great—certainly no very direct—transfusion of the immense verhanging presence. It had to save as it could its own life, to keep ght hold of the tenuous silver thread, the one hope for which was at it shouldn't be tangled or clipped. This earnest grasp of the lver thread was doubtless an easier business in other places—ough as I remount the stream of composition I see it faintly bloured again: with the bright protection of the Normandy coast I worked away a few weeks at Êtretat); with the stronger glow of uthernmost France, breaking in during a stay at Bayonne; then ith the fine historic and other "psychic" substance of Saint-Germain-en-Laye, a purple patch of terraced October before re-ırning to Paris. There comes after that the memory of a last brief ıtense invocation of the enclosing scene, of the pious effort to nwind my tangle, with a firm hand, in the very light (that light of igh, narrowish French windows in old rooms, the light somehow, s one always feels, of "style" itself) that had quickened my orig-ıal vision. I was to pass over to London that autumn; which was a eason the more for considering the matter—the matter of New-ıan's final predicament—with due intensity: to let a loose end angle over into alien air would so fix upon the whole, I strenu-usly felt, the dishonour of piecemeal composition. Therefore I trove to finish—first in a small dusky hotel of the Rive Gauche, vhere, though the windows again were high, the days were dim and he crepuscular court, domestic, intimate, "quaint," testified to an-

wrapped in fine, too wrapped above all in *other* and intenser, reflex-ions for the assertion of his "rights." This last point was of the essence and constituted in fact the subject: there would be no subject at all, obviously,—or simply the commonest of the common,—if my gentleman should enjoy his advantage. I was charmed with my idea, which would take, however, much working out; and precisely because it had so much to give, I think, must I have dropped it for the time into the deep well of unconscious cerebration: not without the hope, doubtless, that it might eventually emerge from that reservoir, as one had already known the buried treasure to come to light, with a firm iridescent surface and a notable increase of weight.

This resurrection then took place in Paris, where I was at the moment living, and in December, 1875; my good fortune being apparently that Paris had ever so promptly offered me, and with an immediate directness at which I now marvel (since I had come back there, after earlier visitations, but a few weeks before), every-thing that was needed to make my conception concrete. I seem again at this distant day to see it become so quickly and easily, quite as if filling itself with life in that air. The objectivity it had wanted it promptly put on, and if the questions had been, with the usual intensity, for my hero and his crisis—the whole formidable list, the who? the what? the where? the when? the why? the how?—they gathered their answers in the cold shadow of the Arc de Triomphe, for fine reasons, very much as if they had been plucking spring flowers for the weaving of a frolic garland. I saw from one day to another my particular cluster of circumstances, with the life of the splendid city playing up in it like a flashing fountain in a marble basin. The very splendour seemed somehow to witness and intervene; it was important for the effect of my friend's discom-fiture that it should take place on a high and lighted stage, and that his original ambition, the project exposing him, should have sprung from beautiful and noble suggestions—those that, at certain hours and under certain impressions, we feel the many-tinted medium by the Seine irresistibly to communicate. It was all charmingly simple, this conception, and the current must have gushed, full and clear, to my imagination, from the moment Christopher Newman rose before me, on a perfect day of the divine Paris spring, in the great gilded Salon Carré of the Louvre. Under this strong contagion of the place he would, by the happiest of hazards, meet his old com-rade, now initiated and domiciled; after which the rest would go of itself. If he was to be wronged he would be wronged with just that conspicuity, with his felicity at just that pitch and with the highest aggravation of the general effect of misery mocked at. Great and gilded the whole trap set, in fine, for his wary freshness and into which it would blunder upon its fate. I have, I confess, no memory of a disturbing doubt; once the man himself was imaged to me (and *that* germination is a process almost always untraceable) he must have walked into the situation as by taking a pass-key from his pocket.

But what then meanwhile would be the affront one would see him as most feeling—the affront of course done him as a lover; and yet not that done by his mistress herself, since injuries of this order are the stalest stuff of romance. I was not to have him jilted, any more than I was to have him successfully vindictive: both his wrong and his right would have been in these cases of too vulgar a type. I doubtless even then felt that the conception of Paris as the consecrated scene of rash infatuations and bold bad treacheries belongs, in the Anglo-Saxon imagination, to the infancy of art. The right renovation of any such theme as *that* would place it in Boston or at Cleveland, at Hartford or at Utica—give it some local connexion in which we had not already had so much of it. No, I should make my heroine herself, if heroine there was to be, an equal victim—just as Romeo was not less the sport of fate for not having been interestedly sacrificed by Juliet; and to this end I had but to imagine "great people" again, imagine my hero confronted and involved with them, and impute to them, with a fine free hand, the arrogance and cruelty, the tortuous behaviour, in given conditions, of which great people have been historically so often capable. But as this was the light in which they were to show, so the essence of the matter would be that he should at the right moment find them in his power, and so the situation would reach its highest interest with the question of his utilisation of that knowledge. It would be here, in the possession and application of his power, that he would come out strong and would so deeply appeal to our sympathy. Here above all it really was, however, that my conception unfurled, with the best conscience in the world, the emblazoned flag of romance; which venerable ensign it had, though quite unwittingly, from the first and at every point sported in perfect good faith. I had been plotting arch-romance without knowing it, just as I began to write it that December day without recognising it and just as I all serenely and blissfully pursued the process from month to month and from place to place; just as I now, in short, reading the book over, find it yields me no interest and no reward comparable to the fond perception of this truth.

The thing is consistently, consummately—and I would fain really make bold to say charmingly—romantic; and all without intention, presumption, hesitation, contrition. The effect is equally undesigned and unabashed, and I lose myself, at this late hour, I am bound to

add, in a certain sad envy of the free play of so much uncha instinct. One would like to woo back such hours of fine pr tion. They represent to the critical sense which the exercise c *whole* faculty has, with time, so inevitably and so tho waked up, the happiest season of surrender to the invoke and the projected fable: the season of images so free and co and ready that they brush questions aside and disport ther like the artless schoolboys of Gray's beautiful Ode, in ecstasy of the ignorance attending them. The time doubtless soon enough when questions, as I call them, rule the ro when the little victim, to adjust Gray's term again to the cre frolic fancy, doesn't dare propose a gambol till they have all board of trustees discussing a new outlay) sat on the scandalous case. I somehow feel, accordingly, that it was l have sacrificed on this particular altar while one still could; it is perhaps droll—in a yet higher degree—to have done simply because one was guileless, but even quite under the tion, in a general way, that, since no "rendering" of any ob no painting of any picture can take effect without some reference and control, so these guarantees could but resi high probity of observation. I must decidedly have supposed while, that I was acutely observing—and with a blest ab wonder at its being so easy. Let me certainly at present r that absence; for I ask myself how without it I could have "The American."

Was it indeed meanwhile my excellent conscience that charm as unbroken as it appears to me, in rich retrospect, remained?—or is it that I suffer the mere influence of rem of associated places and hours, all acute impressions, to pa off as the sign of a finer confidence than I could justly clain pleasure to perceive how again and again the shrunken d old work yet permit themselves to be sounded or—even terrible the image—"dragged": the long pole of memory rummages the bottom, and we fish up such fragments and the submerged life and the extinct consciousness as tem piece them together. My windows looked into the Rue de bourg—since then meagrely re-named Rue Cambon—and ticular light Parisian click of the small cab-horse on asphalt, with its sharpness of detonation between the hig makes for the faded page to-day a sort of interlineation This sound rises to a martial clatter at the moment a cuirassiers charges down the narrow street, each mornin directly opposite my house, through the plain portal of the occupying part of the vast domain attached in a rearwar cient manners almost as if it had been that of Balzac's Maison Vauquer in "Le Père Goriot": and then once more in the Rue de Luxembourg, where a black-framed Empire portrait-medallion, suspended in the centre of each white panel of my almost noble old salon, made the coolest, discreetest, most measured decoration, and where, through casements open to the last mildness of the year, a belated Saint Martin's summer, the tale was taken up afresh by the charming light click and clatter, that sound as of the thin, quick, quite feminine surface-breathing of Paris, the shortest of rhythms for so huge an organism.

I shall not tell whether I did there bring my book to a close—and indeed I shrink, for myself, from putting the question to the test of memory. I follow it so far, the old urgent ingenious business, and then I lose sight of it: from which I infer—all exact recovery of the matter failing—that I did not in the event drag over the Channel a lengthening chain; which would have been detestable. I reduce to the absurd perhaps, however, by that small subjective issue, any undue measure of the interest of this insistent recovery of what I have called attendant facts. There always has been, for the valid work of art, a history—though mainly inviting, doubtless, but to the curious critic, for whom such things grow up and are formed very much in the manner of attaching young lives and characters, those conspicuous cases of happy development as to which evidence and anecdote are always in order. The development indeed must be certain to have been happy, the life sincere, the character fine: the work of art, to create or repay critical curiosity, must in short have been very "valid" indeed. Yet there is on the other hand no mathematical measure of that importance—it may be a matter of widely-varying appreciation; and I am willing to grant, assuredly, that this interest, in a given relation, will nowhere so effectually kindle as on the artist's own part. And I am afraid that after all even his best excuse for it must remain the highly personal plea—the joy of living over, as a chapter of experience, the particular intellectual adventure. Here lurks an immense homage to the general privilege of the artist, to that constructive, that creative passion—portentous words, but they are convenient—the exercise of which finds so many an occasion for appearing to him the highest of human fortunes, the rarest boon of the gods. He values it, all sublimely and perhaps a little fatuously, for itself—as the great extension, great beyond all others, of experience and of consciousness; with the toil and trouble a mere sun-cast shadow that falls, shifts and vanishes, the result of his living in so large a light. On the constant nameless felicity of this Robert Louis Stevenson has, in an admirable passage and as in so many other connexions, said the right word: that the partaker of the "life of art" who repines at the absence of the rewards, as they are called, of the pursuit might surely be better occupied. Much rather should he endlessly wonder at his not having to pay half his substance for his luxurious immersion. He enjoys it, so to speak, without a tax; the effort of labour involved, the torment of expression, of which we have heard in our time so much, being after all but the last refinement of his privilege. It may leave him weary and worn; but how, after his fashion, he will have lived! As if one were to expect at once freedom and ease! That silly safety is but the sign of bondage and forfeiture. Who can imagine free selection—which is the beautiful, terrible *whole* of art—without free difficulty? This is the very franchise of the city and high ambition of the citizen. The vision of the difficulty, as one looks back, bathes one's course in a golden glow by which the very objects along the road are transfigured and glorified; so that one exhibits them to other eyes with an elation possibly presumptuous.

Since I accuse myself at all events of these complacencies I take advantage of them to repeat that I value, in my retrospect, nothing so much as the lively light on the romantic property of my subject that I had not expected to encounter. If in "The American" I invoked the romantic association without malice prepense, yet with a production of the romantic effect that is for myself unmistakeable, the occasion is of the best perhaps for penetrating a little the obscurity of that principle. By what art or mystery, what craft of selection, omission or commission, does a given picture of life appear to us to surround its theme, its figures and images, with the air of romance while another picture close beside it may affect us as steeping the whole matter in the element of reality? It is a question, no doubt, on the painter's part, very much more of perceived effect, effect *after* the fact, than of conscious design—though indeed I have ever failed to see how a coherent picture of anything is producible save by a complex of fine measurements. The cause of the deflexion, in one pronounced sense or the other, must lie deep, however; so that for the most part we recognise the character of our interest only after the particular magic, as I say, has thoroughly operated—and then in truth but if we be a bit critically minded, if we find our pleasure, that is, in these intimate appreciations (for which, as I am well aware, ninety-nine readers in a hundred have no use whatever). The determining condition would at any rate seem so latent that one may well doubt if the full artistic consciousness ever reaches it; leaving the matter thus a case, ever, not of an author's plotting and planning and calculating, but just of his feeling and seeing, of his conceiving, in a word, and of his thereby inevitably expressing himself, under the influence of one value or the other. These values represent different sorts and degrees of the communicable thrill, and I doubt if any novelist, for instance, ever proposed to commit himself to one kind or the other with as little mitigation as we are sometimes able to find for him. The interest is greatest—the interest of his genius, I mean, and of his general wealth—when he commits himself in both directions; not quite at the same time or to the same effect, of course, but by some need of performing his whole possible revolution, by the law of some rich passion in him for extremes.

Of the men of largest responding imagination before the human scene, of Scott, of Balzac, even of the coarse, comprehensive, prodigious Zola, we feel, I think, that the deflexion toward either quarter has never taken place; that neither the nature of the man's faculty nor the nature of his experience has ever quite determined it. His current remains therefore extraordinarily rich and mixed, washing us successively with the warm wave of the near and familiar and the tonic shock, as may be, of the far and strange. (In making which opposition I suggest not that the strange and the far are at all necessarily romantic; they happen to be simply the unknown, which is quite a different matter. The real represents to my perception the things we cannot possibly *not* know, sooner or later, in one way or another; it being but one of the accidents of our hampered state, and one of the incidents of their quantity and number, that particular instances have not yet come our way. The romantic stands, on the other hand, for the things that, with all the facilities in the world, all the wealth and all the courage and all the wit and all the adventure, we never *can* directly know; the things that can reach us only through the beautiful circuit and subterfuge of our thought and our desire.) There have been, I gather, many definitions of romance, as a matter indispensably of boats, or of caravans, or of tigers, or of "historical characters," or of ghosts, or of forgers, or of detectives, or of beautiful wicked women, or of pistols and knives, but they appear for the most part reducible to the idea of the facing of danger, the acceptance of great risks for the fascination, the very love, of their uncertainty, the joy of success if possible and of battle in any case. This would be a fine formula if it bore examination; but it strikes me as weak and inadequate, as by no means covering the true ground and yet as landing us in strange confusions.

The panting pursuit of danger is the pursuit of life itself, in which danger awaits us possibly at every step and faces us at every turn; so that the dream of an intenser experience easily becomes rather some vision of a sublime security like that enjoyed on the flowery plains of heaven, where we may conceive ourselves proceeding in ecstasy from one prodigious phase and form of it to another. And if it be insisted that the measure of the type is then in the *appreciation* of danger—the sign of our projection of the real being the smallness of its dangers, and that of our projection of the romantic the hugeness, the mark of the distinction being in short, as they say of collars and gloves and shoes, the size and "number" of the danger—this discrimination again surely fails, since it makes our difference not a difference of kind, which is what we want, but a difference only of degree, and subject by that condition to the indignity of a sliding scale and a shifting measure. There are immense and flagrant dangers that are but sordid and squalid ones, as we feel, tainting with their quality the very defiances they provoke; while there are common and covert ones, that "look like nothing" and that can be but inwardly and occultly dealt with, which involve the sharpest hazards to life and honour and the highest instant decisions and intrepidities of action. It is an arbitrary stamp that keeps these latter prosaic and makes the former heroic; and yet I should still less subscribe to a mere "subjective" division—I mean one that would place the difference wholly in the temper of the imperilled agent. It would be impossible to have a more romantic temper than Flaubert's Madame Bovary, and yet nothing less resembles a romance than the record of her adventures. To classify it by that aspect—the definition of the spirit that happens to animate her—is like settling the question (as I have seen it witlessly settled) by the presence or absence of "costume." Where again then does costume begin or end?—save with the "run" of one or another sort of play? We must reserve vague labels for artless mixtures.

The only *general* attribute of projected romance that I can see, the only one that fits all its cases, is the fact of the kind of experience with which it deals—experience liberated, so to speak; experience disengaged, disembroiled, disencumbered, exempt from the conditions that we usually know to attach to it and, if we wish so to put the matter, drag upon it, and operating in a medium which relieves it, in a particular interest, of the inconvenience of a *related*, a measurable state, a state subject to all our vulgar communities. The greatest intensity may so be arrived at evidently—when the sacrifice of community, of the "related" sides of situations, has not been too rash. It must to this end not flagrantly betray itself; we must even be kept if possible, for our illusion, from suspecting any sacrifice at all. The balloon of experience is in fact of course tied to the earth, and under that necessity we swing, thanks to a rope of remarkable length, in the more or less commodious car of the imagination; but it is by the rope we know where we are, and from the moment that cable is cut we are at large and unrelated: we only swing apart from the globe—though remaining as exhilarated, naturally, as we like, especially when all goes well. The art of the romancer is, "for the fun of it," insidiously to cut the cable, to cut it without our detecting him. What I have recognised then in "The American," much to my surprise and after long years, is that the experience here represented is the disconnected and uncontrolled experience—uncontrolled by our general sense of "the way things happen"—which romance alone more or less successfully palms off on us. It is a case of Newman's own intimate experience all, that being my subject, the thread of which, from beginning to end, is not once exchanged, however momentarily, for any other thread; and the experience of others concerning us, and concerning him, only so far as it touches him and as he recognises, feels or divines it. There is our general sense of the way things happen—it abides with us indefeasibly, as readers of fiction, from the moment we demand that our fiction shall be intelligible; and there is our particular sense of the way they don't happen, which is liable to wake up unless reflexion and criticism, in us, have been skilfully and successfully drugged. There are drugs enough, clearly—it is all a question of applying them with tact; in which case the way things don't happen may be artfully made to pass for the way things do.

Amusing and even touching to me, I profess, at this time of day, the ingenuity (worthy, with whatever lapses, of a better cause) with which, on behalf of Newman's adventure, this hocus-pocus is attempted: the value of the instance not being diminished either, surely, by its having been attempted in such evident good faith. Yes, all is romantic to my actual vision here, and not least so, I hasten to add, the fabulous felicity of my candour. The way things happen is frankly not the way in which they are represented as having happened, in Paris, to my hero: the situation I had conceived only saddled me with that for want of my invention of something better. The great house of Bellegarde, in a word, would, I now feel, given the circumstances, given the *whole* of the ground, have comported itself in a manner as different as possible from the manner to which my narrative commits it; of which truth, moreover, I am by no means sure that, in spite of what I have called my serenity, I had not all the while an uneasy suspicion. I had dug in my path, alas, a hole into which I was destined to fall. I was so possessed of my idea that Newman should be ill-used—which was the essence of my subject—that I attached too scant an importance to its fashion of coming about. Almost any fashion would serve, I appear to have assumed, that would give me my main chance for him; a matter depending not so much on the particular trick played him as on the interesting face presented by him to *any* damnable trick. So where I part company with *terra-firma* is in making that projected, that performed outrage so much more showy, dramatically speaking, than sound. Had I patched it up to a greater apparent soundness my own trick, artistically speaking, would have been played; I should have cut the cable without my reader's suspecting it. I doubtless at the time, I repeat, believed I had taken my precautions; but truly they should have been greater, to impart the air of truth to the attitude—that is first to the pomp and circumstance, and second to the queer falsity—of the Bellegardes.

They would positively have jumped then, the Bellegardes, at my rich and easy American, and not have "minded" in the least any drawback—especially as, after all, given the pleasant palette from which I have painted him, there were few drawbacks to mind. My subject imposed on me a group of closely-allied persons animated by immense pretensions—which was all very well, which might be full of the promise of interest: only of interest felt most of all in the light of comedy and of irony. This, better understood, would have dwelt in the idea not in the least of their not finding Newman good enough for their alliance and thence being ready to sacrifice him, but in that of their taking with alacrity everything he could give them, only asking for more and more, and then adjusting their pretensions and their pride to it with all the comfort in life. Such accommodation of the theory of a noble indifference to the practice of a deep avidity is the real note of policy in forlorn aristocracies—and I meant of course that the Bellegardes should be virtually forlorn. The perversion of truth is by no means, I think, in the displayed acuteness of their remembrance of "who" and "what" they are, or at any rate take themselves for; since it is the misfortune of all insistence on "worldly" advantages—and the situation of such people bristles at the best (by which I mean under whatever invocation of a superficial simplicity) with emphasis, accent, assumption—to produce at times an effect of grossness. The picture of their tergiversation, at all events, however it may originally have seemed to me to hang together, has taken on this rococo appearance precisely because their preferred course, a thousand times preferred, would have been to haul him and his fortune into their boat under cover of night perhaps, in any case as quietly and with as little bumping and splashing as possible, and there accommodate him with the very safest and most convenient seat. Given Newman, given the fact that the thing constitutes itself organically as *his* adventure, that too might very well be a situation and a subject: only it wouldn't have been the theme of "The American" as the book stands, the theme to which I was from so early pledged. Since I had wanted a "wrong" this other turn might even have been arranged to give me *that*, might even have been arranged to meet my requirement that somebody or something should be "in his power" so delightfully; and with the signal effect, after all, of "defining" everything. (It is as difficult, I said above, to trace the dividing-line between the real and the romantic as to plant a milestone between north and south; but I am not sure an infallible sign of the latter is not this rank vegetation of the "power" of bad people that good get into, or *vice versa*. It is so rarely, alas, into *our* power that any one gets!)

It is difficult for me to-day to believe that I had not, as my work went on, *some* shade of the rueful sense of my affront to verisimilitude; yet I catch the memory at least of no great sharpness, no true critical anguish, of remorse: an anomaly the reason of which in fact now glimmers interestingly out. My concern, as I saw it, was to make and to keep Newman consistent; the picture of his consistency was all my undertaking, and the memory of *that* infatuation perfectly abides with me. He was to be the lighted figure, the others—even doubtless to an excessive degree the woman who is made the agent of his discomfiture—were to be the obscured; by which I should largely get the very effect most to be invoked, that of a generous nature engaged with forces, with difficulties and dangers, that it but half understands. If Newman was attaching enough, I must have argued, his tangle would be sensible enough; for the interest of everything is all that it is *his* vision, *his* conception, *his* interpretation: at the window of his wide, quite sufficiently wide, consciousness we are seated, from that admirable position we "assist." He therefore supremely matters; all the rest matters only as he feels it, treats it, meets it. A beautiful infatuation this, always, I think, the intensity of the creative effort to get into the skin of the creature; the act of personal possession of one being by another at its completest—and with the high enhancement, ever, that it is, by the same stroke, the effort of the artist to preserve for his subject that unity, and for his use of it (in other words for the interest he desires to excite) that effect of a *centre*, which most economise its value. Its value is most discussable when that economy has most operated; the content and the "importance" of a work of art are in fine wholly dependent on its *being* one: outside of which all prate of its representative character, its meaning and its bearing, its morality and humanity, are an impudent thing. Strong in that character, which is the condition of its really bearing witness at all, it is strong every way. So much remains true then on behalf of my instinct of multiplying the fine touches by which Newman should live and communicate life; and yet I still ask myself, I confess, what I can have made of "life," in my picture, at such a juncture as the interval offered as elapsing between my hero's first accepted state and the nuptial rites that are to crown it. Nothing here is in truth "offered"—everything is evaded, and the effect of this, I recognise, is of the oddest. His relation to Madame de Cintré takes a great stride, but the author appears to view that but as a signal for letting it severely alone.

I have been stupefied, in so thoroughly revising the book, to find, on turning a page, that the light in which he is presented immediately after Madame de Bellegarde has conspicuously introduced him to all her circle as her daughter's husband-to-be is that of an evening at the opera quite alone; as if he wouldn't surely spend his leisure, and especially those hours of it, with his intended. Instinctively, from that moment, one would have seen them intimately and, for one's interest, beautifully together; with some illustration of the beauty incumbent on the author. The truth was that at this point the author, all gracelessly, could but hold his breath and pass; lingering was too difficult—he had made for himself a crushing complication. Since Madame de Cintré was after all to "back out" every touch in the picture of her apparent loyalty would add to her eventual shame. She had acted in clear good faith, but how could I give the *detail* of an attitude, on her part, of which the foundation was yet so weak? I preferred, as the minor evil, to shirk the attempt —at the cost evidently of a signal loss of "charm"; and with this lady, altogether, I recognise, a light plank, too light a plank, is laid for the reader over a dark "psychological" abyss. The delicate clue to her conduct is never definitely placed in his hand: I must have liked verily to think it *was* delicate and to flatter myself it was to be felt with finger-tips rather than heavily tugged at. Here then, at any rate, is the romantic *tout craché*—the fine flower of Newman's experience blooming in a medium "cut off" and shut up to itself. I don't for a moment pronounce any spell proceeding from it necessarily the less workable, to a rejoicing ingenuity, for that; beguile the reader's suspicion of *his* being shut up, transform it for *him* into a positive illusion of the largest liberty, and the success will ever be proportionate to the chance. Only all this gave me, I make out, a great deal to look to, and I was perhaps wrong in thinking that Newman by himself, and for any occasional extra inch or so I might smuggle into his measurements, would see me through my wood. Anything more liberated and disconnected, to repeat my terms, than his prompt general profession, before the Tristrams, of aspiring to a "great" marriage, for example, could surely not well be imagined. I had to take that over with the rest of him and fit it in—I had indeed to exclude the outer air. Still, I find on re-perusal that I have been able to breathe at least in my aching void; so that, clinging to my hero as to a tall, protective, good-natured elder brother in a rough place, I leave the record to stand or fall by his more or less convincing image.

The American

Chapter I

On a brilliant day in May, in the year 1868, a gentleman was reclining at his ease on the great circular divan which at that period occupied the centre of the Salon Carré, in the Museum of the Louvre.[1] This commodious ottoman has since been removed, to the extreme regret of all weak-kneed lovers of the fine arts; but the gentleman in question had taken serene possession of its softest spot, and, with his head thrown back and his legs outstretched, was staring at Murillo's[2] beautiful moon-borne Madonna in profound enjoyment of his posture. He had removed his hat, and flung down beside him a little red guide-book and an opera-glass. The day was warm; he was heated with walking, and he repeatedly passed his handkerchief over his forehead, with a somewhat wearied gesture. And yet he was evidently not a man to whom fatigue was familiar; long, lean, and muscular, he suggested the sort of vigour that is commonly known as "toughness." But his exertions on this particular day had been of an unwonted sort, and he had often performed great physical feats which left him less jaded than his tranquil stroll through the Louvre. He had looked out all the pictures to which an asterisk was affixed in those formidable pages of fine print in his Bädeker;[3] his attention had been strained and his eyes dazzled, and he had sat down with an æsthetic headache. He had looked, moreover, not only at all the pictures, but at all the copies that were going forward around them, in the hands of those innumerable young women in irreproachable toilets who devote themselves, in France, to the propagation of masterpieces; and if the truth must be told, he had often admired the copy much more than the original. His physiognomy would have sufficiently indicated that he was a shrewd and capable fellow, and in truth he had often sat up all night over a bristling bundle of accounts, and heard the cock crow without a yawn. But Raphael and Titian and Rubens[4] were a new kind of arithmetic, and they inspired our friend, for the first time in his life, with a vague self-mistrust.

An observer, with anything of an eye for national types, would

1. A gallery in the most famous of Parisian museums, especially notable for its collection of old masters.

2. Bartolomé Estéban Murillo (1617?–82), Spanish religious and portrait painter.

3. A travel guide, named for the Coblenz publisher who developed it, Karl Baedeker (1801–59).

4. Famous old masters whose works hang in the Louvre; Raphael (1483–1520), Titian (1490–1576), Rubens (1577–1640).

have had no difficulty in determining the local origin of this undeveloped connoisseur, and indeed such an observer might have felt a certain humorous relish of the almost ideal completeness with which he filled out the national mould. The gentleman on the divan was a powerful specimen of an American. But he was not only a fine American; he was in the first place, physically, a fine man. He appeared to possess that kind of health and strength which, when found in perfection, are the most impressive—the physical capital which the owner does nothing to "keep up." If he was a muscular Christian, it was quite without knowing it. If it was necessary to walk to a remote spot, he walked, but he had never known himself to "exercise." He had no theory with regard to cold bathing or the use of Indian clubs; he was neither an oarsman, a rifleman, nor a fencer—he had never had time for these amusements—and he was quite unaware that the saddle is recommended for certain forms of indigestion. He was by inclination a temperate man; but he had supped the night before his visit to the Louvre at the Café Anglais—someone had told him it was an experience not to be omitted—and he had slept none the less the sleep of the just. His usual attitude and carriage were of a rather relaxed and lounging kind, but when, under a special inspiration, he straightened himself, he looked like a grenadier on parade. He never smoked. He had been assured—such things are said—that cigars were excellent for the health, and he was quite capable of believing it; but he knew as little about tobacco as about homœopathy. He had a very well-formed head, with a shapely, symmetrical balance of the frontal and the occipital development, and a good deal of straight, rather dry brown hair. His complexion was brown, and his nose had a bold, well-marked arch. His eye was of a clear, cold gray, and, save for a rather abundant moustache, he was clean-shaved. He had the flat jaw and sinewy neck which are frequent in the American type; but the traces of national origin are a matter of expression even more than of feature, and it was in this respect that our friend's countenance was supremely eloquent. The discriminating observer we have been supposing might, however, perfectly have measured its expressiveness, and yet have been at a loss to describe it. It had that typical vagueness which is not vacuity, that blankness which is not simplicity, that look of being committed to nothing in particular, of standing in an attitude of general hospitality to the chances of life, of being very much at one's own disposal, so characteristic of many American faces. It was our friend's eye that chiefly told his story; an eye in which innocence and experience were singularly blended. It was full of contradictory suggestions; and though it was by no means the glowing orb of a hero of romance, you could find in it almost anything you looked for. Frigid and yet friendly, frank yet cautious, shrewd yet credulous, positive yet sceptical, confident yet shy, extremely intelligent and extremely good-humoured, there was something vaguely defiant in its concessions, and something profoundly reassuring in its reserve. The cut of this gentleman's moustache, with the two premature wrinkles in the cheek above it, and the fashion of his garments, in which an exposed shirt-front and a cerulean cravat played perhaps an obtrusive part, completed the conditions of his identity. We have approached him, perhaps, at a not especially favourable moment; he is by no means sitting for his portrait. But listless as he lounges there, rather baffled on the æsthetic question, and guilty of the damning fault (as we have lately discovered it to be) of confounding the merit of the artist with that of his work (for he admires the squinting Madonna of the young lady with the boyish coiffure, because he thinks the young lady herself uncommonly taking), he is a sufficiently promising acquaintance. Decision, salubrity, jocosity, prosperity, seem to hover within his call; he is evidently a practical man, but the idea, in his case, has undefined and mysterious boundaries, which invite the imagination to bestir itself on his behalf.

As the little copyist proceeded with her work, she sent every now and then a responsive glance toward her admirer. The cultivation of the fine arts appeared to necessitate, to her mind, a great deal of by-play, a great standing off with folded arms and head drooping from side to side, stroking of a dimpled chin with a dimpled hand, sighing and frowning and patting of the foot, fumbling in disordered tresses for wandering hair-pins. These performances were accompanied by a restless glance, which lingered longer than elsewhere upon the gentleman we have described. At last he rose abruptly, put on his hat, and approached the young lady. He placed himself before her picture and looked at it for some moments, during which she pretended to be quite unconscious of his inspection. Then, addressing her with the single word which constituted the strength of his French vocabulary, and holding up one finger in a manner which appeared to him to illuminate his meaning, "*Combien?*"[5] he abruptly demanded.

The artist stared a moment, gave a little pout, shrugged her shoulders, put down her palette and brushes, and stood rubbing her hands.

"How much?" said our friend, in English. "*Combien?*"

"Monsieur wishes to buy it?" asked the young lady, in French.

"Very pretty, *splendide. Combien?*" repeated the American.

"It pleases monsieur, my little picture? It's a very beautiful subject," said the young lady.

5. "How much?"

"The Madonna, yes; I am not a Catholic, but I want to buy it. *Combien?* Write it here." And he took a pencil from his pocket, and showed her the fly-leaf of his guidebook. She stood looking at him and scratching her chin with the pencil. "Is it not for sale?" he asked. And as she still stood reflecting, and looking at him with an eye which, in spite of her desire to treat this avidity of patronage as a very old story, betrayed an almost touching incredulity, he was afraid he had offended her. She was simply trying to look indifferent, and wondering how far she might go. "I haven't made a mistake—*pas insulté,*[6] no?" her interlocutor continued. "Don't you understand a little English?"

The young lady's aptitude for playing a part at short notice was remarkable. She fixed him with her conscious, perceptive eye, and asked him if he spoke no French. Then, "*Donnez!*"[7] she said briefly, and took the open guide-book. In the upper corner of the fly-leaf she traced a number, in a minute and extremely neat hand. Then she handed back the book, and took up her palette again.

Our friend read the number: "2,000 francs." He said nothing for a time, but stood looking at the picture, while the copyist began actively to dabble with her paint. "For a copy, isn't that a good deal?" he asked at last. "*Pas beaucoup?*"[8]

The young lady raised her eyes from her palette, scanned him from head to foot, and alighted with admirable sagacity upon exactly the right answer. "Yes, it's a good deal. But my copy has remarkable qualities; it is worth nothing less."

The gentleman in whom we are interested understood no French, but I have said he was intelligent, and here is a good chance to prove it. He apprehended, by a natural instinct, the meaning of the young woman's phrase, and it gratified him to think that she was so honest. Beauty, talent, virtue; she combined everything! "But you must finish it," he said. "*Finish*, you know," and he pointed to the unpainted hand of the figure.

"Oh, it shall be finished in perfection—in the perfection of perfections!" cried mademoiselle; and to confirm her promise, she deposited a rosy blotch in the middle of the Madonna's cheek.

But the American frowned. "Ah, too red, too red!" he rejoined. "Her complexion," pointing to the Murillo, "is more delicate."

"Delicate? Oh, it shall be delicate, monsieur; delicate as Sèvres *biscuit*. I am going to tone that down; I know all the secrets of my art. And where will you allow us to send it to you? Your address?"

"My address? Oh yes!" And the gentleman drew a card from his pocket-book and wrote something upon it. Then hesitating a mo-

6. "Not insulted?"
7. "Give!"
8. "Not a lot?"

ment he said: "If I don't like it when it is finished, you know, I shall not be obliged to take it."

The young lady seemed as good a guesser as himself. "Oh, I am very sure that monsieur is not capricious," she said with a roguish smile.

"Capricious?" And at this monsieur began to laugh. "Oh no, I'm not capricious. I am very faithful. I am very constant. *Comprenez?*"[9]

"Monsieur is constant; I understand perfectly. It's a rare virtue. To recompense you, you shall have your picture on the first possible day; next week—as soon as it is dry. I will take the card of monsieur." And she took it and read his name: "Christopher Newman." Then she tried to repeat it aloud, and laughed at her bad accent. "Your English names are so droll!"

"Droll?" said Mr. Newman, laughing too. "Did you ever hear of Christopher Columbus?"

"*Bien sûr!*[1] He invented America; a very great man. And is he your patron?"

"My patron?"

"Your patron-saint, in the calendar."[2]

"Oh, exactly; my parents named me for him."

"Monsieur is American?"

"Don't you see it?" monsieur inquired.

"And you mean to carry my little picture away over there?" and she explained her phrase with a gesture.

"Oh, I mean to buy a great many pictures—*beaucoup, beaucoup*,"[3] said Christopher Newman.

"The honour is not less for me," the young lady answered, "for I am sure monsieur has a great deal of taste."

"But you must give me your card," Newman said; "your card, you know."

The young lady looked severe for an instant, and then said: "My father will wait upon you."

But this time Mr. Newman's powers of divination were at fault. "Your card, your address," he simply repeated.

"My address?" said mademoiselle. Then, with a little shrug: "Happily for you, you are an American! It is the first time I ever gave my card to a gentleman." And, taking from her pocket a rather greasy portemonnaie, she extracted from it a small glazed visiting card, and presented the latter to her patron. It was neatly inscribed in pencil, with a great many flourishes: "Mlle. Noémie Nioche." But Mr. Newman, unlike his companion, read the name

9. "Understand?"
1. "Of course!"
2. In the Christian religion, a tutelary guardian of a person, institution, or place.
3. "A lot, a lot."

with perfect gravity; all French names to him were equally droll.

"And precisely, here is my father, who has come to escort me home," said Mademoiselle Noémie. "He speaks English. He will arrange with you." And she turned to welcome a little old gentleman who came shuffling up, peering over his spectacles at Newman.

M. Nioche wore a glossy wig, of an unnatural colour, which overhung his little meek, white, vacant face, and left it hardly more expressive than the unfeatured block upon which these articles are displayed in the barber's window. He was an exquisite image of shabby gentility. His little ill-made coat, desperately brushed, his darned gloves, his highly-polished boots, his rusty, shapely hat, told the story of a person who had "had losses," and who clung to the spirit of nice habits, though the letter had been hopelessly effaced. Among other things M. Nioche had lost courage. Adversity had not only ruined him, it had frightened him, and he was evidently going through his remnant of life on tiptoe, for fear of waking up the hostile fates. If this strange gentleman was saying anything improper to his daughter, M. Nioche would entreat him huskily, as a particular favour, to forbear; but he would admit at the same time that he was very presumptuous to ask for particular favours.

"Monsieur has bought my picture," said Mademoiselle Noémie. "When it is finished you will carry it to him in a cab."

"In a cab!" cried M. Nioche; and he stared, in a bewildered way, as if he had seen the sun rising at midnight.

"Are you the young lady's father?" said Newman. "I think she said you speak English."

"Speak English—yes," said the old man, slowly rubbing his hands. "I will bring it in a cab."

"Say something, then," cried his daughter. "Thank him a little—not too much."

"A little, my daughter, a little," said M. Nioche, perplexed. "How much?"

"Two thousand!" said Mademoiselle Noémie. "Don't make a fuss, or he will take back his word."

"Two thousand!" cried the old man; and he began to fumble for his snuff-box. He looked at Newman, from head to foot, at his daughter, and then at the picture. "Take care you don't spoil it!" he cried, almost sublimely.

"We must go home," said Mademoiselle Noémie. "This is a good day's work. Take care how you carry it!" And she began to put up her utensils.

"How can I thank you?" said M. Nioche. "My English does not suffice."

"I wish I spoke French as well," said Newman, good-naturedly. "Your daughter is very clever."

"Oh sir!" and M. Nioche looked over his spectacles with tearful eyes and nodded several times with a world of sadness. "She has had an education—*très-supérieure!*[4] Nothing was spared. Lessons in pastel at ten francs the lesson, lessons in oil at twelve francs. I didn't look at the francs then. She's an *artiste*, eh?"

"Do I understand you to say that you have had reverses?" asked Newman.

"Reverses? Oh sir, misfortunes—terrible!"

"Unsuccessful in business, eh?"

"Very unsuccessful, sir."

"Oh, never fear, you'll get on your legs again," said Newman cheerily.

The old man drooped his head on one side and looked at him with an expression of pain, as if this were an unfeeling jest.

"What does he say?" demanded Mademoiselle Noémie.

M. Nioche took a pinch of snuff. "He says I will make my fortune again."

"Perhaps he will help you. And what else?"

"He says thou art very clever."

"It is very possible. You believe it yourself, my father?"

"Believe it, my daughter? With this evidence!" and the old man turned afresh, with a staring, wondering homage, to the audacious daub on the easel.

"Ask him, then, if he would not like to learn French."

"To learn French?"

"To take lessons."

"To take lessons, my daughter? From thee?"

"From you!"

"From me, my child? How should I give lessons?"

"*Pas de raisons!*[5] Ask him immediately!" said Mademoiselle Noémie, with soft brevity.

M. Nioche stood aghast, but under his daughter's eye he collected his wits, and, doing his best to assume an agreeable smile, he executed her commands. "Would it please you to receive instruction in our beautiful language?" he inquired, with an appealing quaver.

"To study French?" asked Newman, staring.

M. Nioche pressed his finger-tips together and slowly raised his shoulders. "A little conversation!"

"Conversation—that's it!" murmured Mademoiselle Noémie, who had caught the word. "The conversation of the best society."

"Our French conversation is famous, you know," M. Nioche ventured to continue. "It's a great talent."

4. "Very high class."

5. "No excuses!"

"But isn't it awfully difficult?" asked Newman, very simply.

"Not to a man of *esprit*,[6] like monsieur, an admirer of beauty in every form!" and M. Nioche cast a significant glance at his daughter's Madonna.

"I can't fancy myself chattering French!" said Newman with a laugh. "And yet, I suppose that the more a man knows the better."

"Monsieur expresses that very happily. *Hélas, oui!*"[7]

"I suppose it would help me a great deal, knocking about Paris, to know the language."

"Ah, there are so many things monsieur must want to say: difficult things!"

"Everything I want to say is difficult. But you give lessons?"

Poor M. Nioche was embarrassed; he smiled more appealingly. "I am not a regular professor," he admitted. "I can't nevertheless tell him that I'm a professor," he said to his daughter.

"Tell him it's a very exceptional chance," answered Mademoiselle Noémie; "an *homme du monde*[8]—one gentleman conversing with another! Remember what you are—what you have been!"

"A teacher of languages in neither case! Much more formerly and much less to-day! And if he asks the price of the lessons?"

"He won't ask it," said Mademoiselle Noémie.

"What he pleases, I may say?"

"Never! That's bad style."

"If he asks, then?"

Mademoiselle Noémie had put on her bonnet and was tying the ribbons. She smoothed them out, with her soft little chin thrust forward. "Ten francs," she said quickly.

"Oh, my daughter! I shall never dare."

"Don't dare, then! He won't ask till the end of the lessons, and then I will make out the bill."

M. Nioche turned to the confiding foreigner again, and stood rubbing his hands, with an air of seeming to plead guilty which was not intenser only because it was habitually so striking. It never occurred to Newman to ask him for a guarantee of his skill in imparting instruction; he supposed of course M. Nioche knew his own language, and his appealing forlornness was quite the perfection of what the American, for vague reasons, had always associated with all elderly foreigners of the lesson-giving class. Newman had never reflected upon philological processes. His chief impression with regard to ascertaining those mysterious correlatives of his familiar English vocables which were current in this extraordinary city of Paris was, that it was simply a matter of a good deal of

6. Wit.
7. "Alas, yes!"
8. "A man of the world."

unwonted and rather ridiculous muscular effort on his own part. "How did you learn English?" he asked of the old man.

"When I was young, before my miseries. Oh, I was wide awake, then. My father was a great *commerçant*;[9] he placed me for a year in a counting-house in England. Some of it stuck to me; but I have forgotten!"

"How much French can I learn in a month?"

"What does he say?" asked Mademoiselle Noémie.

M. Nioche explained.

"He will speak like an angel!" said his daughter.

But the native integrity which had been vainly exerted to secure M. Nioche's commercial prosperity flickered up again. "*Dame*,[1] monsieur!" he answered. "All I can teach you!" And then, recovering himself at a sign from his daughter, "I will wait upon you at your hotel."

"Oh yes, I should like to learn French," Newman went on, with democratic confidingness. "Hang me if I should ever have thought of it! I took for granted it was impossible. But if you learned my language, why shouldn't I learn yours?" and his frank, friendly laugh drew the sting from the jest. "Only, if we are going to converse, you know, you must think of something cheerful to converse about."

"You are very good, sir; I am overcome!" said M. Nioche, throwing out his hands. "But you have cheerfulness and happiness for two!"

"Oh no," said Newman more seriously. "You must be bright and lively; that's part of the bargain."

M. Nioche bowed, with his hand on his heart. "Very well, sir; you have already made me lively."

"Come and bring me my picture then; I will pay you for it, and we will talk about that. That will be a cheerful subject!"

Mademoiselle Noémie had collected her accessories, and she gave the precious Madonna in charge to her father, who retreated backwards out of sight, holding it at arm's-length and reiterating his obeisances. The young lady gathered her shawl about her like a perfect Parisienne, and it was with the smile of a Parisienne that she took leave of her patron.

Chapter II

He wandered back to the divan and seated himself on the other side, in view of the great canvas on which Paul Veronese has

9. Merchant.
1. An exclamatory word, the literal meaning of which is "lady!"

depicted the marriage feast of Cana.[2] Wearied as he was he found the picture entertaining; it had an illusion for him; it satisfied his conception, which was ambitious, of what a splendid banquet should be. In the left-hand corner of the picture is a young woman with yellow tresses confined in a golden head-dress; she is bending forward and listening, with the smile of a charming woman at a dinner-party, to her neighbour. Newman detected her in the crowd, admired her, and perceived that she too had her votive copyist—a young man with his hair standing on end. Suddenly he became conscious of the germ of the mania of the "collector;" he had taken the first step; why should he not go on? It was only twenty minutes before that he had bought the first picture of his life, and now he was already thinking of art-patronage as a fascinating pursuit. His reflections quickened his good-humour, and he was on the point of approaching the young man with another "*Combien?*" Two or three facts in this relation are noticeable, although the logical chain which connects them may seem imperfect. He knew Mademoiselle Nioche had asked too much; he bore her no grudge for doing so, and he was determined to pay the young man exactly the proper sum. At this moment, however, his attention was attracted by a gentleman who had come from another part of the room, and whose manner was that of a stranger to the gallery, although he was equipped with neither guide-book nor opera-glass. He carried a white sun-umbrella, lined with blue silk, and he strolled in front of the Paul Veronese, vaguely looking at it, but much too near to see anything but the grain of the canvas. Opposite to Christopher Newman he paused and turned, and then our friend, who had been observing him, had a chance to verify a suspicion aroused by an imperfect view of his face. The result of this larger scrutiny was that he presently sprang to his feet, strode across the room, and, with an outstretched hand, arrested the gentleman with the blue-lined umbrella. The latter stared, but put out his hand at a venture. He was corpulent and rosy; and though his countenance, which was ornamented with a beautiful flaxen beard, carefully divided in the middle and brushed outward at the sides, was not remarkable for intensity of expression, he looked like a person who would willingly shake hands with anyone. I know not what Newman thought of his face, but he found a want of response in his grasp.

"Oh, come, come," he said, laughing; "don't say, now, you don't know me—if I have *not* got a white parasol!"

The sound of his voice quickened the other's memory, his face expanded to its fullest capacity, and he also broke into a laugh.

2. Paolo Caliari (1528–88), Italian painter of the Venetian school, so named from his birthplace, Verona. *The Marriage at Cana* (1562) hangs in the Louvre.

"Why, Newman—I'll be blowed! Where in the world—I declare—who would have thought? You know you have changed."

"You haven't," said Newman.

"Not for the better, no doubt. When did you get here?"

"Three days ago."

"Why didn't you let me know?"

"I had no idea *you* were here."

"I have been here these six years."

"It must be eight or nine since we met."

"Something of that sort. We were very young."

"It was in St. Louis, during the war. You were in the army."

"Oh no, not I. But you were."

"I believe I was."

"You came out all right?"

"I came out with my legs and arms—and with satisfaction. All that seems very far away."

"And how long have you been in Europe?"

"Seventeen days."

"First time?"

"Yes, very much so."

"Made your everlasting fortune?"

Christopher Newman was silent a moment, and then, with a tranquil smile, he answered: "Yes."

"And come to Paris to spend it, eh?"

"Well, we shall see. So they carry those parasols here—the men-folk?"

"Of course they do. They're great things. They understand comfort out here."

"Where do you buy them?"

"Anywhere, everywhere."

"Well, Tristram, I'm glad to get hold of you. You can show me the ropes. I suppose you know Paris inside out."

Mr. Tristram gave a mellow smile of self-gratulation. "Well, I guess there are not many men that can show me much. I'll take care of you."

"It's a pity you were not here a few minutes ago. I have just bought a picture. You might have put the thing through for me."

"Bought a picture?" said Mr. Tristram, looking vaguely round at the walls. "Why, do they sell them?"

"I mean a copy."

"Oh, I see. These," said Mr. Tristram, nodding at the Titians and Vandykes,[3] "these, I suppose, are originals?"

"I hope so," cried Newman. "I don't want a copy of a copy."

3. Sir Anthony Vandyke (1599–1641), Flemish portrait and religious painter.

"Ah," said Mr. Tristram, mysteriously, "you can never tell. They imitate, you know, so deucedly well. It's like the jewellers, with their false stones. Go into the Palais Royal, there; you see 'Imitation' on half the windows. The law obliges them to stick it on, you know; but you can't tell the things apart. To tell the truth," Mr. Tristram continued, with a wry face, "I don't do much in pictures. I leave that to my wife."

"Ah, you have got a wife?"

"Didn't I mention it? She's a very nice woman; you must know her. She's up there in the Avenue d'Iéna."

"So you are regularly fixed—house and children and all?"

"Yes; a tip-top house, and a couple of youngsters."

"Well," said Christopher Newman, stretching his arms a little, with a sigh, "I envy you."

"Oh no, you don't," answered Mr. Tristram, giving him a little poke with his parasol.

"I beg your pardon; I do."

"Well, you won't, then, when—when——"

"You don't certainly mean when I have seen your establishment?"

"When you have seen Paris, my boy. You want to be your own master here."

"Oh, I have been my own master all my life, and I'm tired of it."

"Well, try Paris. How old are you?"

"Thirty-six."

"*C'est le bel âge*,[4] as they say here."

"What does that mean?"

"It means that a man shouldn't send away his plate till he has eaten his fill."

"All that? I have just made arrangements to take French lessons."

"Oh, you don't want any lessons. You'll pick it up. I never took any."

"I suppose you speak French as well as English?"

"Better!" said Mr. Tristram, roundly. "It's a splendid language. You can say all sorts of bright things in it."

"But I suppose," said Christopher Newman, with an earnest desire for information, "that you must be bright to begin with."

"Not a bit; that's just the beauty of it."

The two friends, as they exchanged these remarks, had remained standing where they met, and leaning against the rail which protected the pictures. Mr. Tristram at last declared that he was overcome with fatigue, and should be happy to sit down. Newman

4. "It's the right age."

recommended in the highest terms the great divan on which he had been lounging, and they prepared to seat themselves. "This is a great place; isn't it?" said Newman, with ardour.

"Great place, great place. Finest thing in the world." And then, suddenly, Mr. Tristram hesitated and looked about him. "I suppose they won't let you smoke here?"

Newman stared. "Smoke? I'm sure I don't know. You know the regulations better than I."

"I? I never was here before!"

"Never! in six years?"

"I believe my wife dragged me here once when we first came to Paris, but I never found my way back."

"But you say you know Paris so well!"

"I don't call this Paris!" cried Mr. Tristram, with assurance. "Come; let's go over to the Palais Royal and have a smoke."

"I don't smoke," said Newman.

"A drink, then."

And Mr. Tristram led his companion away. They passed through the glorious halls of the Louvre, down the staircases, along the cool, dim galleries of sculpture, and out into the enormous court. Newman looked about him as he went, but he made no comments; and it was only when they at last emerged into the open air that he said to his friend: "It seems to me that in your place I should have come here once a week."

"Oh no, you wouldn't!" said Mr. Tristram. "You think so, but you wouldn't. You wouldn't have had time. You would always mean to go, but you never would go. There's better fun than that, here in Paris. Italy's the place to see pictures; wait till you get there. There you have to go; you can't do anything else. It's an awful country; you can't get a decent cigar. I don't know why I went in there to-day. I was strolling along, rather hard up for amusement. I sort of noticed the Louvre as I passed, and I thought I would go in and see what was going on. But if I hadn't found you there I should have felt rather sold. Hang it, I don't care for pictures; I prefer the reality!" And Mr. Tristram tossed off this happy formula with an assurance which the numerous class of persons suffering from an overdose of "culture" might have envied him.

The two gentlemen proceeded along the Rue de Rivoli and into the Palais Royal, where they seated themselves at one of the little tables stationed at the door of the café which projects into the great open quadrangle. The place was filled with people, the fountains were spouting, a band was playing, clusters of chairs were gathered beneath all the lime-trees, and buxom, white-capped nurses, seated along the benches, were offering to their infant charges the amplest facilities for nutrition. There was an easy, homely gaiety in the whole scene, and Christopher Newman felt that it was most characteristically Parisian.

"And now," began Mr. Tristram, when they had tasted the decoction which he had caused to be served to them, "now just give an account of yourself. What are your ideas, what are your plans, where have you come from and where are you going? In the first place, where are you staying?"

"At the Grand Hotel," said Newman.

"Mr. Tristram puckered his plump visage. "That won't do! You must change."

"Change?" demanded Newman. "Why, it's the finest hotel I ever was in."

"You don't want a 'fine' hotel; you want something small and quiet and elegant, where your bell is answered and your—your person is recognised."

"They keep running to see if I have rung before I have touched the bell," said Newman, "and as for my person, they are always bowing and scraping to it."

"I suppose you are always tipping them. That's very bad style."

"Always? By no means. A man brought me something yesterday, and then stood loafing about in a beggarly manner. I offered him a chair and asked him if he wouldn't sit down. Was that bad style?"

"Very!"

"But he bolted, instantly. At any rate, the place amuses me. Hang your elegance, if it bores me. I sat in the court of the Grand Hotel last night until two o'clock in the morning, watching the coming and going, and the people knocking about."

"You're easily pleased. But you can do as you choose—a man in your shoes. You have made a pile of money, eh?"

"I have made enough."

"Happy the man who can say that! Enough for what?"

"Enough to rest awhile, to forget the confounded thing, to look about me, to see the world, to have a good time, to improve my mind, and, if the fancy takes me, to marry a wife." Newman spoke slowly, with a certain dryness of accent and with frequent pauses. This was his habitual mode of utterance, but it was especially marked in the words I have just quoted.

"Jupiter! There's a programme!" cried Mr. Tristram. "Certainly, all that takes money, especially the wife; unless indeed she gives it, as mine did. And what's the story? How have you done it?"

Newman had pushed his hat back from his forehead, folded his arms, and stretched his legs. He listened to the music, he looked about him at the bustling crowd, at the plashing fountains, at the nurses and the babies. "I have worked!" he answered at last.

Tristram looked at him for some moments, and allowed his

placid eyes to measure his friend's generous longitude and rest upon his comfortably contemplative face. "What have you worked at?" he asked.

"Oh, at several things."

"I suppose you're a smart fellow, eh?"

Newman continued to look at the nurses and babies; they imparted to the scene a kind of primordial, pastoral simplicity. "Yes," he said at last, "I suppose I am." And then, in answer to his companion's inquiries, he related briefly his history since their last meeting. It was an intensely Western story, and it dealt with enterprises which it will be needless to introduce to the reader in detail. Newman had come out of the war with a brevet of brigadier-general,[5] an honour which in this case—without invidious comparisons—had lighted upon shoulders amply competent to bear it. But though he could manage a fight, when need was, Newman heartily disliked the business; his four years in the army had left him with an angry, bitter sense of the waste of precious things—life and time and money and "smartness" and the early freshness of purpose; and he had addressed himself to the pursuits of peace with passionate zest and energy. He was of course as penniless when he plucked off his shoulder-straps as when he put them on, and the only capital at his disposal was his dogged resolution and his lively perception of ends and means. Exertion and action were as natural to him as respiration; a more completely healthy mortal had never trod the elastic soil of the West. His experience, moreover, was as wide as his capacity; when he was fourteen years old, necessity had taken him by his slim young shoulders and pushed him into the street, to earn that night's supper. He had not earned it; but he had earned the next night's, and afterwards, whenever he had had none, it was because he had gone without it to use the money for something else, a keener pleasure or a finer profit. He had turned his hand, with his brain in it, to many things; he had been enterprising, in an eminent sense of the term; he had been adventurous and even reckless, and he had known bitter failure as well as brilliant success; but he was a born experimentalist, and he had always found something to enjoy in the pressure of necessity, even when it was as irritating as the haircloth shirt of the mediæval monk. At one time failure seemed inexorably his portion; ill-luck became his bedfellow, and whatever he touched he turned, not to gold, but to ashes. His most vivid conception of a supernatural element in the world's affairs had come to him once when this pertinacity of misfortune was at its climax; there seemed to him something stronger in life than his own will. But the mysterious something

5. A commission giving a higher nominal rank than that for which the officer receives pay.

could only be the devil, and he was accordingly seized with an intense personal enmity to this impertinent force. He had known what it was to have utterly exhausted his credit, to be unable to raise a dollar, and to find himself at nightfall in a strange city, without a penny to mitigate its strangeness. It was under these circumstances that he made his entrance into San Francisco, the scene, subsequently, of his happiest strokes of fortune. If he did not, like Dr. Franklin in Philadelphia, march along the street munching a penny loaf,[6] it was only because he had not the penny loaf necessary to the performance. In his darkest days he had had but one simple, practical impulse—the desire, as he would have phrased it, to see the thing through. He did so at last, buffeted his way into smooth waters, and made money largely. It must be admitted, rather nakedly, that Christopher Newman's sole aim in life had been to make money; what he had been placed in the world for was, to his own perception, simply to wrest a fortune, the bigger the better, from defiant opportunity. This idea completely filled his horizon and satisfied his imagination. Upon the uses of money, upon what one might do with a life into which one had succeeded in injecting the golden stream, he had up to his thirty-fifth year very scantily reflected. Life had been for him an open game, and he had played for high stakes. He had won at last and carried off his winnings; and now what was he to do with them? He was a man to whom, sooner or later, the question was sure to present itself, and the answer to it belongs to our story. A vague sense that more answers were possible than his philosophy had hitherto dreamt of had already taken possession of him, and it seemed softly and agreeably to deepen as he lounged in this brilliant corner of Paris with his friend.

"I must confess," he presently went on, "that here I don't feel at all smart. My remarkable talents seem of no use. I feel as simple as a little child and a little child might take me by the hand and lead me about."

"Oh, I'll be your little child," said Tristram, jovially; "I'll take you by the hand. Trust yourself to me."

"I am a good worker," Newman continued, "but I rather think I am a poor loafer. I have come abroad to amuse myself, but I doubt whether I know how."

"Oh, that's easily learned."

"Well, I may perhaps learn it, but I am afraid I shall never do it by rote. I have the best will in the world about it, but my genius doesn't lie in that direction. As a loafer I shall never be original, as I take it that you are."

6. In his *Autobiography*, Benjamin Franklin (1706–90) narrates his arrival in Philadelphia, as a young man, with only some rolls of bread.

"Yes," said Tristram, "I suppose I am original; like all those immoral pictures in the Louvre."

"Besides," Newman continued, "I don't want to work at pleasure, any more than I played at work. I want to take it easily. I feel deliciously lazy, and I should like to spend six months as I am now, sitting under a tree and listening to a band. There's only one thing; I want to hear some good music."

"Music and pictures! Lord, what refined tastes! You are what my wife calls intellectual. I ain't, a bit. But we can find something better for you to do than to sit under a tree. To begin with, you must come to the club."

"What club?"

"The Occidental. You will see all the Americans there; all the best of them, at least. Of course you play poker?"

"Oh, I say," cried Newman, with energy, "you are not going to lock me up in a club and stick me down at a card-table! I haven't come all this way for that."

"What the deuce *have* you come for! You were glad enough to play poker in St. Louis, I recollect, when you cleaned me out."

"I have come to see Europe, to get the best out of it I can. I want to see all the great things, and do what the clever people do."

"The clever people? Much obliged. You set me down as a blockhead, then?"

Newman was sitting sidewise in his chair, with his elbow on the back and his head leaning on his hand. Without moving he looked awhile at his companion, with his dry, guarded, half-inscrutable, and yet altogether good-natured smile. "Introduce me to your wife!" he said at last.

Tristram bounced about in his chair. "Upon my word, I won't. She doesn't want any help to turn up her nose at me, nor do you, either!"

"I don't turn up my nose at you, my dear fellow; nor at anyone, or anything. I'm not proud, I assure you I'm not proud. That's why I am willing to take example by the clever people."

"Well, if I'm not the rose, as they say here, I have lived near it. I can show you some clever people, too. Do you know General Packard? Do you know C. P. Hatch? Do you know Miss Kitty Upjohn?"

"I shall be happy to make their acquaintance; I want to cultivate society."

Tristram seemed restless and suspicious; he eyed his friend askance, and then: "What are you up to, any way?" he demanded. "Are you going to write a book?"

Christopher Newman twisted one end of his moustache awhile, in silence, and at last he made answer. "One day, a couple of months ago, something very curious happened to me. I had come on to New York on some important business; it was rather a long story—a question of getting ahead of another party, in a certain particular way, in the stock-market. This other party had once played me a very mean trick. I owed him a grudge, I felt awfully savage at the time, and I vowed that, when I got a chance, I would, figuratively speaking, put his nose out of joint. There was a matter of some sixty thousand dollars at stake. If I put it out of his way, it was a blow the fellow would feel, and he really deserved no quarter. I jumped into a hack[7] and went about my business, and it was in this hack—this immortal, historical hack—that the curious thing I speak of occurred. It was a hack like any other, only a trifle dirtier, with a greasy line along the top of the drab cushions, as if it had been used for a great many Irish funerals. It is possible I took a nap; I had been travelling all night, and though I was excited with my errand, I felt the want of sleep. At all events I woke up suddenly, from a sleep or from a kind of a reverie, with the most extraordinary feeling in the world—a mortal disgust for the thing I was going to do. It came upon me like *that!*"—and he snapped his fingers—"as abruptly as an old wound that begins to ache. I couldn't tell the meaning of it; I only felt that I loathed the whole business and wanted to wash my hands of it. The idea of losing that sixty thousand dollars, of letting it utterly slide and scuttle and never hearing of it again, seemed the sweetest thing in the world. And all this took place quite independently of my will, and I sat watching it as if it were a play at the theatre. I could feel it going on inside of me. You may depend upon it that there are things going on inside of us that we understand mighty little about."

"Jupiter! you make my flesh creep!" cried Tristram. "And while you sat in your hack, watching the play, as you call it, the other man marched in and bagged your sixty thousand dollars?"

"I have not the least idea. I hope so, poor devil! but I never found out. We pulled up in front of the place I was going to in Wall Street,[8] but I sat still in the carriage, and at last the driver scrambled down off his seat to see whether his carriage had not turned into a hearse. I couldn't have got out, any more than if I had been a corpse. What was the matter with me? Momentary idiocy, you'll say. What I wanted to get out of was Wall Street. I told the man to drive down to the Brooklyn ferry and to cross over. When we were over, I told him to drive me out into the country. As I had told him originally to drive for dear life down town, I suppose he thought me insane. Perhaps I was, but in that case I am insane still. I spent the morning looking at the first green leaves on

7. Taxicab.
8. New York center of commerce and stock transactions.

Long Island. I was sick of business; I wanted to throw it all up and break off short; I had money enough, or if I hadn't I ought to have. I seemed to feel a new man[9] inside my old skin, and I longed for a new world. When you want a thing so very badly you had better treat yourself to it. I didn't understand the matter, not in the least; but I gave the old horse the bridle and let him find his way. As soon as I could get out of the game I sailed for Europe. That is how I come to be sitting here."

"You ought to have bought up that hack," said Tristram; "it isn't a safe vehicle to have about. And you have really sold out, then; you have retired from business?"

"I have made over my hand to a friend; when I feel disposed, I can take up the cards again. I daresay that a twelvemonth hence the operation will be reversed. The pendulum will swing back again. I shall be sitting in the gondola or on a dromedary, and all of a sudden I shall want to clear out. But for the present I am perfectly free. I have even bargained that I am to receive no business letters."

"Oh, it's a real *caprice de prince*,"[1] said Tristram. "I back out; a poor devil like me can't help you to spend such very magnificent leisure as that. You should get introduced to the crowned heads."

Newman looked at him a moment, and then, with his easy smile: "How does one do it?" he asked.

"Come, I like that!" cried Tristram. "It shows you are in earnest."

"Of course I am in earnest. Didn't I say I wanted the best? I know the best can't be had for mere money, but I rather think money will do a good deal. In addition, I am willing to take a good deal of trouble."

"You are not bashful, eh?"

"I haven't the least idea. I want the biggest kind of entertainment a man can get. People, places, art, nature, everything! I want to see the tallest mountains, and the bluest lakes, and the finest pictures, and the handsomest churches, and the most celebrated men, and the most beautiful women."

"Settle down in Paris, then. There are no mountains that I know of, and the only lake is in the Bois de Boulogne,[2] and not particularly blue. But there is everything else: plenty of pictures and churches, no end of celebrated men, and several beautiful women."

"But I can't settle down in Paris at this season, just as summer is coming on."

"Oh, for the summer go up to Trouville."[3]

9. A play on Newman's name, indicating the moral transformation which has occurred in him.
1. Princely caprice.
2. A public park in Paris, noted for its promenades and bridle paths.
3. A popular beach resort on the Normandy coast.

"What is Trouville?"

"The French Newport. Half the Americans go."

"Is it anywhere near the Alps?"

"About as near as Newport is to the Rocky Mountains."

"Oh, I want to see Mont Blanc,"[4] said Newman, "and Amsterdam, and the Rhine, and a lot of places. Venice in particular. I have great ideas about Venice."

"Ah," said Mr. Tristram, rising, "I see I shall have to introduce you to my wife!"

Chapter III

He performed this ceremony on the following day, when, by appointment, Christopher Newman went to dine with him. Mr. and Mrs. Tristram lived behind one of those chalk-coloured façades which decorate with their pompous sameness the broad avenues manufactured by Baron Haussmann[5] in the neighbourhood of the Arc de Triomphe.[6] Their apartment was rich in the modern conveniences, and Tristram lost no time in calling his visitor's attention to their principal household treasures, the gas-lamps and the furnace-holes. "Whenever you feel homesick," he said, "you must come up here. We'll stick you down before a register, under a good big burner, and——"

"And you will soon get over your homesickness," said Mrs. Tristram.

Her husband stared; his wife often had a tone which he found inscrutable; he could not tell for his life whether she was in jest or in earnest. The truth is that circumstances had done much to cultivate in Mrs. Tristram a marked tendency to irony. Her taste on many points differed from that of her husband; and though she made frequent concessions, it must be confessed that her concessions were not always graceful. They were founded upon a vague project she had of some day doing something very positive, something a trifle passionate. What she meant to do she could by no means have told you; but meanwhile, nevertheless, she was buying a good conscience, by instalments.

It should be added, without delay, to anticipate misconception, that her little scheme of independence did not definitely involve the assistance of another person, of the opposite sex; she was not saving up virtue to cover the expenses of a flirtation. For this there were various reasons. To begin with, she had a very plain face, and

4. An alpine massif on the French-Italian border, southeast of Geneva.

5. Baron Georges Eugène Haussmann (1809–91), city planner chiefly responible for the present design of Paris's streets, parks, and vistas.

6. The Arch of Triumph, famous Paris monument at the head of the Champs Élysées.

she was entirely without illusions as to her appearance. She had taken its measure to a hair's breadth, she knew the worst and the best, she had accepted herself. It had not been, indeed, without a struggle. As a young girl, she had spent hours with her back to her mirror, crying her eyes out; and later she had, from desperation and bravado, adopted the habit of proclaiming herself the most ill-favoured of women, in order that she might—as in common politeness was inevitable—be contradicted and reassured. It was since she had come to live in Europe that she had begun to take the matter philosophically. Her observation, acutely exercised here, had suggested to her that a woman's first duty is not to be beautiful, but to be pleasing; and she encountered so many women who pleased without beauty, that she began to feel that she had discovered her mission. She had once heard an enthusiastic musician, out of patience with a gifted bungler, declare that a fine voice is really an obstacle to singing properly; and it occurred to her that it might perhaps be equally true that a beautiful face is an obstacle to the acquisition of charming manners. Mrs. Tristram, then, undertook to be exquisitely agreeable, and she brought to the task a really touching devotion. How well she would have succeeded I am unable to say; unfortunately she broke off in the middle. Her own excuse was the want of encouragement in her immediate circle. But I am inclined to think that she had not a real genius for the matter, or she would have pursued the charming art for itself. The poor lady was very incomplete. She fell back upon the harmonies of the toilet, which she thoroughly understood, and contented herself with dressing in perfection. She lived in Paris, which she pretended to detest, because it was only in Paris that one could find things to exactly suit one's complexion. Besides, out of Paris it was always more or less of a trouble to get ten-button gloves. When she railed at this serviceable city, and you asked her where she would prefer to reside, she returned some very unexpected answer. She would say in Copenhagen, or in Barcelona; having, while making the tou of Europe, spent a couple of days at each of these places. On th whole, with her poetic furbelows,[7] and her misshapen, intelliger little face, she was, when you knew her, a decidedly interestir woman. She was naturally shy, and if she had been born a beaut she would (having no vanity) probably have remained shy. No she was both diffident and importunate; extremely reserved son times with her friends, and strangely expansive with strangers. S despised her husband; despised him too much, for she had b perfectly at liberty not to marry him. She had been in love wit clever man, who had slighted her, and she had married a fool

7. Ruffles or pleats.

the hope that this thankless wit, reflecting on it, would conclude that she had no appreciation of merit, and that he had flattered himself in supposing that she cared for his own. Restless, discontented, visionary, without personal ambitions, but with a certain avidity of imagination, she was, as I have said before, eminently incomplete. She was full—both for good and for ill—of beginnings that came to nothing; but she had nevertheless, morally, a spark of the sacred fire.

Newman was fond, under all circumstances, of the society of women; and now that he was out of his native element, and deprived of his habitual interests, he turned to it for compensation. He took a great fancy to Mrs. Tristram; she frankly repaid it, and after their first meeting he passed a great many hours in her drawing-room. After two or three talks, they were fast friends. Newman's manner with women was peculiar, and it required some ingenuity on a lady's part to discover that he admired her. He had no gallantry, in the usual sense of the term; no compliments, no graces, no speeches. Very fond of what is called chaffing, in his dealings with men, he never found himself on a sofa beside a member of the softer sex without feeling extremely serious. He was not shy, and, so far as awkwardness proceeds from a struggle with shyness, he was not awkward; grave, attentive, submissive, often silent, he was simply swimming in a sort of rapture of respect. This emotion was not at all theoretic, it was not even in a high degree sentimental; he had thought very little about the "position" of women, and he was not familiar, either sympathetically or otherwise, with the image of a President in petticoats. His attitude was simply the flower of his general good-nature, and a part of his instinctive and genuinely democratic assumption of everyone's right to lead an easy life. If a shaggy pauper had a right to bed and board and wages and a vote, women, of course, who were weaker than paupers, and whose physical tissue was in itself an appeal, should be maintained, sentimentally, at the public expense. Newman was willing to be taxed for this purpose, largely, in proportion to his means. Moreover, many of the common traditions with regard to women were with him fresh personal impressions; he had never read a novel! He had been struck with their acuteness, their subtlety, their tact, their felicity of judgment. They seemed to him exquisitely organised. If it is true that one must always have in one's work here below a religion, or at least an ideal, of some sort, Newman found his metaphysical inspiration in a vague acceptance of final responsibility to some illumined feminine brow.

He spent a great deal of time in listening to advice from Mrs. Tristram; advice, it must be added, for which he had never asked.

He would have been incapable of asking for it, for he had no perception of difficulties, and consequently no curiosity about remedies. The complex Parisian world about him seemed a very simple affair; it was an immense, amazing spectacle, but it neither inflamed his imagination nor irritated his curiosity. He kept his hands in his pockets, looked on good-humouredly, desired to miss nothing important, observed a great many things narrowly, and never reverted to himself. Mrs. Tristram's "advice" was a part of the show, and a more entertaining element, in her abundant gossip, than the others. He enjoyed her talking about himself; it seemed a part of her beautiful ingenuity; but he never made an application of anything she said, or remembered it when he was away from her. For herself, she appropriated him; he was the most interesting thing she had had to think about in many a month. She wished to do something with him—she hardly knew what. There was so much of him; he was so rich and robust, so easy, friendly, well-disposed, that he kept her fancy constantly on the alert. For the present, the only thing she could do was to like him. She told him that he was "horribly Western," but in this compliment the adverb was tinged with insincerity. She led him about with her, introduced him to fifty people, and took extreme satisfaction in her conquest. Newman accepted every proposal, shook hands universally and promiscuously, and seemed equally unfamiliar with trepidation or with elation. Tom Tristram complained of his wife's avidity, and declared that he could never have a clear five minutes with his friend. If he had known how things were going to turn out, he never would have brought him to the Avenue d'Iéna. The two men, formerly, had not been intimate, but Newman remembered his earlier impression of his host, and did Mrs. Tristram, who had by no means taken him into her confidence, but whose secret he presently discovered, the justice to admit that her husband was a rather degenerate mortal. At twenty-five he had been a good fellow, and in this respect he was unchanged; but of a man of his age one expected something more. People said he was sociable, but this was as much a matter of course as for a dipped sponge to expand; and it was not a high order of sociability. He was a great gossip and tattler, and to produce a laugh would hardly have spared the reputation of his aged mother. Newman had a kindness for old memories, but he found it impossible not to perceive that Tristram was nowadays a very light weight. His only aspirations were to hold out at poker, at his club, to know the names of all the *cocottes*,[8] to shake hands all round, to ply his rosy gullet with truffles and champagne, and to

8. "Chicks."

create uncomfortable eddies and obstructions among the constituent atoms of the American colony. He was shamefully idle, spiritless, sensual, snobbish. He irritated our friend by the tone of his allusions to their native country, and Newman was at a loss to understand why the United States were not good enough for Mr. Tristram. He had never been a very conscious patriot, but it vexed him to see them treated as little better than a vulgar smell in his friend's nostrils, and he finally broke out and swore that they were the greatest country in the world, that they could put all Europe into their breeches' pockets, and that an American who spoke ill of them ought to be carried home in irons and compelled to live in Boston. (This, for Newman, was putting it very vindictively.) Tristram was a comfortable man to snub; he bore no malice, and he continued to insist on Newman's finishing his evenings at the Occidental Club.

Christopher Newman dined several times in the Avenue d'Iéna, and his host always proposed an early adjournment to this institution. Mrs. Tristram protested, and declared that her husband exhausted his ingenuity in trying to displease her.

"Oh no, I never try, my love," he answered. "I know you loathe me quite enough when I take my chance."

Newman hated to see a husband and wife on these terms, and he was sure one or other of them must be very unhappy. He knew it was not Tristram. Mrs. Tristram had a balcony before her windows, upon which, during the June evenings, she was fond of sitting, and Newman used frankly to say that he preferred the balcony to the club. It had a fringe of perfumed plants in tubs, and enabled you to look up the broad street and see the Arch of Triumph vaguely massing its heroic sculptures in the summer starlight. Sometimes Newman kept his promise of following Mr. Tristram, in half an hour, to the Occidental, and sometimes he forgot it. His hostess asked him a great many questions about himself, but on this subject he was an indifferent talker. He was not what is called subjective, though when he felt that her interest was sincere, he made an almost heroic attempt to be. He told her a great many things he had done, and regaled her with anecdotes of Western life; she was from Philadelphia, and with her eight years in Paris, talked of herself as a languid Oriental. But some other person was always the hero of the tale, by no means always to his advantage; and Newman's own emotions were but scantily chronicled. She had an especial wish to know whether he had ever been in love—seriously, passionately—and, failing to gather any satisfaction from his allusions, she at last directly inquired. He hesitated awhile, and at last he said: "No!" She declared that she was delighted to hear it, as it confirmed her private conviction that he was a man of no feeling.[9]

"Really?" he asked, very gravely. "Do you think so? How do you recognise a man of feeling?"

"I can't make out," said Mrs. Tristram, "whether you are very simple or very deep."

"I'm very deep. That's a fact."

"I believe that if I were to tell you with a certain air that you have no feeling, you would implicitly believe me."

"A certain air?" said Newman. "Try it and see."

"You would believe me, but you would not care," said Mrs. Tristram.

"You have got it all wrong. I should care immensely, but I shouldn't believe you. The fact is I have never had time to feel things. I have had to *do* them, to make myself felt."

"I can imagine that you may have done that tremendously, sometimes."

"Yes, there's no mistake about that."

"When you are in a fury it can't be pleasant."

"I am never in a fury."

"Angry, then, or displeased."

"I am never angry, and it is so long since I have been displeased that I have quite forgotten it."

"I don't believe," said Mrs. Tristram, "that you are never angry. A man ought to be angry sometimes, and you are neither good enough nor bad enough always to keep your temper."

"I lose it perhaps once in five years."

"The time is coming round, then," said his hostess. "Before I have known you six months I shall see you in a fine fury."

"Do you mean to put me into one?"

"I should not be sorry. You take things too coolly. It exasperates me. And then you are too happy. You have what must be the most agreeable thing in the world—the consciousness of having bought your pleasure beforehand, and paid for it. You have not a day of reckoning staring you in the face. Your reckonings are over."

"Well, I suppose I am happy," said Newman, meditatively.

"You have been odiously successful."

"Successful in copper," said Newman, "only so-so in railroads, and a hopeless fizzle in oil."

"It is very disagreeable to know how Americans have made their money. Now you have the world before you. You have only to enjoy."

9. To be a man of feeling, or sensibility, had been an ideal of the previous century. Cf. Henry Mackenzie's *The Man of Feeling* (1771), a novel of extravagant sentimentality.

"Oh, I suppose I am very well off," said Newman. "Only I am tired of having it thrown up at me. Besides, there are several drawbacks. I am not intellectual."

"One doesn't expect it of you," Mrs. Tristram answered. Then in a moment: "Besides, you are!"

"Well, I mean to have a good time, whether or no," said Newman. "I am not cultivated, I am not even educated; I know nothing about history, or art, or foreign tongues, or any other learned matters. But I am not a fool, either, and I shall undertake to know something about Europe by the time I have done with it. I feel something under my ribs here," he added in a moment, "that I can't explain—a sort of a mighty hankering, a desire to stretch out and haul in."

"Bravo!" said Mrs. Tristram, "that is very fine. You are the great Western Barbarian, stepping forth in his innocence and might, gazing awhile at this poor effete Old World, and then swooping down on it."

"Oh come," said Newman. "I am not a barbarian, by a good deal. I am very much the reverse. I have seen barbarians; I know what they are."

"I don't mean that you are a Comanche chief, or that you wear a blanket and feathers. There are different shades."

"I am a highly civilised man," said Newman. "I stick to that. If you don't believe it, I should like to prove it to you."

Mrs. Tristram was silent awhile. "I should like to make you prove it," she said, at last. "I should like to put you in a difficult place."

"Pray do," said Newman.

"That has a little conceited sound!" his companion rejoined.

"Oh," said Newman, "I have a very good opinion of myself."

"I wish I could put it to the test. Give me time, and I will." And Mrs. Tristram remained silent for some time afterwards, as if she was trying to keep her pledge. It did not appear that evening that she succeeded; but as he was rising to take his leave, she passed suddenly, as she was very apt to do, from the tone of unsparing persiflage to that of almost tremulous sympathy. "Speaking seriously," she said, "I believe in you, Mr. Newman. You flatter my patriotism."

"Your patriotism?" Christopher demanded.

"Even so. It would take too long to explain, and you probably would not understand. Besides, you might take it—really, you might take it for a declaration. But it has nothing to do with you personally; it's what you represent. Fortunately you don't know all that, or your conceit would increase insufferably."

Newman stood staring and wondering what under the sun he "represented."

"Forgive all my meddlesome chatter, and forget my advice. It is very silly in me to undertake to tell you what to do. When you are embarrassed, do as you think best, and you will do very well. When you are in a difficulty, judge for yourself."

"I shall remember everything you have told me," said Newman. "There are so many forms and ceremonies over here——"

"Forms and ceremonies are what I mean, of course."

"Ah, but I want to observe them," said Newman. "Haven't I as good a right as another? They don't scare me, and you needn't give me leave to violate them. I won't take it."

"That is not what I mean. I mean, observe them in your own way. Settle nice questions for yourself. Cut the knot or untie it, as you choose."

"Oh, I am sure I shall never fumble over it," said Newman.

The next time that he dined in the Avenue d'Iéna was a Sunday, a day on which Mr. Tristram left the cards unshuffled, so that there was a trio in the evening on the balcony. The talk was of many things, and at last Mrs. Tristram suddenly observed to Christopher Newman that it was high time he should take a wife.

"Listen to her; she has the audacity!" said Tristram, who on Sunday evenings was always rather acrimonious.

"I don't suppose you have made up your mind not to marry?" Mrs. Tristram continued.

"Heaven forbid!" cried Newman. "I am sternly resolved on it."

"It's very easy," said Tristram; "fatally easy!"

"Well, then, I suppose you do not mean to wait till you are fifty."

"On the contrary, I am in a great hurry."

"One would never suppose it. Do you expect a lady to come and propose to you?"

"No; I am willing to propose. I think a great deal about it."

"Tell me some of your thoughts."

"Well," said Newman, slowly, "I want to marry very well."

"Marry a woman of sixty, then," said Tristram.

" 'Well' in what sense?"

"In every sense. I shall be hard to please."

"You must remember that, as the French proverb says, the most beautiful girl in the world can give but what she has."

"Since you ask me," said Newman, "I will say frankly that I want extremely to marry. It is time, to begin with; before I know it I shall be forty. And then I'm lonely and helpless and dull. But if I marry now, so long as I didn't do it in hot haste when I was twenty,

I must do it with my eyes open. I want to do the thing in handsome style. I not only want to make no mistakes, but I want to make a great hit. I want to take my pick. My wife must be a magnificent woman."

"*Voilà ce qui s'appelle parler!*"[1] cried Mrs. Tristram.

"Oh, I have thought an immense deal about it."

"Perhaps you think too much. The best thing is simply to fall in love."

"When I find the woman who pleases me, I shall love her enough. My wife shall be very comfortable."

"You are superb! There's a chance for the magnificent women."

"You are not fair," Newman rejoined. "You draw a fellow out and put him off his guard, and then you laugh at him."

"I assure you," said Mrs. Tristram, "that I am very serious. To prove it, I will make you a proposal. Should you like me, as they say here, to marry you?"

"To hunt up a wife for me?"

"She is already found. I will bring you together."

"Oh come," said Tristram, "we don't keep a matrimonial bureau. He will think you want your commission."

"Present me to a woman who comes up to my notions," said Newman, "and I will marry her to-morrow."

"You have a strange tone about it, and I don't quite understand you. I didn't suppose you would be so cold-blooded and calculating."

Newman was silent a while. "Well," he said, at last, "I want a great woman. I stick to that. That's one thing I *can* treat myself to, and if it is to be had I mean to have it. What else have I toiled and struggled for all these years? I have succeeded, and now what am I to do with my success? To make it perfect, as I see it, there must be a beautiful woman perched on the pile, like a statue on a monument. She must be as good as she is beautiful, and as clever as she is good. I can give my wife a good deal, so I am not afraid to ask a good deal myself. She shall have everything a woman can desire; I shall not even object to her being too good for me; she may be cleverer and wiser than I can understand, and I shall only be the better pleased. I want to possess, in a word, the best article in the market."

"Why didn't you tell a fellow all this at the outset?" Tristram demanded. "I have been trying so to make you fond of *me!*"

"This is very interesting," said Mrs. Tristram. "I like to see a man know his own mind."

"I have known mine for a long time," Newman went on. "I made

1. "That's what's called talking," or "That's the way to talk!"

up my mind tolerably early in life that a beautiful wife was the thing best worth having, here below. It is the greatest victory over circumstances. When I say beautiful, I mean beautiful in mind and in manners, as well as in person. It is a thing every man has an equal right to; he may get it if he can. He doesn't have to be born with certain faculties on purpose; he needs only to be a man. Then he needs only to use his will and such wits as he has, and to try."

"It strikes me that your marriage is to be rather a matter of vanity."

"Well, it is certain," said Newman, "that if people notice my wife and admire her, I shall be mightily tickled."

"After this," cried Mrs. Tristram, "call any man modest!"

"But none of them will admire her so much as I."

"I see you have a taste for splendour."

Newman hesitated a little; and then: "I honestly believe I have!" he said.

"And I suppose you have already looked about you a good deal."

"A good deal, according to opportunity."

"And you have seen nothing that satisfied you?"

"No," said Newman, half reluctantly, "I am bound to say in honesty that I have seen nothing that really satisfied me."

"You remind me of the heroes of the French romantic poets, Rolla and Fortunio and all those other insatiable gentlemen for whom nothing in this world was handsome enough. But I see you are in earnest, and I should like to help you."

"Who the deuce is it, darling, that you are going to put upon him?" Tristram cried. "We know a good many pretty girls, thank Heaven, but magnificent women are not so common."

"Have you any objections to a foreigner?" his wife continued, addressing Newman, who had tilted back his chair, and, with his feet on a bar of the balcony railing and his hands in his pockets, was looking at the stars.

"No Irish need apply,"[2] said Tristram.

Newman meditated awhile. "As a foreigner, no," he said at last; "I have no prejudices."

"My dear fellow, you have no suspicions!" cried Tristram. "You don't know what terrible customers these foreign women are; especially the 'magnificent' ones. How should you like a fair Circassian,[3] with a dagger in her belt?"

2. A note frequently added to employment advertisements in nineteenth-century America, during the great period of Irish immigration.

3. Literally, a resident of the region between the Black Sea, the Kuban River, and the greater Caucasus; here used as a symbol of a beautiful but dangerous woman.

Newman administered a vigorous slap to his knee. "I would marry a Japanese, if she pleased me," he affirmed.

"We had better confine ourselves to Europe," said Mrs. Tristram. "The only thing is, then, that the person be in herself to your taste?"

"She is going to offer you an unappreciated governess!" Tristram groaned.

"Assuredly. I won't deny that, other things being equal, I should prefer one of my own countrywomen. We should speak the same language, and that would be a comfort. But I am not afraid of a foreigner. Besides, I rather like the idea of taking in Europe, too. It enlarges the field of selection. When you choose from a greater number, you can bring your choice to a finer point."

"You talk like Sardanapalus!"[4] exclaimed Tristram.

"You say all this to the right person," said Newman's hostess. "I happen to number among my friends the loveliest woman in the world. Neither more nor less. I don't say a very charming person or a very estimable woman or a very great beauty; I say simply the loveliest woman in the world."

"The deuce!" cried Tristram, "you have kept very quiet about her. Were you afraid of me?"

"You have seen her," said his wife, "but you have no perception of such merit as Claire's."

"Ah, her name is Claire? I give it up."

"Does your friend wish to marry?" asked Newman.

"Not in the least. It is for you to make her change her mind. It will not be easy; she has had one husband, and he gave her a low opinion of the species."

"Oh, she is a widow, then?" said Newman.

"Are you already afraid? She was married at eighteen, by her parents, in the French fashion, to a disagreeable old man. But he had the good taste to die a couple of years afterward, and she is now twenty-five."

"So she is French?"

"French by her father, English by her mother. She is really more English than French, and she speaks English as well as you or I—or rather much better. She belongs to the very top of the basket, as they say here. Her family, on each side, is of fabulous antiquity; her mother is the daughter of an English Catholic earl. Her father is dead, and since her widowhood she has lived with her mother and a married brother. There is another brother, younger, who I believe is wild. They have an old hotel in the Rue de l'Université,

4. An ancient Assyrian monarch who burnt up himself and his court, rather than be captured by the Medes. Byron wrote a tragedy on the theme.

but their fortune is small, and they make a common household, for economy's sake. When I was a girl I was put into a convent here for my education, while my father made the tour of Europe. It was a silly thing to do with me, but it had the advantage that it made me acquainted with Claire de Bellegarde. She was younger than I, but we became fast friends. I took a tremendous fancy to her, and she returned my passion as far as she could. They kept such a tight rein on her that she could do very little, and when I left the convent she had to give me up. I was not of her *monde*;[5] I am not now, either, but we sometimes meet. They are terrible people—her *monde*; all mounted upon stilts a mile high, and with pedigrees long in proportion. It is the skim of the milk of the old *noblesse*.[6] Do you know what a Legitimist[7] is, or an Ultramontane?[8] Go into Madame de Cintré's drawing-room some afternoon, at five o'clock, and you will see the best-preserved specimens. I say go, but no one is admitted who can't show his fifty quarterings."[9]

"And this is the lady you propose to me to marry?" asked Newman. "A lady I can't even approach?"

"But you said just now that you recognised no obstacles."

Newman looked at Mrs. Tristram a while, stroking his moustache. "Is she a beauty?" he demanded.

"No."

"Oh, then it's no use——"

"She is not a beauty, but she is beautiful, two very different things. A beauty has no faults in her face; the face of a beautiful woman may have faults that only deepen its charm."

"I remember Madame de Cintré, now," said Tristram. "She is as plain as a pikestaff. A man wouldn't look at her twice."

"In saying that *he* would not look at her twice, my husband sufficiently describes her," Mrs. Tristram rejoined.

"Is she good; is she clever?" Newman asked.

"She is perfect! I won't say more than that. When you are praising a person to another who is to know her, it is bad policy to go into details. I won't exaggerate. I simply recommend her. Among all women I have known she stands alone; she is of a different clay."

"I should like to see her," said Newman, simply.

"I will try to manage it. The only way will be to invite her to dinner. I have never invited her before, and I don't know that she

5. In her social set.
6. Nobility.
7. A proponent of the right of Henry V (1820–83), Bourbon claimant, to the throne of France.
8. A proponent of the view that the pope is the supreme head of the Roman Catholic church, as distinct from a Gallicianist, who asserted the special rights of the French monarch in the French church.
9. That is, his long pedigree. An allusion to the marshalling (or quarterings) of various coats of arms on an escutcheon.

will come. Her old feudal countess of a mother rules the family with an iron hand, and allows her to have no friends but of her own choosing, and to visit only in a certain sacred circle. But I can at least ask her."

At this moment Mrs. Tristram was interrupted; a servant stepped out upon the balcony and announced that there were visitors in the drawing-room. When Newman's hostess had gone in to receive her friends, Tom Tristram approached his guest.

"Don't put your foot into *this,* my boy," he said, puffing the last whiffs of his cigar. "There's nothing in it!"

Newman looked askance at him, inquisitive. "You tell another story, eh?"

"I say simply that Madame de Cintré is a great white doll of a woman, who cultivates quiet haughtiness."

"Ah, she's haughty, eh?"

"She looks at you as if you were so much thin air, and cares for you about as much."

"She is very proud, eh!"

"Proud? As proud as I'm humble."

"And not good-looking?"

Tristram shrugged his shoulders: "It's a kind of beauty you must be intellectual to understand. But I must go in and amuse the company."

Some time elapsed before Newman followed his friends into the drawing-room. When he at last made his appearance there he remained but a short time, and during this period sat perfectly silent, listening to a lady to whom Mrs. Tristram had straightway introduced him and who chattered, without a pause, with the full force of an extraordinarily high-pitched voice. Newman gazed and attended. Presently he came to bid good-night to Mrs. Tristram.

"Who is that lady?" he asked.

"Miss Dora Finch. How do you like her?"

"She's too noisy."

"She is thought so bright! Certainly, you are fastidious," said Mrs. Tristram.

Newman stood a moment, hesitating. Then at last, "Don't forget about your friend," he said; "Madame What's-her-name? the proud beauty. Ask her to dinner, and give me good notice." And with this he departed.

Some days later he came back; it was in the afternoon. He found Mrs. Tristram in her drawing-room; with her was a visitor, a woman young and pretty, dressed in white. The two ladies had risen and the visitor was apparently taking her leave. As Newman approached, he received from Mrs. Tristram a glance of the most vivid significance, which he was not immediately able to interpret.

"This is a good friend of ours," she said, turning to her companion, "Mr. Christopher Newman. I have spoken of you to him and he has an extreme desire to make your acquaintance. If you had consented to come and dine, I should have offered him an opportunity."

The stranger turned her face toward Newman, with a smile. He was not embarrassed, for his unconscious *sang-froid*[1] was boundless; but as he became aware that this was the proud and beautiful Madame de Cintré, the loveliest woman in the world, the promised perfection, the proposed ideal, he made an instinctive movement to gather his wits together. Through the slight preoccupation that it produced he had a sense of a long, fair face, and of two eyes that were both brilliant and mild.

"I should have been most happy," said Madame de Cintré. "Unfortunately, as I have been telling Mrs. Tristram, I go on Monday to the country."

Newman had made a solemn bow. "I am very sorry," he said.

"Paris is getting too warm," Madame de Cintré added, taking her friend's hand again in farewell.

Mrs. Tristram seemed to have formed a sudden and somewhat venturesome resolution, and she smiled more intensely, as women do when they take such resolutions. "I want Mr. Newman to know you," she said, dropping her head on one side and looking at Madame de Cintré's bonnet ribbons.

Christopher Newman stood gravely silent, while his native penetration admonished him. Mrs. Tristram was determined to force her friend to address him a word of encouragement which should be more than one of the common formulas of politeness; and if she was prompted by charity, it was by the charity that begins at home. Madame de Cintré was her dearest Claire, and her especial admiration; but Madame de Cintré had found it impossible to dine with her, and Madame de Cintré should for once be forced gently to render tribute to Mrs. Tristram.

"It would give me great pleasure," she said, looking at Mrs. Tristram.

"That's a great deal," cried the latter, "for Madame de Cintré to say!"

"I am very much obliged to you," said Newman. "Mrs. Tristram can speak better for me than I can speak for myself."

Madame de Cintré looked at him again, with the same soft brightness. "Are you to be long in Paris?" she asked.

1. Self-possession.

"We shall keep him," said Mrs. Tristram.

"But you are keeping *me!*" and Madame de Cintré shook her friend's hand.

"A moment longer," said Mrs. Tristram.

Madame de Cintré looked at Newman again; this time without her smile. Her eyes lingered a moment. "Will you come and see me?" she asked.

Mrs. Tristram kissed her. Newman expressed his thanks, and she took her leave. Her hostess went with her to the door, and left Newman alone a moment. Presently she returned, rubbing her hands. "It was a fortunate chance," she said. "She had come to decline my invitation. You triumphed on the spot, making her ask you, at the end of three minutes, to her house."

"It was you who triumphed," said Newman. "You must not be too hard upon her."

Mrs. Tristram stared. "What do you mean?"

"She did not strike me as so proud. I should say she was shy."

"You are very discriminating. And what do you think of her face?"

"It's handsome!" said Newman.

"I should think it was! Of course you will go and see her."

"To-morrow!" cried Newman.

"No, not to-morrow; the next day. That will be Sunday; she leaves Paris on Monday. If you don't see her, it will at least be a beginning." And she gave him Madame de Cintré's address.

He walked across the Seine, late in the summer afternoon, and made his way through those gray and silent streets of the Faubourg St. Germain,[2] whose houses present to the outer world a face as impassive and as suggestive of the concentration of privacy within as the blank walls of Eastern seraglios. Newman thought it a queer way for rich people to live; his ideal of grandeur was a splendid façade, diffusing its brilliancy outward too, irradiating hospitality. The house to which he had been directed had a dark, dusty, painted portal, which swung open in answer to his ring. It admitted him into a wide, gravelled court, surrounded on three sides with closed windows, and with a doorway facing the street, approached by three steps and surmounted by a tin canopy. The place was all in the shade; it answered to Newman's conception of a convent. The portress could not tell him whether Madame de Cintré was visible; he would please to apply at the farther door. He crossed the court; a gentleman was sitting, bareheaded, on the steps of the portico, playing with a beautiful pointer. He rose as Newman approached, and, as he laid his hand upon the bell, said with a smile, in English,

2. The aristocratic quarter of Paris.

that he was afraid Newman would be kept waiting; the servants were scattered; he himself had been ringing; he didn't know what the deuce was in them. He was a young man; his English was excellent, and his smile very frank. Newman pronounced the name of Madame de Cintré.

"I think," said the young man, "that my sister is visible. Come in, and if you will give me your card I will carry it to her myself."

Newman had been accompanied on his present errand by a slight sentiment, I will not say of defiance—a readiness for aggression or defence, as they might prove needful—but of reflective good-humoured suspicion. He took from his pocket, while he stood on the portico, a card upon which, under his name, he had written the words "San Francisco," and while he presented it he looked warily at his interlocutor. His glance was singularly reassuring; he liked the young man's face; it strongly resembled that of Madame de Cintré. He was evidently her brother. The young man, on his side, had made a rapid inspection of Newman's person. He had taken the card and was about to enter the house with it when another figure appeared on the threshold—an older man, of a fine presence, wearing evening dress. He looked hard at Newman, and Newman looked at him. "Madame de Cintré," the younger man repeated, as an introduction of the visitor. The other took the card from his hand, read it in a rapid glance, looked again at Newman from head to foot, hesitated a moment, and then said, gravely, but urbanely, "Madame de Cintré is not at home."

The younger man made a gesture, and then turning to Newman: "I am very sorry, sir," he said.

Newman gave him a friendly nod, to show that he bore him no malice, and retraced his steps. At the porter's lodge he stopped; the two men were still standing on the portico.

"Who is the gentleman with the dog?" he asked of the old woman who reappeared. He had begun to learn French.

"That is Monsieur le Comte."

"And the other?"

"That is Monsieur le Marquis."

"A marquis?" said Christopher in English, which the old woman fortunately did not understand. "Oh, then he's not the butler!"

Chapter IV

Early one morning, before Christopher Newman was dressed, a little old man was ushered into his apartment, followed by a youth in a blouse, bearing a picture in a brilliant frame. Newman, among the distractions of Paris, had forgotten M. Nioche and his accomplished daughter; but this was an effective reminder.

"I am afraid you had given me up, sir," said the old man, after many apologies and salutations. "We have made you wait so many days. You accused us, perhaps, of inconstancy, of bad faith. But behold me at last! And behold also the pretty 'Madonna.' Place it on a chair, my friend, in a good light, so that monsieur may admire it." And M. Nioche, addressing his companion, helped him to dispose the work of art.

It had been endued with a layer of varnish an inch thick, and its frame, of an elaborate pattern, was at least a foot wide. It glittered and twinkled in the morning light, and looked, to Newman's eyes, wonderfully splendid and precious. It seemed to him a very happy purchase, and he felt rich in the possession of it. He stood looking at it complacently, while he proceeded with his toilet, and M. Nioche, who had dismissed his own attendant, hovered near, smiling and rubbing his hands.

"It has wonderful *finesse*,"[3] he murmured, caressingly. "And here and there are marvellous touches; you probably perceive them, sir. It attracted great attention on the Boulevard, as we came along. And then a gradation of tones! That's what it is to know how to paint. I don't say it because I am her father, sir; but as one man of taste addressing another I cannot help observing that you have there an exquisite work. It is hard to produce such things and to have to part with them. If our means only allowed us the luxury of keeping it! I really may say, sir"—and M. Nioche gave a little feebly insinuating laugh—"I really may say that I envy you! You see," he added in a moment, "we have taken the liberty of offering you a frame. It increases by a trifle the value of the work, and it will save you the annoyance—so great for a person of your delicacy—of going about to bargain at the shops."

The language spoken by M. Nioche was a singular compound, which I shrink from the attempt to reproduce in its integrity. He had apparently once possessed a certain knowledge of English, and his accent was oddly tinged with the cockneyism of the British metropolis. But his learning had grown rusty with disuse, and his vocabulary was defective and capricious. He had repaired it with large patches of French, with words anglicised by a process of his own, and with native idioms literally translated. The result, in the form in which he in all humility presented it, would be scarcely comprehensible to the reader, so that I have ventured to trim and sift it. Newman only half understood it, but it amused him, and the old man's decent forlornness appealed to his democratic instincts.

3. Delicacy.

The assumption of a fatality in misery always irritated his strong good-nature—it was almost the only thing that did so; and he felt the impulse to wipe it out, as it were, with the sponge of his own prosperity. The papa of Mademoiselle Noémie, however, had apparently on this occasion been vigorously indoctrinated, and he showed a certain tremulous eagerness to cultivate unexpected opportunities.

"How much do I owe you, then, with the frame?" asked Newman.

"It will make in all three thousand francs," said the old man, smiling agreeably, but folding his hands in instinctive suppliance.

"Can you give me a receipt?"

"I have brought one," said M. Nioche. "I took the liberty of drawing it up in case monsieur should happen to desire to discharge his debt." And he drew a paper from his pocket-book and presented it to his patron. The document was written in a minute, fantastic hand, and couched in the choicest language.

Newman laid down the money, and M. Nioche dropped the napoleons[4] one by one, solemnly and lovingly, into an old leathern purse.

"And how is your young lady?" asked Newman. "She made a great impression on me."

"An impression? Monsieur is very good. Monsieur admires her appearance?"

"She is very pretty, certainly."

"Alas, yes, she is very pretty!"

"And what is the harm in her being pretty?"

M. Nioche fixed his eyes upon a spot on the carpet and shook his head. Then looking up at Newman with a gaze that seemed to brighten and expand, "Monsieur knows what Paris is. She is dangerous to beauty, when beauty hasn't the sou."[5]

"Ah, but that is not the case with your daughter. She is rich, now."

"Very true; we are rich for six months. But if my daughter were a plain girl I should sleep better, all the same."

"You are afraid of the young men?"

"The young and the old!"

"She ought to get a husband."

"Ah, monsieur, one doesn't get a husband for nothing. Her husband must take her as she is; I can't give her a sou. But the young men don't see with that eye."

"Oh," said Newman, "her talent is in itself a dowry."

"Ah, sir, it needs first to be converted into specie!"[6] and M.

4. Former gold coins of France, each equal to twenty francs, bearing the portrait of either Napoleon I or Napoleon III.

5. A bronze coin equal to five centimes.

6. Cash.

Nioche slapped his purse tenderly before he stowed it away. "The operation doesn't take place every day."

"Well, your young men are very shabby," said Newman; "that's all I can say. They ought to pay for your daughter, and not ask money themselves."

"Those are very noble ideas, monsieur; but what will you have? They are not the ideas of this country. We want to know what we are about when we marry."

"How big a portion does your daughter want?"

M. Nioche stared, as if he wondered what was coming next; but he promptly recovered himself, at a venture, and replied that he knew a very nice young man, employed by an insurance company, who would content himself with fifteen thousand francs.

"Let your daughter paint half-a-dozen pictures for me, and she shall have her dowry."

"Half-a-dozen pictures—her dowry! Monsieur is not speaking inconsiderately?"

"If she will make me six or eight copies in the Louvre as pretty as that 'Madonna,' I will pay her the same price," said Newman.

Poor M. Nioche was speechless a moment, with amazement and gratitude, and then he seized Newman's hand, pressed it between his own ten fingers, and gazed at him with watery eyes. "As pretty as that? They shall be a thousand times prettier—they shall be magnificent, sublime. Ah, if I only knew how to paint myself, sir, so that I might lend a hand! What can I do to thank you? *Voyons*!"[7] and he pressed his forehead while he tried to think of something.

"Oh, you have thanked me enough," said Newman.

"Ah, here it is, sir!" cried M. Nioche. "To express my gratitude, I will charge you nothing for the lessons in French conversation."

"The lessons? I had quite forgotten them. Listening to your English," added Newman, laughing, "is almost a lesson in French."

"Ah, I don't profess to teach English, certainly," said M. Nioche. "But for my own admirable tongue I am still at your service."

"Since you are here, then," said Newman, "we will begin. This is a very good hour. I am going to have my coffee; come every morning at half-past nine and have yours with me."

"Monsieur offers me my coffee, also?" cried M. Nioche. "Truly, my *beaux jours*[8] are coming back."

"Come," said Newman, "let us begin. The coffee is almighty hot. How do you say that in French?"

Every day, then, for the following three weeks, the minutely respectable figure of M. Nioche made its appearance, with a series

7. "Let's see!"

8. "Good old days."

of little inquiring and apologetic obeisances, among the aromatic fumes of Newman's morning beverage. I don't know how much French our friend learned; but, as he himself said, if the attempt did him no good, it could at any rate do him no harm. And it amused him; it gratified that irregularly sociable side of his nature which had always expressed itself in a relish for ungrammatical conversation, and which often, even in his busy and preoccupied days, had made him sit on rail fences in young Western towns, in the twilight, in gossip hardly less than fraternal with humorous loafers and obscure fortune-seekers. He had notions, wherever he went, about talking with the natives; he had been assured, and his judgment approved the advice, that in travelling abroad it was an excellent thing to look into the life of the country. M. Nioche was very much of a native, and, though his life might not be particularly worth looking into, he was a palpable and smoothly-rounded unit in that picturesque Parisian civilisation which offered our hero so much easy entertainment and propounded so many curious problems to his inquiring and practical mind. Newman was fond of statistics; he liked to know how things were done; it gratified him to learn what taxes were paid, what profits were gathered, what commercial habits prevailed, how the battle of life was fought. M. Nioche, as a reduced capitalist, was familiar with these considerations, and he formulated his information, which he was proud to be able to impart, in the neatest possible terms and with a pinch of snuff between finger and thumb. As a Frenchman—quite apart from Newman's napoleons—M. Nioche loved conversation, and even in his decay his urbanity had not grown rusty. As a Frenchman, too, he could give a clear account of things, and—still as a Frenchman—when his knowledge was at fault he could supply its lapses with the most convenient and ingenious hypotheses. The little shrunken financier was intensely delighted to have questions asked him, and he scraped together information, by frugal processes, and took notes, in his little greasy pocket-book, of incidents which might interest his munificent friend. He read old almanacs at the book-stalls on the quays, and he began to frequent another *café*, where more newspapers were taken and his post-prandial *demitasse*[9] cost him a penny extra, and where he used to con the tattered sheets[1] for curious anecdotes, freaks of nature, and strange coincidences. He would relate with solemnity the next morning that a child of five years of age had lately died at Bordeaux, whose brain had been found to weigh sixty ounces—the brain of a Napoleon or a Washington! or that Madame P——, *charcutière*[2] in the Rue de

9. After-dinner coffee.
1. Slang for "read the daily newspapers."
2. Clerk in a butcher-shop.

Clichy, had found in the wadding of an old petticoat the sum of three hundred and sixty francs, which she had lost five years before. He pronounced his words with great distinctness and sonority, and Newman assured him that his way of dealing with the French tongue was very superior to the bewildering chatter that he heard in other mouths. Upon this M. Nioche's accent became more finely trenchant than ever; he offered to read extracts from Lamartine,[3] and he protested that, although he did endeavour according to his feeble lights to cultivate refinement of diction, monsieur, if he wanted the real thing, should go to the Théâtre Français.[4]

Newman took an interest in French thriftiness and conceived a lively admiration for Parisian economies. His own economic genius was so entirely for operations on a larger scale, and, to move at his ease, he needed so imperatively the sense of great risks and great prizes, that he found an ungrudging entertainment in the spectacle of fortunes made by the aggregation of copper coins, and in the minute subdivision of labour and profit. He questioned M. Nioche about his own manner of life, and felt a friendly mixture of compassion and respect over the recital of his delicate frugalities. The worthy man told him how, at one period, he and his daughter had supported existence, comfortably, upon the sum of fifteen sous *per diem*;[5] recently, having succeeded in hauling ashore the last floating fragments of the wreck of his fortune, his budget had been a trifle more ample. But they still had to count their sous very narrowly, and M. Nioche intimated with a sigh that Mademoiselle Noémie did not bring to this task that zealous co-operation which might have been desired.

"But what will you have?" he asked, philosophically. "One is young, one is pretty, one needs new dresses and fresh gloves; one can't wear shabby gowns among the splendours of the Louvre."

"But your daughter earns enough to pay for her own clothes," said Newman.

M. Nioche looked at him with weak, uncertain eyes. He would have liked to be able to say that his daughter's talents were appreciated, and that her crooked little daubs commanded a market; but it seemed a scandal to abuse the credulity of this free-handed stranger, who, without a suspicion or a question, had admitted him to equal social rights. He compromised, and declared that while it was obvious that Mademoiselle Noémie's reproductions of the old masters had only to be seen to be coveted, the prices which, in consideration of their altogether peculiar degree of finish she felt obliged to ask for them, had kept purchasers at a respectful distance. "Poor

3. Alphonse Lamartine (1790–1869), French poet, novelist, and statesman.
4. The national theater of France, on the Rue de Richelieu in Paris; also known as the Comédie Française.
5. Per day.

little one!" said M. Nioche, with a sigh; "it is almost a pity that her work is so perfect! It would be in her interest to paint less well."

"But if Mademoiselle Noémie has this devotion to her art," Newman once observed, "why should you have those fears for her that you spoke of the other day?"

M. Nioche meditated; there was an inconsistency in his position; it made him chronically uncomfortable. Though he had no desire to destroy the goose with the golden eggs—Newman's benevolent confidence—he felt a tremulous impulse to speak out all his trouble. "Ah, she is an artist, my dear sir, most assuredly," he declared. "But to tell you the truth, she is also a *franche coquette*.[6] I am sorry to say," he added in a moment, shaking his head with a world of harmless bitterness, "that she comes honestly by it. Her mother was one before her!"

"You were not happy with your wife?" Newman asked.

M. Nioche gave half-a-dozen little backward jerks of his head. "She was my purgatory, monsieur!"

"She deceived you?"

"Under my nose, year after year. I was too stupid, and the temptation was too great. But I found her out at last. I have only been once in my life a man to be afraid of; I know it very well: it was in that hour! Nevertheless I don't like to think of it. I loved her—I can't tell you how much. She was a bad woman."

"She is not living?"

"She has gone to her account."

"Her influence on your daughter, then," said Newman encouragingly, "is not to be feared."

"She cared no more for her daughter than for the sole of her shoe! But Noémie has no need of influence. She is sufficient to herself. She is stronger than I."

"She doesn't obey you, eh?"

"She can't obey, monsieur, since I don't command. What would be the use? It would only irritate her and drive her to some *coup de tête*.[7] She is very clever, like her mother; she would waste no time about it. As a child—when I was happy, or supposed I was—she studied drawing and painting with first-class professors, and they assured me she had a talent. I was delighted to believe it, and when I went into society I used to carry her pictures with me in a portfolio and hand them round to the company. I remember, once, a lady thought I was offering them for sale, and I took it very ill. We don't know what we may come to! Then came my dark days, and my explosion with Madame Nioche. Noémie had no more twenty-franc lessons; but in the course of time, when she grew

6. Open flirt.

7. Rash impulse.

older, and it became highly expedient that she should do something that would help to keep us alive, she bethought herself of her palette and brushes. Some of our friends in the *quartier*[8] pronounced the idea fantastic; they recommended her to try bonnet-making, to get a situation in a shop, or—if she was more ambitious—to advertise for a place of *dame de compagnie*.[9] She did advertise, and an old lady wrote her a letter and bade her come and see her. The old lady liked her, and offered her her living and six hundred francs a year; but Noémie discovered that she passed her life in her arm-chair and had only two visitors, her confessor and her nephew: the confessor very strict, and the nephew a man of fifty, with a broken nose and a government clerkship of two thousand francs. She threw her old lady over, bought a paint-box, a canvas, and a new dress, and went and set up her easel in the Louvre. There, in one place and another, she has passed the last two years; I can't say it has made us millionaires. But Noémie tells me that Rome was not built in a day, that she is making great progress, that I must leave her to her own devices. The fact is, without prejudice to her genius, that she has no idea of burying herself alive. She likes to see the world, and to be seen. She says, herself, that she can't work in the dark. With her appearance it is very natural. Only, I can't help worrying and trembling and wondering what may happen to her there all alone, day after day, amid all that coming and going of strangers. I can't be always at her side. I go with her in the morning, and I come to fetch her away, but she won't have me near her in the interval; she says I make her nervous. As if it didn't make me nervous to wander about all day without her! Ah, if anything were to happen to her!" cried M. Nioche, clenching his two fists and jerking back his head again, portentously.

"Oh, I guess nothing will happen," said Newman.

"I believe I should shoot her!" said the old man solemnly.

"Oh, we'll marry her," said Newman, "since that's how you manage it; and I will go and see her to-morrow at the Louvre and pick out the pictures she is to copy for me."

M. Nioche had brought Newman a message from his daughter, in acceptance of his magnificent commission, the young lady declaring herself his most devoted servant, promising her most zealous endeavour, and regretting that the proprieties forbade her coming to thank him in person. The morning after the conversation just narrated, Newman reverted to his intention of meeting Mademoiselle Noémie at the Louvre. M. Nioche appeared preoc-

8. Neighborhood.

9. "Lady's companion."

cupied, and left his budget of anecdotes unopened; he took a great deal of snuff, and sent certain oblique, appealing glances toward his stalwart pupil. At last, when he was taking his leave, he stood a moment, after he had polished his hat with his calico pocket-handkerchief, with his small, pale eyes fixed strangely upon Newman.

"What's the matter?" our hero demanded.

"Excuse the solicitude of a father's heart!" said M. Nioche. "You inspire me with boundless confidence, but I can't help giving you a warning. After all, you are a man, you are young and at liberty. Let me beseech you, then, to respect the innocence of Mademoiselle Nioche!"

Newman had wondered what was coming, and at this he broke into a laugh. He was on the point of declaring that his own innocence struck him as the more exposed, but he contented himself with promising to treat the young girl with nothing less than veneration. He found her waiting for him, seated upon the great divan in the Salon Carré. She was not in her working-day costume, but wore her bonnet and gloves and carried her parasol, in honour of the occasion. These articles had been selected with unerring taste, and a fresher, prettier image of youthful alertness and blooming discretion was not to be conceived. She made Newman a most respectful curtsy and expressed her gratitude for his liberality in a wonderfully graceful little speech. It annoyed him to have a charming young girl stand there thanking him, and it made him feel uncomfortable to think that this perfect young lady, with her excellent manners and her finished intonation, was literally in his pay. He assured her, in such French as he could muster, that the thing was not worth mentioning, and that he considered her services a great favour.

"Whenever you please, then," said Mademoiselle Noémie, "we will pass the review."

They walked slowly round the room, then passed into the others and strolled about for half an hour. Mademoiselle Noémie evidently relished her situation, and had no desire to bring her public interview with her striking-looking patron to a close. Newman perceived that prosperity agreed with her. The little thin-lipped, peremptory air with which she had addressed her father on the occasion of their former meeting had given place to the most lingering and caressing tones.

"What sort of pictures do you desire?" she asked. "Sacred, or profane?"

"Oh, a few of each," said Newman. "But I want something bright and gay."

"Something gay? There is nothing very gay in this solemn old Louvre. But we will see what we can find. You speak French to-day like a charm. My father has done wonders."

"Oh, I am a bad subject," said Newman. "I am too old to learn a language."

"Too old? *Quelle folie!*"[1] cried Mademoiselle Noémie, with a clear, shrill laugh. "You are a very young man. And how do you like my father?"

"He is a very nice old gentleman. He never laughs at my blunders."

"He is very *comme il faut*,[2] my papa," said Mademoiselle Noémie, "and as honest as the day. Oh, an exceptional probity! You could trust him with millions."

"Do you always obey him?" asked Newman.

"Obey him?"

"Do you do what he bids you?"

The young girl stopped and looked at him; she had a spot of colour in either cheek, and in her expressive French eye, which projected too much for perfect beauty, there was a slight gleam of audacity. "Why do you ask me that?" she demanded.

"Because I want to know."

"You think me a bad girl?" And she gave a strange smile.

Newman looked at her a moment; he saw that she was pretty, but he was not in the least dazzled. He remembered poor M. Nioche's solicitude for her "innocence," and he laughed out again as his eyes met hers. Her face was the oddest mixture of youth and maturity, and beneath her candid brow her searching little smile seemed to contain a world of ambiguous intentions. She was pretty enough, certainly, to make her father nervous; but, as regards her innocence, Newman felt ready on the spot to affirm that she had never parted with it. She had simply never had any; she had been looking at the world since she was ten years old, and he would have been a wise man who could tell her any secrets. In her long mornings at the Louvre she had not only studied Madonnas and St. Johns; she had kept an eye upon all the variously embodied human nature around her, and she had formed her conclusions. In a certain sense, it seemed to Newman, M. Nioche might be at rest; his daughter might do something very audacious, but she would never do anything foolish. Newman, with his long-drawn, leisurely smile, and his even, unhurried utterance, was always, mentally, taking his time; and he asked himself, now, what she was looking at him in that way for. He had an idea that she would like him to confess that he did think her a bad girl.

1. "What nonsense!"

2. Proper.

"Oh no," he said at last; "it would be very bad manners in me to judge you that way. I don't know you."

"But my father has complained to you," said Mademoiselle Noémie.

"He says you are a coquette."

"He shouldn't go about saying such things to gentlemen! But you don't believe it?"

"No," said Newman gravely, "I don't believe it."

She looked at him again, gave a shrug and a smile, and then pointed to a small Italian picture, a Marriage of St. Catherine.[3] "How should you like that?" she asked.

"It doesn't please me," said Newman. "The young lady in the yellow dress is not pretty."

"Ah, you are a great connoisseur," murmured Mademoiselle Noémie.

"In pictures? Oh no; I know very little about them."

"In pretty women, then?"

"In that I am hardly better."

"What do you say to that, then?" the young girl asked, indicating a superb Italian portrait of a lady. "I will do it for you on a smaller scale."

"On a smaller scale? Why not as large as the original?"

Mademoiselle Noémie glanced at the glowing splendour of the Venetian masterpiece and gave a little toss of her head. "I don't like that woman. She looks stupid."

"I do like her," said Newman. "Decidedly, I must have her, as large as life. And just as stupid as she is there."

The young girl fixed her eyes on him again, and with her mocking smile, "It certainly ought to be easy for me to make her look stupid!" she said.

"What do you mean?" asked Newman, puzzled.

She gave another little shrug. "Seriously, then, you want that portrait—the golden hair, the purple satin, the pearl necklace, the two magnificent arms?"

"Everything—just as it is."

"Would nothing else do, instead?"

"Oh, I want some other things, but I want that too."

Mademoiselle Noémie turned away a moment, walked to the other side of the hall, and stood there, looking vaguely about her. At last she came back. "It must be charming to be able to order pictures at such a rate. Venetian portraits, as large as life! You go at it *en prince*.[4] And you are going to travel about Europe that way?"

3. Possibly that of Murillo, painted in 1682.

4. "Like a prince."

"Yes, I intend to travel," said Newman.

"Ordering, buying, spending money?"

"Of course I shall spend some money."

"You are very happy to have it. And you are perfectly free?"

"How do you mean, free?"

"You have nothing to bother you—no family, no wife, no *fiancée*?"

"Yes, I am tolerably free."

"You are very happy," said Mademoiselle Noémie gravely.

"*Je le veux bien!*"[5] said Newman, proving that he had learned more French than he admitted.

"And how long shall you stay in Paris?" the young girl went on.

"Only a few days more."

"Why do you go away?"

"It is getting hot, and I must go to Switzerland."

"To Switzerland? That's a fine country. I would give my new parasol to see it! Lakes and mountains, romantic valleys and icy peaks! Oh, I congratulate you. Meanwhile, I shall sit here through all the hot summer, daubing at your pictures."

"Oh, take your time about it," said Newman. "Do them at your convenience."

They walked farther and looked at a dozen other things. Newman pointed out what pleased him, and Mademoiselle Noémie generally criticised it, and proposed something else. Then suddenly she diverged and began to talk about some personal matter.

"What made you speak to me the other day in the Salon Carré?" she abruptly asked.

"I admired your picture."

"But you hesitated a long time."

"Oh, I do nothing rashly," said Newman.

"Yes, I saw you watching me. But I never supposed you were going to speak to me. I never dreamed I should be walking about here with you to-day. It's very curious."

"It is very natural," observed Newman.

"Oh, I beg your pardon; not to me. Coquette as you think me, I have never walked about in public with a gentleman before. What was my father thinking of when he consented to our interview?"

"He was repenting of his unjust accusations," replied Newman.

Mademoiselle Noémie remained silent; at last she dropped into a seat. "Well, then, for those five it is fixed," she said. "Five copies as brilliant and beautiful as I can make them. We have one more to choose. Shouldn't you like one of those great Rubenses—the mar-

5. "I am willing to admit it!"

riage of Marie de Médicis?[6] Just look at it and see how handsome it is."

"Oh yes; I should like that," said Newman. "Finish off with that."

"Finish off with that—good!" And she laughed. She sat a moment, looking at him, and then she suddenly rose and stood before him, with her hands hanging and clasped in front of her. "I don't understand you," she said with a smile. "I don't understand how a man can be so ignorant."

"Oh, I am ignorant, certainly," said Newman, putting his hands into his pockets.

"It's ridiculous! I don't know how to paint."

"You don't know how?"

"I paint like a cat; I can't draw a straight line. I never sold a picture until you bought that thing the other day." And as she offered this surprising information she continued to smile.

Newman burst into a laugh. "Why do you tell me this?" he asked.

"Because it irritates me to see a clever man blunder so. My pictures are grotesque."

"And the one I possess——"

"That one is rather worse than usual."

"Well," said Newman, "I like it all the same!"

She looked at him askance. "That is a very pretty thing to say," she answered; "but it is my duty to warn you before you go farther. This order of yours is impossible, you know. What do you take me for? It is work for ten men. You pick out the six most difficult pictures in the Louvre, and you expect me to go to work as if I were sitting down to hem a dozen pocket-handkerchiefs. I wanted to see how far you would go."

Newman looked at the young girl in some perplexity. In spite of the ridiculous blunder of which he stood convicted, he was very far from being a simpleton, and he had a lively suspicion that Mademoiselle Noémie's sudden frankness was not essentially more honest than her leaving him in error would have been. She was playing a game; she was not simply taking pity on his æsthetic verdancy. What was it she expected to win? The stakes were high and the risk was great; the prize therefore must have been commensurate. But even granting that the prize might be great, Newman could not resist a movement of admiration for his companion's intrepidity. She was throwing away with one hand, whatever she might intend to do with the other, a very handsome sum of money.

6. Works of Peter Paul Rubens (1577–1640), Flemish painter; Rubens painted a marriage portrait of Marie de Médicis, wife of King Henry IV and Queen of France.

"Are you joking," he said, "or are you serious?"

"Oh, serious!" cried Mademoiselle Noémie, but with her extraordinary smile.

"I know very little about pictures, or how they are painted. If you can't do all that, of course you can't. Do what you can, then."

"It will be very bad," said Mademoiselle Noémie.

"Oh," said Newman, laughing, "if you are determined it shall be bad, of course it will. But why do you go on painting badly?"

"I can do nothing else; I have no real talent."

"You are deceiving your father, then."

The young girl hesitated a moment. "He knows very well!"

"No," Newman declared; "I am sure he believes in you."

"He is afraid of me. I go on painting badly, as you say, because I want to learn. I like it, at any rate. And I like being here; it is a place to come to every day; it is better than sitting in a little dark damp room, on a court, or selling buttons and whalebones over a counter."

"Of course it is much more amusing," said Newman. "But for a poor girl isn't it rather an expensive amusement?"

"Oh, I am very wrong, there is no doubt about that," said Mademoiselle Noémie. "But rather than earn my living as some girls do—toiling with a needle, in little black holes, out of the world—I would throw myself into the Seine."[7]

"There is no need of that," Newman answered; "your father told you my offer?"

"Your offer?"

"He wants you to marry, and I told him I would give you a chance to earn your *dot*."[8]

"He told me all about it, and you see the account I make of it! Why should you take such an interest in my marriage?"

"My interest was in your father. I hold to my offer; do what you can, and I will buy what you paint."

She stood for some time, meditating, with her eyes on the ground. At last, looking up: "What sort of a husband can you get for twelve thousand francs?" she asked.

"Your father tells me he knows some very good young men."

"Grocers and butchers and little *maîtres de cafés*![9] I will not marry at all if I can't marry well."

"I would advise you not to be too fastidious," said Newman. "That's all the advice I can give you."

"I am very much vexed at what I have said!" cried the young girl. "It has done me no good. But I couldn't help it."

7. A principal river of France, the Seine flows through Paris.

8. Dowry.

9. Headwaiters.

"What good did you expect it to do you?"

"I couldn't help it, simply."

Newman looked at her a moment. "Well, your pictures may be bad," he said, "but you are too clever for me, nevertheless. I don't understand you. Good-bye!" And he put out his hand.

She made no response, and offered him no farewell. She turned away and seated herself sidewise on a bench, leaning her head on the back of her hand, which clasped the rail in front of the pictures. Newman stood a moment and then turned on his heel and retreated. He had understood her better than he confessed; this singular scene was a practical commentary upon her father's statement that she was a frank coquette.[1]

Chapter V

When Newman related to Mrs. Tristram his fruitless visit to Madame de Cintré, she urged him not to be discouraged, but to carry out his plan of "seeing Europe" during the summer, and return to Paris in the autumn and settle down comfortably for the winter. "Madame de Cintré will keep," she said; "she is not a woman who will marry from one day to another." Newman made no distinct affirmation that he would come back to Paris; he even talked about Rome and the Nile, and abstained from professing any especial interest in Madame de Cintré's continued widowhood. This circumstance was at variance with his habitual frankness, and may perhaps be regarded as characteristic of the incipient stage of that passion which is more particularly known as the mysterious one. The truth is that the expression of a pair of eyes, that were at once brilliant and mild, had become very familiar to his memory, and he would not easily have resigned himself to the prospect of never looking into them again. He communicated to Mrs. Tristram a number of other facts, of greater or less importance, as you choose; but on this particular point he kept his own counsel. He took a kindly leave of M. Nioche, having assured him that, so far as he was concerned, the blue-cloaked Madonna herself might have been present at his interview with Mademoiselle Noémie; and left the old man nursing his breast-pocket, in an ecstasy which the acutest misfortune might have been defied to dissipate. Newman then started on his travels with all his usual appearance of slow-strolling leisure, and all his essential directness and intensity of aim. No man seemed less in a hurry, and yet no man achieved more in brief periods. He had certain practical instincts which served him excellently in his trade of tourist. He found his way in foreign cities by

1. Flirt.

divination, his memory was excellent when once his attention had been at all cordially given, and he emerged from dialogues in foreign tongues, of which he had, formally, not understood a word, in full possession of the particular fact he had desired to ascertain. His appetite for facts was capacious, and although many of those which he noted would have seemed woefully dry and colourless to the ordinary sentimental traveller, a careful inspection of the list would have shown that he had a soft spot in his imagination. In the charming city of Brussels—his first stopping-place after leaving Paris—he asked a great many questions about the street-cars, and took extreme satisfaction in the reappearance of this familiar symbol of American civilisation; but he was also greatly struck with the beautiful Gothic tower of the Hôtel de Ville, and wondered whether it would not be possible to "get up" something like it in San Francisco. He stood for half an hour in the crowded square before this edifice, in imminent danger from carriage-wheels, listening to a toothless old cicerone[2] mumble in broken English the touching history of Counts Egmont and Horn;[3] and he wrote the names of these gentlemen—for reasons best known to himself—on the back of an old letter.

At the outset, on his leaving Paris, his curiosity had not been intense; passive entertainment, in the Champs Élysées[4] and at the theatres, seemed about as much as he need expect of himself, and although, as he had said to Tristram, he wanted to see the mysterious, satisfying *best*, he had not the Grand Tour[5] in the least on his conscience, and was not given to cross-questioning the amusement of the hour. He believed that Europe was made for him, and not he for Europe. He had said that he wanted to improve his mind, but he would have felt a certain embarrassment, a certain shame, even —a false shame, possibly—if he had caught himself looking intellectually into the mirror. Neither in this nor in any other respect had Newman a high sense of responsibility; it was his prime conviction that a man's life should be easy, and that he should be able to resolve privilege into a matter of course. The world, to his sense, was a great bazaar, where one might stroll about and purchase handsome things; but he was no more conscious, individually, of social pressure than he admitted the existence of such a thing as an obligatory purchase. He had not only a dislike, but a sort of moral mistrust, of uncomfortable thoughts, and it was both uncomfort-

2. A sight-seeing guide.
3. Political opponents of the Spanish Inquisition in the Netherlands; both were beheaded by the Duke of Alba in 1562. Goethe's *Egmont* is a historical drama on the theme.
4. A major Parisian boulevard, leading from the Place de la Concorde to the Arc de Triomphe; celebrated for its tree-lined beauty.
5. An extended tour of Europe, formerly regarded as a necessary part of the education of a young British aristocrat.

able and slightly contemptible to feel obliged to square oneself with a standard. One's standard was the ideal of one's own good-humoured prosperity, the prosperity which enabled one to give as well as take. To expand, without bothering about it—without shiftless timidity on one side, or loquacious eagerness on the other—to the full compass of what he would have called a "pleasant" experience, was Newman's most definite programme of life. He had always hated to hurry to catch railroad trains, and yet he had always caught them; and just so an undue solicitude for "culture" seemed a sort of silly dawdling at the station, a proceeding properly confined to women, foreigners, and other unpractical persons. All this admitted, Newman enjoyed his journey, when once he had fairly entered the current, as profoundly as the most zealous *dilettante*. One's theories, after all, matter little; it is one's humour that is the great thing. Our friend was intelligent, and he could not help that. He lounged through Belgium and Holland and the Rhineland, through Switzerland and Northern Italy, planning about nothing, but seeing everything. The guides and *valets de place*[6] found him an excellent subject. He was always approachable, for he was much addicted to standing about in the vestibules and porticoes of inns, and he availed himself little of the opportunities for impressive seclusion which are so liberally offered in Europe to gentlemen who travel with long purses. When an excursion, a church, a gallery, a ruin was proposed to him, the first thing Newman usually did, after surveying his postulant in silence, from head to foot, was to sit down at a little table and order something to drink. The cicerone, during this process, usually retreated to a respectful distance; otherwise I am not sure that Newman would not have bidden him sit down and have a glass also, and tell him as an honest fellow whether his church or his gallery was really worth a man's trouble. At last he rose and stretched his long legs, beckoned to the man of monuments, looked at his watch, and fixed his eye on his adversary. "What is it?" he asked. "How far?" And whatever the answer was, although he seemed to hesitate, he never declined. He stepped into an open cab, made his conductor sit beside him to answer questions, bade the driver go fast (he had a particular aversion to slow driving), and rolled, in all probability through a dusty suburb, to the goal of his pilgrimage. If the goal was a disappointment, if the church was meagre, or the ruin a heap of rubbish, Newman never protested or berated his cicerone; he looked with an impartial eye upon great monuments and small, made the guide recite his lesson, listened to it religiously, asked if there was nothing else to be seen in the neighbourhood, and drove back again at a rattling

6. Inn-servants.

pace. It is to be feared that his perception of the difference between good architecture and bad was not acute, and that he might sometimes have been seen gazing with culpable serenity at inferior productions. Ugly churches were a part of his pastime in Europe, as well as beautiful ones, and his tour was altogether a pastime. But there is sometimes nothing like the imagination of those people who have none, and Newman, now and then, in an unguided stroll in a foreign city, before some lonely, sad-towered church, or some angular image of one who had rendered civic service in an unknown past, had felt a singular inward tremor. It was not an excitement or a perplexity; it was a placid, fathomless sense of diversion.

He encountered by chance in Holland a young American, with whom, for a time, he formed a sort of traveller's partnership. They were men of a very different cast, but each, in his way, was so good a fellow that, for a few weeks at least, it seemed something of a pleasure to share the chances of the road. Newman's comrade, whose name was Babcock, was a young Unitarian minister; a small, spare, neatly-attired man, with a strikingly candid physiognomy. He was a native of Dorchester, Massachusetts, and had spiritual charge of a small congregation in another suburb of the New England metropolis. His digestion was weak, and he lived chiefly on Graham bread and hominy—a regimen to which he was so much attached that his tour seemed to him destined to be blighted when, on landing on the Continent, he found that these delicacies did not flourish under the *table d'hôte*[7] system. In Paris he had purchased a bag of hominy at an establishment which called itself an American Agency, and at which the New York illustrated papers were also to be procured, and he had carried it about with him, and shown extreme serenity and fortitude in the somewhat delicate position of having his hominy prepared for him and served at anomalous hours, at the hotels he successively visited. Newman had once spent a morning, in the course of business, at Mr. Babcock's birthplace, and, for reasons too recondite to unfold, his visit there always assumed in his mind a jocular cast. To carry out his joke, which certainly seems poor so long as it is not explained, he used often to address his companion as "Dorchester." Fellow-travellers very soon grow intimate; but it is highly improbable that at home these extremely dissimilar characters would have found any very convenient points of contact. They were, indeed, as different as possible. Newman, who never reflected on such matters, accepted the situation with great equanimity, but Babcock used to

7. A restaurant meal served to all guests at a fixed hour and a fixed price.

meditate over it privately; used often, indeed, to retire to his room early in the evening for the express purpose of considering it conscientiously and impartially. He was not sure that it was a good thing for him to associate with our hero, whose way of taking life was so little his own. Newman was an excellent, generous fellow; Mr. Babcock sometimes said to himself that he was a *noble* fellow, and, certainly, it was impossible not to like him. But would it not be desirable to try to exert an influence upon him, to try to quicken his moral life and sharpen his sense of duty? He liked everything, he accepted everything, he found amusement in everything; he was not discriminating, he had not a high tone. The young man from Dorchester accused Newman of a fault which he considered very grave, and which he did his best to avoid: what he would have called a want of "moral reaction." Poor Mr. Babcock was extremely fond of pictures and churches, and carried Mrs. Jameson's works[8] about in his trunk; he delighted in æsthetic analysis, and received peculiar impressions from everything he saw. But nevertheless in his secret soul he detested Europe, and he felt an irritating need to protest against Newman's gross intellectual hospitality. Mr. Babcock's moral *malaise*,[9] I am afraid, lay deeper than where any definition of mine can reach it. He mistrusted the European temperament, he suffered from the European climate, he hated the European dinner-hour; European life seemed to him unscrupulous and impure. And yet he had an exquisite sense of beauty; and as beauty was often inextricably associated with the above displeasing conditions, as he wished, above all, to be just and dispassionate, and as he was, furthermore, extremely devoted to "culture," he could not bring himself to decide that Europe was utterly bad. But he thought it was very bad indeed, and his quarrel with Newman was that this unregulated epicure had a sadly insufficient perception of the bad. Babcock himself really knew as little about the bad, in any quarter of the world, as a nursing infant; his most vivid realisation of evil had been the discovery that one of his college classmates, who was studying architecture in Paris, had a love affair with a young woman who did not expect him to marry her. Babcock had related this incident to Newman, and our hero had applied an epithet of an unflattering sort to the young girl. The next day his companion asked him whether he was very sure he had used exactly the right word to characterise the young architect's mistress. Newman stared and laughed. "There are a great many words to express that idea," he said; "you can take your choice!"

8. Anna Brownell Jameson (1794–1860), author of works on art, travel, and history. Now largely forgotten, she was the author of *Sacred and Legendary Art* (1848–60).

9. Uneasiness.

"Oh, I mean," said Babcock, "was she possibly not to be considered in a different light? Don't you think she *really* expected him to marry her?"

"I am sure I don't know," said Newman. "Very likely she did; I have no doubt she is a grand woman." And he began to laugh again.

"I didn't mean that either," said Babcock; "I was only afraid that I might have seemed yesterday not to remember—not to consider; well, I think I will write to Percival about it."

And he had written to Percival (who answered him in a really impudent fashion), and he had reflected that it was, somehow, raw and reckless in Newman to assume in that off-hand manner that the young woman in Paris might be "grand." The brevity of Newman's judgments very often shocked and discomposed him. He had a way of damning people without farther appeal, or of pronouncing them capital company in the face of uncomfortable symptoms, which seemed unworthy of a man whose conscience had been properly cultivated. And yet poor Babcock liked him, and remembered that even if he was sometimes perplexing and painful, this was not a reason for giving him up. Goethe[1] recommended seeing human nature in the most various forms, and Mr. Babcock thought Goethe perfectly splendid. He often tried, in odd half-hours of conversation, to infuse into Newman a little of his own spiritual starch, but Newman's personal texture was too loose to admit of stiffening. His mind could no more hold principles than a sieve can hold water. He admired principles extremely, and thought Babcock a mighty fine little fellow for having so many. He accepted all that his high-strung companion offered him, and put them away in what he supposed to be a very safe place; but poor Babcock never afterwards recognised his gifts among the articles that Newman had in daily use.

They travelled together through Germany and into Switzerland, where for three or four weeks they trudged over passes and lounged upon blue lakes. At last they crossed the Simplon[2] and made their way to Venice. Mr. Babcock had become gloomy and even a trifle irritable; he seemed moody, absent, preoccupied; he got his plans into a tangle, and talked one moment of doing one thing and the next of doing another. Newman led his usual life, made acquaintances, took his ease in the galleries and churches, spent an unconscionable amount of time in strolling in the Piazza San Marco,[3] bought a great many bad pictures, and for a fortnight

1. Johann Wolfgang von Goethe (1749–1832), German poet, novelist, and scientist, author of *Dichtung and Wahrheit* (1811), *Faust* (1808), and the historical drama *Egmont* (1788).

2. A famous pass in the Alps between Switzerland and Italy.

3. The principal plaza in Venice, at St. Mark's Church.

enjoyed Venice grossly. One evening, coming back to his inn, he found Babcock waiting for him in the little garden beside it. The young man walked up to him, looking very dismal, thrust out his hand, and said with solemnity that he was afraid they must part. Newman expressed his surprise and regret, and asked why a parting had become necessary. "Don't be afraid I'm tired of you," he said.

"You are not tired of me?" demanded Babcock, fixing him with his clear gray eye.

"Why the deuce should I be? You are a very plucky fellow. Besides, I don't grow tired of things."

"We don't understand each other," said the young minister.

"Don't I understand you?" cried Newman. "Why, I hoped I did. But what if I don't; where's the harm?"

"I don't understand *you*," said Babcock. And he sat down and rested his head on his hand, and looked up mournfully at his immeasurable friend.

"Oh Lord, I don't mind that!" cried Newman, with a laugh.

"But it's very distressing to me. It keeps me in a state of unrest. It irritates me; I can't settle anything. I don't think it's good for me."

"You worry too much; that's what's the matter with you," said Newman.

"Of course it must seem so to you. You think I take things too hard, and I think you take things too easily. We can never agree."

"But we have agreed very well all along."

"No, I haven't agreed," said Babcock, shaking his head. "I am very uncomfortable. I ought to have separated from you a month ago."

"Oh, horrors! I'll agree to anything!" cried Newman.

Mr. Babcock buried his head in both hands. At last, looking up, "I don't think you appreciate my position," he said. "I try to arrive at the truth about everything. And then you go too fast. For me, you are too passionate, too extravagant. I feel as if I ought to go over all this ground we have traversed again, by myself, alone. I am afraid I have made a great many mistakes."

"Oh, you needn't give so many reasons," said Newman. "You are simply tired of my company. You have a good right to be."

"No, no, I am not tired!" cried the pestered young divine. "It is very wrong to be tired."

"I give it up!" laughed Newman. "But of course it will never do to go on making mistakes. Go your way, by all means. I shall miss you; but you have seen I make friends very easily. You will be lonely yourself; but drop me a line, when you feel like it, and I will wait for you anywhere."

"I think I will go back to Milan. I am afraid I didn't do justice to Luini."[4]

"Poor Luini!" said Newman.

"I mean that I am afraid I over-estimated him. I don't think that he is a painter of the first rank."

"Luini?" Newman exclaimed; "why, he's enchanting—he's magnificent! There is something in his genius that is like a beautiful woman. It gives one the same feeling."

Mr. Babcock frowned and winced. And it must be added that this was, for Newman, an unusually metaphysical flight; but in passing through Milan he had taken a great fancy to the painter. "There you are again!" said Mr. Babcock. "Yes, we had better separate." And on the morrow he retraced his steps and proceeded to tone down his impressions of the great Lombard[5] artist.

A few days afterwards Newman received a note from his late companion which ran as follows:

> "My dear Mr. Newman,—I am afraid that my conduct at Venice, a week ago, seemed to you strange and ungrateful, and I wish to explain my position, which, as I said at the time, I do not think you appreciate. I had long had it on my mind to propose that we should part company, and this step was not really so abrupt as it seemed. In the first place, you know, I am travelling in Europe on funds supplied by my congregation, who kindly offered me a vacation and an opportunity to enrich my mind with the treasures of nature and art in the Old World. I feel, therefore, as if I ought to use my time to the very best advantage. I have a high sense of responsibility. You appear to care only for the pleasure of the hour, and you give yourself up to it with a violence which I confess I am not able to emulate. I feel as if I must arrive at some conclusion and fix my belief on certain points. Art and life seem to me intensely serious things, and in our travels in Europe we should especially remember the immense seriousness of Art. You seem to hold that if a thing amuses you for the moment, that is all you need ask for it; and your relish for mere amusement is also much higher than mine. You put, moreover, a kind of reckless confidence into your pleasure which at times, I confess, has seemed to me—shall I say it?—almost cynical. Your way at any rate is not my way, and it is unwise that we should attempt any longer to pull together. And yet, let me add, that I know there is a great deal to be said for your way; I have felt its attraction, in your society, very strongly. But for this I should have left you long ago. But I was so perplexed. I hope I have not done wrong. I feel as if I had a

4. Bernardino Luini (ca. 1480–1532), Italian painter of the school of Leonardo da Vinci.

5. Luini was born in Lombardy, a region of Northern Italy.

great deal of lost time to make up. I beg you take all this as I mean it, which, Heaven knows, is not invidiously. I have a great personal esteem for you, and hope that some day, when I have recovered my balance, we shall meet again. I hope you will continue to enjoy your travels; only *do* remember that Life and Art *are* extremely serious. Believe me your sincere friend and well-wisher, BENJAMIN BABCOCK.

"P.S.—I am greatly perplexed by Luini."

This letter produced in Newman's mind a singular mixture of exhilaration and awe. At first, Mr. Babcock's tender conscience seemed to him a capital farce, and his travelling back to Milan only to get into a deeper muddle appeared, as the reward of his pedantry, exquisitely and ludicrously just. Then Newman reflected that these are mighty mysteries; that possibly he himself was indeed that baleful and barely mentionable thing, a cynic, and that his manner of considering the treasures of art and the privileges of life was probably very base and immoral. Newman had a great contempt for immorality, and that evening, for a good half hour, as he sat watching the star-sheen on the warm Adriatic,[6] he felt rebuked and depressed. He was at a loss how to answer Babcock's letter. His good nature checked his resenting the young minister's lofty admonitions, and his tough, inelastic sense of humour forbade his taking them seriously. He wrote no answer at all, but a day or two afterward he found in a curiosity-shop a grotesque little statuette in ivory, of the sixteenth century, which he sent off to Babcock without a commentary. It represented a gaunt, ascetic-looking monk, in a tattered gown and cowl, kneeling with clasped hands and pulling a portentously long face. It was a wonderfully delicate piece of carving, and in a moment, through one of the rents of his gown, you espied a fat capon hung round the monk's waist. In Newman's intention what did the figure symbolise? Did it mean that he was going to try to be as "high-toned" as the monk looked at first, but that he feared he should succeed no better than the friar, on a closer inspection, proved to have done? It is not supposable that he intended a satire upon Babcock's own asceticism, for this would have been a truly cynical stroke. He made his late companion, at any rate, a very valuable little present.

Newman, on leaving Venice, went through the Tyrol[7] to Vienna, and then returned westward, through Southern Germany. The autumn found him at Baden-Baden,[8] where he spent several weeks. The place was charming, and he was in no hurry to depart; besides, he was looking about him and deciding what to do for the winter.

6. The sea between Italy and the Balkan Peninsula.
7. An alpine province of Austria, bordering on northern Italy.
8. A resort in the Black Forest, in southwestern Germany.

His summer had been very full, and as he sat under the great trees beside the miniature river that trickles past the Baden flower-beds, he slowly rummaged it over. He had seen and done a great deal, enjoyed and observed a great deal; he felt older, and yet he felt younger too. He remembered Mr. Babcock and his desire to form conclusions, and he remembered also that he had profited very little by his friend's exhortation to cultivate the same respectable habit. Could he not scrape together a few conclusions? Baden-Baden was the prettiest place he had seen yet, and orchestral music in the evening, under the stars, was decidedly a great institution. This was one of his conclusions! But he went on to reflect that he had done very wisely to pull up stakes and come abroad; this seeing of the world was a very interesting thing. He had learned a great deal; he couldn't say just what, but he had it there under his hat-band. He had done what he wanted; he had seen the great things, and he had given his mind a chance to "improve," if it would. He cheerfully believed that it had improved. Yes, this seeing of the world was very pleasant, and he would willingly do a little more of it. Thirty-six years old as he was, he had a handsome stretch of life before him yet, and he need not begin to count his weeks. Where should he take the world next? I have said he remembered the eyes of the lady whom he had found standing in Mrs. Tristram's drawing-room; four months had elapsed, and he had not forgotten them yet. He had looked—he had made a point of looking—into a great many other eyes in the interval, but the only ones he thought of now were Madame de Cintré's. If he wanted to see more of the world, should he find it in Madame de Cintré's eyes? He would certainly find something there, call it this world or the next. Throughout these rather formless meditations he sometimes thought of his past life and the long array of years (they had begun so early) during which he had had nothing in his head but "enterprise." They seemed far away now, for his present attitude was more than a holiday, it was almost a rupture. He had told Tristram that the pendulum was swinging back, and it appeared that the backward swing had not yet ended. Still "enterprise," which was over in the other quarter, wore to his mind a different aspect at different hours. In its train a thousand forgotten episodes came trooping back into his memory. Some of them he looked complacently enough in the face; from some he averted his head. They were old efforts, old exploits, antiquated examples of "smartness" and sharpness. Some of them, as he looked at them, he felt decidedly proud of; he admired himself as if he had been looking at another man. And, in fact, many of the qualities that make a great deed were there; the decision, the resolution, the courage, the celerity, the clear eye, and the strong hand. Of certain other achievements it would be going too far to say that he was ashamed of them, for Newman had never had a stomach for dirty work. He was blessed with a natural impulse to disfigure with a direct, unreasoning blow the comely visage of temptation. And, certainly, in no man could a want of integrity have been less excusable. Newman knew the crooked from the straight at a glance, and the former had cost him, first and last, a great many moments of lively disgust. But none the less some of his memories seemed to wear at present a rather graceless and sordid mien, and it struck him that if he had never done anything very ugly, he had never, on the other hand, done anything particularly beautiful. He had spent his years in the unremitting effort to add thousands to thousands, and, now that he stood well outside of it, the business of money-getting appeared extremely dry and sterile. It is very well to sneer at money-getting after you have filled your pockets, and Newman, it may be said, should have begun somewhat earlier to moralise thus delicately. To this it may be answered that he might have made another fortune, if he chose; and we ought to add that he was not exactly moralising. It had come back to him simply that what he had been looking at all the summer was a very rich and beautiful world, and that it had not all been made by sharp railroad men and stock-brokers.

During his stay at Baden-Baden he received a letter from Mrs. Tristram, scolding him for the scanty tidings he had sent to his friends of the Avenue d'Iéna, and begging to be definitely informed that he had not concocted any horrid scheme for wintering in outlying regions, but was coming back sanely and promptly to the most comfortable city in the world. Newman's answer ran as follows:

"I supposed you knew I was a miserable letter-writer, and didn't expect anything of me. I don't think I have written twenty letters of pure friendship in my whole life; in America I conducted my correspondence altogether by telegrams. This is a letter of pure friendship; you have got hold of a curiosity, and I hope you will value it. You want to know everything that has happened to me these three months. The best way to tell you, I think, would be to send you my half-dozen guide-books, with my pencil-marks in the margin. Wherever you find a scratch, or a cross, or a 'Beautiful' or a 'So true!' or a 'Too thin!' you may know that I have had a sensation of some sort or other. That has been about my history, ever since I left you. Belgium, Holland, Switzerland, Germany, Italy—I have been through the whole list, and I don't think I am any the worse for it. I know more about Madonnas and church-steeples than I supposed any man could. I have seen some very pretty things, and shall perhaps talk them over this winter, by your fireside. You see, my face is not altogether set against Paris. I have had all kinds of plans and visions, but your letter has blown most of them away. '*L'appétit vient en mangeant*,'[9] says the French proverb, and I find that the more I see of the world the more I want to see. Now that I am in the shafts, why shouldn't I trot to the end of the course? Sometimes I think of the far East, and keep rolling the names of Eastern cities under my tongue; Damascus and Bagdad, Medina and Mecca. I spent a week last month in the company of a returned missionary, who told me I ought to be ashamed to be loafing about Europe when there are such big things to be seen out there. I do want to explore, but I think I would rather explore over in the Rue de l'Université. Do you ever hear from that pretty lady? If you can get her to promise she will be at home the next time I call, I will go back to Paris straight. I am more than ever in the state of mind I told you about that evening; I want a first-class wife. I have kept an eye on all the pretty girls I have come across this summer, but none of them came up to my notion, or anywhere near it. I should have enjoyed all this a thousand times more if I had had the lady just mentioned by my side. The nearest approach to her was a Unitarian minister from Boston, who very soon demanded a separation, for incompatibility of temper. He told me I was low-minded, immoral, a devotee of 'art for art'—whatever that is: all of which greatly afflicted me, for he was really a sweet little fellow. But shortly afterwards I met an Englishman, with whom I struck up an acquaintance which at first seemed to promise well—a very bright man, who writes in the London papers and knows Paris nearly as well as Tristram. We knocked about for a week together, but he very soon gave me up in disgust. I was too virtuous by half; I was too stern a moralist. He told me, in a friendly way, that I was cursed with a conscience; that I judged things like a Methodist and talked about them like an old lady. This was rather bewildering. Which of my two critics was I to believe? I didn't worry about it, and very soon made up my mind they were both idiots. But there is one thing in which no one will ever have the impudence to pretend I am wrong; that is, in being your faithful friend,

C.N."

Chapter VI

Newman gave up Damascus and Bagdad and returned to Paris before the autumn was over. He established himself in some rooms selected for him by Tom Tristram, in accordance with the latter's estimate of what he called his social position. When Newman learned that his social position was to be taken into account, he professed himself utterly incompetent, and begged Tristram to relieve him of the care. "I didn't know I had a social position," he

9. "The appetite comes while one is eating."

said, "and if I have, I haven't the smallest idea what it is. Isn't a social position knowing some two or three thousand people and inviting them to dinner? I know you and your wife and little old Mr. Nioche, who gave me French lessons last spring. Can I invite you to dinner to meet each other? If I can, you must come to-morrow."

"That is not very grateful to me," said Mrs. Tristram, "who introduced you last year to every creature I know."

"So you did; I had quite forgotten. But I thought you wanted me to forget," said Newman, with that tone of simple deliberateness which frequently marked his utterance, and which an observer would not have known whether to pronounce a somewhat mysteriously humorous affectation of ignorance or a modest aspiration to knowledge; "you told me you disliked them all."

"Ah, the way you remember what I say is at least very flattering. But in future," added Mrs. Tristram, "pray forget all the wicked things and remember only the good ones. It will be easily done, and it will not fatigue your memory. But I forewarn you that if you trust my husband to pick out your rooms, you are in for something hideous."

"Hideous, darling?" cried Tristram.

"To-day I must say nothing wicked; otherwise I should use stronger language."

"What do you think she would say, Newman?" asked Tristram. "If she really tried, now? She can express displeasure, volubly, in two or three languages; that's what it is to be intellectual. It gives her the start of me completely, for I can't swear, for the life of me, except in English. When I get mad I have to fall back on our dear old mother tongue. There's nothing like it, after all."

Newman declared that he knew nothing about tables and chairs, and that he would accept, in the way of a lodging, with his eyes shut, anything that Tristram should offer him. This was partly pure veracity on our hero's part, but it was also partly charity. He knew that to pry about and look at rooms, and make people open windows, and poke into sofas with his cane, and gossip with landladies, and ask who lived above and who below—he knew that this was of all pastimes the dearest to Tristram's heart, and he felt the more disposed to put it in his way as he was conscious that, as regards his obliging friend, he had suffered the warmth of ancient good-fellowship somewhat to abate. Besides, he had no taste for upholstery; he had even no very exquisite sense of comfort or convenience. He had a relish for luxury and splendour, but it was satisfied by rather gross contrivances. He scarcely knew a hard chair from a soft one, and he possessed a talent for stretching his legs which quite dispensed with adventitious facilities. His idea of comfort was to inhabit very large rooms, have a great many of them, and be conscious of their possessing a number of patented mechanical devices—half of which he should never have occasion to use. The apartments should be light and brilliant and lofty; he had once said that he liked rooms in which you wanted to keep your hat on. For the rest, he was satisfied with the assurance of any respectable person that everything was "handsome." Tristram accordingly secured for him an apartment to which this epithet might be lavishly applied. It was situated on the Boulevard Haussmann,[1] on a first-floor, and consisted of a series of rooms, gilded from floor to ceiling a foot thick, draped in various light shades of satin, and chiefly furnished with mirrors and clocks. Newman thought them magnificent, thanked Tristram heartily, immediately took possession, and had one of his trunks standing for three months in his drawing-room.

One day Mrs. Tristram told him that her beautiful friend, Madame de Cintré, had returned from the country; that she had met her three days before, coming out of the Church of St. Sulpice; she herself having journeyed to that distant quarter in quest of an obscure lace-mender, of whose skill she had heard high praise.

"And how were those eyes?" Newman asked.

"Those eyes were red with weeping, if you please!" said Mrs. Tristram. "She had been to confession."

"It doesn't tally with your account of her," said Newman, "that she should have sins to confess."

"They were not sins; they were sufferings."

"How do you know that?"

"She asked me to come and see her; I went this morning."

"And what does she suffer from?"

"I didn't ask her. With her, somehow, one is very discreet. But I guessed, easily enough. She suffers from her wicked old mother and her Grand Turk[2] of a brother. They persecute her. But I can almost forgive them, because, as I told you, she is a saint, and a persecution is all that she needs to bring out her saintliness and make her perfect."

"That's a comfortable theory for her. I hope you will never impart it to the old folks. Why does she let them bully her? Is she not her own mistress?"

"Legally, yes, I suppose; but morally, no. In France you must never say Nay to your mother, whatever she requires of you. She may be the most abominable old woman in the world, and make

1. A principal thoroughfare in Paris, named after Baron Georges Eugène Haussmann, the city planner of modern Paris.

2. Tyrant.

your life a purgatory; but after all she is *ma mère*,[3] and you have no right to judge her. You have simply to obey. The thing has a fine side to it. Madame de Cintré bows her head and folds her wings."

"Can't she at least make her brother leave off?"

"Her brother is the *chef de la famille*,[4] as they say; he is the head of the clan. With those people the family is everything; you must act, not for your own pleasure, but for the advantage of the family."

"I wonder what *my* family would like me to do!" exclaimed Tristram.

"I wish you had one!" said his wife.

"But what do they want to get out of that poor lady?" Newman asked.

"Another marriage. They are not rich, and they want to bring more money into the family."

"There's your chance, my boy!" said Tristram.

"And Madame de Cintré objects," Newman continued.

"She has been sold once; she naturally objects to being sold again. It appears that the first time they made rather a poor bargain; M. de Cintré left a scanty property."

"And to whom do they want to marry her now?"

"I thought it best not to ask; but you may be sure it is to some horrid old nabob,[5] or to some dissipated little duke."

"There's Mrs. Tristram, as large as life!" cried her husband. "Observe the richness of her imagination. She has not asked a single question—it's vulgar to ask questions—and yet she knows everything.[6] She has the history of Madame de Cintré's marriage at her fingers' ends. She has seen the lovely Claire on her knees, with loosened tresses and streaming eyes, and the rest of them standing over her with spikes and goads and red-hot irons, ready to come down on her if she refuses the tipsy duke. The simple truth is that they have made a fuss about her milliner's bill or refused her an opera-box."

Newman looked from Tristram to his wife with a certain mistrust in each direction. "Do you really mean," he asked of Mrs. Tristram, "that your friend is being forced into an unhappy marriage?"

"I think it extremely probable. Those people are very capable of that sort of thing."

3. "My mother."
4. "Head of the family."
5. A personage of great wealth.
6. A fair description of how James's "super-subtle fry" in the later novels of the "major phase" guess the unseen from the seen, trace the implication of things, and judge the whole piece by the pattern. Cf. James's *The Art of Fiction*.

"It is like something in a play," said Newman; "that dark old house over there looks as if wicked things had been done in it, and might be done again."

"They have a still darker old house in the country, Madame de Cintré tells me, and there, during the summer, this scheme must have been hatched."

"*Must* have been; mind that!" said Tristram.

"After all," suggested Newman, after a silence, "she may be in trouble about something else."

"If it is something else, then it is something worse," said Mrs. Tristram, with rich decision.

Newman was silent awhile, and seemed lost in meditation. "Is it possible," he asked at last, "that they do that sort of thing over here? that helpless women are bullied into marrying men they hate?"

"Helpless women, all over the world, have a hard time of it," said Mrs. Tristram. "There is plenty of bullying everywhere."

"A great deal of that kind goes on in New York," said Tristram. "Girls are bullied or coaxed or bribed, or all three together, into marrying nasty fellows. There is no end of that always going on in the Fifth Avenue, and other bad things besides. The Mysteries of the Fifth Avenue! Someone ought to show them up."

"I don't believe it!" said Newman, very gravely. "I don't believe that, in America, girls are ever subjected to compulsion. I don't believe there have been a dozen cases of it since the country began."

"Listen to the voice of the spread eagle!"[7] cried Tristram.

"The spread eagle ought to use his wings," said Mrs. Tristram. "Fly to the rescue of Madame de Cintré!"

"To her rescue?"

"Pounce down, seize her in your talons, and carry her off. Marry her yourself."

Newman, for some moments, answered nothing; but presently, "I should suppose she had heard enough of marrying," he said. "The kindest way to treat her would be to admire her, and yet never to speak of it. But that sort of thing is infamous," he added; "it makes me feel savage to hear of it."

He heard of it, however, more than once afterward. Mrs. Tristram again saw Madame de Cintré, and again found her looking very sad. But on these occasions there had been no tears; her beautiful eyes were clear and still. "She is cold, calm, and hopeless," Mrs. Tristram declared, and she added that on her mentioning that her friend Mr. Newman was again in Paris and was faithful in his desire to make Madame de Cintré's acquaintance, this

7. A parodic symbol of the United States.

lovely woman had found a smile in her despair, and declared that she was sorry to have missed his visit in the spring and that she hoped he had not lost courage. "I told her something about you," said Mrs. Tristram.

"That's a comfort," said Newman, placidly. "I like people to know about me."

A few days after this, one dusky autumn afternoon, he went again to the Rue de l'Université. The early evening had closed in as he applied for admittance at the stoutly guarded Hôtel de Bellegarde.[8] He was told that Madame de Cintré was at home; he crossed the court, entered the farther door, and was conducted through a vestibule, vast, dim, and cold, up a broad stone staircase with an ancient iron balustrade, to an apartment on the second-floor. Announced and ushered in, he found himself in a sort of panelled boudoir, at one end of which a lady and gentleman were seated before the fire. The gentleman was smoking a cigarette; there was no light in the room save that of a couple of candles and the glow from the hearth. Both persons rose to welcome Newman, who, in the firelight, recognised Madame de Cintré. She gave him her hand with a smile which seemed in itself an illumination, and, pointing to her companion, said softly, "My brother." The gentleman offered Newman a frank, friendly greeting, and our hero then perceived him to be the young man who had spoken to him in the court of the hotel on his former visit and who had struck him as a good fellow.

"Mrs. Tristram has spoken to me a great deal of you," said Madame de Cintré gently, as she resumed her former place.

Newman, after he had seated himself, began to consider what, in truth, was his errand. He had an unusual, unexpected sense of having wandered into a strange corner of the world. He was not given, as a general thing, to anticipating danger, or forecasting disaster, and he had had no social tremors on this particular occasion. He was not timid and he was not impudent. He felt too kindly toward himself to be the one, and too good-naturedly toward the rest of the world to be the other. But his native shrewdness sometimes placed his ease of temper at its mercy; with every disposition to take things simply, it was obliged to perceive that some things were not so simple as others. He felt as one does in missing a step, in an ascent, where one expected to find it. This strange, pretty woman, sitting in fireside talk with her brother, in the gray depths of her inhospitable-looking house—what had he to say to her? She seemed enveloped in a sort of fantastic privacy; on what grounds had he pulled away the curtain? For a moment he felt as if he had

8. The family's private residence; not a "hotel" in the American sense.

plunged into some medium as deep as the ocean, and as if he must exert himself to keep from sinking. Meanwhile he was looking at Madame de Cintré, and she was settling herself in her chair and drawing in her long dress and turning her face towards him. Their eyes met; a moment afterwards she looked away and motioned to her brother to put a log on the fire. But the moment, and the glance which traversed it, had been sufficient to relieve Newman of the first and the last fit of personal embarrassment he was ever to know. He performed the movement which was so frequent with him, and which was always a sort of symbol of his taking mental possession of a scene—he extended his legs. The impression Madame de Cintré had made upon him on their first meeting came back in an instant; it had been deeper than he knew. She was pleasing, she was interesting; he had opened a book and the first lines held his attention.

She asked him several questions: how lately he had seen Mrs. Tristram, how long he had been in Paris, how long he expected to remain there, how he liked it. She spoke English without an accent, or rather with that distinctively British accent which, on his arrival in Europe, had struck Newman as an altogether foreign tongue, but which, in women, he had come to like extremely. Here and there Madame de Cintré's utterance had a faint shade of strangeness, but at the end of ten minutes Newman found himself waiting for these soft roughnesses. He enjoyed them and he marvelled to see that gross thing, error, brought down to so fine a point.

"You have a beautiful country," said Madame de Cintré, presently.

"Oh, magnificent!" said Newman. "You ought to see it."

"I shall never see it," said Madame de Cintré with a smile.

"Why not?" asked Newman.

"I don't travel; especially so far."

"But you go away sometimes; you are not always here?"

"I go away in summer, a little way, to the country."

Newman wanted to ask her something more, something personal, he hardly knew what. "Don't you find it rather—rather quiet here?" he said; "so far from the street?" Rather "gloomy," he was going to say, but he reflected that that would be impolite.

"Yes, it is very quiet," said Madame de Cintré; "but we like that."

"Ah, you like that," repeated Newman slowly.

"Besides, I have lived here all my life."

"Lived here all your life," said Newman, in the same way.

"I was born here, and my father was born here before me, and my grandfather, and my great-grandfathers. Were they not, Valentin?" and she appealed to her brother.

"Yes, it's a family habit to be born here!" the young man said with a laugh, and rose and threw the remnant of his cigarette into the fire, and then remained leaning against the chimney-piece. An observer would have perceived that he wished to take a better look at Newman, whom he covertly examined, while he stood, stroking his moustache.

"Your house is tremendously old, then," said Newman.

"How old is it, brother?" asked Madame de Cintré.

The young man took the two candles from the mantelshelf, lifted one high in each hand, and looked up toward the cornice of the room, above the chimney-piece. This latter feature of the apartment was of white marble, and in the familiar rococo style of the last century; but above it was a panelling of an earlier date, quaintly carved, painted white, and gilded here and there. The white had turned to yellow, and the gilding was tarnished. On the top, the figures ranged themselves into a sort of shield, on which an armorial device was cut. Above it, in relief, was a date—1627. "There you have it," said the young man. "That is old or new, according to your point of view."

"Well, over here," said Newman, "one's point of view gets shifted round considerably." And he threw back his head and looked about the room. "Your house is of a very curious style of architecture," he said.

"Are you interested in architecture?" asked the young man at the chimney-piece.

"Well, I took the trouble, this summer," said Newman, "to examine—as well as I can calculate—some four hundred and seventy churches. Do you call that interested?"

"Perhaps you are interested in theology," said the young man.

"Not particularly. Are you a Roman Catholic, madam?" And he turned to Madame de Cintré.

"Yes, sir," she answered, gravely.

Newman was struck with the gravity of her tone; he threw back his head and began to look round the room again. "Had you never noticed that number up there?" he presently asked.

She hesitated a moment, and then, "In former years," she said.

Her brother had been watching Newman's movement. "Perhaps you would like to examine the house," he said.

Newman slowly brought down his eyes and looked at him; he had a vague impression that the young man at the chimney-piece was inclined to irony. He was a handsome fellow, his face wore a smile, his moustachios were curled up at the ends, and there was a little dancing gleam in his eye. "Damn his French impudence!" Newman was on the point of saying to himself. "What the deuce is he grinning at?" He glanced at Madame de Cintré; she was sitting with her eyes fixed on the floor. She raised them, they met his, and she looked at her brother. Newman turned again to this young man and observed that he strikingly resembled his sister. This was in his favour, and our hero's first impression of the Count Valentin, moreover, had been agreeable. His mistrust expired, and he said he would be very glad to see the house.

The young man gave a frank laugh, and laid his hand on one of the candlesticks. "Good, good!" he exclaimed. "Come, then."

But Madame de Cintré rose quickly and grasped his arm. "Ah, Valentin!" she said. "What do you mean to do?"

"To show Mr. Newman the house. It will be very amusing."

She kept her hand on his arm and turned to Newman with a smile. "Don't let him take you," she said; "you will not find it amusing. It is a musty old house like any other."

"It is full of curious things," said the count, resisting. "Besides, I want to do it; it is a rare chance."

"You are very wicked, brother," Madame de Cintré answered.

"Nothing venture, nothing have!" cried the young man. "Will you come?"

Madame de Cintré stepped toward Newman, gently clasping her hands and smiling softly. "Would you not prefer my society, here, by my fire, to stumbling about dark passages after my brother?"

"A hundred times!" said Newman. "We will see the house some other day."

The young man put down his candlestick with mock solemnity, and shaking his head, "Ah, you have defeated a great scheme, sir!" he said.

"A scheme? I don't understand," said Newman.

"You would have played your part in it all the better. Perhaps some day I shall have a chance to explain it."

"Be quiet, and ring for the tea,' said Madame de Cintré.

The young man obeyed, and presently a servant brought in the tea, placed the tray on a small table, and departed. Madame de Cintré, from her place, busied herself with making it. She had but just begun, when the door was thrown open and a lady rushed in, making a loud rustling sound. She stared at Newman, gave a little nod and a "Monsieur!" and then quickly approached Madame de Cintré, and presented her forehead to be kissed. Madame de Cintré saluted her, and continued to make tea. The new-comer was young and pretty, it seemed to Newman; she wore her bonnet and cloak, and a train of royal proportions. She began to talk rapidly in French. "Oh, give me some tea, my beautiful one, for the love of God! I'm exhausted, mangled, massacred." Newman found himself quite unable to follow her; she spoke much less distinctly than M. Nioche.

"That is my sister-in-law," said the Count Valentin, leaning towards him.

"She is very pretty," said Newman.

"Exquisite," answered the young man, and this time, again, Newman suspected him of irony.

His sister-in-law came round to the other side of the fire with her cup of tea in her hand, holding it out at arm's-length, so that she might not spill it on her dress, and uttering little cries of alarm. She placed the cup on the mantelshelf and began to unpin her veil and pull off her gloves, looking meanwhile at Newman.

"Is there anything I can do for you, my dear lady?" the Count Valentin asked, in a sort of mock-caressing tone.

"Present monsieur," said his sister-in-law.

The young man answered, "Mr. Newman!"

"I can't curtsy to you, monsieur, or I shall spill my tea," said the lady. "So Claire receives strangers, like that?" she added in a low voice, in French, to her brother-in-law.

"Apparently!" he answered, with a smile. Newman stood a moment, and then he approached Madame de Cintré. She looked up at him as if she were thinking of something to say. But she seemed to think of nothing; so she simply smiled. He sat down near her and she handed him a cup of tea. For a few moments they talked about that, and meanwhile he looked at her. He remembered what Mrs. Tristram had told him of her "perfection," and of her having, in combination, all the brilliant things that he dreamed of finding. This made him observe her not only without mistrust, but without uneasy conjectures; the presumption, from the first moment he looked at her, had been in her favour. And yet, if she was beautiful, it was not a dazzling beauty. She was tall and moulded in long lines; she had thick, fair hair, a wide forehead, and features with a sort of harmonious irregularity. Her clear gray eyes were strikingly expressive; they were both gentle and intelligent, and Newman liked them immensely; but they had not those depths of splendour—those many-coloured rays—which illumine the brow of famous beauties. Madame de Cintré was rather thin, and she looked younger than probably she was. In her whole person there was something both youthful and subdued, slender and yet ample, tranquil yet shy; a mixture of immaturity and repose, of innocence and dignity. What had Tristram meant, Newman wondered, by calling her proud? She was certainly not proud now, to him; or if she was, it was of no use, it was lost upon him; she must pile it up higher if she expected him to mind it. She was a beautiful woman, and it was very easy to get on with her. Was she a countess, a *marquise*, a kind of historical formation? Newman, who had rarely heard these words used, had never been at pains to attach any particular image to them; but they occurred to him now and seemed charged with a sort of melodious meaning. They signified something fair and softly bright, that had easy motions and spoke very agreeably.

"Have you many friends in Paris; do you go out?" asked Madame de Cintré, who had at last thought of something to say.

"Do you mean do I dance, and all that?"

"Do you go *dans le monde*,[9] as we say?"

"I have seen a good many people. Mrs. Tristram has taken me about. I do whatever she tells me."

"By yourself, you are not fond of amusements?"

"Oh yes, of some sorts. I am not fond of dancing, and that sort of thing; I am too old and sober. But I want to be amused; I came to Europe for that."

"But you can be amused in America, too."

"I couldn't; I was always at work. But, after all, that was my amusement."

At this moment Madame de Bellegarde came back for another cup of tea, accompanied by the Count Valentin. Madame de Cintré, when she had served her, began to talk again with Newman, and recalling what he had last said, "In your own country you were very much occupied?" she asked.

"I was in business. I have been in business since I was fifteen years old."

"And what was your business?" asked Madame de Bellegarde, who was decidedly not so pretty as Madame de Cintré.

"I have been in everything," said Newman. "At one time I sold leather; at one time I manufactured wash-tubs."

Madame de Bellegarde made a little grimace. "Leather? I don't like that. Wash-tubs are better. I prefer the smell of soap. I hope at least they made your fortune." She rattled this off with the air of a woman who had the reputation of saying everything that came into her head, and with a strong French accent.

Newman had spoken with cheerful seriousness, but Madame de Bellegarde's tone made him go on, after a meditative pause, with a certain light grimness of jocularity. "No, I lost money on wash-tubs, but I came out pretty square on leather."

"I have made up my mind, after all," said Madame de Bellegarde, "that the great point is—how do you call it?—to come out square. I am on my knees to money; I don't deny it. If you have it, I ask no questions. For that I am a real democrat—like you, monsieur. Madame de Cintré is very proud; but I find that one gets much more pleasure in this sad life if one doesn't look too close."

9. **"Into society."**

"Just Heaven, dear madam, how you go at it," said the Count Valentin, lowering his voice.

"He's a man one can speak to, I suppose, since my sister receives him," the lady answered. "Besides, it's very true; those are my ideas."

"Ah, you call them ideas," murmured the young man.

"But Mrs. Tristram told me you had been in the army—in your war," said Madame de Cintré.

"Yes, but that is not business!" said Newman.

"Very true!" said M. de Bellegarde. "Otherwise perhaps I should not be penniless."

"Is it true," asked Newman in a moment, "that you are so proud? I had already heard it."

Madame de Cintré smiled. "Do you find me so?"

"Oh," said Newman, "I am no judge. If you are proud with me, you will have to tell me. Otherwise I shall not know it."

Madame de Cintré began to laugh. "That would be pride in a sad position!" she said.

"It would be partly," Newman went on, "because I shouldn't want to know it. I want you to treat me well."

Madame de Cintré, whose laugh had ceased, looked at him with her head half averted, as if she feared what he was going to say.

"Mrs. Tristram told you the literal truth," he went on; "I want very much to know you. I didn't come here simply to call to-day; I came in the hope that you might ask me to come again."

"Oh, pray come often," said Madame de Cintré.

"But will you be at home?" Newman insisted. Even to himself he seemed a trifle "pushing," but he was, in truth, a trifle excited.

"I hope so!" said Madame de Cintré.

Newman got up. "Well, we shall see," he said, smoothing his hat with his coat-cuff.

"Brother," said Madame de Cintré, "invite Mr. Newman to come again."

The Count Valentin looked at our hero from head to foot with his peculiar smile, in which impudence and urbanity seemed perplexingly commingled. "Are you a brave man?" he asked, eyeing him askance.

"Well, I hope so," said Newman.

"I rather suspect so. In that case, come again."

"Ah, what an invitation!" murmured Madame de Cintré, with something painful in her smile.

"Oh, I want Mr. Newman to come—particularly," said the young man. "It will give me great pleasure. I shall be desolate if I miss one of his visits. But I maintain he must be brave. A stout heart, sir!" And he offered Newman his hand.

"I shall not come to see you; I shall come to see Madame de Cintré," said Newman.

"You will need all the more courage."

"Ah, Valentin!" said Madame de Cintré, appealingly.

"Decidedly," cried Madame de Bellegarde, "I am the only person here capable of saying something polite! Come to see me; you will need no courage," she said.

Newman gave a laugh which was not altogether an assent, and took his leave. Madame de Cintré did not take up her sister's challenge to be gracious, but she looked with a certain troubled air at the retreating guest.

Chapter VII

One evening, very late, about a week after his visit to Madame de Cintré, Newman's servant brought him a card. It was that of young M. de Bellegarde. When, a few moments later, he went to receive his visitor, he found him standing in the middle of his great gilded parlour and eyeing it from cornice to carpet. M. de Bellegarde's face, it seemed to Newman, expressed a sense of lively entertainment. "What the devil is he laughing at now?" our hero asked himself. But he put the question without acrimony, for he felt that Madame de Cintré's brother was a good fellow, and he had a presentiment that on this basis of good fellowship they were destined to understand each other. Only, if there was anything to laugh at, he wished to have a glimpse of it too.

"To begin with," said the young man, as he extended his hand, "have I come too late?"

"Too late for what?" asked Newman.

"To smoke a cigar with you."

"You would have to come early to do that," said Newman. "I don't smoke."

"Ah, you are a strong man!"

"But I keep cigars," Newman added. "Sit down."

"Surely, I may not smoke here," said M. de Bellegarde.

"What is the matter? Is the room too small?"

"It is too large. It is like smoking in a ball-room, or a church."

"That is what you were laughing at just now?" Newman asked; "the size of my room?"

"It is not size only," replied M. de Bellegarde, "but splendour, and harmony, and beauty of detail. It was the smile of admiration."

Newman looked at him a moment, and then, "So it *is* very ugly?" he inquired.

"Ugly, my dear sir? It is magnificent."

"That is the same thing, I suppose," said Newman. "Make yourself comfortable. Your coming to see me, I take it, is an act of friendship. You were not obliged to. Therefore, if anything around here amuses you, it will be all in a pleasant way. Laugh as loud as you please; I like to see my visitors cheerful. Only, I must make this request: that you explain the joke to me as soon as you can speak. I don't want to lose anything, myself."

M. de Bellegarde stared, with a look of unresentful perplexity. He laid his hand on Newman's sleeve and seemed on the point of saying something, but he suddenly checked himself, leaned back in his chair, and puffed at his cigar. At last, however, breaking silence, "Certainly," he said, "my coming to see you is an act of friendship. Nevertheless I was in a measure obliged to do so. My sister asked me to come, and a request from my sister is, for me, a law. I was near you, and I observed lights in what I supposed were your rooms. It was not a ceremonious hour for making a call, but I was not sorry to do something that would show I was not performing a mere ceremony."

"Well, here I am as large as life," said Newman, extending his legs.

"I don't know what you mean," the young man went on, "by giving me unlimited leave to laugh. Certainly I am a great laugher, and it is better to laugh too much than too little. But it is not in order that we may laugh together—or separately—that I have, I may say, sought your acquaintance. To speak with almost impudent frankness, you interest me!" All this was uttered by M. de Bellegarde with the modulated smoothness of the man of the world, and, in spite of his excellent English, of the Frenchman; but Newman, at the same time that he sat noting its harmonious flow, perceived that it was not mere mechanical urbanity. Decidedly, there was something in his visitor that he liked. M. de Bellegarde was a foreigner to his finger-tips, and if Newman had met him on a Western prairie he would have felt it proper to address him with a "How-d'ye-do, Mosseer?" But there was something in his physiognomy which seemed to cast a sort of aerial bridge over the impassable gulf produced by difference of race. He was below the middle height, and robust and agile in figure. Valentin de Bellegarde, Newman afterwards learned, had a mortal dread of the robustness overtaking the agility; he was afraid of growing stout; he was too short, as he said, to afford a belly. He rode and fenced and practiced gymnastics with unremitting zeal, and if you greeted him with a "How well you are looking!" he started and turned pale. In your *well* he read a grosser monosyllable. He had a round head, high above the ears, a crop of hair at once dense and silky, a broad, low forehead, a short nose, of the ironical and inquiring rather than of the dogmatic or sensitive cast, and a moustache as delicate as that of a page in a romance. He resembled his sister not in feature, but in the expression of his clear bright eye, completely void of introspection, and in the way he smiled. The great point in his face was that it was intensely alive—frankly, ardently, gallantly alive. The look of it was like a bell, of which the handle might have been in the young man's soul: at a touch of the handle it rang with a loud silver sound. There was something in his quick, light brown eye which assured you that he was not economising his consciousness. He was not living in a corner of it to spare the furniture of the rest. He was squarely encamped in the centre, and he was keeping open house. When he smiled, it was like the movement of a person who in emptying a cup turns it upside down: he gave you the last drop of his jollity. He inspired Newman with something of the same kindness that our hero used to feel in his earlier years for those of his companions who could perform strange and clever tricks—make their joints crack in queer places or whistle at the back of their mouths.

"My sister told me," M. de Bellegarde continued, "that I ought to come and remove the impression that I had taken such great pains to produce upon you; the impression that I am a lunatic. Did it strike you that I behaved very oddly the other day?"

"Rather so," said Newman.

"So my sister tells me." And M. de Bellegarde watched his host for a moment through his smoke-wreaths. "If that is the case, I think we had better let it stand. I didn't try to make you think I was a lunatic, at all; on the contrary, I wanted to produce a favourable impression. But if, after all, I made a fool of myself, it was the intention of Providence. I should injure myself by protesting too much, for I should seem to set up a claim for wisdom which, in the sequel of our acquaintance, I could by no means justify. Set me down as a lunatic with intervals of sanity."

"Oh, I guess you know what you are about," said Newman.

"When I am sane, I am very sane; that I admit," M. de Bellegarde answered. "But I didn't come here to talk about myself. I should like to ask you a few questions. You allow me?"

"Give me a specimen," said Newman.

"You live here all alone?"

"Absolutely. With whom should I live?"

"For the moment," said M. de Bellegarde with a smile, "I am asking questions, not answering them. You have come to Paris for your pleasure?"

Newman was silent awhile. Then, at last, "Everyone asks me that!" he said with his mild slowness. "It sounds so awfully foolish."

"But at any rate you had a reason."

"Oh, I came for my pleasure!" said Newman. "Though it is foolish, it is true."

"And you are enjoying it?"

Like any other good American, Newman thought it as well not to truckle to the foreigner. "Oh, so-so," he answered.

M. de Bellegarde puffed his cigar again in silence. "For myself," he said at last, "I am entirely at your service. Anything I can do for you I shall be very happy to do. Call upon me at your convenience. Is there anyone you desire to know—anything you wish to see? It is a pity you should not enjoy Paris."

"Oh, I do enjoy it!" said Newman, good-naturedly. "I'm much obliged to you."

"Honestly speaking," M. de Bellegarde went on, "there is something absurd to me in hearing myself make you these offers. They represent a great deal of good-will, but they represent little else. You are a successful man and I am a failure, and it's a turning of the tables to talk as if I could lend you a hand."

"In what way are you a failure?" asked Newman.

"Oh, I'm not a tragical failure!" cried the young man with a laugh. "I have not fallen from a height, and my fiasco has made no noise. You, evidently, are a success. You have made a fortune, you have built up an edifice, you are a financial, commercial power, you can travel about the world until you have found a soft spot, and lie down in it with the consciousness of having earned your rest. Is not that true? Well, imagine the exact reverse of all that, and you have me. I have done nothing—I can do nothing!"

"Why not?"

"It's a long story. Some day I will tell you. Meanwhile, I'm right, eh? You are a success? You have made a fortune? It's none of my business, but, in short, you are rich?"

"That's another thing that it sounds foolish to say," said Newman. "Hang it, no man is rich!"

"I have heard philosophers affirm," laughed M. de Bellegarde, "that no man was poor; but your formula strikes me as an improvement. As a general thing, I confess, I don't like successful people, and I find clever men who have made great fortunes very offensive. They tread on my toes; they make me uncomfortable. But as soon as I saw you, I said to myself, 'Ah, there is a man with whom I shall get on. He has the good-nature of success and none of the *morgue*;[1] he has not our confoundedly irritable French vanity.' In short, I took a fancy to you. We are very different, I'm sure; I don't believe there is a subject on which we think or feel

1. Arrogance.

alike. But I rather think we shall get on, for there is such a thing, you know, as being too different to quarrel."

"Oh, I never quarrel," said Newman.

"Never? Sometimes it's a duty—or at least it's a pleasure. Oh, I have had two or three delicious quarrels in my day!" and M. de Bellegarde's handsome smile assumed, at the memory of these incidents, an almost voluptuous intensity.

With the preamble embodied in his share of the foregoing fragment of dialogue, he paid our hero a long visit; as the two men sat with their heels on Newman's glowing hearth, they heard the small hours of the morning striking larger from a far-off belfry. Valentin de Bellegarde was, by his own confession, at all times a great chatterer, and on this occasion he was evidently in a particularly loquacious mood. It was a tradition of his race that people of its blood always conferred a favour by their smiles, and as his enthusiasms were as rare as his civility was constant, he had a double reason for not suspecting that his friendship could ever be importunate. Moreover, the flower of an ancient stem as he was, tradition (since I have used the word) had in his temperament nothing of disagreeable rigidity. It was muffled in sociability and urbanity, as an old dowager in her laces and strings of pearls. Valentin was what is called in France a *gentilhomme*,[2] of the purest source, and his rule of life, so far as it was definite, was to play the part of a *gentilhomme*. This, it seemed to him, was enough to occupy comfortably a young man of ordinary good parts. But all that he was he was by instinct and not by theory, and the amiability of his character was so great that certain of the aristocratic virtues, which in some aspects seem rather brittle and trenchant, acquired in his application of them an extreme geniality. In his younger years he had been suspected of low tastes, and his mother had greatly feared he would make a slip in the mud of the highway and bespatter the family shield. He had been treated, therefore, to more than his share of schooling and drilling, but his instructors had not succeeded in mounting him upon stilts. They could not spoil his safe spontaneity, and he remained the least cautious and the most lucky of young nobles. He had been tied with so short a rope in his youth that he had now a mortal grudge against family discipline. He had been known to say, within the limits of the family, that, lightheaded as he was, the honour of the name was safer in his hands than in those of some of its other members, and that if a day ever came to try it, they should see. His talk was an odd mixture of almost boyish garrulity and of the reserve and discretion of the man of the world, and he seemed to Newman, as afterwards young

2. Gentleman.

members of the Latin races often seemed to him, now amusingly juvenile and now appallingly mature. In America, Newman reflected, lads of twenty-five and thirty have old heads and young hearts, or at least young morals; here they have young heads and very aged hearts, morals the most grizzled and wrinkled.

"What I envy you is your liberty," observed M. de Bellegarde, "your wide range, your freedom to come and go, your not having a lot of people, who take themselves awfully seriously, expecting something of you. I live," he added with a sigh, "beneath the eyes of my admirable mother."

"It is your own fault; what is to hinder you ranging?" said Newman.

"There is a delightful simplicity in that remark! Everything is to hinder me. To begin with, I have not a penny."

"I had not a penny when I began to range."

"Ah, but your poverty was your capital. Being an American, it was impossible you should remain what you were born, and being born poor—do I understand it?—it was therefore inevitable that you should become rich. You were in a position that makes one's mouth water; you looked round you and saw a world full of things you had only to step up and take hold of. When I was twenty, I looked around me and saw a world with everything ticketed 'Hands off!' and the deuce of it was that the ticket seemed meant only for me. I couldn't go into business, I couldn't make money, because I was a Bellegarde. I couldn't go into politics, because I was a Bellegarde—the Bellegardes don't recognise the Bonapartes.[3] I couldn't go into literature, because I was a dunce. I couldn't marry a rich girl, because no Bellegarde had ever married a *roturière*,[4] and it was not proper that I should begin. We shall have to come to it, yet. Marriageable heiresses, *de notre bord*,[5] are not to be had for nothing; it must be name for name, and fortune for fortune. The only thing I could do was to go and fight for the Pope. That I did, punctiliously, and received an apostolic flesh-wound at Castelfidardo. It did neither the Holy Father nor me any good, that I could see. Rome was doubtless a very amusing place in the days of Caligula,[6] but it has sadly fallen off since. I passed three years in the Castle of St. Angelo, and then came back to secular life."

"So you have no profession—you do nothing!" said Newman.

"I do nothing! I am supposed to amuse myself, and, to tell the truth, I have amused myself. One can, if one knows how. But you can't keep it up for ever. I am good for another five years, perhaps,

3. The family name of Napoleon I, Emperor of France; the Bonapartes were socially ostracized by the conservative royalists.

4. Commoner.

5. "In our circle."

6. Roman emperor (A.D. 12–41).

but I foresee that after that I shall lose my appetite. Then what shall I do? I think I shall turn monk. Seriously, I think I shall tie a rope round my waist and go into a monastery. It was an old custom, and the old customs were very good. People understood life quite as well as we do. They kept the pot boiling till it cracked, and then they put it on the shelf altogether."

"Are you very religious?" asked Newman, in a tone which gave the inquiry a grotesque effect.

M. de Bellegarde evidently appreciated the comical element in the question, but he looked at Newman a moment with extreme soberness. "I am a very good Catholic. I respect the Church. I adore the blessed Virgin. I fear the Devil."

"Well, then," said Newman, "you are well fixed. You have got pleasure in the present and religion in the future; what do you complain of?"

"It's a part of one's pleasure to complain. There is something in your own circumstances that irritates me. You are the first man I have ever envied. It's singular, but so it is. I have known many men who besides any factitious advantages that I may possess, had money and brains into the bargain; but somehow they have never disturbed my good-humour. But you have got something that I should have liked to have. It is not money, it is not even brains—though no doubt yours are excellent. It is not your six feet of height, though I should have rather liked to be a couple of inches taller. It's a sort of air you have of being thoroughly at home in the world. When I was a boy, my father told me that it was by such an air as that that people recognised a Bellegarde. He called my attention to it. He didn't advise me to cultivate it; he said that as we grew up it always came of itself. I supposed it had come to me, because I think I have always had the feeling. My place in life was made for me, and it seemed easy to occupy it. But you who, as I understand it, have made your own place, you who, as you told us the other day, have manufactured wash-tubs—you strike me, somehow, as a man who stands at his ease, who looks at things from a height. I fancy you going about the world like a man travelling on a railroad in which he owns a large amount of stock. You make me feel as if I had missed something. What is it?"

"It is the proud consciousness of honest toil—of having manufactured a few wash-tubs," said Newman, at once jocose and serious.

"Oh no; I have seen men who had done even more, men who had made not only wash-tubs, but soap—strong-smelling yellow soap, in great bars; and they never made me the least uncomfortable."

"Then it's the privilege of being an American citizen," said Newman. "That sets a man up."

"Possibly," rejoined M. de Bellegarde. "But I am forced to say that I have seen a great many American citizens who didn't seem at all set up or in the least like large stockholders. I never envied them. I rather think the thing is an accomplishment of your own."

"Oh, come," said Newman, "you will make me proud!"

"No, I shall not. You have nothing to do with pride, or with humility—that is a part of this easy manner of yours. People are proud only when they have something to lose, and humble when they have something to gain."

"I don't know what I have to lose," said Newman, "but I certainly have something to gain."

"What is it?" asked his visitor.

Newman hesitated awhile. "I will tell you when I know you better."

"I hope that will be soon! Then, if I can help you to gain it, I shall be happy."

"Perhaps you may," said Newman.

"Don't forget, then, that I am your servant," M. de Bellegarde answered; and shortly afterwards he took his departure.

During the next three weeks Newman saw Bellegarde several times, and without formally swearing an eternal friendship the two men established a sort of comradeship. To Newman, Bellegarde was the ideal Frenchman, the Frenchman of tradition and romance, so far as our hero was acquainted with these mystical influences. Gallant, expansive, amusing, more pleased himself with the effect he produced than those (even when they were well pleased) for whom he produced it; a master of all the distinctively social virtues and a votary of all agreeable sensations; a devotee of something mysterious and sacred to which he occasionally alluded in terms more ecstatic even than those in which he spoke of the last pretty woman, and which was simply the beautiful though somewhat superannuated image of *honour*; he was irresistibly entertaining and enlivening; and he formed a character to which Newman was as capable of doing justice when he had once been placed in contact with it, as he was unlikely, in musing upon the possible mixtures of our human ingredients, mentally to have foreshadowed it. Bellegarde did not in the least cause him to modify his needful premise that all Frenchmen are of a frothy and imponderable substance; he simply reminded him that light materials may be beaten up into a most agreeable compound. No two companions could be more different, but their differences made a capital basis for a friendship of which the distinctive characteristic was that it was extremely amusing to each.

Valentin de Bellegarde lived in the basement of an old house in the Rue d'Anjou St. Honoré, and his small apartments lay between the court of the house and an old garden which spread itself behind it—one of those large, sunless, humid gardens into which you look unexpectingly in Paris from back windows, wondering how among the grudging habitations they find their space. When Newman returned Bellegarde's visit, he hinted that *his* lodging was at least as much a laughing matter as his own. But its oddities were of a different cast from those of our hero's gilded saloons on the Boulevard Haussmann: the place was low, dusky, contracted, and crowded with curious bric-à-brac. Bellegarde, penniless patrician as he was, was an insatiable collector, and his walls were covered with rusty arms and ancient panels and platters, his doorways draped in faded tapestries, his floors muffled in the skins of beasts. Here and there was one of those uncomfortable tributes to elegance in which the upholsterer's art, in France, is so prolific; a curtained recess with a sheet of looking-glass in which, among the shadows, you could see nothing; a divan on which, for its festoons and furbelows, you could not sit: a fireplace draped, flounced, and frilled to the complete exclusion of fire. The young man's possessions were in picturesque disorder, and his apartment was pervaded by the odour of cigars, mingled with perfumes more inscrutable. Newman thought it a damp, gloomy place to live in, and was puzzled by the obstructive and fragmentary character of the furniture.

Bellegarde, according to the custom of his country, talked very generously about himself, and unveiled the mysteries of his private history with an unsparing hand. Inevitably, he had a vast deal to say about women, and he used frequently to indulge in sentimental and ironical apostrophes to these authors of his joys and woes. "Oh, the women, the women, and the things they have made me do!" he would exclaim with a lustrous eye. "*C'est égal*,[7] of all the follies and stupidities I have committed for them I would not have missed one!" On this subject Newman maintained an habitual reserve; to expatiate largely upon it had always seemed to him a proceeding vaguely analogous to the cooing of pigeons and the chatterings of monkeys, and even inconsistent with a fully-developed human character. But Bellegarde's confidences greatly amused him, and rarely displeased him, for the generous young Frenchman was not a cynic. "I really think," he had once said, "that I am not more depraved than most of my contemporaries. They are tolerably depraved, my contemporaries!" He said wonderfully pretty things about his female friends, and, numerous and various as they had been, declared that on the whole there was more good in them than

7. "All the same."

harm. "But you are not to take that as advice," he added. "As an authority I am very untrustworthy. I'm prejudiced in their favour; I'm an *idealist!*" Newman listened to him with his impartial smile, and was glad, for his own sake, that he had fine feelings; but he mentally repudiated the idea of a Frenchman having discovered any merit in the amiable sex which he himself did not suspect. M. de Bellegarde, however, did not confine his conversation to the autobiographical channel; he questioned our hero largely as to the events of his own life, and Newman told him some better stories than any that Bellegarde carried in his budget. He narrated his career, in fact, from the beginning, through all its variations, and whenever his companion's credulity, or his habits of gentility, appeared to protest, it amused him to heighten the colour of the episode. Newman had sat with Western humorists in knots, round cast-iron stoves, and seen "tall" stories grow taller without toppling over, and his own imagination had learned the trick of piling up consistent wonders. Bellegarde's regular attitude at last became that of laughing self-defence; to maintain his reputation as an all-knowing Frenchman, he doubted of everything, wholesale. The result of this was that Newman found it impossible to convince him of certain time-honoured verities.

"But the details don't matter," said M. de Bellegarde. "You have evidently had some surprising adventures; you have seen some strange sides of life, you have revolved to and fro over a whole continent as I walk up and down the Boulevard. You are a man of the world with a vengeance! You have spent some deadly dull hours, and you have done some extremely disagreeable things: you have shovelled sand, as a boy, for supper, and you have eaten roast dog in a gold-diggers' camp. You have stood casting up figures for ten hours at a time, and you have sat through Methodist sermons for the sake of looking at a pretty girl in another pew. All that is rather stiff, as we say. But at any rate you have done something and you are something; you have used your will and you have made your fortune. You have not stupefied yourself with debauchery and you have not mortgaged your fortune to social conveniences. You take things easily, and you have fewer prejudices even than I, who pretend to have none, but who in reality have three or four. Happy man, you are strong and you are free. But what the deuce," demanded the young man in conclusion, "do you propose to do with such advantages? Really to use them you need a better world than this. There is nothing worth your while here."

"Oh, I think there is something," said Newman.

"What is it?"

"Well," murmured Newman, "I will tell you some other time!"

In this way our hero delayed from day to day broaching a

subject which he had very much at heart. Meanwhile, however, he was growing practically familiar with it; in other words, he had called again, three times, on Madame de Cintré. On only two of these occasions had he found her at home, and on each of them she had other visitors. Her visitors were numerous and extremely loquacious, and they exacted much of their hostess's attention. She found time, however, to bestow a little of it on Newman, in an occasional vague smile, the very vagueness of which pleased him, allowing him as it did to fill it out mentally, both at the time and afterwards, with such meanings as most pleased him. He sat by without speaking, looking at the entrances and exits, the greetings and chatterings, of Madame de Cintré's visitors. He felt as if he were at the play, and as if his own speaking would be an interruption; sometimes he wished he had a book to follow the dialogue; he half expected to see a woman in a white cap and pink ribbons come and offer him one for two francs. Some of the ladies looked at him very hard—or very soft, as you please; others seemed profoundly unconscious of his presence. The men only looked at Madame de Cintré. This was inevitable; for whether one called her beautiful or not, she entirely occupied and filled one's vision, just as an agreeable sound fills one's ear. Newman had but twenty distinct words with her, but he carried away an impression to which solemn promises could not have given a higher value. She was part of the play that he was seeing acted, quite as much as her companions; but how she filled the stage, and how much better she did it! Whether she rose or seated herself; whether she went with her departing friends to the door and lifted up the heavy curtain as they passed out, and stood an instant looking after them and giving them the last nod; or whether she leaned back in her chair with her arms crossed and her eyes resting, listening and smiling; she gave Newman the feeling that he should like to have her always before him, moving slowly to and fro along the whole scale of expressive hospitality. If it might be *to* him, it would be well; if it might be *for* him, it would be still better! She was so tall and yet so light, so active and yet so still, so elegant and yet so simple, so frank and yet so mysterious! It was the mystery—it was what she was off the stage, as it were—that interested Newman most of all. He could not have told you what warrant he had for talking about mysteries; if it had been his habit to express himself in poetic figures he might have said that in observing Madame de Cintré he seemed to see the vague circle which sometimes accompanies the partly-filled disc of the moon. It was not that she was reserved; on the contrary, she was as frank as flowing water. But he was sure she had qualities which she herself did not suspect.

He had abstained for several reasons from saying some of these things to Bellegarde. One reason was that before proceeding to any act he was always circumspect, conjectural, contemplative; he had little eagerness, as became a man who felt that whenever he really began to move he walked with long steps. And then it simply pleased him not to speak—it occupied him, it excited him. But one day Bellegarde had been dining with him, at a restaurant, and they had sat long over their dinner. On rising from it, Bellegarde proposed that, to help them through the rest of the evening, they should go and see Madame Dandelard. Madame Dandelard was a little Italian lady who had married a Frenchman who proved to be a rake and a brute and the torment of her life. Her husband had spent all her money, and then, lacking the means of obtaining more expensive pleasures, had taken, in his duller hours, to beating her. She had a blue spot somewhere, which she showed to several persons, including Bellegarde. She had obtained a separation from her husband, collected the scraps of her fortune (they were very meagre) and come to live in Paris, where she was staying at a *hôtel garni*.[8] She was always looking for an apartment, and visiting inquiringly, those of other people. She was very pretty, very childlike, and she made very extraordinary remarks. Bellegarde had made her acquaintance, and the source of his interest in her was, according to his own declaration, a curiosity as to what would become of her. "She is poor, she is pretty, and she is silly," he said; "it seems to me she can go only one way. It's a pity, but it can't be helped. I will give her six months. She has nothing to fear from me, but I am watching the process. I am curious to see just how things will go. Yes, I know what you are going to say: this horrible Paris hardens one's heart. But it quickens one's wits, and it ends by teaching one a refinement of observation! To see this little woman's little drama play itself out, now, is, for me, an intellectual pleasure."

"If she is going to throw herself away," Newman had said, "you ought to stop her."

"Stop her? How stop her?"

"Talk to her; give her some good advice."

Bellegarde laughed. "Heaven deliver us both! Imagine the situation! Go and advise her yourself."

It was after this that Newman had gone with Bellegarde to see Madame Dandelard. When they came away, Bellegarde reproached his companion. "Where was your famous advice?" he asked. "I didn't hear a word of it."

"Oh, I give it up," said Newman, simply.

"Then you are as bad as I!" said Bellegarde.

"No, because I don't take an 'intellectual pleasure' in her pro-

8. In furnished rooms.

spective adventures. I don't in the least want to see her going down hill. I had rather look the other way. But why," he asked, in a moment, "don't you get your sister to go and see her?"

Bellegarde stared. "Go and see Madame Dandelard—my sister?"

"She might talk to her to very good purpose."

Bellegarde shook his head with sudden gravity. "My sister can't see that sort of person. Madame Dandelard is nothing at all; they would never meet."

"I should think," said Newman, "that your sister might see whom she pleased." And he privately resolved that after he knew her a little better, he would ask Madame de Cintré to go and talk to the foolish little Italian lady.

After his dinner with Bellegarde, on the occasion I have mentioned, he demurred to his companion's proposal that they should go again and listen to Madame Dandelard describe her sorrows and her bruises. "I have something better in mind," he said; "come home with me and finish the evening before my fire."

Bellegarde always welcomed the prospect of a long stretch of conversation, and before long the two men sat watching the great blaze which scattered its scintillations over the high adornments of Newman's ballroom.

Chapter VIII

"Tell me something about your sister," Newman began, abruptly.

Bellegarde turned and gave him a quick look. "Now that I think of it, you have never yet asked me a question about her."

"I know that very well."

"If it is because you don't trust me, you are very right," said Bellegarde. "I can't talk of her rationally. I admire her too much."

"Talk of her as you can," rejoined Newman. "Let yourself go."

"Well, we are very good friends; we are such a brother and sister as have not been seen since Orestes and Electra.[9] You have seen her; you know what she is: tall, thin, light, imposing, and gentle, half a *grande dame*[1] and half an angel; a mixture of pride and humility, of the eagle and the dove. She looks like a statue which had failed as stone, resigned itself to its grave defects, and come to life as flesh and blood, to wear white capes and long trains. All I can say is that she really possesses every merit that her face, her glance, her smile, the tone of her voice, lead you to expect; it is saying a great deal. As a general thing, when a woman seems very charming, I should say 'Beware!' But in proportion as Claire seems

9. In Greek mythology, the children of Agamemnon and Clytemnestra. Their closeness to each other, and to their parents, is dramatically rendered in the plays of Sophocles and Euripides, and especially by Aeschylus in the *Oresteia*.

1. "Great lady."

charming you may fold your arms and let yourself float with the current; you are safe. She is so good! I have never seen a woman half so perfect or so complete. She has everything; that is all I can say about her. There!" Bellegarde concluded: "I told you I should rhapsodize."

Newman was silent awhile, as if he were turning over his companion's words. "She is very good, eh?" he repeated at last.

"Divinely good!"

"Kind, charitable, gentle, generous?"

"Generosity itself; kindness double-distilled!"

"Is she clever?"

"She is the most intelligent woman I know. Try her, some day, with something difficult, and you will see."

"Is she fond of admiration?"

"*Parbleu!*"[2] cried Bellegarde; "what woman is not?"

"Ah, when they are too fond of admiration they commit all kinds of follies to get it."

"I did not say she was too fond!" Bellegarde exclaimed. "Heaven forbid I should say anything so idiotic. She is not *too* anything! If I were to say she was ugly, I should not mean she was too ugly. She is fond of pleasing, and if you are pleased she is grateful. If you are not pleased, she lets it pass and thinks the worse neither of you nor of herself. I imagine, though, she hopes the saints in heaven are, for I am sure she is incapable of trying to please by any means of which they would disapprove."

"Is she grave or gay?" asked Newman.

"She is both; not alternately, for she is always the same. There is gravity in her gaiety, and gaiety in her gravity. But there is no reason why she should be particularly gay."

"Is she unhappy?"

"I won't say that, for unhappiness is according as one takes things, and Claire takes them according to some receipt communicated to her by the Blessed Virgin in a vision. To be unhappy is to be disagreeable, which, for her, is out of the question. So she has arranged her circumstances so as to be happy in them."

"She is a philosopher," said Newman.

"No, she is simply a very nice woman."

"Her circumstances, at any rate, have been disagreeable."

Bellegarde hesitated a moment—a thing he very rarely did. "Oh, my dear fellow, if I go into the history of my family I shall give you more than you bargain for."

"No, on the contrary, I bargain for that," said Newman.

"We shall have to appoint a special séance, then, beginning early.

2. "I should say so!"

Suffice it for the present that Claire has not slept on roses. She made, at eighteen, a marriage that was expected to be brilliant, but that turned out like a lamp that goes out; all smoke and bad smell. M. de Cintré was sixty years old, and an odious old gentleman. He lived, however, but a short time, and after his death his family pounced upon his money, brought a lawsuit against his widow, and pushed things very hard. Their case was a good one, for M. de Cintré, who had been trustee for some of his relatives, appeared to have been guilty of some very irregular practices. In the course of the suit some revelations were made as to his private history which my sister found so displeasing that she ceased to defend herself and washed her hands of the property. This required some pluck, for she was between two fires, her husband's family opposing her and her own family forcing her. My mother and my brother wished her to cleave to what they regarded as her rights. But she resisted firmly, and at last bought her freedom—obtained my mother's assent to dropping the suit at the price of a promise."

"What was the promise?"

"To do anything else, for the next ten years, that was asked of her—anything, that is, but marry."

"She had disliked her husband very much?"

"No one knows how much!"

"The marriage had been made in your horrible French way," Newman continued, "made by the two families without her having any voice?"

"It was a chapter for a novel. She saw M. de Cintré for the first time a month before the wedding, after everything, to the minutest detail, had been arranged. She turned white when she looked at him, and white she remained till her wedding-day. The evening before the ceremony she swooned away, and she spent the whole night in sobs. My mother sat holding her two hands, and my brother walked up and down the room. I declared it was revolting, and told my sister publicly that if she would refuse downright, I would stand by her. I was told to go about my business, and she became Comtesse de Cintré."

"Your brother," said Newman reflectively, "must be a very nice young man."

"He is very nice, though he is not young. He is upwards of fifty; fifteen years my senior. He has been a father to my sister and me. He is a very remarkable man; he has the best manners in France. He is extremely clever; indeed he is very learned. He is writing a history of The Princesses of France who never Married." This was said by Bellegarde with extreme gravity, looking straight at Newman, and with an eye that betokened no mental reservation; or that, at least, almost betokened none.

Newman perhaps discovered there what little there was, for he presently said: "You don't love your brother."

"I beg your pardon," said Bellegarde ceremoniously; "well-bred people always love their brothers."

"Well, I don't love him, then!" Newman answered.

"Wait till you know him!" rejoined Bellegarde, and this time he smiled.

"Is your mother also very remarkable?" Newman asked, after a pause.

"For my mother," said Bellegarde, now with intense gravity, "I have the highest admiration. She is a very extraordinary woman. You cannot approach her without perceiving it."

"She is the daughter, I believe, of an English nobleman."

"Of the Earl of St. Dunstan's."

"Is the Earl of St. Dunstan's a very old family?"

"So-so; the sixteenth century. It is on my father's side that we go back—back, back, back. The family antiquaries themselves lose breath. At last they stop, panting and fanning themselves, somewhere in the ninth century, under Charlemagne.[3] That is where we begin."

"There is no mistake about it?" said Newman.

"I'm sure I hope not. We have been mistaken at least for several centuries."

"And you have always married into old families?"

"As a rule; though in so long a stretch of time there have been some exceptions. Three or four Bellegardes, in the seventeenth and eighteenth centuries, took wives out of the *bourgeoisie*—married lawyers' daughters."

"A lawyer's daughter; that's very bad, is it?" asked Newman.

"Horrible! one of us, in the Middle Ages, did better: he married a beggar-maid, like King Cophetua.[4] That was really better; it was like marrying a bird or a monkey; one didn't have to think about her family at all. Our women have always done well; they have never even gone into the *petite noblesse*.[5] There is, I believe, not a case on record of a misalliance among the women."

Newman turned this over awhile, and then at last he said: "You offered, the first time you came to see me, to render me any service you could. I told you that some time I would mention something you might do. Do you remember?"

"Remember? I have been counting the hours."

"Very well; here's your chance. Do what you can to make your sister think well of me."

3. Frankish king (742–814), emperor of the Holy Roman Empire.
4. Legendary king who fell in love with a beggar maid.
5. Petty nobility.

Bellegarde stared, with a smile. "Why, I'm sure she thinks as well of you as possible, already."

"An opinion founded on seeing me three or four times? That is putting me off with very little. I want something more. I have been thinking of it a good deal, and at last I have decided to tell you. I should like very much to marry Madame de Cintré."

Bellegarde had been looking at him with quickened expectancy, and with the smile with which he had greeted Newman's allusion to his promised request. At this last announcement he continued to gaze; but his smile went through two or three curious phases. It felt, apparently, a momentary impulse to broaden; but this it immediately checked. Then it remained for some instants taking counsel with itself, at the end of which it decreed a retreat. It slowly effaced itself and left a look of seriousness modified by the desire not to be rude. Extreme surprise had come into the Count Valentin's face; but he had reflected that it would be uncivil to leave it there. And yet, what the deuce was he to do with it? He got up, in his agitation, and stood before the chimney-piece, still looking at Newman. He was a longer time thinking what to say than one would have expected.

"If you can't render me the service I ask," said Newman, "say it out!"

"Let me hear it again, distinctly," said Bellegarde. "It's very important, you know. I shall plead your cause with my sister, because you want—you want to marry her? That's it, eh?"

"Oh, I don't say plead my cause, exactly; I shall try and do that myself. But say a good word for me, now and then—let her know that you think well of me."

At this, Bellegarde gave a little light laugh.

"What I want chiefly, after all," Newman went on, "is just to let you know what I have in mind. I suppose that is what you expect, isn't it? I want to do what is customary over here. If there is anything particular to be done, let me know and I will do it. I wouldn't for the world approach Madame de Cintré without all the proper forms. If I ought to go and tell your mother, why I will go and tell her. I will go and tell your brother, even. I will go and tell anyone you please. As I don't know anyone else, I begin by telling you. But that, if it is a social obligation, is a pleasure as well."

"Yes, I see—I see," said Bellegarde, lightly stroking his chin. "You have a very right feeling about it, but I'm glad you have begun with me." He paused, hesitated, and then turned away and walked slowly the length of the room. Newman got up and stood leaning against the mantelshelf, with his hands in his pockets, watching Bellegarde's promenade. The young Frenchman came back and stopped in front of him. "I give it up," he said; "I will not pretend I am not surprised. I am—hugely! *Ouf!*[6] It's a relief."

"That sort of news is always a surprise," said Newman. "No matter what you have done, people are never prepared. But if you are so surprised, I hope at least you are pleased."

"Come!" said Bellegarde. "I am going to be tremendously frank. I don't know whether I am pleased or horrified."

"If you are pleased, I shall be glad," said Newman, "and I shall be—encouraged. If you are horrified, I shall be sorry, but I shall not be discouraged. You must make the best of it."

"That is quite right—that is your only possible attitude. You are perfectly serious?"

"Am I a Frenchman, that I should not be?" asked Newman. "But why is it, by-the-bye, that you should be horrified?"

"Bellegarde raised his hand to the back of his head and rubbed his hair quickly up and down, thrusting out the tip of his tongue as he did so. "Why, you are not noble, for instance," he said.

"The devil I am not!" exclaimed Newman.

"Oh," said Bellegarde, a little more seriously, "I did not know you had a title."

"A title? What do you mean by a title?" asked Newman. "A count, a duke, a marquis? I don't know anything about that, I don't know who is and who is not. But I say I am noble. I don't exactly know what you mean by it, but it's a fine word and a fine idea; I put in a claim to it."

"But what have you to show, my dear fellow; what proofs?"

"Anything you please! But you don't suppose I am going to undertake to prove that I am noble. It is for you to prove the contrary."

"That's easily done. You have manufactured wash-tubs."

Newman stared a moment. "Therefore I am not noble? I don't see it. Tell me something I have *not* done—something I cannot do."

"You cannot marry a woman like Madame de Cintré for the asking."

"I believe you mean," said Newman slowly, "that I am not good enough."

"Brutally speaking—yes!"

Bellegarde had hesitated a moment, and while he hesitated Newman's attentive glance had grown somewhat eager. In answer to these last words he for a moment said nothing. He simply blushed a little. Then he raised his eyes to the ceiling and stood

6. An exclamation meaning "Whew!"

looking at one of the rosy cherubs that was painted upon it. "Of course I don't expect to marry any woman for the asking," he said at last; "I expect first to make myself acceptable to her. She must like me, to begin with. But that I am not good enough to make a trial is rather a surprise."

Bellegarde wore a look of mingled perplexity, sympathy, and amusement. "You should not hesitate, then, to go up to-morrow and ask a duchess to marry you?"

"Not if I thought she would suit me. But I am very fastidious; she might not at all."

Bellegarde's amusement began to prevail. "And you should be surprised if she refused you?"

Newman hesitated a moment. "It sounds conceited to say Yes; but, nevertheless, I think I should. For I should make a very handsome offer."

"What would it be?"

"Everything she wishes. If I get hold of a woman that comes up to my standard, I shall think nothing too good for her. I have been a long time looking, and I find such women are rare. To combine the qualities I require seems to be difficult, but when the difficulty is vanquished it deserves a reward. My wife shall have a good position, and I am not afraid to say that I shall be a good husband."

"And these qualities that you require—what are they?"

"Goodness, beauty, intelligence, a fine education, personal elegance—everything, in a word, that makes a splendid woman."

"And noble birth, evidently," said Bellegarde.

"Oh, throw that in, by all means, if it's there. The more the better!"

"And my sister seems to you to have all these things?"

"She is exactly what I have been looking for. She is my dream realised."

"And you would make her a very good husband?"

"That is what I wanted you to tell her."

Bellegarde laid his hand on his companion's arm a moment, looked at him with his head on one side, from head to foot, and then, with a loud laugh, and shaking the other hand in the air, turned away. He walked again the length of the room, and again he came back and stationed himself in front of Newman. "All this is very interesting—it is very curious. In what I said just now I was speaking, not for myself, but for my traditions, my superstitions. For myself, really, your proposal tickles me. It startled me at first, but the more I think of it the more I see in it. It's no use attempting to explain anything; you don't understand me. After all, I don't see why you need; it's no great loss."

"Oh, if there is anything more to explain, try it! I want to proceed with my eyes open. I will do my best to understand."

"No," said Bellegarde, "it's disagreeable to me; I give it up. I liked you the first time I saw you, and I will abide by that. It would be quite odious for me to come talking to you as if I could patronise you. I have told you before that I envy you; *vous m'imposez,*[7] as we say. I didn't know you much until within five minutes. So we will let things go, and I will say nothing to you that, if our positions were reversed, you would not say to me."

I do not know whether, in renouncing the mysterious opportunity to which he alluded, Bellegarde felt that he was doing something very generous. If so, he was not rewarded; his generosity was not appreciated. Newman quite failed to recognise the young Frenchman's power to wound his feelings, and he had now no sense of escaping or coming off easily. He did not thank his companion even with a glance. "My eyes are open, though," he said, "so far as that you have practically told me that your family and your friends will turn up their noses at me. I have never thought much about the reasons that make it proper for people to turn up their noses, and so I can only decide the question off-hand. Looking at it in that way I can't see anything in it. I simply think, if you want to know, that I'm as good as the best. Who the best are, I don't pretend to say. I have never thought much about that either. To tell the truth, I have always had rather a good opinion of myself; a man who is successful can't help it. But I will admit that I was conceited. What I don't say Yes to is that I don't stand high—as high as any one else. This is a line of speculation I should not have chosen, but you must remember you began it yourself. I should never have dreamed that I was on the defensive, or that I had to justify myself; but if your people will have it so, I will do my best."

"But you offered, awhile ago, to make your court, as we say, to my mother and my brother."

"Damn it!" cried Newman, "I want to be polite."

"Good!" rejoined Bellegarde; "this will go far, it will be very entertaining. Excuse my speaking of it in that cold-blooded fashion, but the matter must, of necessity, be for me something of a spectacle. It's positively exciting. But apart from that I sympathise with you, and I shall be actor, so far as I can, as well as spectator. You are a capital fellow; I believe in you and I back you. The simple fact that you appreciate my sister will serve as the proof I was asking for. All men are equal—especially men of taste!"

7. "You overwhelm me."

"Do you think," asked Newman presently, "that Madame de Cintré is determined not to marry?"

"That is my impression. But that is not against you; it's for you to make her change her mind."

"I am afraid it will be hard," said Newman gravely.

"I don't think it will be easy. In a general way I don't see why a widow should ever marry again. She has gained the benefits of matrimony—freedom and consideration—and she has got rid of the drawbacks. Why should she put her head into the noose again? Her usual motive is ambition; if a man can offer her a great position, make her a princess or an ambassadress, she may think the compensation sufficient."

"And—in that way—is Madame de Cintré ambitious?"

"Who knows?" said Bellegarde, with a profound shrug. "I don't pretend to say all that she is or all that she is not. I think she might be touched by the prospect of becoming the wife of a great man. But in a certain way, I believe, whatever she does will be the *improbable*. Don't be too confident, but don't absolutely doubt. Your best chance for success will be precisely in being, to her mind, unusual, unexpected, original. Don't try to be any one else; be simply yourself, out and out. Something or other can't fail to come of it; I am very curious to see what."

"I am much obliged to you for your advice," said Newman. "And," he added, with a smile, "I am glad, for your sake, I am going to be so amusing."

"It will be more than amusing," said Bellegarde; "it will be inspiring. I look at it from my point of view, and you from yours. After all, anything for a change! And only yesterday I was yawning so as to dislocate my jaw, and declaring that there was nothing new under the sun! If it isn't new to see you come into the family as a suitor, I am very much mistaken. Let me say that, my dear fellow; I won't call it anything else, bad or good; I will simply call it *new*." And overcome with a sense of the novelty thus foreshadowed, Valentin de Bellegarde threw himself into a deep armchair before the fire, and with a fixed intense smile, seemed to read a vision of it in the flame of the logs. After awhile he looked up. "Go ahead, my boy; you have my good wishes," he said. "But it is really a pity you don't understand me, that you don't know just what I am doing."

"Oh," said Newman laughing, "don't do anything wrong. Leave me to myself, rather, or defy me, out and out. I wouldn't lay any load on your conscience."

Bellegarde sprang up again; he was evidently excited; there was a warmer spark even than usual in his eye. "You never will understand—you never will know," he said; "and if you succeed, and I turn out to have helped you, you will never be grateful, not as I shall deserve you should be. You will be an excellent fellow always, but you will not be grateful. But it doesn't matter, for I shall get my own fun out of it." And he broke into an extravagant laugh. "You look puzzled," he added; "you look almost frightened."

"It *is* a pity," said Newman, "that I don't understand you. I shall lose some very good jokes."

"I told you, you remember, that we were very strange people," Bellegarde went on. "I give you warning again. We are! My mother is strange, my brother is strange, and I verily believe that I am stranger than either. You will even find my sister a little strange. Old trees have crooked branches, old houses have queer cracks, old races have odd secrets. Remember that we are eight hundred years old!"

"Very good," said Newman; "that's the sort of thing I came to Europe for. You come into my programme."

"*Touchez-là*,[8] then," said Bellegarde, putting out his hand. "It's a bargain: I accept you; I espouse your cause. It's because I like you, in a great measure; but that is not the only reason." And he stood holding Newman's hand and looking at him askance.

"What is the other one?"

"I am in the Opposition. I dislike someone else."

"Your brother?" asked Newman, in his unmodulated voice.

Bellegarde laid his finger on his lips with a whispered *hush!* "Old races have strange secrets!" he said. "Put yourself into motion, come and see my sister, and be assured of my sympathy!" And on this he took his leave.

Newman dropped into a chair before his fire, and sat a long time staring into the blaze.

Chapter IX

He went to see Madame de Cintré the next day, and was informed by the servant that she was at home. He passed as usual up the large cold staircase, and through a spacious vestibule above, where the walls seemed all composed of small door panels, touched with long-faded gilding; whence he was ushered into the sitting-room in which he had already been received. It was empty, and the servant told him that Madame la Comtesse would presently appear. He had time, while he waited, to wonder whether Bellegarde had seen his sister since the evening before, and whether in this case he had spoken to her of their talk. In this case Madame de Cintré's receiving him was an encouragement. He felt a certain trepidation

8. "Shake hands on it!"

as he reflected that she might come in with the knowledge of his supreme admiration and of the project he had built upon it in her eyes; but the feeling was not disagreeable. Her face could wear no look that would make it less beautiful, and he was sure beforehand that however she might take the proposal he had in reserve, she would not take it in scorn or in irony. He had a feeling that if she could only read the bottom of his heart, and measure the extent of his good will toward her, she would be entirely kind.

She came in at last, after so long an interval that he wondered whether she had been hesitating. She smiled with her usual frankness, and held out her hand; she looked at him straight with her soft and luminous eyes, and said, without a tremor in her voice, that she was glad to see him, and that she hoped he was well. He found in her what he had found before—that faint perfume of a personal shyness worn away by contact with the world, but the more perceptible the more closely you approached her. This lingering diffidence seemed to give a peculiar value to what was definite and assured in her manner; it made it seem like an accomplishment, a beautiful talent, something that one might compare to an exquisite touch in a pianist. It was, in fact, Madame de Cintré's "authority," as they say of artists, that especially impressed and fascinated Newman; he always came back to the feeling that when he should complete himself by taking a wife, that was the way he should like his wife to interpret him to the world. The only trouble, indeed, was that when the instrument was so perfect it seemed to interpose too much between you and the genius that used it. Madame de Cintré gave Newman the sense of an elaborate education, of her having passed through mysterious ceremonies and processes of culture in her youth, of her having been fashioned and made flexible to certain exalted social needs. All this, as I have affirmed, made her seem rare and precious—a very expensive article, as he would have said, and one which a man with an ambition to have everything about him of the best would find it highly agreeable to possess. But looking at the matter with an eye to private felicity, Newman wondered where, in so exquisite a compound, nature and art showed their dividing line. Where did the special intention separate from the habit of good manners? Where did urbanity end and sincerity begin? Newman asked himself these questions even while he stood ready to accept the admired object in all its complexity; he felt that he could do so in profound security, and examine its mechanism afterwards, at leisure.

"I am very glad to find you alone," he said. "You know I have never had such good luck before."

"But you have seemed before very well contented with your luck," said Madame de Cintré. "You have sat and watched my visitors with an air of quiet amusement. What have you thought of them?"

"Oh, I have thought the ladies were very elegant and very graceful, and wonderfully quick at repartee. But what I have chiefly thought has been that they only help me to admire you." This was not gallantry on Newman's part—an art in which he was quite unversed. It was simply the instinct of the practical man, who had quite made up his mind what he wanted, and was now beginning to take active steps to obtain it.

Madame de Cintré started slightly, and raised her eyebrows; she had evidently not expected so fervid a compliment. "Oh, in that case," she said, with a laugh, "your finding me alone is not good luck for me. I hope some one will come in quickly."

"I hope not," said Newman. "I have something particular to say to you. Have you seen your brother?"

"Yes; I saw him an hour ago."

"Did he tell you that he had seen me last night?"

"He said so."

"And did he tell you what we had talked about?"

Madame de Cintré hesitated a moment. As Newman asked these questions she had grown a little pale, as if she regarded what was coming as necessary, but not as agreeable. "Did you give him a message to me?" she asked.

"It was not exactly a message—I asked him to render me a service."

"The service was to sing your praises, was it not?" And she accompanied this question with a little smile, as if to make it easier to herself.

"Yes, that is what it really amounts to," said Newman. "Did he sing my praises?"

"He spoke very well of you. But when I know that it was by your special request, of course I must take his eulogy with a grain of salt."

"Oh, that makes no difference," said Newman. "Your brother would not have spoken well of me unless he believed what he was saying. He is too honest for that."

"Are you very deep?" said Madame de Cintré. "Are you trying to please me by praising my brother? I confess it is a good way."

"For me, any way that succeeds will be good. I will praise your brother all day, if that will help me. He is a noble little fellow. He has made me feel, in promising to do what he can to help me, that I can depend upon him."

"Don't make too much of that," said Madame de Cintré. "He can help you very little."

"Of course I must work my way myself. I know that very well; I only want a chance to. In consenting to see me, after what he told you, you almost seem to be giving me a chance."

"I am seeing you," said Madame de Cintré, slowly and gravely, "because I promised my brother I would."

"Blessings on your brother's head!" cried Newman. "What I told him last evening was this: that I admired you more than any woman I had ever seen, and that I should like immensely to make you my wife." He uttered these words with great directness and firmness, and without any sense of confusion. He was full of his idea, he had completely mastered it, and he seemed to look down on Madame de Cintré, with all her gathered elegance, from the height of his bracing good conscience. It is probable that this particular tone and manner were the very best he could have hit upon. Yet the light, just visibly forced smile, with which his companion had listened to him died away, and she sat looking at him with her lips parted and her face as solemn as a tragic mask. There was evidently something very painful to her in the scene to which he was subjecting her, and yet her impatience of it found no angry voice. Newman wondered whether he was hurting her; he could not imagine why the liberal devotion he meant to express should be disagreeable. He got up and stood before her, leaning one hand on the chimney-piece. "I know I have seen you very little to say this," he said, "so little that it may make what I say seem disrespectful. That is my misfortune! I could have said it the first time I saw you. Really, I had seen you before; I had seen you in imagination; you seemed almost an old friend. So what I say is not mere gallantry and compliments and nonsense—I can't talk that way, I don't know how, and I wouldn't to you if I could. It's as serious as such words can be. I feel as if I knew you and knew what a beautiful admirable woman you are. I shall know better perhaps, some day, but I have a general notion now. You are just the woman I have been looking for, except that you are far more perfect. I won't make any protestations and vows, but you can trust me. It is very soon, I know, to say all this; it is almost offensive. But why not gain time if one can? And if you want time to reflect—of course you do—the sooner you begin the better for me. I don't know what you think of me; but there is no great mystery about me; you see what I am. Your brother told me that my antecedents and occupations were against me; that your family stands somehow on a higher level than I do. That is an idea which, of course, I don't understand and don't accept. But you don't care anything about that. I can assure you that I am a very solid fellow, and that if I give my mind to it I can arrange things so that in a very few years I shall not need to waste time in explaining who I am and what I am. You will decide for yourself whether you like me or not. What there is you see before you. I honestly believe I have no hidden vices or nasty tricks. I am kind, kind, kind! Everything that a man can give a woman I will give you. I have a large fortune, a very large fortune; some day, if you will allow me, I will go into details. If you want brilliancy, everything in the way of brilliancy that money can give you, you shall have. And as regards anything you may give up, don't take for granted too much that its place cannot be filled. Leave that to me; I'll take care of you; I shall know what you need. Energy and ingenuity can arrange everything. I'm a strong man! There, I have said what I had on my heart! It was better to get it off. I am very sorry if it's disagreeable to you; but think how much better it is that things should be clear. Don't answer me now, if you don't wish it. Think about it; think about it as slowly as you please. Of course I hav'n't said, I can't say, half I mean, especially about my admiration for you. But take a favourable view of me; it will only be just."

During this speech, the longest that Newman had ever made, Madame de Cintré kept her gaze fixed upon him, and it expanded at the last into a sort of fascinated stare. When he ceased speaking she lowered her eyes and sat for some moments looking down and straight before her. Then she slowly rose to her feet, and a pair of exceptionally keen eyes would have perceived that she was trembling a little in the movement. She still looked extremely serious. "I am very much obliged to you for your offer," she said. "It seems very strange, but I am glad you spoke without waiting any longer. It is better the subject should be dismissed. I appreciate all you say; you do me great honour. But I have decided not to marry."

"Oh, don't say that!" cried Newman, in a tone absolutely *naïf*[9] from its pleading and caressing cadence. She had turned away, and it made her stop a moment with her back to him. "Think better of that. You are too young, too beautiful, too much made to be happy and to make others happy. If you are afraid of losing your freedom, I can assure you that this freedom here, this life you now lead, is a dreary bondage to what I will offer you. You shall do things that I don't think you have ever thought of. I will take you to live anywhere in the wide world that you propose. Are you unhappy? You give me a feeling that you *are* unhappy. You have no right to be, or to be made so. Let me come in and put an end to it."

Madame de Cintré stood there a moment longer, looking away from him. If she was touched by the way he spoke, the thing was conceivable. His voice, always very mild and interrogative, gradually became as soft and as tenderly argumentative as if he had been

9. Naive, ingenuous.

talking to a much-loved child. He stood watching her, and she presently turned round again, but this time she did not look at him, and she spoke with a quietness in which there was a visible trace of effort.

"There are a great many reasons why I should not marry," she said, "more than I can explain to you. As for my happiness, I am very happy. Your offer seems strange to me, for more reasons also than I can say. Of course you have a perfect right to make it. But I cannot accept it—it is impossible. Please never speak of this matter again. If you cannot promise me this, I must ask you not to come back."

"Why is it impossible?" Newman demanded. "You may think it is, at first, without its really being so. I didn't expect you to be pleased at first, but I do believe that if you will think of it a good while, you may be satisfied."

"I don't know you," said Madame de Cintré. "Think how little I know you."

"Very little, of course, and therefore I don't ask for your ultimatum on the spot. I only ask you not to say No, and to let me hope. I will wait as long as you desire. Meanwhile you can see more of me and know me better, look at me as a possible husband—as a candidate—and make up your mind."

Something was going on, rapidly, in Madame de Cintré's thoughts; she was weighing a question there, beneath Newman's eyes, weighing it and deciding it. "From the moment I don't very respectfully beg you to leave the house and never return," she said, "I listen to you, I seem to give you hope. I *have* listened to you—against my judgment. It is because you are eloquent. If I had been told this morning that I should consent to consider you as a possible husband, I should have thought my informant a little crazy. I *am* listening to you, you see!" And she threw her hands out for a moment and let them drop with a gesture in which there was just the slightest expression of appealing weakness.

"Well, as far as saying goes, I have said everything," said Newman. "I believe in you, without restriction, and I think all the good of you that it is possible to think of a human creature. I firmly believe that in marrying me you will be *safe*. As I said just now," he went on with a smile, "I have no bad ways. I can *do* so much for you. And if you are afraid that I am not what you have been accustomed to, not refined and delicate and punctilious, you may easily carry that too far. I *am* delicate! You shall see!"

Madame de Cintré walked some distance away, and paused before a great plant, an azalea, which was flourishing in a porcelain tub before her window. She plucked off one of the flowers and, twisting it in her fingers, retraced her steps. Then she sat down in silence, and her attitude seemed to be a consent that Newman should say more.

"Why should you say it is impossible you should marry?" he continued. "The only thing that could make it really impossible would be your being already married. Is it because you have been unhappy in marrriage? That is all the more reason. Is it because your family exert a pressure upon you, interfere with you, annoy you? That is still another reason; you ought to be perfectly free, and marriage will make you so. I don't say anything against your family—understand that!" added Newman, with an eagerness which might have made a perspicacious observer smile. "Whatever way you feel toward them is the right way, and anything that you should wish me to do to make myself agreeable to them I will do as well as I know how. Depend upon that!"

Madame de Cintré rose again and came toward the fireplace, near which Newman was standing. The expression of pain and embarrassment had passed out of her face, and it was illuminated with something which, this time at least, Newman need not have been perplexed whether to attribute to habit or to intention, to art or to nature. She had the air of a woman who had stepped across the frontier of friendship and, looking round her, finds the region vast. A certain checked and controlled exaltation seemed mingled with the usual level radiance of her glance. "I will not refuse to see you again," she said, "because much of what you have said has given me pleasure. But I will see you only on this condition: that you say nothing more in the same way for a long time."

"For how long?"

"For six months. It must be a solemn promise."

"Very well; I promise."

"Good-bye, then," she said, and extended her hand.

He held it a moment, as if he were going to say something more. But he only looked at her; then he took his departure.

That evening, on the Boulevard, he met Valentin de Bellegarde. After they had exchanged greetings, Newman told him that he had seen Madame de Cintré a few hours before.

"I know it," said Bellegarde. "I dined in the Rue de l'Université." And then, for some moments, both men were silent. Newman wished to ask Bellegarde what visible impression his visit had made, and the Count Valentin had a question of his own. Bellegarde spoke first.

"It's none of my business, but what the deuce did you say to my sister?"

"I am willing to tell you," said Newman, "that I made her an offer of marriage."

"Already!" And the young man gave a whistle. " 'Time is money!'

Is that what you say in America? And Madame de Cintré?" he added, with an interrogative inflection.

"She did not accept my offer."

"She couldn't, you know, in that way."

"But I'm to see her again," said Newman.

"Oh the strangeness of woman!" exclaimed Bellegarde. Then he stopped, and held Newman off at arms'-length. "I look at you with respect!" he exclaimed. "You have achieved what we call a personal success! Immediately, now, I must present you to my brother."

"Whenever you please!" said Newman.

Chapter X

Newman continued to see his friends the Tristrams with a good deal of frequency, though, if you had listened to Mrs. Tristram's account of the matter, you would have supposed that they had been cynically repudiated for the sake of grander acquaintance. "We were all very well so long as we had no rivals—we were better than nothing. But now that you have become the fashion, and have your pick every day of three invitations to dinner, we are tossed into the corner. I am sure it is very good of you to come and see us once a month; I wonder you don't send us your cards in an envelope. When you do, pray have them with black edges; it will be for the death of my last illusion." It was in this incisive strain that Mrs. Tristram moralised over Newman's so-called neglect, which was in reality a most exemplary constancy. Of course she was joking, but there was always something ironical in her jokes, as there was always something jocular in her gravity.

"I know no better proof that I have treated you very well," Newman had said, "than the fact that you make so free with my character. Familiarity breeds contempt; I have made myself too cheap. If I had a little proper pride I would stay away awhile, and when you asked me to dinner say I was going to the Princess Borealska's. But I have not any pride where my pleasure is concerned, and to keep you in the humour to see me—if you must see me only to call me bad names—I will agree to anything you choose; I will admit that I am the biggest snob in Paris." Newman, in fact, had declined an invitation personally given by the Princess Borealska, an inquiring Polish lady to whom he had been presented, on the ground that on that particular day he always dined at Mrs. Tristram's; and it was only a tenderly perverse theory of his hostess of the Avenue d'Iéna that he was faithless to his early friendships. She needed the theory to explain a certain moral irritation by which she was often visited; though, if this explanation was unsound, a deeper analyst than I must give the right one. Having launched our hero upon the current which was bearing him so rapidly along, she appeared but half-pleased at its swiftness. She had succeeded too well; she had played her game too cleverly, and she wished to mix up the cards. Newman had told her, in due season, that her friend was "satisfactory." The epithet was not romantic, but Mrs. Tristram had no difficulty in perceiving that, in essentials, the feeling which lay beneath it was. Indeed, the mild expansive brevity with which it was uttered, and a certain look, at once appealing and inscrutable, that issued from Newman's half-closed eyes as he leaned his head against the back of his chair, seemed to her the most eloquent attestation of a mature sentiment that she had ever encountered. Newman was, according to the French phrase, only abounding in her own sense, but his temperate raptures exerted a singular effect upon that ardour which she herself had so freely manifested a few months before. She now seemed inclined to take a purely critical view of Madame de Cintré, and wished to have it understood that she did not in the least answer for her being a compendium of all the virtues. "No woman was ever so good as that woman seems," she said. "Remember what Shakespeare calls Desdemona: 'A supersubtle Venetian.'[1] Madame de Cintré is a supersubtle Parisian. She is a charming woman, and she has five hundred merits; but you had better keep that in mind." Was Mrs. Tristram simply finding out that she was jealous of her dear friend on the other side of the Seine, and that in undertaking to provide Newman with an ideal wife she had counted too much on her own disinterestedness? We may be permitted to doubt it. The inconsistent little lady of the Avenue d'Iéna had an insuperable need of changing her place, intellectually. She had a lively imagination, and she was capable, at certain times, of imagining the direct reverse of her most cherished beliefs, with a vividness more intense than that of conviction. She got tired of thinking aright; but there was no serious harm in it, as she got equally tired of thinking wrong. In the midst of her mysterious perversities she had admirable flashes of justice. One of these occurred when Newman related to her that he had made a formal proposal to Madame de Cintré. He repeated in a few words what he had said, and in a great many what she had answered. Mrs. Tristram listened with extreme interest.

"But after all," said Newman, "there is nothing to congratulate me upon. It is not a triumph."

"I beg your pardon," said Mrs. Tristram; "it is a great triumph.

1. Iago tells Roderigo: "Make all the money thou canst: if sanctimony and a frail vow betwixt an erring barbarian and a super-subtle Venetian be not too hard for my wits and all the tribe of hell, thou shalt enjoy her; therefore make money." Act I, scene 3 of Shakespeare's *Othello*.

It is a great triumph that she did not silence you at the first word, and request you never to speak to her again."

"I don't see that," observed Newman.

"Of course you don't; heaven forbid you should! When I told you to go your own way and do what came into your head, I had no idea you would go over the ground so fast. I never dreamed you would offer yourself after five or six morning-calls. As yet, what had you done to make her like you? You had simply sat—not very straight—and stared at her. But she does like you."

"That remains to be seen."

"No, that is proved. What will come of it remains to be seen. That you should propose to marry her, without more ado, could never have come into her head. You can form very little idea of what passed through her mind as you spoke; if she ever really marries you, the affair will be characterised by the usual justice of all human things towards women. You will think you take generous views of her; but you will never begin to know through what a strange sea of feeling she passed before she accepted you. As she stood there in front of you the other day, she plunged into it. She said, 'Why not?' to something which, a few hours earlier, had been inconceivable. She turned about on a thousand gathered prejudices and traditions as on a pivot, and looked where she had never looked hitherto. When I think of it—when I think of Claire de Cintré and all that she represents; there seems to me something very fine in it. When I recommended you to try your fortune with her I of course thought well of you, and in spite of your sins I think so still. But I confess I don't see quite what you are and what you have done, to make such a woman do this sort of thing for you."

"Oh, there is something very fine in it!" said Newman, with a laugh, repeating her words. He took an extreme satisfaction in hearing that there was something fine in it. He had not the least doubt of it himself, but he had already begun to value the world's admiration of Madame de Cintré, as adding to the prospective glory of possession.

It was immediately after this conversation that Valentin de Bellegarde came to conduct his friend to the Rue de l'Université to present him to the other members of his family. "You are already introduced," he said, "and you have begun to be talked about. My sister has mentioned your successive visits to my mother, and it was an accident that my mother was present at none of them. I have spoken of you as an American of immense wealth, and the best fellow in the world, who is looking for something very superior in the way of a wife."

"Do you suppose," asked Newman, "that Madame de Cintré has related to your mother the last conversation I had with her?"

"I am very certain that she has not; she will keep her own counsel. Meanwhile you must make your way with the rest of the family. Thus much is known about you: you have made a great fortune in trade; you are a little eccentric; and you frankly admire our dear Claire. My sister-in-law, whom you remember seeing in Madame de Cintré's sitting-room, took, it appears, a fancy to you; she has described you as having *beaucoup de cachet*.[2] My mother, therefore, is curious to see you."

"She expects to laugh at me, eh?" said Newman.

"She never laughs. If she does not like you, don't hope to purchase favour by being amusing. Take warning by me!"

This conversation took place in the evening, and half an hour later Valentin ushered his companion into an apartment of the house of the Rue de l'Université into which he had not yet penetrated, the salon of the dowager Marquise de Bellegarde. It was a vast high room, with elaborate and ponderous mouldings, painted a whitish gray, along the upper portion of the walls and the ceiling; with a great deal of faded and carefully-repaired tapestry in the doorways and chair-backs; a Turkey carpet in light colours, still soft and deep, in spite of great antiquity, on the floor; and portraits of each of Madame de Bellegarde's children, at the age of ten, suspended against an old screen of red silk. The room was illumined, exactly enough for conversation, by half-a-dozen candles, placed in odd corners, at a great distance apart. In a deep armchair, near the fire, sat an old lady in black; at the other end of the room another person was seated at the piano, playing a very expressive waltz. In this latter person Newman recognised the young Marquise de Bellegarde.

Valentin presented his friend, and Newman walked up to the old lady by the fire and shook hands with her. He received a rapid impression of a white, delicate, aged face, with a high forehead, a small mouth, and a pair of cold blue eyes which had kept much of the freshness of youth. Madame de Bellegarde looked hard at him, and returned his handshake with a sort of British positiveness which reminded him that she was the daughter of the Earl of St. Dunstan's. Her daughter-in-law stopped playing and gave him an agreeable smile. Newman sat down and looked about him, while Valentin went and kissed the hand of the young marquise.

"I ought to have seen you before," said Madame de Bellegarde. "You have paid several visits to my daughter."

"Oh yes," said Newman, smiling; "Madame de Cintré and I are old friends by this time."

"You have gone fast," said Madame de Bellegarde.

2. A great deal of "charisma," "style," or "distinction."

"Not so fast as I should like," said Newman bravely.

"Oh, you are very ambitious," answered the old lady.

"Yes, I confess I am," said Newman, smiling.

Madame de Bellegarde looked at him with her cold fine eyes, and he returned her gaze, reflecting that she was a possible adversary and trying to take her measure. Their eyes remained in contact for some moments. Then Madame de Bellegarde looked away, and without smiling: "I am very ambitious, too," she said.

Newman felt that taking her measure was not easy; she was a formidable, inscrutable little woman. She resembled her daughter, and yet she was utterly unlike her. The colouring in Madame de Cintré was the same, and the high delicacy of her brow and nose was hereditary. But her face was a larger and freer copy, and her mouth in especial a happy divergence from that conservative orifice, a little pair of lips at once plump and pinched, that looked, when closed, as if they could not open wider than to swallow a gooseberry or to emit an "Oh dear, no!" which probably had been thought to give the finishing touch to the aristocratic prettiness of the Lady Emmeline Atheling as represented, forty years before, in several Books of Beauty. Madame de Cintré's face had, to Newman's eye, a range of expression as delightfully vast as the wind-streaked, cloud-flecked distance on a Western prairie. But her mother's white, intense, respectable countenance, with its formal gaze, and its circumscribed smile, suggested a document signed and sealed; a thing of parchment, ink, and ruled lines. "She is a woman of conventions and proprieties," he said to himself as he looked at her; "her world is the world of things immutably decreed. But how she is at home in it, and what a paradise she finds it! She walks about in it as if it were a blooming park, a Garden of Eden; and when she sees 'This is genteel,' or 'This is improper,' written on a milestone she stops ecstatically, as if she were listening to a nightingale or smelling a rose." Madame de Bellegarde wore a little black velvet hood tied under her chin, and she was wrapped in an old black cashmere shawl.

"You are an American?" she said presently. "I have seen several Americans."

"There are several in Paris," said Newman jocosely.

"Oh, really?" said Madame de Bellegarde. "It was in England I saw these, or somewhere else; not in Paris. I think it must have been in the Pyrenees,[3] many years ago. I am told your ladies are very pretty. One of these ladies was very pretty! such a wonderful complexion! She presented me a note of introduction from some one—I forget whom—and she sent with it a note of her own. I kept

3. A mountain chain of southwestern Europe, between France and Spain.

her letter a long time afterwards, it was so strangely expressed. I used to know some of the phrases by heart. But I have forgotten them now, it is so many years ago. Since then I have seen no more Americans. I think my daughter-in-law has; she is a great gad-about, she sees everyone."

At this the young lady came rustling forward, pinching in a very slender waist, and casting idly preoccupied glances over the front of her dress, which was apparently designed for a ball. She was, in a singular way, at once ugly and pretty; she had protuberant eyes, and lips that were strangely red. She reminded Newman of his friend, Mademoiselle Nioche; this was what that much-obstructed young lady would have liked to be. Valentin de Bellegarde walked behind her at a distance, hopping about to keep off the far-spreading train of her dress.

"You ought to show more of your shoulders behind," he said, very gravely. "You might as well wear a standing ruff as such a dress as that."

The young woman turned her back to the mirror over the chimney-piece, and glanced behind her, to verify Valentin's assertion. The mirror descended low, and yet it reflected nothing but a large unclad flesh surface. The young marquise put her hands behind her and gave a downward pull to the waist of her dress. "Like that, you mean?" she asked.

"That is a little better," said Bellegarde, in the same tone, "but it leaves a good deal to be desired."

"Oh, I never go to extremes," said his sister-in-law. And then, turning to Madame de Bellegarde: "What were you calling me just now, madame?"

"I called you a gad-about," said the old lady. "But I might call you something else, too."

"A gad-about? What an ugly word! What does it mean?"

"A very beautiful person," Newman ventured to say, seeing that it was in French.

"That is a pretty compliment but a bad translation," said the young marquise. And then, looking at him a moment: "Do you dance?"

"Not a step."

"You are very wrong," she said simply. And with another look at her back in the mirror she turned away.

"Do you like Paris?" asked the old lady, who was apparently wondering what was the proper way to talk to an American.

"Yes, rather," said Newman. And then he added, with a friendly intonation: "Don't you?"

"I can't say I know it. I know my house—I know my friends—I don't know Paris."

"Oh, you lose a great deal," said Newman sympathetically.

Madame de Bellegarde stared; it was presumably the first time she had been condoled with on her losses.

"I am content with what I have," she said, with dignity.

Newman's eyes, at this moment, were wandering round the room, which struck him as rather sad and shabby; passing from the high casements, with their small thickly-framed panes, to the sallow tints of two or three portraits in pastel, of the last century, which hung between them. He ought obviously to have answered that the contentment of his hostess was quite natural—she had a great deal; but the idea did not occur to him during the pause of some moments which followed.

"Well, my dear mother," said Valentin, coming and leaning against the chimney-piece, "what do you think of my dear friend Newman? Is he not the excellent fellow I told you?"

"My acquaintance with Mr. Newman has not gone very far," said Madame de Bellegarde. "I can as yet only appreciate his great politeness."

"My mother is a great judge of these matters," said Valentin to Newman. "If you have satisfied her, it is a triumph."

"I hope I shall satisfy you, some day," said Newman, looking at the old lady. "I have done nothing yet."

"You must not listen to my son; he will bring you into trouble. He is a sad scatterbrain."

"Oh, I like him—I like him," said Newman genially.

"He amuses you, eh?"

"Yes, perfectly."

"Do you hear that, Valentin?" said Madame de Bellegarde. "You amuse Mr. Newman."

"Perhaps we shall all come to that!" Valentin exclaimed.

"You must see my other son," said Madame de Bellegarde. "He is much better than this one. But he will not amuse you."

"I don't know—I don't know!" murmured Valentin reflectively. "But we shall very soon see. Here comes *Monsieur mon frère*."[4]

The door had just opened to give ingress to a gentleman who stepped forward and whose face Newman remembered. He had been the author of our hero's discomfiture the first time he tried to present himself to Madame de Cintré. Valentin de Bellegarde went to meet his brother, looked at him a moment, and then, taking him by the arm, led him up to Newman.

"This is my excellent friend Mr. Newman," he said very blandly. "You must know him."

4. "My honorable brother."

"I am delighted to know Mr. Newman," said the marquis, with a low bow, but without offering his hand.[5]

"He is the old woman at second-hand," Newman said to himself, as he returned M. de Bellegarde's greeting. And this was the starting-point of a speculative theory, in his mind, that the late marquis had been a very amiable foreigner, with an inclination to take life easily and a sense that it was difficult for the husband of the stilted little lady by the fire to do so. But if he had taken little comfort in his wife he had taken much in his two younger children, who were after his own heart, while Madame de Bellegarde had paired with her eldest-born.

"My brother has spoken to me of you," said M. de Bellegarde; "and as you are also acquainted with my sister, it was time we should meet." He turned to his mother and gallantly bent over her hand, touching it with his lips, and then he assumed an attitude before the chimney-piece. With his long lean face, his high-bridged nose, and his small opaque eyes, he looked much like an Englishman. His whiskers were fair and glossy, and he had a large dimple, of unmistakable British origin, in the middle of his handsome chin. He was "distinguished" to the tips of his polished nails, and there was not a movement of his fine perpendicular person that was not noble and majestic. Newman had never yet been confronted with such an incarnation of the art of taking oneself seriously; he felt a sort of impulse to step backward, as you do to get a view of a great façade.

"Urbain," said young Madame de Bellegarde, who had apparently been waiting for her husband to take her to her ball, "I call your attention to the fact that I am dressed."

"That is a good idea," murmured Valentin.

"I am at your orders, my dear friend," said M. de Bellegarde. "Only, you must allow me first the pleasure of a little conversation with Mr. Newman."

"Oh, if you are going to a party, don't let me keep you," objected Newman. "I am very sure we shall meet again. Indeed, if you would like to converse with me I will gladly name an hour." He was eager to make it known that he would readily answer all questions and satisfy all exactions.

M. de Bellegarde stood in a well-balanced position before the fire, caressing one of his fair whiskers with one of his white hands, and looking at Newman, half askance, with eyes from which a particular ray of observation made its way through a general meaningless smile. "It is very kind of you to make such an offer," he

5. The custom of the handshake, at an introduction, was an American novelty.

said. "If I am not mistaken, your occupations are such as to make your time precious. You are in—a—as we say, *dans les affaires*."[6]

"In business, you mean? Oh no, I have thrown business overboard for the present. I am 'loafing,' as *we* say. My time is quite my own."

"Ah, you are taking a holiday," rejoined M. de Bellegarde. " 'Loafing.' Yes, I have heard that expression."

"Mr. Newman is American," said Madame de Bellegarde.

"My brother is a great ethnologist," said Valentin.

"An ethnologist?" said Newman. "Ah, you collect negroes' skulls, and that sort of thing."

The marquis looked hard at his brother, and began to caress his other whisker. Then, turning to Newman, with sustained urbanity: "You are travelling for your pleasure?" he asked.

"Oh, I am knocking about to pick up one thing and another. Of course I get a good deal of pleasure out of it."

"What especially interests you?" inquired the marquis.

"Well, everything interests me," said Newman. "I am not particular. Manufactures are what I care most about."

"That has been your specialty?"

"I can't say I have had any specialty. My specialty has been to make the largest possible fortune in the shortest possible time." Newman made this last remark very deliberately; he wished to open the way, if it were necessary, to an authoritative statement of his means.

M. de Bellegarde laughed agreeably. "I hope you have succeeded," he said.

"Yes, I have made a fortune in a reasonable time. I am not so old, you see."

"Paris is a very good place to spend a fortune. I wish you great enjoyment of yours." And M. de Bellegarde drew forth his gloves and began to put them on.

Newman for a few moments watched him sliding his white hands into the white kid, and as he did so his feelings took a singular turn. M. de Bellegarde's good wishes seemed to descend out of the white expanse of his sublime serenity with the soft scattered movement of a shower of snow-flakes. Yet Newman was not irritated; he did not feel that he was being patronised; he was conscious of no especial impulse to introduce a discord into so noble a harmony. Only he felt himself suddenly in personal contact with the forces with which his friend Valentin had told him that he would have to contend, and he became sensible of their intensity. He wished to make some answering manifestations, to stretch himself out at his own length,

6. "In business."

to sound a note at the uttermost end of *his* scale. It must be added that if this impulse was not vicious or malicious, it was by no means void of humorous expectancy. Newman was quite as ready to give play to that loosely-adjusted smile of his, if his hosts should happen to be shocked, as he was far from deliberately planning to shock them.

"Paris is a very good place for idle people," he said, "or it is a very good place if your family has been settled here for a long time, and you have made acquaintances and got your relations round you; or if you have got a big house like this, and a wife and children and mother and sister, and everything comfortable. I don't like that way of living all in rooms next door to each other. But I am not an idler. I try to be, but I can't manage it; it goes against the grain. My business habits are too deep-seated. Then, I hav'n't any house to call my own, or anything in the way of a family. My sisters are five thousand miles away, my mother died when I was a youngster, and I hav'n't any wife; I wish I had! So, you see, I don't exactly know what to do with myself. I am not fond of books, as you are, sir, and I get tired of dining out and going to the opera. I miss my business activity. You see, I began to earn my living when I was almost a baby, and until a few months ago I have never had my hand off the plow. Elegant leisure comes hard."

This speech was followed by a profound silence of some moments, on the part of Newman's entertainers. Valentin stood looking at him fixedly, with his hands in his pockets, and then he slowly, with a half-sidling motion, went out of the room. The marquis continued to draw on his gloves and to smile benignantly.

"You began to earn your living when you were a mere baby?" said the marquise.

"Hardly more—a small boy."

"You say you are not fond of books," said M. de Bellegarde; "but you must do yourself the justice to remember that your studies were interrupted early."

"That is very true; on my tenth birthday I stopped going to school. I thought it was a grand way to keep it. But I picked up some information afterwards," said Newman, reassuringly.

"You have some sisters?" asked old Madame de Bellegarde.

"Yes, two sisters. Splendid women!"

"I hope that for them the hardships of life commenced less early."

"They married very early, if you call that a hardship, as girls do in our Western country. One of them is married to the owner of the largest india-rubber house in the West."[7]

7. A product of the *Ficus elastica* rubber tree, produced in Assam; India rubber, a novelty at the time, became popular for overshoes and raincoats.

"Ah, you make houses also of india-rubber?" inquired the marquise.

"You can stretch them as your family increases," said young Madame de Bellegarde, who was muffling herself in a long white shawl.

Newman indulged in a burst of hilarity, and explained that the house in which his brother-in-law lived was a large wooden structure, but that he manufactured and sold india-rubber on a colossal scale.

"My children have some little india-rubber shoes which they put on when they go to play in the Tuileries[8] in damp weather," said the young marquise. "I wonder whether your brother-in-law made them?"

"Very likely," said Newman; "if he did, you may be very sure that they are well made."

"Well, you must not be discouraged," said M. de Bellegarde, with vague urbanity.

"Oh, I don't mean to be. I have a project which gives me plenty to think about, and that is an occupation." And then Newman was silent a moment, hesitating, yet thinking rapidly; he wished to make his point, and yet to do so forced him to speak out in a way that was disagreeable to him. "Nevertheless," he continued, addressing himself to old Madame de Bellegarde, "I will tell you my project; perhaps you can help me. I want to take a wife."

"It is a very good project, but I am no matchmaker," said the old lady.

Newman looked at her an instant, and then, with perfect sincerity: "I should have thought you were," he declared.

Madame de Bellegarde appeared to think him too sincere. She murmured something sharply in French, and fixed her eyes on her son. At this moment the door of the room was thrown open, and with a rapid step Valentin reappeared.

"I have a message for you," he said to his sister-in-law. "Claire bids me to request you not to start for your ball. She will go with you."

"Claire will go with us!" cried the young marquise. "*En voilà, du nouveau!*"[9]

"She has changed her mind; she decided half an hour ago, and she is sticking the last diamond into her hair!" said Valentin.

"What has taken possession of my daughter?" demanded Madame de Bellegarde sternly. "She has not been into the world

8. The royal palace in Paris, destroyed by fire during the time of the Commune of Paris in 1871; still noted for its splendid formal gardens designed by Lenôtre.

9. "There's something new!"

these three years. Does she take such a step at half-an-hour's notice and without consulting me?"

"She consulted me, dear mother, five minutes since," said Valentin, "and I told her that such a beautiful woman—she is beautiful, you will see—had no right to bury herself alive."

"You should have referred Claire to her mother, my brother," said M. de Bellegarde, in French. "This is very strange."

"I refer her to the whole company!" said Valentin. "Here she comes!" and he went to the open door, met Madame de Cintré on the threshold, took her by the hand, and led her into the room. She was dressed in white; but a long blue cloak, which hung almost to her feet, was fastened across her shoulders by a silver clasp. She had tossed it back, however, and her long white arms were uncovered. In her dense fair hair there glittered a dozen diamonds. She looked serious and, Newman thought, rather pale; but she glanced round her, and, when she saw him, smiled and put out her hand. He thought her tremendously handsome. He had a chance to look at her full in the face, for she stood a moment in the centre of the room, hesitating, apparently, what she should do, without meeting his eyes. Then she went up to her mother, who sat in her deep chair by the fire, looking at Madame de Cintré almost fiercely. With her back turned to the others, Madame de Cintré held her cloak apart to show her dress.

"What do you think of me?" she asked.

"I think you are audacious," said the marquise. "It was but three days ago, when I asked you, as a particular favour to myself, to go to the Duchess de Lusignan's, that you told me you were going nowhere, and that one must be consistent. Is this your consistency? Why should you distinguish Madame Robineau? Who is it you wish to please to-night?"

"I wish to please myself, dear mother," said Madame de Cintré. And she bent over and kissed the old lady.

"I don't like surprises, my sister," said Urbain de Bellegarde; "especially when one is on the point of entering a drawing-room."

Newman at this juncture felt inspired to speak. "Oh, if you are going into a room with Madame de Cintré, you needn't be afraid of being noticed yourself!"

M. de Bellegarde turned to his sister with a smile too intense to be easy. "I hope you appreciate a compliment that is paid you at your brother's expense," he said. "Come, come, madam." And offering Madame de Cintré his arm he led her rapidly out of the room. Valentin rendered the same service to young Madame de Bellegarde, who had apparently been reflecting on the fact that the ball-dress of her sister-in-law was much less brilliant than her own, and yet had failed to derive absolute comfort from the reflection. With a farewell smile she sought the complement of her consolation in the eyes of the American visitor, and perceiving in them a certain mysterious brilliancy, it is not improbable that she may have flattered herself she had found it.

Newman, left alone with old Madame de Bellegarde, stood before her a few moments in silence. "Your daughter is very beautiful," he said, at last.

"She is very strange," said Madame de Bellegarde.

"I am glad to hear it," Newman rejoined, smiling. "It makes me hope."

"Hope what?"

"That she will consent, some day, to marry me."

The old lady rose slowly to her feet. "That really is your project, then?"

"Yes; will you favour it?"

"Favour it?" Madame de Bellegarde looked at him a moment and then shook her head. "No!" she said softly.

"Will you suffer it then? Will you let it pass?"

"You don't know what you ask. I am a very proud and meddlesome old woman."

"Well, I am very rich," said Newman.

Madame de Bellegarde fixed her eyes on the floor, and Newman thought it probable she was weighing the reasons in favour of resenting the brutality of this remark. But at last looking up, she said simply: "How rich?"

Newman expressed his income in a round number which had the magnificent sound that large aggregations of dollars put on when they are translated into francs. He added a few remarks of a financial character, which completed a sufficiently striking presentment of his resources.

Madame de Bellegarde listened in silence. "You are very frank," she said finally. "I will be the same. I would rather favour you, on the whole, than suffer you. It will be easier."

"I am thankful for any terms," said Newman. "But, for the present, you have suffered me long enough. Good night!" And he took his leave.

Chapter XI

Newman, on his return to Paris, had not resumed the study of French conversation with M. Nioche; he found that he had too many other uses for his time. M. Nioche, however, came to see him very promptly, having learned his whereabouts by a mysterious process to which his patron never obtained the key. The shrunken little capitalist repeated his visit more than once. He seemed oppressed by a humiliating sense of having been overpaid, and wished apparently to redeem his debt by the offer of grammatical and statistical information in small instalments. He wore the same decently melancholy aspect as a few months before; a few months more or less of brushing could make little difference in the antique lustre of his coat and hat. But the poor old man's spirit was a trifle more threadbare; it seemed to have received some hard rubs during the summer. Newman inquired with interest about Mademoiselle Noémie; and M. Nioche, at first, for answer, simply looked at him in lachrymose silence.

"Don't ask me, sir," he said at last. "I sit and watch her, but I can do nothing."

"Do you mean that she misconducts herself?"

"I don't know, I am sure. I can't follow her. I don't understand her. She has something in her head; I don't know what she is trying to do. She is too deep for me."

"Does she continue to go to the Louvre? Has she made any of those copies for me?"

"She goes to the Louvre, but I see nothing of the copies. She has something on her easel; I suppose it is one of the pictures you ordered. Such a magnificent order ought to give her fairy-fingers. But she is not in earnest. I can't say anything to her; I am afraid of her. One evening, last summer, when I took her to walk in the Champs Élysées, she said some things to me that frightened me."

"What were they?"

"Excuse an unhappy father from telling you," said M. Nioche, unfolding his calico pocket-handkerchief.

Newman promised himself to pay Mademoiselle Noémie another visit at the Louvre. He was curious about the progress of his copies, but it must be added that he was still more curious about the progress of the young lady herself. He went one afternoon to the great museum, and wandered through several of the rooms in fruitless quest of her. He was bending his steps to the long hall of the Italian masters, when suddenly he found himself face to face with Valentin de Bellegarde. The young Frenchman greeted him with ardour, and assured him that he was a godsend. He himself was in the worst of humours and he wanted someone to contradict.

"In a bad humour among all these beautiful things?" said Newman. "I thought you were so fond of pictures, especially the old black ones. There are two or three here that ought to keep you in spirits."

"Oh, to-day," answered Valentin, "I am not in a mood for pictures, and the more beautiful they are the less I like them. Their great staring eyes and fixed positions irritate me. I feel as if I were at some big dull party, in a room full of people I shouldn't wish to speak to. What should I care for their beauty? It's a bore, and, worse still, it's a reproach. I have a great many *ennuis*;[1] I feel vicious."

"If the Louvre has so little comfort for you, why in the world did you come here?" Newman asked.

"That is one of my *ennuis*. I came to meet my cousin—a dreadful English cousin, a member of my mother's family—who is in Paris for a week for her husband, and who wishes me to point out the 'principal beauties.' Imagine a woman who wears a green crape bonnet in December and has straps sticking out of the ankles of her interminable boots! My mother begged I would do something to oblige them. I have undertaken to play *valet de place*[2] this afternoon. They were to have met me here at two o'clock, and I have been waiting for them twenty minutes. Why doesn't she arrive? She has at least a pair of feet to carry her. I don't know whether to be furious at their playing me false, or delighted to have escaped them."

"I think in your place I would be furious," said Newman, "because they may arrive yet, and then your fury will still be of use to you. Whereas if you were delighted and they were afterwards to turn up, you might not know what to do with your delight."

"You give me excellent advice, and I already feel better. I will be furious; I will let them go to the deuce and I myself will go with you—unless by chance you too have a rendezvous."

"It is not exactly a rendezvous," said Newman. "But I have in fact come to see a person, not a picture."

"A woman, presumably?"

"A young lady."

"Well," said Valentin, "I hope for you with all my heart that she is not clothed in green tulle and that her feet are not too much out of focus."

"I don't know much about her feet, but she has very pretty hands."

Valentin gave a sigh. "And on that assurance I must part with you?"

"I am not certain of finding my young lady," said Newman, "and I am not quite prepared to lose your company on the chance. It does not strike me as particularly desirable to introduce you to her, and yet I should rather like to have your opinion of her."

"Is she pretty?"

"I guess you will think so."

Bellegarde passed his arm into that of his companion. "Conduct

1. Annoyances.

2. Guide at an inn or hotel.

me to her on the instant! I should be ashamed to make a pretty woman wait for my verdict."

Newman suffered himself to be gently propelled in the direction in which he had been walking, but his step was not rapid. He was turning something over in his mind. The two men passed into the long gallery of the Italian masters, and Newman, after having scanned for a moment its brilliant vista, turned aside into the smaller apartment devoted to the same school, on the left. It contained very few persons, but at the farther end of it sat Mademoiselle Nioche, before her easel. She was not at work; her palette and brushes had been laid down beside her, her hands were folded in her lap, and she was leaning back in her chair and looking intently at two ladies on the other side of the hall, who, with their backs turned to her, had stopped before one of the pictures. These ladies were apparently persons of high fashion; they were dressed with great splendour, and their long silken trains and furbelows were spread over the polished floor. It was at their dresses Mademoiselle Noémie was looking, though what she was thinking of I am unable to say. I hazard the supposition that she was saying to herself that to be able to drag such a train over a polished floor was a felicity worth any price. Her reflections, at any rate, were disturbed by the advent of Newman and his companion. She glanced at them quickly, and then, colouring a little, rose and stood before her easel.

"I came here on purpose to see you," said Newman in his bad French, offering to shake hands. And then, like a good American, he introduced Valentin formally: "Allow me to make you acquainted with the Comte Valentin de Bellegarde."

Valentin made a bow which must have seemed to Mademoiselle Noémie quite in harmony with the impressiveness of his title, but the graceful brevity of her own response made no concession to underbred surprise. She turned to Newman, putting up her hands to her hair and smoothing its delicately-felt roughness. Then, rapidly, she turned the canvas that was on her easel over upon its face. "You have not forgotten me?" she asked.

"I shall never forget you," said Newman. "You may be sure of that."

"Oh," said the young girl, "there are a great many different ways of remembering a person." And she looked straight at Valentin de Bellegarde, who was looking at her as a gentleman may when a "verdict" is expected of him.

"Have you painted anything for me?" said Newman. "Have you been industrious?"

"No, I have done nothing." And taking up her palette, she began to mix her colours at hazard.

"But your father tells me you have come here constantly."

"I have nowhere else to go! Here, all summer, it was cool, at least."

"Being here, then," said Newman, "you might have tried something."

"I told you before," she answered softly, "that I don't know how to paint."

"But you have something charming on your easel, now," said Valentin, "if you would only let me see it."

She spread out her two hands, with the fingers expanded, over the back of the canvas—those hands which Newman had called pretty, and which, in spite of several paint-stains, Valentin could now admire. "My painting is not charming," she said.

"It is the only thing about you that is not, then, mademoiselle," quoth Valentin gallantly.

She took up her little canvas and silently passed it to him. He looked at it, and in a moment she said, "I am sure you are a judge."

"Yes," he answered, "I am."

"You know, then, that that is very bad."

"*Mon Dieu!*"[3] said Valentin, shrugging his shoulders, "let us distinguish."

"You know that I ought not to attempt to paint," the young girl continued.

"Frankly, then, mademoiselle, I think you ought not."

She began to look at the dresses of the two splendid ladies again—a point on which, having risked one conjecture, I think I may risk another. While she was looking at the ladies she was seeing Valentin de Bellegarde. He, at all events, was seeing her. He put down the roughly-besmeared canvas and addressed a little click with his tongue, accompanied by an elevation of the eyebrows, to Newman.

"Where have you been all these months?" asked Mademoiselle Noémie of our hero. "You took those great journeys, you amused yourself well?"

"Oh yes," said Newman, "I amused myself well enough."

"I am very glad," said Mademoiselle Noémie with extreme gentleness; and she began to dabble in her colours again. She was singularly pretty, with the look of serious sympathy that she threw into her face.

Valentin took advantage of her downcast eyes to telegraph again to his companion. He renewed his mysterious physiognomical play, making at the same time a rapid tremulous movement in the air

3. "Good Lord!"

with his fingers. He was evidently finding Mademoiselle Noémie extremely interesting; the blue devils had departed, leaving the field clear.

"Tell me something about your travels," murmured the young girl.

"Oh, I went to Switzerland—to Geneva, and Zermatt, and Zürich, and all those places, you know; and down to Venice, and all through Germany, and down the Rhine, and into Holland and Belgium—the regular round. How do you say that in French—the regular round?" Newman asked of Valentin.

Mademoiselle Nioche fixed her eyes an instant on Bellegarde, and then with a little smile: "I don't understand, monsieur," she said, "when he says so much at once. Would you be so good as to translate?"

"I would rather talk to you out of my own head," Valentin declared.

"No," said Newman gravely, still in his bad French, "you must not talk to Mademoiselle Nioche, because you say discouraging things. You ought to tell her to work, to persevere."

"And we French, mademoiselle," said Valentin, "are accused of being false flatterers!"

"I don't want any flattery, I want only the truth. But I know the truth."

"All I say is that I suspect there are some things that you can do better than paint," said Valentin.

"I know the truth—I know the truth," Mademoiselle Noémie repeated. And, dipping a brush into a clot of red paint, she drew a great horizontal daub across her unfinished picture.

"What is that?" asked Newman.

Without answering, she drew another long crimson daub, in a vertical direction, down the middle of her canvas, and so, in a moment, completed the rough indication of a cross. "It is the sign of the truth," she said at last.

The two men looked at each other, and Valentin indulged in another flash of physiognomical eloquence. "You have spoiled your picture," said Newman.

"I know that very well. It was the only thing to do with it. I had sat looking at it all day without touching it. I had begun to hate it. It seemed to me something was going to happen."

"I like it better that way than as it was before," said Valentin. "Now it is more interesting. It tells a story. Is it for sale, mademoiselle?"

"Everything I have is for sale," said Mademoiselle Noémie.

"How much is this thing?"

"Ten thousand francs," said the young girl, without a smile.

"Everything that Mademoiselle Nioche may do at present is mine in advance," said Newman. "It makes part of an order I gave her some months ago. So you can't have this."

"Monsieur will lose nothing by it," said the young girl, looking at Valentin. And she began to put up her utensils.

"I shall have gained a charming memory," said Valentin. "You are going away? your day is over?"

"My father is coming to fetch me," said Mademoiselle Noémie.

She had hardly spoken when, through the door behind her, which opens on one of the great white stone staircases of the Louvre, M. Nioche made his appearance. He came in with his usual patient shuffle, and he made a low salute to the two gentlemen who were standing before his daughter's easel. Newman shook his hand with muscular friendliness, and Valentin returned his greeting with extreme deference. While the old man stood waiting for Noémie to make a parcel of her implements, he let his mild oblique gaze hover towards Bellegarde, who was watching Mademoiselle Noémie put on her bonnet and mantle. Valentin was at no pains to disguise his scrutiny. He looked at a pretty girl as he would have listened to a piece of music. Attention, in each case, was simple good manners. M. Nioche at last took his daughter's paint-box in one hand and the bedaubed canvas, after giving it a solemn puzzled stare, in the other, and led the way to the door. Mademoiselle Noémie made the young men the salute of a duchess, and followed her father.

"Well," said Newman, "what do you think of her?"

"She is very remarkable. *Diable, diable, diable!*"[4] repeated M. de Bellegarde, reflectively; "she is very remarkable."

"I am afraid she is a sad little adventuress," said Newman.

"Not a little one—a great one. She has the material." And Valentin began to walk away slowly, looking vaguely at the pictures on the walls, with a thoughtful illumination in his eye. Nothing could have appealed to his imagination more than the possible adventures of a young lady endowed with the "material" of Mademoiselle Nioche. "She is very interesting," he went on. "She is a beautiful type."

"A beautiful type? What the deuce do you mean?" asked Newman.

"I mean from the artistic point of view. She is an artist—outside of her painting, which obviously is execrable."

"But she is not beautiful. I don't even think her very pretty."

"She is quite pretty enough for her purposes, and it is a face and

4. **"The devil, the devil, the devil!"**

figure in which everything tells. If she were prettier she would be less intelligent, and her intelligence is half of her charm."

"In what way," asked Newman, who was much amused at his companion's immediate philosophisation of Mademoiselle Nioche, "does her intelligence strike you as so remarkable?"

"She has taken the measure of life, and she has determined to *be* something—to succeed at any cost. Her painting, of course, is a mere trick to gain time. She is waiting for her chance; she wishes to launch herself, and to do it well. She knows her Paris. She is one of fifty thousand, so far as the mere ambition goes; but I am very sure that in the way of resolution and capacity she is a rarity. And in one gift—perfect heartlessness—I will warrant she is unsurpassed. She has not as much heart as will go on the point of a needle. That is an immense virtue. Yes, she is one of the celebrities of the future."

"Heaven help us!" said Newman, "how far the artistic point of view may take a man! But in this case I must request that you don't let it take you too far. You have learned a wonderful deal about Mademoiselle Noémie in a quarter of an hour. Let that suffice; don't follow up your researches."

"My dear fellow," cried Bellegarde, with warmth, "I hope I have too good manners to intrude."

"You are not intruding. The girl is nothing to me. In fact, I rather dislike her. But I like her poor old father, and for his sake I beg you to abstain from any attempt to verify your theories."

"For the sake of that seedy old gentleman who came to fetch her?" demanded Valentin, stopping short. And on Newman's assenting, "Ah no, ah no," he went on with a smile. "You are quite wrong, my dear fellow; you needn't mind him."

"I verily believe that you are accusing the poor gentleman of being capable of rejoicing in his daughter's dishonour."

"*Voyons!*"[5] said Valentin; "who is he? what is he?"

"He is what he looks like: as poor as a rat, but very high-toned."

"Exactly. I noticed him perfectly; be sure I do him justice. He has had losses, *des malheurs*,[6] as we say. He is very low-spirited, and his daughter is too much for him. He is the pink of respectability, and he has sixty years of honesty on his back. All this I perfectly appreciate. But I know my fellow-men and my fellow-Parisians, and I will make a bargain with you." Newman gave ear to his bargain and he went on. "He would rather his daughter were a good girl than a bad one, but if the worst comes to the worst, the

5. "Let's see!"

6. Misfortunes.

old man will not do what Virginius did.[7] Success justifies everything. If Mademoiselle Noémie makes a figure, her papa will feel—well, we will call it relieved. And she will make a figure. The old gentleman's future is assured."

"I don't know what Virginius did, but M. Nioche will shoot Miss Noémie," said Newman. "After that, I suppose his future will be assured in some snug prison."

"I am not a cynic; I am simply an observer," Valentin rejoined. "Mademoiselle Noémie interests me; she is extremely remarkable. If there is a good reason, in honour or decency, for dismissing her from my thoughts forever, I am perfectly willing to do it. Your estimate of the papa's sensibilities is a good reason until it is invalidated. I promise you not to look at the young girl again until you tell me that you have changed your mind about the papa. When he has given distinct proof of being a philosopher, you will raise your interdict. Do you agree to that?"

"Do you mean to bribe him?"

"Oh, you admit, then, that he is bribable? No, he would ask too much, and it would not be exactly fair. I mean simply to wait. You will continue, I suppose, to see this interesting couple, and you will give me the news yourself."

"Well," said Newman, "if the old man turns out a humbug, you may do what you please. I wash my hands of the matter."[8]

"For the girl herself, you may be at rest. I don't know what harm she may do to me, but I certainly can't hurt her."

"It seems to me," said Newman, "that you are very well matched. You are both hard cases, and M. Nioche and I, I believe, are the only virtuous men to be found in Paris."

Soon after this M. de Bellegarde, in punishment for his levity, received a stern poke in the back from a pointed instrument. Turning quickly round he found the weapon to be a parasol wielded by a lady in a green gauze bonnet. Valentin's English cousins had been drifting about unpiloted, and evidently deemed that they had a grievance. Newman left him to their mercies, but with a boundless faith in his power to plead his cause.

Chapter XII

Three days after his introduction to the family of Madame de Cintré, Newman, coming in toward evening, found upon his table

7. Virginius murdered his daughter in order to prevent her virtue from being corrupted by Appius. The story is told by Livy; it reappears in *The Romance of the Rose* and in Chaucer's "Physician's Tale."

8. The words of Pontius Pilate, in delivering Jesus to the mob for crucifixion.

the card of the Marquis de Bellegarde. On the following day he received a note informing him that the Marquise de Bellegarde would be grateful for the honour of his company at dinner.

He went, of course, though he had to break another engagement to do it. He was ushered into the room in which Madame de Bellegarde had received him before, and here he found his venerable hostess, surrounded by her entire family. The room was lighted only by the crackling fire, which illumined the very small pink slippers of a lady who, seated in a low chair, was stretching out her toes before it. This lady was the younger Madame de Bellegarde. Madame de Cintré was seated at the other end of the room, holding a little girl against her knee, the child of her brother Urbain, to whom she was apparently relating a wonderful story. Valentin was sitting on a puff close to his sister-in-law, into whose ear he was certainly distilling the finest nonsense. The marquis was stationed before the fire, with his head erect and his hands behind him, in an attitude of formal expectancy.

Old Madame de Bellegarde stood up to give Newman her greeting, and there was that in the way she did so which seemed to measure narrowly the extent of her condescension. "We are all alone, you see; we have asked no one else," she said austerely.

"I am very glad you didn't; this is much more sociable," said Newman. "Good evening, sir," and he offered his hand to the marquis.

M. de Bellegarde was affable, but in spite of his dignity he was restless. He began to pace up and down the room, he looked out of the long windows, he took up books and laid them down again. Young Madame de Bellegarde gave Newman her hand without moving and without looking at him.

"You may think that is coldness," exclaimed Valentin; "but it is not, it is warmth. It shows she is treating you as an intimate. Now she detests me, and yet she is always looking at me."

"No wonder I detest you if I am always looking at you!" cried the lady. "If Mr. Newman does not like my way of shaking hands, I will do it again."

But this charming privilege was lost upon our hero, who was already making his way across the room to Madame de Cintré. She looked at him as she shook hands, but she went on with the story she was telling her little niece. She had only two or three phrases to add, but they were apparently of great moment. She deepened her voice, smiling as she did so, and the little girl gazed at her with round eyes.

"But in the end the young prince married the beautiful Florabella," said Madame de Cintré, "and carried her off to live with him in the Land of the Pink Sky.[9] There she was so happy that she forgot all her troubles, and went out to drive every day of her life in an ivory coach drawn by five hundred white mice. Poor Florabella," she explained to Newman, "had suffered terribly."

"She had had nothing to eat for six months," said little Blanche.

"Yes, but when the six months were over, she had a plum-cake as big as that ottoman," said Madame de Cintré. "That quite set her up again."

"What a checkered career!" said Newman. "Are you very fond of children?" He was certain that she was, but he wished to make her say it.

"I like to talk with them," she answered; "we can talk with them so much more seriously than with grown persons. That is great nonsense that I have been telling Blanche, but it is a great deal more serious than most of what we say in society."

"I wish you would talk to me, then, as if I were Blanche's age," said Newman laughing. "Were you happy at your ball the other night?"

"Ecstatically!"

"Now you are talking the nonsense that we talk in society," said Newman. "I don't believe that."

"It was my own fault if I was not happy. The ball was very pretty, and everyone very amiable."

"It was on your conscience," said Newman, "that you had annoyed your mother and your brother."

Madame de Cintré looked at him a moment without answering. "That is true," she replied at last. "I had undertaken more than I could carry out. I have very little courage; I am not a heroine." She said this with a certain soft emphasis; but then, changing her tone: "I could never have gone through the sufferings of the beautiful Florabella," she added, "not even for her prospective rewards."

Dinner was announced, and Newman betook himself to the side of old Madame de Bellegarde. The dining-room, at the end of a cold corridor, was vast and sombre; the dinner was simple and delicately excellent. Newman wondered whether Madame de Cintré had had something to do with ordering the repast, and greatly hoped she had. Once seated at table, with the various members of the ancient house of Bellegarde around him, he asked himself the meaning of his position. Was the old lady responding to his advances? Did the fact that he was a solitary guest augment his credit or diminish it? Were they ashamed to show him to other people, or

9. The fairy-tale quality of Newman's ambition underlines James's remark, in the Preface, on the romancelike aspect of the story.

did they wish to give him a sign of sudden adoption into their last reserve of favour? Newman was on his guard; he was watchful and conjectural; and yet at the same time he was vaguely indifferent. Whether they gave him a long rope or a short one he was there now, and Madame de Cintré was opposite to him. She had a tall candlestick on each side of her; she would sit there for the next hour, and that was enough. The dinner was extremely solemn and measured; he wondered whether this was always the state of things in "old families." Madame de Bellegarde held her head very high, and fixed her eyes, which looked peculiarly sharp in her little finely-wrinkled white face, very intently upon the table-service. The marquis appeared to have decided that the fine arts offered a safe subject of conversation, as not leading to startling personal revelations. Every now and then, having learned from Newman that he had been through the museums of Europe, he uttered some polished aphorism upon the flesh-tints of Rubens and the good-taste of Sansovino.[1] His manners seemed to indicate a fine nervous dread that something disagreeable might happen if the atmosphere were not purified by allusions of a thoroughly superior cast. "What under the sun is the man afraid of?" Newman asked himself. "Does he think I am going to offer to swap jack-knives with him?" It was useless to shut his eyes to the fact that the marquis was profoundly disagreeable to him. He had never been a man of strong personal aversions; his nerves had not been at the mercy of the mystical qualities of his neighbours. But here was a man towards whom he was irresistibly in opposition; a man of forms and phrases and postures; a man full of possible impertinences and treacheries. M. de Bellegarde made him feel as if he were standing barefooted on a marble floor; and yet, to gain his desire, Newman felt perfectly able to stand. He wondered what Madame de Cintré thought of his being accepted, if accepted it was. There was no judging from her face, which expressed simply the desire to be gracious in a manner which should require as little explicit recognition as possible. Young Madame de Bellegarde had always the same manners; she was always preoccupied, distracted, listening to everything and hearing nothing, looking at her dress, her rings, her finger-nails, seeming rather bored, and yet puzzling you to decide what was her ideal of social diversion. Newman was enlightened on this point later. Even Valentin did not quite seem master of his wits; his vivacity was fitful and forced, yet Newman observed that in the lapses of his talk he appeared excited. His eyes had an intenser

1. Jacopo Sansovino (1486–1570), Italian sculptor and architect, famed for his gigantic sculptures of Mars and Neptune outside the Doge's palace in Venice.

spark than usual. The effect of all this was that Newman, for the first time in his life, was not himself; that he measured his movements, and counted his words, and resolved that if the occasion demanded that he should appear to have swallowed a ramrod, he would meet the emergency.

After dinner M. de Bellegarde proposed to his guest that they should go into the smoking-room, and he led the way toward a small somewhat musty apartment, the walls of which were ornamented with old hangings of stamped leather and trophies of rusty arms. Newman refused a cigar, but he established himself upon one of the divans, while the marquis puffed his own weed before the fireplace, and Valentin sat looking through the light fumes of a cigarette from one to the other.

"I can't keep quiet any longer," said Valentin, at last. "I must tell you the news and congratulate you. My brother seems unable to come to the point; he revolves around his announcement like the priest around the altar. You are accepted as a candidate for the hand of our sister."

"Valentin, be a little proper!" murmured the marquis, with a look of the most delicate irritation contracting the bridge of his high nose.

"There has been a family council," the young man continued; "my mother and Urbain have put their heads together, and even my testimony has not been altogether excluded. My mother and the marquis sat at a table covered with green cloth; my sister-in-law and I were on a bench against the wall. It was like a committee at the Corps Législatif.[2] We were called up, one after the other, to testify. We spoke of you very handsomely. Madame de Bellegarde said that if she had not been told who you were, she would have taken you for a duke—an American duke, the Duke of California. I said that I could warrant you grateful for the smallest favours—modest, humble, unassuming. I was sure that you would know your own place always, and never give us occasion to remind you of certain differences. After all, you couldn't help it if you were not a duke. There were none in your country; but if there had been, it was certain that, smart and active as you are, you would have got the pick of the titles. At this point I was ordered to sit down, but I think I made an impression in your favour."

M. de Bellegarde looked at his brother with dangerous coldness, and gave a smile as thin as the edge of a knife. Then he removed a spark of cigar-ash from the sleeve of his coat; he fixed his eyes for a while on the cornice of the room, and at last he inserted one of

2. Legislature.

his white hands into the breast of his waistcoat. "I must apologise to you for the deplorable levity of my brother," he said, "and I must notify you that this is probably not the last time that his want of tact will cause you serious embarrassment."

"No, I confess I have no tact," said Valentin. "Is your embarrassment really painful, Newman? The marquis will put you right again; his own touch is deliciously delicate."

"Valentin, I am sorry to say," the marquis continued, "has never possessed the tone, the manner, that belong to a young man in his position. It has been a great affliction to his mother, who is very fond of the old traditions. But you must remember that he speaks for no one but himself."

"Oh, I don't mind him, sir," said Newman good-humouredly. "I know what he amounts to."

"In the good old times," said Valentin, "marquises and counts used to have their appointed fools and jesters, to crack jokes for them. Nowadays we see a great strapping democrat keeping a count about him to play the fool. It's a good situation, but I certainly am very degenerate."

M. de Bellegarde fixed his eyes for some time on the floor. "My mother informed me," he said presently, "of the announcement that you made to her the other evening."

"That I desired to marry your sister?" said Newman.

"That you wished to arrange a marriage," said the marquis slowly, "with my sister, the Comtesse de Cintré. The proposal was serious, and required, on my mother's part, a great deal of reflection. She naturally took me into her counsels, and I gave my most zealous attention to the subject. There was a great deal to be considered; more than you appear to imagine. We have viewed the question on all its faces, we have weighed one thing against another. Our conclusion has been that we favour your suit. My mother has desired me to inform you of our decision. She will have the honour of saying a few words to you on the subject herself. Meanwhile, by us, the heads of the family, you are accepted."

Newman got up and came nearer to the marquis. "You will do nothing to hinder me, and all you can to help me, eh?"

"I will recommend my sister to accept you."

Newman passed his hand over his face, and pressed it for a moment upon his eyes. This promise had a great sound, and yet the pleasure he took in it was embittered by his having to stand there so and receive his passport from M. de Bellegarde. The idea of having this gentleman mixed up with his wooing and wedding was more and more disagreeable to him. But Newman had resolved to go through the mill, as he imaged it, and he would not cry out at the first turn of the wheel. He was silent a while, and then he said, with a certain dryness which Valentin told him afterwards had a very grand air: "I am much obliged to you."

"I take note of the promise," said Valentin, "I register the vow."

M. de Bellegarde began to gaze at the cornice again; he apparently had something more to say. "I must do my mother the justice," he resumed, "I must do myself the justice, to say that our decision was not easy. Such an arrangement was not what we had expected. The idea that my sister should marry a gentleman—ah—in business, was something of a novelty."

"So I told you, you know," said Valentin, raising his finger at Newman.

"The novelty has not quite worn away, I confess," the marquis went on; "perhaps it never will, entirely. But possibly that is not altogether to be regretted," and he gave his thin smile again. "It may be that the time has come when we should make some concession to novelty. There had been no novelties in our house for a great many years. I made the observation to my mother, and she did me the honour to admit that it was worthy of attention."

"My dear brother," interrupted Valentin, "is not your memory just here leading you the least bit astray? Our mother is, I may say, distinguished for her small respect for abstract reasoning. Are you very sure that she replied to your striking proposition in the gracious manner you describe? You know how terribly incisive she is sometimes. Didn't she, rather, do you the honour to say: 'A fiddlestick for your phrases! There are better reasons than that?' "

"Other reasons were discussed," said the marquis, without looking at Valentin, but with an audible tremor in his voice; "some of them possibly were better. We are conservative, Mr. Newman, but we are not also bigots. We judged the matter liberally. We have no doubt that everything will be comfortable."

Newman had stood listening to these remarks with his arms folded and his eyes fastened upon M. de Bellegarde. "Comfortable?" he said, with a sort of grim flatness of intonation. "Why shouldn't we be comfortable? If you are not, it will be your own fault; I have everything to make *me* so."

"My brother means that with the lapse of time you may get used to the change," and Valentin paused, to light another cigarette.

"What change?" asked Newman, in the same tone.

"Urbain," said Valentin, very gravely, "I am afraid that Mr. Newman does not quite realise the change. We ought to insist upon that."

"My brother goes too far," said M. de Bellegarde. "It is his fatal want of tact again. It is my mother's wish, and mine, that no such allusions should be made. Pray never make them yourself. We prefer to assume that the person accepted as the possible husband of my sister is one of ourselves, and that he should have no explanations to make. With a little discretion on both sides, everything, I think, will be easy. That is exactly what I wished to say—that we quite understand what we have undertaken, and that you may depend upon our adhering to our resolution."

Valentin shook his hands in the air and then buried his face in them. "I have less tact than I might have, no doubt; but oh, my brother, if you knew what you yourself were saying!" And he went off into a long laugh.

M. de Bellegarde's face flushed a little, but he held his head higher, as if to repudiate this concession to vulgar perturbability. "I am sure you understand me," he said to Newman.

"Oh no, I don't understand you at all," said Newman. "But you needn't mind that. I don't care. In fact, I think I had better not understand you. I might not like it. That wouldn't suit me at all, you know. I want to marry your sister, that's all; to do it as quickly as possible, and to find fault with nothing. I don't care how I do it. I am not marrying you, you know, sir. I have got my leave, and that is all I want."

"You had better receive the last word from my mother," said the marquis.

"Very good; I will go and get it," said Newman; and he prepared to return to the drawing-room.

M. de Bellegarde made a motion for him to pass first, and when Newman had gone out he shut himself into the room with Valentin. Newman had been a trifle bewildered by the audacious irony of the younger brother, and he had not needed its aid to point the moral of M. de Bellegarde's transcendent patronage. He had wit enough to appreciate the force of that civility which consists in calling your attention to the impertinences it spares you. But he had felt warmly the delicate sympathy with himself that underlay Valentin's fraternal irreverence, and he was most unwilling that his friend should pay a tax upon it. He paused a moment in the corridor, after he had gone a few steps, expecting to hear the resonance of M. de Bellegarde's displeasure; but he detected only a perfect stillness. The stillness itself seemed a trifle portentous; he reflected, however, that he had no right to stand listening, and he made his way back to the salon. In his absence several persons had come in. They were scattered about the room in groups, two or three of them having passed into a small boudoir, next to the drawing-room, which had now been lighted and opened. Old Madame de Bellegarde was in her place by the fire, talking to a very old gentleman in a wig and a profuse white neckcloth of the fashion of 1820. Madame de Cintré was bending a listening head to the historic confidences of an old lady who was presumably the wife of the old gentleman in the neckcloth, an old lady in a red satin dress and an ermine cape, who wore across her forehead a band with a topaz set in it. Young Madame de Bellegarde, when Newman came in, left some people among whom she was sitting, and took the place that she had occupied before dinner. Then she gave a little push to the puff that stood near her, and by a glance at Newman seemed to indicate that she had placed it in position for him. He went and took possession of it; the marquis's wife amused and puzzled him.

"I know your secret," she said, in her bad but charming English; "you need make no mystery of it. You wish to marry my sister-in-law. *C'est un beau choix.*[3] A man like you ought to marry a tall thin woman. You must know that I have spoken in your favour; you owe me a famous taper!"

"You have spoken to Madame de Cintré?" said Newman.

"Oh no, not that. You may think it strange, but my sister-in-law and I are not so intimate as that. No; I spoke to my husband and my mother-in-law; I said I was sure we could do what we chose with you."

"I am much obliged to you," said Newman, laughing; "but you can't."

"I know that very well; I didn't believe a word of it. But I wanted you to come into the house; I thought we should be friends."

"I am very sure of it," said Newman.

"Don't be too sure. If you like Madame de Cintré so much, perhaps you will not like me. We are as different as blue and pink. But you and I have something in common. I have come into this family by marriage; you want to come into it in the same way."

"Oh no, I don't!" interrupted Newman. "I only want to take Madame de Cintré out of it."

"Well, to cast your nets you have to go into the water. Our positions are alike; we shall be able to compare notes. What do you think of my husband? It's a strange question, isn't it? But I shall ask you some stranger ones yet."

"Perhaps a stranger one will be easier to answer," said Newman. "You might try me."

"Oh, you get off very well; the old Comte de la Rochefidèle, yonder, couldn't do it better. I told them that if we only gave you a chance you would be a perfect *talon rouge.*[4] I know something about men. Besides, you and I belong to the same camp. I am a ferocious democrat. By birth I am *vielle roche*;[5] a good little bit of the history of France is the history of my family. Oh, you never

3. "It's a good choice."
4. A perfect aristocrat. (Courtiers frequently wore boots with red heels; *talon rouge* means "red heels.")
5. One of the old school (literally, "old rock").

heard of us, of course! *Ce que c'est que la gloire!*[6] We are much better than the Bellegardes, at any rate. But I don't care a pin for my pedigree; I want to belong to my time. I'm a revolutionist, a radical, a child of the age! I am sure I go beyond you. I like clever people, wherever they come from, and I take my amusement wherever I find it. I don't pout at the Empire; here all the world pouts at the Empire. Of course I have to mind what I say; but I expect to take my revenge with you." Madame de Bellegarde discoursed for some time longer in this sympathetic strain, with an eager abundance which seemed to indicate that her opportunities for revealing her esoteric philosophy were indeed rare. She hoped that Newman would never be afraid of her, however he might be with the others, for, really, she went very far indeed. "Strong people"—*les gens forts*[7]—were in her opinion equal, all the world over. Newman listened to her with an attention at once beguiled and irritated. He wondered what the deuce she, too, was driving at, with her hope that he would not be afraid of her and her protestations of equality. In so far as he could understand her, she was wrong; a silly rattling woman was certainly not the equal of a sensible man, preoccupied with an ambitious passion. Madame de Bellegarde stopped suddenly, and looked at him sharply, shaking her fan. "I see you don't believe me," she said, "you are too much on your guard. You will not form an alliance, offensive or defensive? You are very wrong; I could help you."

Newman answered that he was very grateful and that he would certainly ask for help; she should see. "But first of all," he said, "I must help myself." And he went to join Madame de Cintré.

"I have been telling Madame de la Rochefidèle that you are an American," she said, as he came up. "It interests her greatly. Her father went over with the French troops to help you in your battles in the last century,[8] and she has always, in consequence, wanted greatly to see an American. But she has never succeeded till to-night. You are the first—to her knowledge—that she has ever looked at."

Madame de la Rochefidèle had an aged cadaverous face, with a falling of the lower jaw which prevented her from bringing her lips together, and reduced her conversation to a series of impressive but inarticulate gutturals. She raised an antique eyeglass, elaborately mounted in chased silver, and looked at Newman from head to foot. Then she said something to which he listened deferentially, but which he completely failed to understand.

"Madame de la Rochefidèle says that she is convinced that she must have seen Americans without knowing it," Madame de Cintré

6. "That's all that glory amount to."
7. "Solid citizens."
8. The American Revolutionary War.

explained. Newman thought it probable she had seen a great many things without knowing it; and the old lady, again addressing herself to utterance, declared—as interpreted by Madame de Cintré—that she wished she had known it.

At this moment the old gentleman who had been talking to the elder Madame de Bellegarde drew near, leading the marquise on his arm. His wife pointed out Newman to him, apparently explaining his remarkable origin. M. de la Rochefidèle, whose old age was rosy and rotund, spoke very neatly and clearly; almost as prettily, Newman thought, as M. Nioche. When he had been enlightened, he turned to Newman with an inimitable elderly grace.

"Monsieur is by no means the first American that I have seen," he said. "Almost the first person I ever saw—to notice him—was an American."

"Ah!" said Newman, sympathetically.

"The great Dr. Franklin,"[9] said M. de la Rochefidèle. "Of course I was very young. He was received very well in our *monde*."[1]

"Not better than Mr. Newman," said Madame de Bellegarde. "I beg he will offer me his arm into the other room. I could have offered no higher privilege to Dr. Franklin."

Newman, complying with Madame de Bellegarde's request, perceived that her two sons had returned to the drawing-room. He scanned their faces an instant for traces of the scene that had followed his separation from them, but the marquis seemed neither more nor less frigidly grand than usual, and Valentin was kissing ladies' hands with at least his habitual air of self-abandonment to the act. Madame de Bellegarde gave a glance at her eldest son, and by the time she had crossed the threshold of her boudoir he was at her side. The room was now empty and offered a sufficient degree of privacy. The old lady disengaged herself from Newman's arm and rested her hand on the arm of the marquis; and in this position she stood a moment, holding her head high and biting her small under-lip. I am afraid the picture was lost upon Newman, but Madame de Bellegarde was, in fact, at this moment a striking image of the dignity which—even in the case of a little time-shrunken old lady—may reside in the habit of unquestioned authority and the absoluteness of a social theory favourable to yourself.

"My son has spoken to you as I desired," she said, "and you understand that we shall not interfere. The rest will lie with yourself."

"M. de Bellegarde told me several things I didn't understand," said Newman, "but I made out that. You will leave me an open field. I am much obliged."

9. Benjamin Franklin (1706–90) was diplomatic representative of the new American government in Paris in the 1770s.

1. "Social circle."

"I wish to add a word that my son probably did not feel at liberty to say," the marquise rejoined. "I must say it for my own peace of mind. We are stretching a point; we are doing you a great favour."

"Oh, your son said it very well; didn't you?" said Newman.

"Not so well as my mother," declared the marquis.

"I can only repeat—I am much obliged."

"It is proper I should tell you," Madame de Bellegarde went on, "that I am very proud, and that I hold my head very high. I may be wrong, but I am too old to change. At least I know it, and I don't pretend to anything else. Don't flatter yourself that my daughter is not proud. She is proud in her own way—a somewhat different way from mine. You will have to make your terms with that. Even Valentin is proud, if you touch the right spot—or the wrong one. Urbain is proud—that you see for yourself. Sometimes I think he is a little too proud; but I wouldn't change him. He is the best of my children; he cleaves to his old mother. But I have said enough to show you that we are all proud together. It is well that you should know the sort of people you have come among."

"Well," said Newman, "I can only say, in return, that I am *not* proud; I shan't mind you! But you speak as if you intended to be very disagreeable."

"I shall not enjoy having my daughter marry you, and I shall not pretend to enjoy it. If you don't mind that, so much the better."

"If you stick to your own side of the contract we shall not quarrel; that is all I ask of you," said Newman. "Keep your hands off, and give me an open field. I am very much in earnest, and there is not the slightest danger of my getting discouraged or backing out. You will have me constantly before your eyes; if you don't like it, I am sorry for you. I will do for your daughter, if she will accept me, everything that a man can do for a woman. I am happy to tell you that, as a promise—a pledge. I consider that on your side you make me an equal pledge. You will not back out, eh?"

"I don't know what you mean by 'backing out,'" said the marquise. "It suggests a movement of which I think no Bellegarde has ever been guilty."

"Our word is our word," said Urbain. "We have given it."

"Well, now," said Newman, "I am very glad you are so proud; it makes me believe you will keep it."

The marquise was silent a moment, and then, suddenly, "I shall always be polite to you, Mr. Newman," she declared, "but, decidedly, I shall never like you."

"Don't be too sure," said Newman, laughing.

"I am so sure that I will ask you to take me back to my armchair without the least fear of having my sentiments modified by the service you render me." And Madame de Bellegarde took his arm, and returned to the salon and to her customary place.

M. de la Rochefidèle and his wife were preparing to take their leave, and Madame de Cintré's interview with the mumbling old lady was at an end. She stood looking about her, asking herself, apparently, to whom she should next speak, when Newman came up to her.

"Your mother has given me leave—very solemnly—to come here often," he said. "I mean to come often."

"I shall be glad to see you," she answered simply. And then, in a moment: "You probably think it very strange that there should be such a solemnity—as you say—about your coming."

"Well, yes; I do, rather."

"Do you remember what my brother Valentin said, the first time you came to see me—that we were a strange, strange family?"

"It was not the first time I came, but the second," said Newman.

"Very true. Valentin annoyed me at the time; but now I know you better, I may tell you he was right. If you come often, you will see!" and Madame de Cintré turned away.

Newman watched her awhile, talking with other people, and then he took his leave. He shook hands last with Valentin de Bellegarde, who came out with him to the top of the staircase. "Well, you have got your permit," said Valentin. "I hope you liked the process."

"I like your sister more than ever. But don't worry your brother any more, for my sake," Newman added. "I don't mind him. I am afraid he came down on you in the smoking-room, after I went out."

"When my brother comes down on me," said Valentin, "he falls hard. I have a peculiar way of receiving him. I must say," he continued, "that they came up to the mark much sooner than I expected. I don't understand it; they must have had to turn the screw pretty tight. It's a tribute to your millions."

"Well, it's the most precious one they have ever received," said Newman.

He was turning away when Valentin stopped him, looking at him with a brilliant softly-cynical glance. "I should like to know whether, within a few days, you have seen your venerable friend M. Nioche."

"He was yesterday at my rooms," Newman answered.

"What did he tell you?"

"Nothing particular."

"You didn't see the muzzle of a pistol sticking out of his pocket?"

"What are you driving at?" Newman demanded. "I thought he seemed rather cheerful, for him."

Valentin broke into a laugh. "I am delighted to hear it! I win my bet. Mademoiselle Noémie has thrown her cap over the mill, as we say. She has left the paternal domicile. She is launched! And M. Nioche is rather cheerful—*for him!* Don't brandish your tomahawk at that rate; I have not seen her nor communicated with her since that day at the Louvre. Andromeda has found another Perseus than I.[2] My information is exact; on such matters it always is. I suppose that now you will raise your protest?"

"My protest be hanged!" murmured Newman, disgustedly.

But his tone found no echo in that in which Valentin, with his hand on the door, to return to his mother's apartment, exclaimed: "But I shall see her now! She is very remarkable—she is very remarkable!"

Chapter XIII

Newman kept his promise, or his menace, of going often to the Rue de l'Université, and during the next six weeks he saw Madame de Cintré more times than he could have numbered. He flattered himself that he was not in love, but his biographer[3] may be supposed to know better. He claimed, at least, none of the exemptions and emoluments of the romantic passion. Love, he believed, made a fool of a man, and his present emotion was not folly but wisdom—wisdom sound, serene, well-directed. What he felt was an intense all-consuming tenderness, which had for its object an extraordinarily graceful and delicate, and at the same time impressive woman, who lived in a large gray house on the left bank of the Seine. This tenderness turned very often into a positive heartache; a sign in which, certainly, Newman ought to have read the appellation which science has conferred upon his sentiment. When the heart has a heavy weight upon it, it hardly matters whether the weight be of gold or of lead; when, at any rate, happiness passes into that place in which it becomes identical with pain, a man may admit that the reign of wisdom is temporarily suspended. Newman wished Madame de Cintré so well that nothing he could think of doing for her in the future rose to the high standard which his present mood had set itself. She seemed to him so felicitious a product of nature and circumstance, that his invention, musing on future combinations, was constantly catching its breath with the fear of stumbling into some brutal compression or mutilation of her beautiful personal harmony. This is what I mean by Newman's tenderness: Madame de Cintré pleased him so, exactly as she was, that his desire to interpose between her and the troubles of life had the

2. In Greek mythology, Perseus rescued Andromeda from a sea monster and married her.

3. One of James's characteristic metaphors for the novelist.

quality of a young mother's eagerness to protect the sleep of her first-born child. Newman was simply charmed, and he handled his charm as if it were a music-box which would stop if one shook it. There can be no better proof of the hankering epicure that is hidden in every man's temperament, waiting for a signal from some divine confederate that he may safely peep out. Newman at last was enjoying, purely, freely, deeply. Certain of Madame de Cintré's personal qualities—the luminous sweetness of her eyes, the delicate mobility of her face, the deep liquidity of her voice—filled all his consciousness. A rose-crowned Greek of old, gazing at a marble goddess with his whole bright intellect resting satisfied in the act, could not have been a more complete embodiment of the wisdom that loses itself in the enjoyment of quiet harmonies.

He made no violent love to her—no sentimental speeches. He never trespassed on what she had made him understand was for the present forbidden ground. But he had, nevertheless, a comfortable sense that she knew better from day to day how much he admired her. Though in general he was no great talker, he talked much, and he succeeded perfectly in making her say many things. He was not afraid of boring her, either by his discourse or by his silence; and whether or no he did occasionally bore her, it is probable that on the whole she liked him only the better for his absence of embarrassed scruples. Her visitors, coming in often while Newman sat there, found a tall, lean, silent man, in a half-lounging attitude, who laughed out sometimes when no one had meant to be droll, and remained grave in the presence of calculated witticisms, for the appreciation of which he had apparently not the proper culture.

It must be confessed that the number of subjects upon which Newman had no ideas was extremely large, and it must be added that as regards those subjects upon which he was without ideas he was also perfectly without words. He had little of the small change of conversation, and his stock of ready-made formulas and phrases was the scantiest. On the other hand he had plenty of attention to bestow, and his estimate of the importance of a topic did not depend upon the number of clever things he could say about it. He himself was almost never bored, and there was no man with whom it would have been a greater mistake to suppose that silence meant displeasure. What it was that entertained him during some of his speechless sessions I must, however, confess myself unable to determine. We know in a general way that a great many things which were old stories to a great many people had the charm of novelty to him, but a complete list of his new impressions would probably contain a number of surprises for us. He told Madame de Cintré a hundred long stories; he explained to her, in talking of the United States, the working of various local institutions and mercantile customs. Judging by the sequel, she was interested, but one would not have been sure of it beforehand. As regards her own talk, Newman was very sure himself that she herself enjoyed it: this was as a sort of amendment to the portrait that Mrs. Tristram had drawn of her. He discovered that she had naturally an abundance of gaiety. He had been right at first in saying she was shy; her shyness, in a woman whose circumstances and tranquil beauty afforded every facility for well-mannered hardihood, was only a charm the more. For Newman it had lasted some time, and even when it went it left something behind it which for awhile performed the same office. Was this the tearful secret of which Mrs. Tristram had had a glimpse, and of which, as of her friend's reserve, her high-breeding, and her profundity, she had given a sketch of which the outlines were, perhaps, rather too heavy? Newman supposed so, but he found himself wondering less every day what Madame de Cintré's secrets might be, and more convinced that secrets were, in themselves, hateful things to her. She was a woman for the light, not for the shade; and her natural line was not picturesque reserve and mysterious melancholy, but frank, joyous, brilliant action, with just so much meditation as was necessary, and not a grain more. To this, apparently, he had succeeded in bringing her back. He felt, himself, that he was an antidote to oppressive secrets; what he offered her was, in fact, above all things a vast sunny immunity from the need of having any. He often passed his evenings, when Madame de Cintré had so appointed it, at the chilly fireside of Madame de Bellegarde, contenting himself with looking across the room, through narrowed eyelids, at his mistress, who always made a point, before her family, of talking to someone else. Madame de Bellegarde sat by the fire conversing neatly and coldly with whosoever approached her, and glancing round the room with her slowly-restless eye, the effect of which, when it lighted upon him, was to Newman's sense identical with that of a sudden spurt of damp air. When he shook hands with her he always asked her with a laugh whether she could "stand him" another evening, and she replied, without a laugh, that, thank God, she had always been able to do her duty. Newman, talking once of the marquise to Mrs. Tristram, said that after all it was very easy to get on with her; it always was easy to get on with out-and-out rascals.

"And is it by that elegant term," said Mrs. Tristram, "that you designate the Marquise de Bellegarde?"

"Well," said Newman, "she is wicked, she is an old sinner."

"What is her crime?" asked Mrs. Tristram.

"I shouldn't wonder if she had murdered some one—all from a sense of duty, of course."

"How can you be so dreadful?" sighed Mrs. Tristram.

"I am not dreadful. I am speaking of her favourably."

"Pray what will you say when you want to be severe?"

"I shall keep my severity for someone else—for the marquis. There's a man I can't swallow, mix the drink as I will."

"And what has *he* done?"

"I can't quite make out; it is something dreadfully bad, something mean and underhand, and not redeemed by audacity, as his mother's misdemeanours may have been. If he has never committed murder, he has at least turned his back and looked the other way while someone else was committing it."

In spite of this invidious hypothesis, which must be taken for nothing more than an example of the capricious play of "American humour," Newman did his best to maintain an easy and friendly style of communication with M. de Bellegarde. So long as he was in personal contact with people, he disliked extremely to have anything to forgive them, and he was capable of a good deal of unsuspected imaginative effort (for the sake of his own personal comfort) to assume for the time that they were good fellows. He did his best to treat the marquis as one; he believed honestly, moreover, that he could not, in reason, be such a confounded fool as he seemed. Newman's familiarity was never importunate; his sense of human equality was not an aggressive taste or an æsthetic theory, but something as natural and organic as a physical appetite which had never been put on a scanty allowance, and consequently was innocent of ungraceful eagerness. His tranquil unsuspectingness of the relativity of his own place in the social scale was probably irritating to M. de Bellegarde, who saw himself reflected in the mind of his potential brother-in-law in a crude and colourless form, unpleasantly dissimilar to the impressive image projected upon his own intellectual mirror. He never forgot himself for an instant, and replied to what he must have considered Newman's "advances" with mechanical politeness. Newman, who was constantly forgetting himself, and indulging in an unlimited amount of irresponsible inquiry and conjecture, now and then found himself confronted by the conscious ironical smile of his host. What the deuce M. de Bellegarde was smiling at he was at a loss to divine. M. de Bellegarde's smile may be supposed to have been, for himself, a compromise between a great many emotions. So long as he smiled he was polite, and it was proper he should be polite. A smile, moreover, committed him to nothing more than politeness, and left the degree of politeness agreeably vague. A smile, too, was neither dissent—which was too serious—nor agreement, which might have brought on terrible complications. And then a smile covered his own personal dignity, which in this critical situation he was resolved to keep immaculate; it was quite enough that the glory of his house should pass into eclipse. Between him and Newman, his whole manner seemed to declare, there could be no interchange of opinion; he was holding his breath so as not to inhale the odour of democracy. Newman was far from being versed in European politics, but he liked to have a general idea of what was going on about him, and he accordingly asked M. de Bellegarde several times what he thought of public affairs. M. de Bellegarde answered with suave concision that he thought as ill of them as possible, that they were going from bad to worse, and that the age was rotten to its core. This gave Newman, for the moment, an almost kindly feeling for the marquis; he pitied a man for whom the world was so cheerless a place, and the next time he saw M. de Bellegarde he attempted to call his attention to some of the brilliant features of the time. The marquis presently replied that he had but a single political conviction, which was enough for him: he believed in the divine right of Henry of Bourbon, Fifth of his name, to the throne of France.[4] Newman stared, and after this he ceased to talk politics with M. de Bellegarde. He was not horrified nor scandalised, he was not even amused; he felt as he should have felt if he had discovered in M. de Bellegarde a taste for certain oddities of diet; an appetite, for instance, for fishbones or nutshells. Under these circumstances, of course, he would never have broached dietary questions with him.

One afternoon, on his calling on Madame de Cintré, Newman was requested by the servant to wait a few moments, as his hostess was not at liberty. He walked about the room awhile, taking up her books, smelling her flowers, and looking at her prints and photographs (which he thought prodigiously pretty), and at last he heard the opening of a door to which his back was turned. On the threshold stood an old woman whom he remembered to have met several times in entering and leaving the house. She was tall and straight, and dressed in black, and she wore a cap which, if Newman had been initiated into such mysteries, would have been a sufficient assurance that she was not a Frenchwoman; a cap of pure British composition. She had a pale, decent, depressed-looking face, and a clear, dull, English eye. She looked at Newman a moment, both intently and timidly, and then she dropped a short, straight English curtsy.

"Madame de Cintré begs you will kindly wait," she said. "She has just come in; she will soon have finished dressing."

"Oh, I will wait as long as she wants," said Newman. "Pray tell her not to hurry."

"Thank you, sir," said the woman softly; and then, instead of

4. Henry Charles Ferdinand Marie Dieudonné Chambord (1820–83), Bourbon claimant to the French throne, spent his life in exile. To the Legitimists, he was known as Henry V, although he never held the throne of France.

retiring with the message, she advanced into the room. She looked about her for a moment, and presently went to the table and began to arrange certain books and knick-knacks. Newman was struck with the high respectability of her appearance; he was afraid to address her as a servant. She busied herself for some moments with putting the table in order and pulling the curtains straight, while Newman walked slowly to and fro. He perceived at last, from her reflection in the mirror, as he was passing, that her hands were idle and that she was looking at him intently. She evidently wished to say something, and Newman perceiving it, helped her to begin.

"You are English?" he asked.

"Yes, sir, please," she answered quickly and softly; "I was born in Wiltshire."[5]

"And what do you think of Paris?"

"Oh, I don't think of Paris, sir," she said, in the same tone. "It is so long since I have been here."

"Ah, you have been here very long?"

"It is more than forty years, sir. I came over with Lady Emmeline."

"You mean with old Madame de Bellegarde?"

"Yes, sir. I came with her when she was married. I was my lady's own woman."

"And you have been with her ever since?"

"I have been in the house ever since. My lady has taken a younger person. You see I am very old. I do nothing regular now. But I keep about."

"You look very strong and well," said Newman, observing the erectness of her figure, and a certain venerable rosiness in her cheek.

"Thank God I am not ill, sir; I hope I know my duty too well to go panting and coughing about the house. But I am an old woman, sir, and it is as an old woman that I venture to speak to you."

"Oh, speak out," said Newman, curiously. "You needn't be afraid of me."

"Yes, sir. I think you are kind. I have seen you before."

"On the stairs, you mean?"

"Yes, sir. When you have been coming to see the countess. I have taken the liberty of noticing that you come often."

"Oh yes; I come very often," said Newman, laughing. "You need not have been very wide awake to notice that."

"I have noticed it with pleasure, sir," said the ancient tirewoman gravely. And she stood looking at Newman with a strange expression of face. The old instinct of deference and humility was there;

5. A county in southern England.

the habit of decent self-effacement and knowledge of her "own place." But there mingled with it a certain mild audacity, born of the occasion and of a sense, probably, of Newman's unprecedented approachableness, and, beyond this, a vague indifference to the old proprieties; as if my lady's own woman had at last begun to reflect that, since my lady had taken another person, she had a slight reversionary property in herself.

"You take a great interest in the family?" said Newman.

"A deep interest, sir. Especially in the countess."

"I am glad of that," said Newman. And in a moment he added, smiling: "So do I!"

"So I supposed, sir. We can't help noticing these things and having our ideas; can we, sir?"

"You mean as a servant?" said Newman.

"Ah, there it is, sir. I am afraid that when I let my thoughts meddle with such matters I am no longer a servant. But I am so devoted to the countess; if she were my own child I couldn't love her more. That is how I come to be so bold, sir. They say you want to marry her."

Newman eyed his interlocutress and satisfied himself that she was not a gossip, but a zealot; she looked anxious, appealing, discreet. "It is quite true," he said. "I want to marry Madame de Cintré."

"And to take her away to America?"

"I will take her wherever she wants to go."

"The farther away the better, sir!" exclaimed the old woman with sudden intensity. But she checked herself, and, taking up a paper-weight in mosaic, began to polish it with her black apron. "I don't mean anything against the house or the family, sir. But I think a great change would do the poor countess good. It is very sad here."

"Yes, it's not very lively," said Newman. "But Madame de Cintré is gay herself."

"She is everything that is good. You will not be vexed to hear that she has been gayer for a couple of months past than she had been in many a day before."

Newman was delighted to gather this testimony to the prosperity of his suit, but he repressed all violent marks of elation. "Has Madame de Cintré been in bad spirits before this?" he asked.

"Poor lady, she has good reason. M. de Cintré was no husband for a sweet young lady like that. And then, as I say, it has been a sad house. It is better, in my humble opinion, that she were out of it. So, if you will excuse me for saying so, I hope she will marry you."

"I hope she will!" said Newman.

"But you must not lose courage, sir, if she doesn't make up her mind at once. That is what I wanted to beg of you, sir. Don't give it up, sir. You will not take it ill if I say it's a great risk for any lady at any time; all the more when she has got rid of one bad bargain. But if she can marry a good, kind, respectable gentleman, I think she had better make up her mind to it. They speak very well of you, sir, in the house, and, if you will allow me to say so, I like your face. You have a very different appearance from the late count; he wasn't five feet high. And they say your fortune is beyond everything. There's no harm in that. So I beseech you to be patient, sir, and bide your time. If I don't say this to you, sir, perhaps no one will. Of course it is not for me to make any promises. I can answer for nothing. But I think your chance is not so bad, sir. I am nothing but a weary old woman in my quiet corner, but one woman understands another, and I think I make out the countess. I received her in my arms when she came into the world, and her first wedding-day was the saddest of my life. She owes it to me to show me another and a brighter one. If you will hold firm, sir—and you look as if you would—I think we may see it."

"I am much obliged to you for your encouragement," said Newman heartily. "One can't have too much. I mean to hold firm. And if Madame de Cintré marries me, you must come and live with her."

The old woman looked at him strangely, with her soft lifeless eyes. "It may seem a heartless thing to say, sir, when one has been forty years in a house, but I may tell you that I should like to leave this place."

"Why, it's just the time to say it," said Newman fervently. "After forty years one wants a change."

"You are very kind, sir;" and this faithful servant dropped another curtsy and seemed disposed to retire. But she lingered a moment, and gave a timid joyless smile. Newman was disappointed, and his fingers stole half shyly half irritably into his waistcoat-pocket. His informant noticed the movement. "Thank God I am not a Frenchwoman," she said. "If I were, I would tell you with a brazen simper, old as I am, that if you please, monsieur, my information is worth something. Let me tell you so in my own decent English way. It *is* worth something."

"How much, please?" said Newman.

"Simply this: a promise not to hint to the countess that I have said these things."

"If that is all, you have it," said Newman.

"That is all, sir. Thank you, sir. Good-day, sir." And having once more slid down telescope-wise into her scanty petticoats, the old woman departed. At the same moment Madame de Cintré came in by an opposite door. She noticed the movement of the other *portiére*[6] and asked Newman who had been entertaining him.

"The British female!" said Newman. "An old lady in a black dress and a cap, who curtsies up and down, and expresses herself ever so well."

"An old lady who curtsies and expresses herself? . . . . Ah, you mean poor Mrs. Bread. I happen to know that you have made a conquest of her."

"Mrs. Cake, she ought to be called," said Newman. "She is very sweet. She is a delicious old woman."

Madame de Cintré looked at him a moment. "What can she have said to you? She is an excellent creature, but we think her rather dismal."

"I suppose," Newman answered presently, "that I like her because she has lived near you so long. Since your birth, she told me."

"Yes," said Madame de Cintré, simply; "she is very faithful; I can trust her."

Newman had never made any reflections to this lady upon her mother and her brother Urbain; had given no hint of the impression they made upon him. But, as if she had guessed his thoughts, she seemed careful to avoid all occasion for making him speak of them. She never alluded to her mother's domestic decrees; she never quoted the opinions of the marquis. They had talked, however, of Valentin, and she had made no secret of her extreme affection for her younger brother. Newman listened sometimes with a certain harmless jealousy; he would have liked to divert some of her tender allusions to his own credit. Once Madame de Cintré told him, with a little air of triumph, about something that Valentin had done which she thought very much to his honour. It was a service he had rendered to an old friend of the family; something more "serious" than Valentin was usually supposed capable of being. Newman said he was glad to hear of it, and then began to talk about something which lay upon his own heart. Madame de Cintré listened, but after awhile she said: "I don't like the way you speak of my brother Valentin." Hereupon Newman, surprised, said that he had never spoken of him but kindly.

"It is too kindly," said Madame de Cintré. "It is a kindness that costs nothing; it is the kindness you show to a child. It is as if you didn't respect him."

"Respect him? Why, I think I do."

"You think? If you are not sure, it is no respect."

"Do you respect him?" said Newman. "If you do, I do."

6. A door curtain or drape hanging across a doorway in place of a door.

"If one loves a person, that is a question one is not bound to answer," said Madame de Cintré.

"You should not have asked it of me, then. I am very fond of your brother."

"He amuses you. But you would not like to resemble him."

"I shouldn't like to resemble anyone. It is hard enough work resembling oneself."

"What do you mean," asked Madame de Cintré, "by resembling oneself?"

"Why, doing what is expected of one. Doing one's duty."

"But that is only when one is very good."

"Well, a great many people are good," said Newman. "Valentin is quite good enough for me."

Madame de Cintré was silent for a short time. "He is not good enough for me," she said at last. "I wish he would do something."

"What can he do?" asked Newman.

"Nothing. Yet he is very clever."

"It is a proof of cleverness," said Newman, "to be happy without doing anything."

"I don't think Valentin is happy, in reality. He is clever, generous, brave—but what is there to show for it? To me there is something sad in his life, and sometimes I have a sort of foreboding about him. I don't know why, but I fancy he will have some great trouble—perhaps an unhappy end."

"Oh, leave him to me," said Newman jovially. "I will watch over him and keep harm away."

One evening, in Madame de Bellegarde's salon, the conversation had flagged most sensibly. The marquis walked up and down in silence, like a sentinel at the door of some smooth-fronted citadel of the proprieties; his mother sat staring at the fire; young Madame de Bellegarde worked at an enormous band of tapestry. Usually there were three or four visitors, but on this occasion a violent storm sufficiently accounted for the absence of even the most devoted habitués. In the long silences the howling of the wind and the beating of the rain were distinctly audible. Newman sat perfectly still, watching the clock, determined to stay till the stroke of eleven, but not a moment longer. Madame de Cintré had turned her back to the circle, and had been standing for some time within the uplifted curtain of a window, with her forehead against the pane, gazing out into the deluged darkness. Suddenly she turned round toward her sister-in-law.

"For heaven's sake," she said, with peculiar eagerness, "go to the piano and play something."

Madame de Bellegarde held up her tapestry and pointed to a

little white flower. "Don't ask me to leave this. I am in the midst of a masterpiece. My flower is going to smell very sweet; I am putting in the smell with his gold-coloured silk. I am holding my breath; I can't leave off. Play something yourself."

"It is absurd for me to play when you are present," said Madame de Cintré. But the next moment she went to the piano and began to strike the keys with vehemence. She played for some time, rapidly and brilliantly; when she stopped, Newman went to the piano and asked her to begin again. She shook her head, and, on his insisting, she said: "I have not been playing for you; I have been playing for myself." She went back to the window again and looked out, and shortly afterwards left the room. When Newman took leave, Urbain de Bellegarde accompanied him, as he always did, just three steps down the staircase. At the bottom stood a servant with his overcoat. He had just put it on when he saw Madame de Cintré coming towards him across the vestibule.

"Shall you be at home on Friday?" Newman asked.

She looked at him a moment before answering his question. "You don't like my mother and my brother," she said.

He hesitated a moment, and then he said softly: "No."

She laid her hand on the balustrade and prepared to ascend the stairs, fixing her eyes on the first step.

"Yes, I shall be at home on Friday," and she passed up the wide dusky staircase.

On the Friday, as soon as he came in, she asked him to please to tell her why he disliked her family.

"Dislike your family?" he exclaimed. "That has a horrid sound. I didn't say so, did I? I didn't mean it, if I did."

"I wish you would tell me what you think of them," said Madame de Cintré.

"I don't think of any of them but you."

"That is because you dislike them. Speak the truth; you can't offend me."

"Well, I don't exactly love your brother," said Newman. "I remember now. But what is the use of my saying so? I had forgotten it."

"You are too good-natured," said Madame de Cintré, gravely. Then, as if to avoid the appearance of inviting him to speak ill of the marquis, she turned away, motioning him to sit down.

But he remained standing before her and said presently: "What is of much more importance is that they don't like me."

"No—they don't," she said.

"And don't you think they are wrong?" Newman asked. "I don't believe I am a man to dislike."

"I suppose that a man who may be liked, may also be disliked. And my brother—my mother," she added, "have not made you angry?"

"Yes, sometimes."

"You have never shown it."

"So much the better."

"Yes, so much the better. They think they have treated you very well."

"I have no doubt they might have handled me much more roughly," said Newman. "I am much obliged to them. Honestly."

"You are generous," said Madame de Cintré. "It's a disagreeable position."

"For them, you mean. Not for me."

"For me," said Madame de Cintré.

"Not when their sins are forgiven!" said Newman. "They don't think I am as good as they are. I do. But we shan't quarrel about it."

"I can't even agree with you without saying something that has a disagreeable sound. The presumption was against you. That you probably don't understand."

Newman sat down and looked at her for some time. "I don't think I really understand it. But when you say it, I believe it."

"That's a poor reason," said Madame de Cintré, smiling.

"No, it's a very good one. You have a high spirit, a high standard; but with you it's all natural and unaffected; you don't seem to have stuck your head into a vice, as if you were sitting for the photograph of propriety. You think of me as a fellow who has had no idea in life but to make money and drive sharp bargains. That's a fair description of me, but it is not the whole story. A man ought to care for something else, though I don't know exactly what. I cared for money-making, but I never cared particularly for the money. There was nothing else to do, and it was impossible to be idle. I have been very easy to others, and to myself. I have done most of the things that people asked me—I don't mean rascals. As regards your mother and your brother," Newman added, "there is only one point upon which I feel that I might quarrel with them. I don't ask them to sing my praises to you, but I ask them to let you alone. If I thought they talked ill of me to you, I should come down upon them."

"They have let me alone, as you say. They have not talked ill of you."

"In that case," cried Newman, "I declare they are only too good for this world!"

Madame de Cintré appeared to find something startling in his exclamation. She would, perhaps, have replied, but at this moment the door was thrown open, and Urbain de Bellegarde stepped across the threshold. He appeared surprised at finding Newman, but his surprise was but a momentary shadow across the surface of an unwonted joviality. Newman had never seen the marquis so exhilarated; his pale unlighted countenance had a sort of thin transfiguration. He held open the door for someone else to enter, and presently appeared old Madame de Bellegarde, leaning on the arm of a gentleman whom Newman had not seen before. He had already risen, and Madame de Cintré rose, as she always did before her mother. The marquis, who had greeted Newman almost genially, stood apart, slowly rubbing his hands. His mother came forward with her companion. She gave a majestic little nod at Newman, and then she released the strange gentleman, that he might make his bow to her daughter.

"My daughter," she said, "I have brought you an unknown relative, Lord Deepmere. Lord Deepmere is our cousin, but he has done only to-day what he ought to have done long ago—come to make our acquaintance."

Madame de Cintré smiled, and offered Lord Deepmere her hand. "It is very extraordinary," said this noble laggard, "but this is the first time that I have ever been in Paris for more than three or four weeks."

"And how long have you been here now?" asked Madame de Cintré.

"Oh, for the last two months," said Lord Deepmere.

These two remarks might have constituted an impertinence; but a glance at Lord Deepmere's face would have satisfied you, as it apparently satisfied Madame de Cintré, that they constituted only a *naïveté*. When his companions were seated, Newman, who was out of the conversation, occupied himself with observing the newcomer. Observation, however, as regards Lord Deepmere's person, had no great range. He was a small meagre man, of some three-and-thirty years of age, with a bald head, a short nose, and no front teeth in the upper jaw; he had round, candid, blue eyes, and several pimples on his chin. He was evidently very shy, and he laughed a great deal, catching his breath with an odd startling sound, as the most convenient imitation of repose. His physiognomy denoted great simplicity, a certain amount of brutality, and a probable failure in the past to profit by rare educational advantages. He remarked that Paris was awfully jolly, but that for real, thorough-paced entertainment it was nothing to Dublin. He even preferred Dublin to London. Had Madame de Cintré ever been to Dublin? They must all come over there some day, and he would show them some Irish sport. He always went to Ireland for the fishing, and he came to Paris for the new Offenbach things.[7] They always brought them out in Dublin, but he couldn't wait. He had been nine times to hear La Pomme de Paris. Madame de Cintré, leaning back, with her arms folded, looked at Lord Deepmere with a more visibly puzzled face than she usually showed to society. Madame de Bellegarde, on the other hand, wore a fixed smile. The marquis said that among light operas his favourite was the "Gazza Ladra." The marquise then began a series of inquiries about the duke and the cardinal, the old countess and Lady Barbara, after listening to which, and to Lord Deepmere's somewhat irreverent responses, for a quarter of an hour, Newman rose to take his leave. The marquis went with him three steps into the hall.

"Is he Irish?" asked Newman, nodding in the direction of the visitor.

"His mother was the daughter of Lord Finucane," said the marquis; "he has great Irish estates. Lady Bridget, in the complete absence of male heirs, either direct or collateral—a most extraordinary circumstance—came in for everything. But Lord Deepmere's title is English, and his English property is immense. He is a charming young man."

Newman answered nothing, but he detained the marquis as the latter was beginning gracefully to recede. "It is a good time for me to thank you," he said, "for sticking so punctiliously to our bargain, for doing so much to help me on with your sister."

The marquis stared. "Really, I have done nothing that I can boast of," he said.

"Oh, don't be modest," Newman answered, laughing. "I can't flatter myself that I am doing so well simply by my own merit. And thank your mother for me, too!" And he turned away, leaving M. de Bellegarde looking after him.

Chapter XIV

The next time Newman came to the Rue de l'Université he had the good fortune to find Madame de Cintré alone. He had come with a definite intention, and he lost no time in executing it. She wore, moreover, a look which he eagerly interpreted as expectancy.

"I have been coming to see you for six months, now," he said, "and I have never spoken to you a second time of marriage. That was what you asked me; I obeyed. Could any man have done better?"

"You have acted with great delicacy," said Madame de Cintré.

7. Jacques Levy Offenbach (1819–1880), composer of light French operettas and musical comedies.

"Well, I am going to change now," said Newman. "I don't mean that I am going to be indelicate; but I am going to go back to where I began. I *am* back there. I have been all round the circle. Or rather, I have never been away from there. I have never ceased to want what I wanted then. Only now I am more sure of it, if possible; I am more sure of myself, and more sure of you. I know you better, though I don't know anything I didn't believe three months ago. You are everything—you are beyond everything—I can imagine or desire. You know me now; you *must* know me. I won't say that you have seen the best—but you have seen the worst. I hope you have been thinking all this while. You must have seen that I was only waiting; you can't suppose that I was changing. What will you say to me, now? Say that everything is clear and reasonable, and that I have been very patient and considerate, and deserve my reward. And then give me your hand. Madame de Cintré, do that. Do it."

"I knew you were only waiting," she said; "and I was very sure this day would come. I have thought about it a great deal. At first I was half afraid of it. But I am not afraid of it now." She paused a moment, and then she added: "It's a relief."

She was sitting on a low chair, and Newman was on an ottoman, near her. He leaned a little and took her hand, which for an instant she let him keep. "That means that I have not waited for nothing," he said. She looked at him for a moment, and he saw her eyes fill with tears. "With me," he went on, "you will be as safe—as safe"—and even in his ardour he hesitated a moment for a comparison—"as safe," he said, with a kind of simple solemnity, "as in your father's arms."

Still she looked at him and her tears increased. Then, abruptly, she buried her face on the cushioned arm of the sofa beside her chair, and broke into noiseless sobs. "I am weak—I am weak," he heard her say.

"All the more reason why you should give yourself up to me," he answered. "Why are you troubled? There is nothing here that should trouble you. I offer you nothing but happiness. Is that so hard to believe?"

"To you everything seems so simple," she said, raising her head. "But things are not so. I like you extremely. I liked you six months ago, and now I am sure of it, as you say you are sure. But it is not easy, simply for that, to decide to marry you. There are a great many things to think about."

"There ought to be only one thing to think about—that we love each other," said Newman. And as she remained silent he quickly added: "Very good; if you can't accept that, don't tell me so."

"I should be very glad to think of nothing," she said at last; "not to think at all; only to shut both my eyes and give myself up. But I can't. I'm cold, I'm old, I'm a coward; I never supposed I should marry again, and it seems to me very strange I should ever have listened to you. When I used to think, as a girl, of what I should do if I were to marry freely by my own choice, I thought of a very different man from you."

"That's nothing against me," said Newman, with an immense smile; "your taste was not formed."

His smile made Madame de Cintré smile. "Have you formed it?" she asked. And then she said, in a different tone: "Where do you wish to live?"

"Anywhere in the wide world you like. We can easily settle that."

"I don't know why I ask you," she presently continued. "I care very little. I think if I were to marry you I could live almost anywhere. You have some false ideas about me; you think that I need a great many things—that I must have a brilliant worldly life. I am sure you are prepared to take a great deal of trouble to give me such things. But that is very arbitrary; I have done nothing to prove that." She paused again, looking at him, and her mingled sound and silence were so sweet to him that he had no wish to hurry her, any more than he would have had a wish to hurry a golden sunrise. "Your being so different, which at first seemed a difficulty, a trouble, began one day to seem to me a pleasure, a great pleasure. I was glad you were different. And yet, if I had said so, no one would have understood me; I don't mean simply to my family."

"They would have said I was a queer monster, eh?" said Newman.

"They would have said I could never be happy with you—you were too different; and I would have said it was just *because* you were so different that I might be happy. But they would have given better reasons than I. My only reason——" and she paused again.

But this time, in the midst of his golden sunrise, Newman felt the impulse to grasp at a rosy cloud. "Your only reason is that you love me!" he murmured, with an eloquent gesture, and for want of a better reason Madame de Cintré reconciled herself to this one.

Newman came back the next day, and in the vestibule, as he entered the house, he encountered his friend Mrs. Bread. She was wandering about in honourable idleness, and when his eyes fell upon her she delivered him one of her curtsies. Then turning to the servant who had admitted him, she said, with the combined majesty of her native superiority and of a rugged English accent: "You may retire; I will have the honour of conducting monsieur." In spite of this combination, however, it appeared to Newman that her voice had a slight quaver, as if the tone of command were not habitual to it. The man gave her an impertinent stare, but he walked slowly away, and she led Newman upstairs. At half its course the staircase gave a bend, forming a little platform. In the angle of the wood stood an indifferent statue of an eighteenth-century nymph, simpering, sallow, and cracked. Here Mrs. Bread stopped and looked with shy kindness at her companion.

"I know the good news, sir," she murmured.

"You have a good right to be first to know it," said Newman. "You have taken such a friendly interest."

Mrs. Bread turned away and began to blow the dust off the statue, as if this might be mockery.

"I suppose you want to congratulate me," said Newman. "I am greatly obliged." And then he added: "You gave me much pleasure the other day."

She turned round, apparently reassured. "You are not to think that I have been told anything," she said; "I have only guessed. But when I looked at you, as you came in, I was sure I had guessed aright."

"You are very sharp," said Newman. "I am sure that in your quiet way you see everything."

"I am not a fool, sir, thank God. I have guessed something else beside," said Mrs. Bread.

"What's that?"

"I needn't tell you that, sir; I don't think you would believe it. At any rate it wouldn't please you."

"Oh, tell me nothing but what will please me," laughed Newman. "That is the way you began."

"Well, sir, I suppose you won't be vexed to hear that the sooner everything is over the better."

"The sooner we are married, you mean? The better for me, certainly."

"The better for everyone."

"The better for you, perhaps. You know you are coming to live with us," said Newman.

"I am extremely obliged to you, sir, but it is not of myself I was thinking. I only wanted, if I might take the liberty, to recommend you to lose no time."

"Whom are you afraid of?"

Mrs. Bread looked up the staircase and then down, and then she looked at the undusted nymph, as if she possibly had sentient ears. "I am afraid of everyone," she said.

"What an uncomfortable state of mind!" said Newman. "Does 'every one' wish to prevent my marriage?"

"I am afraid of already having said too much," Mrs. Bread replied. "I won't take it back, but I won't say any more." And she took her way up the staircase again and led him into Madame de Cintré's salon.

Newman indulged in a brief and silent imprecation when he found that Madame de Cintré was not alone. With her sat her mother, and in the middle of the room stood young Madame de Bellegarde, in her bonnet and mantle. The old marquise, who was leaning back in her chair with a hand clasping the knob of each arm, looked at him fixedly, without moving. She seemed barely conscious of his greeting; she appeared to be musing intently. Newman said to himself that her daughter had been announcing her engagement, and that the old lady found the morsel hard to swallow. But Madame de Cintré, as she gave him her hand, gave him also a look by which she appeared to mean that he should understand something. Was it a warning or a request? Did she wish to enjoin speech or silence? He was puzzled, and young Madame de Bellegarde's pretty grin gave him no information.

"I have not told my mother," said Madame de Cintré, abruptly, looking at him.

"Told me what?" demanded the marquise. "You tell me too little; you should tell me everything."

"That is what I do," said Madame Urbain, with a little laugh.

"Let *me* tell your mother," said Newman.

The old lady stared at him again, and then turned to her daughter. "You are going to marry him?" she cried softly.

"*Oui, ma mère,*"[8] said Madame de Cintré.

"Your daughter has consented, to my great happiness," said Newman.

"And when was this arrangement made?" asked Madame de Bellegarde. "I seem to be picking up the news by chance!"

"My suspense came to an end yesterday," said Newman.

"And how long was mine to have lasted?" said the marquise to her daughter. She spoke without irritation; with a sort of cold noble displeasure.

Madame de Cintré stood silent, with her eyes on the ground. "It is over now," she said.

"Where is my son—where is Urbain?" asked the marquise. "Send for your brother and inform him."

Young Madame de Bellegarde laid her hand on the bell-rope. "He was to make some visits with me, and I was to go and knock—very softly, very softly—at the door of his study. But he can come

8. "Yes, mother."

to me!" She pulled the bell, and in a few moments Mrs. Bread appeared, with a face of calm inquiry.

"Send for your brother," said the old lady.

But Newman felt an irresistible impulse to speak, and to speak in a certain way. "Tell the marquis we want him," he said to Mrs. Bread, who quietly retired.

Young Madame de Bellegarde went to her sister-in-law and embraced her. Then she turned to Newman, with an intense smile. "She is charming. I congratulate you."

"I congratulate you, sir," said Madame de Bellegarde, with extreme solemnity. "My daughter is an extraordinarily good woman. She may have faults, but I don't know them."

"My mother does not often make jokes," said Madame de Cintré; "but when she does they are terrible."

"She is ravishing," the Marquise Urbain resumed, looking at her sister-in-law, with her head on one side. "Yes, I congratulate you."

Madame de Cintré turned away, and, taking up a piece of tapestry, began to ply the needle. Some minutes of silence elapsed, which were interrupted by the arrival of M. de Bellegarde. He came in with his hat in his hand, gloved, and was followed by his brother Valentin, who appeared to have just entered the house. M. de Bellegarde looked around the circle and greeted Newman with his usual finely-measured courtesy. Valentin saluted his mother and his sisters, and, as he shook hands with Newman, gave him a glance of acute interrogation.

"*Arrivez donc, messieurs!*"[9] cried young Madame de Bellegarde. "We have great news for you."

"Speak to your brother, my daughter," said the old lady.

Madame de Cintré had been looking at her tapestry. She raised her eyes to her brother. "I have accepted Mr. Newman."

"Your sister has consented," said Newman. "You see, after all, I knew what I was about."

"I am charmed!" said M. de Bellegarde, with superior benignity.

"So am I," said Valentin to Newman. "The marquis and I are charmed. I can't marry, myself, but I can understand it. I can't stand on my head, but I can applaud a clever acrobat. My dear sister, I bless your union."

The marquis stood looking for awhile into the crown of his hat. "We have been prepared," he said at last, "but it is inevitable that in the face of the event one should experience a certain emotion." And he gave a most unhilarious smile.

"I feel no emotion that I was not perfectly prepared for, " said his mother.

9. "Come on in, sirs!"

"I can't say that for myself," said Newman, smiling, but differently from the marquis. "I am happier than I expected to be. I suppose it's the sight of your happiness!"

"Don't exaggerate that," said Madame de Bellegarde, getting up and laying her hand upon her daughter's arm. "You can't expect an honest old woman to thank you for taking away her beautiful only daughter."

"You forget me, dear madame," said the young marquise, demurely.

"Yes, she is very beautiful," said Newman.

"And when is the wedding, pray?" asked young Madame de Bellegarde; "I must have a month to think over a dress."

"That must be discussed," said the marquise.

"Oh, we will discuss it, and let you know!" Newman exclaimed.

"I have no doubt we shall agree," said Urbain.

"If you don't agree with Madame de Cintré, you will be very unreasonable."

"Come, come, Urbain," said young Madame de Bellegarde. "I must go straight to my tailor's."

The old lady had been standing with her hand on her daughter's arm, looking at her fixedly. She gave a little sigh and murmured, "No, I did *not* expect it! You are a fortunate man," she added, turning to Newman, with an expressive nod.

"Oh, I know that!" he answered. "I feel tremendously proud. I feel like crying it on the housetops—like stopping people in the street to tell them."

Madame de Bellegarde narrowed her lips. "Pray don't," she said.

"The more people that know it, the better," Newman declared. "I haven't yet announced it here, but I telegraphed it this morning to America."

"Telegraphed it to America?" the old lady murmured.

"To New York, to St. Louis, and to San Francisco; those are the principal cities, you know. To-morrow I shall tell my friends here."

"Have you many?" asked Madame de Bellegarde, in a tone of which I am afraid that Newman but partly measured the impertinence.

"Enough to bring me a great many hand-shakes and congratulations. To say nothing," he added, in a moment, "of those I shall receive from your friends."

"They will not use the telegraph," said the marquise, taking her departure.

M. de Bellegarde, whose wife, her imagination having apparently taken flight to the tailor's, was fluttering her silken wings in emulation, shook hands with Newman, and said, with a more persuasive accent than the latter had ever heard him use: "You may count upon me." Then his wife led him away.

Valentin stood looking from his sister to our hero.

"I hope you have both reflected seriously," he said.

Madame de Cintré smiled. "We have neither your powers of reflection nor your depth of seriousness; but we have done our best."

"Well, I have a great regard for each of you," Valentin continued. "You are charming young people. But I am not satisfied, on the whole, that you belong to that small and superior class—that exquisite group—composed of persons who are worthy to remain unmarried. These are rare souls; they are the salt of the earth. But I don't mean to be invidious; the marrying people are often very nice."

"Valentin holds that women should marry, and that men should not," said Madame de Cintré. "I don't know how he arranges it."

"I arrange it by adoring you, my sister," said Valentin, ardently. "Good-bye."

"Adore some one whom you can marry," said Newman. "I will arrange that for you some day. I foresee that I am going to turn apostle."

Valentin was on the threshold; he looked back a moment, with a face that had turned grave. "I adore some one I can't marry!" he said. And he dropped the *portière* and departed.

"They don't like it," said Newman, standing alone before Madame de Cintré.

"No," she said, after a moment; "they don't like it."

"Well, now do you mind that?" asked Newman.

"Yes!" she said after another interval.

"That's a mistake."

"I can't help it. I should prefer that my mother were pleased."

"Why the deuce," demanded Newman, "is she not pleased? She gave you leave to marry me."

"Very true; I don't understand it. And yet I do 'mind it,' as you say. You will call it superstitious."

"That will depend upon how much you let it bother you. Then I shall call it an awful bore."

"I will keep it to myself," said Madame de Cintré. "It shall not bother you." And they then talked of their marriage-day, and Madame de Cintré assented unreservedly to Newman's desire to have it fixed for an early date.

Newman's telegrams were answered with interest. Having despatched but three electric missives, he received no less than eight gratulatory bulletins in return. He put them into his pocketbook, and the next time he encountered old Madame de Bellegarde drew them forth and displayed them to her. This, it must be confessed, was a slightly malicious stroke; the reader must judge in what degree the offence was venial. Newman knew that the marquise disliked his telegrams, though he could see no sufficient reason for it. Madame de Cintré, on the other hand, liked them; and, most of them being of a humorous cast, laughed at them immoderately, and inquired into the character of their authors. Newman, now that his prize was gained, felt a peculiar desire that his triumph should be manifest. He more than suspected that the Bellegardes were keeping quiet about it, and allowing it, in their select circle, but a limited resonance; and it pleased him to think that if he were to take the trouble he might, as he phrased it, break all the windows. No man likes being repudiated, and yet Newman, if he was not flattered, was not exactly offended. He had not this good excuse for his somewhat aggressive impulse to promulgate his felicity; his sentiment was of another quality. He wanted for once to make the heads of the house of Bellegarde *feel* him; he knew not when he should have another chance. He had had for the past six months a sense of the old lady and her son looking straight over his head, and he was now resolved that they should toe a mark which he would give himself the satisfaction of drawing.

"It is like seeing a bottle emptied when the wine is poured too slowly," he said to Mrs. Tristram. "They make me want to joggle their elbows and force them to spill their wine."

To this Mrs. Tristram answered that he had better leave them alone, and let them do things in their own way. "You must make allowances for them," she said. "It is natural enough that they should hang fire a little. They thought they accepted you when you made your application; but they are not people of imagination, they could not project themselves into the future, and now they will have to begin again. But they *are* people of honour, and they will do whatever is necessary."

Newman spent a few moments in narrow-eyed meditation.

"I am not hard on them," he presently said; "and to prove it I will invite them all to a festival."

"To a festival?"

"You have been laughing at my great gilded rooms all winter; I will show you that they are good for something. I will give a party. What is the grandest thing one can do here? I will hire all the great singers from the opera, and all the first people from the Théâtre Française, and I will give an entertainment."

"And whom will you invite?"

"You, first of all. And then the old lady and her son. And then everyone among her friends whom I have met at her house or elsewhere, everyone who has shown me the minimum of politeness, every duke of them and his wife. And then all my friends, without exception—Miss Kitty Upjohn, Miss Dora Finch, General Packard, C. P. Hatch, and all the rest. And everyone shall know what it is about; that is, to celebrate my engagement to the Countess de Cintré. What do you think of the idea?"

"I think it is odious!" said Mrs. Tristram. And then in a moment: "I think it is delicious!"

The very next evening Newman repaired to Madame de Bellegarde's salon, where he found her surrounded by her children, and invited her to honour his poor dwelling by her presence on a certain evening a fortnight distant.

The marquise stared a moment. "My dear sir," she cried, "what do you want to do to me?"

"To make you acquainted with a few people, and then to place you in a very easy chair and ask you to listen to Madame Frezzolini's singing."

"You mean to give a concert?"

"Something of that sort."

"And to have a crowd of people?"

"All my friends, and I hope some of yours and your daughter's. I want to celebrate my engagement."

It seemed to Newman that Madame de Bellegarde turned pale. She opened her fan, a fine old painted fan of the last century, and looked at the picture, which represented a *fête champêtre*[1]—a lady with a guitar, singing, and a group of dancers round a garlanded Hermes.[2]

"We go out so little," murmured the marquis, "since my poor father's death."

"But *my* dear father is still alive, my friend," said his wife. "I am only waiting for my invitation to accept it," and she glanced with amiable confidence at Newman. "It will be magnificent; I am very sure of that."

I am sorry to say, to the discredit of Newman's gallantry, that this lady's invitation was not then and there bestowed; he was giving all his attention to the old marquise. She looked up at last smiling. "I can't think of letting you offer me a fête," she said, "until I have offered you one. We want to present you to our friends; we will invite them all. We have it very much at heart. We must do things in order. Come to me about the 25th; I will let you know the exact day immediately. We shall not have anyone so fine as Madame Frezzolini, but we shall have some very good people. After that you may talk of your own fête." The old lady spoke with

1. A country revel.
2. In Greek religion, Hermes was the son of Zeus. Known as the giver of fertility, Hermes was celebrated at the Hermaea, a riotous festival of sexual activity. His monument was often phallus-shaped.

a certain quick eagerness, smiling more agreeably as she went on.

It seemed to Newman a handsome proposal, and such proposals always touched the sources of his good-nature. He said to Madame de Bellegarde that he should be glad to come on the 25th or any other day, and that it mattered very little whether he met his friends at her house or at his own. I have said that Newman was observant, but it must be admitted that on this occasion he failed to notice a certain delicate glance which passed between Madame de Bellegarde and the marquis, and which we may presume to have been a commentary upon the innocence displayed in that latter clause of his speech.

Valentin de Bellegarde walked away with Newman that evening, and when they had left the Rue de l'Université some distance behind them he said reflectively: "My mother is very strong—very strong." Then in answer to an interrogative movement of Newman's he continued: "She was driven to the wall; but you would never have thought it. Her fête of the 25th was an invention of the moment. She had no idea whatever of giving a fête, but finding it the only issue from your proposal, she looked straight at the dose—excuse the expression—and bolted it, as you saw, without winking. She is very strong."

"Dear me!" said Newman, divided between relish and compassion. "I don't care a straw for her fête; I am willing to take the will for the deed."

"No, no," said Valentin, with a little inconsequent touch of family pride. "The thing will be done now, and done handsomely."

Chapter XV

Valentin de Bellegarde's announcement of the secession of Mademoiselle Nioche from her father's domicile, and his irreverent reflections upon the attitude of this anxious parent in so grave a catastrophe, received a practical commentary in the fact that M. Nioche was slow to seek another interview with his late pupil. It had cost Newman some disgust to be forced to assent to Valentin's somewhat cynical interpretation of the old man's philosophy, and, though circumstances seemed to indicate that he had not given himself up to a noble despair, Newman thought it very possible he might be suffering more keenly than was apparent. M. Nioche had been in the habit of paying him a respectful little visit every two or three weeks, and his absence might be a proof quite as much of extreme depression as of a desire to conceal the success with which he had patched up his sorrow. Newman presently learned from Valentin several details touching this new phase of Mademoiselle Noémie's career.

"I told you she was remarkable," this unshrinking observer declared, "and the way she has managed this performance proves it. She has had other chances, but she was resolved to take none but the best. She did you the honour to think for awhile that you might be such a chance. You were not; so she gathered up her patience and waited awhile longer. At last her occasion came along, and she made her move with her eyes wide open. I am very sure she had no innocence to lose, but she had all her respectability. Dubious little damsel as you thought her, she had kept a firm hold of that; nothing could be proved against her, and she was determined not to let her reputation go till she had got her equivalent. About her equivalent she had high ideas. Apparently her ideal has been satisfied. It is fifty years old, bald-headed, and deaf, but it is very easy about money."

"And where in the world," asked Newman, "did you pick up this valuable information?"

"In conversation. Remember my frivolous habits. In conversation with a young woman engaged in the humble trade of glove-cleaner, who keeps a small shop in the Rue St. Roch. M. Nioche lives in the same house, up six pair of stairs, across the court, in and out of whose ill-swept doorway Miss Noémie has been flitting for the last five years. The little glove-cleaner was an old acquaintance; she used to be the friend of a friend of mine, who has married and dropped such friends. I often saw her in his society. As soon as I espied her behind her clear little windowpane, I recollected her. I had on a spotlessly fresh pair of gloves, but I went in and held up my hands, and said to her: 'Dear mademoiselle, what will you ask me for cleaning these?' 'Dear count,' she answered immediately, 'I will clean them for you for nothing.' She had instantly recognised me, and I had to hear her history for the last six years. But after that, I put her upon that of her neighbours. She knows and admires Noémie, and she told me what I have just repeated."

A month elapsed without M. Nioche reappearing, and Newman, who every morning read two or three suicides in the *Figaro*,[3] began to suspect that, mortification proving stubborn, he had sought a balm for his wounded pride in the waters of the Seine. He had a note of M. Nioche's address in his pocketbook, and finding himself one day in the *quartier*,[4] he determined, in so far as he might, to clear up his doubts. He repaired to the house in the Rue St. Roch which bore the recorded number, and observed in a neighbouring basement, behind a dangling row of neatly inflated gloves, the attentive physiognomy of Bellegarde's informant—a sallow person

3. A Paris newspaper.

4. Neighborhood.

in a dressing-gown—peering into the street as if she were expecting that amiable nobleman to pass again. But it was not to her that Newman applied; he simply asked of the portress if M. Nioche were at home. The portress replied, as the portress invariably replies, that her lodger had gone out barely three minutes before; but then, through the little square hole of her lodge-window taking the measure of Newman's fortunes, and seeing them, by an unspecified process, refresh the dry places of servitude to occupants of fifth floors on courts, she added that M. Nioche would have had just time to reach the Café de la Patrie, round the second corner to the left, at which establishment he regularly spent his afternoons. Newman thanked her for the information, took the second turning to the left, and arrived at the Café de la Patrie. He felt a momentary hesitation to go in; was it not rather mean to "follow up" poor old Nioche at that rate? But there passed across his vision an image of a haggard little septuagenarian taking measured sips of a glass of sugar and water, and finding them quite impotent to sweeten his desolation. He opened the door and entered, perceiving nothing at first but a dense cloud of tobacco-smoke. Across this, however, in a corner, he presently descried the figure of M. Nioche, stirring the contents of a deep glass, with a lady seated in front of him. The lady's back was turned to Newman, but M. Nioche very soon perceived and recognised his visitor. Newman had gone toward him, and the old man rose slowly, gazing at him with a more blighted expression even than usual.

"If you are drinking hot punch," said Newman, "I suppose you are not dead. That's all right. Don't move."

M. Nioche stood staring, with a fallen jaw, not daring to put out his hand. The lady, who sat facing him, turned round in her place and glanced upward with a spirited toss of her head, displaying the agreeable features of his daughter. She looked at Newman sharply, to see how he was looking at her, then—I don't know what she discovered—she said graciously: "How d'ye do, monsieur? won't you come into our little corner?"

"Did you come—did you come after *me*?" asked M. Nioche, very softly.

"I went to your house to see what had become of you. I thought you might be sick," said Newman.

"It is very good of you, as always," said the old man. "No, I am not well. Yes, I am *seek*."

"Ask monsieur to sit down," said Mademoiselle Nioche. "Garçon,[5] bring a chair."

"Will you do us the honour to *seat*?" said M. Nioche, timorously, and with a double foreignness of accent.

5. "Waiter."

Newman said to himself that he had better see the thing out, and he took a chair at the end of the table, with Mademoiselle Nioche on his left and her father on the other side. "You will take something, of course," said Miss Noémie, who was sipping a glass of madeira. Newman said that he believed not, and then she turned to her papa with a smile. "What an honour, eh? he has come only for us." M. Nioche drained his pungent glass at a long draught, and looked out from eyes more lachrymose in consequence. "But you didn't come for me, eh?" Mademoiselle Noémie went on. "You didn't expect to find me here?"

Newman observed the change in her appearance. She was very elegant, and prettier than before; she looked a year or two older, and it was noticeable that, to the eye, she had only gained in respectability. She looked "lady-like." She was dressed in quiet colours, and she wore her expensively unobtrusive toilet with a grace that might have come from years of practice. Her present self-possession and *aplomb*[6] struck Newman as really infernal, and he inclined to agree with Valentin de Bellegarde that the young lady was very remarkable. "No, to tell the truth, I didn't come for you," he said, "and I didn't expect to find you. I was told," he added in a moment, "that you had left your father."

"*Quelle horreur*!"[7] cried Mademoiselle Nioche, with a smile. "Does one leave one's father? You have the proof of the contrary."

"Yes, convincing proof," said Newman, glancing at M. Nioche. The old man caught his glance obliquely, with his faded deprecating eye, and then, lifting his empty glass, pretended to drink again.

"Who told you that?" Noémie demanded. "I know very well. It was M. de Bellegarde. Why don't you say yes? You are not polite."

"I am embarrassed," said Newman.

"I set you a better example. I know M. de Bellegarde told you. He knows a great deal about me—or he thinks he does. He has taken a great deal of trouble to find out, but half of it isn't true. In the first place, I haven't left my father; I am much too fond of him. Isn't it so, little father? M. de Bellegarde is a charming young man; it is impossible to be cleverer. I know a good deal about him too; you can tell him that when you next see him."

"No," said Newman, with a sturdy grin; "I won't carry any messages for you."

"Just as you please," said Mademoiselle Nioche. "I don't depend upon you, nor does M. de Bellegarde either. He is very much interested in me; he can be left to his own devices. He is a contrast to you."

"Oh, he is a great contrast to me, I have no doubt," said Newman. "But I don't exactly know how you mean it."

6. Poise.

7. "What a horrible thing!"

"I mean it in this way. First of all, he never offered to help me to a *dot*[8] and a husband." And Mademoiselle Nioche paused, smiling. "I won't say that is in his favour, for I do you justice. What led you, by the way, to make me such a queer offer? You didn't care for me."

"Oh yes, I did," said Newman.

"How so?"

"It would have given me real pleasure to see you married to a respectable young fellow."

"With six thousand francs of income!" cried Mademoiselle Nioche. "Do you call that caring for me? I'm afraid you know little about women. You were not *galant*;[9] you were not what you might have been."

Newman flushed, a trifle fiercely. "Come!" he exclaimed, "that's rather strong. I had no idea I had been so shabby."

Mademoiselle Nioche smiled as she took up her muff. "It is something, at any rate, to have made you angry."

Her father had leaned both his elbows on the table, and his head, bent forward, was supported in his hands, the thin white fingers of which were pressed over his ears. In this position he was staring fixedly at the bottom of his empty glass, and Newman supposed he was not hearing. Mademoiselle Noémie buttoned her furred jacket and pushed back her chair, casting a glance charged with the consciousness of an expensive appearance first down over her flounces and then up at Newman.

"You had better have remained an honest girl," Newman said quietly.

M. Nioche continued to stare at the bottom of his glass, and his daughter got up, still bravely smiling. "You mean that I look so much like one? That's more than most women do nowadays. Don't judge me yet awhile," she added. "I mean to succeed; that's what I mean to do. I leave you; I don't mean to be seen in cafés, for one thing. I can't think what you want of my poor father; he's very comfortable now. It isn't his fault either. *Au revoir*,[1] little father." And she tapped the old man on the head with her muff. Then she stopped a minute, looking at Newman. "Tell M. de Bellegarde, when he wants news of me, to come and get it from *me*!" And she turned and departed, the white-aproned waiter, with a bow, holding the door wide open for her.

M. Nioche sat motionless, and Newman hardly knew what to say to him. The old man looked dismally foolish. "So you determined not to shoot her, after all," Newman said presently.

8. Dowry.
9. "Gallant" or "chivalrous."
1. "Good-bye."

M. Nioche, without moving, raised his eyes and gave him a long peculiar look. It seemed to confess everything, and yet not to ask for pity, nor to pretend, on the other hand, to a rugged ability to do without it. It might have expressed the state of mind of an innocuous insect, flat in shape, and conscious of the impending pressure of a boot-sole, and reflecting that he was perhaps too flat to be crushed. M. Nioche's gaze was a profession of moral flatness. "You despise me terribly," he said, in the weakest possible voice.

"Oh no," said Newman; "it is none of my business. It's a good plan to take things easily."

"I made you too many fine speeches," M. Nioche added. "I meant them at the time."

"I am sure I am very glad you didn't shoot her," said Newman. "I was afraid you might have shot yourself. That is why I came to look you up." And he began to button his coat.

"Neither," said M. Nioche. "You despise me, and I can't explain to you. I hoped I shouldn't see you again."

"Why, that's rather shabby," said Newman. "You shouldn't drop your friends that way. Besides, the last time you came to see me I thought you particularly jolly."

"Yes, I remember," said M. Nioche musingly; "I was in a fever. I didn't know what I said, what I did. It was delirium."

"Ah well, you are quieter now."

M. Nioche was silent a moment. "As quiet as the grave," he whispered softly.

"Are you very unhappy?" asked Newman.

M. Nioche rubbed his forehead slowly, and even pushed back his wig a little, looking askance at his empty glass. "Yes—yes. But that's an old story. I have always been unhappy. My daughter does what she will with me. I take what she gives me, good or bad. I have no spirit, and when you have no spirit you must keep quiet. I shan't trouble you any more."

"Well," said Newman, rather disgusted at the smooth operation of the old man's philosophy, "that's as you please."

M. Nioche seemed to have been prepared to be despised, but nevertheless he made a feeble movement of appeal from Newman's faint praise. "After all," he said, "she is my daughter, and I can still look after her. If she will do wrong, why she will. But there are many different paths, there are degrees. I can give her the benefit—give her the benefit"—and M. Nioche paused, staring vaguely at Newman, who began to suspect that his brain had softened—"the benefit of my experience," M. Nioche added.

"Your experience?" inquired Newman, both amused and amazed.

"My experience of business," said M. Nioche gravely.

"Ah yes," said Newman, laughing, "that will be a great advantage to her!" And then he said good-bye, and offered the poor foolish old man his hand.

M. Nioche took it and leaned back against the wall, holding it a moment and looking up at him. "I suppose you think my wits are going," he said. "Very likely; I have always a pain in my head. That's why I can't explain, I can't tell you. And she's so strong, she makes me walk as she will, anywhere! But there's this—there's this." And he stopped, still staring up at Newman. His little white eyes expanded and glittered for a moment like those of a cat in the dark. "It's not as it seems. I haven't forgiven her. Oh no!"

"That's right; don't," said Newman. "She's a bad case."

"It's horrible, it's terrible," said M. Nioche; "but do you want to know the truth? I hate her! I take what she gives me, and I hate her more. To-day she brought me three hundred francs; they are here in my waistcoat-pocket. Now I hate her almost cruelly. No, I haven't forgiven her."

"Why did you accept the money?" Newman asked.

"If I hadn't," said M. Nioche, "I should have hated her still more. That's what misery is. No, I haven't forgiven her."

"Take care you don't hurt her!" said Newman, laughing again. And with this he took his leave. As he passed along the glazed side of the café, on reaching the street, he saw the old man motioning the waiter, with a melancholy gesture, to replenish his glass.

One day, a week after his visit to the Café de la Patrie, he called upon Valentin de Bellegarde, and by good fortune found him at home. Newman spoke of his interview with M. Nioche and his daughter, and said he was afraid Valentin had judged the old man correctly. He had found the couple hobnobbing together in amity; the old gentleman's rigour was purely theoretic. Newman confessed that he was disappointed; he should have expected to see M. Nioche take high ground.

"High ground, my dear fellow," said Valentin, laughing; "there is no high ground for him to take. The only perceptible eminence in M. Nioche's horizon is Montmartre,[2] which is not an edifying quarter. You can't go mountaineering in a flat country."

"He remarked, indeed," said Newman, "that he had not forgiven her. But she'll never find it out."

"We must do him the justice to suppose he doesn't like the thing," Valentin rejoined. "Mademoiselle Nioche is like the great artists whose biographies we read, who at the beginning of their career have suffered opposition in the domestic circle. Their voca-

2. A hilly district in Paris, on the bank of the Seine, known for its night life.

tion has not been recognised by their families, but the world has done it justice. Mademoiselle Nioche has a vocation."

"Oh, come," said Newman impatiently, "you take the little baggage[3] too seriously."

"I know I do; but when one has nothing to think about, one must think of little baggages. I suppose it is better to be serious about light things than not to be serious at all. This little baggage entertains me."

"Oh, she has discovered that. She knows you have been hunting her up and asking questions about her. She is very much tickled by it. That's rather annoying."

"Annoying, my dear fellow," laughed Valentin; "not the least!"

'Hanged if I should want to have a greedy little adventuress like that know I was giving myself such pains about her!" said Newman.

"A pretty woman is always worth one's pains," objected Valentin. "Mademoiselle Nioche is welcome to be tickled by my curiosity, and to know that I am tickled that she is tickled. She is not so much tickled, by the way."

"You had better go and tell her," Newman rejoined. "She gave me a message for you of some such drift."

"Bless your quiet imagination," said Valentin, "I have been to see her—three times in five days. She is a charming hostess; we talk of Shakespeare and the musical-glasses. She is extremely clever and a very curious type; not at all coarse or wanting to be coarse—determined not to be. She means to take very good care of herself. She is extremely perfect; she is as hard and clear-cut as some little figure of a sea-nymph in an antique intaglio, and I will warrant that she has not a grain more of sentiment or heart than if she were scooped out of a big amethyst. You can't scratch her even with a diamond. Extremely pretty—really, when you know her, she is wonderfully pretty—intelligent, determined, ambitious, unscrupulous, capable of looking at a man strangled without changing colour, she is, upon my honour, extremely entertaining."

"It's a fine list of attractions," said Newman; "they would serve as a police-detective's description of a favourite criminal. I should sum them up by another word than 'entertaining.' "

"Why, that is just the word to use. I don't say she is laudable or lovable. I don't want her as my wife or my sister. But she is a very curious and ingenious piece of machinery; I like to see it in operation."

"Well, I have seen some very curious machines, too," said Newman; "and once, in a needle factory, I saw a gentleman from the

3. Slang for "worthless woman."

city, who had stepped too near one of them, picked up as neatly as if he had been prodded by a fork, swallowed down straight, and ground into small pieces."

Re-entering his domicile, late in the evening, three days after Madame de Bellegarde had made her bargain with him—the expression is sufficiently correct—touching the entertainment at which she was to present him to the world, he found on his table a card of goodly dimensions bearing an announcement that this lady would be at home on the 27th of the month, at ten o'clock in the evening. He stuck it into the frame of his mirror and eyed it with some complacency; it seemed an agreeable emblem of triumph, documentary evidence that his prize was gained. Stretched out on a chair, he was looking at it lovingly, when Valentin de Bellegarde was shown into the room. Valentin's glance presently followed the direction of Newman's, and he perceived his mother's invitation.

"And what have they put into the corner?" he asked. "Not the customary 'music,' 'dancing,' or '*tableaux vivants*'?[4] They ought at least to put 'An American.' "

"Oh, there are to be several of us," said Newman. "Mrs. Tristram told me to-day that she had received a card and sent an acceptance."

"Ah, then, with Mrs. Tristram and her husband you will have support. My mother might have put on her card 'Three Americans.' But I suspect you will not lack amusement. You will see a great many of the best people in France. I mean the long pedigrees and the high noses, and all that. Some of them are awful idiots; I advise you to take them up cautiously."

"Oh, I guess I shall like them," said Newman. "I am prepared to like everyone and everything in these days; I am in high good-humour."

Valentin looked at him a moment in silence, and then dropped himself into a chair with an unwonted air of weariness. "Happy man!" he said with a sigh. "Take care you don't become offensive."

"If anyone chooses to take offense, he may. I have a good conscience," said Newman.

"So you are really in love with my sister?"

"Yes, sir!" said Newman, after a pause.

"And she also?"

"I guess she likes me," said Newman.

"What is the witchcraft you have used?" Valentin asked. "How do *you* make love?"

"Oh, I haven't any general rules," said Newman. "In any way that seems acceptable."

4. Theatrical performances in which living actors reproduce celebrated paintings or historical scenes.

"I suspect that, if one knew it," said Valentin, laughing, "you are a terrible customer. You walk in seven-league boots."

"There is something the matter with you to-night," Newman said in response to this. "You are vicious. Spare me all discordant sounds until after my marriage. Then, when I have settled down for life, I shall be better able to take things as they come."

"And when does your marriage take place?"

"About six weeks hence."

Valentin was silent awhile, and then he said: "And you feel very confident about the future?"

"Confident. I knew what I wanted, exactly, and I know what I have got."

"You are sure you are going to be happy?"

"Sure?" said Newman. "So foolish a question deserves a foolish answer. Yes!"

"You are not afraid of anything?"

"What should I be afraid of? You can't hurt me unless you kill me by some violent means. That I should indeed consider a tremendous sell.[5] I want to live and I mean to live. I can't die of illness, I am too ridiculously tough; and the time for dying of old age won't come round yet awhile. I can't lose my wife, I shall take too good care of her. I may lose my money, or a large part of it; but that won't matter, for I shall make twice as much again. So what have I to be afraid of?"

"You are not afraid it may be rather a mistake for an American man of business to marry a French countess?"

"For the countess, possibly; but not for the man of business, if you mean me! But my countess shall not be disappointed; I answer for her happiness!" And as if he felt the impulse to celebrate his happy certitude by a bonfire, he got up to throw a couple of logs upon the already blazing hearth. Valentin watched for a few moments the quickened flame, and then, with his head leaning on his hand, gave a melancholy sigh. "Got a headache?" Newman asked.

"*Je suis triste*,"[6] said Valentin, with Gallic simplicity.

"You are sad, eh? Is it about the lady you said the other night that you adored and that you couldn't marry?"

"Did I really say that? It seemed to me afterwards that the words had escaped me. Before Claire it was bad taste. But I felt gloomy as I spoke, and I feel gloomy still. Why did you ever introduce me to that girl?"

"Oh, it's Noémie, is it? Lord deliver us! You don't mean to say you are lovesick about her?"

"Lovesick, no; it's not a grand passion. But the cold-blooded

5. Sellout or betrayal.

6. "I am sad."

little demon sticks in my thoughts; she has bitten me with those even little teeth of hers; I feel as if I might turn rabid and do something crazy in consequence. It's very low; it's disgustingly low. She's the most mercenary little jade in Europe. Yet she really affects my peace of mind; she is always running in my head. It's a striking contrast to your noble and virtuous attachment—a vile contrast! It is rather pitiful that it should be the best I am able to do for myself at my present respectable age. I am a nice young man, eh, *en somme?*[7] You can't warrant my future, as you do your own."

"Drop that girl, short," said Newman; "don't go near her again, and your future will do. Come over to America and I will get you a place in a bank."

"It is easy to say drop her," said Valentin, with a light laugh. "You can't drop a pretty woman like that. One must be polite, even with Noémie. Besides, I'll not have her suppose I am afraid of her."

"So, between politeness and vanity, you will get deeper into the mud? Keep them both for something better. Remember, too, that I didn't want to introduce you to her; you insisted. I had a sort of uneasy feeling about it."

"Oh, I don't reproach you," said Valentin. "Heaven forbid! I wouldn't for the world have missed knowing her. She is really extraordinary. The way she has already spread her wings is amazing. I don't know when a woman has amused me more. But excuse me," he added in an instant; "she doesn't amuse you, at second hand, and the subject is an impure one. Let us talk of something else." Valentin introduced another topic, but within five minutes Newman observed that, by a bold transition, he had reverted to Mademoiselle Nioche, and was giving pictures of her manners and quoting specimens of her *mots*.[8] These were very witty, and, for a young woman who six months before had been painting the most artless madonnas, startlingly cynical. But at last, abruptly, he stopped, became thoughtful, and for some time afterwards said nothing. When he rose to go it was evident that his thoughts were still running upon Mademoiselle Nioche. "Yes, she's a frightful little monster!" he said.

Chapter XVI

The next ten days were the happiest that Newman had ever known. He saw Madame de Cintré every day, and never saw either old Madame de Bellegarde or the elder of his prospective brothers-

7. "In short."

8. Clever remarks.

in-law. Madame de Cintré at last seemed to think it becoming to apologise for their never being present. "They are much taken up," she said, "with doing the honours of Paris to Lord Deepmere." There was a smile in her gravity as she made this declaration, and it deepened as she added: "He is our seventh cousin, you know, and blood is thicker than water. And then, he is so interesting!" And with this she laughed.

Newman met young Madame de Bellegarde two or three times, always roaming about with graceful vagueness, as if in search of an unattainable ideal of amusement. She always reminded him of a painted perfume-bottle with a crack in it; but he had grown to have a kindly feeling for her, based on the fact of her owing conjugal allegiance to Urbain de Bellegarde. He pitied M. de Bellegarde's wife, especially since she was a silly, thirstily-smiling little brunette, with a suggestion of an unregulated heart. The small marquise sometimes looked at him with an intensity too marked not to be innocent, for coquetry is more finely shaded. She apparently wanted to ask him something or tell him something; he wondered what it was. But he was shy of giving her an opportunity, because, if her communication bore upon the aridity of her matrimonial lot, he was at a loss to see how he could help her. He had a fancy, however, of her coming up to him some day and saying (after looking round behind her) with a little passionate hiss: "I know you detest my husband; let me have the pleasure of assuring you for once you are right. Pity a poor woman who is married to a clock-image in *papier-mâché!*" Possessing, however, in default of a competent knowledge of the principles of etiquette, a very downright sense of the "meanness" of certain actions, it seemed to him to belong to his position to keep on his guard; he was not going to put it into the power of these people to say that in their house he had done anything unpleasant. As it was, Madame de Bellegarde used to give him news of the dress she meant to wear at his wedding, and which had not yet, in her creative imagination, in spite of many interviews with the tailor, resolved itself into its composite totality. "I told you pale blue bows on the sleeves, at the elbows," she said. "But to-day I don't see my blue bows at all. I don't know what has become of them. To-day I see pink—a tender pink. And then I pass through strange dull phases in which neither blue nor pink says anything to me. And yet I must have the bows."

"Have them green or yellow," said Newman.

"*Malheureux!*"[9] the little marquise would cry. "Green bows would break your marriage—your children would be illegitimate!"

Madame de Cintré was calmly happy before the world, and

9. "You poor thing!"

Newman had the felicity of fancying that before him, when the world was absent, she was almost agitatedly happy. She said very tender things. "I take no pleasure in you. You never give me a chance to scold you, to correct you. I bargained for that; I expected to enjoy it. But you won't do anything dreadful; you are dismally inoffensive. It is very stupid; there is no excitement for me; I might as well be marrying someone else."

"I am afraid it's the worst I can do," Newman would say in answer to this. "Kindly overlook the deficiency." He assured her that he, at least, would never scold her; she was perfectly satisfactory. "If you only knew," he said, "how exactly you are what I coveted! And I am beginning to understand why I coveted it; the having it makes all the difference that I expected. Never was a man so pleased with his good fortune. You have been holding your head for a week past just as I wanted my wife to hold hers. You say just the things I want her to say. You walk about the room just as I want her to walk. You have just the taste in dress that I want her to have. In short, you come up to the mark; and, I can tell you, my mark was high."

These observations seemed to make Madame de Cintré rather grave. At last she said: "Depend upon it, I don't come up to the mark; your mark is too high. I am not all that you suppose; I am a much smaller affair. She is a magnificent woman, your ideal. Pray, how did she come to such perfection?"

"She was never anything else," Newman said.

"I really believe," Madame de Cintré went on, "that she is better than my own ideal. Do you know that is a very handsome compliment? Well, sir, I will make her my own!"

Mrs. Tristram came to see her dear Claire after Newman had announced his engagement, and she told our hero the next day that his good fortune was simply absurd. "For the ridiculous part of it is," she said, "that you are evidently going to be as happy as if you were marrying Miss Smith or Miss Thompson. I call it a brilliant match for you, but you get brilliancy without paying any tax upon it. Those things are usually a compromise, but here you have everything, and nothing crowds anything else out. You will be brilliantly happy as well." Newman thanked her for her pleasant encouraging way of saying things; no woman could encourage or discourage better. Tristram's way of saying things was different; he had been taken by his wife to call upon Madame de Cintré, and he gave an account of the expedition.

"You don't catch me giving an opinion on your countess this time," he said; "I put my foot in it once. That's a d——d underhand thing to do, by the way—coming round to sound a fellow upon the woman you are going to marry. You deserve anything you get. Then of course you rush and tell her, and she takes care to make it pleasant for the poor spiteful wretch the first time he calls. I will do you the justice to say, however, that you don't seem to have told Madame de Cintré; or, if you have, she's uncommonly magnanimous. She was very nice; she was tremendously polite. She and Lizzie sat on the sofa, pressing each other's hands and calling each other *chère belle*,[1] and Madame de Cintré sent me with every third word a magnificent smile, as if to give me to understand that I too was a handsome dear. She quite made up for past neglect, I assure you; she was very pleasant and sociable. Only in an evil hour it came into her head to say that she must present us to her mother—her mother wished to know your friends. I didn't want to know her mother, and I was on the point of telling Lizzie to go in alone and let me wait for her outside. But Lizzie, with her usual infernal ingenuity, guessed my purpose and reduced me by a glance of her eye. So they marched off arm-in-arm, and I followed as I could. We found the old lady in her armchair, twiddling her aristocratic thumbs. She looked at Lizzie from head to foot; but at that game Lizzie, to do her justice, was a match for her. My wife told her we were great friends of Mr. Newman. The marquise stared a moment, and then said: 'Oh, Mr. Newman! My daughter has made up her mind to marry a Mr. Newman.' Then Madame de Cintré began to fondle Lizzie again, and said it was this dear lady that had planned the match and brought them together. 'Oh, 'tis you I have to thank for my American son-in-law,' the old lady said to Mrs. Tristram. 'It was a very clever thought of yours. Be sure of my gratitude.' And then she began to look at me, and presently said: 'Pray, are you engaged in some species of manufacture?' I wanted to say that I manufactured broomsticks for old witches to ride on, but Lizzie got in ahead of me. 'My husband, Madame la Marquise,' she said, 'belongs to that unfortunate class of persons who have no profession and no business, and do very little good in the world.' To get her poke at the old woman she didn't care where she shoved me. 'Dear me,' said the marquise, 'we all have our duties.' 'I am sorry mine compel me to take leave of you,' said Lizzie. And we bundled out again. But you have a mother-in-law, in all the force of the term."

"Oh," said Newman, "my mother-in-law desires nothing better than to let me alone."

Betimes, on the evening of the 27th, he went to Madame de Bellegarde's ball. The old house in the Rue de l'Université looked strangely brilliant. In the circle of light projected from the outer gate a detachment of the populace stood watching the carriages roll

1. "You beautiful dear."

in; the court was illumined with flaring torches and the portico carpeted with crimson. When Newman arrived there were but a few people present. The marquise and her two daughters were at the top of the staircase, where the sallow old nymph in the angle peeped out from a bower of plants. Madame de Bellegarde, in purple and fine laces, looked like an old lady painted by Vandyke; Madame de Cintré was dressed in white. The old lady greeted Newman with majestic formality, and, looking round her, called several of the persons who were standing near. They were elderly gentlemen, of what Valentin de Bellegarde had designated as the high-nosed category; two or three of them wore cordons and stars.[2] They approached with measured alertness, and the marquise said that she wished to present them to Mr. Newman, who was going to marry her daughter. Then she introduced successively three dukes, three counts, and a baron. These gentlemen bowed and smiled most agreeably, and Newman indulged in a series of impartial hand shakes, accompanied by a "Happy to make your acquaintance, sir." He looked at Madame de Cintré, but she was not looking at him. If his personal self-consciousness had been of a nature to make him constantly refer to her, as the critic before whom, in company, he played his part, he might have found it a flattering proof of her confidence that he never caught her eyes resting upon him. It is a reflection Newman did not make, but we may nevertheless risk it, that in spite of this circumstance she probably saw every movement of his little finger. Young Madame de Bellegarde was dressed in an audacious toilet of crimson crape, bestrewn with huge silver moons —thin crescents and full discs.

"You don't say anything about my dress," she said to Newman.

"I feel," he answered, "as if I were looking at you through a telescope. It is very strange."

"If it is strange it matches the occasion. But I am not a heavenly body."

"I never saw the sky at midnight that particular shade of crimson," said Newman.

"That is my originality; anyone could have chosen blue. My sister-in-law would have chosen a lovely shade of blue, with a dozen little delicate moons. But I think crimson is much more amusing. And I give my idea, which is moonshine."

"Moonshine and bloodshed," said Newman.

"A murder by moonlight," laughed Madame de Bellegarde. "What a delicious idea for a toilet! To make it complete, there is a dagger of diamonds, you see, stuck into my hair. But here comes Lord Deepmere," she added in a moment; "I must find out what he

2. Ribbons and military or government decorations.

thinks of it." Lord Deepmere came up, looking very red in the face, and laughing. "Lord Deepmere can't decide which he prefers, my sister-in-law or me," said Madame de Bellegarde. "He likes Claire because she is his cousin, and me because I am not. But he has no right to make love to Claire, whereas I am perfectly *disponible*.[3] It is very wrong to make love to a woman who is engaged, but it is very wrong not to make love to a woman who is married."

"Oh, it's very jolly making love to married women," said Lord Deepmere, "because they can't ask you to marry them."

"Is that what the others do—the spinsters?" Newman inquired.

"Oh dear yes," said Lord Deepmere; "in England all the girls ask a fellow to marry them."

"And a fellow brutally refuses," said Madame de Bellegarde.

"Why, really, you know, a fellow can't marry any girl that asks him," said his lordship.

"Your cousin won't ask you. She is going to marry Mr. Newman."

"Oh, that's a very different thing!" laughed Lord Deepmere.

"You would have accepted *her*, I suppose. That makes me hope that after all you prefer me."

"Oh, when things are nice I never prefer one to the other," said the young Englishman. "I take them all."

"Ah, what a horror! I won't be taken in that way; I must be kept apart," cried Madame de Bellegarde. "Mr. Newman is much better; he knows how to choose. Oh, he chooses as if he were threading a needle. He prefers Madame de Cintré to any conceivable creature or thing."

"Well, you can't help my being her cousin," said Lord Deepmere to Newman, with candid hilarity.

"Oh no, I can't help that," said Newman, laughing back; "neither can she!"

"And you can't help my dancing with her," said Lord Deepmere, with sturdy simplicity.

"I could prevent that only by dancing with her myself," said Newman. "But unfortunately I don't know how to dance."

"Oh, you may dance without knowing how; may you not, milord?" said Madame de Bellegarde. But to this Lord Deepmere replied that a fellow ought to know how to dance if he didn't want to make an ass of himself; and at this same moment Urbain de Bellegarde joined the group, slow-stepping and with his hands behind him.

"This is a very splendid entertainment," said Newman cheerfully. "The old house looks very bright."

3. Available.

"If *you* are pleased, we are content," said the marquis, lifting his shoulders and bending them forward.

"Oh, I suspect everyone is pleased," said Newman. "How can they help being pleased when the first thing they see as they come in is your sister, standing there as beautiful as an angel?"

"Yes, she is very beautiful," rejoined the marquis solemnly. "But that is not so great a source of satisfaction to other people, naturally, as to you."

"Yes, I am satisfied, marquis, I am satisfied," said Newman, with his protracted enunciation. "And now tell me," he added, looking round, "who some of your friends are."

M. de Bellegarde looked about him in silence, with his head bent and his hand raised to his lower lip, which he slowly rubbed. A stream of people had been pouring into the salon in which Newman stood with his host, the rooms were filling up and the spectacle had become brilliant. It borrowed its splendour chiefly from the shining shoulders and profuse jewels of the women, and from the voluminous elegance of their dresses. There were no uniforms, as Madame de Bellegarde's door was inexorably closed against the myrmidons of the upstart power which then ruled the fortunes of France, and the great company of smiling and chattering faces was not graced by any very frequent suggestions of harmonious beauty. It is a pity, nevertheless, that Newman had not been a physiognomist, for a great many of the faces were irregularly agreeable, expressive, and suggestive. If the occasion had been different they would hardly have pleased him; he would have thought the women not pretty enough and the men too smirking; but he was now in a humour to receive none but agreeable impressions, and he looked no more narrowly than to perceive that everyone was brilliant, and to feel that the sum of their brilliancy was a part of his credit. "I will present you to some people," said M. de Bellegarde after awhile. "I will make a point of it, in fact. You will allow me?"

"Oh, I will shake hands with anyone you want," said Newman. "Your mother just introduced me to half-a-dozen old gentlemen. Take care you don't pick up the same parties again."

"Who are the gentlemen to whom my mother presents you?"

"Upon my word, I forget them," said Newman, laughing. "The people here look very much alike."

"I suspect they have not forgotten you," said the marquis, and he began to walk through the rooms. Newman, to keep near him in the crowd, took his arm; after which, for some time, the marquis walked straight along, in silence. At last, reaching the farther end of the suite of reception-rooms, Newman found himself in the presence of a lady of monstrous proportions, seated in a very capacious armchair, with several persons standing in a semicircle round her. This little group had divided as the marquis came up, and M. de Bellegarde stepped forward and stood for an instant silent and obsequious, with his hat raised to his lips, as Newman had seen some gentlemen stand in churches as soon as they entered their pews. The lady, indeed, bore a very fair likeness to a reverend effigy in some idolatrous shrine. She was monumentally stout and imperturbably serene. Her aspect was to Newman almost formidable; he had a troubled consciousness of a triple chin, a small piercing eye, a vast expanse of uncovered bosom, a nodding twinkling tiara of plumes and gems, and an immense circumference of satin petticoat. With her little circle of beholders this remarkable woman reminded him of the Fat Lady at a fair. She fixed her small, unwinking eyes at the new-comers.

"Dear duchess," said the marquis, "let me present you our good friend Mr. Newman, of whom you have heard us speak. Wishing to make Mr. Newman known to those who are dear to us, I could not possibly fail to begin with you."

"Charmed, dear friend; charmed, monsieur," said the duchess in a voice which, though small and shrill, was not disagreeable, while Newman executed his obeisance. "I came on purpose to see monsieur. I hope he appreciates the compliment. You have only to look at me to do so, sir," she continued, sweeping her person with a much-encompassing glance. Newman hardly knew what to say, though it seemed that to a duchess who joked about her corpulence one might say almost anything. On hearing that the duchess had come on purpose to see Newman, the gentlemen who surrounded her turned a little and looked at him with sympathetic curiosity. The marquis with supernatural gravity mentioned to him the name of each, while the gentleman who bore it bowed; they were all what are called in France *beaux noms*.[4] "I wanted extremely to see you," the duchess went on. "*C'est positif*.[5] In the first place, I am very fond of the person you are going to marry; she is the most charming creature in France. Mind you treat her well, or you shall hear some news of me. But you look as if you were good. I am told you are very remarkable. I have heard all sorts of extraordinary things about you. *Voyons*,[6] are they true?"

"I don't know what you can have heard," said Newman.

"Oh, you have your *légende*. We have heard that you have had a career the most chequered, the most *bizarre*. What is that about your having founded a city some ten years ago in the great West, a city which contains to-day half a million of inhabitants? Isn't it half a million, messieurs? You are exclusive proprietor of this flourishing settlement, and are consequently fabulously rich, and you

4. "Prestigious names."
5. "That's certain."
6. "Let's see."

would be richer still if you didn't grant lands and houses free of rent to all new-comers who will pledge themselves never to smoke cigars. At this game, in three years, we are told, you are going to be made president of America."

The duchess recited this amusing "legend" with a smooth self-possession which gave the speech, to Newman's mind, the air of being a bit of amusing dialogue in a play, delivered by a veteran comic actress. Before she had ceased speaking he had burst into loud, irrepressible laughter. "Dear duchess, dear duchess," the marquis began to murmur, soothingly. Two or three persons came to the door of the room to see who was laughing at the duchess. But the lady continued with the soft, serene assurance of a person who, as a duchess, was certain of being listened to, and, as a garrulous woman, was independent of the pulse of her auditors. "But I know you are very remarkable. You must be, to have endeared yourself to this good marquis and to his admirable mother. They don't bestow their esteem on all the world. They are very exacting. I myself am not very sure at this hour of really possessing it. Eh, Bellegarde? To please you, I see, one must be an American millionaire. But your real triumph, my dear sir, is pleasing the countess; she is as difficult as a princess in a fairy tale. Your success is a miracle. What is your secret? I don't ask you to reveal it before all these gentlemen, but come and see me some day and give me a specimen of your talents."

"The secret is with Madame de Cintré," said Newman. "You must ask her for it. It consists in her having a great deal of charity."

"Very pretty!" said the duchess. "That's a very nice specimen, to begin with. What, Bellegarde, are you already taking monsieur away?"

"I have a duty to perform, dear friend," said the marquis, pointing to the other groups.

"Ah, for you I know what that means. Well, I have seen monsieur; that is what I wanted. He can't persuade me that he isn't very clever. Farewell."

As Newman passed on with his host, he asked who the duchess was. "The greatest lady in France," said the marquis. M. de Bellegarde then presented his prospective brother-in-law to some twenty other persons of both sexes, selected apparently for their typically august character. In some cases this character was written in a good round hand upon the countenance of the wearer; in others Newman was thankful for such help as his companion's impressively brief intimation contributed to the discovery of it. There were large, majestic men, and small, demonstrative men; there were ugly ladies in yellow lace and quaint jewels, and pretty ladies with white shoulders from which jewels and everything else were absent.

Everyone gave Newman extreme attention, everyone smiled, everyone was charmed to make his acquaintance, everyone looked at him with that soft hardness of good society which puts out its hand but keeps its fingers closed over the coin. If the marquis was going about as a bear-leader, if the fiction of Beauty and the Beast[7] was supposed to have found its companion-piece, the general impression appeared to be that the bear was a very fair imitation of humanity. Newman found his reception among the marquis's friends very "pleasant;" he could not have said more for it. It was pleasant to be treated with so much explicit politeness; it was pleasant to hear neatly-turned civilities, with a flavour of wit, uttered from beneath carefully-shaped moustaches; it was pleasant to see clever Frenchwomen—they all seemed clever—turn their backs to their partners to get a good look at the strange American whom Claire de Cintré was to marry, and reward the object of the exhibition with a charming smile. At last, as he turned away from a battery of smiles and other amenities, Newman caught the eye of the marquis looking at him heavily; and thereupon, for a single instant, he checked himself. "Am I behaving like a d——d fool?" he asked himself. "Am I stepping about like a terrier on his hind legs?" At this moment he perceived Mrs. Tristram at the other side of the room, and he waved his hand in farewell to M. de Bellegarde and made his way toward her.

"Am I holding my head too high?" he asked. "Do I look as if I had the lower end of a pulley fastened to my chin?"

"You look like all happy men, very ridiculous," said Mrs. Tristram. "It's the usual thing, neither better nor worse. I have been watching you for the last ten minutes, and I have been watching M. de Bellegarde. He doesn't like it."

"The more credit to him for putting it through," replied Newman. "But I shall be generous. I shan't trouble him any more. But I am very happy. I can't stand still here. Please to take my arm and we will go for a walk."

He led Mrs. Tristram through all the rooms. There were a great many of them, and, decorated for the occasion and filled with a stately crowd, their somewhat tarnished nobleness recovered its lustre. Mrs. Tristram, looking about her, dropped a series of softly-incisive comments upon her fellow-guests. But Newman made vague answers; he hardly heard her; his thoughts were elsewhere. They were lost in a cheerful sense of success, of attainment and victory. His momentary care as to whether he looked like a fool passed away, leaving him simply with a rich contentment. He had got what he wanted. The savour of success had always been highly

7. A folktale and fairy story, probably derived from the Greek myth of Psyche and Cupid, in which a beautiful young woman is bound in love to a monster.

agreeable to him, and it had been his fortune to know it often. But it had never before been so sweet, been associated with so much that was brilliant and suggestive and entertaining. The lights, the flowers, the music, the crowd, the splendid women, the jewels, the strangeness even of the universal murmur of a clever foreign tongue, were all a vivid symbol and assurance of his having grasped his purpose and forced along his groove. If Newman's smile was larger than usual, it was not tickled vanity that pulled the strings; he had no wish to be shown with the finger or to achieve a personal success. If he could have looked down at the scene, invisible, from a hole in the roof, he would have enjoyed it quite as much. It would have spoken to him about his own prosperity and deepened that easy feeling about life to which, sooner or later, he made all experience contribute. Just now the cup seemed full.

"It is a very pretty party," said Mrs. Tristram, after they had walked awhile. "I have seen nothing objectionable except my husband leaning against the wall and talking to an individual whom I suppose he takes for a duke, but whom I more than suspect to be the functionary who attends to the lamps. Do you think you could separate them? Knock over a lamp!"

I doubt whether Newman, who saw no harm in Tristram's conversing with an ingenious mechanic, would have complied with this request; but at this moment Valentin de Bellegarde drew near. Newman, some weeks previously, had presented Madame de Cintré's youngest brother to Mrs. Tristram, for whose merits Valentin professed a discriminating relish and to whom he had paid several visits.

"Did you ever read Keats' 'Belle Dame sans Merci'?" asked Mrs. Tristram. "You remind me of the hero of the ballad:

"Oh, what can ail thee, knight-at-arms,
Alone and palely loitering?"

"If I am alone, it is because I have been deprived of your society," said Valentin. "Besides, it is good manners for no man except Newman to look happy. This is all to his address. It is not for you and me to go before the curtain."

"You promised me last spring," said Newman to Mrs. Tristram, "that six months from that time I should get into a monstrous rage. It seems to me the time's up, and yet the nearest I can come to doing anything rough now is to offer you a *café glacé*."[8]

"I told you we should do things grandly," said Valentin. "I don't

8. Iced coffee.

allude to the *cafés glacés*. But everyone is here, and my sister told me just now that Urbain had been adorable."

"He's a good fellow, he's a good fellow," said Newman. "I love him as a brother. That reminds me that I ought to go and say something polite to your mother."

"Let it be something very polite indeed," said Valentin. "It may be the last time you will feel so much like it!"

Newman walked away, almost disposed to clasp old Madame de Bellegarde round the waist. He passed through several rooms and at last found the old marquise in the first saloon, seated on a sofa, with her young kinsman, Lord Deepmere, beside her. The young man looked somewhat bored; his hands were thrust into his pockets and his eyes were fixed upon the toes of his shoes, his feet being thrust out in front of him. Madame de Bellegarde appeared to have been talking to him with some intensity and to be waiting for an answer to what she had said, or for some sign of the effect of her words. Her hands were folded in her lap, and she was looking at his lordship's simple physiognomy with an air of politely suppressed irritation.

Lord Deepmere looked up as Newman approached, met his eyes, and changed colour.

"I am afraid I disturb an interesting interview," said Newman.

Madame de Bellegarde rose, and her companion rising at the same time, she put her hand into his arm. She answered nothing for an instant, and then, as he remained silent, she said with a smile: "It would be polite for Lord Deepmere to say it was very interesting."

"Oh, I'm not polite!" cried his lordship. "But it *was* interesting."

"Madame de Bellegarde was giving you some good advice, eh?" said Newman; "toning you down a little?"

"I was giving him some excellent advice," said the marquise, fixing her fresh cold eyes upon our hero. "It's for him to take it."

"Take it, sir, take it!" Newman exclaimed. "Any advice the marquise gives you to-night must be good; for to-night, marquise, you must speak from a cheerful, comfortable spirit, and that makes good advice. You see everything going on so brightly and successfully round you. Your party is magnificent; it was a very happy thought. It is much better than that thing of mine would have been."

"If you are pleased I am satisfied," said Madame de Bellegarde. "My desire was to please you."

"Do you want to please me a little more?" said Newman. "Just drop our lordly friend; I am sure he wants to be off and shake his heels a little. Then take my arm and walk through the rooms."

"My desire was to please you," the old lady repeated. And she liberated Lord Deepmere, Newman rather wondering at her docility. "If this young man is wise," she added, "he will go and find my daughter and ask her to dance."

"I have been endorsing your advice," said Newman, bending over her and laughing, "I suppose I must swallow that!"

Lord Deepmere wiped his forehead and departed, and Madame de Bellegarde took Newman's arm. "Yes, it's a very pleasant, sociable entertainment," the latter declared, as they proceeded on their circuit. "Everyone seems to know everyone and to be glad to see everyone. The marquis has made me acquainted with ever so many people, and I feel quite like one of the family. It's an occasion," Newman continued, wanting to say something thoroughly kind and comfortable, "that I shall always remember, and remember very pleasantly."

"I think it is an occasion that we shall none of us forget," said the marquise, with her pure, neat enunciation.

People made way for her as she passed, others turned round and looked at her, and she received a great many greetings and pressings of the hand, all of which she accepted with the most delicate dignity. But though she smiled upon everyone, she said nothing until she reached the last of the rooms, where she found her elder son. Then, "This is enough, sir," she declared with measured softness to Newman, and turned to the marquis. He put out both his hands and took both hers, drawing her to a seat with an air of the tenderest veneration. It was a most harmonious family group, and Newman discreetly retired. He moved through the rooms for some time longer, circulating freely, overtopping most people by his great height, renewing acquaintance with some of the groups to which Urbain de Bellegarde had presented him, and expending generally the surplus of his equanimity. He continued to find it all extremely agreeable; but the most agreeable things have an end, and the revelry on this occasion began to deepen to a close. The music was sounding its ultimate strains and people were looking for the marquise, to make their farewells. There seemed to be some difficulty in finding her, and Newman heard a report that she had left the ball, feeling faint. "She has succumbed to the emotions of the evening," he heard a lady say. "Poor, dear marquise; I can imagine all that they may have been for her!"

But he learned immediately afterwards that she had recovered herself and was seated in an armchair near the doorway, receiving parting compliments from great ladies who insisted upon her not rising. He himself set out in quest of Madame de Cintré. He had seen her move past him many times in the rapid circles of a waltz, but in accordance with her explicit instructions he had exchanged no words with her since the beginning of the evening. The whole house having been thrown open, the apartments of the *rez-de-chaussée*[9] were also accessible, though a smaller number of persons had gathered there. Newman wandered through them, observing a few scattered couples to whom this comparative seclusion appeared grateful, and reached a small conservatory which opened into the garden. The end of the conservatory was formed by a clear sheet of glass, unmasked by plants, and admitting the winter starlight so directly that a person standing there would seem to have passed into the open air. Two persons stood there now, a lady and a gentleman; the lady Newman, from within the room, and although she had turned her back to it, immediately recognised as Madame de Cintré. He hesitated as to whether he would advance, but as he did so she looked round, feeling apparently that he was there. She rested her eyes on him a moment, and then turned again to her companion.

"It is almost a pity not to tell Mr. Newman," she said softly, but in a tone that Newman could hear.

"Tell him if you like!" the gentleman answered, in the voice of Lord Deepmere.

"Oh, tell me by all means!" said Newman, advancing.

Lord Deepmere, he observed, was very red in the face, and he had twisted his gloves into a tight cord as if he had been squeezing them dry. These, presumably, were tokens of violent emotion, and it seemed to Newman that the traces of a corresponding agitation were visible in Madame de Cintré's face. The two had been talking with much vivacity. "What I should tell you is only to my lord's credit," said Madame de Cintré, smiling frankly enough.

"He wouldn't like it any better for that," said my lord, with his awkward laugh.

"Come; what's the mystery?" Newman demanded. "Clear it up. I don't like mysteries."

"We must have some things we don't like, and go without some we do," said the ruddy young nobleman, laughing still.

"It is to Lord Deepmere's credit, but it is not to every one's," said Madame de Cintré. "So I shall say nothing about it. You may be sure," she added; and she put out her hand to the Englishman, who took it half shyly, half impetuously. "And now go and dance!" she said.

"Oh yes, I feel awfully like dancing!" he answered. "I shall go and get tipsy." And he walked away with a gloomy guffaw.

"What has happened between you?" Newman asked.

"I can't tell you—now," said Madame de Cintré. "Nothing that need make you unhappy."

9. Ground floor.

"Has the little Englishman been trying to make love to you?"

She hesitated, and then she uttered a grave "No! he's a very honest little fellow."

"But you are agitated. Something is the matter."

"Nothing, I repeat, that need make you unhappy. My agitation is over. Some day I will tell you what it was; not now. I can't now!"

"Well, I confess," remarked Newman, "I don't want to hear anything unpleasant. I am satisfied with everything—most of all with you. I have seen all the ladies and talked with a great many of them; but I am satisfied with you." Madame de Cintré covered him for a moment with her large, soft glance, and then turned her eyes away into the starry night. So they stood silent a moment, side by side. "Say you are satisfied with me," said Newman.

He had to wait a moment for the answer; but it came at last, low yet distinct: "I am very happy."

It was presently followed by a few words from another source, which made them both turn round. "I am sadly afraid Madame de Cintré will take a chill. I have ventured to bring a shawl." Mrs. Bread stood there softly solicitous, holding a white drapery in her hand.

"Thank you," said Madame de Cintré, "the sight of those cold stars gives one a sense of frost. I won't take your shawl, but we will go back into the house."

She passed back and Newman followed her, Mrs. Bread standing respectfully aside to make way for them. Newman paused an instant before the old woman, and she glanced up at him with a silent greeting. "Oh yes," he said, "you must come and live with us."

"Well then, sir, if you will," she answered, "you have not seen the last of me!"

Chapter XVII

Newman was fond of music and went often to the opera. A couple of evenings after Madame de Bellegarde's ball he sat listening to "Don Giovanni,"[1] having in honour of this work, which he had never yet seen represented, come to occupy his orchestra-chair before the rising of the curtain. Frequently he took a large box and invited a party of his compatriots; this was a mode of recreation to which he was much addicted. He liked making up parties of his friends and conducting them to the theatre, and taking them to drive on high drags or to dine at remote restaurants. He liked doing things which involved his paying for people; the vulgar truth is that he enjoyed "treating" them. This was not because he was what is

1. An opera by Mozart (1787), in which a licentious seducer is dragged off to hell.

called purse-proud; handling money in public was on the contrary positively disagreeable to him; he had a sort of personal modesty about it, akin to what he would have felt about making a toilet before spectators. But just as it was a gratification to him to be handsomely dressed, just so it was a private satisfaction to him (he enjoyed it very clandestinely) to have interposed, pecuniarily, in a scheme of pleasure. To set a large group of people in motion and transport them to a distance, to have special conveyances, to charter railway-carriages and steamboats, harmonised with his relish for bold processes, and made hospitality seem more active and more to the purpose. A few evenings before the occasion of which I speak he had invited several ladies and gentlemen to the opera to listen to Madame Alboni[2]—a party which included Miss Dora Finch. It befell, however, that Miss Dora Finch, sitting near Newman in the box, discoursed brilliantly, not only during the entr'actes, but during many of the finest portions of the performance, so that Newman had really come away with an irritated sense that Madame Alboni had a thin, shrill voice, and that her musical phrase was much garnished with a laugh of the giggling order. After this he promised himself to go for awhile to the opera alone.

When the curtain had fallen upon the first act of "Don Giovanni," he turned round in his place to observe the house. Presently, in one of the boxes, he perceived Urbain de Bellegarde and his wife. The little marquise was sweeping the house very busily with a glass, and Newman, supposing that she saw him, determined to go and bid her good-evening. M. de Bellegarde was leaning against a column, motionless, looking straight in front of him, with one hand in the breast of his white waistcoat and the other resting his hat on his thigh. Newman was about to leave his place when he noticed in that obscure region devoted to the small boxes which in France are called, not inaptly, "bathing-tubs," a face which even the dim light and the distance could not make wholly indistinct. It was the face of a young and pretty woman, and it was surmounted with a *coiffure*[3] of pink roses and diamonds. This person was looking round the house, and her fan was moving to and fro with the most practised grace; when she lowered it, Newman perceived a pair of plump white shoulders and the edge of a rose-coloured dress. Beside her, very close to the shoulders, and talking, apparently with an earnestness which it pleased her scantily to heed, sat a young man with a red face and a very low shirt-collar. A moment's gazing left Newman with no doubts; the pretty young woman was Noémie Nioche. He looked hard into the depths of the box, thinking her father might perhaps be in attendance, but from what he

2. Marietta Alboni (1823–94), Italian opera singer, the most famous contralto of the nineteenth century.
3. Hairdo.

could see the young man's eloquence had no other auditor. Newman at last made his way out, and in doing so he passed beneath the *baignoire*[4] of Mademoiselle Noémie. She saw him as he approached, and gave him a nod and smile which seemed meant as an assurance that she was still a good-natured girl, in spite of her enviable rise in the world. Newman passed into the *foyer*[5] and walked through it. Suddenly he paused in front of a gentleman seated on one of the divans. The gentleman's elbows were on his knees; he was leaning forward and staring at the pavement, lost apparently in meditations of a somewhat gloomy cast. But in spite of his bent head Newman recognised him, and in a moment sat down beside him. Then the gentleman looked up and displayed the expressive countenance of Valentin de Bellegarde.

"What in the world are you thinking of so hard?" asked Newman.

"A subject that requires hard thinking to do it justice," said Valentin. "My immeasurable idiocy."

"What is the matter now?"

"The matter now is that I am a man again, and no more a fool than usual. But I came within an inch of taking that girl *au sérieux*."[6]

"You mean the young lady below stairs, in a *baignoire*, in a pink dress?" said Newman.

"Did you notice what a brilliant kind of pink it was?" Valentin inquired, by way of answer. "It makes her look as white as new milk."

"White or black, as you please. But you have stopped going to see her?"

"Oh, bless you, no. Why should I stop? I have changed, but she hasn't," said Valentin. "I see she is a vulgar little wretch, after all. But she is as amusing as ever, and one *must* be amused."

"Well, I am glad she strikes you so unpleasantly," Newman rejoined. "I suppose you have swallowed all those fine words you used about her the other night. You compared her to a sapphire, or a topaz, or an amethyst—some precious stone; what was it?"

"I don't remember," said Valentin, "it may have been to a carbuncle! But she won't make a fool of me now. She has no real charm. It's an awfully low thing to make a mistake about a person of that sort."

"I congratulate you," Newman declared, "upon the scales having fallen from your eyes. It's a great triumph; it ought to make you feel better."

"Yes, it makes me feel better!" said Valentin gaily. Then, check-

4. A theater or orchestra box on one of the lower levels of the theater.

5. Lobby

6. Seriously.

ing himself, he looked askance at Newman. "I rather think you are laughing at me. If you were not one of the family I would take it up."

"Oh no, I'm not laughing, any more than I am one of the family. You make me feel badly. You are too clever a fellow, you are made of too good stuff, to spend your time in ups and downs over that class of goods. The idea of splitting hairs about Miss Nioche! It seems to me awfully foolish. You say you have given up taking her seriously; but you take her seriously so long as you take her at all."

Valentin turned round in his place and looked awhile at Newman, wrinkling his forehead and rubbing his knees. "*Vous parlez d'or.*[7] But she has wonderfully pretty arms. Would you believe I didn't know it till this evening?"

"But she is a vulgar little wretch, remember, all the same," said Newman.

"Yes; the other day she had the bad taste to begin to abuse her father, to his face, in my presence. I shouldn't have expected it of her; it was a disappointment; heigho!"

"Why, she cares no more for her father than for her doormat," said Newman. "I discovered that the first time I saw her."

"Oh, that's another affair; she may think of the poor old beggar what she pleases. But it was low in her to call him bad names; it quite threw me off. It was about a frilled petticoat that he was to have fetched from the washer-woman's; he appeared to have neglected this graceful duty. She almost boxed his ears. He stood there staring at her with his little blank eyes and smoothing his old hat with his coat-tail. At last he turned round and went out without a word. Then I told her it was in very bad taste to speak so to one's papa. She said she should be so thankful to me if I would mention it to her whenever her taste was at fault; she had immense confidence in mine. I told her I couldn't have the bother of forming her manners; I had had an idea they were already formed, after the best models. She had disappointed me. But I shall get over it," said Valentin gaily.

"Oh, time's a great consoler!" Newman answered with humorous sobriety. He was silent a moment, and then he added in another tone: "I wish you would think of what I said to you the other day. Come over to America with us, and I will put you in the way of doing some business. You have got a very good head if you will only use it."

Valentin made a genial grimace. "My head is much obliged to you. Do you mean the place in a bank?"

"There are several places, but I suppose you would consider the bank the most aristocratic."

7. "Your words are as good as gold"; or "You speak truly."

Valentin burst into a laugh. "My dear fellow, at night all cats are gray! When one derogates there are no degrees."

Newman answered nothing for a minute. Then, "I think you will find there are degrees in success," he said with a certain dryness.

Valentin had leaned forward again, with his elbows on his knees, and he was scratching the pavement with his stick. At last he said, looking up: "Do you really think I ought to do something!"

Newman laid his hand on his companion's arm and looked at him a moment through sagaciously-narrowed eyelids. "Try it and see. You are not good enough for it, but we will stretch a point."

"Do you really think I can make some money? I should like to see how it feels to have a little."

"Do what I tell you, and you shall be rich," said Newman. "Think of it." And he looked at his watch and prepared to resume his way to Madame de Bellegarde's box.

"Upon my word I will think of it," said Valentin. "I will go and listen to Mozart another half hour—I can always think better to music—and profoundly meditate upon it."

The marquis was with his wife when Newman entered their box; he was bland, remote, and correct as usual; or, as it seemed to Newman, even more than usual.

"What do you think of the opera?" asked our hero. "What do you think of the Don?"

"We all know what Mozart is," said the marquis; "our impressions don't date from this evening. Mozart is youth, freshness, brilliancy, facility—a little too great facility, perhaps. But the execution is here and there deplorably rough."

"I am very curious to see how it ends," said Newman.

"You speak as if it were a *feuilleton* in the *Figaro*,"[8] observed the marquis. "You have surely seen the opera before?"

"Never," said Newman. "I am sure I should have remembered it. Donna Elvira[9] reminds me of Madame de Cintré; I don't mean in her circumstances, but in the music she sings."

"It is a very nice distinction," laughed the marquis lightly. "There is no great possibility, I imagine, of Madame de Cintré being forsaken."

"Not much!" said Newman. "But what becomes of the Don?"

"The devil comes down—or comes up," said Madame de Bellegarde, "and carries him off. I suppose Zerlina[1] reminds you of me."

"I will go to the *foyer* for a few moments," said the marquis,

8. A serialized story in the Paris newspaper, *Figaro*.

9. One of Don Juan's discarded sweethearts in Mozart's *Don Giovanni*.

1. A peasant girl whom Don Juan attempts to seduce on the eve of her wedding with Masetto, a villager.

"and give you a chance to say that the Commander—the man of stone[2]—resembles me." And he passed out of the box.

The little marquise stared an instant at the velvet ledge of the balcony, and then murmured: "Not a man of stone, a man of wood." Newman had taken her husband's empty chair. She made no protest, and then she turned suddenly and laid her closed fan upon his arm. "I am very glad you came in," she said. "I want to ask you a favour. I wanted to do so on Thursday, at my mother-in-law's ball, but you would give me no chance. You were in such very good spirits that I thought you might grant my little favour then; not that you look particularly doleful now. It is something you must promise me; now is the time to take you; after you are married you will be good for nothing. Come, promise!"

"I never sign a paper without reading it first," said Newman. "Show me your document."

"No, you must sign with your eyes shut; I will hold your hand. Come, before you put your head into the noose. You ought to be thankful for me giving you a chance to do something amusing."

"If it is so amusing," said Newman, "it will be in even better season after I am married."

"In other words," cried Madame de Bellegarde, "you will not do it at all. You will be afraid of your wife."

"Oh, if the thing is intrinsically improper," said Newman, "I won't go into it. If it is not, I will do it after my marriage."

"You talk like a treatise on logic, and English logic into the bargain!" exclaimed Madame de Bellegarde. "Promise, then, after you are married. After all, I shall enjoy keeping you to it."

"Well, then, after I am married," said Newman serenely.

The little marquise hesitated a moment, looking at him, and he wondered what was coming. "I suppose you know what my life is," she presently said. "I have no pleasure, I see nothing, I do nothing. I live in Paris as I might live at Poitiers.[3] My mother-in-law calls me—what is the pretty word?—a gadabout? accuses me of going to unheard-of places, and thinks it ought to be joy enough for me to sit at home and count over my ancestors on my fingers. But why should I bother about my ancestors? I am sure they never bothered about me. I don't propose to live with a green shade on my eyes; I hold that things were made to look at. My husband, you know, has principles, and the first on the list is that the Tuileries are dreadfully vulgar. If the Tuileries are vulgar, his principles are tiresome. If I chose I might have principles quite as well as he. If they grew on one's family tree I should only have to give mine a shake to

2. Don Pedro. After he is killed by Don Juan his statue comes to life, in the final scene of Don *Giovanni*, and he transports Don Juan down to hell.

3. A city in west central France.

bring down a shower of the finest. At any rate, I prefer clever Bonapartes to stupid Bourbons."

"Oh, I see; you want to go to court," said Newman, vaguely conjecturing that she might wish him to appeal to the United States legation to smooth her way to the imperial halls.

The marquise gave a little sharp laugh. "You are a thousand miles away. I will take care of the Tuileries myself; the day I decide to go they will be very glad to have me. Sooner or later I shall dance in an imperial quadrille. I know what you are going to say: 'How will you dare?' But I *shall* dare. I am afraid of my husband; he is soft, smooth, irreproachable, everything that you know; but I am afraid of him—horribly afraid of him. And yet I shall arrive at the Tuileries. But that will not be this winter, nor perhaps next, and meantime I must live. For the moment, I want to go somewhere else; it's my dream. I want to go to the Bal Bullier."

"To the Bal Bullier?" repeated Newman, for whom the words at first meant nothing.

"The ball in the Latin Quarter, where the students dance with their mistresses. Don't tell me you have not heard of it."

"Oh yes," said Newman; "I have heard of it; I remember now. I have even been there. And you want to go there?"

"It is silly, it is low, it is anything you please. But I want to go. Some of my friends have been, and they say it is awfully *drôle*.[4] My friends go everywhere; it is only I who sit moping at home."

"It seems to me you are not at home now," said Newman, "and I shouldn't exactly say you were moping."

"I am bored to death. I have been to the opera twice a week for the last eight years. Whenever I ask for anything my mouth is stopped with that: Pray, madam, haven't you an opera-box? Could a woman of taste want more? In the first place, my opera-box was down in my *contrat*;[5] they have to give it to me. To-night, for instance, I should have preferred a thousand times to go to the Palais Royal. But my husband won't go to the Palais Royal because the ladies of the court go there so much. You may imagine, then, whether he would take me to Bullier's; he says it is a mere imitation —and a bad one—of what they do at the Princess Kleinfuss's. But as I don't go to the Princess Kleinfuss's, the next best thing is to go to Bullier's. It is my dream, at any rate; it's a fixed idea. All I ask of you is to give me your arm; you are less compromising than anyone else. I don't know why, but you are. I can arrange it. I shall risk something, but that is my own affair. Besides, fortune favours the bold. Don't refuse me; it is my dream!"

4. Amusing.

5. Marriage contract. In France, part of the ceremony of marriage consists in drawing up a legal contract between the two partners, each of whom brings a witness to the agreement.

Newman gave a loud laugh. It seemed to him hardly worth while to be the wife of the Marquis de Bellegarde, a daughter of the crusaders, heiress of six centuries of glories and traditions, to have centred one's aspirations upon the sight of a couple of hundred young ladies kicking off young men's hats. It struck him as a theme for the moralist; but he had no time to moralise upon it. The curtain rose again; M. de Bellegarde returned, and Newman went back to his seat.

He observed that Valentin de Bellegarde had taken his place in the *baignoire*[6] of Mademoiselle Nioche, behind this young lady and her companion, where he was visible only if one carefully looked for him. In the next act Newman met him in the lobby and asked him if he had reflected upon possible emigration. "If you really meant to meditate," he said, "you might have chosen a better place for it."

"Oh, the place was not bad," said Valentin. "I was not thinking of that girl. I listened to the music, and without thinking of the play or looking at the stage, I turned over your proposal. At first it seemed quite fantastic. And then a certain fiddle in the orchestra—I could distinguish it—began to say as it scraped away: 'Why not, why not?' And then, in that rapid movement, all the fiddles took it up, and the conductor's stick seemed to beat it in the air: 'Why not, why not?' I'm sure I can't say! I don't see why not. I don't see why I shouldn't do something. It appears to me really a very bright idea. This sort of thing is certainly very stale. And then I could come back with a trunk full of dollars. Besides, I might possibly find it amusing. They call me a *raffiné*;[7] who knows but that I might discover an unsuspected charm in shop-keeping? It would really have a certain romantic, picturesque side; it would look well in my biography. It would look as if I were a strong man, a first-rate man, a man who dominated circumstances."

"Never mind how it would look," said Newman. "It always looks well to have half a million of dollars. There is no reason why you shouldn't have them if you will mind what I tell you—I alone—and not talk to other parties." He passed his arm into that of his companion, and the two walked for some time up and down one of the less frequented corridors. Newman's imagination began to glow with the idea of converting his bright, impracticable friend into a first-class man of business. He felt for the moment a sort of spiritual zeal, the zeal of the propagandist. Its ardour was in part the result of that general discomfort which the sight of all uninvested capital produced in him; so fine an intelligence as Bellegarde's ought to be dedicated to high uses. The highest uses known to

6. Stall or theater box.

7. A man of extreme refinement.

Newman's experience were certain transcendent sagacities in the handling of railway stock. And then his zeal was quickened by his personal kindness for Valentin; he had a sort of pity for him which he was well aware he never could have made the Comte de Bellegarde understand. He never lost a sense of its being pitiable that Valentin should think it a large life to revolve in varnished boots between the Rue d'Anjou and the Rue de l'Université, taking the Boulevard des Italiens on the way, when over there in America one's promenade was a continent, and one's boulevard stretched from New York to San Francisco. It mortified him, moreover, to think that Valentin lacked money; there was a painful grotesqueness in it. It affected him as the ignorance of a companion, otherwise without reproach, touching some rudimentary branch of learning would have done. There were things that one knew about as a matter of course, he would have said in such a case. Just so, if one pretended to be easy in the world, one had money as a matter of course; one had made it! There was something almost ridiculously anomalous to Newman in the sight of lively pretensions unaccompanied by large investments in railroads; though I may add that he would not have maintained that such investments were in themselves a proper ground for pretensions. "I will make you do something," he said to Valentin; "I will put you through. I know half-a-dozen things in which we can make a place for you. You will see some lively work. It will take you a little while to get used to the life, but you will work in before long, and at the end of six months—after you have done a thing or two on your own account—you will like it. And then it will be very pleasant for you, having your sister over there. It will be pleasant for her to have you, too. Yes, Valentin," continued Newman, pressing his friend's arm genially, "I think I see just the opening for you. Keep quiet, and I'll push you right in."

Newman pursued this favouring strain for some time longer. The two men strolled about for a quarter of an hour. Valentin listened and questioned, many of his questions making Newman laugh loud at the *naïveté* of his ignorance of the vulgar processes of money-getting; smiling himself, too, half ironical and half curious. And yet he was serious; he was fascinated by Newman's plain prose version of the legend of El Dorado.[8] It is true, however, that though to accept an "opening" in an American mercantile house might be a bold, original, and in its consequences extremely agreeable thing to do, he did not quite see himself objectively doing it. So that when the bell rang to indicate the close of the entr'acte,[9] there was a certain mock-heroism in his saying, with his brilliant smile: "Well,

8. A mythical country, rich in gold and plenty, sought by the conquistadors in South America.
9. Intermission.

then, put me through; push me in! I make myself over to you. Dip me into the pot and turn me into gold."

They had passed into the corridor which encircled the row of *baignoires,* and Valentin stopped in front of the dusky little box in which Mademoiselle Nioche had bestowed herself, laying his hand on the door-knob. "Oh, come, are you going back there?" asked Newman.

"*Mon Dieu, oui,*"[1] said Valentin.

"Haven't you another place?"

"Yes, I have my usual place, in the stalls."

"You had better go and occupy it, then."

"I see her very well from there, too," added Valentin serenely; "and to-night she is worth seeing. But," he added in a moment, "I have a particular reason for going back just now."

"Oh, I give you up," said Newman. "You are infatuated!"

"No, it is only this. There is a young man in the box whom I shall annoy by going in, and I want to annoy him."

"I am sorry to hear it," said Newman. "Can't you leave the poor fellow alone?"

"No, he has given me cause. The box is not his; Noémie came in alone and installed herself. I went and spoke to her, and in a few moments she asked me to go and get her fan from the pocket of her cloak, which the *ouvreuse*[2] had carried off. In my absence this gentleman came in and took the chair beside Noémie in which I had been sitting. My reappearance disgusted him, and he had the grossness to show it. He came within an ace of being impertinent. I don't know who he is; he is some vulgar wretch. I can't think where she picks up such acquaintances. He has been drinking, too, but he knows what he is about. Just now, in the second act, he was unmannerly again. I shall put in another appearance for ten minutes—time enough to give him an opportunity to commit himself, if he feels inclined. I really can't let the brute suppose that he is keeping me out of the box."

"My dear fellow," said Newman remonstrantly, "what child's play! You are not going to pick a quarrel about that girl, I hope."

"That girl has nothing to do with it, and I have no intention of picking a quarrel. I am not a bully nor a fire-eater.[3] I simply wish to make a point that a gentleman must."

"Oh, damn your point!" said Newman. "That is the trouble with you Frenchmen; you must be always making points. Well," he added, "be short. But if you are going in for this kind of thing, we must ship you off to America in advance."

"Very good," Valentin answered, "whenever you please. But if I

1. "Good heavens, yes."
2. Usherette.
3. A rash, intemperate person.

go to America, I must not let this gentleman suppose that it is to run away from him."

And they separated. At the end of the act Newman observed that Valentin was still in the *baignoire*. He strolled into the corridor again, expecting to meet him, and when he was within a few yards of Mademoiselle Nioche's box, saw his friend pass out, accompanied by the young man who had been seated beside its fair occupant. The two gentlemen walked with some quickness of step to a distant part of the lobby, where Newman perceived them stop and stand talking. The manner of each was perfectly quiet, but the stranger, who looked flushed, had begun to wipe his face very emphatically with his pocket-handkerchief. By this time Newman was abreast of the *baignoire*; the door had been left ajar, and he could see a pink dress inside. He immediately went in. Mademoiselle Nioche turned and greeted him with a brilliant smile.

"Ah, you have at last decided to come and see me?" she exclaimed. "You just save your politeness. You find me in a fine moment. Sit down." There was a very becoming little flush in her cheek, and her eye had a noticeable spark. You would have said that she had received some very good news.

"Something has happened here!" said Newman, without sitting down.

"You find me in a very fine moment," she repeated. "Two gentlemen—one of them is M. de Bellegarde, the pleasure of whose acquaintance I owe to you—have just had words about your humble servant. Very big words too. They can't come off without crossing swords. A duel—that will give me a push!" cried Mademoiselle Noémie, clapping her little hands. "*C'est ça qui pose une femme!*"[4]

"You don't mean to say that Bellegarde is going to fight about *you*!" exclaimed Newman disgustedly.

"Nothing less!" and she looked at him with a hard little smile. "No, no, you are not *galant*![5] And if you prevent this affair I shall owe you a grudge—and pay my debt!"

Newman uttered an imprecation which, though brief—it consisted simply of the interjection "Oh!" followed by a geographical, or more correctly, perhaps, a theological noun in four letters—had better not be transferred to these pages. He turned his back without more ceremony upon the pink dress and went out of the box. In the corridor he found Valentin and his companion walking towards him. The latter was thrusting a card into his waistcoat-pocket. Mademoiselle Noémie's jealous votary was a tall robust young man with a thick nose, a prominent blue eye, a Germanic physiognomy, and a massive watch-chain. When they reached the box, Valentin

4. "That really sets a woman up!"

5. Chivalrous.

with an emphasised bow made way for him to pass in first. Newman touched Valentin's arm as a sign that he wished to speak with him, and Bellegarde answered that he would be with him in an instant. Valentin entered the box after the robust young man, but a couple of minutes afterwards he reappeared, largely smiling.

"She is immensely tickled," he said. "She says we will make her fortune. I don't want to be fatuous, but I think it is very possible."

"So you are going to fight?" said Newman.

"My dear fellow, don't look so mortally disgusted. It was not my own choice. The thing is all arranged."

"I told you so!" groaned Newman.

"I told *him* so," said Valentin, smiling.

"What did he do to you?"

"My good friend, it doesn't matter what. He used an expression —I took it up."

"But I insist upon knowing; I can't, as your elder brother, have you rushing into this sort of nonsense."

"I am very much obliged to you," said Valentin. "I have nothing to conceal, but I can't go into particulars now and here."

"We will leave this place, then. You can tell me outside."

"Oh no, I can't leave this place; why should I hurry away? I will go to my orchestra-stall and sit out the opera."

"You will not enjoy it; you will be preoccupied."

Valentin looked at him a moment, coloured a little, smiled, and patted him on the arm. "You are delightfully simple! Before an affair a man is quiet. The quietest thing I can do is to go straight to my place."

"Ah," said Newman, "you want her to see you there—you and your quietness. I am not so simple! It is a poor business."

Valentin remained, and the two men, in their respective places, sat out the rest of the performance, which was also enjoyed by Mademoiselle Nioche and her truculent admirer. At the end Newman joined Valentin again, and they went into the street together. Valentin shook his head at his friend's proposal that he should get into Newman's own vehicle, and stopped on the edge of the pavement. "I must go off alone," he said; "I must look up a couple of friends who will take charge of this matter."

"I will take charge of it," Newman declared. "Put it into my hands."

"You are very kind, but that is hardly possible. In the first place, you are, as you said just now, almost my brother; you are about to marry my sister. That alone disqualifies you; it casts doubts on your impartiality. And if it didn't, it would be enough for me that I strongly suspect you of disapproving of the affair. You would try to prevent a meeting."

"Of course I should," said Newman. "Whoever your friends are, I hope they will do that."

"Unquestionably they will. They will urge that excuses be made, proper excuses. But you would be too good-natured. You won't do."

Newman was silent a moment. He was keenly annoyed, but he saw it was useless to attempt interference. "When is this precious performance to come off?" he asked.

"The sooner the better," said Valentin. "The day after to-morrow, I hope."

"Well," said Newman, "I have certainly a claim to know the facts. I can't consent to shut my eyes to the matter."

"I shall be most happy to tell you the facts," said Valentin. "They are very simple, and it will be quickly done. But now everything depends on my putting my hands on my friends without delay. I will jump into a cab; you had better drive to my room and wait for me there. I will turn up at the end of an hour."

Newman assented protestingly, let his friend go, and then betook himself to the picturesque little apartment in the Rue d'Anjou. It was more than an hour before Valentin returned, but when he did so he was able to announce that he had found one of his desired friends, and that this gentleman had taken upon himself the care of securing an associate. Newman had been sitting without lights by Valentin's faded fire, upon which he had thrown a log; the blaze played over the richly-encumbered little sitting-room and produced fantastic gleams and shadows. He listened in silence to Valentin's account of what had passed between him and the gentleman whose card he had in his pocket—M. Stanislas Kapp, of Strasbourg[6]—after his return to Mademoiselle Nioche's box. This hospitable young lady had espied an acquaintance on the other side of the house, and had expressed her displeasure at his not having the civility to come and pay her a visit. "Oh, let him alone!" M. Stanislas Kapp had hereupon exclaimed. "There are too many people in the box already." And he had fixed his eyes with a demonstrative stare upon M. de Bellegarde. Valentin had promptly retorted that if there were too many people in the box it was easy for M. Kapp to diminish the number. "I shall be most happy to open the door for *you*!" M. Kapp exclaimed. "I shall be delighted to fling you into the pit!" Valentin had answered. "Oh, do make a rumpus and get into the papers!" Miss Noémie had gleefully ejaculated. "M. Kapp, turn him out; or, M. de Bellegarde, pitch him into the pit, into the orchestra—anywhere! I don't care who does which, so long as you make a scene." Valentin answered that they would

6. The capital of Bas-Rhine (formerly Lower Alsace), in northeastern France.

make no scene, but that the gentleman would be so good as to step into the corridor with him. In the corridor, after a brief further exchange of words, there had been an exchange of cards. M. Stanislas Kapp was very stiff. He evidently meant to force his offence home.

"The man, no doubt, was insolent," Newman said; "but if you hadn't gone back into the box the thing wouldn't have happened."

"Why, don't you see," Valentin replied, "that the event proves the extreme propriety of my going back into the box? M. Kapp wished to provoke me; he was awaiting his chance. In such a case—that is, when he has been, so to speak, notified—a man must be on hand to receive the provocation. My not returning would simply have been tantamount to my saying to M. Stanislas Kapp: 'Oh, if you are going to be disagreeable'——"

" 'You must manage it by yourself; damned if I'll help you!' That would have been a thoroughly sensible thing to say. The only attraction for you seems to have been the prospect of M. Kapp's impertinence," Newman went on. "You told me you were not going back for that girl."

"Oh, don't mention that girl any more," murmured Valentin. "She's a bore."

"With all my heart. But if that is the way you feel about her, why couldn't you let her alone?"

Valentin shook his head with a fine smile. "I don't think you quite understand, and I don't believe I can make you. She understood the situation; she knew what was in the air; she was watching us."

"A cat may look at a king! What difference does that make?"

"Why, a man can't back down before a woman."

"I don't call her a woman. You said yourself she was a stone," cried Newman.

"Well," Valentin rejoined, "there is no disputing about tastes. It's a matter of feeling; it's measured by one's sense of honour."

"Oh, confound your sense of honour!" cried Newman.

"It is vain talking," said Valentin; "words have passed, and the thing is settled."

Newman turned away, taking his hat. Then pausing with his hand on the door, "What are you going to use?" he asked.

"That is for M. Stanislas Kapp, as the challenged party, to decide. My own choice would be a short, light sword. I handle it well. I'm an indifferent shot."

Newman had put on his hat; he pushed it back, gently scratching his forehead high up. "I wish it were pistols," he said. "I could show you how to lodge a bullet!"

Valentin broke into a laugh. "What is it some English poet says about consistency? It's a flower, or a star, or a jewel.[7] Yours has the beauty of all three!" But he agreed to see Newman again on the morrow, after the details of his meeting with M. Stanislas Kapp should have been arranged.

In the course of the day Newman received three lines from him, saying that it had been decided that he should cross the frontier, with his adversary, and that he was to take the night express to Geneva. He should have time, however, to dine with Newman. In the afternoon Newman called upon Madame de Cintré, but his visit was brief. She was as gracious and sympathetic as he had ever found her, but she was sad, and she confessed, on Newman's charging her with her red eyes, that she had been crying. Valentin had been with her a couple of hours before, and his visit had left her with a painful impression. He had laughed and gossiped, he had brought her no bad news, he had only been, in his manner, rather more affectionate than usual. His fraternal tenderness had touched her, and on his departure she had burst into tears. She had felt as if something strange and sad were going to happen; she had tried to reason away the fancy, and the effort had only given her a headache. Newman, of course, was perforce tongue-tied about Valentin's projected duel, and his dramatic talent was not equal to satirising Madame de Cintré's presentiment as pointedly as perfect security demanded. Before he went away he asked Madame de Cintré whether Valentin had seen his mother.

"Yes," she said, "but he didn't make her cry."

It was in Newman's own apartment that Valentin dined, having brought his portmanteau,[8] so that he might adjourn directly to the railway. M. Stanislas Kapp had positively declined to make excuses, and he, on his side, obviously, had none to offer. Valentin had found out with whom he was dealing. M. Stanislas Kapp was the son and heir of a rich brewer of Strasbourg, a youth of a sanguineous—and sanguinary—temperament. He was making ducks and drakes of the paternal brewery,[9] and although he passed in a general way for a good fellow, he had already been observed to be quarrelsome after dinner. "*Que voulez-vous?*"[1] said Valentin. "Brought up on beer, he can't stand champagne." He had chosen pistols. Valentin, at dinner, had an excellent appetite; he made a point, in view of his long journey, of eating more than usual. He took the liberty of suggesting to Newman a slight modification in the composition of a certain fish-sauce; he thought it would be worth mentioning to the cook. But Newman had no thoughts for

7. John Bartlett's *Familiar Quotations* lists the saying as of unknown, popular origin.
8. Traveling bag.
9. Playing idly with. To play ducks and drakes is to skip flat stones over water.
1. "What do you expect?"

fish-sauce; he felt thoroughly discontented. As he sat and watched his amiable and clever companion going through his excellent repast with the delicate deliberation of hereditary epicurism, the folly of so charming a fellow travelling off to expose his agreeable young life for the sake of M. Stanislas and Mademoiselle Noémie struck him with intolerable force. He had grown fond of Valentin, he felt now how fond; and his sense of helplessness only increased his irritation.

"Well, this sort of thing may be all very well," he cried at last, "but I declare I don't see it. I can't stop you, perhaps, but at least I can protest. I do protest, violently."

"My dear fellow, don't make a scene," said Valentin. "Scenes in these cases are in very bad taste."

"Your duel itself is a scene," said Newman; "that's all it is! It's a wretched theatrical affair. Why don't you take a band of music with you outright? It's d——d barbarous and it's d——d corrupt, both."

"Oh, I can't begin, at this time of day, to defend the theory of duelling," said Valentin. "It is our custom, and I think it is a good thing. Quite apart from the goodness of the cause in which a duel may be fought, it has a kind of picturesque charm which in this age of vile prose seems to me greatly to recommend it. It's a remnant of a higher-tempered time; one ought to cling to it. Depend upon it; a duel is never amiss."

"I don't know what you mean by a higher-tempered time," said Newman. "Because your great-grandfather was an ass, is that any reason why you should be? For my part, I think we had better let our temper take care of itself; it generally seems to me quite high enough; I am not afraid of being too meek. If your great-grandfather were to make himself unpleasant to me, I think I could manage him yet."

"My dear friend," said Valentin, smiling, "you can't invent anything that will take the place of satisfaction for an insult. To demand it and to give it are equally excellent arrangements."

"Do you call this sort of thing satisfaction?" Newman asked. "Does it satisfy you to receive a present of the carcass of that coarse fop? does it gratify you to make him a present of yours? If a man hits you, hit him back; if a man libels you, haul him up."

"Haul him up, into court? Oh, that is very nasty!" said Valentin.

"The nastiness is his—not yours. And for that matter, what you are doing is not particularly nice. You are too good for it. I don't say you are the most useful man in the world, or the cleverest, or the most amiable. But you are too good to go and get your throat cut for a prostitute."

Valentin flushed a little, but he laughed. "I shan't get my throat cut if I can help it. Moreover, one's honour hasn't two different measures. It only knows that it is hurt; it doesn't ask when, or how, or where."

"The more fool it is!" said Newman.

Valentin ceased to laugh; he looked grave. "I beg you not to say any more," he said. "If you do I shall almost fancy you don't care about—about"—and he paused.

"About what?"

"About that matter—about one's honour."

"Fancy what you please," said Newman. "Fancy while you are at it that I care about *you*—though you are not worth it. But come back without damage," he added in a moment, "and I will forgive you. And then," he continued, as Valentin was going: "I will ship you straight off to America."

"Well," answered Valentin, "if I am to turn over a new page, this may figure as a tail-piece to the old." And then he lit another cigar and departed.

"Blast that girl!" said Newman, as the door closed upon Valentin.

Chapter XVIII

Newman went the next morning to see Madame de Cintré, timing his visit so as to arrive after the noonday breakfast. In the court of the *hôtel*,[2] before the portico, stood Madame de Bellegarde's old square carriage. The servant who opened the door answered Newman's inquiry with a slightly embarrassed and hesitating murmur, and at the same moment Mrs. Bread appeared in the background, dim-visaged as usual, and wearing a large black bonnet and shawl.

"What is the matter?" asked Newman. "Is Madame la Comtesse at home, or not?"

Mrs. Bread advanced, fixing her eyes upon him; he observed that she held a sealed letter, very delicately, in her fingers. "The countess has left a message for you, sir; she has left this," said Mrs. Bread, holding out the letter, which Newman took.

"Left it? Is she out? Is she gone away?"

"She is going away, sir; she is leaving town," said Mrs. Bread.

"Leaving town!" exclaimed Newman. "What has happened?"

"It is not for me to say, sir," said Mrs. Bread, with her eyes on the ground. "But I thought it would come."

"What would come, pray?" Newman demanded. He had broken

2. Residence.

the seal of the letter, but he still questioned. "She is in the house? She is visible?"

"I don't think she expected you this morning," the old waiting-woman replied. "She was to leave immediately."

"Where is she going?"

"To Fleurières."

"To Fleurières? But surely I can see her?"

Mrs. Bread hesitated a moment, and then clasping together her two hands, "I will take you!" she said. And she led the way upstairs. At the top of the staircase she paused and fixed her dry, sad eyes upon Newman. "Be very easy with her," she said; "she is most unhappy!" Then she went on to Madame de Cintré's apartment; Newman, perplexed and alarmed, followed her rapidly. Mrs. Bread threw open the door, and Newman pushed back the curtain at the farther side of its deep embrasure. In the middle of the room stood Madame de Cintré; her face was pale and she was dressed for travelling. Behind her, before the fireplace, stood Urbain de Bellegarde, looking at his finger-nails; near the marquis sat his mother, buried in an armchair, and with her eyes immediately fixing themselves upon Newman. He felt, as soon as he entered the room, that he was in the presence of something evil; he was startled and pained, as he would have been by a threatening cry in the stillness of the night. He walked straight to Madame de Cintré and seized her by the hand.

"What is the matter?" he asked commandingly; "what is happening?"

Urbain de Bellegarde stared, then left his place and came and leaned upon his mother's chair, behind. Newman's sudden irruption had evidently discomposed both mother and son. Madame de Cintré stood silent, with her eyes resting upon Newman's. She had often looked at him with all her soul, as it seemed to him; but in this present gaze there was a sort of bottomless depth. She was in distress; it was the most touching thing he had ever seen. His heart rose into his throat, and he was on the point of turning to her companions with an angry challenge; but she checked him, pressing the hand that held her own.

"Something very grave has happened," she said. "I cannot marry you."

Newman dropped her hand and stood staring, first at her and then at the others. "Why not?" he asked, as quietly as possible.

Madame de Cintré almost smiled, but the attempt was strange. "You must ask my mother, you must ask my brother."

"Why can't she marry me?" said Newman, looking at them.

Madame de Bellegarde did not move in her place, but she was as pale as her daughter. The marquis looked down at her. She said nothing for some moments, but she kept her keen clear eyes upon Newman bravely. The marquis drew himself up and looked at the ceiling. "It's impossible!" he said softly.

"It's improper," said Madame de Bellegarde.

Newman began to laugh. "Oh, you are fooling!" he exclaimed.

"My sister, you have no time; you are losing your train," said the marquis.

"Come, is he mad?" asked Newman.

"No; don't think that," said Madame de Cintré. "But I am going away."

"Where are you going?"

"To the country, to Fleurières; to be alone."

"To leave me?" said Newman slowly.

"I can't see you, now," said Madame de Cintré.

"*Now*—why not?"

"I am ashamed," said Madame de Cintré simply.

Newman turned toward the marquis. "What have you done to her—what does it mean?" he asked with the same effort at calmness, the fruit of his constant practice in taking things easily. He was excited, but excitement with him was only an intenser deliberateness; it was the swimmer stripped.

"It means that I have given you up," said Madame de Cintré. "It means that."

Her face was too charged with tragic expression not fully to confirm her words. Newman was profoundly shocked, but he felt as yet no resentment against her. He was amazed, bewildered, and the presence of the old marquise and her son seemed to smite his eyes like the glare of a watchman's lantern. "Can't I see you alone?" he asked.

"It would be only more painful. I hoped I should not see you—I should escape. I wrote to you. Good-bye." And she put out her hand again.

Newman put both his own into his pockets. "I will go with you," he said.

She laid her two hands on his arm. "Will you grant me a last request?" and as she looked at him, urging this, her eyes filled with tears. "Let me go alone—let me go in peace. I can't call it peace—it's death. But let me bury myself. So—good-bye."

Newman passed his hand into his hair and stood slowly rubbing his head and looking through his keenly-narrowed eyes from one to the other of the three persons before him. His lips were compressed, and the two lines which had formed themselves beside his mouth might have made it appear at a first glance that he was smiling. I have said that his excitement was an intenser deliberateness, and now he looked grimly deliberate. "It seems very much as if you had interfered, marquis," he said slowly. "I thought you said you wouldn't interfere. I know you don't like me; but that doesn't make any difference. I thought you promised me you wouldn't interfere. I thought you swore on your honour that you wouldn't interfere. Don't you remember, marquis?"

The marquis lifted his eyebrows; but he was apparently determined to be even more urbane than usual. He rested his two hands upon the back of his mother's chair and bent forward, as if he were leaning over the edge of a pulpit or a lecture-desk. He did not smile, but he looked softly grave. "Excuse me, sir," he said, "I assured you that I would not influence my sister's decision. I adhered, to the letter, to my engagement. Did I not, sister?"

"Don't appeal, my son," said the marquise, "your word is sufficient."

"Yes—she accepted me," said Newman. "That is very true; I can't deny that. At least," he added, in a different tone, turning to Madame de Cintré, "you *did* accept me?"

Something in the tone seemed to move her strongly. She turned away, burying her face in her hands.

"But you have interfered now, haven't you?" inquired Newman of the marquis.

"Neither then nor now have I attempted to influence my sister. I used no persuasion then, I have used no persuasion to-day."

"And what have you used?"

"We have used authority," said Madame de Bellegarde in a rich, bell-like voice.

"Ah, you have used authority," Newman exclaimed. "They have used authority," he went on, turning to Madame de Cintré. "What is it? how did they use it?"

"My mother commanded," said Madame de Cintré.

"Commanded you to give me up—I see. And you obey—I see. But why do you obey?" asked Newman.

Madame de Cintré looked across at the old marquise; her eyes slowly measured her from head to foot. "I am afraid of my mother," she said.

Madame de Bellegarde rose with a certain quickness, crying: "This is a most indecent scene!"

"I have no wish to prolong it," said Madame de Cintré; and turning to the door she put out her hand again. "If you can pity me a little, let me go alone."

Newman shook her hand quietly and firmly. "I'll come down there," he said. The *portière*[3] dropped behind her, and Newman sank with a long breath into the nearest chair. He leaned back in it,

3. Curtain.

resting his hands on the knobs of the arms and looking at Madame de Bellegarde and Urbain. There was a long silence. They stood side by side, with their heads high and their handsome eyebrows arched.

"So you make a distinction?" Newman said at last. "You make a distinction between persuading and commanding? It's very neat. But the distinction is in favour of commanding. That rather spoils it."

"We have not the least objection to defining our position," said M. de Bellegarde. "We understand that it should not at first appear to you quite clear. We rather expect, indeed, that you should not do us justice."

"Oh, I'll do you justice," said Newman. "Don't be afraid. Please proceed."

The marquise laid her hand on her son's arm, as if to deprecate the attempt to define their position. "It is quite useless," she said, "to try and arrange this matter so as to make it agreeable to you. It can never be agreeable to you. It is a disappointment, and disappointments are unpleasant. I thought it over carefully and tried to arrange it better; but I only gave myself a headache and lost my sleep. Say what we will, you will think yourself ill-treated, and you will publish your wrongs among your friends. But we are not afraid of that. Besides, your friends are not our friends, and it will not matter. Think of us as you please. I only beg you not to be violent. I have never in my life been present at a violent scene of any kind, and at my age I can't be expected to begin."

"Is *that* all you have got to say?" asked Newman, slowly rising out of his chair. "That's a poor show for a clever lady like you, marquise. Come, try again."

"My mother goes to the point, with her usual honesty and intrepidity," said the marquis, toying with his watch-guard. "But it is perhaps well to say a little more. We of course quite repudiate the charge of having broken faith with you. We left you entirely at liberty to make yourself agreeable to my sister. We left her quite at liberty to entertain your proposal. When she accepted you we said nothing. We therefore quite observed our promise. It was only at a later stage of the affair, and on quite a different basis, as it were, that we determined to speak. It would have been better, perhaps, if we had spoken before. But really, you see, nothing has yet been done."

"Nothing has yet been done?" Newman repeated the words, unconscious of their comical effect. He had lost the sense of what the marquis was saying; M. de Bellegarde's superior style was a mere humming in his ears. All that he understood, in his deep and simple indignation, was that the matter was not a violent joke, and that the people before him were perfectly serious. "Do you suppose I can take this?" he asked. "Do you suppose it can matter to me what you say? Do you suppose I can seriously listen to you? You are simply crazy!"

Madame de Bellegarde gave a rap with her fan in the palm of her hand. "If you don't take it you can leave it, sir. It matters very little what you do. My daughter has given you up."

"She doesn't mean it," Newman declared after a moment.

"I think I can assure you that she does," said the marquis.

"Poor woman, what damnable thing have you done to her?" cried Newman.

"Gently, gently!" murmured M. de Bellegarde.

"She told you," said the old lady. "I commanded her."

Newman shook his head heavily. "This sort of thing can't be, you know," he said. "A man can't be used in this fashion. You have got no right; you have got no power."

"My power," said Madame de Bellegarde, "is in my children's obedience."

"In their fear, your daughter said. There is something very strange in it. Why should your daughter be afraid of you?" added Newman, after looking a moment at the old lady. "There is some foul play."

The marquise met his gaze without flinching, and as if she did not hear or heed what he said. "I did my best," she said quietly. "I could endure it no longer."

"It was a bold experiment!" said the marquis.

Newman felt disposed to walk to him, clutch his neck with his fingers and press his windpipe with his thumb. "I needn't tell you how you strike me," he said, "of course you know that. But I should think you would be afraid of your friends—all those people you introduced me to the other night. There were some very nice people among them; you may depend upon it there were some honest men and women."

"Our friends approve us," said M. de Bellegarde; "there is not a family among them that would have acted otherwise. And however that may be, we take the cue from no one. The Bellegardes have been used to set the example, not to wait for it."

"You would have waited long before anyone would have set you such an example as this," exclaimed Newman. "Have I done anything wrong?" he demanded. "Have I given you reason to change your opinion? Have you found out anything against me? I can't imagine."

"Our opinion," said Madame de Bellegarde, "is quite the same as at first—exactly. We have no ill-will towards yourself; we are very far from accusing you of misconduct. Since your relations with us began you have been, I frankly confess, less—less peculiar than I expected. It is not your disposition that we object to, it is your antecedents. We really cannot reconcile ourselves to a commercial person. We fancied in an evil hour that we could; it was a great misfortune. We determined to persevere to the end, and to give you every advantage. I was resolved that you should have no reason to accuse me of a want of loyalty. We let the thing certainly go very far—we introduced you to our friends. To tell the truth, it was that, I think, that broke me down. I succumbed to the scene that took place on Thursday night in these rooms. You must excuse me if what I say is disagreeable to you, but we cannot release ourselves without an explanation."

"There can be no better proof of our good faith," said the marquis, "than our committing ourselves to you in the eyes of the world the other evening. We endeavoured to bind ourselves—to tie our hands, as it were."

"But it was that," added his mother, "that opened our eyes and broke our bonds. We should have been most uncomfortable! You know," she added in a moment, "that you were forewarned. I told you we were very proud."

Newman took up his hat and began mechanically to smooth it; the very fierceness of his scorn kept him from speaking. "You are not proud enough," he observed at last.

"In all this matter," said the marquis, smiling, "I really see nothing but our humility."

"Let us have no more discussion than is necessary," resumed Madame de Bellegarde. "My daughter told you everything when she said she gave you up."

"I am not satisfied about your daughter," said Newman; "I want to know what you did to her. It is all very easy talking about authority and saying you commanded her. She didn't accept me blindly, and she wouldn't have given me up blindly. Not that I believe yet she has really given me up; she will talk it over with me. But you have frightened her, you have bullied her, you have *hurt* her. What was it you did to her?"

"I did very little!" said Madame de Bellegarde, in a tone which gave Newman a chill when he afterwards remembered it.

"Let me remind you that we offered you these explanations," the marquis observed, "with the express understanding that you should abstain from violence of language."

"I am not violent," Newman answered, "it is you who are violent! But I don't know that I have much more to say to you. What you expect of me, apparently, is to go my way, thanking you for favours received, and promising never to trouble you again."

"We expect of you to act like a clever man," said Madame de

Bellegarde. "You have shown yourself that already, and what we have done is altogether based upon your being so. When one must submit, one must. Since my daughter absolutely withdraws, what will be the use of your making a noise?"

"It remains to be seen whether your daughter absolutely withdraws. Your daughter and I are still very good friends; nothing is changed in that. As I say, I will talk it over with her."

"That will be of no use," said the old lady. "I know my daughter well enough to know that words spoken as she just now spoke to you are final. Besides, she has promised me."

"I have no doubt her promise is worth a good deal more than your own," said Newman; "nevertheless I don't give her up."

"Just as you please! But if she won't even see you—and she won't—your constancy must remain purely Platonic."

Poor Newman was feigning a greater confidence than he felt. Madame de Cintré's strange intensity had in fact struck a chill to his heart; her face, still impressed upon his vision, had been a terribly vivid image of renunciation. He felt sick, and suddenly helpless. He turned away and stood for a moment with his hand on the door; then he faced about, and after the briefest hesitation broke out with a different accent. "Come, think of what this must be to me, and let her alone! Why should you object to me so—what's the matter with me? I can't hurt you, I wouldn't if I could. I'm the most unobjectionable fellow in the world. What if I am a commercial person? What under the sun do you mean? A commercial person? I will be any sort of person you want. I never talk to you about business. Let her go, and I will ask no questions. I will take her away, and you shall never see me or hear of me again. I will stay in America if you like. I'll sign a paper promising never to come back to Europe! All I want is not to lose her!"

Madame de Bellegarde and her son exchanged a glance of lucid irony, and Urbain said: "My dear sir, what you propose is hardly an improvement. We have not the slightest objection to seeing you, as an amiable foreigner, and we have every reason for not wishing to be eternally separated from my sister. We object to the marriage; and in that way," and M. de Bellegarde gave a small, thin laugh, "she would be more married than ever."

"Well, then," said Newman, "where is this place of yours—Fleurières? I know it is near some old city on a hill."

"Precisely. Poitiers is on a hill," said Madame de Bellegarde. "I don't know how old it is. We are not afraid to tell you."

"It is Poitiers, is it? Very good," said Newman. "I shall immediately follow Madame de Cintré."

"The trains after this hour won't serve you," said Urbain.

"I shall hire a special train!"

"That will be a very silly waste of money," said Madame de Bellegarde.

"It will be time enough to talk about waste three days hence," Newman answered; and clapping his hat on his head, he departed.

He did not immediately start for Fleurières; he was too stunned and wounded for consecutive action. He simply walked; he walked straight before him, following the river, till he got out of the *enceinte*[4] of Paris. He had a burning, tingling sense of personal outrage. He had never in his life received so absolute a check; he had never been pulled up, or, as he would have said, "let down," so short; and he found the sensation intolerable; he strode along, tapping the trees and lamp-posts fiercely with his stick and inwardly raging. To lose Madame de Cintré after he had taken such jubilant and triumphant possession of her was as great an affront to his pride as it was an injury to his happiness. And to lose her by the interference and the dictation of others, by an impudent old woman and a pretentious fop stepping in with their "authority!" It was too preposterous, it was too pitiful. Upon what he deemed the unblushing treachery of the Bellegardes, Newman wasted little thought; he consigned it, once for all, to eternal perdition. But the treachery of Madame de Cintré herself amazed and confounded him; there was a key to the mystery, of course, but he groped for it in vain. Only three days had elapsed since she stood beside him in the starlight, beautiful and tranquil as the trust with which he had inspired her, and told him that she was happy in the prospect of their marriage. What was the meaning of the change? of what infernal potion had she tasted? Poor Newman had a terrible apprehension that she had really changed. His very admiration for her attached the idea of force and weight to her rupture. But he did not rail at her as false, for he was sure she was unhappy. In his walk he had crossed one of the bridges of the Seine, and he still followed, unheedingly, the long, unbroken quay. He had left Paris behind him, and he was almost in the country; he was in the pleasant suburb of Auteuil. He stopped at last, looked around him without seeing or caring for its pleasantness, and then slowly turned and at a slower pace retraced his steps. When he came abreast of the fantastic embankment known as the Trocadero, he reflected, through his throbbing pain, that he was near Mrs. Tristram's dwelling, and that Mrs. Tristram, on particular occasions, had much of a woman's kindness in her utterance. He felt that he needed to pour out his ire, and took the road to her house. Mrs. Tristram was at home and alone, and as soon as she had looked at him, on his entering the room, she told

4. City limits.

him that she knew what he had come for. Newman sat down heavily, in silence, looking at her.

"They have backed out!" she said. "Well, you may think it strange, but I felt something the other night in the air." Presently he told her his story; she listened, with her eyes fixed on him. When he had finished she said quietly: "They want her to marry Lord Deepmere." Newman stared. He did not know that she knew any thing about Lord Deepmere. "But I don't think she will," Mrs. Tristram added.

"*She* marry that poor little cub!" cried Newman. "Oh, Lord! And yet, why did she refuse me?"

"But that isn't the only thing," said Mrs. Tristram. "They really couldn't endure you any longer. They had overrated their courage. I must say, to give the devil his due, that there is something rather fine in that. It was your commercial quality in the abstract they couldn't swallow. That is really aristocratic. They wanted your money, but they have given you up for an idea."

Newman frowned most ruefully, and took up his hat again. "I thought you would encourage me!" he said, with almost childlike sadness.

"Excuse me," she answered very gently. "I feel none the less sorry for you, especially as I am at the bottom of your troubles. I have not forgotten that I suggested the marriage to you. I don't believe that Madame de Cintré has any intention of marrying Lord Deepmere. It is true he is not younger than she, as he looks. He is thirty-three years old; I looked in the Peerage.[5] But no—I can't believe her so horribly, cruelly false."

"Please say nothing against her," said Newman.

"Poor woman, she *is* cruel. But of course you will go after her and you will plead powerfully. Do you know that as you are now," Mrs. Tristram pursued with characteristic audacity of comment, "you are extremely eloquent, even without speaking? To resist you a woman must have a very fixed idea in her head. I wish I had done you a wrong, that you might come to me in that fine fashion! But go to Madame de Cintré at any rate, and tell her that she is a puzzle even to me. I am very curious to see how far family discipline will go."

Newman sat awhile longer, leaning his elbows on his knees and his head in his hands, and Mrs. Tristram continued to temper charity with philosophy, and compassion with criticism. At last she inquired: "And what does the Count Valentin say to it?" Newman

5. John Burke's *A Genealogical and Heraldic Dictionary of the Peerage and Baronetage of the United Kingdom.* Known as *Burke's Peerage,* this work contains a genealogical record of aristocratic families.

started; he had not thought of Valentin and his errand on the Swiss frontier since the morning. The reflection made him restless again, and he took his leave. He went straight to his apartment, where, upon the table of the vestibule, he found a telegram. It ran (with the date and place) as follows: "I am seriously ill; please to come to me as soon as possible. V. B." Newman groaned at this miserable news, and at the necessity of deferring his journey to the Château de Fleurières. But he wrote to Madame de Cintré these few lines; they were all he had time for:

> "I don't give you up, and I don't really believe you give me me up. I don't understand it, but we shall clear it up together. I can't follow you to-day, as I am called to see a friend at a distance who is very ill, perhaps dying. But I shall come to you as soon as I can leave my friend. Why shouldn't I say that he is your brother?—C. N."

After this he had only time to catch the night express to Geneva.

Chapter XIX

Newman possessed a remarkable talent for sitting still when it was necessary, and he had an opportunity to use it on his journey to Switzerland. The successive hours of the night brought him no sleep; but he sat motionless in his corner of the railway-carriage, with his eyes closed, and the most observant of his fellow-travellers might have envied him his apparent slumber. Toward morning slumber really came, as an effect of mental rather than of physical fatigue. He slept for a couple of hours, and at last, waking, found his eyes resting upon one of the snow-powdered peaks of the Jura,[6] behind which the sky was just reddening with the dawn. But he saw neither the cold mountain nor the warm sky; his consciousness began to throb again, on the very instant, with a sense of his wrong. He got out of the train half an hour before it reached Geneva, in the cold morning twilight, at the station indicated in Valentin's telegram. A drowsy station-master was on the platform with a lantern, and the hood of his overcoat over his head, and near him stood a gentleman who advanced to meet Newman. This personage was a man of forty, with a tall lean figure, a sallow face, a dark eye, a neat moustache, and a pair of fresh gloves. He took off his hat, looking very grave, and pronounced Newman's name. Our hero assented and said: "You are M. de Bellegarde's friend?"

"I unite with you in claiming that sad honour," said the gentleman. "I had placed myself at M. de Bellegarde's service in this

6. A range of mountains at the border of Switzerland and France.

melancholy affair, together with M. de Grosjoyaux, who is now at his bedside. M. de Grosjoyaux, I believe, has had the honour of meeting you in Paris, but as he is a better nurse than I he remained with our poor friend. Bellegarde has been eagerly expecting you."

"And how is Bellegarde?" said Newman. "He was badly hit?"

"The doctor has condemned him; we brought a surgeon with us. But he will die in the best sentiments. I sent last evening for the curé[7] of the nearest French village, who spent an hour with him. The curé was quite satisfied."

"Heaven forgive us!" groaned Newman. "I would rather the doctor were satisfied! And can he see me—shall he know me?"

"When I left him, half an hour ago, he had fallen asleep, after a feverish, wakeful night. But we shall see." And Newman's companion proceeded to lead the way out of the station to the village, explaining as he went that the little party was lodged in the humblest of Swiss inns, where, however, they had succeeded in making M. de Bellegarde much more comfortable than could at first have been expected. "We are old companions-in-arms," said Valentin's second; "it is not the first time that one of us has helped the other to lie easily. It is a very nasty wound, and the nastiest thing about it is that Bellegarde's adversary was no shot. He put his bullet where he could. It took it into its head to walk straight into Bellegarde's left side, just below the heart."

As they picked their way in the gray, deceptive dawn, between the manure-heaps of the village street, Newman's new acquaintance narrated the particulars of the duel. The conditions of the meeting had been that if the first exchange of shots should fail to satisfy one of the two gentlemen, a second should take place. Valentin's first bullet had done exactly what Newman's companion was convinced he had intended it to do; it had grazed the arm of M. Stanislas Kapp, just scratching the flesh. M. Kapp's own projectile, meanwhile, had passed at ten good inches from the person of Valentin. The representatives of M. Stanislas had demanded another shot, which was granted. Valentin had then fired aside and the young Alsatian had done effective execution. "I saw, when we met him on the ground," said Newman's informant, "that he was not going to be *commode*.[8] It is a kind of bovine temperament." Valentin had immediately been installed at the inn, and M. Stanislas and his friends had withdrawn to regions unknown. The police authorities of the canton had waited upon the party at the inn, had been extremely majestic, and had drawn up a long *procès-verbal*;[9] but it was probable that they would wink at so very gentlemanly a bit of bloodshed. Newman asked whether a message had not been sent to

7. The parish priest.
8. Easy to deal with.
9. Oral deposition.

Valentin's family, and learned that up to a late hour on the preceding evening Valentin had opposed it. He had refused to believe his wound was dangerous. But after his interview with the curé he had consented, and a telegram had been despatched to his mother. "But the marquise had better hurry," said Newman's conductor.

"Well, it's an abominable affair!" said Newman. "That's all I have got to say!" To say this, at least, in a tone of infinite disgust, was an irresistible need.

"Ah, you don't approve?" questioned his conductor, with curious urbanity.

"Approve?" cried Newman. "I wish that when I had him there, night before last, I had locked him up in my *cabinet de toilette!*"[1]

Valentin's late second opened his eyes, and shook his head up and down two or three times, gravely, with a little flute-like whistle. But they had reached the inn, and a stout maid-servant in a night-cap was at the door with a lantern, to take Newman's travelling-bag from the porter who trudged behind him. Valentin was lodged on the ground-floor at the back of the house, and Newman's companion went along a stone-faced passage and softly opened a door. Then he beckoned to Newman, who advanced and looked into the room, which was lighted by a single shaded candle. Beside the fire sat M. de Grosjoyaux asleep in his dressing-gown—a little plump fair man whom Newman had seen several times in Valentin's company. On the bed lay Valentin, pale and still, with his eyes closed—a figure very shocking to Newman, who had seen it hitherto awake to its finger-tips. M. de Grosjoyaux's colleague pointed to an open door beyond, and whispered that the doctor was within, keeping guard. So long as Valentin slept, or seemed to sleep, of course Newman could not approach him; so our hero withdrew for the present, committing himself to the care of the half-waked *bonne.*[2] She took him to a room above-stairs, and introduced him to a bed on which a magnified bolster, in yellow calico, figured as a counterpane. Newman lay down, and, in spite of his counterpane, slept for three or four hours. When he awoke, the morning was advanced and the sun was filling his window, and he heard, outside of it, the clucking of hens.

While he was dressing there came to his door a messenger from M. de Grosjoyaux and his companion, proposing that he should breakfast with them. Presently he went down-stairs to the little stone-paved dining-room, where the maid-servant, who had taken off her night-cap, was serving the repast. M. de Grosjoyaux was there, surprisingly fresh for a gentleman who had been playing sick-nurse half the night, rubbing his hands and watching the

1. Dressing room.

2. Maidservant.

breakfast-table attentively. Newman renewed acquaintance with him, and learned that Valentin was still sleeping; the surgeon, who had had a fairly tranquil night, was at present sitting with him. Before M. de Grosjoyaux's associate reappeared, Newman learned that his name was M. Ledoux, and that Bellegarde's acquaintance with him dated from the days when they served together in the Pontifical Zouaves.[3] M. Ledoux was the nephew of a distinguished Ultramontane bishop. At last the bishop's nephew came in with a toilet in which an ingenious attempt at harmony with the peculiar situation was visible, and with a gravity tempered by a decent deference to the best breakfast that the Croix Helvétique had ever set forth. Valentin's servant, who was allowed only in scanty measure the honour of watching with his master, had been lending a light Parisian hand in the kitchen. The two Frenchmen did their best to prove that if circumstances might overshadow, they could not really obscure the national talent for conversation, and M. Ledoux delivered a neat little eulogy on poor Bellegarde, whom he pronounced the most charming Englishman he had ever known.

"Do you call him an Englishman?" Newman asked.

M. Ledoux smiled a moment and then made an epigram. "*C'est plus qu'un Anglais—c'est un Anglomane!*"[4] Newman said soberly that he had never noticed it; and M. de Grosjoyaux remarked that it was really too soon to deliver a funeral oration upon poor Bellegarde. "Evidently," said M. Ledoux. "But I couldn't help observing this morning to Mr. Newman that when a man has taken such excellent measures for his salvation as our dear friend did last evening, it seems almost a pity he should put it in peril again by returning to the world." M. Ledoux was a great Catholic, and Newman thought him a queer mixture. His countenance, by daylight, had a sort of amiably saturnine cast; he had a very large thin nose, and looked like a Spanish picture. He appeared to think duelling a very perfect arrangement, provided, if one should get hit, one could promptly see the priest. He seemed to take a great satisfaction in Valentin's interview with the curé, and yet his conversation did not at all indicate a sanctimonious habit of mind. M. Ledoux had evidently a high sense of the becoming, and was prepared to be urbane and tasteful on all points. He was always furnished with a smile (which pushed his moustache up under his nose) and an explanation. *Savoir-vivre*—knowing how to live—was his specialty, in which he included knowing how to die; but, as Newman reflected, with a good deal of dumb irritation, he seemed disposed to delegate to others the application of his learning on this latter point. M. de Grosjoyaux was of quite another complexion,

3. A military unit, noted for its colorful costumes, in the service of the pope.

4. "He's more than an Englishman; he's an Anglomaniac."

and appeared to regard his friend's theological unction as the sign of an inaccessibly superior mind. He was evidently doing his utmost, with a kind of jovial tenderness, to make life agreeable to Valentin to the last, and help him as little as possible to miss the Boulevard des Italiens; but what chiefly occupied his mind was the mystery of a bungling brewer's son making so neat a shot. He himself could snuff a candle, &c., and yet he confessed that he could not have done better than this. He hastened to add that on the present occasion he would have made a point of not doing so well. It was not an occasion for that sort of murderous work, *que diable*![5] He would have picked out some quiet fleshy spot and just tapped it with a harmless ball. M. Stanislas Kapp had been deplorably heavy-handed; but really, when the world had come to that pass that one granted a meeting to a brewer's son! . . . . This was M. de Grosjoyaux's nearest approach to a generalisation. He kept looking through the window, over the shoulder of M. Ledoux, at a slender tree which stood at the end of a lane, opposite to the inn, and seemed to be measuring its distance from his extended arm and secretly wishing that, since the subject had been introduced, propriety did not forbid a little speculative pistol-practice.

Newman was in no humour to enjoy good company. He could neither eat nor talk; his soul was sore with grief and anger, and the weight of his double sorrow was intolerable. He sat with his eyes fixed upon his plate, counting the minutes, wishing at one moment that Valentin would see him and leave him free to go in quest of Madame de Cintré and his lost happiness, and mentally calling himself a vile brute the next, for the impatient egotism of the wish. He was very poor company, himself, and even his acute preoccupation and his general lack of the habit of pondering the impression he produced did not prevent him from reflecting, that his companions must be puzzled to see how poor Bellegarde came to take such a fancy to this taciturn Yankee that he must needs have him at his death-bed. After breakfast he strolled forth alone into the village and looked at the fountain, the geese, the open barn doors, the brown, bent old women, showing their hugely darned stocking-heels at the ends of their slowly-clicking sabots, and the beautiful view of snowy Alp and purple Jura at either end of the little street. The day was brilliant; early spring was in the air and sunshine, and the winter's damp was trickling out of the cottage eaves. It was birth and brightness for all nature, even for chirping chickens and waddling goslings, and it was to be death and burial for poor, foolish, generous, delightful Bellegarde. Newman walked as far as the village church, and went into the small graveyard beside it,

5. "Damn it!"

where he sat down and looked at the awkward tablets which were planted around. They were all sordid and hideous, and Newman could feel nothing but the hardness and coldness of death. He got up and came back to the inn, where he found M. Ledoux having coffee and a cigarette at a little green table which he had caused to be carried into the small garden. Newman, learning that the doctor was still sitting with Valentin, asked M. Ledoux if he might not be allowed to relieve him; he had a great desire to be useful to his poor friend. This was easily arranged; the doctor was very glad to go to bed. He was a youthful and rather jaunty practitioner, but he had a clever face, and the ribbon of the Legion of Honour[6] in his button-hole; Newman listened attentively to the instructions he gave him before retiring, and took mechanically from his hand a small volume which the surgeon recommended as a help to wakefulness, and which turned out to be an old copy of "Les Liaisons Dangereuses."[7]

Valentin was still lying with his eyes closed, and there was no visible change in his condition. Newman sat down near him, and for a long time narrowly watched him. Then his eyes wandered away with his thoughts upon his own situation, and rested upon the chain of the Alps, disclosed by the drawing of the scant white cotton curtain of the window, through which the sunshine passed and lay in squares upon the red-tiled floor. He tried to interweave his reflections with hope, but he only half succeeded. What had happened to him seemed to have, in its violence and audacity, the force of a real calamity—the strength and insolence of Destiny herself. It was unnatural and monstrous, and he had no arms against it. At last a sound struck upon the stillness, and he heard Valentin's voice.

"It can't be about *me* you are pulling that long face!" He found, when he turned, that Valentin was lying in the same position; but his eyes were open, and he was even trying to smile. It was with a very slender strength that he returned the pressure of Newman's hand. "I have been watching you for a quarter of an hour," Valentin went on; "you have been looking as black as thunder. You are greatly disgusted with me, I see. Well, of course! So am I!"

"Oh, I shall not scold you," said Newman. "I feel too badly. And how are you getting on?"

"Oh, I'm getting off! They have quite settled that; haven't they?"

"That's for you to settle; you can get well if you try," said Newman with resolute cheerfulness.

6. An award given for service to the nation.

7. Choderlos de Laclos, *Les Liaisons Dangereuses* (1782). As noted below, in the Boston 1877 edition James used the title *Faublas*, a shortened form of *Les Amours du Chevalier de Faublas*, by Jean Baptiste Louvet de Couvray (Paris, 1821). In revising the text for the London edition of 1879, by Macmillan, he substituted *Les Liaisons Dangereuses* for *Faublas*.

"My dear fellow, how can I try? Trying is violent exercise, and that sort of thing isn't in order for a man with a hole in his side as big as your hat, that begins to bleed if he moves a hair's-breadth. I knew you would come," he continued; "I knew I should wake up and find you here; so I'm not surprised. But last night I was very impatient. I didn't see how I could keep still until you came. It was a matter of keeping still, just like this; as still as a mummy in his case. You talk about trying; I tried that! Well, here I am yet—these twenty hours. It seems like twenty days." Bellegarde talked slowly and feebly, but distinctly enough. It was visible, however, that he was in extreme pain, and at last he closed his eyes. Newman begged him to remain silent and spare himself; the doctor had left urgent orders. "Oh," said Valentin, "let us eat and drink, for to-morrow—to-morrow"[8]—and he paused again. "No, not to-morrow, perhaps, but to-day. I can't eat and drink, but I can talk. What's to be gained, at this pass, by renun—renunciation? I mustn't use such big words. I was always a chatterer; Lord, how I have talked in my day!"

"That's a reason for keeping quiet now," said Newman. "We know how well you talk, you know."

But Valentin, without heeding him, went on in the same weak dying drawl. "I wanted to see you because you have seen my sister. Does she know—will she come?"

Newman was embarrassed. "Yes, by this time she must know."

"Didn't you tell her?" Valentin asked. And then, in a moment: "Didn't you bring me any message from her?" His eyes rested upon Newman's with a certain soft keenness.

"I didn't see her after I got your telegram," said Newman. "I wrote to her."

"And she sent you no answer?"

Newman was obliged to reply that Madame de Cintré had left Paris. "She went yesterday to Fleurières."

"Yesterday—to Fleurières? Why did she go to Fleurières? What day is this? What day was yesterday? Ah, then I shan't see her," said Valentin sadly. "Fleurières is too far!" And then he closed his eyes again. Newman sat silent, summoning pious invention to his aid, but he was relieved at finding that Valentin was apparently too weak to reason or to be curious. Bellegarde, however, presently went on. "And my mother—and my brother—will they come? Are they at Fleurières?"

"They were in Paris, but I didn't see them, either," Newman

8. A familiar hedonistic, or epicurean, proverb; it ends ". . . for tomorrow we die."

answered. "If they received your telegram in time, they will have started this morning. Otherwise they will be obliged to wait for the night-express, and they will arrive at the same hour as I did."

"They won't thank me—they won't thank me," Valentin murmured. "They will pass an atrocious night, and Urbain doesn't like the early morning air. I don't remember ever in my life to have seen him before noon—before breakfast. No one ever saw him. We don't know how he is then. Perhaps he's different. Who knows? Posterity, perhaps, will know. That's the time he works, in his *cabinet*,[9] at the history of the Princesses. But I had to send for them—hadn't I? And then I want to see my mother sit there where you sit, and say good-bye to her. Perhaps, after all, I don't know her, and she will have some surprise for me. Don't think you know her yet, yourself; perhaps, she may surprise *you*. But if I can't see Claire, I don't care for anything. I have been thinking of it—and in my dreams, too. Why did she go to Fleurières to-day? She never told me. What has happened? Ah, she ought to have guessed I was here—this way. It is the first time in her life she ever disappointed me. Poor Claire!"

"You know we are not man and wife quite yet—your sister and I," said Newman. "She doesn't yet account to me for all her actions." And, after a fashion, he smiled.

Valentin looked at him a moment. "Have you quarrelled?"

"Never, never, never!" Newman exclaimed.

"How happily you say that!" said Valentin. "You are going to be happy—*va*!"[1] In answer to this stroke of irony, none the less powerful for being so unconscious, all poor Newman could do was to give a helpless and transparent stare. Valentin continued to fix him with his own rather over-bright gaze, and presently he said: "But something *is* the matter with you. I watched you just now; you haven't a bridegroom's face."

"My dear fellow," said Newman, "how can I show *you* a bridegroom's face? If you think I enjoy seeing you lie there and not being able to help you——"

"Why, you are just the man to be cheerful; don't forfeit your rights! I'm a proof of your wisdom. When was a man ever gloomy when he could say: 'I told you so?' You told me so, you know. You did what you could about it. You said some very good things; I have thought them over. But, my dear friend, I was right, all the same. This is the regular way."

"I didn't do what I ought," said Newman. "I ought to have done something else."

9. Study.

1. "Good!"

"For instance?"

"Oh, something or other. I ought to have treated you as a small boy."

"Well, I'm a very small boy, now," said Valentin. "I'm rather less than an infant. An infant is helpless, but it's generally voted promising. I'm not promising, eh? Society can't lose a less valuable member."

Newman was strongly moved. He got up and turned his back upon his friend and walked away to the window, where he stood looking out, but only vaguely seeing. "No, I don't like the look of your back," Valentin continued. "I have always been an observer of backs; yours is quite out of sorts."

Newman returned to his bedside and begged him to be quiet. "Be quiet and get well," he said. "That's what you must do. Get well and help me."

"I told you you were in trouble! How can I help you?" Valentin asked.

"I'll let you know when you are better. You were always curious; there is something to get well for!" Newman answered, with resolute animation.

Valentin closed his eyes and lay a long time without speaking. He seemed even to have fallen asleep. But at the end of half an hour he began to talk again. "I am rather sorry about that place in the bank. Who knows but that I might have become another Rothschild?[2] But I wasn't meant for a banker; bankers are not so easy to kill. Don't you think I have been very easy to kill? It's not like a serious man. It's really very mortifying. It's like telling your hostess you must go, when you count upon her begging you to stay, and then finding she does no such thing. 'Really—so soon? You've only just come!' Life doesn't make me any such polite little speech."

Newman for some time said nothing, but at last he broke out. "It's a bad case—it's a bad case—it's the worst case I ever met. I don't want to say anything unpleasant, but I can't help it. I've seen men dying before—and I've seen men shot. But it always seemed more natural; they were not so clever as you. Damnation—damnation! You might have done something better than this. It's about the meanest winding-up of a man's affairs that I can imagine!"

Valentin feebly waved his hand to and fro. "Don't insist—don't insist! It is mean—decidedly mean. For you see at the bottom—down at the bottom, in a little place as small as the end of a wine-funnel—I agree with you!"

A few moments after this the doctor put his head through the half-opened door, and, perceiving that Valentin was awake, came in

2. A famous banking family in Paris.

and felt his pulse. He shook his head and declared that he had talked too much—ten times too much. "Nonsense!" said Valentin; "a man sentenced to death can never talk too much. Have you never read an account of an execution in a newspaper? Don't they always set a lot of people at the prisoner—lawyers, reporters, priests—to make him talk? But it's not Mr. Newman's fault; he sits there as mum as a death's-head."

The doctor observed that it was time his patient's wound should be dressed again; MM. de Grosjoyaux and Ledoux, who had already witnessed this delicate operation, taking Newman's place as assistants. Newman withdrew and learned from his fellow-watchers that they had received a telegram from Urbain de Bellegarde to the effect that their message had been delivered in the Rue de l'Université too late to allow him to take the morning train, but that he would start with his mother in the evening. Newman wandered away into the village again, and walked about restlessly for two or three hours. The day seemed terribly long. At dusk he came back and dined with the doctor and M. Ledoux. The dressing of Valentin's wound had been a very critical operation; the doctor didn't really see how he was to endure a repetition of it. He then declared that he must beg of Mr. Newman to deny himself for the present the satisfaction of sitting with M. de Bellegarde; more than anyone else, apparently, he had the flattering but inconvenient privilege of exciting him. M. Ledoux, at this, swallowed a glass of wine in silence; he must have been wondering what the deuce Bellegarde found so exciting in the American.

Newman, after dinner, went up to his room, where he sat for a long time staring at his lighted candle, and thinking that Valentin was dying downstairs. Late, when the candle had burnt low, there came a soft tap at his door. The doctor stood there with a candlestick and a shrug.

"He must amuse himself still!" said Valentin's medical adviser. "He insists upon seeing you, and I am afraid you must come. I think, at this rate, that he will hardly outlast the night."

Newman went back to Valentin's room, which he found lighted by a taper on the hearth. Valentin begged him to light a candle. "I want to see your face," he said. "They say you excite me," he went on, as Newman complied with this request, "and I confess I do feel excited; but it isn't you—it's my own thoughts. I have been thinking—thinking. Sit down there and let me look at you again." Newman seated himself, folded his arms, and bent a heavy gaze upon his friend. He seemed to be playing a part, mechanically, in a lugubrious comedy. Valentin looked at him for some time. "Yes, this morning I was right; you have something on your mind heavier than Valentin de Bellegarde. Come, I'm a dying man and it's indecent to deceive me. Something happened after I left Paris. It was not for nothing that my sister started off at this season of the year for Fleurières. Why was it? It sticks in my crop. I have been thinking it over, and if you don't tell me I shall guess."

"I had better not tell you," said Newman. "It won't do you any good."

"If you think it will do me any good not to tell me, you are very much mistaken. There is trouble about your marriage."

"Yes," said Newman. "There is trouble about my marriage."

"Good!" And Valentin was silent again. "They have stopped it."

"They have stopped it," said Newman. Now that he had spoken out, he found a satisfaction in it which deepened as he went on. "Your mother and brother have broken faith. They have decided that it can't take place. They have decided that I am not good enough, after all. They have taken back their word. Since you insist, there it is!"

Valentin gave a sort of groan, lifted his hands a moment, and then let them drop.

"I am sorry not to have anything better to tell you about them," Newman pursued. "But it's not my fault. I was, indeed, very unhappy when your telegram reached me; I was quite upside down. You may imagine whether I feel any better now."

Valentin moaned gaspingly, as if his wound were throbbing. "Broken faith, broken faith!" he murmured. "And my sister—my sister?"

"Your sister is very unhappy; she has consented to give me up. I don't know why. I don't know what they have done to her; it must be something pretty bad. In justice to her you ought to know it. They have made her suffer. I haven't seen her alone, but only before them! We had an interview yesterday morning. They came out flat, in so many words. They told me to go about my business. It seems to me a very bad case. I'm angry, I'm sore, I'm sick."

Valentin lay there staring, with his eyes more brilliantly lighted, his lips soundlessly parted, and a flush of colour in his pale face. Newman had never before uttered so many words in the plaintive key, but now, in speaking to Valentin in the poor fellow's extremity, he had a feeling that he was making his complaint somewhere within the presence of the power that men pray to in trouble; he felt his out-gush of resentment as a sort of spiritual privilege.

"And Claire," said Bellegarde, "Claire? She has given you up?"

"I don't really believe it," said Newman.

"No, don't believe it, don't believe it. She is gaining time; excuse her."

"I pity her!" said Newman.

"Poor Claire!" murmured Valentin. "But they—but they"—and he paused again. "You saw them; they dismissed you, face to face?"

"Face to face. They were very explicit."

"What did they say?"

"They said they couldn't stand a commercial person."

Valentin put out his hand and laid it upon Newman's arm. "And about their promise—their engagement with you?"

"They made a distinction. They said it was to hold good only until Madame de Cintré accepted me."

Valentin lay staring awhile, and his flush died away. "Don't tell me any more," he said at last; "I'm ashamed."

"You? You are the soul of honour," said Newman simply.

Valentin groaned and turned away his head. For some time nothing more was said. Then Valentin turned back again and found a certain force to press Newman's arm. "It's very bad—very bad. When my people—when my race—come to that, it is time for me to withdraw. I believe in my sister; she will explain. Excuse her. If she can't—if she can't, forgive her. She has suffered. But for the others it is very bad—very bad. You take it very hard? No, it's a shame to make you say so." He closed his eyes and again there was a silence. Newman felt almost awed; he had evoked a more solemn spirit than he expected. Presently Valentin looked at him again, removing his hand from his arm. "I apologise," he said. "Do you understand? Here on my death-bed. I apologise for my family. For my mother. For my brother. For the ancient house of Bellegarde. *Voilà*!"[3] he added softly.

Newman for all answer took his hand and pressed it with a world of kindness. Valentin remained quiet, and at the end of half an hour the doctor softly came in. Behind him, through the half-open door, Newman saw the two questioning faces of MM. de Grosjoyaux and Ledoux. The doctor laid his hand on Valentin's wrist and sat looking at him. He gave no sign and the two gentlemen came in, M. Ledoux having first beckoned to someone outside. This was M. le Curé, who carried in his hand an object unknown to Newman, and covered with a white napkin. M. le Curé was short, round, and red: he advanced, pulling off his little black cap to Newman, and deposited his burden on the table; and then he sat down in the best armchair, with his hands folded across his person. The other gentlemen had exchanged glances which expressed unanimity as to the timeliness of their presence. But for a long time Valentin neither spoke nor moved. It was Newman's belief, afterwards, that M. le Curé went to sleep. At last, abruptly, Valentin

3. "There!"

pronounced Newman's name. His friend went to him, and he said in French: "You are not alone. I want to speak to you alone." Newman looked at the doctor, and the doctor looked at the curé, who looked back at him; and then the doctor and the curé, together, gave a shrug. "Alone—for five minutes," Valentin repeated. "Please leave us."

The curé took up his burden again and led the way out, followed by his companions. Newman closed the door behind them and came back to Valentin's bedside. Bellegarde had watched all this intently.

"It's very bad, it's very bad," he said, after Newman had seated himself close to him. "The more I think of it the worse it is."

"Oh, don't think of it," said Newman.

But Valentin went on, without heeding him. "Even if they should come round again, the shame—the baseness—is there."

"Oh, they won't come round!" said Newman.

"Well, you can make them."

"Make them?"

"I can tell you something—a great secret—an immense secret. You can use it against them—frighten them, force them."

"A secret!" Newman repeated. The idea of letting Valentin, on his death-bed, confide to him an "immense secret" shocked him, for the moment, and made him draw back. It seemed an illicit way of arriving at information, and even had a vague analogy with listening at a keyhole. Then, suddenly, the thought of "forcing" Madame de Bellegarde and her son became attractive, and Newman bent his head closer to Valentin's lips. For some time, however, the dying man said nothing more. He only lay and looked at his friend with his kindled, expanded, troubled eye, and Newman began to believe that he had spoken in delirium. But at last he said:

"There was something done—something done at Fleurières. It was foul play. My father—something happened to him. I don't know; I have been ashamed—afraid to know. But I know there is something. My mother knows—Urbain knows."

"Something happened to your father?" said Newman urgently.

Valentin looked at him, still more wide-eyed. "He didn't get well."

"Get well of what?"

But the immense effort which Valentin had made, first to decide to utter these words, and then to bring them out, appeared to have taken his last strength. He lapsed again into silence, and Newman sat watching him. "Do you understand?" he began again presently. "At Fleurières. You can find out. Mrs. Bread knows. Tell her I begged you to ask her. Then tell them that, and see. It may help you. If not, tell everyone. It will—it will"—here Valentin's voice sank to the feeblest murmur—"it will avenge you!"

The words died away in a long soft groan. Newman stood up, deeply impressed, not knowing what to say; his heart was beating violently. "Thank you," he said at last. "I am much obliged." But Valentin seemed not to hear him; he remained silent, and his silence continued. At last Newman went and opened the door. M. le Curé re-entered, bearing his sacred vessel,[4] and followed by the three gentlemen and by Valentin's servant. It was almost processional.

Chapter XX

Valentin de Bellegarde died tranquilly, just as the cold faint March dawn began to illumine the faces of the little knot of friends gathered about his bedside. An hour afterwards Newman left the inn and drove to Geneva; he was naturally unwilling to be present at the arrival of Madame de Bellegarde and her first-born. At Geneva, for the moment, he remained. He was like a man who has had a fall and wants to sit still and count his bruises. He instantly wrote to Madame de Cintré, relating to her the circumstances of her brother's death—with certain exceptions—and asking her what was the earliest moment at which he might hope that she would consent to see him. M. Ledoux had told him that he had reason to know that Valentin's will—Bellegarde had a great deal of elegant personal property to dispose of—contained a request that he should be buried near his father in the churchyard of Fleurières, and Newman intended that the state of his own relations with the family should not deprive him of the satisfaction of helping to pay the last earthly honours to the best fellow in the world. He reflected that Valentin's friendship was older than Urbain's enmity, and that at a funeral it was easy to escape notice. Madame de Cintré's answer to his letter enabled him to time his arrival at Fleurières. This answer was very brief; it ran as follows:

> "I thank you for your letter, and for your being with Valentin. It is a most inexpressible sorrow to me that I was not. To see you will be nothing but a distress to me; there is no need, therefore, to wait for what you call brighter days. It is all one now, and I shall have no brighter days. Come when you please; only notify me first. My brother is to be buried here on Friday, and my family is to remain.—C. DE C."

4. The vessel with which the priest administers extreme unction, the sacrament in which a critically ill or injured person is annointed and prayers are said for his recovery and salvation.

As soon as he received this letter Newman went straight to Paris and to Poitiers. The journey took him far southward, through green Touraine[5] and across the far-shining Loire,[6] into a country where the early spring deepened about him as he went; but he had never made a journey during which he heeded less what he would have called the lay of the land. He obtained lodging at an inn at Poitiers, and the next morning drove in a couple of hours to the village of Fleurières. But here, preoccupied though he was, he could not fail to notice the picturesqueness of the place. It was what the French call a *petit bourg;*[7] it lay at the base of a sort of huge mound, on the summit of which stood the crumbling ruins of a feudal castle, much of whose sturdy material, as well as that of the wall which dropped along the hill, to enclose the clustered houses defensively, had been absorbed into the very substance of the village. The church was simply the former chapel of the castle, fronting upon its grass-grown court, which, however, was of generous enough width to have given up its quaintest corner to a little graveyard. Here the very headstones themselves seemed to sleep, as they slanted into the grass; the patient elbow of the rampart held them together on one side, and in front, far beneath their mossy lids, the green plains and blue distances stretched away. The way to church, up the hill, was impracticable to vehicles. It was lined with peasants two or three rows deep, who stood watching old Madame de Bellegarde slowly ascend it, on the arm of her elder son, behind the pall-bearers of the other. Newman chose to lurk among the common mourners, who murmured "Madame la Comtesse" as a tall figure veiled in black passed before them. He stood in the dusky little church while the service was going forward, but at the dismal tomb-side, he turned away and walked down the hill. He went back to Poitiers, and spent two days in which patience and impatience were singularly commingled. On the third day he sent Madame de Cintré a note, saying that he would call upon her in the afternoon, and in accordance with this he again took his way to Fleurières. He left his vehicle at the tavern in the village street, and obeyed the simple instructions which were given him for finding the château.

"It is just beyond there," said the landlord, and pointed to the tree-tops of the park above the opposite houses. Newman followed the first cross-road to the right—it was bordered with mouldy cottages—and in a few moments saw before him the peaked roofs of the towers. Advancing farther he found himself before a vast iron gate, rusty and closed; here he paused a moment, looking through the bars. The château was near the road; this was at once its merit and its defect; but its aspect was extremely impressive.

5. A region of west central France.
6. The longest river of France.
7. Small town.

Newman learned afterwards, from a guide-book of the province, that it dated from the time of Henry IV.[8] It presented to the wide paved area which preceded it, and which was edged with shabby farm-buildings, an immense façade of dark time-stained brick, flanked by two low wings, each of which terminated in a little Dutch-looking pavilion, capped with a fantastic roof. Two towers rose behind, and behind the towers was a mass of elms and beeches, now just faintly green.

But the great feature was a wide green river, which washed the foundations of the château. The building rose from an island in the circling stream, so that this formed a perfect moat, spanned by a two-arched bridge without a parapet. The dull brick walls, which here and there made a grand straight sweep, the ugly little cupolas of the wings, the deep-set windows, the long steep pinnacles of mossy slate, all mirrored themselves in the quiet water. Newman rang at the gate, and was almost frightened at the tone with which a big rusty bell above his head replied to him. An old woman came out from the gate-house and opened the creaking portal just wide enough for him to pass, and he went in, across the dry bare court and the little cracked white slabs of the causeway on the moat. At the door of the château he waited for some moments, and this gave him a chance to observe that Fleurières was not "kept up," and to reflect that it was a melancholy place of residence. "It looks," said Newman to himself—and I give the comparison for what it is worth—"like a Chinese penitentiary." At last the door was opened by a servant whom he remembered to have seen in the Rue de l'Université. The man's dull face brightened as he perceived our hero, for Newman, for indefinable reasons, enjoyed the confidence of the liveried gentry.[9] The footman led the way across a great central vestibule, with a pyramid of plants in tubs in the middle, and glass doors all around, to what appeared to be the principal drawing-room of the château. Newman crossed the threshold of a room of superb proportions, which made him feel at first like a tourist with a guide-book and a cicerone awaiting a fee. But when his guide had left him alone, with the observation that he would call Madame la Comtesse, Newman perceived that the salon contained little that was remarkable, save a dark ceiling with curiously-carved rafters, some curtains of elaborate antiquated tapestry, and a dark oaken floor, polished like a mirror. He waited some minutes, walking up and down; but at length, as he turned at the end of the room, he saw that Madame de Cintré had come in by a distant door. She wore a black dress, and she stood looking at him. As the

8. King Henry IV (1553–1610) ruled France from 1589–1610.

9. The servant classes.

length of the immense room lay between them he had time to look at her before they met in the middle of it.

He was dismayed at the change in her appearance. Pale, heavy-browed, almost haggard, with a sort of monastic rigidity in her dress, she had little but her pure features in common with the woman whose radiant good grace he had hitherto admired. She let her eyes rest on his own, and she let him take her hand; but her eyes looked like two rainy autumn moons, and her touch was portentously lifeless.

"I was at your brother's funeral," Newman said. "Then I waited three days. But I could wait no longer."

"Nothing can be lost or gained by waiting," said Madame de Cintré. "But it was very considerate of you to wait, wronged as you have been."

"I'm glad you think I have been wronged," said Newman, with that oddly humorous accent with which he often uttered words of the gravest meaning.

"Do I need to say so?" she asked. "I don't think I have wronged, seriously, many persons; certainly not consciously. To you, to whom I have done this hard and cruel thing, the only reparation I can make is to say: 'I know it, I feel it!' The reparation is pitifully small!"

"Oh, it's a great step forward!" said Newman, with a gracious smile of encouragement. He pushed a chair towards her and held it, looking at her urgently. She sat down mechanically, and he seated himself near her; but in a moment he got up, restlessly, and stood before her. She remained seated, like a troubled creature who had passed through the stage of restlessness.

"I say nothing is to be gained by my seeing you," she went on, "and yet I am very glad you came. Now I can tell you what I feel. It is a selfish pleasure, but it is one of the last I shall have." And she paused, with her great misty eyes fixed upon him. "I know how I have deceived and injured you; I know how cruel and cowardly I have been. I see it as vividly as you do—I feel it to the ends of my fingers." And she unclasped her hands, which were locked together in her lap, lifted them, and dropped them at her side. "Anything that you may have said of me in your angriest passion is nothing to what I have said to myself."

"In my angriest passion," said Newman, "I have said nothing hard of you. The very worst thing I have said of you yet is that you are the loveliest of women." And he seated himself before her again abruptly.

She flushed a little, but even her flush was pale. "That is because you think I will come back. But I will not come back. It is in that hope you have come here, I know; I am very sorry for you. I would do almost anything for you. To say that, after what I have done, seems simply impudent; but what can I say that will not seem impudent? To wrong you and apologise—that is easy enough. I should not have wronged you." She stopped a moment, looking at him, and motioned him to let her go on. "I ought never to have listened to you at first; that was the wrong. No good could come of it. I felt it, and yet I listened; that was your fault. I liked you too much; I believed in you."

"And don't you believe in me now?"

"More than ever. But now it doesn't matter. I have given you up."

Newman gave a powerful thump with his clenched fist upon his knee. "Why, why, why?" he cried. "Give me a reason—a decent reason. You are not a child—you are not a minor, nor an idiot. You are not obliged to drop me because your mother told you to. Such a reason isn't worthy of you."

"I know that; it's not worthy of me. But it's the only one I have to give. After all," said Madame de Cintré, throwing out her hands, "think me an idiot and forget me! That will be the simplest way."

Newman got up and walked away with a crushing sense that his cause was lost, and yet with an equal inability to give up fighting. He went to one of the great windows, and looked out at the stiffly embanked river and the formal gardens which lay beyond it. When he turned round, Madame de Cintré had risen; she stood there silent and passive. "You are not frank," said Newman; "you are not honest. Instead of saying that you are imbecile, you should say that other people are wicked. Your mother and your brother have been false and cruel; they have been so to me, and I am sure they have been so to you. Why do you try to shield them? Why do you sacrifice me to them? I'm not false; I'm not cruel. You don't know what you give up; I can tell you that—you don't. They bully you and plot about you; and I—I——" And he paused, holding out his hands. She turned away and began to leave him. "You told me the other day that you were afraid of your mother," he said, following her. "What did you mean?"

Madame de Cintré shook her head. "I remember; I was sorry afterwards."

"You were sorry when she came down and put on the thumbscrews. In God's name, what *is* it she does to you?"

"Nothing. Nothing that you can understand. And now that I have given you up, I must not complain of her to you."

"That's no reasoning!" cried Newman. "Complain of her, on the contrary. Tell me all about it, frankly and trustfully, as you ought, and we will talk it over so satisfactorily that you won't give me up."

Madame de Cintré looked down some moments, fixedly; and then, raising her eyes, she said: "One good at least has come of this: I have made you judge me more fairly. You thought of me in a way that did me great honour; I don't know why you had taken it into your head. But it left me no loophole for escape—no chance to be the common weak creature I am. It was not my fault; I warned you from the first. But I ought to have warned you more. I ought to have convinced you that I was doomed to disappoint you. But I *was*, in a way, too proud. You see what my superiority amounts to, I hope!" she went on, raising her voice with a tremor which even then and there Newman thought beautiful. "I am too proud to be honest, I am not too proud to be faithless. I am timid and cold and selfish. I am afraid of being uncomfortable."

"And you call marrying me uncomfortable!" said Newman, staring.

Madame de Cintré blushed a little, and seemed to say that if begging his pardon in words was impudent, she might at least thus mutely express her perfect comprehension of his finding her conduct odious. "It is not marrying you; it is doing all that would go with it. It's the rupture, the defiance, the insisting upon being happy in my own way. What right have I to be happy when—when——" And she paused.

"When what?" said Newman.

"When others have been most unhappy."

"What others?" Newman asked. "What have you to do with any others but me? Besides, you said just now that you wanted happiness, and that you should find it by obeying your mother. You contradict yourself."

"Yes, I contradict myself; that shows you that I am not even intelligent."

"You are laughing at me!" cried Newman. "You are mocking me!"

She looked at him intently, and an observer might have said that she was asking herself whether she might not most quickly end their common pain by confessing that she was mocking him. "No; I am not," she presently said.

"Granting that you are not intelligent," he went on, "that you are weak, that you are common, that you are nothing that I have believed you were—what I ask of you is not an heroic effort, it is a very common effort. There is a great deal on my side to make it easy. The simple truth is that you don't care enough about me to make it."

"I am cold," said Madame de Cintré. "I am as cold as that flowing river."

Newman gave a great rap on the floor with his stick, and a long grim laugh. "Good, good!" he cried. "You go altogether too far—you overshoot the mark. There isn't a woman in the world as bad as you would make yourself out. I see your game; it's what I said. You are blackening yourself to whiten others. You don't want to give me up at all; you like me—you like me. I know you do; you have shown it, and I have felt it. After that you may be as cold as you please! They have bullied you, I say; they have tortured you. It's an outrage, and I insist upon saving you from the extravagance of your own generosity. Would you chop off your hand if your mother requested it?"

Madame de Cintré looked a little frightened. "I spoke of my mother too blindly the other day. I am my own mistress, by law and by her approval. She can do nothing to me; she has done nothing. She has never alluded to those hard words I used about her."

"She has made you feel them, I'll promise you!" said Newman.

"It's my conscience that makes me feel them."

"Your conscience seems to me to be rather mixed!" exclaimed Newman passionately.

"It has been in great trouble, but now it is very clear," said Madame de Cintré. "I don't give you up for any worldly advantage or for any worldly happiness."

"Oh, you don't give me up for Lord Deepmere, I know," said Newman. "I won't pretend, even to provoke you, that I think that. But that's what your mother and your brother wanted, and your mother, at that villainous ball of hers—I liked it at the time, but the very thought of it now makes me rabid—tried to push him on to make up to you."

"Who told you this?" said Madame de Cintré softly.

"Not Valentin. I observed it. I guessed it. I didn't know at the time that I was observing it, but it stuck in my memory. And afterwards, you recollect, I saw Lord Deepmere with you in the conservatory. You said then that you would tell me at another time what he had said to you."

"That was before—before *this*," said Madame de Cintré.

"It doesn't matter," said Newman; "and besides, I think I know. He's an honest little Englishman. He came and told you what your mother was up to—that she wanted him to supplant me; not being a commercial person. If he would make you an offer she would undertake to bring you over and give me the slip. Lord Deepmere isn't very intellectual, so she had to spell it out to him. He said he admired you 'no end,' and that he wanted you to know it; but he didn't like being mixed up with that sort of underhand work, and he came to you and told tales. That was about the amount of it, wasn't it? And then you said you were perfectly happy."

"I don't see why we should talk of Lord Deepmere," said Madame de Cintré. "It was not for that you came here; and about my mother, it doesn't matter what you suspect and what you know. When once my mind has been made up, as it is now, I should not discuss these things. Discussing anything, now, is very idle. We must try and live each as we can. I believe you will be happy again; even, sometimes, when you think of me. When you do so, think this—that it was not easy, and that I did the best I could. I have things to reckon with that you don't know. I mean I have feelings. I must do as they force me—I must, I must. They would haunt me otherwise," she cried, with vehemence; "they would kill me!"

"I know what your feelings are: they are superstitions! They are the feeling that, after all, though I *am* a good fellow, I have been in business; the feeling that your mother's looks are law and your brother's words are gospel; that you all hang together, and that it's a part of the everlasting proprieties that they should have a hand in everything you do. It makes my blood boil. That *is* cold; you are right. And what I feel here," and Newman struck his heart and became more poetical than he knew, "is a glowing fire!"

A spectator less preoccupied than Madame de Cintré's distracted wooer would have felt sure from the first that her appealing calm of manner was the result of violent effort, in spite of which the tide of agitation was rapidly rising. On these last words of Newman's it overflowed, though at first she spoke low, for fear of her voice betraying her. "No, I was not right—I am not cold! I believe that if I am doing what seems so bad, it is not mere weakness and falseness. Mr. Newman, it's like a religion. I can't tell you—I can't! It's cruel of you to insist. I don't see why I shouldn't ask you to believe me—and pity me. It's like a religion. There's a curse upon the house; I don't know what—I don't know why—don't ask me. We must all bear it. I have been too selfish; I wanted to escape from it. You offered me a great chance—besides my liking you. It seemed good to change completely, to break, to go away. And then I admired you. But I can't—it has overtaken and come back to me." Her self-control had now completely abandoned her, and her words were broken with long sobs. "Why do such dreadful things happen to us—why is my brother Valentin killed, like a beast, in the midst of his youth and his gaiety and his brightness and all that we loved him for? Why are there things I can't ask about—that I am afraid to know? Why are there places I can't look at, sounds I can't hear? Why is it given to me to choose, to decide, in a case so hard and so terrible as this? I am not meant for that—I am not made for boldness and defiance. I was made to be happy in a quiet natural way." At this Newman gave a most expressive groan, but Madame de Cintré went on: "I was made to do gladly and gratefully what is expected of me. My mother has always been very good to me; that's all I can say. I must not judge her; I must not criticise her. If I did, it would come back to me. I can't change!"

"No," said Newman bitterly; "*I* must change—if I break in two in the effort!"

"You are different. You are a man; you will get over it. You have all kinds of consolation. You were born—you were trained, to changes. Besides—besides, I shall always think of you."

"I don't care for that!" cried Newman. "You are cruel—you are terribly cruel. God forgive you! You may have the best reasons and the finest feelings in the world; that makes no difference. You are a mystery to me; I don't see how such hardness can go with such loveliness."

Madame de Cintré fixed him a moment with her swimming eyes. "You believe I am hard, then?"

Newman answered her look, and then broke out: "You are a perfect faultless creature! Stay by me!"

"Of course I am hard," she went on. "Whenever we give pain we are hard. And we *must* give pain; that's the world—the hateful miserable world! Ah!" and she gave a long deep sigh, "I can't even say I am glad to have known you—though I am. That too is to wrong you. I can say nothing that is not cruel. Therefore let us part, without more of this. Good-bye!" And she put out her hand.

Newman stood and looked at it without taking it, and then raised his eyes to her face. He felt himself like shedding tears of rage. "What are you going to do?" he asked. "Where are you going?"

"Where I shall give no more pain and suspect no more evil. I am going out of the world."

"Out of the world?"

"I am going into a convent."

"Into a convent!" Newman repeated the words with the deepest dismay; it was as if she had said she was going into a hospital. "Into a convent—*you!*"

"I told you that it was not for my worldly advantage or pleasure I was leaving you."

But still Newman hardly understood. "You are going to be a nun," he went on, "in a cell—for life—with a gown and white veil?"

"A nun—a Carmelite nun,"[1] said Madame de Cintré. "For life, with God's leave."

The idea struck Newman as too dark and horrible for belief, and made him feel as he would have done if she had told him that she was going to mutilate her beautiful face, or drink some potion that

1. A Roman Catholic order of nuns, noted for the contemplative and mystical life.

would make her mad. He clasped his hands and began to tremble visibly.

"Madame de Cintré, don't, don't!" he said, "I beseech you! On my knees, if you like, I'll beseech you."

She laid her hand upon his arm, with a tender, pitying, almost reassuring gesture. "You don't understand," she said. "You have wrong ideas. It's nothing horrible. It is only peace and safety. It is to be out of the world, where such troubles as this come to the innocent, to the best. And for life—that's the blessing of it! They can't begin again."

Newman dropped into a chair and sat looking at her with a long inarticulate murmur. That this superb woman, in whom he had seen all human grace and household force, should turn from him and all the brightness that he offered her—him and his future and his fortune and his fidelity—to muffle herself in ascetic rags and entomb herself in a cell, was a confounding combination of the inexorable and the grotesque. As the image deepened before him the grotesque seemed to expand and overspread it; it was a reduction to the absurd of the trial to which he was subjected. "You—you a nun!" he exclaimed; "you with your beauty defaced—you behind locks and bars! Never, never, if I can prevent it!" And he sprang to his feet with a violent laugh.

"You can't prevent it," said Madame de Cintré, "and it ought—a little—to satisfy you. Do you suppose I will go on living in the world, still beside you, and yet not with you? It is all arranged. Good-bye, good-bye."

This time he took her hand, took it in both his own. "Forever?" he said. Her lips made an inaudible movement and his own uttered a deep imprecation. She closed her eyes, as if with the pain of hearing it; then he drew her towards him and clasped her to his breast. He kissed her white face; for an instant she resisted and for a moment she submitted; then, with force, she disengaged herself and hurried away over the long shining floor. The next moment the door closed behind her.

Newman made his way out as he could.

Chapter XXI

There is a pretty public walk at Poitiers, laid out upon the crest of the high hill around which the little city clusters, planted with thick trees, and looking down upon the fertile fields in which the old English princes fought for their right and held it. Newman paced up and down this quiet promenade for the greater part of the next day, and let his eyes wander over the historic prospect; but he would have been sadly at a loss to tell you afterwards whether the latter was made up of coal-fields or of vineyards. He was wholly given up to his grievance, of which reflection by no means diminished the weight. He feared that Madame de Cintré was irretrievably lost; and yet, as he would have said himself, he didn't see his way clear to giving her up. He found it impossible to turn his back upon Fleurières and its inhabitants; it seemed to him that some germ of hope or reparation must lurk there somewhere, if he could only stretch his arm out far enough to pluck it. It was as if he had his hand on a door-knob and were closing his clenched fist upon it: he had thumped, he had called, he had pressed the door with his powerful knee, and shaken it with all his strength, and dead damning silence had answered him. And yet something held him there—something hardened the grasp of his fingers. Newman's satisfaction had been too intense, his whole plan too deliberate and mature, his prospect of happiness too rich and comprehensive, for this fine moral fabric to crumble at a stroke. The very foundation seemed fatally injured, and yet he felt a stubborn desire still to try to save the edifice. He was filled with a sorer sense of wrong than he had ever known, or than he had supposed it possible he should know. To accept his injury and walk away without looking behind him was a stretch of good-nature of which he found himself incapable. He looked behind him intently and continually, and what he saw there did not assuage his resentment. He saw himself trustful, generous, liberal, patient, easy, pocketing frequent irritation and furnishing unlimited modesty. To have eaten humble pie,[2] to have been snubbed and patronised and satirised, and have consented to take it as one of the conditions of the bargain—to have done this, and done it all for nothing, surely gave one a right to protest. And to be turned off because one was a commercial person! As if he had ever talked or dreamt of the commercial since his connection with the Bellegardes began—as if he had made the least circumstance of the commercial—as if he would not have consented to confound the commercial fifty times a day, if it might have increased by a hair's breadth the chance of the Bellegardes' not playing him a trick! Granted that being commercial was fair ground for having a trick played upon one, how little they knew about the class so designated and its enterprising way of not standing upon trifles! It was in the light of his injury that the weight of Newman's past endurance seemed so heavy; his actual irritation had not been so great, merged as it was in his vision of the cloudless blue that overarched his immediate wooing. But now his sense of outrage was deep, rancorous, and ever present; he felt that he was a good fellow wronged. As for Madame de Cintré's conduct, it struck him

2. To have been humiliated.

with a kind of awe, and the fact that he was powerless to understand it or feel the reality of its motives only deepened the force with which he had attached himself to her. He had never let the fact of her Catholicism trouble him; Catholicism to him was nothing but a name, and to express a mistrust of the form in which her religious feelings had moulded themselves would have seemed to him on his own part a rather pretentious affectation of Protestant zeal. If such superb white flowers as that could bloom in Catholic soil, the soil was not insalubrious. But it was one thing to be a Catholic, and another to turn nun—on your hands! There was something lugubriously comical in the way Newman's thoroughly contemporaneous optimism was confronted with this dusky old-world expedient. To see a woman made for him and for motherhood to his children juggled away in this tragic travesty—it was a thing to rub one's eyes over, a nightmare, an illusion, a hoax. But the hours passed away without disproving the thing, and leaving him only the after-sense of the vehemence with which he had embraced Madame de Cintré. He remembered her words and her looks; he turned them over and tried to shake the mystery out of them, and to infuse them with an endurable meaning. What had she meant by her feeling being a kind of religion? It was the religion simply of the family laws, the religion of which her implacable little mother was the high-priestess. Twist the thing about as her generosity would, the one certain fact was that they had used force against her. Her generosity had tried to screen them, but Newman's heart rose into his throat at the thought that they should go scot-free.

The twenty-four hours wore themselves away, and the next morning Newman sprang to his feet with the resolution to return to Fleurières and demand another interview with Madame de Bellegarde and her son. He lost no time in putting it into practice. As he rolled swiftly over the excellent road in the little calèche furnished him at the inn at Poitiers, he drew forth, as it were, from the very safe place in his mind to which he had consigned it, the last information given him by poor Valentin. Valentin had told him he could do something with it, and Newman thought it would be well to have it at hand. This was of course not the first time, lately, that Newman had given it his attention. It was information in the rough—it was dark and puzzling; but Newman was neither helpless nor afraid. Valentin had evidently meant to put him in possession of a powerful instrument, though he could not be said to have placed the handle very securely within his grasp. But if he had not really told him the secret, he had at least given him the clew to it—a clew of which that queer old Mrs. Bread held the other end. Mrs. Bread had always looked to Newman as if she knew secrets; and as he apparently enjoyed her esteem, he suspected she might be induced to share her knowledge with him. So long as there was only Mrs. Bread to deal with, he felt easy. As to what there was to find out, he had only one fear—that it might not be bad enough. Then, when the image of the marquise and her son rose before him again, standing side by side, the old woman's hand in Urbain's arm, and the same cold unsociable fixedness in the eyes of each, he cried out to himself that the fear was groundless. There was blood in the secret at the very least! He arrived at Fleurières almost in a state of elation; he had satisfied himself, logically, that in the presence of his threat of exposure they would, as he mentally phrased it, rattle down like unwound buckets. He remembered indeed that he must first catch his hare—first ascertain what there was to expose; but after that, why shouldn't his happiness be as good as new again? Mother and son would drop their lovely victim in terror, and take to hiding, and Madame de Cintré, left to herself, would surely come back to him. Give her a chance and she would rise to the surface, return to the light. How could she fail to perceive that his house would be much the most comfortable sort of convent?

Newman, as he had done before, left his conveyance at the inn and walked the short remaining distance to the château. When he reached the gate, however, a singular feeling took possession of him—a feeling which, strange as it may seem, had its source in its unfathomable good-nature. He stood there awhile, looking through the bars of the large time-stained face of the edifice, and wondering to what crime it was that the dark old house, with its flowery name, had given convenient occasion. It had given occasion, first and last, to tyrannies and sufferings enough, Newman said to himself; it was an evil-looking place to live in. Then, suddenly, came the reflection: What a horrible rubbish-heap of iniquity to fumble in! The attitude of inquisitor turned its ignoble face, and with the same movement Newman declared that the Bellegardes should have another chance. He would appeal once more directly to their sense of fairness, and not to their fear; and if they should be accessible to reason, he need know nothing worse about them than what he already knew. That was bad enough.

The gate-keeper let him in through the same stiff crevice as before, and he passed through the court and over the little rustic bridge on the moat. The door was opened before he had reached it, and, as if to put his clemency to rout with the suggestion of a richer opportunity, Mrs. Bread stood there awaiting him. Her face, as usual, looked as hopelessly blank as the tide-smoothed sea-sand, and her black garments seemed of an intenser sable. Newman had already learned that her strange inexpressiveness could be a vehicle for emotion, and he was not surprised at the muffled vivacity with which she whispered: "I thought you would try again, sir. I was looking out for you."

"I am glad to see you," said Newman; "I think you are my friend."

Mrs. Bread looked at him opaquely. "I wish you well, sir; but it's vain wishing now."

"You know, then, how they have treated me?"

"Oh sir," said Mrs. Bread dryly, "I know everything."

Newman hesitated a moment. "Everything?"

Mrs. Bread gave him a glance somewhat more lucent. "I know at least too much, sir."

"One can never know too much. I congratulate you. I have come to see Madame de Bellegarde and her son," Newman added. "Are they at home? If they are not, I will wait."

"My lady is always at home," Mrs. Bread replied, "and the marquis is mostly with her."

"Please then tell them—one or the other, or both—that I am here and that I desire to see them."

Mrs. Bread hesitated. "May I take a great liberty, sir?"

"You have never taken a liberty but you have justified it," said Newman, with diplomatic urbanity.

Mrs. Bread dropped her wrinkled eyelids as if she were curtsying; but the curtsy stopped there; the occasion was too grave. "You have come to plead with them again, sir? Perhaps you don't know this—that Madame de Cintré returned this morning to Paris."

"Ah, she's gone!" And Newman, groaning, smote the pavement with his stick.

"She has gone straight to the convent—the Carmelites they call it. I see you know, sir. My lady and the marquis take it very ill. It was only last night she told them."

"Ah, she had kept it back, then?" cried Newman. "Good, good! And they are very fierce?"

"They are not pleased," said Mrs. Bread. "But they may well dislike it. They tell me it's most dreadful, sir; of all the nuns in Christendom the Carmelites are the worst. You may say they are really not human, sir; they make you give up everything—forever. And to think of *her* there! If I was one that cried, sir, I could cry."

Newman looked at her an instant. "We mustn't cry, Mrs. Bread; we must act. Go and call them!" And he made a movement to enter farther.

But Mrs. Bread gently checked him. "May I take another liberty? I am told you were with my dearest Mr. Valentin, in his last hours. If you would tell me a word about him! The poor count was my own boy, sir; for the first year of his life he was hardly out of my arms; I taught him to speak. And the count spoke so well, sir! He always spoke well to his poor old Bread. When he grew up and took his pleasure he always had a kind word for me. And to die in that wild way! They have a story that he fought with a wine merchant. I can't believe that, sir! And was he in great pain?"

"You are a wise kind old woman, Mrs. Bread," said Newman. "I hoped I might see you with my own children in your arms. Perhaps I shall yet." And he put out his hand. Mrs. Bread looked for a moment at his open palm, and then, as if fascinated by the novelty of the gesture, extended her own ladylike fingers. Newman held her hand firmly and deliberately, fixing his eyes upon her. "You want to know all about Mr. Valentin?" he said.

"It would be a sad pleasure, sir."

"I can tell you everything. Can you sometimes leave this place?"

"The château, sir? I really don't know. I never tried."

"Try, then; try hard. Try this evening, at dusk. Come to me in the old ruin there on the hill, in the court before the church. I will wait for you there; I have something very important to tell you. An old woman like you can do as she pleases."

Mrs. Bread stared, wondering, with parted lips. "Is it from the count, sir?" she asked.

"From the count—from his death-bed," said Newman.

"I will come, then. I will be bold, for once, for *him*."

She led Newman into the great drawing-room with which he had already made acquaintance, and retired to execute his commands. Newman waited a long time; at last he was on the point of ringing and repeating his request. He was looking round him for a bell when the marquis came in with his mother on his arm. It will be seen that Newman had a logical mind when I say that he declared to himself, in perfect good faith, as a result of Valentin's dark hints, that his adversaries looked grossly wicked. "There is no mistake about it now," he said to himself as they advanced. "They're a bad lot; they have pulled off the mask." Madame de Bellegarde and her son certainly bore in their faces the signs of extreme perturbation; they looked like people who had passed a sleepless night. Confronted, moreover, with an annoyance which they hoped they had disposed of, it was not natural that they should have any very tender glances to bestow upon Newman. He stood before them, and such eyebeams as they found available they levelled at him; Newman feeling as if the door of a sepulchre had suddenly been opened, and the damp darkness were being exhaled.

"You see I have come back," he said. "I have come to try again."

"It would be ridiculous," said M. de Bellegarde, "to pretend that we are glad to see you or that we don't question the taste of your visit."

"Oh, don't talk about taste," said Newman with a laugh, "or that will bring us round to yours! If I consulted my taste I certainly shouldn't come to see you. Besides, I will make as short work as you please. Promise me to raise the blockade—to set Madame de Cintré at liberty—and I will retire instantly."

"We hesitated as to whether we would see you," said Madame de Bellegarde; "and we were on the point of declining the honour. But it seemed to me that we should act with civility, as we have always done, and I wished to have the satisfaction of informing you that there are certain weaknesses that people of our way of feeling can be guilty of but once."

"You may be weak but once, but you will be audacious many times, madam," Newman answered. "I didn't come, however, for conversational purposes. I came to say this simply: That if you will write immediately to your daughter that you withdraw your opposition to her marriage, I will take care of the rest. You don't want her to turn nun—you know more about the horrors of it than I do. Marrying a commercial person is better than that. Give me a letter to her, signed and sealed, saying you retract, and that she may marry me with your blessing, and I will take it to her at the convent and bring her out. There's your chance—I call those easy terms."

"We look at the matter otherwise, you know. We call them very hard terms," said Urbain de Bellegarde. They had all remained standing rigidly in the middle of the room. "I think my mother will tell you that she would rather her daughter should become Sœur Catherine[3] than Mrs. Newman."

But the old lady, with the serenity of supreme power, let her son make her epigrams for her. She only smiled, almost sweetly, shaking her head and repeating: "But once, Mr. Newman; but once!"

Nothing that Newman had ever seen or heard gave him such a sense of marble hardness as this movement and the tone that accompanied it. "Could anything compel you?" he asked. "Do you know of anything that would force you?"

"This language, sir," said the marquis, "addressed to people in bereavement and grief is beyond all qualification."

"In most cases," Newman answered, "your objection would have some weight, even admitting that Madame de Cintré's present intentions make time precious. But I have thought of what you speak of, and I have come here to-day without scruple simply because I consider your brother and you two very different parties. I see no

3. "Sister Catherine."

connection between you. Your brother was ashamed of you. Lying there wounded and dying, the poor fellow apologised to me for your conduct. He apologised to me for that of his mother."

For a moment the effect of these words was as if Newman had struck a physical blow. A quick flush leaped into the faces of Madame de Bellegarde and her son, and they exchanged a glance like a twinkle of steel. Urbain uttered two words which Newman but half heard, but of which the sense came to him as it were in the reverberation of the sound, "*Le misérable!*"[4]

"You show little respect for the living," said Madame de Bellegarde, "but at least respect the dead. Don't profane—don't insult—the memory of my innocent son."

"I speak the simple truth," Newman declared, "and I speak it for a purpose. I repeat it—distinctly. Your son was utterly disgusted—your son apologised."

Urbain de Bellegarde was frowning portentously, and Newman supposed he was frowning at poor Valentin's invidious image. Taken by surprise, his scant affection for his brother had made a momentary concession to dishonour. But not for an appreciable instant did his mother lower her flag. "You are immensely mistaken, sir," she said. "My son was sometimes light, but he was never indecent. He died faithful to his name."

"You simply misunderstood him," said the marquis, beginning to rally. "You affirm the impossible."

"Oh, I don't care for poor Valentin's apology," said Newman. "It was far more painful than pleasant to me. This atrocious thing was not his fault; he never hurt me, or anyone else; he was the soul of honour. But it shows how he took it."

"If you wish to prove that my poor brother, in his last moments, was out of his head, we can only say that under the melancholy circumstances nothing was more possible. But confine yourself to that."

"He was quite in his right mind," said Newman, with gentle but dangerous doggedness; "I have never seen him so bright and clever. It was terrible to see that witty capable fellow dying such a death. You know I was very fond of your brother. And I have further proof of his sanity," Newman concluded.

The marquise gathered herself together majestically. "This is too gross!" she cried. "We decline to accept your story, sir—we repudiate it. Urbain, open the door." She turned away, with an imperious motion to her son, and passed rapidly down the length of the room. The marquis went with her and held the door open. Newman was left standing.

4. "The wretch!"

He lifted his finger, as a sign to M. de Bellegarde, who closed the door behind his mother and stood waiting. Newman slowly advanced, more silent, for the moment, than life. The two men stood face to face. Then Newman had a singular sensation; he felt his sense of injury almost brimming over into jocularity. "Come," he said, "you don't treat me well; at least admit that."

M. de Bellegarde looked at him from head to foot, and then, in the most delicate best-bred voice: "I detest you personally," he said.

"That's the way I feel to you, but for politeness' sake I don't say it," said Newman. "It's singular I should want so much to be your brother-in-law, but I can't give it up. Let me try once more." And he paused a moment. "You have a secret—you have a skeleton in the closet." M. de Bellegarde continued to look at him hard, but Newman could not see whether his eyes betrayed anything; the look of his eyes was always so strange. Newman paused again, and then went on. "You and your mother have committed a crime." At this M. de Bellegarde's eyes certainly did change; they seemed to flicker, like blown candles. Newman could see that he was profoundly startled; but there was something admirable in his self-control.

"Continue," said M. de Bellegarde.

Newman lifted a finger and made it waver a little in the air. "Need I continue? You are trembling."

"Pray where did you obtain this interesting information?" M. de Bellegarde asked very softly.

"I shall be strictly accurate," said Newman. "I won't pretend to know more than I do. At present that is all I know. You have done something that you must hide, something that would damn you if it were known, something that would disgrace the name you are so proud of. I don't know what it is, but I can find out. Persist in your present course and I *will* find out. Change it, let your sister go in peace, and I will leave you alone. It's a bargain?"

The marquis almost succeeded in looking untroubled; the breaking up of the ice in his handsome countenance was an operation that was necessarily gradual. But Newman's mildly-syllabled argumentation seemed to press, and press, and presently he averted his eyes. He stood some moments, reflecting.

"My brother told you this," he said, looking up.

Newman hesitated a moment. "Yes, your brother told me."

The marquis smiled, handsomely. "Didn't I say that he was out of his mind?"

"He was out of his mind if I don't find out. He was very much in it if I do."

M. de Bellegarde gave a shrug. "Eh, sir, find out or not, as you please."

"I don't frighten you?" demanded Newman.

"That's for you to judge."

"No, it's for you to judge, at your leisure. Think it over, feel yourself all round. I will give you an hour or two. I can't give you more, for how do we know how fast they may be making Madame de Cintré a nun? Talk it over with your mother; let her judge whether she is frightened. I don't believe she is as easily frightened, in general, as you; but you will see. I will go and wait in the village, at the inn, and I beg you to let me know as soon as possible. Say by three o'clock. A simple *yes* or *no* on paper will do. Only, you know, in case of a *yes* I shall expect you, this time, to stick to your bargain." And with this Newman opened the door and let himself out. The marquis did not move, and Newman, retiring, gave him another look. "At the inn, in the village," he repeated. Then he turned away altogether and passed out of the house.

He was extremely excited by what he had been doing, for it was inevitable that there should be a certain emotion in calling up the spectre of dishonour before a family a thousand years old. But he went back to the inn and contrived to wait there, deliberately, for the next two hours. He thought it more than probable that Urbain de Bellegarde would give no sign; for an answer to his challenge, in either sense, would be a confession of guilt. What he most expected was silence—in other words defiance. But he prayed that, as he imaged it, his shot might bring them down. It did bring, by three o'clock, a note, delivered by a footman; a note addressed in Urbain de Bellegarde's handsome English hand. It ran as follows:

> "I cannot deny myself the satisfaction of letting you know that I return to Paris, to-morrow, with my mother, in order that we may see my sister and confirm her in the resolution which is the most effectual reply to your audacious pertinacity.
>
> "HENRI-URBAIN DE BELLEGARDE."

Newman put the letter into his pocket, and continued his walk up and down the inn-parlour. He had spent most of his time, for the past week, in walking up and down. He continued to measure the length of the little *salle*[5] of the Armes de France until the day began to wane, when he went out to keep his rendezvous with Mrs. Bread. The path which led up the hill to the ruin was easy to find, and Newman in a short time had followed it to the top. He passed beneath the rugged arch of the castle-wall, and looked about him in the early dusk for an old woman in black. The castle-yard was

5. Room.

empty, but the door of the church was open. Newman went into the little nave and of course found a deeper dusk than without. A couple of tapers, however, twinkled on the altar and just enabled him to perceive a figure seated by one of the pillars. Closer inspection helped him to recognise Mrs. Bread, in spite of the fact that she was dressed with unwonted splendour. She wore a large black silk bonnet, with imposing bows of crape, and an old black satin dress disposed itself in vaguely lustrous folds about her person. She had judged it proper to the occasion to appear in her stateliest apparel. She had been sitting with her eyes fixed upon the ground, but when Newman passed before her she looked up at him, and then she rose.

"Are you a Catholic, Mrs. Bread?" he asked.

"No, sir; I'm a good Church of England woman, very Low,"[6] she answered. "But I thought I should be safer in here than outside. I was never out in the evening before, sir."

"We shall be safer," said Newman, "where no one can hear us." And he led the way back into the castle-court and then followed a path beside the church, which he was sure must lead into another part of the ruin. He was not deceived. It wandered along the crest of the hill and terminated before a fragment of wall pierced by a rough aperture which had once been a door. Through this aperture Newman passed and found himself in a nook peculiarly favourable to quiet conversation, as probably many an earnest couple, otherwise assorted than our friends, had assured themselves. The hill sloped abruptly away, and on the remnant of its crest were scattered two or three fragments of stone. Beneath, over the plain, lay the gathered twilight, through which, in the near distance, gleamed two or three lights from the château. Mrs. Bread rustled slowly after her guide, and Newman, satisfying himself that one of the fallen stones was steady, proposed to her to sit upon it. She cautiously complied, and he placed himself upon another, near her.

Chapter XXII

"I am very much obliged to you for coming," Newman said. "I hope it won't get you into trouble."

"I don't think I shall be missed. My lady, in these days, is not fond of having me about her." This was said with a certain fluttered eagerness which increased Newman's sense of having inspired the old woman with confidence.

"From the first, you know," he answered, "you took an interest

6. The Church of England had three "levels" in the nineteenth century. The "High Church" was very near to Roman Catholicism in doctrine and liturgy; the "Broad Church" was latitudinarian; the "Low Church" was very near to the Protestant fundamentalism of the Methodist church.

in my prospects. You were on my side. That gratified me, I assure you. And now that you know what they have done to me, I am sure you are with me all the more."

"They have not done well—I must say it," said Mrs. Bread. "But you mustn't blame the poor countess; they pressed her hard."

"I would give a million of dollars to know what they did to her!" cried Newman.

Mrs. Bread sat with a dull, oblique gaze fixed upon the lights of the château. "They worked on her feelings; they knew that was the way. She is a delicate creature. They made her feel wicked. She is only too good."

"Ah, they made her feel wicked," said Newman slowly; and then he repeated it. "They made her feel wicked—they made her feel wicked." The words seemed to him for the moment a vivid description of infernal ingenuity.

"It was because she was so good that she gave up—poor sweet lady!" added Mrs. Bread.

"But she was better to them than to me," said Newman.

"She was afraid," said Mrs. Bread, very confidently; "she has always been afraid, or at least for a long time. That was the real trouble, sir. She was like a fair peach, I may say, with just one little speck. She had one little sad spot. You pushed her into the sunshine, sir, and it almost disappeared. Then they pulled her back into the shade and in a moment it began to spread. Before we knew it she was gone. She was a delicate creature."

This singular attestation of Madame de Cintré's delicacy, for all its singularity, set Newman's wound aching afresh. "I see," he presently said; "she knew something bad about her mother."

"No, sir, she knew nothing," said Mrs. Bread, holding her head very stiff and keeping her eyes fixed upon the glimmering windows of the château.

"She guessed something, then, or suspected it."

"She was afraid to know," said Mrs. Bread.

"But *you* know, at any rate," said Newman.

She slowly turned her vague eyes upon Newman, squeezing her hands together in her lap. "You are not quite faithful, sir. I thought it was to tell me about Mr. Valentin you asked me to come here."

"Oh, the more we talk of Mr. Valentin the better," said Newman. "That's exactly what I want. I was with him, as I told you, in his last hour. He was in a great deal of pain, but he was quite himself. You know what that means; he was bright and lively and clever."

"Oh, he would always be clever, sir," said Mrs. Bread. "And did he know of your trouble?"

"Yes, he guessed it of himself."

"And what did he say to it?"

"He said it was a disgrace to his name—but it was not the first."

"Lord, Lord!" murmured Mrs. Bread.

"He said that his mother and his brother had once put their heads together and invented something even worse."

"You shouldn't have listened to that, sir."

"Perhaps not. But I *did* listen, and I don't forget it. Now I want to know what it is they did."

Mrs. Bread gave a soft moan. "And you have enticed me up into this strange place to tell you?"

"Don't be alarmed," said Newman. "I won't say a word that shall be disagreeable to you. Tell me as it suits you, and when it suits you. Only remember that it was Mr. Valentin's last wish that you should."

"Did he say that?"

"He said it with his last breath: 'Tell Mrs. Bread I told you to ask her.' "

"Why didn't he tell you himself?"

"It was too long a story for a dying man; he had no breath left in his body. He could only say that he wanted me to know—that, wronged as I was, it was my right to know."

"But how will it help you, sir?" said Mrs. Bread.

"That's for me to decide. Mr. Valentin believed it would, and that's why he told me. Your name was almost the last word he spoke."

Mrs. Bread was evidently awe-struck by this statement; she shook her clasped hands slowly up and down. "Excuse me, sir," she said, "if I take a great liberty. Is it the solemn truth you are speaking? I *must* ask you that; must I not, sir?"

"There's no offence. It *is* the solemn truth; I solemnly swear it. Mr. Valentin himself would certainly have told me more if he had been able."

"Oh, sir, if he knew more!"

"Don't you suppose he did?"

"There's no saying what he knew about anything," said Mrs. Bread, with a mild head-shake. "He was so mightily clever. He could make you believe he knew things that he didn't, and that he didn't know others that he had better not have known."

"I suspect he knew something about his brother that kept the marquis civil to him," Newman propounded; "he made the marquis feel him. What he wanted now was to put me in his place; he wanted to give me a chance to make the marquis feel *me*."

"Mercy on us!" cried the old waiting-woman, "how wicked we all are!"

"I don't know," said Newman; "some of us are wicked, certainly. I am very angry, I am very sore, and I am very bitter, but I don't know that I am wicked. I have been cruelly injured. They have hurt me, and I want to hurt them. I don't deny that; on the contrary, I tell you plainly that that is the use I want to make of your secret."

Mrs. Bread seemed to hold her breath. "You want to publish them—you want to shame them?"

"I want to bring them down—down, down, down! I want to turn the tables upon them—I want to mortify them as they mortified me. They took me up into a high place and made me stand there for all the world to see me, and then they stole behind me and pushed me into this bottomless pit, where I lie howling and gnashing my teeth! I made a fool of myself before all their friends; but I shall make something worse of them."

This passionate sally, which Newman uttered with the greater fervour that it was the first time he had had a chance to say all this aloud, kindled two small sparks in Mrs. Bread's fixed eyes. "I suppose you have a right to your anger, sir; but think of the dishonour you will draw down on Madame de Cintré."

"Madame de Cintré is buried alive," cried Newman. "What are honour or dishonour to her? The door of the tomb is at this moment closing behind her."

"Yes, it is most awful," moaned Mrs. Bread.

"She has moved off, like her brother Valentin, to give me room to work. It's as if it were done on purpose."

"Surely," said Mrs. Bread, apparently impressed by the ingenuity of this reflection. She was silent for some moments; then she added: "And would you bring my lady before the courts?"

"The courts care nothing for my lady," Newman replied. "If she has committed a crime, she will be nothing for the courts but a wicked old woman."

"And will they hang her, sir?"

"That depends upon what she has done." And Newman eyed Mrs. Bread intently.

"It would break up the family most terribly, sir!"

"It's time such a family should be broken up!" said Newman, with a laugh.

"And me at my age out of place, sir!" sighed Mrs. Bread.

"Oh, I will take care of you! You shall come and live with me. You shall be my housekeeper, or anything you like. I will pension you for life."

"Dear, dear, sir, you think of everything." And she seemed to fall a-brooding.

Newman watched her awhile, and then he said suddenly: "Ah, Mrs. Bread, you are too fond of my lady!"

She looked at him as quickly. "I wouldn't have you say that, sir. I don't think it any part of my duty to be fond of my lady. I have served her faithfully this many a year; but if she were to die to-morrow, I believe, before Heaven, I shouldn't shed a tear for her." Then after a pause, "I have no reason to love her!" Mrs. Bread added. "The most she has done for me has been not to turn me out of the house." Newman felt that decidedly his companion was more and more confidential—that if luxury is corrupting, Mrs. Bread's conservative habits were already relaxed by the spiritual comfort of this preconcerted interview, in a remarkable locality, with a free-spoken millionaire. All his native shrewdness admonished him that his part was simply to let her take her time—let the charm of the occasion work. So he said nothing; he only looked at her kindly. Mrs. Bread sat nursing her lean elbows. "My lady once did me a great wrong," she went on at last. "She has a terrible tongue when she is vexed. It was many a year ago, but I have never forgotten it. I have never mentioned it to a human creature; I have kept my grudge to myself. I daresay I have been wicked, but my grudge has grown old with me. It has grown good for nothing, too, I daresay; but it has lived along, as I have lived. It will die when I die—not before!"

"And what *is* your grudge?" Newman asked.

Mrs. Bread dropped her eyes and hesitated. "If I were a foreigner, sir, I should make less of telling you; it comes harder to a decent Englishwoman. But I sometimes think I have picked up too many foreign ways. What I was telling you belongs to a time when I was much younger and very different looking to what I am now. I had a very high colour, sir, if you can believe it; indeed I was a very smart lass. My lady was younger, too, and the late marquis was youngest of all—I mean in the way he went on, sir; he had a very high spirit; he was a magnificent man. He was fond of his pleasure, like most foreigners, and it must be owned that he sometimes went rather below him to take it. My lady was often jealous, and, if you'll believe it, sir, she did me the honour to be jealous of me. One day I had a red ribbon in my cap, and my lady flew out at me and ordered me to take it off. She accused me of putting it on to make the marquis look at me. I don't know that I was impertinent, but I spoke up like an honest girl and didn't count my words. A red ribbon indeed! As if it was my ribbons the marquis looked at! My lady knew afterwards that I was perfectly respectable, but she never said a word to show that she believed it. But the marquis did!" Mrs. Bread presently added: "I took off my red ribbon and put it away in a drawer, where I have kept it to this day. It's faded, now, it's a very pale pink; but there it lies. My grudge has faded, too; the red has all gone out of it; but it lies here yet." And Mrs. Bread stroked her black satin bodice.

Newman listened with interest to this decent narrative, which seemed to have opened up the deeps of memory to his companion. Then, as she remained silent, and seemed to be losing herself in retrospective meditation upon her perfect respectability, he ventured upon a short cut to his goal. "So Madame de Bellegarde was jealous; I see. And M. de Bellegarde admired pretty women, without distinction of class. I suppose one mustn't be hard upon him, for they probably didn't all behave so properly as you. But years afterwards it could hardly have been jealousy that turned Madame de Bellegarde into a criminal."

Mrs. Bread gave a weary sigh. "We are using dreadful words, sir, but I don't care now. I see you have your idea, and I have no will of my own. My will was the will of my children, as I called them; but I have lost my children now. They are dead—I may say it of both of them; and what should I care for the living? What is anyone in the house to me now—what am I to them? My lady objects to me—she has objected to me these thirty years. I should have been glad to be something to young Madame de Bellegarde, though I never was nurse to the present marquis. When he was a baby I was too young; they wouldn't trust me with him. But his wife told her own maid, Mamselle Clarisse, the opinion she had of me. Perhaps you would like to hear it, sir."

"Oh, immensely," said Newman.

"She said that if I would sit in her children's schoolroom I should do very well for a penwiper! When things have come to that I don't think I need stand upon ceremony."

"Decidedly not," said Newman. "Go on, Mrs. Bread."

Mrs. Bread, however, relapsed again into troubled dumbness, and all Newman could do was to fold his arms and wait. But at last she appeared to have set her memories in order. "It was when the late marquis was an old man and his eldest son had been two years married. It was when the time came on for marrying Mademoiselle Claire; that's the way they talk of it here, you know, sir. The marquis's health was bad; he was very much broken down. My lady had picked out M. de Cintré, for no good reason that I could see. But there are reasons, I very well know, that are beyond me, and you must be high in the world to understand them. Old M. de Cintré was very high, and my lady thought him almost as good as herself; that's saying a good deal. Mr. Urbain took sides with his mother, as he always did. The trouble, I believe, was that my lady would give very little money, and all the other gentlemen asked more. It was only M. de Cintré that was satisfied. The Lord willed it he should have that one soft spot; it was the only one he had. He may have been very grand in his birth, and he certainly was very grand in his bows and speeches; but that was all the grandeur he had. I think he was like what I have heard of comedians; not that I have ever seen one. But I know he painted his face. He might paint it all he would; he could never make me like it! The marquis couldn't abide him, and declared that sooner than take such a husband as that, Mademoiselle Claire should take none at all. He and my lady had a great scene; it came even to our ears in the servants' hall. It was not their first quarrel, if the truth must be told. They were not a loving couple, but they didn't often come to words, because, I think, neither of them thought the other's doings worth the trouble. My lady had long ago got over her jealousy, and she had taken to indifference. In this, I must say, they were well matched. The marquis was very easy-going; he had a most gentlemanly temper. He got angry only once a year, but then it was very bad. He always took to bed directly afterwards. This time I speak of he took to bed as usual, but he never got up again. I'm afraid the poor gentleman was paying for his dissipation; isn't it true they mostly do, sir, when they get old? My lady and Mr. Urbain kept quiet, but I know my lady wrote letters to M. de Cintré. The marquis got worse and the doctors gave him up. My lady she gave him up too, and if the truth must be told, she gave him up gladly. When once he was out of the way she could do what she pleased with her daughter, and it was all arranged that my poor innocent child should be handed over to M. de Cintré. You don't know what mademoiselle was in those days, sir; she was the sweetest young creature in France, and knew as little of what was going on around her as the lamb does of the butcher. I used to nurse the marquis, and I was always in his room. It was here at Fleurières, in the autumn. We had a doctor from Paris, who came and stayed two or three weeks in the house. Then there came two others, and there was a consultation, and these two others, as I said, declared that the marquis couldn't be saved. After this they went off, pocketing their fees, but the other one stayed and did what he could. The marquis himself kept crying out that he wouldn't die, that he didn't want to die, that he would live and look after his daughter. Mademoiselle Claire and the viscount—that was Mr. Valentin, you know—were both in the house. The doctor was a clever man—that I could see myself—and I think he believed that the marquis might get well. We took good care of him, he and I, between us, and one day, when my lady had almost ordered her mourning, my patient suddenly began to mend. He got better and better, till the doctor said he was out of danger. What was killing him was the dreadful fits of pain in his stomach. But little by little they stopped, and the poor marquis began to make his jokes again. The doctor found something that gave him great comfort—some white stuff that we kept in a great bottle on the chimney-piece. I used to give it to the marquis through a glass tube; it always made him easier. Then the doctor went away, after telling me to keep on giving him the mixture whenever he was bad. After that there was a little doctor from Poitiers, who came every day. So we were alone in the house—my lady and her poor husband and their three children. Young Madame de Bellegarde had gone away, with her little girl, to her mother's. You know she is very lively, and her maid told me that she didn't like to be where people were dying." Mrs. Bread paused a moment, and then she went on with the same quiet consistency. "I think you have guessed, sir, that when the marquis began to turn my lady was disappointed." And she paused again, bending upon Newman a face which seemed to grow whiter as the darkness settled down upon them.

Newman had listened eagerly—with an eagerness greater even than that with which he had bent his ear to Valentin de Bellegarde's last words. Every now and then, as his companion looked up at him, she reminded him of an ancient tabby cat, protracting the enjoyment of a dish of milk. Even her triumph was measured and decorous; the faculty of exultation had been chilled by disuse. She presently continued. "Late one night I was sitting by the marquis in his room, the great red room in the west tower. He had been complaining a little, and I gave him a spoonful of the doctor's dose. My lady had been there in the early part of the evening; she sat for more than an hour by his bed. Then she went away and left me alone. After midnight she came back, and her eldest son was with her. They went to the bed and looked at the marquis, and my lady took hold of his hand. Then she turned to me and said he was not so well; I remember how the marquis, without saying anything, lay staring at her. I can see his white face, at this moment, in the great black square between the bed-curtains. I said I didn't think he was very bad; and she told me to go to bed—she would sit a while with him. When the marquis saw me going he gave a sort of groan, and called out to me not to leave him; but Mr. Urbain opened the door for me and pointed the way out. The present marquis—perhaps you have noticed, sir—has a very proud way of giving orders, and I was there to take orders. I went to my room, but I wasn't easy; I couldn't tell you why. I didn't undress; I sat there waiting and listening. For what would you have said, sir? I couldn't have told you; for surely a poor gentleman might be comfortable with his wife and his son. It was as if I expected to hear the marquis moaning after me again. I listened, but I heard nothing. It was a very still night; I never knew a night so still. At last the very stillness itself seemed to frighten me, and I came out of my room and went very softly downstairs. In the anteroom, outside of the marquis's chamber, I found Mr. Urbain walking up and down. He asked me what I wanted, and I said I came back to relieve my lady. He said *he* would relieve my lady, and ordered me back to bed; but as I stood there, unwilling to turn away, the door of the room opened and my lady came out. I noticed she was very pale; she was very strange. She looked a moment at the count and at me, and then she held out her arms to the count. He went to her, and she fell upon him and hid her face. I went quickly past her into the room, and to the marquis's bed. He was lying there, very white, with his eyes shut, like a corpse. I took hold of his hand and spoke to him, and he felt to me like a dead man. Then I turned round; my lady and Mr. Urbain were there. 'My poor Bread,' said my lady, 'M. le Marquis is gone.' Mr. Urbain knelt down by the bed and said softly, '*Mon père, mon père*.'[7] I thought it wonderful strange, and asked my lady what in the world had happened, and why she hadn't called me. She said nothing had happened; that she had only been sitting there with the marquis, very quiet. She had closed her eyes, thinking she might sleep, and she had slept she didn't know how long. When she woke up he was dead. 'It's death, my son, it's death,' she said to the count. Mr. Urbain said they must have the doctor immediately, from Poitiers, and that he would ride off and fetch him. He kissed his father's face, and then he kissed his mother and went away. My lady and I stood there at the bedside. As I looked at the poor marquis it came into my head that he was not dead, that he was in a kind of swoon. And then my lady repeated, 'My poor Bread, it's death, it's death;' and I said, 'Yes, my lady, it's certainly death.' I said just the opposite to what I believed; it was my notion. Then my lady said we must wait for the doctor, and we sat there and waited. It was a long time; the poor marquis neither stirred nor changed. 'I have seen death before,' said my lady, 'and it's terribly like this.' 'Yes, please, my lady,' said I; and I kept thinking. The night wore away without the count's coming back, and my lady began to be frightened. She was afraid he had had an accident in the dark, or met with some wild people. At last she got so restless that she went below to watch in the court for her son's return. I sat there alone and the marquis never stirred."

Here Mrs. Bread paused again, and the most artistic of romancers could not have been more effective. Newman made a movement as if he were turning over the page of a novel. "So he *was* dead!" he exclaimed.

"Three days afterwards he was in his grave," said Mrs. Bread

7. **"My father, my father."**

sententiously. "In a little while I went away to the front of the house and looked out into the court, and there, before long, I saw Mr. Urbain ride in alone. I waited a bit, to hear him come upstairs with his mother, but they stayed below, and I went back to the marquis's room. I went to the bed and held up the light to him, but I don't know why I didn't let the candlestick fall. The marquis's eyes were open—open wide! they were staring at me. I knelt down beside him and took his hands, and begged him to tell me, in the name of wonder, whether he was alive or dead. Still he looked at me a long time, and then he made me a sign to put my ear close to him: 'I am dead,' he said, 'I am dead. The marquise has killed me.' I was all in a tremble. I didn't understand him. I didn't know what had become of him. He seemed both a man and a corpse if you can fancy, sir. 'But you'll get well, now, sir,' I said. And then he whispered again, ever so weak: 'I wouldn't get well, for a kingdom. I wouldn't be that woman's husband again. And then he said more; he said she had murdered him. I asked him what she had done to him, but he only replied: 'Murder, murder. And she'll kill my daughter,' he said; 'my poor unhappy child.' And he begged me to prevent that, and then he said that he was dying, that he was dead. I was afraid to move or to leave him; I was almost dead myself. All of a sudden he asked me to get a pencil and write for him; and then I had to tell him that I couldn't manage a pencil. He asked me to hold him up in bed while he wrote himself, and I said he could never, never do such a thing. But he seemed to have a kind of terror that gave him strength. I found a pencil in the room and a piece of paper and a book, and I put the paper on the book and the pencil into his hand, and moved the candle near him. You will think all this very strange, sir; and very strange it was. The strangest part of it was that I believed he was dying, and that I was eager to help him to write. I sat on the bed and put my arm round him, and held him up. I felt very strong; I believe I could have lifted him and carried him. It was a wonder how he wrote, but he did write, in a big scratching hand; he almost covered one side of the paper. It seemed a long time; I suppose it was three or four minutes. He was groaning, terribly, all the while. Then he said it was ended, and I let him down upon his pillows, and he gave me the paper and told me to fold it, and hide it, and to give it to those who would act upon it. 'Whom do you mean?' I said. 'Who are those who will act upon it?' But he only groaned, for an answer; he couldn't speak, for weakness. In a few minutes he told me to go and look at the bottle on the chimney-piece. I knew the bottle he meant; the white stuff that was good for his stomach. I went and looked at it, but it was empty. When I came back his eyes were open and he was staring at me; but soon he closed them and he said no more. I hid the paper in my dress; I didn't look at what was written upon it, though I can read very well, sir, if I haven't any hand-writing. I sat down near the bed, but it was nearly half an hour before my lady and the count came in. The marquis looked as he did when they left him, and I never said a word about his having been otherwise. Mr. Urbain said that the doctor had been called to a person in child-birth, but that he promised to set out for Fleurieres immediately. In another half hour he arrived, and as soon as he had examined the marquis he said that we had had a false alarm. The poor gentleman was very low, but he was still living. I watched my lady and her son when he said this, to see if they looked at each other, and I am obliged to admit that they didn't. The doctor said there was no reason he should die; he had been going on so well. And then he wanted to know how he had suddenly fallen off; he had left him so very hearty. My lady told her little story again—what she had told Mr. Urbain and me—and the doctor looked at her and said nothing. He stayed all the next day at the château, and hardly left the marquis. I was always there. Mademoiselle and Mr. Valentin came and looked at their father, but he never stirred. It was a strange, deathly stupor. My lady was always about; her face was as white as her husband's, and she looked very proud, as I had seen her look when her orders or her wishes had been disobeyed. It was as if the poor marquis had defied her; and the way she took it made me afraid of her. The apothecary from Poitiers kept the marquis along through the day, and we waited for the other doctor from Paris, who, as I told you, had been staying at Fleurières. They had telegraphed for him early in the morning, and in the evening he arrived. He talked a bit outside with the doctor from Poitiers, and then they came in to see the marquis together. I was with him, and so was Mr. Urbain. My lady had been to receive the doctor from Paris, and she didn't come back with him into the room. He sat down by the marquis—I can see him there now, with his hand on the marquis's wrist, and Mr. Urbain watching him with a little looking-glass in his hand. 'I'm sure he's better,' said the little doctor from Poitiers; 'I'm sure he'll come back.' A few moments after he had said this the marquis opened his eyes, as if he were waking up, and looked at us, from one to the other. I saw him look at me very softly, as you'd say. At the same moment my lady came in on tiptoe; she came up to the bed and put in her head between me and the count. The marquis saw her and gave a long, most wonderful moan. He said something we couldn't understand, and he seemed to have a kind of spasm. He shook all over and then closed his eyes, and the doctor jumped up and took hold of my lady. He held her for a moment a bit roughly. The marquis was stone dead! This time there were those there that knew."

Newman felt as if he had been reading by starlight the report of highly important evidence in a great murder case. "And the paper —the paper!" he said, excitedly. "What was written upon it?"

"I can't tell you, sir," answered Mrs. Bread. "I couldn't read it; it was in French."

"But could no one else read it?"

"I never asked a human creature."

"No one has ever seen it?"

"If you see it you'll be the first."

Newman seized the old woman's hand in both his own and pressed it vigorously. "I thank you ever so much for that," he cried. "I want to be the first; I want it to be my property and no one else's! You're the wisest old woman in Europe. And what did you do with the paper?" This information had made him feel extraordinarily strong. "Give it to me quick!"

Mrs. Bread got up with a certain majesty. "It is not so easy as that, sir. If you want the paper, you must wait."

"But waiting is horrible, you know," urged Newman.

"I am sure *I* have waited; I have waited these many years," said Mrs. Bread.

"That is very true. You have waited for me. I won't forget it. And yet, how comes it you didn't do as M. de Bellegarde said, show the paper to someone?"

"To whom should I show it?" answered Mrs. Bread mournfully. "It was not easy to know, and many's the night I have lain awake thinking of it. Six months afterwards, when they married Mademoiselle to her vicious old husband, I was very near bringing it out. I thought it was my duty to do something with it, and yet I was mightily afraid. I didn't know what was written on the paper, or how bad it might be, and there was no one I could trust enough to ask. And it seemed to me a cruel kindness to do that sweet young creature, letting her know that her father had written her mother down so shamefully; for that's what he did I suppose. I thought she would rather be unhappy with her husband than be unhappy that way. It was for her and for my dear Mr. Valentin I kept quiet. Quiet I call it, but for me it was a weary quietness. It worried me terribly, and it changed me altogether. But for others I held my tongue, and no one, to this hour, knows what passed between the poor marquis and me."

"But evidently there were suspicions," said Newman. "Where did Mr. Valentin get his ideas?"

"It was the little doctor from Poitiers. He was very ill-satisfied, and he made a great talk. He was a sharp Frenchman, and coming to the house, as he did, day after day, I suppose he saw more than he seemed to see. And indeed the way the poor marquis went off as soon as his eyes fell on my lady was a most shocking sight for anyone. The medical gentleman from Paris was much more accommodating, and he hushed up the other. But for all he could do Mr. Valentin and Mademoiselle heard something; they knew their father's death was somehow against nature. Of course they couldn't accuse their mother, and, as I tell you, I was as dumb as that stone. Mr. Valentin used to look at me sometimes, and his eyes seemed to shine, as if he were thinking of asking me something. I was dreadfully afraid he would speak, and I always looked away and went about my business. If I were to tell him, I was sure he would hate me afterwards, and that I could never have borne. Once I went up to him and took a great liberty; I kissed him, as I had kissed him when he was a child. 'You oughtn't to look so sad, sir,' I said; 'believe your poor old Bread. Such a gallant, handsome young man can have nothing to be sad about.' And I think he understood me; he understood that I was begging off, and he made up his mind in his own way. He went about with his unasked question in his mind, as I did with my untold tale; we were both afraid of bringing dishonour on a great house. And it was the same with Mademoiselle. She didn't know what had happened; she wouldn't know. My lady and Mr. Urbain asked me no questions because they had no reason. I was as still as a mouse. When I was younger my lady thought me a hussy, and now she thought me a fool. How should I have any ideas?"

"But you say the little doctor from Poitiers made a talk," said Newman. "Did no one take it up?"

"I heard nothing of it, sir. They are always talking scandal in these foreign countries—you may have noticed—and I suppose they shook their heads over Madame de Bellegarde. But after all, what could they say? The marquis had been ill, and the marquis had died; he had as good a right to die as anyone. The doctor couldn't say he had not come honestly by his cramps. The next year the little doctor left the place and bought a practice in Bordeaux, and if there has been any gossip it died out. And I don't think there could have been much gossip about my lady that anyone would listen to. My lady is so very respectable."

Newman, at this last affirmation, broke into an immense, resounding laugh. Mrs. Bread had begun to move away from the spot where they were sitting, and he helped her through the aperture in the wall and along the homeward path. "Yes," he said, "my lady's respectability is delicious; it will be a great crash!" They reached the empty space in front of the church, where they stopped a moment, looking at each other with something of an air of closer fellowship—like two sociable conspirators. "But what was it," said

Newman, "what was it she did to her husband? She didn't stab him or poison him."

"I don't know, sir; no one saw it."

"Unless it was Mr. Urbain. You say he was walking up and down, outside the room. Perhaps he looked through the keyhole. But no; I think that with his mother he would take it on trust."

"You may be sure I have often thought of it," said Mrs. Bread. "I am sure she didn't touch him with her hands. I saw nothing on him, anywhere. I believe it was in this way. He had a fit of his great pain, and he asked her for his medicine. Instead of giving it to him she went and poured it away, before his eyes. Then he saw what she meant, and, weak and helpless as he was, he was frightened, he was terrified. 'You want to kill me,' he said. 'Yes, M. le Marquis, I want to kill you,' says my lady, and sits down and fixes her eyes upon him. You know my lady's eyes, I think, sir; it was with them she killed him; it was with the terrible strong will she put into them. It was like a frost on flowers."

"Well, you are a very intelligent woman; you have shown great discretion," said Newman. "I shall value your services as housekeeper extremely."

They had begun to descend the hill, and Mrs. Bread said nothing until they reached the foot. Newman strolled lightly beside her; his head was thrown back as he was gazing at all the stars; he seemed to himself to be riding his vengeance along the Milky Way. "So you are serious, sir, about that?" said Mrs. Bread, softly.

"About your living with me? Why of course I take care of you to the end of your days. You can't live with those people any longer. And you oughtn't to, you know, after this. You give me the paper, and you move away."

"It seems very flighty in me to be taking a new place at this time of life," observed Mrs. Bread lugubriously. "But if you are going to turn the house upside down, I would rather be out of it."

"Oh," said Newman, in the cheerful tone of a man who feels rich in alternatives, "*I* don't think I shall bring in the constables, if that's what you mean. Whatever Madame de Bellegarde did, I am afraid the law can't take hold of it. But I am glad of that; it leaves it altogether to me!"

"You are a mighty bold gentleman, sir," murmured Mrs. Bread, looking at him round the edge of her great bonnet.

He walked with her back to the château; the curfew had tolled for the laborious villagers of Fleurières, and the street was unlighted and empty. She promised him that he should have the marquis's manuscript in half an hour. Mrs. Bread choosing not to go in by the great gate, they passed round by a winding lane to a door in the wall of the park, of which she had the key, and which would enable her to enter the château from behind. Newman arranged with her that he should await outside the wall her return with the coveted document.

She went in, and his half hour in the dusky lane seemed very long. But he had plenty to think about. At last the door in the wall opened and Mrs. Bread stood there, with one hand on the latch and the other holding out a scrap of white paper, folded small. In a moment he was master of it, and it had passed into his waistcoat-pocket. "Come and see me in Paris," he said; "we are to settle your future, you know; and I will translate poor M. de Bellegarde's French to you." Never had he felt so grateful as at this moment for M. Nioche's instructions.

Mrs. Bread's dull eyes had followed the disappearance of the paper, and she gave a heavy sigh. "Well, you have done what you would with me, sir, and I suppose you will do it again. You *must* take care of me now. You are a terribly positive gentleman."

"Just now," said Newman, "I'm a terribly impatient gentleman!" And he bade her good-night and walked rapidly back to the inn. He ordered his vehicle to be prepared for his return to Poitiers, and then he shut the door of the common salle and strode towards the solitary lamp on the chimney-piece. He pulled out the paper and quickly unfolded it. It was covered with pencil-marks, which at first, in the feeble light, seemed indistinct. But Newman's fierce curiosity forced a meaning from the tremulous signs. The English of them was as follows:

> "My wife has tried to kill me, and she has done it; I am dying, dying horribly. It is to marry my dear daughter to M. de Cintré. With all my soul I protest—I forbid it. I am not insane—ask the doctors, ask Mrs. B——. It was alone with me here, to-night; she attacked me and put me to death. It is murder, if murder ever was. Ask the doctors.
>
> "Henri-Urbain de Bellegarde."

Chapter XXIII

Newman returned to Paris the second day after his interview with Mrs. Bread. The morrow he had spent at Poitiers, reading over and over again the little document which he had lodged in his pocketbook, and thinking what he would do in the circumstances and how he would do it. He would not have said that Poitiers was an amusing place; yet the day seemed very short. Domiciled once more in the Boulevard Haussmann, he walked over to the Rue de l'Université and inquired of Madame de Bellegarde's portress whether the marquise had come back. The portress told him that she had arrived, with M. le Marquis, on the preceding day, and further informed him that if he desired to enter, Madame de Bellegarde and her son were both at home. As she said these words the little white-faced old woman who peered out of the dusky gatehouse of the Hôtel de Bellegarde gave a small wicked smile—a smile which seemed to Newman to mean, "Go in if you dare!" She was evidently versed in the current domestic history; she was placed where she could feel the pulse of the house. Newman stood a moment, twisting his moustache and looking at her; then he abruptly turned away. But this was not because he was afraid to go in—though he doubted whether, if he did so, he should be able to make his way, unchallenged, into the presence of Madame de Cintré's relatives. Confidence—excessive confidence, perhaps—quite as much as timidity prompted his retreat. He was nursing his thunderbolt; he loved it; he was unwilling to part with it. He seemed to be holding it aloft in the rumbling, vaguely-flashing air, directly over the heads of his victims, and he fancied he could see their pale upturned faces. Few specimens of the human countenance had ever given him such pleasure as these, lighted in the lurid fashion I have hinted at, and he was disposed to sip the cup of contemplative revenge in a leisurely fashion. It must be added, too, that he was at a loss to see exactly how he could arrange to witness the operation of his thunder. To send in his card to Madame de Bellegarde would be a waste of ceremony; she would certainly decline to receive him. On the other hand he could not force his way into her presence. It annoyed him keenly to think that he might be reduced to the blind satisfaction of writing her a letter; but he consoled himself in a measure with the reflection that a letter might lead to an interview. He went home, and feeling rather tired—nursing a vengeance was, it must be confessed, a rather fatiguing process; it took a good deal out of one—flung himself into one of his brocaded fauteuils, stretched his legs, thrust his hands into his pockets, and, while he watched the reflected sunset fading from the ornate house-tops on the opposite side of the Boulevard, began mentally to compose a cool epistle to Madame de Bellegarde. While he was so occupied his servant threw open the door and announced ceremoniously, "Madame Brett!"

Newman roused himself, expectantly, and in a few moments perceived upon his threshold the worthy woman with whom he had conversed to such good purpose on the starlit hill-top of Fleurières. Mrs. Bread had made for this visit the same toilet as for her former expedition. Newman was struck with her distinguished appearance. His lamp was not lit, and as her large grave face gazed at him through the light dusk from under the shadow of her ample bonnet, he felt the incongruity of such a person presenting herself as a servant. He greeted her with high geniality, and bade her come in and sit down and make herself comfortable. There was something which might have touched the springs both of mirth and of melancholy in the ancient maidenliness with which Mrs. Bread endeavoured to comply with these directions. She was not playing at being fluttered, which would have been simply ridiculous; she was doing her best to carry herself as a person so humble that, for her, even embarrassment would have been pretentious; but evidently she had never dreamed of its being in her horoscope to pay a visit, at nightfall, to a friendly single gentleman who lived in theatrical-looking rooms on one of the new boulevards.

"I truly hope I am not forgetting my place, sir," she murmured.

"Forgetting your place?" cried Newman. "Why, you are remembering it. This is your place, you know. You are already in my service; your wages, as housekeeper, began a fortnight ago. I can tell you my house wants keeping! Why don't you take off your bonnet and stay?"

"Take off my bonnet?" said Mrs. Bread, with timid literalness. "Oh sir, I haven't my cap. And with your leave, sir, I couldn't keep house in my best gown."

"Never mind your gown," said Newman cheerfully. "You shall have a better gown than that."

Mrs. Bread stared solemnly and then stretched her hands over her lustreless satin skirt, as if the perilous side of her situation was defining itself. "Oh sir, I am fond of my own clothes," she murmured.

"I hope you have left those wicked people, at any rate," said Newman.

"Well, sir, here I am!" said Mrs. Bread. "That's all I can tell you. Here I sit, poor Catherine Bread. It's a strange place for me to be. I don't know myself; I never supposed I was so bold. But indeed, sir, I have gone as far as my own strength will bear me."

"Oh come, Mrs. Bread," said Newman, almost caressingly, "don't make yourself uncomfortable. Now's the time to feel lively, you know."

She began to speak again with a trembling voice. "I think it would be more respectable if I could—if I could——" and her voice trembled to a pause.

"If you could give up this sort of thing altogether?" said Newman kindly, trying to anticipate her meaning, which he supposed might be a wish to retire from service.

"If I could give up everything, sir! All I should ask is a decent Protestant burial."

"Burial!" cried Newman, with a burst of laughter. "Why, to bury you now would be a sad piece of extravagance. It's only rascals who have to be buried to get respectable. Honest folks like you and me can live our time out—and live together. Come! did you bring your baggage?"

"My box is locked and corded; but I haven't yet spoken to my lady."

"Speak to her, then, and have done with it. I should like to have your chance!" cried Newman.

"I would gladly give it you, sir. I have passed some weary hours in my lady's dressing-room; but this will be one of the longest. She will tax me with ingratitude."

"Well," said Newman, "so long as you can tax her with murder——"

"Oh sir, I can't; not I," sighed Mrs. Bread.

"You don't mean to say anything about it? So much the better. Leave that to me."

"If she calls me a thankless old woman," said Mrs. Bread, "I shall have nothing to say. But it is better so," she softly added. "She shall be my lady to the last. That will be more respectable."

"And then you will come to me and I shall be your gentleman," said Newman; "that will be more respectable still!"

Mrs. Bread rose, with lowered eyes, and stood a moment; then, looking up, she rested her eyes upon Newman's face. The disordered proprieties were somehow settling to rest. She looked at Newman so long and so fixedly, with such a dull intense devotedness, that he himself might have had a pretext for embarrassment. At last she said gently: "You are not looking well, sir."

"That's natural enough," said Newman. "I have nothing to feel well about. To be very indifferent and very fierce, very dull and very jovial, very sick and very lively, all at once—why, it rather mixes one up."

Mrs. Bread gave a noiseless sigh. "I can tell you something that will make you feel duller still, if you want to feel all one way. About Madame de Cintré."

"What can you tell me?" Newman demanded. "Not that you have seen her?"

She shook her head. "No, indeed, sir, nor ever shall. That's the dulness of it. Nor my lady. Nor M. de Bellegarde."

"You mean that she is kept so close."

"Close, close," said Mrs. Bread, very softly.

These words, for an instant, seemed to check the beating of Newman's heart. He leaned back in his chair, staring up at the old woman. "They have tried to see her, and she wouldn't—she couldn't?"

"She refused—forever! I had it from my lady's own maid," said Mrs. Bread, "who had it from my lady. To speak of it to such a person my lady must have felt the shock. Madame de Cintré won't see them now, and now is her only chance. A while hence she will have no chance."

"You mean the other women—the mothers, the daughters, the sister; what is it they call them?—won't let her?"

"It is what they call the rule of the house—or of the order, I believe," said Mrs. Bread. "There is no rule so strict as that of the Carmelites. The bad women in the reformatories are fine ladies to them. They wear old brown cloaks—so the *femme de chambre*[8] told me—that you wouldn't use for a horse blanket. And the poor countess was so fond of soft-feeling dresses; she would never have anything stiff! They sleep on the ground," Mrs. Bread went on; "they are no better, no better"—and she hesitated for a comparison—"they are no better than tinkers' wives. They give up everything, down to the very name their poor old nurses called them by. They give up father and mother, brother and sister—to say nothing of other persons," Mrs. Bread delicately added. "They wear a shroud under their brown cloaks and a rope round their waists, and they get up on winter nights and go off into cold places to pray to the Virgin Mary. The Virgin Mary is a hard mistress!"

Mrs. Bread, dwelling on these terrible facts, sat dry-eyed and pale, with her hands clasped in her satin lap. Newman gave a melancholy groan and fell forward, leaning his head in his hands. There was a long silence, broken only by the ticking of the great gilded clock on the chimney-piece.

"Where is this place—where is the convent?" Newman asked at last, looking up.

"There are two houses," said Mrs. Bread. "I found out; I thought you would like to know—though it's poor comfort, I think. One is the Avenue de Messine; they have learned that Madame de Cintré is there. The other is in the Rue d'Enfer.[9] That's a terrible name; I suppose you know what it means."

Newman got up and walked away to the end of his long room. When he came back Mrs. Bread had got up, and stood by the fire with folded hands. "Tell me this," he said. "Can I get near her—even if I don't see her? Can I look through a grating, or some such thing, at the place where she is?"

It is said that all women love a lover, and Mrs. Bread's sense of the pre-established harmony which kept servants in their "place," even as planets in their orbits (not that Mrs. Bread had ever consciously likened herself to a planet), barely availed to temper the

8. Housemaid.

9. "Hell Street."

maternal melancholy with which she leaned her head on one side and gazed at her new employer. She probably felt for the moment as if, forty years before, she had held him also in her arms. "That wouldn't help you, sir. It would only make her seem farther away."

"I want to go there, at all events," said Newman. "Avenue de Messine, you say? And what is it they call themselves?"

"Carmelites," said Mrs. Bread.

"I shall remember that."

Mrs. Bread hesitated a moment, and then: "It's my duty to tell you this, sir," she went on. "The convent has a chapel, and some people are admitted on Sunday to the mass. You don't see the poor creatures that are shut up there, but I am told you can hear them sing. It's a wonder they have any heart for singing! Some Sunday I shall make bold to go. It seems to me I should know *her* voice in fifty."

Newman looked at his visitor very gratefully; then he held out his hand and shook hers. "Thank you," he said. "If anyone can get in, I will." A moment later Mrs. Bread proposed, deferentially, to retire, but he checked her and put a lighted candle into her hand. "There are half-a-dozen rooms there I don't use," he said, pointing through an open door. "Go and look at them and take your choice. You can live in the one you like best." From this bewildering opportunity Mrs. Bread at first recoiled; but finally, yielding to Newman's gentle, reassuring push, she wandered off into the dusk with her tremulous taper. She remained absent a quarter of an hour, during which Newman paced up and down, stopped occasionally to look out of the window at the lights on the Boulevard, and then resumed his walk. Mrs. Bread's relish for her investigations apparently increased as she proceeded; but at last she reappeared and deposited her candlestick on the chimney-piece.

"Well, have you picked one out?" asked Newman.

"A room, sir? They are all too fine for a dingy old body like me. There isn't one that hasn't a bit of gilding."

"It's only tinsel, Mrs. Bread," said Newman. "If you stay there a while it will all peel off of itself." And he gave a dismal smile.

"Oh, sir, there are things enough peeling off already!" rejoined Mrs. Bread, with a head-shake. "Since I was there I thought I would look about me. I don't believe you know, sir. The corners are most dreadful. You do want a house-keeper, that you do; you want a tidy Englishwoman that isn't above taking hold of a broom."

Newman assured her that he suspected, if he had not measured, his domestic abuses, and that to reform them was a mission worthy of her powers. She held her candlestick aloft again and looked round the salon with compassionate glances; then she intimated that she accepted the mission, and that its sacred character would sustain her in her rupture with Madame de Bellegarde. With this she curtsied herself away.

She came back the next day with her worldly goods, and Newman going into his drawing-room, found her upon her aged knees before a divan, sewing up some detached fringe. He questioned her as to her leave-taking with her late mistress, and she said it had proved easier than she feared. "I was perfectly civil, sir, but the Lord helped me to remember that a good woman has no call to tremble before a bad one."

"I should think so!" cried Newman. "And does she know you have come to me?"

"She asked me where I was going, and I mentioned your name," said Mrs. Bread.

"What did she say to that?"

"She looked at me very hard, and she turned very red. Then she bade me leave her. I was all ready to go, and I had got the coachman, who is an Englishman, to bring down my poor box, and to fetch me a cab. But when I went down myself to the gate I found it closed. My lady had sent orders to the porter not to let me pass, and by the same orders the porter's wife—she is a dreadful sly old body—had gone out in a cab to fetch home M. de Bellegarde from his club.

Newman slapped his knee. "She *is* scared! she *is* scared!" he cried exultantly.

"I was frightened too, sir," said Mrs. Bread, "but I was also mightily vexed. I took it very high with the porter, and asked him by what right he used violence to an honourable Englishwoman who had lived in the house for thirty years before he was heard of. Oh, sir, I was very grand, and I brought the man down. He drew his bolts, and let me out, and I promised the cabman something handsome if he would drive fast. But he was terribly slow; it seemed as if we should never reach your blessed door. I am all of a tremble still; it took me five minutes, just now, to thread my needle."

Newman told her, with a gleeful laugh, that if she chose she might have a little maid on purpose to thread her needles; and he went away murmuring to himself again that the old woman *was* scared—she *was* scared!

He had not shown Mrs. Tristram the little paper that he carried in his pocket-book, but since his return to Paris he had seen her several times, and she had told him that he seemed to her to be in a strange way—an even stranger way than his sad situation made natural. Had his disappointment gone to his head? He looked like a man who was going to be ill, and yet she had never seen him more restless and active. One day he would sit hanging his head and looking as if he were firmly resolved never to smile again; another he would indulge in laughter that was almost unseemly and made jokes that were bad even for him. If he was trying to carry off his sorrow, he at such times really went too far. She begged him of all things not to be "strange." Feeling in a measure responsible as she did for the affair which had turned out so ill for him, she could endure anything but his strangeness. He might be melancholy if he would, or he might be stoical; he might be cross and cantankerous with her and ask her why she had ever dared to meddle with his destiny: to this she would submit; for this she would make allowances. Only, for Heaven's sake, let him not be incoherent. That would be extremely unpleasant. It was like people talking in their sleep; they always frightened her. And Mrs. Tristram intimated that, taking very high ground as regards the moral obligation which events had laid upon her, she proposed not to rest quiet until she should have confronted him with the least inadequate substitute for Madame de Cintré that the two hemispheres contained.

"Oh," said Newman, "we are even now, and we had better not open a new account! You may bury me some day, but you shall never marry me. It's too rough. I hope, at any rate," he added, "that there is nothing incoherent in this—that I want to go next Sunday to the Carmelite chapel in the Avenue de Messine. You know one of the Catholic ministers—an abbé, is that it?—I have seen him here, you know; that motherly old gentleman with the big waistband. Please ask him if I need a special leave to go in, and if I do, beg him to obtain it for me."

Mrs. Tristram gave expression to the liveliest joy. "I am so glad you have asked me to do something!" she cried. "You shall get into the chapel if the abbé is disfrocked for his share in it." And two days afterwards she told him that it was all arranged; the abbé was enchanted to serve him, and if he would present himself civilly at the convent-gate there would be no difficulty.

Chapter XXIV

Sunday was as yet two days off; but meanwhile, to beguile his impatience, Newman took his way to the Avenue de Messine and got what comfort he could in staring at the blank outer wall of Madame de Cintré's present residence. The street in question, as some travellers will remember, adjoins the Parc Monceau, which is one of the prettiest corners of Paris. The quarter has an air of modern opulence and convenience which seems at variance with the ascetic institution, and the impression made upon Newman's gloomily-irritated gaze by the fresh-looking, windowless expanse behind which the woman he loved was perhaps even then pledging herself to pass the rest of her days was less exasperating than he had feared. The place suggested a convent with the modern improvements—an asylum in which privacy, though unbroken, might be not quite identical with privation, and meditation, though monotonous, might be of a cheerful cast. And yet he knew the case was otherwise; only at present it was not a reality to him. It was too strange and too mocking to be real; it was like a page torn out of a romance, with no context in his own experience.

On Sunday morning, at the hour which Mrs. Tristram had indicated, he rang at the gate in the blank wall. It instantly opened and admitted him into a clean, cold-looking court, from beyond which a dull, plain edifice looked down upon him. A robust lay sister with a cheerful complexion emerged from a porter's lodge, and, on his stating his errand, pointed to the open door of the chapel, an edifice which occupied the right side of the court and was preceded by a high flight of steps. Newman ascended the steps and immediately entered the open door. Service had not yet begun; the place was dimly lighted, and it was some moments before he could distinguish its features. Then he saw it was divided by a large close iron screen into two unequal portions. The altar was on the hither side of the screen, and between it and the entrance were disposed several benches and chairs. Three or four of these were occupied by vague, motionless figures—figures that he presently perceived to be women, deeply absorbed in their devotion. The place seemed to Newman very cold; the smell of the incense itself was cold. Besides this there was a twinkle of tapers and here and there a glow of coloured glass. Newman seated himself; the praying women kept still, with their backs turned. He saw they were visitors like himself, and he would have liked to see their faces; for he believed that they were the mourning mothers and sisters of other women who had had the same pitiless courage as Madame de Cintré. But they were better off than he, for they at least shared the faith to which the others had sacrificed themselves. Three or four persons came in; two of them were elderly gentlemen. Everyone was very quiet. Newman fastened his eyes upon the screen behind the altar. That was the convent, the real convent, the place where she was. But he could see nothing; no light came through the crevices. He got up and approached the partition very gently, trying to look through. But behind it there was darkness, with nothing stirring. He went back to his place, and after that a priest and two altar-boys came in and began to say mass.

Newman watched their genuflections and gyrations with a grim, still enmity; they seemed aids and abettors of Madame de Cintré's desertion; they were mouthing and droning out their triumph. The priest's long, dismal intonings acted upon his nerves and deepened his wrath; there was something defiant in his unintelligible drawl; it seemed meant for Newman himself. Suddenly there arose from the depths of the chapel, from behind the inexorable grating, a sound which drew his attention from the altar—the sound of a strange, lugubrious chant uttered by women's voices. It began softly, but it presently grew louder, and as it increased it became more of a wail and a dirge. It was the chant of the Carmelite nuns, their only human utterance. It was their dirge over their buried affections and over the vanity of earthly desires. At first Newman was bewildered—almost stunned—by the strangeness of the sound; then, as he comprehended its meaning, he listened intently and his heart began to throb. He listened for Madame de Cintré's voice, and in the very heart of the tuneless harmony he imagined he made it out. (We are obliged to believe that he was wrong, inasmuch as she had obviously not yet had time to become a member of the invisible sisterhood.) The chant kept on, mechanical and monotonous, with dismal repetitions and despairing cadences. It was hideous, it was horrible; as it continued, Newman felt that he needed all his self-control. He was growing more agitated; he felt tears in his eyes. At last, as in its full force the thought came over him that this confused, impersonal wail was all that he or the world she had deserted should ever hear of the voice he had found so sweet, he felt that he could bear it no longer. He rose abruptly and made his way out. On the threshold he paused, listened again to the dreary strain, and then hastily descended into the court. As he did so he saw that the good sister with the high-coloured cheeks and the fan-like frill to her coiffure, who had admitted him, was in conference at the gate with two persons who had just come in. A second glance informed him that these persons were Madame de Bellegarde and her son, and that they were about to avail themselves of that method of approach to Madame de Cintré which Newman had found but a mockery of consolation. As he crossed the court M. de Bellegarde recognised him; the marquis was coming to the steps, leading his mother. The old lady also gave Newman a look, and it resembled that of her son. Both faces expressed a franker perturbation, something more akin to the humbleness of dismay than Newman had yet seen in them. Evidently he startled the Bellegardes, and they had not their grand behaviour immediately in hand. Newman hurried past them, guided only by the desire to get out of the convent-walls into the street. The gate opened itself at his approach; he strode over the threshold and it closed behind him. A carriage, which appeared to have been standing there, was just turning away from the sidewalk. Newman looked at it for a moment, blankly; then he became conscious, through the dusky mist that swam before his eyes, that a lady seated in it was bowing to him. The vehicle had turned away before he recognised her; it was an ancient landau with one half the cover lowered. The lady's bow was very positive and accompanied with a smile; a little girl was seated beside her. He raised his hat, and then the lady bade the coachman stop.

The carriage halted again beside the pavement, and she sat there and beckoned to Newman—beckoned with the demonstrative grace of Madame Urbain de Bellegarde. Newman hesitated a moment before he obeyed her summons; during this moment he had time to curse his stupidity for letting the others escape him. He had been wondering how he could get at them; fool that he was for not stopping them then and there! What better place than beneath the very prison-walls to which they had consigned the promise of his joy? He had been too bewildered to stop them, but now he felt ready to wait for them at the gate. Madame Urbain, with a certain attractive petulance, beckoned to him again, and this time he went over to the carriage. She leaned out and gave him her hand, looking at him kindly, and smiling.

"Ah monsieur," she said, "you don't include me in your wrath? I had nothing to do with it."

"Oh, I don't suppose *you* could have prevented it!" Newman answered in a tone which was not that of studied gallantry.

"What you say is too true for me to resent the small account it makes of my influence. I forgive you, at any rate, because you look as if you had seen a ghost."

"I have!" said Newman.

"I am glad, then, I didn't go in with Madame de Bellegarde and my husband. You must have seen them, eh? Was the meeting affectionate? Did you hear the chanting? They say it's like the lamentations of the damned. I wouldn't go in: one is certain to hear that soon enough. Poor Claire—in a white shroud and a big brown cloak! That's the *toilette*[1] of the Carmelites, you know. Well, she was always fond of long, loose things. But I must not speak of her to you; only I must say that I am very sorry for you, that if I could have helped you I would, and that I think everyone has been very shabby. I was afraid of it, you know; I felt it in the air for a fortnight before it came. When I saw you at my mother-in-law's ball, taking it all so easily, I felt as if you were dancing on your grave. But what could I do? I wish you all the good I can think of. You will say that isn't much! Yes; they have been very shabby; I am not a bit afraid to say it; I assure you everyone thinks so. We are not all like that. I am sorry I am not going to see you again; you know I think you very good company. I would prove it by

1. Attire; habit.

asking you to get into the carriage and drive with me for a quarter of an hour, while I wait for my mother-in-law. Only if we were seen—considering what has passed, and everyone knows you have been turned away—it might be thought I was going a little too far, even for me. But I shall see you sometimes—somewhere, eh? You know"—this was said in English—"we have a plan for a little amusement."

Newman stood there with his hand on the carriage-door, listening to this consolatory murmur with an unlighted eye. He hardly knew what Madame de Bellgarde was saying; he was only conscious that she was chattering ineffectively. But suddenly it occurred to him that, with her pretty professions, there was a way of making her effective; she might help him to get at the old woman and the marquis. "They are coming back soon—your companions?" he said. "You are waiting for them?"

"They will hear the mass out; there is nothing to keep them longer. Claire has refused to see them."

"I want to speak to them," said Newman; "and you can help me, you can do me a favour. Delay your return for five minutes and give me a chance at them. I will wait for them here."

Madame de Bellegarde clasped her hands with a tender grimace. "My poor friend, what do you want to do to them? To beg them to come back to you? It will be wasted words. They will never come back!"

"I want to speak to them, all the same. Pray do what I ask you. Stay away and leave them to me for five minutes; you needn't be afraid; I shall not be violent; I am very quiet."

"Yes, you look very quiet! If they had *le cœur tendre*[2] you would move them. But they haven't! However, I will do better for you than what you propose. The understanding is not that I shall come back for them. I am going to the Parc Monceau with my little girl to give her a walk, and my mother-in-law, who comes so rarely into this quarter, is to profit by the same opportunity to take the air. We are to wait for her in the park, where my husband is to bring her to us. Follow me now; just within the gates I shall get out of my carriage. Sit down on a chair in some quiet corner and I will bring them near you. There's devotion for you! *Le reste vous regarde.*"[3]

This proposal seemed to Newman extremely felicitous; it revived his drooping spirit, and he reflected that Madame Urbain was not such a goose as she seemed. He promised immediately to overtake her, and the carriage drove away.

The Parc Monceau is a very pretty piece of landscape-gardening, but Newman, passing into it, bestowed little attention upon its

2. "The tender heart"—meaning, "If they were tenderhearted."

3. "The rest is your business."

elegant vegetation, which was full of the freshness of spring. He found Madame de Bellegarde promptly, seated in one of the quiet corners of which she had spoken, while before her, in the alley, her little girl, attended by the footman and the lap-dog, walked up and down as if she were taking a lesson in deportment. Newman sat down beside the mamma, and she talked a great deal, apparently with the design of convincing him that—if he would only see it—poor dear Claire did not belong to the most fascinating type of woman. She was too tall and thin, too stiff and cold; her mouth was too wide and her nose too narrow. She had no dimples anywhere. And then she was eccentric, eccentric in cold blood; she was an Anglaise, after all. Newman was very impatient; she was counting the minutes until his victims should reappear. He sat silent, leaning upon his cane, looking absently and insensibly at the little marquise. At length Madame de Bellegarde said she would walk toward the gate of the park and meet her companions; but before she went she dropped her eyes, and, after playing a moment with the lace of her sleeve, looked up again at Newman.

"Do you remember," she asked, "the promise you made me three weeks ago?" And then, as Newman, vainly consulting his memory, was obliged to confess that the promise had escaped it, she declared that he had made her, at the time, a very queer answer—an answer at which, viewing it in the light of the sequel, she had fair ground for taking offence. "You promised to take me to Bullier's[4] after your marriage. After your marriage—you made a great point of that. Three days after that your marriage was broken off. Do you know, when I heard the news, the first thing I said to myself? 'Oh heaven, now he won't go with me to Bullier's!' And I really began to wonder if you had not been expecting the rupture."

"Oh, my dear lady," murmured Newman, looking down the path to see if the others were not coming.

"I shall be good-natured," said Madame de Bellegarde. "One must not ask too much of a gentleman who is in love with a cloistered nun. Besides, I can't go to Bullier's while we are in mourning. But I haven't given it up for that. The *partie*[5] is arranged; I have my cavalier. Lord Deepmere, if you please! He has gone back to his dear Dublin; but a few months hence I am to name any evening and he will come over from Ireland on purpose. That's what I call gallantry!"

Shortly after this Madame de Bellegarde walked away with her little girl. Newman sat in his place; the time seemed terribly long. He felt how fiercely his quarter of an hour in the convent chapel had raked over the glowing coals of his resentment. Madame de Belle-

4. A dance, the Bal Bullier.

5. Match.

garde kept him waiting, but she proved as good as her word. At last she reappeared at the end of the path, with her little girl and her footman; beside her slowly walked her husband, with his mother on his arm. They were a long time advancing, during which Newman sat unmoved. Tingling as he was with passion, it was extremely characteristic of him that he was able to moderate his expression of it, as he would have turned down a flaring gas-burner. His native coolness, shrewdness, and deliberateness, his life-long submissiveness to the sentiment that words were acts and acts were steps in life, and that in this matter of taking steps curveting and prancing were exclusively reserved for quadrupeds and foreigners—all this admonished him that rightful wrath had no connection with being a fool and indulging in spectacular violence. So as he rose, when old Madame de Bellegarde and her son were close to him, he only felt very tall and light. He had been sitting beside some shrubbery, in such a way as not to be noticeable at a distance; but M. de Bellegarde had evidently already perceived him. His mother and he were holding their course, but Newman stepped in front of them, and they were obliged to pause. He lifted his hat slightly, and looked at them for a moment; they were pale with amazement and disgust.

"Excuse me for stopping you," he said in a low tone, "but I must profit by the occasion. I have ten words to say to you. Will you listen to them?"

The marquis glared at him and then turned to his mother. "Can Mr. Newman possibly have anything to say that is worth our listening to?"

"I assure you I have something," said Newman; "besides, it is my duty to say it. It's a notification—a warning."

"Your duty?" said old Madame de Bellegarde, her thin lips curving like scorched paper. "This is your affair, not ours."

Madame Urbain meanwhile had seized her little girl by the hand, with a gesture of surprise and impatience which struck Newman, intent as he was upon his own words, with its dramatic effectiveness. "If Mr. Newman is going to make a scene in public," she exclaimed, "I will take my poor child out of the *mêlée*.[6] She is too young to see such naughtiness!" and she instantly resumed her walk.

"You had much better listen to me," Newman went on. "Whether you do or not, things will be disagreeable for you; but at any rate you will be prepared."

"We have already heard something of your threats," said the marquis, "and you know what we think of them."

"You think a good deal more than you admit. A moment,"

6. Dispute.

Newman added in reply to an exclamation of the old lady. "I remember perfectly that we are in a public place, and you see I am very quiet. I am not going to tell your secret to the passers-by; I shall keep it, to begin with, for certain picked listeners. Anyone who observes us will think that we are having a friendly chat, and that I am complimenting you, madam, on your venerable virtues."

The marquis gave three short sharp raps on the ground with his stick. "I demand of you to step out of our path!" he hissed.

Newman instantly complied, and M. de Bellegarde stepped forward with his mother. Then Newman said: "Half an hour hence Madame de Bellegarde will regret that she didn't learn exactly what I mean."

The marquise had taken a few steps, but at these words she paused, looking at Newman with eyes like two scintillating globules of ice. "You are like a peddler with something to sell," she said, with a little cold laugh which only partially concealed the tremor in her voice.

"Oh no, not to sell," Newman rejoined; "I give it to you for nothing." And he approached nearer to her, looking her straight in the eyes. "You killed your husband," he said, almost in a whisper. "That is, you tried once and failed, and then, without trying, you succeeded."

Madame de Bellegarde closed her eyes and gave a little cough, which, as a piece of dissimulation, struck Newman as really heroic. "Dear mother," said the marquis, "does this stuff amuse you so much?"

"The rest is more amusing," said Newman. "You had better not lose it."

Madame de Bellegarde opened her eyes; the scintillations had gone out of them; they were fixed and dead. But she smiled superbly with her narrow little lips, and repeated Newman's word. "Amusing? Have I killed someone else?"

"I don't count your daughter," said Newman, "though I might! Your husband knew what you were doing. I have a proof of it, whose existence you have never suspected." And he turned to the marquis, who was terribly white—whiter than Newman had ever seen anyone out of a picture. "A paper written by the hand, and signed with the name of Henri-Urbain de Bellegarde. Written after you, madam, had left him for dead, and while you, sir, had gone—not very fast—for the doctor."

The marquis looked at his mother; she turned away, looking vaguely round her. "I must sit down," she said in a low tone, going toward the bench on which Newman had been sitting.

"Couldn't you have spoken to me alone?" said the marquis to Newman, with a strange look.

"Well, yes, if I could have been sure of speaking to your mother alone, too," Newman answered. "But I have had to take you as I could get you."

Madame de Bellegarde, with a movement very eloquent of what he would have called her "grit," her steel-cold pluck and her instinctive appeal to her own personal resources, drew her hand out of her son's arm and went and seated herself upon the bench. There she remained, with her hands folded in her lap, looking straight at Newman. The expression of her face was such that he fancied at first that she was smiling; but he went and stood in front of her, and saw that her elegant features were distorted by agitation. He saw, however, equally, that she was resisting her agitation with all the rigour of her inflexible will, and there was nothing like either fear or submission in her stony stare. She had been startled, but she was not terrified. Newman had an exasperating feeling that she would get the better of him still; he would not have believed it possible that he could so utterly fail to be touched by the sight of a woman (criminal or other) in so tight a place. Madame de Bellegarde gave a glance at her son which seemed tantamount to an injunction to be silent and leave her to her own devices. The marquis stood beside her, with his hands behind him, looking at Newman.

"What paper is this you speak of?" asked the old lady, with an imitation of tranquillity which would have been applauded in a veteran actress.

"Exactly what I have told you," said Newman. "A paper written by your husband after you had left him for dead, and during the couple of hours before you returned. You see he had the time; you shouldn't have stayed away so long. It declares distinctly his wife's murderous intent."

"I should like to see it," Madame de Bellegarde observed.

"I thought you might," said Newman, "and I have taken a copy." And he drew from his waistcoat-pocket a small folded sheet.

"Give it to my son," said Madame de Bellegarde. Newman handed it to the marquis, whose mother, glancing at him, said simply, "Look at it." M. de Bellegarde's eyes had a pale eagerness which it was useless for him to try to dissimulate; he took the paper in his light-gloved fingers and opened it. There was a silence, during which he read it. He had more than time to read it, but still he said nothing; he stood staring at it. "Where is the original?" asked Madame de Bellegarde, in a voice which was really a consummate negation of impatience.

"In a very safe place. Of course I can't show you that," said Newman. "You might want to take hold of it," he added with conscious quaintness. "But that's a very correct copy—except, of course, the handwriting. I am keeping the original to show someone else."

M. de Bellegarde at last looked up, and his eyes were still very eager. "To whom do you mean to show it?"

"Well, I'm thinking of beginning with the duchess," said Newman; "that stout lady I saw at your ball. She asked me to come and see her, you know. I thought at the moment I shouldn't have much to say to her; but my little document will give us something to talk about."

"You had better keep it, my son," said Madame de Bellegarde.

"By all means," said Newman; "keep it and show it to your mother when you get home."

"And after showing it to the duchess?" asked the marquis, folding the paper and putting it away.

"Well, I'll take up the dukes," said Newman. "Then the counts and the barons—all the people you had the cruelty to introduce me to in a character of which you meant immediately to deprive me. I have made out a list."

For a moment neither Madame de Bellegarde nor her son said a word; the old lady sat with her eyes upon the ground; M. de Bellegarde's blanched pupils were fixed upon her face. Then, looking at Newman, "Is that all you have to say?" she asked.

"No, I want to say a few words more. I want to say that I hope you quite understand what I'm about. This is my revenge, you know. You have treated me before the world—convened for the express purpose—as if I were not good enough for you. I mean to show the world that however bad I may be, you are not quite the people to say it."

Madame de Bellegarde was silent again, and then she broke her silence. Her self-possession continued to be extraordinary. "I needn't ask you who has been your accomplice. Mrs. Bread told me that you had purchased her services."

"Don't accuse Mrs. Bread of venality," said Newman. "She has kept your secret all these years. She had given you a long respite. It was beneath her eyes your husband wrote that paper; he put it into her hands with a solemn injunction that she was to make it public. She was too good-hearted to make use of it."

The old lady appeared for an instant to hesitate, and then, "She was my husband's mistress," she said softly. This was the only concession to self-defence that she condescended to make.

"I doubt that," said Newman.

Madame de Bellegarde got up from her bench. "It was not to your opinions I undertook to listen, and if you have nothing left but them to tell me I think this remarkable interview may terminate."

And turning to the marquis she took his arm again. "My son," she said, "say something!"

M. de Bellegarde looked down at his mother, passing his hand over his forehead, and then, tenderly, caressingly, "What shall I say?" he asked.

"There is only one thing to say," said the marquise. "That it was really not worth while to have interrupted our walk."

But the marquis thought he could improve this. "Your paper's a forgery," he said to Newman.

Newman shook his head a little, with a tranquil smile. "M. de Bellegarde," he said, "your mother does better. She has done better all along, from the first of my knowing you. You're a mighty plucky woman, madam," he continued. "It's a great pity you have made me your enemy. I should have been one of your greatest admirers."

"*Mon pauvre ami,*"[7] said Madame de Bellegarde to her son in French, and as if she had not heard these words, "you must take me immediately to my carriage."

Newman stepped back and let them leave him; he watched them a moment and saw Madame Urbain, with her little girl, come out of a by-path to meet them. The old lady stooped and kissed her grandchild. "Damn it, she *is* plucky!" said Newman, and he walked home with a slight sense of being balked. She was so inexpressively defiant! But on reflection he decided that what he had witnessed was no real sense of security, still less a real innocence. It was only a very superior style of brazen assurance. "Wait till she reads the paper!" he said to himself; and he concluded that he should hear from her soon.

He heard sooner than he expected. The next morning, before midday, when he was about to give orders for his breakfast to be served, M. de Bellegarde's card was brought to him. "She has read the paper and she has passed a bad night," said Newman. He instantly admitted his visitor, who came in with the air of the ambassador of a great power meeting the delegate of a barbarous tribe whom an absurd accident had enabled for the moment to be abominably annoying. The ambassador, at all events, had passed a bad night, and his faultlessly careful toilet only threw into relief the frigid rancour in his eyes and the mottled tones of his refined complexion. He stood before Newman a moment, breathing quickly and softly, and shaking his forefinger curtly as his host pointed to a chair.

7. "My poor dear" (literally, "My poor friend").

"What I have come to say is soon said," he declared, "and can only be said without ceremony."

"I am good for as much or for as little as you desire," said Newman.

The marquis looked round the room a moment, and then: "On what terms will you part with your scrap of paper?"

"On none!" And while Newman, with his head on one side and his hands behind him sounded the marquis's turbid gaze with his own, he added: "Certainly, that is not worth sitting down about."

M. de Bellegarde meditated a moment, as if he had not heard Newman's refusal. "My mother and I, last evening," he said, "talked over your story. You will be surprised to learn that we think your little document is—a"—and he held back his word a moment—"is genuine."

"You forget that with you I am used to surprises!" exclaimed Newman, with a laugh.

"The very smallest amount of respect that we owe to my father's memory," the marquis continued, "makes us desire that he should not be held up to the world as the author of so—so infernal an attack upon the reputation of a wife whose only fault was that she had been submissive to accumulated injury."

"Oh, I see," said Newman. "It's for your father's sake." And he laughed the laugh in which he indulged when he was most amused —a noiseless laugh, with his lips closed.

But M. de Bellegarde's gravity held good. "There are a few of my father's particular friends for whom the knowledge of so—so unfortunate an—inspiration—would be a real grief. Even say we firmly established by medical evidence the presumption of a mind disordered by fever, *il en resterait quelque chose*.[8] At the best it would look ill in him. Very ill!"

"Don't try medical evidence," said Newman. "Don't touch the doctors and they won't touch you. I don't mind your knowing that I have not written to them."

Newman fancied that he saw signs in M. de Bellegarde's discoloured mask that this information was extremely pertinent. But it may have been merely fancy; for the marquis remained majestically argumentative. "For instance, Madame d'Outreville," he said, "of whom you spoke yesterday. I can imagine nothing that would shock her more."

"Oh, I am quite prepared to shock Madame d'Outreville, you know. That's on the cards. I expect to shock a great many people."

M. de Bellegarde examined for a moment the stitching on the back of one of his gloves. Then, without looking up, "We don't offer you money," he said. "That we suppose to be useless."

8. "There would still remain a suspicion."

Newman, turning away, took a few turns about the room, and then came back. "What *do* you offer me? By what I can make out, the generosity is all to be on my side."

The marquis dropped his arms at his side and held his head a little higher. "What we offer you is a chance—a chance that a gentleman should appreciate. A chance to abstain from inflicting a terrible blot upon the memory of a man who certainly had his faults, but who, personally, had done you no wrong."

"There are two things to say to that," said Newman. "The first is, as regards appreciating your 'chance,' that you don't consider me a gentleman. That's your great point, you know. It's a poor rule that won't work both ways. The second is that—well, in a word, you are talking great nonsense!"

Newman, who in the midst of his bitterness had, as I have said, kept well before his eyes a certain ideal of saying nothing rude, was immediately somewhat regretfully conscious of the sharpness of these words. But he speedily observed that the marquis took them more quietly than might have been expected. M. de Bellegarde, like the stately ambassador that he was, continued the policy of ignoring what was disagreeable in his adversary's replies. He gazed at the gilded arabesques on the opposite wall, and then presently transferred his glance to Newman, as if he too were a large grotesque in a rather vulgar system of chamber-decoration. "I suppose you know that as regards yourself, it won't do at all."

"How do you mean it won't do?"

"Why, of course you damn yourself. But I suppose that's in your programme. You propose to throw mud at us; you believe, you hope, that some of it may stick. We know, of course, it can't," explained the marquis in a tone of conscious lucidity; "but you take the chance, and are willing at any rate to show that you yourself have dirty hands."

"That's a good comparison; at least half of it is," said Newman. "I take the chance of something sticking. But as regards my hands, they are clean. I have taken the matter up with my finger-tips."

M. de Bellegarde looked a moment into his hat. "All our friends are quite with us," he said. "They would have done exactly as we have done."

"I shall believe that when I hear them say it. Meanwhile I shall think better of human nature."

The marquis looked into his hat again. "Madame de Cintré was extremely fond of her father. If she knew of the existence of the few written words of which you propose to make this scandalous use, she would demand of you proudly for his sake to give it up to her, and she would destroy it without reading it."

"Very possibly," Newman rejoined. "But she will not know. I

was in that convent yesterday, and I know what *she* is doing. Lord deliver us! You can guess whether it made me feel forgiving!"

M. de Bellegarde appeared to have nothing more to suggest; but he continued to stand there, rigid and elegant, as a man who believed that his mere personal presence had an argumentative value. Newman watched him, and, without yielding an inch on the main issue, felt an incongruously good-natured impulse to help him to retreat in good order.

"Your visit's a failure, you see," he said. "You offer too little."

"Propose something yourself," said the marquis.

"Give me back Madame de Cintré in the same state in which you took her from me."

"M. de Bellegarde threw back his head and his pale face flushed. "Never!" he said.

"You can't!"

"We wouldn't if we could! In the sentiment which led us to deprecate her marriage nothing is changed."

" 'Deprecate' is good!" cried Newman. "It was hardly worth while to come here only to tell me that you are not ashamed of yourselves. I could have guessed that!"

The marquis slowly walked toward the door, and Newman, following, opened it for him. "What you propose to do will be very disagreeable," M. de Bellegarde said. "That is very evident. But it will be nothing more."

"As I understand it," Newman answered, "that will be quite enough!"

M. de Bellegarde stood a moment looking on the ground, as if he were ransacking his ingenuity to see what else he could do to save his father's reputation. Then, with a little cold sigh, he seemed to signify that he regretfully surrendered the late marquis to the penalty of his turpitude. He gave a hardly perceptible shrug, took his neat umbrella from the servant in the vestibule, and, with his gentlemanly walk, passed out. Newman stood listening till he heard the door close; then he slowly exclaimed: "Well, I ought to begin to be satisfied now!"

Chapter XXV

Newman called upon the comical duchess and found her at home. An old gentleman with a high nose and a gold-headed cane was just taking leave of her; he made Newman a protracted obeisance as he retired, and our hero supposed that he was one of the mysterious grandees with whom he had shaken hands at Madame de Bellegarde's ball. The duchess, in her armchair, from which she did not move, with a great flower-pot on one side of her, a pile of pink-covered novels on the other, and a large piece of tapestry depending from her lap, presented an expansive and imposing front; but her aspect was in the highest degree gracious, and there was nothing in her manner to check the effusion of his confidence. She talked to him about flowers and books, getting launched with marvellous promptitude; about the theatres, about the peculiar institutions of his native country, about the humidity of Paris, about the pretty complexions of the American ladies, about his impressions of France and his opinion of its female inhabitants. All this was a brilliant monologue on the part of the duchess, who, like many of her countrywomen, was a person of an affirmative rather than an interrogative cast of mind, who made *mots*[9] and put them herself into circulation, and who was apt to offer you a present of a convenient little opinion, neatly enveloped in the gilt paper of a happy Gallicism.[1] Newman had come to her with a grievance, but he found himself in an atmosphere in which apparently no cognisance was taken of grievances; an atmosphere into which the chill of discomfort had never penetrated, and which seemed exclusively made up of mild, sweet, stale intellectual perfumes. The feeling with which he had watched Madame d'Outreville at the treacherous festival of the Bellegardes came back to him; she struck him as a wonderful old lady in a comedy, particularly well up in her part. He observed before long that she asked him no questions about their common friends; she made no allusion to the circumstances under which he had been presented to her. She neither feigned ignorance of a change in these circumstances nor pretended to condole with him upon it; but she smiled and discoursed and compared the tender-tinted wools of her tapestry, as if the Bellegardes and their wickedness were not of this world. "She is fighting shy!" said Newman to himself; and, having made the observation, he was prompted to observe, further, how the duchess would carry off her indifference. She did so in a masterly manner. There was not a gleam of disguised consciousness in those small, clear, demonstrative eyes which constituted her nearest claim to personal loveliness; there was not a symptom of apprehension that Newman would trench upon the ground she proposed to avoid. "Upon my word, she does it very well," he tacitly commented. "They all hold together bravely, and, whether anyone else can trust them or not, they can certainly trust each other."

Newman, at this juncture, fell to admiring the duchess for her fine manners. He felt, most accurately, that she was not a grain less urbane than she would have been if his marriage were still in prospect; but he felt also that she was not a particle more urbane.

9. Witty remarks.

1. A felicitous turn of phrase in French.

He had come, so reasoned the duchess—Heaven knew why he had come, after what had happened; and for the half hour, therefore, she would be *charmante*.[2] But she would never see him again. Finding no ready-made opportunity to tell his story, Newman pondered these things more dispassionately than might have been expected; he stretched his legs, as usual, and even chuckled a little, appreciatively and noiselessly. And then as the duchess went on relating a *mot* with which her mother had snubbed the great Napoleon, it occurred to Newman that her evasion of a chapter of French history more interesting to himself might possibly be the result of an extreme consideration for his feelings. Perhaps it was delicacy on the duchess's part—not policy. He was on the point of saying something himself, to make the chance which he had determined to give her still better, when the servant announced another visitor. The duchess, on hearing the name—it was that of an Italian prince—gave a little imperceptible pout, and said to Newman, rapidly: "I beg you to remain; I desire this visit to be short." Newman said to himself, at this, that Madame d'Outreville intended, after all, that they should discuss the Bellegardes together.

The prince was a short stout man, with a head disproportionately large. He had a dusky complexion and a bushy eyebrow, beneath which his eye wore a fixed and somewhat defiant expression; he seemed to be challenging you to insinuate that he was top-heavy. The duchess, judging from her charge to Newman, regarded him as a bore; but this was not apparent from the unchecked flow of her conversation. She made a fresh series of *mots,* characterised with great felicity the Italian intellect and the taste of the figs at Sorrento, predicted the ultimate future of the Italian kingdom (disgust with the brutal Sardinian rule[3] and complete reversion, throughout the peninsula, to the sacred sway of the Holy Father),[4] and, finally, gave a history of the love affairs of the Princess X——. This narrative provoked some rectifications on the part of the prince, who, as he said, pretended to know something about that matter; and having satisfied himself that Newman was in no laughing mood, either with regard to the size of his head or anything else, he entered into the controversy with an animation for which the duchess, when she set him down as a bore, could not have been prepared. The sentimental vicissitudes of the Princess X—— led to a discussion of the heart-history of Florentine nobility in general; the duchess had spent five weeks in Florence and had gathered much information on the subject. This was merged, in turn, in an

2. Charming.
3. After the annexation in 1861 of the Two Sicilies, Victor Emmanuel II of Sardinia was proclaimed King of Italy.
4. The pope.

examination of the Italian heart *per se*.[5] The duchess took a brilliantly heterodox view—thought it the least susceptible organ of its kind that she had ever encountered, related examples of its want of susceptibility, and at last declared that for her the Italians were a people of ice. The prince became flame to refute her, and his visit really proved charming. Newman was naturally out of the conversation; he sat with his head a little on one side watching the interlocutors. The duchess, as she talked, frequently looked at him with a smile, as if to intimate, in the charming manner of her nation, that it lay only with him to say something very much to the point. But he said nothing at all, and at last his thoughts began to wander. A singular feeling came over him—a sudden sense of the folly of his errand. What under the sun had he to say to the duchess, after all? Wherein would it profit him to tell her that the Bellegardes were traitors and that the old lady, into the bargain, was a murderess? He seemed morally to have turned a sort of somersault, and to find things looking differently in consequence. He felt a sudden stiffening of his will and quickening of his reserve. What in the world had he been thinking of when he fancied the duchess could help him, and that it would conduce to his comfort to make her think ill of the Bellegardes? What did her opinion of the Bellegardes matter to him? It was only a shade more important than the opinion the Bellegardes entertained of her. The duchess help him—that cold, stout, soft, artificial woman help him?—she who in the last twenty minutes had built up between them a wall of polite conversation in which she evidently flattered herself that he would never find a gate. Had it come to that—that he was asking favours of conceited people, and appealing for sympathy where he had no sympathy to give? He rested his arms on his knees, and sat for some minutes staring into his hat. As he did so his ears tingled—he had come very near being an ass. Whether or no the duchess would hear his story, he wouldn't tell it. Was he to sit there another half hour for the sake of exposing the Bellegardes? The Bellegardes be hanged! He got up abruptly, and advanced to shake hands with his hostess.

"You can't stay longer?" she asked very graciously.

"I am afraid not," he said.

She hesitated a moment, and then, "I had an idea you had something particular to say to me," she declared.

Newman looked at her; he felt a little dizzy; for the moment he seemed to be turning his somersault again. The little Italian prince came to his help: "Ah, madam, who has not that?" he softly sighed.

5. In and of itself, intrinsically.

"Don't teach Mr. Newman to say *fadaises*,"[6] said the duchess. "It is his merit that he doesn't know how."

"Yes, I don't know how to say *fadaises*," said Newman, "and I don't want to say anything unpleasant."

"I am sure you are very considerate," said the duchess with a smile; and she gave him a little nod for good-bye, with which he took his departure.

Once in the street, he stood for some time on the pavement, wondering whether, after all, he was not an ass not to have discharged his pistol. And then he decided that to talk to anyone whomsoever about the Bellegardes would be extremely disagreeable to him. The least disagreeable thing, under the circumstances, was to banish them from his mind, and never think of them again. Indecision had not hitherto been one of Newman's weaknesses, and in this case it was not of long duration. For three days after this he did not, or at least he tried not to, think of the Bellegardes. He dined with Mrs. Tristram, and on her mentioning their name, he begged her almost severely to desist. This gave Tom Tristram a much-coveted opportunity to offer his condolences.

He leaned forward, laying his hand on Newman's arm, compressing his lips, and shaking his head. "The fact is, my dear fellow, you see, that you ought never to have gone into it. It was not your doing, I know—it was all my wife. If you want to come down on her, I'll stand off: I give you leave to hit her as hard as you like. You know she has never had a word of reproach from me in her life, and I think she is in need of something of the kind. Why didn't you listen to *me?* You know I didn't believe in the thing. I thought it at the best an amiable delusion. I don't profess to be a Don Juan or a gay Lothario[7]—that class of man, you know; but I do pretend to know something about the harder sex. I have never disliked a woman in my life that she has not turned out badly. I was not at all deceived in Lizzie, for instance; I always had my doubts about her. Whatever you may think of my present situation, I must at least admit that I got into it with my eyes open. Now suppose you had got into something like this box with Madame de Cintré. You may depend upon it she would have turned out a stiff one. And upon my word I don't see where you could have found your comfort. Not from the marquis, my dear Newman; he wasn't a man you could go and talk things over with in a sociable, common-sense way. Did he ever seem to want to have you on the premises—did he ever try to see you alone? Did he ever ask you to come and smoke a cigar with him of an evening, or step in, when you had been calling on the

6. Nonsense.

7. A romantic lover or seducer.

ladies, and take something? I don't think you would have got much encouragement out of *him*. And as for the old lady, she struck one as an uncommonly strong dose. They have a great expression here, you know; they call it 'sympathetic.' Everything is sympathetic—or ought to be. Now Madame de Bellegarde is about as sympathetic as that mustard-pot. They're a d——d cold-blooded lot, any way; I felt it awfully at that ball of theirs. I felt as if I were walking up and down in the Armoury, in the Tower of London! My dear boy, don't think me a vulgar brute for hinting at it, but you may depend upon it, all they wanted was your money. I know something about that; I can tell when people want one's money! Why they stopped wanting yours I don't know; I suppose because they could get someone else's without working so hard for it. It isn't worth finding out. It may be that it was not Madame de Cintré that backed out first; very likely the old woman put her up to it. I suspect she and her mother are really as thick as thieves, eh? You are well out of it, my boy; make up your mind to that. If I express myself strongly it is all because I love you so much; and from that point of view I may say I should as soon have thought of making up to that piece of pale high-mightiness as I should have thought of making up to the Obelisk in the Place de la Concorde."[8]

Newman sat gazing at Tristram during this harangue with a lack-lustre eye; never yet had he seemed to himself to have outgrown so completely the phase of equal comradeship with Tom Tristram. Mrs. Tristram's glance at her husband had more of a spark; she turned to Newman with a slightly lurid smile. "You must at least do justice," she said, "to the felicity with which Mr. Tristram repairs the indiscretions of a too zealous wife."

But even without the aid of Tom Tristram's conversational felicities, Newman would have begun to think of the Bellegardes again. He could cease to think of them only when he ceased to think of his loss and privation, and the days had as yet but scantily lightened the weight of this incommodity. In vain Mrs. Tristram begged him to cheer up; she assured him that the sight of his countenance made her miserable.

"How can I help it?" he demanded with a trembling voice. "I feel like a widower—and a widower who has not even the consolation of going to stand beside the grave of his wife—who has not the right to wear so much mourning as a weed on his hat. I feel," he added in a moment, "as if my wife had been murdered and her assassins were still at large."

Mrs. Tristram made no immediate rejoinder, but at last she said,

8. The Obelisk is a slender, four-sided tapering monument, celebrating Ramses II, carried off from Luxor, Egypt, and erected in Paris.

with a smile which, in so far as it was a forced one, was less successfully simulated than such smiles, on her lips, usually were: "Are you very sure that you would have been happy?"

Newman stared a moment, and then shook his head. "That's weak," he said; "that won't do."

"Well," said Mrs. Tristram with a more triumphant bravery, "I don't believe you would have been happy."

Newman gave a little laugh. "Say I should have been miserable, then; it's a misery I should have preferred to any happiness."

Mrs. Tristram began to muse. "I should have been curious to see; it would have been very strange."

"Was it from curiosity that you urged me to try and marry her?"

"A little," said Mrs. Tristram, growing still more audacious. Newman gave her the one angry look he had been destined ever to give her, turned away and took up his hat. She watched him a moment, and then she said, "That sounds very cruel, but it is less so than it sounds. Curiosity has a share in almost everything I do. I wanted very much to see, first, whether such a marriage could actually take place; second, what would happen if it should take place."

"So you didn't believe," said Newman, resentfully.

"Yes, I believed—I believed that it would take place, and that you would be happy. Otherwise I should have been, among my speculations, a very heartless creature. *But*," she continued, laying her hand upon Newman's arm and hazarding a grave smile, "it was the highest flight ever taken by a tolerably bold imagination!"

Shortly after this she recommended him to leave Paris and travel for three months. Change of scene would do him good, and he would forget his misfortune sooner in absence from the objects which had witnessed it. "I really feel," Newman rejoined, "as if to leave *you*, at least, would do me good—and cost me very little effort. You are growing cynical; you shock me and pain me."

"Very good," said Mrs. Tristram, good-naturedly or cynically, as may be thought most probable. "I shall certainly see you again."

Newman was very willing to get away from Paris; the brilliant streets he had walked through in his happier hours, and which then seemed to wear a higher brilliancy in honour of his happiness, appeared now to be in the secret of his defeat and to look down upon it in shining mockery. He would go somewhere; he cared little where; and he made his preparations. Then, one morning, at haphazard, he drove to the train that would transport him to Boulogne[9] and despatch him thence to the shores of Britain. As he

9. French city on the English Channel.

rolled along in the train he asked himself what had become of his revenge, and he was able to say that it was provisionally pigeon-holed in a very safe place; it would keep till called for.

He arrived in London in the midst of what is called "the season," and it seemed to him at first that he might here put himself in the way of being diverted from his heavy-heartedness. He knew no one in all England, but the spectacle of the mighty metropolis roused him somewhat from his apathy. Anything that was enormous usually found favour with Newman, and the multitudinous energies and industries of England stirred within him a dull vivacity of contemplation. It is on record that the weather, at that moment, was of the finest English quality; he took long walks and explored London in every direction; he sat by the hour in Kensington Gardens[1] and beside the adjoining Drive, watching the people and the horses and the carriages; the rosy English beauties, the wonderful English dandies, and the splendid flunkies. He went to the opera and found it better than in Paris; he went to the theatre and found a surprising charm in listening to dialogue the finest points of which came within the range of his comprehension. He made several excursions into the country, recommended by the waiter at his hotel, with whom, on this and similar points, he had established confidential relations. He watched the deer in Windsor Forest[2] and admired the Thames from Richmond Hill;[3] he ate whitebait and brown-bread and butter at Greenwich,[4] and strolled in the grassy shadow of the cathedral of Canterbury. He also visited the Tower of London and Madame Tussaud's exhibition.[5] One day he thought he would go to Sheffield, and then, thinking again, he gave it up. Why should he go to Sheffield?[6] He had a feeling that the link which bound him to a possible interest in the manufacture of cutlery was broken. He had no desire for an "inside view" of any successful enterprise whatever, and he would not have given the smallest sum for the privilege of talking over the details of the most "splendid" business with the shrewdest of overseers.

One afternoon he had walked into Hyde Park, and was slowly threading his way through the human maze which edges the Drive. The stream of carriages was no less dense, and Newman, as usual, marvelled at the strange dingy figures which he saw taking the air in some of the stateliest vehicles. They reminded him of what he had read of eastern and southern countries, in which grotesque

1. A park in London, originally the grounds of Kensington palace, adjoining Hyde Park.
2. The grounds adjoining Windsor Castle, the royal residence, in south central England, on the Thames river.
3. A suburb of London.
4. A borough of London on the south bank of the Thames.
5. An exhibition of wax figures, modeled on famous and notorious people throughout history, displayed by Marie Tussaud (1760–1850) in her museum.
6. Town in Yorkshire, northern England, the chief seat of cutlery manufacture since the fourteenth century.

idols and fetiches were sometimes taken out of their temples and carried abroad in golden chariots to be displayed to the multitude. He saw a great many pretty cheeks beneath high-plumed hats as he squeezed his way through serried waves of crumpled muslin; and sitting on little chairs at the base of the great serious English trees, he observed a number of quiet-eyed maidens, who seemed only to remind him afresh that the magic of beauty had gone out of the world with Madame de Cintré: to say nothing of other damsels, whose eyes were not quiet, and who struck him still more as a satire on possible consolation. He had been walking for some time, when, directly in front of him, borne back by the summer breeze, he heard a few words uttered in that bright Parisian idiom from which his ears had begun to alienate themselves. The voice in which the words were spoken made them seem even more like a thing with which he had once been familiar, and as he bent his eyes it lent an identity to the commonplace elegance of the black hair and shoulders of a young lady walking in the same direction as himself. Mademoiselle Nioche, apparently, had come to seek a more rapid advancement in London, and another glance led Newman to suppose that she had found it. A gentleman was strolling beside her, lending a most attentive ear to her conversation and too entranced to open his lips. Newman did not hear his voice, but perceived that he presented the dorsal expression of a well-dressed Englishman. Mademoiselle Nioche was attracting attention: the ladies who passed her turned round to survey the Parisian perfection of her toilet. A great cataract of flounces rolled down from the young lady's waist to Newman's feet; he had to step aside to avoid treading upon them. He stepped aside, indeed, with a decision of movement which the occasion scarcely demanded; for even this imperfect glimpse of Miss Noémie had excited his displeasure. She seemed an odious blot upon the face of nature; he wanted to put her out of his sight. He thought of Valentin de Bellegarde, still green in the earth of his burial—his young life clipped by this flourishing impudence. The perfume of the young lady's finery sickened him; he turned his head and tried to deflect his course; but the pressure of the crowd kept him near her a few minutes longer, so that he heard what she was saying.

"Ah, I'm sure he will miss me," she murmured. "It was very cruel in me to leave him; I am afraid you will think me a very heartless creature. He might perfectly well have come with us. I don't think he is very well," she added; "it seemed to me to-day that he was not very gay."

Newman wondered whom she was talking about, but just then an opening among his neighbours enabled him to turn away, and he said to himself that she was probably paying a tribute to British propriety and playing at tender solicitude about her papa. Was that miserable old man still treading the path of vice in her train? Was he still giving her the benefit of his experience of affairs, and had he crossed the sea to serve as her interpreter? Newman walked some distance farther, and then began to retrace his steps, taking care not to traverse again the orbit of Mademoiselle Nioche. At last he looked for a chair under the trees, but he had some difficulty in finding an empty one. He was about to give up the search when he saw a gentleman rise from the seat he had been occupying, leaving Newman to take it without looking at his neighbours. He sat there for some time without heeding them; his attention was lost in the irritation and bitterness produced by his recent glimpse of Miss Noémie's iniquitous vitality. But at the end of a quarter of an hour, dropping his eyes, he perceived a small pug-dog squatted upon the path near his feet—a diminutive but very perfect specimen of its interesting species. The pug was sniffing at the fashionable world, as it passed him, with his little black muzzle, and was kept from extending his investigation by a large blue ribbon attached to his collar with an enormous rosette,[7] and held in the hand of a person seated next to Newman. To this person Newman transferred his attention, and immediately perceived that he was the object of all that of his neighbour, who was staring up at him from a pair of little fixed white eyes. These eyes Newman instantly recognized; he had been sitting for the last quarter of an hour beside M. Nioche. He had vaguely felt that someone was staring at him. M. Nioche continued to stare; he appeared afraid to move, even to the extent of evading Newman's glance.

"Dear me!" said Newman; "are you here, too?" And he looked at his neighbour's helplessness more grimly than he knew. M. Nioche had a new hat and a pair of kid gloves; his clothes, too, seemed to belong to a more recent antiquity than of yore. Over his arm was suspended a lady's mantilla—a light and brilliant tissue, fringed with white lace—which had apparently been committed to his keeping; and the little dog's blue ribbon was wound tightly round his hand. There was no expression of recognition in his face—or of anything indeed save a sort of feeble fascinated dread. Newman looked at the pug and the lace mantilla, and then he met the old man's eyes again. "You know me, I see," he pursued. "You might have spoken to me before." M. Nioche still said nothing, but it seemed to Newman that his eyes began faintly to water. "I didn't expect," our hero went on, "to meet you so far from—from the Café de la Patrie." The old man remained silent, but decidedly Newman had touched the source of tears. His neighbour sat star-

7. A rose-shaped arrangement of ribbons.

ing, and Newman added: "What's the matter, M. Nioche? You used to talk—to talk very prettily. Don't you remember you even gave lessons in conversation?"

At this M. Nioche decided to change his attitude. He stooped and picked up the pug, lifted it to his face and wiped his eyes on its little soft back. "I am afraid to speak to you," he presently said, looking over the puppy's shoulder. "I hoped you wouldn't notice me. I should have moved away, but I was afraid that if I moved you would notice me. So I sat very still."

"I suspect you have a bad conscience, sir," said Newman.

The old man put down the little dog and held it carefully in his lap. Then he shook his head, with his eyes still fixed upon his interlocutor. "No, Mr. Newman, I have a good conscience," he murmured.

"Then why should you want to slink away from me?"

"Because—because you don't understand my position."

"Oh, I think you once explained it to me," said Newman. "But it seems improved."

"Improved!" exclaimed M. Nioche, under his breath. "Do you call this improvement?" And he glanced at the treasures in his arms.

"Why, you are on your travels," Newman rejoined. "A visit to London in the season is certainly a sign of prosperity."

M. Nioche, in answer to this cruel piece of irony, lifted the puppy up to his face again, peering at Newman with his small blank eye-holes. There was something almost imbecile in the movement, and Newman hardly knew whether he was taking refuge in a convenient affectation of unreason, or whether he had in fact paid for his dishonour by the loss of his wits. In the latter case, just now, he felt little more tenderly to the foolish old man than in the former. Responsible or not, he was equally an accomplice of his detestably mischievous daughter. Newman was going to leave him abruptly, when a ray of entreaty appeared to disengage itself from the old man's misty gaze. "Are you going away?" he asked.

"Do you want me to stay?" said Newman.

"I should have left you—from consideration. But my dignity suffers at your leaving me—that way."

"Have you got anything particular to say to me?"

M. Nioche looked round him to see that no one was listening, and then he said, very softly but distinctly, "I have *not* forgiven her!"

Newman gave a short laugh, but the old man seemed for the moment not to perceive it; he was gazing away, absently, at some metaphysical image of his implacability. "It doesn't much matter whether you forgive her or not," said Newman. "There are other people who won't, I assure you."

"What has she done?" M. Nioche softly questioned, turning round again. "I don't know what she does, you know."

"She has done a devilish mischief; it doesn't matter what," said Newman. "She's a nuisance; she ought to be stopped."

M. Nioche stealthily put out his hand and laid it very gently upon Newman's arm. "Stopped, yes," he whispered. "That's it. Stopped short. She is running away—she must be stopped." Then he paused a moment and looked round him. "I mean to stop her," he went on. "I am only waiting for my chance."

"I see," said Newman, laughing briefly again. "She is running away and you are running after her. You have run a long distance!"

But M. Nioche stared insistently: "I shall stop her!" he softly repeated.

He had hardly spoken when the crowd in front of them separated, as if by the impulse to make way for an important personage. Presently, through the opening, advanced Mademoiselle Nioche, attended by the gentleman whom Newman had lately observed. His face being now presented to our hero, the latter recognised the irregular features, the hardly more regular complexion, and the amiable expression of Lord Deepmere. Noémie, on finding herself suddenly confronted with Newman, who, like M. Nioche, had risen from his seat, faltered for a barely perceptible instant. She gave him a little nod, as if she had seen him yesterday, and then, with a good-natured smile, "*Tiens,*[8] how we keep meeting!" she said. She looked consummately pretty, and the front of her dress was a wonderful work of art. She went up to her father, stretching out her hands for the little dog, which he submissively placed in them, and she began to kiss it and murmur over it: "To think of leaving him all alone—what a wicked, abominable creature he must believe me! He has been very unwell," she added, turning and affecting to explain to Newman, with a spark of infernal impudence, fine as a needle-point, in her eye. "I don't think the English climate agrees with him."

"It seems to agree wonderfully well with his mistress," said Newman.

"Do you mean me? I have never been better, thank you," Miss Noémie declared. "But with *milord,*" and she gave a brilliant glance at her late companion, "how can one help being well?" She seated herself in the chair from which her father had risen, and began to arrange the little dog's rosette.

8. "How amazing."

Lord Deepmere carried off such embarrassment as might be incidental to this unexpected encounter with the inferior grace of a male and a Briton. He blushed a good deal, and greeted the object of his late momentary aspiration to rivalry in the favour of a person other than the mistress of the invalid pug with an awkward nod and a rapid ejaculation—an ejaculation to which Newman, who often found it hard to understand the speech of English people, was able to attach no meaning. Then the young man stood there, with his hand on his hip, and with a conscious grin, staring askance at Miss Noémie. Suddenly an idea seemed to strike him, and he said, turning to Newman, "Oh, you know her?"

"Yes," said Newman, "I know her. I don't believe you do."

"Oh dear, yes, I do!" said Lord Deepmere, with another grin. "I knew her in Paris—by my poor cousin Bellegarde, you know. He knew her, poor fellow, didn't he? It was she, you know, who was at the bottom of his affair. Awfully sad, wasn't it?" continued the young man, talking off his embarrassment as his simple nature permitted. "They got up some story about its being for the Pope; about the other man having said something against the Pope's morals. They always do that, you know. They put it on the Pope because Bellegarde was once in the Zouaves. But it was about *her* morals—*she* was the Pope!" Lord Deepmere pursued, directing an eye illumined by this pleasantry toward Mademoiselle Nioche, who was bending gracefully over her lap-dog, apparently absorbed in conversation with it. "I daresay you think it rather odd that I should—ah—keep up the acquaintance," the young man resumed; "but she couldn't help it, you know, and Bellegarde was only my twentieth cousin. I daresay you think it's rather cheeky, my showing with her in Hyde Park; but you see she isn't known yet, and she's in such very good form——" And Lord Deepmere's conclusion was lost in the attesting glance which he again directed toward the young lady.

Newman turned away; he was having more of her than he relished. M. Nioche had stepped aside on his daughter's approach, and he stood there, within a very small compass, looking down hard at the ground. It had never yet, as between him and Newman, been so apposite to place on record the fact that he had not forgiven his daughter. As Newman was moving away he looked up and drew near to him, and Newman, seeing the old man had something particular to say, bent his head for an instant.

"You will see it some day in the papers," murmured M. Nioche.

Our hero departed to hide his smile, and to this day, though the newspapers form his principal reading, his eyes have not been arrested by any paragraph forming a sequel to this announcement.

Chapter XXVI

In that uninitiated observation of the great spectacle of English life upon which I have touched, it might be supposed that Newman passed a great many dull days. But the dulness of his days pleased him; his melancholy, which was settling into a secondary stage, like a healing wound, had in it a certain acrid, palatable sweetness. He had company in his thoughts, and for the present he wanted no other. He had no desire to make acquaintances, and he left untouched a couple of notes of introduction which had been sent him by Tom Tristram. He thought a great deal of Madame de Cintré—sometimes with a dogged tranquillity which might have seemed, for a quarter of an hour at a time, a near neighbour to forgetfulness. He lived over again the happiest hours he had known—that silver chain of numbered days in which his afternoon visits, tending sensibly to the ideal result, had subtilised his good humour to a sort of spiritual intoxication. He came back to reality, after such reveries, with a somewhat muffled shock; he had begun to feel the need of accepting the unchangeable. At other times the reality became an infamy again and the unchangeable an imposture, and he gave himself up to his angry restlessness till he was weary. But on the whole he fell into a rather reflective mood. Without in the least intending it or knowing it, he attempted to read the moral of his strange misadventure. He asked himself, in his quieter hours, whether perhaps, after all, he *was* more commercial than was pleasant. We know that it was in obedience to a strong reaction against questions exclusively commercial that he had come out to pick up æsthetic entertainment in Europe; it may therefore be understood that he was able to conceive that a man might be too commercial. He was very willing to grant it, but the concession, as to his own case, was not made with any very oppressive sense of shame. If he had been too commercial, he was ready to forget it, for in being so he had done no man any wrong that might not be as easily forgotten. He reflected with sober placidity that at least there were no monuments of his "meanness" scattered about the world. If there was any reason in the nature of things why his connection with business should have cast a shadow upon a connection—even a connection broken—with a woman justly proud, he was willing to sponge it out of his life forever. The thing seemed a possibility; he could not feel it, doubtless, as keenly as some people, and it hardly seemed worth while to flap his wings very hard to rise to the idea; but he could feel it enough to make any sacrifice that still remained to be made. As to what such sacrifice was now to be made to, here

Newman stopped short before a blank wall over which there sometimes played a shadowy imagery. He had a fancy of carrying out his life as he would have directed it if Madame de Cintré had been left to him—of making it a religion to do nothing that she would have disliked. In this, certainly there was no sacrifice; but there was a pale, oblique ray of inspiration. It would be lonely entertainment—a good deal like a man talking to himself in the mirror for want of better company. Yet the idea yielded Newman several half hours' dumb exaltation as he sat, with his hands in his pockets and his legs stretched, over the relics of an expensively poor dinner, in the undying English twilight. If, however, his commercial imagination was dead, he felt no contempt for the surviving actualities begotten by it. He was glad he had been prosperous and had been a great man of business rather than a small one; he was extremely glad he was rich. He felt no impulse to sell all he had and give to the poor, or to retire into meditative economy and asceticism. He was glad he was rich and tolerably young; if it was possible to think too much about buying and selling, it was a gain to have a good slice of life left in which not to think about them. Come, what should he think about now? Again and again Newman could only think of one thing; his thoughts always came back to it, and as they did so, with an emotional rush which seemed physically to express itself in a sudden upward choking, he leaned forward—the waiter having left the room—and, resting his arms on the table, buried his troubled face.

He remained in England till midsummer, and spent a month in the country, wandering about among cathedrals, castles and ruins. Several times, taking a walk from his inn into meadows and parks, he stopped by a well-worn stile, looked across through the early evening at a gray church tower, with its dusky nimbus of thick-circling swallows, and remembered that this might have been part of the entertainment of his honeymoon. He had never been so much alone or indulged so little in accidental dialogue. The period of recreation appointed by Mrs. Tristram had at last expired, and he asked himself what he should do now. Mrs. Tristram had written to him, proposing to him that he should join her in the Pyrenees; but he was not in the humour to return to France. The simplest thing was to repair to Liverpool and embark on the first American steamer. Newman made his way to the great seaport and secured his berth; and the night before sailing he sat in his room at the hotel, staring down, vacantly and wearily, at an open portmanteau. A number of papers were lying upon it, which he had been meaning to look over; some of them might conveniently be destroyed. But at last he shuffled them roughly together, and pushed them into a corner of the valise; they were business papers, and he was in no humour for sifting them. Then he drew forth his pocketbook and took out a paper of smaller size than those he had dismissed. He did not unfold it; he simply sat looking at the back of it. If he had momentarily entertained the idea of destroying it, the idea quickly expired. What the paper suggested was the feeling that lay in his innermost heart and that no reviving cheerfulness could long quench—the feeling that after all and above all he was a good fellow wronged. With it came a hearty hope that the Bellegardes were enjoying their suspense as to what he would do yet. The more it was prolonged the more they would enjoy it! He had hung fire once, yes; perhaps, in his present queer state of mind, he might hang fire again. But he restored the little paper to his pocketbook very tenderly, and felt better for thinking of the suspense of the Bellegardes. He felt better every time he thought of it after that, as he sailed the summer seas. He landed in New York and journeyed across the continent to San Francisco, and nothing that he observed by the way contributed to mitigate his sense of being a good fellow wronged.

He saw a great many other good fellows—his old friends—but he told none of them of the trick that had been played him. He said simply that the lady he was to have married had changed her mind, and when he was asked if he had changed his own, he said, "Suppose we change the subject." He told his friends that he had brought home no "new ideas" from Europe, and his conduct probably struck them as an eloquent proof of failing invention. He took no interest in chatting about his affairs and manifested no desire to look over his accounts. He asked half-a-dozen questions which, like those of an eminent physician inquiring for particular symptoms, showed that he still knew what he was talking about; but he made no comments and gave no directions. He not only puzzled the gentlemen on the Stock Exchange, but he was himself surprised at the extent of his indifference. As it seemed only to increase, he made an effort to combat it; he tried to interest himself and to take up his old occupations. But they appeared unreal to him; do what he would he somehow could not believe in them. Sometimes he began to fear that there was something the matter with his head; that his brain, perhaps, had softened, and that the end of his strong activities had come. This idea came back to him with an exasperating force. A hopeless, helpless loafer, useful to no one and detestable to himself—this was what the treachery of the Bellegardes had made of him. In his restless idleness he came back from San Francisco to New York, and sat for three days in the lobby of his hotel, looking out through a huge wall of plate-glass at the unceasing stream of pretty girls in Parisian-looking dresses, undulating past with little parcels nursed against their neat figures.

At the end of three days he returned to San Francisco, and having arrived there he wished he had stayed away. He had nothing to do, his occupation was gone, and it seemed to him that he should never find it again. He had nothing to do *here*, he sometimes said to himself; but there was something beyond the ocean that he was still to do; something that he had left undone experimentally and speculatively, to see if it could content itself to remain undone. But it was not content: it kept pulling at his heart-strings and thumping at his reason; it murmured in his ears and hovered perpetually before his eyes. It interposed between all new resolutions and their fulfilment; it seemed like a stubborn ghost, dumbly entreating to be laid. Till that was done he should never be able to do anything else.

One day, toward the end of the winter, after a long interval, he received a letter from Mrs. Tristram, who apparently was animated by a charitable desire to amuse and distract her correspondent. She gave him much Paris gossip, talked of General Packard and Miss Kitty Upjohn, enumerated the new plays at the theatre, and enclosed a note from her husband, who had gone down to spend a month at Nice.[9] Then came her signature, and after this her postscript. The latter consisted of these few lines: "I heard three days since from my friend, the Abbé Aubert, that Madame de Cintré last week took the veil at the Carmelites. It was on her twenty-seventh birthday, and she took the name of her patroness, St. Veronica. Sister Veronica has a lifetime before her!"

This letter came to Newman in the morning; in the evening he started for Paris. His wound began to ache with its first fierceness, and during his long bleak journey the thought of Madame de Cintré's "lifetime," passed within prison walls on whose outer side he might stand, kept him perpetual company. Now he would fix himself in Paris forever; he would extort a sort of happiness from the knowledge that if she was not there, at least the stony sepulchre that held her was. He descended, unannounced, upon Mrs. Bread, whom he found keeping lonely watch in his great empty saloons on the Boulevard Haussmann. They were as neat as a Dutch village; Mrs. Bread's only occupation had been removing individual dust-particles. She made no complaint, however, of her loneliness, for in her philosophy a servant was but a mysteriously projected machine, and it would be as fantastic for a housekeeper to comment upon a gentleman's absences as for a clock to remark upon not being wound up. No particular clock, Mrs. Bread supposed, kept all the time, and no particular servant could enjoy all the sunshine diffused by the career of an exacting master. She ventured, nevertheless, to express a modest hope that Newman meant to remain a while in

9. A city on the French Riviera.

Paris. Newman laid his hand on hers and shook it gently. "I mean to remain forever," he said.

He went after this to see Mrs. Tristram, to whom he had telegraphed, and who expected him. She looked at him a moment and shook her head. "This won't do," she said; "you have come back too soon." He sat down and asked about her husband and her children, tried even to inquire about Miss Dora Finch. In the midst of this—"Do you know where she is?" he asked, abruptly.

Mrs. Tristram hesitated a moment; of course he couldn't mean Miss Dora Finch. Then she answered, properly: "She has gone to the other house—in the Rue d'Enfer." After Newman had sat a while longer, looking very sombre, she went on: "You are not so good a man as I thought. You are more—you are more——"

"More what?" Newman asked.

"More unforgiving."

"Good God!" cried Newman; "do you expect me to forgive?"

"No, not that. I have not forgiven, so of course you can't. But you might forget! You have a worse temper about it than I should have expected. You look wicked—you look dangerous."

"I may be dangerous," he said; "but I am not wicked. No, I am not wicked." And he got up to go. Mrs. Tristram asked him to come back to dinner; but he answered that he did not feel like pledging himself to be present at an entertainment, even as a solitary guest. Later in the evening, if he should be able, he would come.

He walked away through the city, beside the Seine and over it, and took the direction of the Rue d'Enfer. The day had the softness of early spring; but the weather was gray and humid. Newman found himself in a part of Paris which he little knew—a region of convents and prisons, of streets bordered by long dead walls and traversed by few wayfarers. At the intersection of two of these streets stood the house of the Carmelites—a dull, plain edifice, with a high-shouldered blank wall all round it. From without Newman could see its upper windows, its steep roof and its chimneys. But these things revealed no symptoms of human life; the place looked dumb, deaf, inanimate. The pale, dead, discoloured wall stretched beneath it far down the empty side street—a vista without a human figure. Newman stood there a long time; there were no passers; he was free to gaze his fill. This seemed the goal of his journey; it was what he had come for. It was a strange satisfaction, and yet it was a satisfaction; the barren stillness of the place seemed to be his own release from ineffectual longing. It told him that the woman within was lost beyond recall, and that the days and years of the future would pile themselves above her like the huge immovable slab of a tomb. These days and years, in this place, would always be just so gray and silent. Suddenly, from the thought of their seeing him stand there, again the charm utterly departed. He would never stand there again; it was gratuitous dreariness. He turned away with a heavy heart, but with a heart lighter than the one he had brought.

Everything was over, and he too at last could rest. He walked down through narrow, winding streets to the edge of the Seine again, and there he saw, close above him, the soft, vast towers of Notre Dame.[1] He crossed one of the bridges and stood a moment in the empty place before the great cathedral; then he went in beneath the grossly-imaged portals. He wandered some distance up the nave and sat down in the splendid dimness. He sat a long time; he heard far-away bells chiming off, at long intervals, to the rest of the world. He was very tired; this was the best place he could be in. He said no prayers; he had no prayers to say. He had nothing to be thankful for, and he had nothing to ask; nothing to ask, because now he must take care of himself. But a great cathedral offers a very various hospitality, and Newman sat in his place, because while he was there he was out of the world. The most unpleasant thing that had ever happened to him had reached its formal conclusion, as it were; he could close the book and put it away. He leaned his head for a long time on the chair in front of him; when he took it up he felt that he was himself again. Somewhere in his mind, a tight knot seemed to have loosened. He thought of the Bellegardes; he had almost forgotten them. He remembered them as people he had meant to do something to. He gave a groan as he remembered what he had meant to do; he was annoyed at having meant to do it; the bottom, suddenly, had fallen out of his revenge. Whether it was Christian charity or unregenerate good nature—what it was, in the background of his soul—I don't pretend to say; but Newman's last thought was that of course he would let the Bellegardes go.

If he had spoken it aloud he would have said that he didn't want to hurt them. He was ashamed of having wanted to hurt them. They had hurt him, but such things were really not his game. At last he got up and came out of the darkening church; not with the elastic step of a man who has won a victory or taken a resolve, but strolling soberly, like a good-natured man who is still a little ashamed.

Going home, he said to Mrs. Bread that he must trouble her to put back his things into the portmanteau she had had unpacked the evening before. His gentle stewardess looked at him through eyes a

1. The principal cathedral in Paris.

trifle bedimmed. "Dear me, sir," she exclaimed, "I thought you said that you were going to stay forever."

"I meant that I was going to stay away forever," said Newman kindly. And since his departure from Paris on the following day he has certainly not returned. The gilded apartments I have so often spoken of stand ready to receive him; but they serve only as a spacious residence for Mrs. Bread, who wanders eternally from room to room, adjusting the tassels of the curtains, and keeps her wages, which are regularly brought her by a banker's clerk, in a great pink Sèvres vase on the drawing-room mantelshelf.

Late in the evening Newman went to Mrs. Tristram's and found Tom Tristram by the domestic fireside. "I'm glad to see you back in Paris," this gentleman declared. "You know it's really the only place for a white man to live." Mr. Tristram made his friend welcome, according to his own rosy light, and offered him a convenient *résumé*[2] of the Franco-American gossip of the last six months. Then at last he got up and said he would go for half an hour to the club. "I suppose a man who has been for six months in California wants a little intellectual conversation. I'll let my wife have a go at you."

Newman shook hands heartily with his host, but did not ask him to remain; and then he relapsed into his place on the sofa, opposite to Mrs. Tristram. She presently asked him what he had done after leaving her. "Nothing particular," said Newman.

"You struck me," she rejoined, "as a man with a plot in his head. You looked as if you were bent on some sinister errand, and after you had left me I wondered whether I ought to have let you go."

"I only went over to the other side of the river—to the Carmelites," said Newman.

Mrs. Tristram looked at him a moment and smiled. "What did you do there? Try to scale the wall?"

"I did nothing. I looked at the place for a few minutes and then came away."

Mrs. Tristram gave him a sympathetic glance. "You didn't happen to meet M. de Bellegarde," she asked, "staring hopelessly at the convent-wall as well? I am told he takes his sister's conduct very hard."

"No, I didn't meet him, I am happy to say," Newman answered, after a pause.

"They are in the country," Mrs. Tristram went on; "at—what is the name of the place?—Fleurières. They returned there at the time you left Paris and have been spending the year in extreme seclu-

2. Summary.

sion. The little marquise must enjoy it; I expect to hear that she has eloped with her daughter's music-master!"

Newman was looking at the light wood-fire; but he listened to this with extreme interest. At last he spoke: "I mean never to mention the name of those people again, and I don't want to hear anything more about them." And then he took out his pocketbook and drew forth a scrap of paper. He looked at it an instant, then got up and stood by the fire. "I am going to burn them up," he said. "I am glad to have you as a witness. There they go!" And he tossed the paper into the flame.

Mrs. Tristram sat with her embroidery-needle suspended. "What is that paper?" she asked.

Newman, leaning against the fireplace, stretched his arms and drew a longer breath than usual. Then after a moment, "I can tell you now," he said. "It was a paper containing a secret of the Bellegardes—something which would damn them if it were known."

Mrs. Tristram dropped her embroidery with a reproachful moan. "Ah, why didn't you show it to me?"

"I thought of showing it to you—I thought of showing it to everyone. I thought of paying my debt to the Bellegardes that way. So I told them, and I frightened them. They have been staying in the country, as you tell me, to keep out of the explosion. But I have given it up."

Mrs. Tristram began to take slow stitches again. "Have you quite given it up?"

"Oh yes."

"Is it very bad, this secret?"

"Yes, very bad."

"For myself," said Mrs. Tristram, "I am sorry you have given it up. I should have liked immensely to see your paper. They have wronged me too, you know, as your sponsor and guarantee, and it would have served for my revenge as well. How did you come into possession of your secret?"

"It's a long story. But honestly, at any rate."

"And they knew you were master of it?"

"Oh, I told them."

"Dear me, how interesting!" cried Mrs. Tristram. "And you humbled them at your feet?"

Newman was silent a moment. "No, not at all. They pretended not to care—not to be afraid. But I know they did care—they were afraid."

"Are you very sure?"

Newman stared a moment. "Yes, I'm sure."

Mrs. Tristram resumed her slow stitches. "They defied you, eh?"

"Yes," said Newman, "it was about that."

"You tried by the threat of exposure to make them retract?" Mrs. Tristram pursued.

"Yes, but they wouldn't. I gave them their choice, and they chose to take their chance of bluffing off the charge and convicting me of fraud. But they *were* frightened," Newman added, "and I have had all the vengeance I want."

"It is most provoking," said Mrs. Tristram, "to hear you talk of the 'charge' when the charge is burnt up. Is it quite consumed?" she asked, glancing at the fire.

Newman assured her that there was nothing left of it.

"Well then," she said, "I suppose there is no harm in saying that you probably did not make them so very uncomfortable. My impression would be that since, as you say, they defied you, it was because they believed that, after all, you would never really come to the point. Their confidence, after counsel taken of each other, was not in their innocence, nor in their talent for bluffing things off; it was in your remarkable good nature! You see they were right."

Newman instinctively turned to see if the little paper was in fact consumed; but there was nothing left of it.

THE END

A Note on the Text

The manuscript of *The American* apparently is no longer extant. The first significant printed form of the novel is *The Atlantic Monthly* serialization in twelve installments between June 1876 and May 1877. (See p. 317 for the chapter grouping of these twelve installments.) James was living in Paris in 1875 and launched the novel under the misapprehension that F. P. Church would publish it in *The Galaxy*, of which Church was then editor. The first two installments of the novel were in fact mailed to Church in early February of 1876 in the expectation that he would accede to James's publication terms. But when Church apparently declined to accept the terms which James reiterated in his letter of March 3, James induced William Dean Howells to accept the novel for *The Atlantic Monthly*.

During this period in Paris, James was in straitened financial circumstances and did not wish to draw on the account of his parents, who could ill afford to stake him between novels. He depended on "perpetual serialization," in one magazine or another—sometimes in more than one—and prompt book editions (ideally timed for the Christmas gift market) to support himself. Very likely the novel began to appear in *The Atlantic* before James had even finished writing it, for he confessed to Howells of having launched his subject "somewhat prematurely." And when he came to write the Preface to the novel for the New York Edition, many years later, he recollected that the novel "started on its course while much was still unwritten," and he remembered the anxiety of "what would happen if anything *should* 'happen,' if one should break one's arm by an accident or make a long illness or suffer, in body, mind, fortune, any other visitation involving a loss of time." Nevertheless, "a degree of joy, an eagerness on behalf of my recital," carried him through his recklessness and must "have overridden anxieties of every sort, including any view of inherent difficulties."[1] In any event, the extant correspondence reveals that after the first two installments had been retrieved from *The Galaxy* offices, James periodically sent batches of manuscript to Howells throughout the spring, fall and early winter of 1876. And the final installment was mailed to *The Atlantic* in February of 1877, just three months before the serial concluded.

There is also considerable evidence to suggest that the text of *The American* was written—or at least shaped—to satisfy the space requirements of *The Atlantic*. James ordinarily liked his serialized novels to appear in six to nine long installments, each of which gave his readers considerably more than a "twenty minutes' nibble."[2] But Howells held out for twelve numbers and complained that the chapters he had retrieved from *The Galaxy* constituted excessively long installments for *The Atlantic*. In May of 1876, about

1. See James's Preface to the New York Edition, p. 1.
2. *Henry James: Letters*, ed. Leon Edel (Cambridge: Harvard University Press, 1975), II, 97; see p. 347.

the time James sent the fourth installment, he conceded that twenty-six pages was "an impossible installment for the magazine" and that he would "endeavour to give you about 14 pp., and to keep doing it for seven or eight months more."[3] Examination of the chapter units as published in the magazine serial confirms Howells's problem: the first installment ran to three chapters; every other, with the exception of the three-chapter September installment of chapters 8–10, is two chapters long. James's obligation to shape the installments to fourteen-page units, moreover, required him to "intensify the interest" of the story at the end of every other chapter; to create, as it were, "cliff-hangers" that would make his serial readers eager for the next month's installment. These manipulations of the plot, as Manfred MacKenzie has shown, invest the novel with much of its melodramatic effect and create those "rude jolts" of the kind which James complained of in his Preface to *The Ambassadors,* which was also serialized.[4]

There is also evidence to suggest that the manuscript may have been "edited" in Cambridge before it went into serial production. For William James, the novelist's brother, complained that some infelicities in James's language—or rather in Newman's—made the "reader's flesh creep." When they were pointed out to him, James conceded his occasional barbarisms and ascribed them to "my not seeing proof." William, who may have read the first two installments before they were delivered to Howells, told his brother that he had been shocked by some of the language and had persuaded Howells "to omit one of two of the same sort." Because he did not wish to offend the sensibilities of his genteel American audience, Henry James in fact told Howells in December of 1876 that he was "very glad" that Howells had deleted the offensive language and "would give you *carte blanche.* It is all along of my not seeing a proof—which is a great disadvantage. There are many things, which, as they stand printed, I should have changed. *Ma che vuole?* Here I have no one to try anything on, or to ask how things sound."[5]

Whether in fact Howells deleted the passages offensive to William or to what extent he may have exercised his editorial *carte blanche,* we shall never know, for the manuscript has been lost. But the likelihood is that Howells did, at least minimally, "clean up" James's style. Certainly Howells was accustomed to cleaning up the "Western" language of Mark Twain's characters. In any event, Henry assured his mother that he would "be easily able in preparing the volume [i.e., the first book edition], to remove effectually, by a few verbal corrections, that Newmanesque taint on which William dwells."[6] Nevertheless, since James had no opportunity to correct the proof of this serial edition, the *Atlantic* version lacks the usual authority of a text set from printer's copy.

On January 1, 1877, Henry James wrote to James Ripley Osgood to propose that Osgood publish the novel in a book edition, one timed to appear, as it turned out, with the termination of the serial in May. Possibly

3. ***The Letters of Henry James,*** **ed. Percy Lubbock (New York: Charles Scribner's, 1920), I, 47;** **see p. 340.**

4. Manfred MacKenzie, "Henry James: Serialist Early and Late," ***Philological Quarterly*** **41 (1962), 494.**

5. ***Henry James: Letters,*** **II, 84;** **see p. 345.**

6. Ibid., II, 87.

to offset any Cambridge gossip about the shocking language of the book, James promised Osgood a revision of the text of the novel. Osgood agreed. Accordingly, the first American book edition was published on April 30, 1877, by the Boston firm of James R. Osgood and Company ("Late Ticknor & Fields, and Fields, Osgood, & Co."). This book text, set in Cambridge by the "printers and stereotypers" H. O. Houghton and Company, was issued in a first printing of 1,008 copies, priced at two dollars each. A second printing of 514 copies was issued on May 18, and a third of 504 on August 29, 1877. There is considerable variation in both substantives, or word changes, and accidentals, or punctuation changes, between the *Atlantic* serialization and the first American book edition. Most, if not all, of the accidentals changes probably represent Osgood house styling. Approximately eighty changes, however, are substantive variants. Do these word changes represent the authorial revisions of the *Atlantic* text which James promised Osgood in his letter of January 1, 1877? It is difficult to say. There is no evidence to suggest that James, by now having moved to London, prepared corrected copy for this first book edition. A natural inference is therefore that the substantive variants represent unauthorized printer's alterations. On the other hand, James did promise his mother that he would make the "verbal corrections" necessary to delete the "Newmanesque taint," and he might have taken the opportunity to send Osgood corrected and revised tear-sheets of the *Atlantic* serial installments as they appeared, especially the early ones, intending them to be used as printer's copy for the first American book edition. Perhaps some of these substantive changes may have been suggested to Osgood by William James or even Howells, as the installments appeared in Boston. Printer's copy for the Osgood edition does not survive. Nor is there any evidence to suggest that James saw the proof of this book text before it was finally printed. Lacking both, one can draw no firm conclusions as to the authority of these substantive changes. Yet since these substantive changes are accepted in later editions of the novel which James did oversee and correct, they are accepted in this Norton Critical Edition as probably reflecting James's intention. At least he acquiesced in them. Whatever the source of these substantive changes in the Osgood edition, the latter in any event is superseded by the 1879 London Macmillan edition. But this is to anticipate the story of the history of this text.

A number of bound copies of the Osgood edition were immediately imported for the English market in June, 1877, by the London firm of Trübner and Company, of 57 and 59 Ludgate Hill, and were sold at ten shillings and sixpence apiece. In December of 1877, the London firm of Ward, Lock & Company, of Warwick House, Dorset Buildings, Salisbury Square, issued an unauthorized version of the Osgood edition; it was printed by the London and Frome printers Butler and Tanner, of the Selwood Printing Works. James wrote to his mother on January 13, 1878: "Did I tell you it has been reprinted here by Ward & Lock, in the railway library, with a wonderful picture on the cover? But this of course is a piracy, and I get no profit from it."[7] This unauthorized edition, bound in multicolored boards, luridly

7. **Leon Edel and Dan Laurence, *A Bibliography of Henry James* (London: Rupert Hart-Davis, 1961), p. 33.**

illustrated, and hawked for two shillings, has no textual authority whatsoever.

James was appalled at the textual corruption of the pirated edition and wrote to Elizabeth Boott on January 30, 1878, that this text—number 30 in the Ward & Lock "Favorite Authors, British and Foreign" series—was "vilely printed" and that "there are whole paragraphs omitted. In fact, it lacks one whole page." Despite the mutilation of this text, it was reissued in 1888 or 1889 at two shillings (in paper) and two shillings and sixpence (in red cloth gilt), as number 519 of the "Select Library of Fiction" series; and in 1894 in the Ward, Lock & Bowden "Copyright Novel Series" at three shillings and sixpence in cloth.

Bernhard Tauchnitz also published *The American* in Leipzig in 1878 in a two-volume "authorised" edition. Numbers 1713–14 of his "Collection of British Authors," this text bore the legend, "The present edition . . . is published with my fullest assent. . . . Paris, Dec. 1877," for Tauchnitz had visited James in Paris, proposed to publish his works, and secured the author's consent to the Leipzig edition. Not authorized, however, was an 1877 German translation published in Stuttgart as *Der Amerikaner oder Marquis und Yankee*. Without James's permission, Heichten-Abenheim, the translator had the "vile impudence" to rewrite the conclusion in order to provide a happy ending. And he had the "cheek" to send this translation to James with his compliments. "If those are your Germans," Henry told William, "I give them up."[8] Less offensive was a French translation by Léon Bochet, published under the title *L'Américain à Paris* by Hachette et cie., in 1884.

To protect himself from the English book pirates, to restore the accuracy of his text, and to introduce himself to the English public through a reputable publisher, James therefore undertook, in 1878, to arrange for the publication of *The American* by the London publisher Macmillan and Company. Set by the printers Charles Dickens and Evans, Crystal Palace Press, the first authorized English edition of the novel was published in March of 1879. Printed in a run of 1,250 copies, the novel sold at six shillings. There has long been a general view that this Macmillan edition of 1879 was an extensively revised text. But in view of James's extraordinary literary productivity during 1878–79, it is not surprising to discover that his revisions for the newly set Macmillan text were minimal. Macmillan house-styled the accidentals, but collation reveals very few substantive variants from the Osgood edition. Nevertheless, James now had a corrected authorized text covered by English copyright.

In 1883 Macmillan further agreed to publish the collected novels of Henry James in a set which included *The American*. This text, however, has no convincing authority. Printer's copy for this new edition was a marked-up copy of the 1879 Macmillan text. It may be observed that there are more than 800 changes in the accidentals between the 1879 and 1883 versions.[9]

8. *Henry James: Letters*, II, 116–17, 121*n*. A more accurate and recent translation has been published by Herta Haas as *Der Amerikaner* (Köln, Berlin: Kiepenheuer & Witsch, 1966).

9. Cf. Matthew J. Bruccoli, "A Note on the Text," in *The American*, by Henry James (Boston: Houghton Mifflin, 1962), p. xxiv.

Most of these alterations, if not all, reflect additional Macmillan house-styling for the uniform edition, for only one substantive variation is introduced into the 1883 text: "hesitated" is substituted for "meditated" at page p. 286, line 10. This single change appears to be a printer's error. For there is no evidence to suggest that James played a role in the preparation of the 1883 text. And, given his manuscript habits, it seems unlikely that, if he *had* revised the text, James would have altered more than 800 accidentals but only one substantive.

In 1905, James revised *The American* for the last time. This edition, published in 1907 as volume 2 of what came to be the twenty-six–volume "New York Edition" (1907–17), was published by Charles Scribner and printed by the Riverside Press in Cambridge, Massachusetts. The new text was issued in a first run of 1,500 copies and sold by subscription for two dollars a volume in cloth and four dollars in half levant. The "New York Edition" of *The American* was extensively revised in both substantives and accidentals. Printer's copy was a set of marked-up sheets of the 1883 London Macmillan edition. James's copy of the 1883 text, containing his extensive revisions in longhand on the margins, between the lines, and on inserted pages of holograph, is now in the Houghton Library at Harvard. A facsimile of the revision for the "New York Edition" has also been published by the Scolar Press in conjunction with the Oxford University Press. James's revisions were so extensive that some readers complained that the final version of the novel lacked the freshness, spontaneity, and immediacy of earlier versions.

Whatever one may think of James's revisions for the "New York Edition," it is clear that the 1907 edition of *The American* is so extensively revised that it is a substantially different book from the novel James composed in the mid-1870s. In reissuing the novel, the editor must therefore choose which of the versions—early or late—should be presented. James, of course, felt justified in markedly altering the novel. As he told Robert Herrick, "I shouldn't have planned the edition at all unless I had felt close revision . . . to be an indispensable part of it."[1] Herrick and many others have nevertheless felt that James's revisions, in the late complicated manner of the "major phase," changed the characterization of Christopher Newman, altered the tone of the novel, and introduced doubtful stylistic improvements into the work. Changing, for example, Newman's "clean shaved" cheek to "he spoke, as to cheek and chin, of the matutinal steel" has seemed to many readers a dubious felicity. For a discussion of the effect of these revisions, see the essays by Isadore Traschen, Max Schulz, Robert Herrick, and William T. Stafford cited in the Bibliography and the essay by Royal Gettmann reprinted in this book.

On reviewing the evidence, and despite James's view that he would eventually be justified in his revision of *The American,* I prefer the directness and immediacy of the early version of the novel, the book as young James essentially wrote it in Paris in the mid-1870s. The copy text for the

1. Robert Herrick, "A Visit to Henry James," *Yale Review* 12 (1923), 735; see p. 384.

Norton Critical Edition is therefore the London Macmillan edition of 1879. A corrected form of the *Atlantic* and Osgood editions, it suffers fewer corruptions than the 1883 Macmillan version, which James apparently did not correct. In preparing this edition, the 1879 text has been read against the serial version, the 1877 Osgood edition, the 1883 Macmillan edition and, for special readings, the 1907 "New York Edition." Demonstrable errors and misprints in the 1879 Macmillan edition are corrected (the emendations are noted below), and the substantive variants between the Osgood and Macmillan editions are tabulated below.

Textual Variants

The following list indicates the substantive variants (i.e., differences in wording) between the London edition of 1879 (from which this Norton Critical Edition is reprinted) and the Boston edition of 1877. The words in boldface, which are preceded by page and line numbers from this Norton Critical Edition, are those of the London edition of 1879: several of these, which are errors, have been emended by the editor, as noted below.

21.41 **Mdlle.** Mlle.
50.16 **yo** you
75.14 **extremely** tolerably
83.15 **curtsy** courtesy
110.27 **Norman** Newman
153.2 **declare, that there** declare, there
186.42 **a dagger of diamonds** the silver dagger
226.38 **and sunshine** and in the sunshine
227.15 **"Les Liaisons Dangereuses"** "Faublas"
237.15 **quiet water** tranquil river
244.34 **him** her
247.4 **with** when
277.39 **convent-walls into** convent-walls and into

Editor's Emendations

The words and punctuation in boldface in the following list, preceded by page and line numbers, are the editor's emendations for this Norton Critical Edition. They are followed by the wording of the 1879 London edition, from which the text of the novel is reprinted.

24.21 **Mlle.** Mdlle.
48.17 **much."** much"
50.16 **you** yo

110.11 **clever?** clever!
105.30 **wash-tubs** washtubs
110.27 **Newman** Norman
113.31 **that.** that."
117.19 **said. "Remember** said. Remember
119.3 **you:** you;
121.31 **word!** word?-
122.30 **that!** that?
126.22 **"Nevertheless,"** "Nevertheless"
127.37 **yourself!** yourself?
128.41 **promptly,** promptly;
134.5 **utensils.** utensils."
136.22 **[Three paragraphs] "Well . . . matter"; "For . . . her"; "It . . . Paris."** [One paragraph] "Well . . . Paris."
137.33 **you!** you?
151.29 **whosoever** whomsoever
153.2 **declare, there** declare, that there
158.18 **Newman."** Newman"
166.2 **more."** more.
185.22 **Newman.'** Newman."
207.13 **you?"** you?'
227.35 **I!"** I!'
243.26 **do?** do!
244.34 **her** him
245.29 **person!** person?
247.4 **when** with
267.23 **stars;** stars:
275.8 **stoical; he** stoical, he
278.21 **it!** it?
291.22 **him?** him!

Installments of *The American* Appearing in *The Atlantic Monthly*

Chapters I–III Volume 37, number 224 (June 1876)
Chapters IV–V Volume 38, number 225 (July 1876)
Chapters VI–VII Volume 38, number 226 (August 1876)
Chapter VIII–X Volume 38, number 227 (September 1876)
Chapters XI–XII Volume 38, number 228 (October 1876)
Chapters XIII–XIV Volume 38, number 229 (November 1876)
Chapters XV–XVI Volume 38, number 230 (December 1876)
Chapters XVII–XVIII Volume 39, number 231 (January 1877)
Chapters XIX–XX Volume 39, number 232 (February 1877)
Chapters XXI–XXII Volume 39, number 233 (March 1877)
Chapters XXIII–XXIV Volume 39, number 234 (April 1877)
Chapters XXV–XXVI Volume 39, number 235 (May 1877)

[illegible] to his mother, who is very fond of the old traditions. But you must remember that he speaks for no one but himself."

"Oh, I don't mind him, ~~sir," said Newman good-humouredly.~~ "I know what [illegible] amount to."

"In the good old times," ~~said Valentin,~~ "marquises and counts used to have their appointed [illegible] and jesters, to crack jokes for them. Nowadays we see a great strapping democrat keeping [illegible] about him to play the fool. It's a good situation, but I certainly am very degenerate."

M. de Bellegarde fixed his eyes for some time on the floor. "My mother ~~informed~~ me," he [illegible] presently, "of the announcement that you made [illegible] her the other evening."

"That I ~~desired to~~ marry your sister?" ~~said Newman.~~

"That you ~~wished to arrange a marriage," said the Marquis, slowly, "with my sister, the Comtesse de Cintré.~~ The proposal ~~was serious, and required, on my mother's part, a great deal of reflection.~~ She naturally took me into her counsels, and ~~I gave my most zealous attention to the subject~~. There was a great deal to be considered; more than you ~~appear to imagine.~~ We have viewed the question on all its faces, we have weighed one thing against another. Our conclusion has been that we [illegible]. My mother has desired me to inform you [illegible]. She will have the honour of saying a few words to you on the subject herself. Meanwhile, [illegible] heads of the family, ~~you are accepted.~~"

Newman got up and came nearer, [illegible] "You ~~will do nothing to hinder me, and all you can to help me, eh?~~"

"I ~~will recommend my sister to accept you.~~"

Newman passed his hand over his face, and pressed it for a moment upon his eyes. This promise had a great sound, and yet the pleasure he took in it was embittered by his having to stand there so and receive ~~his passport~~

Page of *The American* (original version), as revised by Henry James (1906).

Backgrounds and Sources

The following section provides a miscellany of materials from correspondence of and about Henry James, from his notebooks and reviews, and from contemporary magazine journalism. It is intended to illuminate a number of issues which manifestly colored both the writing of and the critical reception of *The American*. The issues dealt with in this section include the composition and publication history of the work; James's attitude toward his native land (including the adequacy of the American scene for the aspiring novelist of manners); his attitude toward Europe and particularly toward France (her social, literary, theatrical, and political life); the spectacle of the American traveler in Europe; James's reasons for becoming an expatriate; literary and dramatic sources for the novel; and the development of James's passion for the theater, which led to his composing a dramatic version of the novel for production in 1891.

Henry James to Mrs. Henry James, Sr., October 13, 1869†

["*. . . the modern man with* culture *quite left out . . .*"]

* * * Willy[1] asked me in one of his recent letters for an 'opinion' of the English, which I haven't yet had time to give—tho' at times I have felt as if it were a theme on which I could write from a full mind. In fact, however, I have very little right to have any opinion on the matter. I've seen far too few specimens and those too superficially. The only thing I'm certain about is that I like them—like them heartily. W. asked if as individuals they 'kill' the individual American. To this I would say that the Englishmen I have met not only kill, but bury in unfathomable depths, the Americans I have met. A set of people less framed to provoke national self-complacency than the latter it would be hard to imagine. There is but one word to use in regard to them—vulgar, vulgar, vulgar. Their ignorance—their stingy, defiant, grudging attitude towards everything European—their perpetual reference of all things to some American standard or precedent which exists only in their own unscrupulous wind-bags—and then our unhappy poverty of voice, of speech and of physiognomy—these things glare at you hideously. On the other hand, we seem a people of *character*, we seem to have energy, capacity and intellectual stuff in ample measure. What I have pointed at as our vices are the elements of the modern man with *culture* quite left out. It's the absolute and incredible lack of *culture* that strikes you in common travelling Americans. The pleasantness of the English, on the other side,

† Written by James to his mother, Mrs. Henry James, Sr., from the Hotel de l'Europe, Florence, October 13, 1869. From *The Letters of Henry James*, ed. Percy Lubbock (New York: Scribner's, 1920), I, 21–23.

1. William James, the novelist's brother. [*Editor.*]

comes in a great measure from the fact of their each having been dipped into the crucible, which gives them a sort of coating of comely varnish and colour. They have been smoothed and polished by mutual social attrition. They have manners and a language. We lack both, but particularly the latter. * * *

16*th, Sunday*. I *have* seen some nice Americans and I still love my country. * * *

Henry James to Charles Eliot Norton, January 16, 1871†

["... *a really* grasping *imagination* ..."]

* * * Cambridge and Boston society still rejoices in that imposing fixedness of outline which is ever so inspiring to contemplate. In Cambridge I see Arthur Sedgwick[2] and Howells;[3] but little of any one else. * * * Howells edits and observes and produces—the latter in his own particular line with more and more perfection. His recent sketches in the *Atlantic*, collected into a volume, belong, I think, by the wondrous cunning of their manner, to very good literature. He seems to have resolved himself, however, [into] one who can write solely of what his fleshly eyes have seen; and for this reason I wish he were 'located' where they would rest upon richer and fairer things than this immediate landscape. Looking about for myself, I conclude that the face of nature and civilization in this our country is to a certain point a very sufficient literary field. But it will yield its secrets only to a really *grasping* imagination. This I think Howells lacks. (Of course I don't!) To write well and worthily of American things one need even more than elsewhere to be a *master*. But unfortunately one is less! * * *

Henry James to Grace Norton, January 14, 1874‡

["... *our poor bare country* ..."]

* * * What Charles[4] says about our civilization seems to me perfectly true, but practically I don't feel as if the facts were so melancholy. The great fact for us all there is that, relish Europe as

† From *The Letters of Henry James*, ed. Percy Lubbock (New York: Scribner's, 1920), I, 30–31. This letter was written by James at Cambridge, Massachusetts, where he was then living. Norton (1827–1908), an art historian, a professor at Harvard, and the author of *Notes of Travel and Study in Italy* (1860), was in Europe at this time. The Nortons were old family friends.

2. Mrs. Norton's brother. [*Editor.*]

3. William Dean Howells, novelist and assistant editor of *The Atlantic Monthly*. [*Editor.*]

‡ Written during James's residence of several months in Florence while he composed *Roderick Hudson*. In the autumn of 1874 he returned to the United States. Grace Norton (1834–1926) was the sister of Charles Eliot Norton. From *The Letters of Henry James*, ed. Percy Lubbock (New York: Scribner's, 1920), I, 36–37.

4. Charles Eliot Norton. [*Editor.*]

we may, we belong much more to that than to this, and stand in a much less factitious and artificial relation to it. I feel forever how Europe keeps holding one at arm's length, and condemning one to a meagre scraping of the surface. I have been nearly a year in Italy and have hardly spoken to an Italian creature save washerwomen and waiters. This, you'll say, is my own stupidity; but granting this gladly, it proves that even a creature addicted as much to sentimentalizing as I am over the whole *mise en scène* of Italian life, doesn't find an easy initiation into what lies behind it. Sometimes I am overwhelmed with the pitifulness of this absurd want of reciprocity between Italy itself and all my rhapsodies about it. * * * But pity our poor bare country and don't revile. England and Italy, with their countless helps to life and pleasure, are the lands for happiness and self-oblivion. It would seem that in our great unendowed, unfurnished, unentertained and unentertaining continent, where we all sit sniffing, as it were, the very earth of our foundations, we ought to have leisure to turn out something handsome from the very heart of simple human nature. * * *

HENRY JAMES

Review of *A Foregone Conclusion*†

["*. . . civilization with us is monotonous . . .*"]

* * * American literature is immature, but it has, in prose and verse alike, a savor of its own, and we have often thought that this might be a theme for various interesting reflections. If we undertook to make a few, we should find Mr. Howells a capital text. He reminds us how much our native-grown imaginative effort is a matter of details, of fine shades, of pale colors, a making of small things do great service. Civilization with us is monotonous, and in the way of contrasts, of salient points, of chiaroscuro, we have to take what we can get. We have to look for these things in fields where a less devoted glance would see little more than an arid blank, and, at the last, we manage to find them. All this refines and sharpens our perceptions, makes us in a literary way, on our own scale, very delicate, and stimulates greatly our sense of proportion and form. Mr. Lowell and Mr. Longfellow among the poets, and

† Henry James, review of William Dean Howells's *A Foregone Conclusion* (Boston: J. R. Osgood & Co., 1875), in *The Nation*, 20 (January 7, 1875), 12–13; reprinted in *Literary Reviews and Essays by Henry James*, ed. Albert Mordell (New York: Vista House Publishers, 1957), 211–15. After two years of off-and-on travel in Europe, James was back in Cambridge with his family when this review was written. His dissatisfaction with America, evident in this review, would result in expatriation nine months later.

Mr. Howells, Bret Harte, and Mr. Aldrich[5] among the story-tellers (the latter writer, indeed, in verse as well as in prose), have all pre-eminently the instinct of style and shape. It is true, in general, that the conditions here indicated give American writing a limited authority, but they often give it a great charm—how great a charm, may be measured in the volume before us. * * *

HENRY JAMES

Review of *Notes on Paris*†

[*Taine's "Perfect Observer" of Parisian Life*]

This is a very clever work, but it is by no means one of the author's most successful. Indeed, though a brilliant failure, no one, we believe, has ever pretended that it was anything but a failure. The author has tried a *tour de force*, and missed his effect. He has attempted to force his talent, but his talent has resisted and proved fatally inflexible. He has wished to be light and graceful, but he has succeeded only in being most elaborately and magnificently grave. * * * Yet one reads the book, as a failure if not as success, and, all abatements made, we feel ourselves to be dealing with a man of extraordinary talent. It is very possible that it may have even more readers in English than in French, and to the American public seem decidedly entertaining. We apparently are capable of consuming an inordinate quantity of information, veracious or the reverse, about Paris, and the present volume is sufficiently free-spoken as to those social mysteries which are deemed typically Parisian. * * *

Exactly what M. Taine desired to do we hardly know; what he has done is to produce a singular compound of Stendhal and Théophile Gautier.[6] * * * M. Taine has proposed to do for Paris what Stendhal did for Milan; but he has come fifty years later, and he is consequently much more complex and needs a great deal more machinery. He is picturesque, for instance, both by necessity and by style, which Stendhal was not at all, in intention; his book overflows with the description of material objects—of face and hair, shoulders and arms, jewels, dresses, and furniture—and it is

5. James Russell Lowell, Henry Wadsworth Longfellow, and Thomas Bailey Aldrich were New England poets. Bret Harte was a California poet and local color writer. [*Editor.*]

† Henry James, review of H. A. Taine's *Notes on Paris: The Life and Opinions of M. Frederic Thomas Graindorge, etc.*, translated by John Austin Stevens (New York: Henry Holt & Co., 1875). The review appeared in *The Nation*, 20 (May 6, 1875), 318–19; and was reprinted in *Literary Reviews and Essays of Henry James*, ed. Albert Mordell (New York: Vista House Publishers, 1957), pp. 68–71.

6. Gautier (1811–72), French poet and critic; Stendhal, pen name of Marie Henri Beyle (1783–1842), author of *La Chartreuse de Parme* and *Le Rouge et le Noir*. [*Editor.*]

evident in all this description that, although M. Taine is a man of too individual a temperament to be an imitator, he has read Théophile Gautier, the master in this line, with great relish and profit. He is shooting in Gautier's premises, and when he brings down a bird we cannot help regarding it as Gautier's property.

M. Taine has endeavored to imagine a perfect observer, and he has given this gentleman's personality as a setting to his own extremely characteristic lucubrations. His observer is M. Frederic-Thomas Graindorge, a Frenchman, a bachelor, a man of fifty, who has made a fortune by hog-packing in Cincinnati, and returns to Paris in the afternoon of his days to take his ease, see the polite world in epitome, and systematize a little his store of observations. He has gone through the mill and been ground very fine; he was at school at Eton, as a boy; he was afterwards at the University of Jena; he has passed twenty years in our own great West, where his adventures have been of the most remarkable description. In his local color, as to this phase of his hero's antecedents, M. Taine is very much at fault; and this is the greater pity, as he has never failed to profess that one should speak only of that which one directly and personally knows. He knows the manners and customs of our Western States in a very roundabout and theoretical fashion; he seems to be under the impression, for instance, that the picturesque art of hog-packing (up to the time of our late war) was carried on in Cincinnati by slave-labor. "I desire only to listen and to look," says M. Graindorge; "I listen and I look; no woman is displeased at being looked at; nor any man at being listened to. Sometimes, as I button up my overcoat, an idea comes to me: I write it down when I go home; hence my notes. You see that this is not a literary matter." It is much more literary than M. Graindorge admits; and his notes have been for M. Taine quite as much an exercise of style as an expression of opinion. He writes admirably; he writes too well; he is simply the very transparent mask of the real author. He is, therefore, as a person, a decidedly ineffective creation, and it was hardly worth while to be at so much labor to construct him. But the point was that M. Taine desired full license to be sceptical and cynical, to prove that he had no prejudices; that he judged things not sentimentally but rationally; that he saw the workings of the *machine humaine* completely *à nu*, and he could do all this under cover of a fictitious M. Graindorge more gracefully than in his own person. M. Graindorge is the most brutal of materialists, and the more he watches the great Parisian spectacle, the greater folly it seems to him to be otherwise. He finds it all excessively ugly, except in so far as it is redeemed by a certain number of pretty women in beautiful dresses, cut very low. But though it is ugly, it is not depressing; exaltation and depression have nothing to do with it; the thing is to see—to see minutely, closely, with your own eyes, not to be a dupe, to find it very convenient that others are, to treat life and your fellow-mortals as a spectacle, to relish a good dinner, and keep yourself in as luxurious a physical good-humor as possible until the "machine" stops working. That of M. Graindorge ceases to operate in the course of the present volume, and the book closes with a statement of his "intimate" personal habits by his secretary, in lieu of a funeral oration.

Henry James to F. P. Church, December 1, 1875†

["*. . . the title of the thing is* The American . . ."]

Paris, Rue de Luxembourg 29
Dec. 1*st* [1875]

My dear Mr. Church

[*the first page of this letter is missing*]

. . . this before I left N.Y.

I propose to take for granted, as soon as I can, that you will be ready to publish, on receipt of them, the opening chapters of a novel. I have got at work upon one sooner than I expected, and particularly desire it to come out without delay. The title of the thing is *The American*. I hope you will not consider that it will interfere with such other serials as you may have under way, nor deem it a drawback if it runs over into next year. I will send you as promptly as possible the first of the MS.

Yours very truly,
H. James Jr.

HENRY JAMES

From *Parisian Sketches*‡

["*. . . to* soigner *an artist or his work . . .*"]*

* * * The Théâtre Français has in rehearsal a piece by the younger Dumas,[7] and this constitutes, from the Parisian point of

† From *Henry James: Letters*, ed. Leon Edel (Cambridge: Harvard University Press, 1975), II, 8–9. Francis P. Church was one of the owners and editors of *The Galaxy* magazine, which published a number of James's essays and stories.

‡ Henry James, *Parisian Sketches: Letters to the New York Tribune, 1875–1876*, eds. Leon Edel and Ilse Dusoir Lind (New York: New York University Press, 1957).

* *Parisian Sketches*, pp. 7–8. James dated this sketch November 22, 1875. [*Editor.*]

7. Alexandre Dumas *fils* (1824–1895), natural son of Alexandre Dumas *père* (1803–70), achieved fame with *La Dame aux Camélias* (1852), one of the great stage successes of the second half of the nineteenth century. His subsequent plays (including *L'Étrangère*) espoused conventional morality. The psychological orientation of Dumas' work, reflecting an unhappy childhood spent in the demimonde atmosphere frequented by his father, was alien to James, who often criticized Dumas' choice of subject matter.

view, a very great event. A *coup d'état* by Marshal MacMahon, an invasion of France by Prussia—it would take something of that sort to equal it. M. Dumas is a great favorite with the *Figaro* newspaper, and the *Figaro*'s compliments—which is saying a great deal—are almost as ingenious as its abuse.[8] Either in good humor or in bad it is, to my sense, a most detestable sheet; but it certainly understands in perfection the art of advertising a man. It has kindled a crackling fire under the *Étrangère*, and it will keep the pot boiling until the play is produced. The greater part of the *Figaro*, the other day, was taken up with an article of many columns about the reading of the play to the actors. Of course the papers could say very little that was definite, for the subject was not to be deflowered. But everything that talking without telling could do the *Figaro* achieved; it even gave the names of the characters—a piece of information which, for Dumas' regular admirers, leaves infinite pasture for the imagination. The French have a particular word for this sort of literary service; they call it to *soigner* an artist or his work—to take care of them. *L'Étrangère* is being very well taken care of. * * *

["*. . . invoking . . . good fortune upon the Republican councils . . .*"] †

Paris, Dec. 16.—There is only one thing talked about just now in Paris—the election of the 75 permanent senators.[9] * * * It was the first day of the voting for the senators at the Assembly; and I repaired to Versailles, invoking as discreetly as a foreigner may in such a matter, good fortune upon the Republican councils. * * * Now that the French legislative body is permanently established there—the new Senate Chamber has just been constructed, with extraordinary celerity—the melancholy of the place is a little less intolerable than formerly, and you may go and enjoy its fine historic flavor with comfortable equanimity. I have just been reading the first installment of the new work by M. Taine,[1] lately so atten-

8. The order of the six leading Parisian newspapers in point of circulation, as estimated in 1858, was: *Siècle*, *Presse*, *Constitutionnel*, *Patrie*, *Débats*, and *Assemblée*. In 1878 the total number of journals of all kinds published in France was 2,200. *Le Figaro* had a circulation of about 70,000.

† *Parisian Sketches*, pp. 23–24, 27–32. The year was 1875. [*Editor*.]

9. The election of the permanent senators marked the beginning of a republican majority in the chamber. President MacMahon had been chosen by the monarchical Right; thus the "victory of the Left" (of the republicans) in the election was indeed "dramatic." It forced MacMahon to follow a republican policy and to select a ministry from the Left Center.

1. Hippolyte Taine (1828–1893), the French critic and historian, became famous with his *Revue de l'Instruction Publique* (1855–1856), a series of articles attacking the French philosophers of the early 19th century and setting forth a system in which the methods of the exact sciences were applied to psychological and metaphysical research. In 1864 Taine was made professor at the École des Beaux Arts, a position which he held for

tively expected—*Les Origines de la France Contemporaine*—in which he sets forth with his usual vividness and vigor the prodigious wastefulness of the manners and customs introduced by Louis XIV. His pompous architecture swallowed up millions of treasure, but in view of the excellent use to which it is now being put we may almost absolve him. Versailles seems to have been made on purpose to offer a haven of security to a Parliament situated as the French Assembly is—a Parliament for which the "emotional" character of the population renders the national capital an unsafe abode.

* * *

One regards the present Assembly with an increase of interest now that it is about to become historical. * * * A great many foolish things have been said there, but one excellent thing has been done. The Republic has been kept along; the silver cord has not been allowed altogether to loose. By hook and by crook, through thick and thin, by something that seemed at times like a clumsy accident, the Republic has been weaned from babyhood and set on its feet. There are plenty of people who promise you it can't walk alone—that it will tumble over and crack its pate. But these are no true friends of the family. The wisest of the doctors and nurses declare that if it is given a chance it will toddle; and now, fortunately, every year its legs are growing longer. In the very place where the monarchs of the last century, as they looked about them at a court that ventured to laugh at honest Molière only when they had given the permissive smile, must have felt peculiarly and transcendently monarchical—beneath that great gilded angel above the proscenium, straddling upon her wrinkled silver cloud and clasping the lilied shield of the Bourbons—under these incongruous circumstances the work has been done. * * *

I just now mentioned M. Taine's new book, which is the literary event of the day, and is very well worth speaking of. The history of the French Revolution, upon which he has so long been engaged, proves to be a work of the somewhat larger scope, which the title I quoted above would indicate. The first volume, a stout octavo of 550 pages, came out two or three days since; it is devoted to the

---

twenty years. His *Histoire de la Littérature Anglaise*, in which his deterministic views were set forth in uncompromising fashion, appeared in 1863. Shocked by the French disasters of 1870–1871, he started to apply his analytical methods to the history of his own country. The first volume of *Les Origines de la France Contemporaine*, begun in 1871, was therefore eagerly awaited. James's dismissal of Taine's philosophic ideas is an interesting reflection of his American intellectual orientation. *Les Origines* has often been admired for its vigor of style, but from the French point of view its importance was ideological; it confronted the public with a criticism of the philosophical abstractions upon which the men of the eighteenth century had built their society and which were still widely current. James had reviewed Taine's work four times previously, in the *Nation* and the *Atlantic Monthly*.

"Ancien Régime." * * * He has given a complete picture of the structure and condition of the French society that preceded the Revolution—its organization, its habits, its occupations, its public and private economy, its diet, its costume, its temper, its ideas, its ways of feeling. The picture is extraordinarily complete, and is executed with that sustained vigor of which M. Taine only is capable. * * * M. Taine is supposed to intend to take a reactionary view of the French Revolution, and to devote himself chiefly to that somewhat neglected province of history, the injury it did to France. It is high time, certainly, that this work were done, from the liberal and philosophical standpoint. In this volume, however, the author is by no means reactionary; a more damning indictment than his picture of the social orders that the Revolution swept away cannot be imagined. The criticism of what it in turn established will come later. The book is a curious mine of facts about the old royal and aristocratic habits—about the expenditure of the court and of those who frequented it. I had marked a great many passages for quotation. Page after page is filled with accounts of the sinecures under Louis XIV and Louis XV. Gentlemen and ladies drew ten and twenty thousand francs a year for performing functions which had not even a name, and others for performing functions which had names which we do not pronounce in English (they do in French), though the functions themselves were strictly nominal. The analysis of the temper and intellectual condition of society is as complete as might have been expected from so keen a psychologist as M. Taine. This is accompanied by a great many characteristic anecdotes. * * * There was doubtless a good deal of reason in Talleyrand's saying that "He who had not lived before 1789 did not know the sweetness of living." There was another point of view, however: the last division of M. Taine's volume, and the most interesting, is on the people. But the whole book is to be read.

* * *

[" . . . *why she married a hunchback* . . ."]†

* * * The *pièce de résistance* on the occasion I mention was a *conférence* by M. Ernest Legouvé,[2] the prince of *conférenciers.* This epithet may be interpreted as a compliment in any degree the

† *Parisian Sketches,* pp. 68–70. James dated this sketch January 28, 1876. [*Editor.*]

2. Ernest Legouvé (1807–1903) was the French dramatist who wrote *Médée* (1855), which gave Ristori a notable part and which led to Legouvé's election to the French Academy. In the middle and late life (he was almost seventy when James heard him) he devoted his energies largely to lecturing and propagandizing for women's rights and children's education, in both of which movements he was a French pioneer. Legouvé was an advocate of physical training, was well known as a fencer, and was long regarded as one of the best shots in France.

reader chooses. A *conférence* (the reader may need to be reminded) is a performance which generally takes place in a very uncomfortable little room on the Boulevard des Capucines, into which curiosity has occasionally beguiled my steps. * * * The only gentleman in whose honor I have ever seen the little room in the Boulevard des Capucines filled is M. Francisque Sarcey,[3] the dramatic critic of the *Temps*, and one of the *maîtres du genre*. M. Sarcey may have begun to prepare his lecture ten minutes before his arrival, but I doubt whether it has taken more of his time. It is generally upon some book which has lately appeared, and it is often very entertaining. There could hardly be a better example of the value of practice and of assurance. If M. Sarcey can once begin he is safe. He rubs his hands, drinks a great many glasses of water, gets under way, drifts from one thing to another, and talks out his hour. But at the end of it, though I may have sat reflecting on the mysterious alchemy of the French tongue, agreeably spoken, I have, in retrospect, felt just a trifle bamboozled. It is, of course, very true that I have not been forced to go there, and it is also to be remembered that the sum taken in at the door is of the slenderest. As the maidservant said, when, on her having saved up thirty crowns, she was asked why she married a hunchback, "What sort of a husband can one get for thirty crowns?"[4]

* * *

["*. . . the good fortune not to be a Frenchman . . .*"]†

* * * Heaven forbid—for simple entertainment's sake—that anyone who has the good fortune not to be a Frenchman should become one, even in thought, at the present hour. They are a sadly perplexed people, and I find the spectacle of the various conflicting embodiments of opinion which I here and there encounter much more interesting than the monotonous interest of having a responsible bundle of doctrines and sticking to it. Without at all pleading guilty to the charge of that exaggeration of versatility known as being of the opinion of the last speaker, I never hear a

3. Francisque Sarcey (1828–1889), dramatic critic for the *Temps*, whose criticism James admired, published a number of volumes on the contemporary theater. * * * He was a master of the art of informal lecture. James's estimate of ten minutes' preparation for a lecture probably undercalculates the effort given by Sarcey to an art form which he developed on the principles of Cicero's *De Oratore*. Sarcey discussed the techniques of his lecture method in *Recollections of Middle Life* (1893).

4. James adapted this amusing anecdote in his novel, *The American*, which he was writing at this time. "What sort of a husband can you get for twelve thousand francs?" asks the little copyist Noémi Nioche of the American, Christopher Newman.

† *Parisian Sketches*, pp. 76–77. James dated this sketch February 11, 1876. [*Editor.*]

political sympathy strongly expressed without desiring at least to understand it—to get inside of the speaker's mind, circumstances, and antecedents. The other day a lady was talking to me of a gentleman whom she had ceased for some time to see—he was so violent a Republican.[5] He had none but Republicans at his house, and they were all horrible people. "No French people," she added in a moment, "are Republicans—at least no one that anyone sees." This seemed to me in its way quite sublime, and it was certainly excusable to desire to pass half an hour in a place so warm and snug and free from uncomfortable drafts as this lady's moral consciousness.

* * *

["... L'Étrangère ... *a disappointment* ..."]†

* * * Without giving up everything for lost, or taking the fall of the Rentes too much to heart, or insisting to—*gagner la frontière*—if one has time, as one of the characters in *L'Étrangère* says—it may be affirmed that the situation is as serious as it has been for many a day. But it is serious in a good and healthy sense. The Republic is now for the first time in Republican hands, and it remains to be seen what they will make of it. The day of speeches and promises and generalities is over, and the day of political conduct has come. It entails a great responsibility, and it will be interesting to see how the party of M. Gambetta[6] meet the occasion. * * *

If it is true that the country is going to the bad, and that the celebrated "era of revolutions" is again to open, people are beguiling the interval in such fashion as they may. A convenient sedative to suspense is found to be an evening at the Théâtre Français, where they are now playing Alexandre Dumas' long-expected drama *L'Étrangère*. Besides your evening, in this case you can get plenty to talk about afterward. The production of this piece has been the event of the winter. Besides its intrinsic importance, there were several accessory reasons for its attracting attention. It is the first play (if I am not mistaken) that Dumas has produced since his

5. James was more intimately acquainted with monarchist than with radical intemperance. To Alice James, on February 22, 1876, he wrote: "I see none but ardent Monarchists and hear everything vile said about the Republic." * * * [Alice James (1848–1892) was the novelist's younger sister.—*Editor.*]

† *Parisian Sketches*, pp. 84–91. James dated this sketch February 28, 1876. [*Editor.*]

6. Léon Gambetta (1838–1882) * * * was first elected to the Assembly in 1869. He rendered heroic service during the crucial years, 1869–1871, and after a brief period of strategic retirement in Spain, returned to France to agitate for the definitive establishment of the Republic. His parliamentary dexterity and eloquence secured the voting of the constitution in February, 1875. . . .

election to the Academy, as well as the first that he has presented to the Théâtre Français. The curiosity of the public, moreover, had been very skillfully stimulated, and the last rehearsal of the play had all the honors of a first representation. *L'Étrangère*, after all, has been but a moderate success—though, certainly, many a poor playwright would be enchanted that "moderation" should deal out his laurels and his percentage in this particular fashion. The great theater is crowded, and for the least little orchestra chairs you have to apply a week in advance. Nevertheless, the play is pronounced indifferent by some people, and shockingly bad by others. No one, as far as I have observed, has had the originality to call it good. I happened to hear it discussed, a few days since, among several gentlemen who are more or less of the same guild as its author, and it was as pretty a cutting up as one could desire to see.[7] The general verdict was that Alexandre Dumas has so much wind in his sails (from former successes) that he will float safely across his present shallows, but that his decline (since decline it is) will be cumulative; that another piece as bad as *L'Étrangère* will have much worse luck, and that the more gentle the public has been for the author hitherto, the more pitiless it will be when he begins to sink. Has he already begun to sink? I confess that *L'Étrangère* strikes me as a rather desperate piece of floundering in the dramatic sea. It is a long story, and I cannot pretend to relate it in detail. Suffice it that the Foreigner who gives its title to the piece, and who is played by that very interesting actress, Mme. Sarah Bernhardt,[8] is a daughter of our own democracy, Mrs. Clarkson by name. She explains, in the second act, by a mortal harangue—the longest, by the watch, I have ever listened to—that she is the daughter of a mulatto slave girl and a Carolinian planter. As she expresses it herself, "My mother was pretty: he remarked her; I was born of the remark." Mrs. Clarkson, however, has next to nothing to do with the action of the play, and she is the least successful figure that the author has ever drawn. Why she should be an American, why she should have Negro blood, why she should be the implacable demon that she is represented, why she should deliver the melodramatic

7. The exact occasion of this discussion is revealed in an unpublished letter to Alice James, February 22: "I went for an hour to Flaubert's * * * they were talking about the great theatrical event, Alexandre Dumas' *L'Étrangère* * * * they all detest Dumas—very properly, and predict for him a great fiasco before long."

8. Sarah Bernhardt (Sarah Henriette Rosine) (1845–1923) began her training for the stage at thirteen, and in 1862 made her first appearance at the Théâtre Français. In 1872, at the Français, she triumphed in *King Lear* and *Ruy Blas*, and shortly thereafter in *Hernani*. She set out on her travels, making her first appearance in London in 1879 in *Phèdre* and in New York in 1880 in *Adrienne Lecouvreur*. James's designation of her as "that very interesting actress" is notable for its lack of enthusiasm. He was always critical of her as being an excessively histrionic personality.

and interminable tirade I have mentioned, why she should come in, why she should go out, why, in short, she should exist—all this is the perfection of mystery. She is like the heroine of an old-fashioned drama of the Boulevard du Crime who has strayed unwittingly into a literary work, in which she is out of time with all her companions. She is, on Dumas' part, an incredible error of taste. It must be confessed, however, that her entrance into the play has a masterly effectiveness. The whole first act indeed is an excellent start, though the goal is never really reached. As one of the characters says, we are *en pleine décomposition sociale*. The Duchess de Sept-Monts is giving a charity ball, and the circle of her particular intimates is collected about her in one of her apartments. The lady in question has been sold by her father, a retired tradesman of immense fortune, to a penniless and exhausted little rake, who, driven to bay by his creditors, has been delighted to raise money on his ducal title by the simple expedient of matrimony. Her father and her husband are present, and the conversation alights upon Mrs. Clarkson, the mysterious American, her beauty, her diamonds, her sinister reputation, her innumerable conquests, and her total absence of female friends. No respectable woman has ever entered her house or has ever received her. It so happens that the Duchess's father, her husband and her lover are all entangled in Mrs. Clarkson's toils, and these facts more or less explicitly transpire. The baleful beauty is moreover even now on the premises; she has been seen in the garden among the visitors present by right of having purchased their ticket—seen on the arm of the Duchess's lover (a lover who is as yet, I hasten to add, sincerely platonic). Abruptly the Duchess is approached by a servant with a card, which she reads in deep agitation. She writes a few words on another card and gives it to the footman; he goes off with it, and then she reads aloud to the company the contents of the first missive. Mrs. Clarkson requests permission to be admitted to the salon in which the Duchess sits apart with her intimates, there to receive from the Duchess's own hands a cup of tea. In compensation, she offers to pay for her cup of tea the sum of 25,000 francs, which the Duchess will make over to the charity for which the ball has been given. At the revelation of this audacity the little circle is aghast, and demands with a single voice what the Duchess has answered. The Duchess has answered that Mrs. Clarkson may be admitted if one of the gentlemen actually about the hostess will go out, offer his arm, and conduct her into the ducal presence. There is a particular silence—half-a-dozen gentlemen are present, but not one of them moves. Finally the shaky, unclean little Duke himself (admirably played by Coquelin)[9] stands forth and declares that he will play the gallant part. The announcement makes a great sensation, for it is his presumed mistress that he proposes to introduce to his wife. He departs and shortly afterward returns, bearing Mrs. Clarkson on his arm, in all the effectiveness of the strange physiognomy and the fantastic toilet of yellow and black which Mme. Sarah Bernhardt has conferred upon her. "A cup!" shouts the outraged Duchess, sticking to her bargain and nothing but her bargain. I must not relate what follows. The real heroine of the play is Mlle. Croizette,[1] who played the Duchess with a great deal of skill and with all that strangely meretricious charm for which she is renowned. She has one really magnificent scene—a scene in which the ill-used (but on her own side by no means unpeccant) heroine, the cup of whose disgust at her husband's turpitude is full, pours it all forth in rage and scorn upon his ignoble head. This is nature caught in the act—Mlle. Croizette's cries and gestures, the passionate reality of her imprecations, electrify the house. The author makes his duchess say things which have never before been said on the stage, but the artistic good faith of the actress carries them off.

I should mention that there is also a Mr. Clarkson in the play—a gentleman engaged in gold-washing in Utah, while his wife drinks tea at five thousand dollars the spoonful in Paris. Half the merit of this figure is with Febvre,[2] who represents it, and who, in particular, has dressed his Yankee with great felicity—quite in the occidental taste, and yet without the least exaggeration. On the whole, as I have said, *L'Étrangère* has been a disappointment, and it is unquestionably a very unsatisfactory piece of work for so clever a man as Dumas. It hangs very loosely together, and the story is both extremely improbable and profoundly disagreeable. Disagreeable, above all, for there is not a person in the play who is not, in one way or another, misbehaving grossly. Everyone is in the wrong, and the author most of all. And then his drama is saturated with that aroma of bad company and loose living which is the distinctive sign of M. Dumas' nurse. This lady is afflicted with a congenital want of perception of certain rudimentary differences between the possible,

9. Benoît Constant Coquelin (1841–1909) entered the Théâtre Français in 1860, becoming *sociétaire* in 1864. He remained with the Français until 1886, shortly before beginning a tour of Europe and America. James, who had been a schoolmate of his at Boulogne-sur-Mer in the 1850s, devoted an article to him in the *Century Magazine*. It was Coquelin who created the part of Cyrano de Bergerac in Rostand's poetic drama. He was one of the actors in France most admired by the novelist.

1. Sophie Alexandrine Croizette (1848–1901) was born in Russia. She entered the Conservatoire in 1867, studied under Bressant, and won first prize for comedy in 1869. She appeared at the Théâtre Français in 1870 and was elected *sociétaire* in 1873.

2. Alexandre-Frédéric Febvre (1853–1916) played in several Paris theaters before joining the Théâtre Français in 1866. He became *sociétaire* in 1867 and retired in 1894.

for decent people, and the impossible. She has also on this occasion abused her characteristic privilege of indulging in pretentious tirades of the would-be philosophic order—explaining that love is physics and marriage is chemistry, &c.

* * *

[". . . *a man with a fixed idea—a monomaniac* . . ."]†

* * * If the Academy has any meaning, one would say that its meaning should be exactly that its honors are not for writers of the Janin[3] family. But has the Academy any meaning? Two or three incidents have lately occurred which make the inquiry proper. The most striking was certainly the admission among the sacred party, last spring, of Alexandre Dumas *fils*. M. Dumas is supremely clever, and he has composed dramas which it is impossible, on certain sides, too highly to admire; but it seems to me that he has about as much business in the Academy as in the Cabinet of the Emperor of China. He is a man with a fixed idea—a monomaniac. He can see nothing in life but the "unfortunate" woman; she is the pivot of his imagination—all his inspiration, his allusions and metaphors are drawn from her. If the Academy were an intellectual asylum, with wards, cells, and keepers, M. Dumas might very well appeal to its hospitality; but as it is, there is something grotesque in his presence there. The prime duty of the Academy ought to be to distinguish between the cracked vessel and the sound;[4] and it seems to me that if she had observed this duty, she would have said to Jules Janin and Alexandre Dumas, alike (dissimilar in talent as they are), that they were welcome to be clever, and popular, and brilliant, but that they were made of precisely the stuff she could not wear—they were deformed, erratic, mistaken. "Here is a certain straight line," she should have said, "you and I can never be on the same side of it."

* * *

† James, *Parisian Sketches*, pp. 97–98. James dated this sketch March 10, 1876. [*Editor.*]

3. Jules Janin (1804–1874), novelist, critic, and journalist, made his chief bid for fame with his collected dramatic criticism from the *Journal des Débats* (1858), under the title, "Histoire de la Littérature Dramatique." He was called in his time "the prince of critics," but James's charge of superficiality has also found its way into the annals. * * *

4. The image of "the cracked vessel and the sound" was to figure in *The Portrait of a Lady* and to be of the essence in *The Golden Bowl*.

Henry James to William Dean Howells, February 3, 1876†

["*. . . to get a novel on the stocks immediately . . .*"]

Paris, Rue de Luxembourg 29
Feb. 3*rd* [1876]

Dear Howells—

Ambiguous tho' it sounds, I was sorry to get your letter of the 16th ult. Shortly after coming to Paris, finding it a matter of prime necessity to get a novel on the stocks immediately, I wrote to F. P. Church, offering him one for the *Galaxy*, to begin in March, and I was just sending off my first instalment of MS. when your letter arrived. (The thing has been delayed to April.) It did not even occur to me to write to you about it, as I took for granted that the *Atlantic* would begin nothing till June or *July*, and it was the money question solely that had to determine me. If I had received your letter some weeks before I think my extreme preference to have the thing appear in the *Atlantic* might have induced me to wait till the time you mention. But even of this I am not sure, as by beginning in April my story, making nine long numbers, may terminate and appear in a volume by next Christmas. This, with the prompter monthly income (I have demanded $150 a number), is a momentous consideration. The story is *The American*—the one I spoke to you about (but which, by the way, runs a little differently from your memory of it). It was the only subject mature enough in my mind to use immediately. It has in fact perhaps been used somewhat prematurely; and I hope you find enough faults in it to console you for not having it in the *Atlantic*. There are two things to add. One is that the insufferable *nonchalance*, neglect and ill-manners of the Churches have left me very much in the dark as to whether my conditions are acceptable to them: and I have written to them that if they are not satisfied they are immediately to forward my parcel to you. The other is that I would, at any rate, rather give a novel to the *Atlantic* next year, (beginning, that is, in January) than this.[5] So far as one party can make a bargain, I hereby covenant to do so. I expect to have the last half of the summer and the autumn to work on such a tale; for I shall have obviously to settle down and produce my yearly romance. I am sorry, on many accounts, that the thing for the present, stands as it

† From *Henry James: Letters*, ed. Leon Edel (Cambridge: Harvard University Press, 1975), II, 22–23.

5. *The American* was published in the *Atlantic Monthly* from June through December 1876 and January through May 1877.

does, but I couldn't wait. I hope you will find something that will serve your turn.

Why didn't you tell me the name of the author of the very charming notice of *Roderick Hudson* in the last *Atlantic*, which I saw today at Galignani's? I don't recognize you, and I don't suspect Mrs. Wister. Was it Lathrop? If so please assure him of my gratitude. I am doing as I would be done by and not reading your story in pieces.[6] Will you mail me the volume when it appears? I should like to notice it.

Yes, I see a good deal of Tourguéneff and am excellent friends with him. He has been very kind to me and has inspired me with an extreme regard. He is everything that one could desire—robust, sympathetic, modest, simple, profound, intelligent, naif—in fine angelic. He has also made me acquainted with G. Flaubert, to whom I have likewise taken a great fancy, and at whose house I have seen the little *coterie* of the young realists in fiction. They are all charming talkers—though as editor of the austere *Atlantic* it would startle you to hear some of their projected subjects. The other day Edmond de Goncourt (the best of them) said he had been lately working very well on his novel—he had got upon an episode that greatly interested him, and into which he was going very far. *Flaubert:* "What is it?" *E. de G.* "A whore-house *de province*." * * *

Yours very truly
H. James Jr.

Henry James to F. P. Church, February 4, 1876†

["*. . . a 1st instalment . . . of my novel . . .*"]

Paris 29 Rue de Luxembourg
Feb. 4th [1876]

My dear Mr. Church,

I sent you a few days since a 1st instalment (in two packages,) of my novel; here is the second, (our number,) in the same form. A safe journey to all!—

Yours very truly
H. James jr

F. P. Church esq.

6. HJ seems to allude here to *Private Theatricals* by Howells, published in the *Atlantic* from November 1875 through May 1876.

† F. P. Church was the editor of *The Galaxy* magazine. James first submitted the manuscript of *The American* to *The Galaxy* on the assumption that it would be promptly serialized and that he would be immediately paid for it.

William Dean Howells to F. P. Church, February 29, 1876†

["... *I should be very glad to get it* ..."]

Editorial Office of
The Atlantic Monthly
The Riverside Press
Cambridge, Mass.

Feb. 29, 1876

My dear M. Church,

If you have found * * * that you can't use Mr. James's new serial, conveniently, won't you turn it over to me? I should be very glad to get it, and you may for editorial reasons, be glad to get rid of it, and so I make bold to ask for it.

Yours truly,
W. D. Howells

Henry James to F. P. Church, March 3, 1876‡

["... *absolute necessity on pecuniary grounds* ..."]

29 Rue de Luxembourg.
March 3*d* [1876]

My dear Mr. Church—

I have just received your letter of Feb. 18th. acknowledging the receipt of Ms.

I hasten to assure you that it is of the very greatest importance to me that the publication of my novel should begin immediately. I thought I made it clear in my letter—I certainly intended to—that I sent you the Ms. only on the understanding that the publication might proceed without delay. This is not only of importance to me, but it is an absolute necessity on pecuniary grounds. If, therefore, you are unable to begin *The American* at the latest in the May *Galaxy*, I must forego the pleasure of having the story appear in the Magazine. I decided it should be plain that this and the price I fixed per number ($150) were the only terms on which I offered it. I greatly hoped you would be able to put it forward in April, and the delay, save for a month, is perforce a matter of regret to me. If these conditions are impossible or inconvenient to you, I beg you to

† Manuscript letter printed with the kind permission of the Manuscript and Archives Division of the New York Public Library, Astor, Lenox, and Tilden Foundations.
‡ From *Henry James: Letters*, ed. Leon Edel (Cambridge: Harvard University Press, 1975), II, 31.

forward the Ms. to my father, 20 Quincy St. Cambridge, *as soon as* you decide such to be the case. Let me repeat with all possible emphasis that the May number is the latest moment to which I can afford to wait, and let me also add that I shall be obliged to you in case you relinquish the Ms., for despatching it, as above without even a day's delay. These then are my terms—$150 a number—to commence in *May*—and failing this to send the copy instantly to Cambridge. But I hope you will be able to accede to them, and I am sorry that this time has been lost in discussion through any ambiguity in my former letter.

Yours very truly
H. James Jr.

William Dean Howells to F. P. Church, March 5, 1876†

["*. . . your decision in regard to Mr. James's story . . .*"]

Editorial Office of
The Atlantic Monthly
The Riverside Press
Cambridge, Mass.

March 5, 1876

Dear Mr. Church:

I should be glad to know within a week what your decision in regard to Mr. James's story is.

Yours truly,
W. D. Howells

Henry James to William Dean Howells, May 28, 1876‡

["*. . . Of pure Parisianism I see absolutely nothing . . .*"]

29 Rue du Luxembourg, Paris.
May 28th [1876]

Dear Howells,

I have just received (an hour ago) your letter of May 14th. I shall be very glad to do my best to divide my story so that it will make twelve numbers, and I think I shall probably succeed. Of

† Manuscript letter printed with the kind permission of the Manuscript and Archives Division of the New York Public Library, Astor, Lenox and Tilden Foundations.

‡ From *The Letters of Henry James*, ed. Percy Lubbock (New York: Scribner's, 1920), I, 47–50.

course 26 pp. is an impossible instalment for the magazine. I had no idea the second number would make so much, though I half expected your remonstrance. I shall endeavour to give you about 14 pp., and to keep doing it for seven or eight months more. I sent you the other day a fourth part, a portion of which, I suppose, you will allot to the fifth.

My heart was touched by your regret that I hadn't given you "a great deal of my news"—though my reason suggested that I could not have given you what there was not to give. "La plus belle fille du monde ne peut donner que ce qu'elle a." I turn out news in very small quantities—it is impossible to imagine an existence less pervaded with any sort of *chiaroscuro*. I am turning into an old, and very contented, Parisian: I feel as if I had struck roots into the Parisian soil, and were likely to let them grow tangled and tenacious there. It is a very comfortable and profitable place, on the whole—I mean, especially, on its general and cosmopolitan side. Of pure Parisianism I see absolutely nothing. The great merit of the place is that one can arrange one's life here exactly as one pleases—that there are facilities for every kind of habit and taste, and that everything is accepted and understood. Paris itself meanwhile is a sort of painted background which keeps shifting and changing, and which is always there, to be looked at when you please, and to be most easily and comfortably ignored when you don't. * * * I have seen a certain number of people all winter who have helped to pass the time, but I have formed but one or two relations of permanent value, and which I desire to perpetuate. I have seen almost nothing of the literary fraternity, and there are fifty reasons why I should not become intimate with them. I don't like their wares, and they don't like any others; and besides, they are not *accueillants*. Turgenev is worth the whole heap of them, and yet he himself swallows them down in a manner that excites my extreme wonder. But he is the most loveable of men and takes all things easily. He is so pure and strong a genius that he doesn't need to be on the defensive as regards his opinions and enjoyments. The mistakes he may make don't hurt him. His modesty and naïveté are simply infantine. I gave him some time since the message you sent him, and he bade me to thank you very kindly and to say that he had the most agreeable memory of your two books. He has just gone to Russia to bury himself for two or three months on his estate, and try and finish a long novel he has for three or four years been working upon. I hope to heaven he may. I suspect he works little here.

I interrupted this a couple of hours since to go out and pay a visit to Gustave Flaubert, it being his time of receiving, and his last Sunday in Paris, and I owing him a farewell. *He* is a very fine old fellow, and the most interesting man and strongest artist of his circle. I had him for an hour alone, and then came in his "following," talking much of Émile Zola's catastrophe—Zola having just had a serial novel for which he was handsomely paid interrupted on account of protests from provincial subscribers against its indecency. The opinion apparently was that it was a bore, but that it could only do the book good on its appearance in a volume. Among your tribulations as editor, I take it that this particular one is not in store for you. On my way down from Flaubert's I met poor Zola climbing the staircase, looking very pale and sombre, and I saluted him with the flourish natural to a contributor who has just been invited to make his novel last longer yet.

Yours very faithfully,
H. James, jr.

Henry James to William James, July 4, 1876†

["... *convinced I am of their bottomless superficiality* ..."]

Paris, July 4 [1876]

Dear William,—

* * * Your remarks on Renan were most refreshing, and (strange as it may appear to you after my worthless account of his book in the *Tribune*)[7] quite in accordance with my own sentiments. I suspected what you say, but as it was only a vague feeling (mingled with a great admiration of his artistry) I attempted to make nothing of it (since I could make so little), and chose the tack of rather wholesale and general praise. But I am ready to believe anything bad of him. The longer I live in France the better I like the French personally, but the more convinced I am of their bottomless superficiality. * * *

Yours ever,
H. James Jr.

William James to Henry James, July 5, 1876‡

["... *your gilded and snobbish heights* ..."]

Cambridge, July 5 [1876]

My dear Harry,—

Your letters breathe more and more a spirit of domestication in

† From Ralph Barton Perry's *The Thought and Character of William James* (Boston: Little, Brown & Co., 1935), I, 369. William (1842–1910), the novelist's elder brother by a year, was a philosopher and psychologist at Harvard.

7. H.J. commented on Renan's *Dialogues et fragments philosophiques* in the *New York Tribune* for June 17, 1876, under the title of "Parisian Topics."

‡ From Ralph Barton Perry's *The Thought and Character of William James* (Boston: Little, Brown & Co., 1935), I, 369–72.

the modern Babylon which is very pleasant to me to receive. I suppose from your gilded and snobbish heights you think of us here with great pity, but for my part I hurl it back at you, being on the whole contented with my outward lot. * * *

Your spiritual condition is evidently felicitous, with your Turgenevs, your de Broglies, your Montargis and your Longchamps. Long may you enjoy them, only keep watch and ward lest in your style you become too Parisian and lose your hold on the pulse of the great American public, to which after all you must pander for support. In your last *Tribune* letter (about the Doudan letters)[8] there were too many traces of Gallicism in manner. It will be a good thing for you to resolve never to use the word "supreme," and to take great care not to use "delicate" in the French sense of a "cultured and fastidious" person. * * *

Your second instalment of *The American* is prime. The morbid little clergyman is worthy of Ivan Sergeitch. I was not a little amused to find some of my own attributes in him,—I think you found my "moral reaction" excessive when I was abroad. But I do detest the monthly, part way of publication, except in George Eliot. * * *

Yours ever,
W. J.

Henry James to William James, July 29, 1876†

["... *third rate Americanism* ..."]

Étretat
July 29*th* [1876]

Dear William,

Your long and charming letter of July 5th came to me just before I left Paris—some ten days since. * * * I am much obliged to you for your literary encouragement and advice—glad especially you like my novel. I can't judge it. Your remarks on my French tricks in my letters are doubtless most just, and shall be heeded. But it's an odd thing that such tricks should grow at a time when my last layer of resistance to a long-encroaching weariness and satiety with the French mind and its utterance has fallen from me like a

8. Victor, Duc de Broglie, statesman and historian. Montargis, a town about thirty miles south of Paris, was where the Lee-Childes were staying and where H.J. was to visit late in July. He had been taken to Longchamps to see the annual military review by Mme. Laugel. The letter referred to appeared in the *New York Tribune*, July 4, 1876, under the heading "Parisian Topics." *Mélanges et lettres*, by Ximénès Doudan, was published in Paris in 1876.

† From *Henry James: Letters*, ed. Leon Edel (Cambridge: Harvard University Press, 1975), II, 57–59.

garment. I have done with 'em forever, and I am turning English all over. I desire only to feed on English life and the contact of English minds—I wish greatly I knew some. Easy and smooth-flowing as life is in Paris, I would throw it over tomorrow for an even very small chance to plant myself for a while in England. If I had but a single good friend in London I would go thither. I have got nothing important out of Paris nor am likely to. My life there makes a much more succulent figure in your letters, as my mention of its thin ingredients comes back to me, than in my own consciousness. A good deal of Boulevard and third rate Americanism: few retributive relations otherwise. I know the Théâtre Français by heart! * * *

Yours always—
H. James Jr.

Henry James to William Dean Howells, October 24, 1876†

["*. . . I couldn't possibly, possibly, have made her do it . . .*"]

29 Rue de Luxembourg
Oct. 24*th* [1876]

Dear Howells—

Many thanks for your letter and the promise of *Hayes,* which I shall expect.[9] Thanks also for your good opinion of the notice of *Daniel Deronda,*[1] which charmed and reassured me. I was rather afraid that you would think its form beneath the majesty of the theme. Many thanks, furthermore, for your continuing to like the *American,* of which I shall send you by the next mail another installment. (I sent you one by the last, and I shall very soon send you the closing pages.) Your appeal on the subject of the *dénouement* fairly set me trembling, and I have to take my courage in both hands to answer you. In a word Mme de Cintré doesn't marry Newman, and I couldn't possibly, possibly, have made her do it. The whole point of the *dénouement* was, in the conception of the tale, in his losing her? I am pretty sure this will make itself clear to you when you read the last quarter of the book. My subject was: an American letting the insolent foreigner go, out of his good

† From *Henry James: Letters,* ed. Leon Edel (Cambridge: Harvard University Press, 1975), II, 70–72.

9. Howells had just written a campaign biography of Rutherford B. Hayes, his wife's cousin, who was elected to the American presidency that autumn.

1. An unsigned note on *Daniel Deronda* had already appeared in the *Nation* in the issue of February 4, 1876; in December of that year Henry James published in the *Atlantic* (XXXVIII, 684–94) "Daniel Deronda: A Conversation," later reprinted in *Partial Portraits* (1888). [*Editor.*]

nature, after the insolent foreigner had wronged him and *he* had held him in his power. To show the good nature I must show the wrong and the wrong of course is that the American is cheated out of Mme de Cintré. That he should only have been scared, and made to fear, for a while, he was going to lose her, would have been insufficient—*non è vero?* The subject is sad certainly but it all holds together. But in my next novel I promise you there shall be much marrying. *Apropos* of this I have it on my conscience to mention that I am in correspondence with Scribner about a serial to begin in this magazine in June next.[2] Nothing is yet settled, but I suppose something will be. The vision of a serial in Scribner does not, I may frankly say, aesthetically delight me; but it is the best thing I can do, so long as having a perpetual serial running has defined itself as a financial necessity for me. When my novels (if they ever do) bring me enough money to carry me over the intervals I shall be very glad to stick to the *Atlantic*. Or I would undertake to do this if I could simply have money down for my MS., leaving the Magazine to publish at its leisure. My novel is to be an *Americana*[3]—the adventures in Europe of a female Newman, who of course equally triumphs over the insolent foreigner. —Yes, I couldn't help translating those [*illegible*]—verses of Turgénieff,[4] tho' I don't share the Russian eagerness for War. T. himself is full of it, and I suspect it is coming. The air is full of it and all the world here expects it.—I think I shall thrive more effectually than here in London, to which city I propose before long to emigrate—if I don't go to Italy. But I shan't, at any rate, winter here. You managed to tell me very little about yourself. What are you writing?

Yours very truly, with love at your fire-side,

H. James Jr.

Henry James to William Dean Howells, December 18, 1876†

[". . . *so shocking as to make the 'reader's flesh creep'* . . ."]

3 Bolton St., Picadilly W.
Dec. 18*th* [1876]

Dear Howells,

Your letter of Nov. 10th lies opened before me, and as I glance over it I derive new satisfaction from your good opinion of my tale.

2. Nothing came of this plan.
3. Here HJ foreshadows *The Portrait of a Lady*.
4. HJ's prose rendering of Turgenev's verses appeared in the *Nation*, XXIII (October 5, 1876), 213.
† From *Henry James: Letters*, ed. Leon Edel (Cambridge: Harvard University Press, 1975), II, 84–85.

I send you herewith the 11th part, which I have been keeping to post in England, as I never feel that I can take precautions enough. It is shorter than any: and the 12th which will soon follow, will likewise be brief. I trust that, to the end, the thing will seem to you to carry itself properly. I received a few days since a letter from my brother William, in which he speaks of some phrases (on Newman's part) as being so shocking as to make the "reader's flesh creep." Two or three that he quotes are indeed infelicitous, as I perceive as soon as my attention is called to them. He mentioned having persuaded you to omit one or two of the same sort. I am very glad you have done so, and would give you *carte blanche*. It is all along of my not seeing a proof—which is a great disadvantage. There are many things, which, as they stand printed, I should have changed. *Ma che vuole?* Here I have no one to try anything on, or to ask how things sound.—

* * *

always faithfully yours
H. James Jr.

Henry James to Mrs. Henry James, Sr., December 24, 1876†

["*. . . that Newmanesque taint . . .*"]

3 Bolton St., Piccadilly W.
Christmas eve [1876]

Dearest mammy—

I lately received your two letters: the one involving William's, and the note enclosing Bob's verses. William will forgive me for addressing my answer to you, rather than to him; but it is meant for both of you. Many thanks for all. * * * I fondly believed he [William] was well again, and I trust he is now. Tell him I thank him much for his strictures on some of Newman's speeches in *The American* of which I quite admit the justice. It is all along of my not seeing proof—I should have let none of those things pass. The story, as it stands, is full of things I should have altered; but I think none of them are so inalterable but that I shall be easily able in preparing the volume, to remove effectually, by a few verbal corrections, that Newmanesque taint on which William dwells. I wish any of you would point out anything more you think subject to modification. * * *

Your fondest
H.J. Jr.

† From *Henry James: Letters*, ed. Leon Edel (Cambridge: Harvard University Press, 1975), II, 85–88.

Henry James to James Ripley Osgood, January 1, 1877†

[". . . *I will promptly send you revised copy* . . ."]

3 Bolton St. Piccadilly W.
Jan 1st [1877]

MY DEAR MR. OSGOOD—

I have delayed writing to you longer than I intended, to ask you whether you are disposed to publish as a volume my novel of *The American* which is at present running in the *Atlantic*. I suppose I may safely assume that you will do so, & that you will offer the same terms as for *Roderick Hudson*. The story is somewhat longer & to make a book of about the same bulk a little more, I suppose, would have to be put upon a page. It terminates in the *Atlantic* in the *May* number, & my desire would be to have it come out as nearly as possible at that moment. If you will let me know your views I will promptly send you revised copy.—Are there no more returns from the sale of *R. H.*? I should be delighted to receive whatever there may be.—I have lately come to England for the winter, & the above is my permanent address. Pray let me hear from you, & believe me yours very truly

H. James Jr.

Henry James to Mrs. Henry James, Sr., January 31, 1877‡

[". . . *the description of the Fleurières* . . ."]

3 Bolton St. Piccadilly.
Jan. 31*st* [1877]

Dearest mother—

* * * The account of Étretat etc. in the January *Galaxy* was most incredibly misprinted.[5] Apropos of such matters don't imagine that in the description of the Fleurières in the *American* I have betrayed the Childes by reproducing Varennes. *Nullement*. It is another and much finer place in that country—Château-Renard. I have lately written a good deal for the *Nation*, and shall, for the present, probably continue, and I suppose you recognise most of my things

† From S. P. Rosenbaum, "Two Henry James Letters on *The American* and *Watch and Ward*," *American Literature*, 30 (1959), 533–37. James Ripley Osgood (1836–1892) was the Boston publisher of *Roderick Hudson* and other early titles by Henry James.

‡ From *Henry James: Letters*, ed. Leon Edel (Cambridge: Harvard University Press, 1975), II, 92–96.

5. "From Normandy to the Pyrenées," *Galaxy*, XXIII (January 1877), 95–109, was reprinted in James's *Portraits of Places* (1883). [*Editor.*]

—but not all.—But I must close, sweet mother, this long letter. I will try and write oftener, more briefly. Give Sarah Sedgwick my love and tell her I hope much she will be able to come out. Love and blessings on everyone else from your fondest

H.J. Jr.

Henry James to William Dean Howells, February 2, 1877†

["*. . . a twenty minutes' nibble . . .*"]

3 Bolton St.
Feb. 2*d* [1877]

Dear Howells.—

I sent you a few lines three days since with my last bundle of copy; but now comes your letter of Jan. 20th which prompts me to send a few more.—I quite understand that you should not be able to begin another serial by H.J. Jr. until after the lapse of a year at least. Your readers and your contributors would alike remonstrate. I shall be glad, however, if you would begin to print a *six-months' tale* sooner than a longer one, to do something of those dimensions. But I should not make use of the subject I had in mind when I last alluded to this matter—that is essentially not compressible into so small a compass. It is the portrait of the character and recital of the adventures of a woman—a great swell, psychologically; a *grande nature*—accompanied with many "developments."[6] I would rather wait and do it when I can have full elbow room. * * * But I think that the real trouble is not that any novel that the *Atlantic* would publish in a year is too long, but that it is chopped up in too fine pieces. Properly such a thing as *The American* should have been put thro' in five or six months, in numbers of thirty or thirty-five pages. To wait a month for a twenty minutes' nibble at it, would, it seems to me, if I were a reader, put me into a fatally bad humor with it. I have just been making this reflection apropos of your little "Comedy"[7]—which is extremely pretty and entertaining. But one wants to go through with it. Your young-lady talk is marvellous—it's as if the devil himself were sitting in your inkstand. *He* only could have made you know that one girl would say that another's walking from the station was *Ghastly!!*

Yours ever
H.J. Jr.

† From *Henry James: Letters*, ed. Leon Edel (Cambridge: Harvard University Press, 1975), II, 96–97.

6. HJ sketches in an early form his plan for *The Portrait of a Lady*.

7. Howells' *Out of the Question*, published in the *Atlantic*, February–April 1877.

Henry James to William Dean Howells, March 30, 1877†

["*. . . an impossible couple . . .*"]

3 Bolton St. W.
March 30*th* [1877]

Dear Howells—

I am supposed to be busily scribbling for lucre this morning; but I must write you three lines of acknowledgment of your welcome long letter. Its most interesting portion was naturally your stricture on the close of my tale, which I accept with saintly meekness. These are matters which one feels about as one may, or as one can. I quite understand that as an editor you should go in for "cheerful endings"; but I am sorry that as a private reader you are not struck with the inevitability of the American dénouement. I fancied that most folks would feel that Mme de Cintré *couldn't*, when the finish came, marry Mr. Newman; and what the few persons who have spoken to me of the tale have expressed to me (e.g. Mrs. Kemble t'other day) was the fear that I should really put the marriage through. *Voyons;* it would have been impossible: they would have been an impossible couple, with an impossible problem before them. For instance—to speak very materially—where would they have lived? It was all very well for Newman to talk of giving her the whole world to choose from: but Asia and Africa being counted out, what would Europe and America have offered? Mme de Cintré couldn't have lived in New York; depend upon it; and Newman, after his marriage (or rather *she*, after it) couldn't have dwelt in France. There would have been nothing left but a farm out West. No, the interest of the subject was, for me, (without my being at all a pessimist) its exemplification of one of those insuperable difficulties which present themselves in people's lives and from which the only issue is by forfeiture—by losing something. It was cruelly hard for poor N. to lose, certainly: but *que diable allait-il faire dans cette galère?* We are each the product of circumstances and there are tall stone walls which fatally divide us. I have written my story from Newman's side of the wall, and I understand so well how Mme de Cintré couldn't really scramble over from *her* side! If I had represented her as doing so I should have made a prettier ending, certainly; but I should have felt as if I were throwing a rather vulgar sop to readers who don't really know the world and who don't measure the merit of a novel by its correspondence to

† From ***Henry James: Letters,*** **ed. Leon Edel (Cambridge: Harvard University Press, 1975), II, 104–7.**

the same. Such readers assuredly have a right to their entertainment, but I don't believe it is in me to give them, in a satisfactory way, what they require.—I don't think that "tragedies" have the presumption against them as much as you appear to; and I see no logical reason why they shouldn't be as *long* as comedies. In the drama they are usually allowed to be longer—*non è vero?*—But whether the *Atlantic* ought to print unlimited tragedy is another question—which you are doubtless quite right in regarding as you do. Of course you couldn't have, for the present, another evaporated marriage from me! I suspect it is the tragedies in life that arrest my attention more than the other things and say more to my imagination; but, on the other hand, if I fix my eyes on a sun-spot I think I am able to see the prismatic colors in it. You shall have the brightest possible sun-spot for the four-number tale of 1878.[8] * * *

Yours always truly
H. James Jr.

Henry James to Thomas Sergeant Perry, June 25, 1877†

["*. . . it was very graceful & sufficient . . .*"]

3 Bolton St. W.
June 25 [1877]

Dear Tom

I heard from Wm, who enclosed your note, about your annoyance over the fate of your notice of the *American* in the *Nation. Allons donc.* I am very sorry they curtailed the article but it was very graceful & sufficient as it was & gave me as much pleasure as your perturbation of mind gives me pain. On its literary side the N. is not ill-disposedly, but simply helplessly & un-cleverly managed. Rather it isn't managed at all, & they never dreamed that it would have been prettier to me (a ten year's servant of the paper) to have in *all* your criticism. Be reassured as to *my* own regrets. I should much have liked to see what else you said: but I am very sorry that the suppression of it should make you any *mauvais sang*. It isn't worth that. I got your letter of 3 weeks (or more) since, with thanks; but this isn't an answer to it. That will come later. Meanwhile will you (if you can) a small service? Walter Pollock (a literary grabb) here who writes in the *Saturday* &c—son of Sir Frederick P. who edited Macready's memoirs & of Lady P. who

8. HJ outlines his plan for *The Europeans*, published in the *Atlantic*, July–October 1878.

† From Virginia Harlow's *Thomas Sergeant Perry: A Biography and Letters to Perry from William, Henry, and Garth Wilkinson James* (Durham, N.C.: Duke University Press, 1950), pp. 296–97. Perry (1845–1928), an editor and critic, was James's Newport schoolmate and lifelong friend. His review of *The American*, reprinted below, was unaccountably shortened by Wendell Phillips Garrison, the editor of *The Nation*.

scribbles in the 19th Cent'y &c) will send you a novel (M——) in the hope that, if you can, you will make a paragraph on it, for the *Atlantic*. If you can decently do. I haven't yet seen the book. He asked me who would or could do it, & as his people have been "civil" to me here, I mentioned you as a person he might experimentally send it to. He is to do (I believe) the *American* (poorly, I ween) in the Saturday.[9] I reserve London gossip for a calmer hour. With love to your wife, in extreme haste

Yours ever
H. James Jr

Henry James to William James, June 28, 1877†

["... *such vile impudence as the translator's performance* ..."]

3 Bolton St. W.
June 28*th* [1877]

Dear Brother—

It is a good while ago now since I received your letter of May 27th; since when also I got a note from father, in which he spoke of sending me a post office order from Osgood, and the German translation of my novel. Both of these have come; for which many thanks. Did you ever see such vile impudence as the translator's performance on the *dénouement* of the tale? and the "cheek" of the man in sending it to me with his "compliments"![1] If those are your Germans I give them up. * * * I enclose a notice of *The American* from the *Daily News*. I esteem it a considerable compliment that Frank Hill, the editor, a fiercely busy man, should have found time to read it, and write me a very good, appreciative little note about it; which I should enclose if I hadn't lost it. (He didn't write the notice.) The *American* will be reviewed (I learned) in the *Saturday Review*; probably indifferently well, as 'tis by Walter Pollock, a very amiable mediocrity. *Apropos* of this matter, I forgot to thank father for enclosing poor T. S. Perry's note of distress to you about the treatment of *his* article in the *Nation*. I am very sorry for his distress, and wrote to him. The notice was respectable; but it was helpless and unperceptive in poor Garrison (as regards *me*) to cut out his comments. * * *

Ever dear brother, your fond
H. J. Jr.

9. "Saturday" refers to the London *Saturday Review*. [*Editor*.]

† From *Henry James: Letters*, ed. Leon Edel (Cambridge: Harvard University Press, 1975), II, 116–21.

1. *The American* was translated as *Der Amerikaner oder Marquis und Yankee* (Stuttgart, 1877). The translator, Heichten-Abenheim, supplied a happy ending and took other liberties with the text.

Henry James to Thomas Sergeant Perry, March 22, 1878†

["*. . . the Freiherr v. Tauchnitz jr. . . .*"]

3 Bolton St.
March 22d 1878

Dear Tom—

* * * I have just (½ hour since) received visits from F. T. Palgrave & the Freiherr v. Tauchnitz jr. The 1st is the biggest talker on record—of any age or clime—& the latter is republishing my "works"—having begun with *The American.* I met last night at dinner old Madame Taglioni, the ex-dancer—a delightful little wizened, ancient, talkative woman; so you see I encounter various specimens. * * * write me soon again, & believe me dear Tommy, faithfully yrs,

H. J. jr

FREDERICK SHELDON

The American Colony in France‡

["*. . . Tout Américain à Paris se croît gentilhomme . . .*"]

Paris, March 20, 1878.

No one can have resided long abroad without noticing that Americans as a people are neither liked nor respected by the French, in spite of their purchasing power and of the pretty speeches made at the Grand Hôtel dinners about Lafayette, Rochambeau & Co. Frenchmen are not prejudiced against us by the stories of our barbarous customs and financial irregularities at home. They only shrug their shoulders when they hear them. "Que voulez-vous! chaque pays a ses usages," as one of them said to a lady who complained that African cannibals had eaten her husband. They judge us by what they see here. Some thoroughly good Americans get to Paris even during life, but what are they compared with the crowd which quick travel and low fares impel every season over Europe? The United States has become the *Officina*

† From Virginia Harlow's *Thomas Sergeant Perry: A Biography and Letters to Perry from William, Henry, and Garth Wilkinson James* (Durham, N.C.: Duke University Press, 1950), pp. 298–99.

‡ "The American Colony in France," *The Nation,* 26 (18 April 1878), 257–59. The author, Frederick Sheldon, signed the article "I.M."

viatorum. Our citizens, male and female, manage to beg, borrow, or steal at least one trip to Europe; and as misfortunes never come single, they bring their children with them—numerous, noisy, and uncontrolled. French and English children are left at home when their parents travel. They also bring with them a wonderful ignorance of the habits, behavior, and feelings of Europeans. Indeed there are many whose untutored minds expect to find here a repetition of the ways and manners of their native town. Everything is compared with home, and nothing that differs seems as good. "Paris is a' very weel, but Peebles for pleasure." The Boulevard is not like Lake Avenue, and at the cafés you cannot get pork and beans or fried ham. We expect the Bon-Marché shop in the Rue de Bac; that is the Caaba of the pilgrimage of American women.

Plato says that a certain brisk pertness and self-assertion is the result of democratic government. For other reasons America is not a good training-school of manners for the multitude. Not that Americans wish to be offensive—on the contrary, they are very good-natured; but they seem not to know the kind of treatment or attention (*égard* is the French word) a civilized being has the right to expect from a stranger. They simply do as they are willing to be done by. But here the standard of out-door manners is very different, and American shortcomings in this respect cause many uncomplimentary remarks. We overheard an exasperated Frenchman assert that no people were so ill-mannered as the Americans, except the Germans. Another difficulty for the American traveller is that he does not know his place in this complex society. In his ignorance of custom and etiquette he will thrust himself even upon royalty, utterly unconscious of the disgust he is producing; or, if ignorant of all languages but his own, he will bestow his company upon hotel servants who speak English, confiding to them his troubles and consulting them about his little wants and purchases. A distinguished New York politician, who missed, no doubt, in Paris his home constituency of ragamuffins, used to address the servants of his hotel, urging them to go to America, where all men were equal and labor respected. Our lucky countrymen who have struck oil or bonanzas have more pretension. They hire a courier, to whom they bow down—an accomplished creature, who speaks six languages unintelligibly, and who knows the best hotels and the best shops all over the Continent. He tells them what to do, what to eat, how to dress; drives with them inside of their landau, pats them on the back when he is good-humored and condescending, smokes in their faces, makes love to the maid, and pockets his ten per cent on everything they buy.

In October, when the summer flood ebbs homeward, numerous

stragglers are left stranded, who give various reasons for stopping. Health, education of children, study of science or art. Some of the students follow the apostolic rule of travel, take neither scrip nor purse, and find it difficult to pay their bills without borrowing, and some are mere adventurers, "gentlemen of independent morals and ladies unattached." One meets single ladies who have come to study for prima donnas or for "general culture," with no visible means of support; married ladies without their husbands (many American families, like their mercantile houses, having branches on this side); widows of the class called *vedova pericolante* in Italy, sometimes alone, sometimes with a daughter pretty, dressy, not bashful, *qui s'habille et babille*; and young girls travelling together without chaperonage or duennage, *sans peur* and all, of course, *sans reproche*; but no amount of conscious rectitude will get them the respect of people who are accustomed to draw certain inferences from certain appearances. Above and beyond these waifs and strays is the "Colonie Américaine," a collection of families who inhabit the Champs Elysées and the quarter about the Arc de Triomphe. Some of them reside abroad to save money, and others because they wish to spend it, and their sudden fortunes have given them no positions at home. The general theory is that they can lead an easier life and get more comfort and luxury from their incomes than they could in the United States, which is probably true. The colonists, in spite of repeated attacks on French society, see very little of it, except, indeed, a few young men attracted by dinners, dances, and daughters with "*dots*." They lead an idle, aimless existence, enlivened for the men by daily visits to Drexel's or Cuvillier's and for the women, by tea-drinking and gossip like that of a small New England village in the winter season—a life not without its attractions for the ladies, especially when they turn Catholic, which is rather the swell thing to do; but, one would think, insufferably dull to a man of energy and character. The Colonie has its little gradations of rank and its *grandes dames*. All unite in sneering at those they call "low Americans." Foreigners do not perceive this distinction, but look upon all Americans as occupying the same social plane, differing only in spending more or less money. Of their own country the Colonie speaks with mild contempt: "Better fifty years of Paris than a cycle of Broadway." New York is provincial; the streets are unswept; men chew tobacco; the servants are not respectful and get very high wages. "It is not fit for a gentleman to live in." All the uses of that new world seem weary, stale, flat, and unprofitable. The Colonie washes its hands of it and addresses new-comers as "You Americans." And yet, in spite of these excellent sentiments, very good apartments, correct servants, strict adherence to the fashions of the natives and prompt payment, the Colonie is not respected. No educated Frenchman or Englishman can understand why a man who is soundly constituted, mentally, morally, and financially, should permanently reside out of his own country, unless as a merchant or a diplomat or an exile for cause.

The critical foreigner is also amused by the love of orders and titles displayed even by the sturdiest American democrats. A red ribbon, or ribbon of any color, is ostentatiously worn, whether derived from a jury position in some International Exposition, or given by the late Emperor as a reward for inventing a clothes-wringer or a new method of making artificial teeth. *Décoré comme un dentiste américain* has become a French proverb. It is said that one of our officials on this side, keenly feeling that this outward and visible sign was wanting to complete the get-up of a great ex-military traveller, invented an order composed of the badges of the different army corps during the war, which was worn both by the great man and himself about their necks on suitable occasions. American girls can marry titles, but they are manifestly unattainable by American men. They try to meet this difficulty by the use of Honorable. A man who has held any office, from President to constable, thinks himself entitled to put this word before his name; or if he has been a volunteer officer, or even honorary aide-de-camp to the governor of his State, he puts Major or Colonel on his visiting cards and conspicuously on his luggage. This particular weakness obtains as much in the aristocratic class of Americans as in the "lower" varieties of the race. There *is* an aristocracy in the United States, although it may be difficult to note in what it consists. Perhaps a rough but tolerable definition is that the father of the American aristocrat kept the shop and bequeathed the fortune. As a consequence, the descendant of the rich family has a better education in the amenities and accomplishments of social life than the fellow-citizen whose head has just appeared above the surface. Indeed, in my opinion there is no nicer person to be found on the planet than a well-bred American of education and sense. But when established here their good sense deserts them on this point. Their sympathy with European manners and social distinctions "o'erleaps itself and falls on the other side." Laboulaye hit the mark when he said, "*Tout Américain à Paris se croît gentilhomme.*" Although they only see society abroad as the Mussulman women do Paradise, through the boundary railings, they wish to live near the upper class and to live like it. They have no other way of asserting their position. Hence many spend more than they can afford; more, certainly, than foreigners of the same fortune would think themselves justified in spending. By some mysterious process of reasoning they consider it necessary to live up to an imaginary social dignity at home. All that the "right people" do they carefully imitate, struggling to avoid sinning against the conventionalities in equipage, dress, and habits. Thinking always what foreigners will think of them begets an uncomfortable self-consciousness, a want of confidence in themselves. They are not genuine; only imitations. The "low" American has here the advantage. He may have little taste or appreciation of art, he may be too ready to assert himself and to boast of his country, but he really believes in himself and in his country. The better-bred man, who looks down upon him, is in his inmost heart ashamed of his country. He will resent any open attack upon it with vigor; he may talk of its wealth, prosperity, ingenuity, and enterprise, but secretly he wishes he had been born elsewhere. If you care to make him your friend for life, tell him he has been taken for an Englishman. It is the greatest compliment you can pay him. Give him time, and ten to one he will tell you himself how often this "odd mistake" has occurred. To England he turns his face when he worships. English opinion decides all social questions for him without appeal. He wears only English clothes, and tries hard to catch the accent. He is familiar with Burke and the history of English families, and does not forget to mention his English friends. If his name is Smith Brown he connects these two aristocratic patronymics with a hyphen, or if it be only Smith, he will spell it with a *y*, trace his descent from the noble family of that name, and adopt their crest on his note-paper and his harness. We are the only powerful nation whose sons and daughters display this lack of moral fibre. Englishmen and Frenchmen are proud of being English and French, and generally proclaim their nationality. The Anglo-American has no confidence in his ability to command respect as an American; he tacitly admits himself to be an inferior creature.

Herein lies a double foolishness. The world, like Alfieri, prefers *originale, anche tristo, a ottima copia*. A certain flavor of the soil is never disagreeable in a well-bred person; rather, it is attractive, as a slight foreign accent is pleasing in a stranger who speaks English well. It is much better form to be American and to have a national individuality of one's own than to offer to foreign eyes a pale imitation of European models.

> "That man's the best cosmopolite
> Who loves his native country best."

In the second place, imitations are always failures. As false teeth and hair-dye deceive nobody, and he who runs may read the age of the person who uses them, so no American, dress, talk, and live as he may, can shake off the land of his birth. The Yankee will show through the London clothes, the carefully studied accent, and the foreign habits. It is impossible long to conceal the melancholy reality.

Henry James to William James, May 1, 1878†

["... *I am still completely an outsider here* ..."]

3 Bolton St., W.
May 1st, '78.

Dear William,

* * * I am still completely an outsider here, and my only chance for becoming a little of an insider (in that limited sense in which an American can ever do so) is to remain here for the present. After that—a couple of years hence—I shall go home for a year, embrace you all, and see everything of the country I can, including Washington. Meanwhile, if one will take what comes, one is by no means cut off from getting impressions here. . . . I know what I am about, and I have always my eyes on my native land.

I am very glad that Howells's play seemed so pretty, on the stage. Much of the dialogue, as it read, was certainly charming; but I should have been afraid of the slimness and un-scenic quality of the plot. For myself (in answer to your adjuration) it has long been my most earnest and definite intention to commence at play-writing as soon as I can. This will be soon, and then I shall astound the world! My inspection of the French theatre will fructify. I have thoroughly mastered Dumas, Augier, and Sardou (whom it is greatly lacking to Howells—by the way—to have studied:) and I know all they know and a great deal more besides. Seriously speaking, I have a great many ideas on this subject, and I sometimes feel tempted to retire to some frugal village, for twelve months, where, my current expenses being inconsiderable, I might have leisure to work them off. Even if I could only find some manager or publisher sufficiently devoted to believe in this and make me an allowance for such a period, I would afterwards make a compact and sign it with my blood, to reimburse him in thousands. But I shall not have to come to this, or to depend upon it. * * *

H. James jr.

† From *The Letters of Henry James*, ed. Percy Lubbock (New York: Scribner's, 1920), I, 59–61.

Henry James to William Dean Howells, July 14 (15?), 1879†

["*. . . a smaller number of long instalments . . .*"]

Reform Club,
[July 14 or 15 1879]

My dear Howells,

Your letter of June 29th, asking me for a novel for next year came to me three days since, and I have been thinking over your proposal. I am under certain pledges to the *Cornhill* and *Macmillan*; but having sifted them out and boiled them down, I have come to the conclusion that I may properly undertake to furnish you a glowing romance about the time you propose. That is if my conditions suit you. These bear on two or three points. For instance I have the desire that the next *long* story I write be *really* a long one—i.e. as long as *The American* at least—though very preferably told in a smaller number of long instalments. As you speak of having *four* novels in one year I am afraid this *won't* suit you. I think that what I should like would be six or seven numbers of twenty-five pages apiece. I should also like to begin about the middle of the year—June or July—hardly before, and not later.—I shall also feel inspired, probably, to ask more for my tale than I have done for any of its predecessors. * * * I must try and seek a larger success than I have yet obtained in doing something on a larger scale than I have yet done. I am greatly in need of it—of the larger success.

Yours ever
H. James Jr.

HENRY JAMES

Americans Abroad‡

["*. . . Americans in Europe are* outsiders . . ."]

Some weeks ago (No. 668) there appeared in these columns a short account of the American colony in Paris, which called forth

† From *Henry James: Letters,* ed. Leon Edel (Cambridge: Harvard University Press, 1975), II, 251–52.

‡ From *The Nation,* 27 (October 3, 1878), 208–9.

at the time a rejoinder, and upon which it has been our fortune to hear privately a good many comments. Some of these comments have been sympathetic; others have been highly dissentient. In every case, however, there was a discussion of the question raised—a discussion which, in the circle in which it took place, could not fail to be extremely interesting. However the question raised may in any case be settled—the question of Americans appearing "to advantage" or otherwise in Europe—there is no doubt that nothing could be well more characteristic of our nationality than the sight of a group of persons more or less earnestly discussing it. We are the only people with whom such a question can be in the least what the French call an actuality. It is hard to imagine two or three Englishmen, two or three Frenchmen, two or three Germans comparing notes and strongly differing as to the impression made upon the civilized world by the collective body of their countrymen. In the first place, the Englishman or the Frenchman sees no reason to suppose that such an impression is in any way peculiar, or that one member of European society distinguishes himself noticeably from another. In the second place, if he were to be made aware that foreigners were criticising him, he would be extremely indifferent to their verdict. He would comfortably assume that the standard of manners—the shaping influences—in his own country are the highest, and that if he is a gentleman according to these canons he may go his way in peace. The season is drawing to a close during which, chiefly, Americans disseminate themselves in foreign lands, and for the last three or four months the national character has had free play in European hotels and railway stations. The impression, whatever it is, produced upon the European community must have been sensibly deepened. In spite of the commercial tribulations at home, the number of American travellers abroad has been very large, and numerous also have been the Americans (more numerous every year) who have betaken themselves to Europe for an indefinite residence. Those observers of whom we just now spoke, who are always ready to be a party to national self-analysis, have probably, in many cases, collected some new ideas. They have encountered, for instance, a few more specimens of the unattached young American lady—the young lady travelling for culture, or relaxation, or economy—and, according to their different points of view, she has seemed to them a touching or a startling phenomenon. The writer of these lines feels that he has added to the number of his own observations; that the data upon which his general conclusions rest have been multiplied; and that, thanks to his having passed some weeks in a great city in which the American tourist is frequently met and easily recognized, he might, in such a discussion as was just now alluded to, be beguiled into giving an even indiscreet extension to remarks originally prompted simply by a friendly interest in that class of Parisians known as Americans.

Americans in Europe are *outsiders*; that is the great point, and the point thrown into relief by all zealous efforts to controvert it. As a people we are out of European society; the fact seems to us incontestable, be it regrettable or not. We are not only out of the European circle politically and geographically; we are out of it socially, and for excellent reasons. We are the only great people of the civilized world that is a pure democracy, and we are the only great people that is exclusively commercial. Add the remoteness represented by these facts to our great and painful geographical remoteness, and it will be easy to see why to be known in Europe as an American is to enjoy an imperfect reciprocity. It may be the Europeans who are the losers by this absence of reciprocity; we do not prejudge that point, and we do not know, indeed, who is to settle it. A great many Americans—by no means all—maintain that the Europeans *are* the losers, and declare that if they don't know us and don't care about us, so much the worse for them. This is in many ways a very proper and very natural attitude; but nothing can be more characteristic of our civilization than the fact that an American may be almost defied to maintain it consistently. Let him be even more patriotic than is necessary, he is constantly lapsing from it, and, when he is in company with Europeans who do nothing to ruffle his usually great good-nature, he constantly takes a tone which indicates that he values their good opinion and that he is rather flattered than otherwise by possessing it. This, however, is a matter to be discussed apart. We wish to mention the last fact which leads Europeans to look upon Americans as aliens—the fact that large and increasing numbers of them elect, as the phrase is, to spend large parts of their lives in foreign lands. When a European sees an American absentee settle down in the country of which he himself is a native it is not surprising that, in the fact of this practical tribute, he should be found doubting whether the country the American has left is as agreeable, as comfortable, as civilized, as desirable a one to belong to as his own. The American may carefully explain that he is living abroad for such and such special and limited reasons—for culture, for music, for art, for the languages, for economy, for the education of his children; the fact remains that in pursuit of some *agrément* or other he has forsaken his native land, and the European retains, ineffaceably, the impression that if America were really a pleasant place he would never do so. He would come to travel—yes, frequently and extensively; but he (or rather *she*, for as a general thing, in this case, that is the proper pronoun) would never take up an abode in a strange city and remain there year after year, looking about, rather hungrily, for social diversion and "trying to get into society." Such a spectacle makes the European take the American, as an American, by so much the less *au sérieux*. An Englishman, a Frenchman, a German finds his intellectual, his aesthetic ideal in living in his own country. A great many Englishmen live out of England for economy; a great many Germans emigrate to make a living. But the ideal in each of these cases is to be rich enough to live at home; the dream of felicity is to have a large income and spend it within one's native borders. If we perhaps except the Russians, who do not altogether come into our category, the Americans are the only highly-civilized people among whom the ideal takes another turn. It will probably never be the case that the country will lack a sufficient number of rich residents to "run" it; but we shall probably for a long time continue to see numbers of Americans absenting themselves from the United States in proportion as fortune puts into their hands the means of what is called enjoying life. A great many of them prefer to enjoy life in Paris, where our correspondent who described the "colony" gave a sketch of their situation. They are naturally a puzzle to many of the people they live among, who are at a loss to imagine the compensation that Americans find in a society with which they do not amalgamate for the forfeiture of those social advantages which, as is supposed, gentlemen and ladies enjoy in their own country. The compensation that comes from shops and theatres and restaurants seems insufficient to the average European mind, preoccupied as that mind is with the belief that nothing can be so agreeable as the *life* of one's native land—the animated circle of which one is a member as a matter of course. The average European mind can never understand that for many enriched Americans life at home has never been strikingly agreeable, and that public amusements in a European capital may not unfairly be held to outweigh the social advantages relinquished even in certain capitals of States.

Curiously combined with that argumentative national self-consciousness of which we began by speaking is a profound, imperturbable, unsuspectingness on the part of many Americans of the impression they produce in foreign lands. With this state of mind it is impossible to find fault; it has always been, we suspect, the mark of great nationalities. It has become a commonplace to say that the English are conspicuous for it, and it is highly probable that the ancient Romans—the *cives Romani*—were equally so. But it may sometimes provoke a smile, when the impression produced is a good deal at variance with European circumstances. There is the conscious and the unconscious American; for we, of course, do not mean that the two characters are combined in the same individual. The conscious American is apologetic, explanatory—a pessimist might sometimes say snobbish. But perhaps, after having traversed a certain phase by a sort of Hegelian unfolding, this type is on its way to become unconscious again. Extremes meet, and that is a symptom of great experiences as well as of great innocence. The great innocence of the usual American tourist is perhaps his most general quality. He takes all sorts of forms, some of them agreeable and some the reverse, and it is probably not unfair to say that by sophisticated Europeans it is harshly interpreted. They waste no time in hair-splitting; they set it down once for all as very vulgar. It may be added that there are a great many cases in which this conclusion hardly seems forced. A very large proportion of the Americans who annually scatter themselves over Europe are by no means flattering to the national vanity. Their merits, whatever they are, are not of a sort that strike the eye—still less the ear. They are ill-made, ill-mannered, ill-dressed. A very good way to get a collective impression of them is to go and sit for half an hour in the waiting-room of any European banker upon whom Americans hold letters of credit. During certain hours of the morning our compatriots swarm, getting their drafts cashed and asking for their letters—those letters which they apparently suspect the banker's clerks of a constitutional indisposition to surrender. The writer of these lines lately enjoyed on several occasions this opportunity of observation, and—from the point of view of amenity—the spectacle was not gratifying. *Are* we the worst-looking people in the world? the sophisticated spectator, on such an occasion, enquires; and lest he should be beguiled into giving an answer too monstrous he abstains from giving any at all. One American (of the "conscious" class) has a way of explaining these things—the common facial types, the vulgar manners, the "mean" voices, the want of acquaintance with the rudiments of the science of dress—to another. He says that in America "every one travels," and that the people at the bankers are much better than the corresponding class in Europe, who languish in downtrodden bondage and never have even a chance to show themselves to the world. The explanation is highly sufficient, for it is very certain that for many Americans a journey to Europe is the reward of a period of sordid toil. An American may take great satisfaction in this circumstance; he may be proud of belonging to a country in which the advantages of foreign travel are open to all, irrespective of "social standing"; instead of being, as in Europe (according at least, to this theory), only within the reach of the luxurious and the privileged. But the

European only perceives that a great many American travellers are remarkably "rough," and quite fails to congratulate either his own country or theirs upon possessing them. The people in question neither know nor care what he thinks about them and, having examined the antiquities of the Old World, they go westward across the Atlantic with a perfectly good conscience. The European critic, however, sometimes opens himself with striking candor to an American of the introspective class. It is a hundred to one that his tone is patronizing; but there are degrees of patronage. If it is grossly patronizing the American is offended, and invites him to keep his approbation for himself; but if it is subtly patronizing the American listens to it with a complacency decidedly at variance with the theory of his more exalted hours—the theory of the sufficiency of the great Republic in every way to itself.

It may be we shall someday become sufficient to ourselves and lose the sense of being the most youthful, most experimental, and, somehow, most irregular of the nations. But until that time comes some of us may occasionally be caught listening without protest to compliments paid us at the expense of some others. It is only just to say, however, that the American in Europe often enters into what we have called the conscious phase by a great deal of irritation. He finds Europeans very ignorant of a country, very indifferent to a country which, in spite of irregularities, he may be pardoned for thinking a magnificent one. A few Englishmen and Germans know a good deal about the United States—a good deal more than most Americans do; but it is hardly too much to say that as a general thing, as regards this subject, the European mind is a perfect blank. A great many Americans are very ignorant of Europe, but in default of knowledge it may be said that they have a certain amount of imagination. In respect to the United States the European imagination is motionless; and it may well seem to an American that there is something ridiculous in a scheme of the universe which leaves out a country as large as an aggregation of European kingdoms. There are many anomalies and crookednesses in the lot of the conscious American, and not the least of them is the fact that the country on whose behalf he is expected to be humble and patient—to wait for further results and withhold inopportune boasts—is an affair which, at times and in certain lights, seems to make this sweet reasonableness an affectation. It is comparatively easy to confess yourself a provincial if you really come from a province; but if you have been brought up among "big things" of every kind the admission requires an effort. On the whole, the American in Europe may be spoken of as a provincial who is terribly bent upon taking, in the fulness of ages, his revenge.

HENRY JAMES

From *Hawthorne*†

[*". . . items of high civilization . . . absent from . . . American life . . ."*]

* * * I know not at what age he [Hawthorne] began to keep a diary; the first entries in the American volumes are of the summer of 1835. There is a phrase in the preface to his novel of *Transformation,*[2] which must have lingered in the minds of many Americans who have tried to write novels, and to lay the scene of them in the Western world. "No author, without a trial, can conceive of the difficulty of writing a romance about a country where there is no shadow, no antiquity, no mystery, no picturesque and gloomy wrong, nor anything but a commonplace prosperity, in broad and simple daylight, as is happily the case with my dear native land." The perusal of Hawthorne's American Note-Books operates as a practical commentary upon this somewhat ominous text. It does so at least to my own mind; it would be too much, perhaps, to say that the effect would be the same for the usual English reader. An American reads between the lines—he completes the suggestions—he constructs a picture. I think I am not guilty of any gross injustice in saying that the picture he constructs from Hawthorne's American diaries, though by no means without charms of its own, is not, on the whole, an interesting one. It is characterised by an extraordinary blankness—a curious paleness of colour and paucity of detail. Hawthorne, as I have said, has a large and healthy appetite for detail, and one is, therefore, the more struck with the lightness of the diet to which his observation was condemned. For myself, as I turn the pages of his journals, I seem to see the image of the crude and simple society in which he lived. I use these epithets, of course, not invidiously, but descriptively; if one desire to enter as closely as possible into Hawthorne's situation, one must endeavour to reproduce his circumstances. We are struck with the large number of elements that were absent from them, and the coldness, the thinness, the blankness, to repeat my epithet, present themselves so vividly that our foremost feeling is that of compassion for a romancer looking for subjects in such a field. It takes so many things, as Hawthorne must have felt later in life, when he made the acquaintance of the denser, richer, warmer European spectacle—it takes such an accumulation of history and custom,

† From *Hawthorne*, by Henry James (New York: Harper and Brothers, 1879), pp. 41–43.

2. The title of the English edition of Hawthorne's *The Marble Faun*. [*Editor.*]

such a complexity of manners and types, to form a fund of suggestion for a novelist. If Hawthorne had been a young Englishman, or a young Frenchman of the same degree of genius, the same cast of mind, the same habits, his consciousness of the world around him would have been a very different affair; however obscure, however reserved, his own personal life, his sense of the life of his fellow-mortals would have been almost infinitely more various. The negative side of the spectacle on which Hawthorne looked out, in his contemplative saunterings and reveries, might, indeed, with a little ingenuity, be made almost ludicrous; one might enumerate the items of high civilization, as it exists in other countries, which are absent from the texture of American life, until it should become a wonder to know what was left. No State, in the European sense of the word, and indeed barely a specific national name. No sovereign, no court, no personal loyalty, no aristocracy, no church, no clergy, no army, no diplomatic service, no country gentlemen, no palaces, no castles, nor manors, nor old country-houses, nor parsonages, nor thatched cottages, nor ivied ruins; no cathedrals, nor abbeys, nor little Norman churches; no great Universities nor public schools—no Oxford, nor Eton, nor Harrow; no literature, no novels, no museums, no pictures, no political society, no sporting class—no Epsom nor Ascot! Some such list as that might be drawn up of the absent things in American life—especially in the American life of forty years ago, the effect of which, upon an English or a French imagination, would probably, as a general thing, be appalling. The natural remark, in the almost lurid light of such an indictment, would be that if these things are left out, everything is left out. The American knows that a good deal remains; what it is that remains—that is his secret, his joke, as one may say. It would be cruel, in this terrible denudation, to deny him the consolation of his natural gift, that "American humour" of which of late years we have heard so much.

Henry James to William Dean Howells, January 31, 1880†

["*. . . It is on manners . . . that a novelist lives . . .*"]

3 Bolton Street, W.
Jan. 31st [1880]

My dear Howells,

Your letter of Jan. 19th and its enclosure (your review of my

† From *The Letters of Henry James*, ed. Percy Lubbock (New York: Scribner's, 1920), I, 71–74.

Hawthorne) came to me last night, and I must thank you without delay for each of them. . . .

Your review of my book is very handsome and friendly and commands my liveliest gratitude. Of course your graceful strictures seem to yourself more valid than they do to me. The little book was a tolerably deliberate and meditated performance, and I should be prepared to do battle for most of the convictions expressed. It is quite true I use the word provincial too many times—I hated myself for't, even while I did it (just as I overdo the epithet "dusky.") But I don't at all agree with you in thinking that "if it is not provincial for an Englishman to be English, a Frenchman French, etc., so it is not provincial for an American to be American." So it is not provincial for a Russian, an Australian, a Portuguese, a Dane, a Laplander, to savour of their respective countries: that would be where the argument would land you. I think it is extremely provincial for a Russian to be very Russian, a Portuguese very Portuguese; for the simple reason that certain national types are essentially and intrinsically provincial. I sympathize even less with your protest against the idea that it takes an old civilization to set a novelist in motion—a proposition that seems to me so true as to be a truism. It is on manners, customs, usages, habits, forms, upon all these things matured and established, that a novelist lives —they are the very stuff his work is made of; and in saying that in the absence of those "dreary and worn-out paraphernalia" which I enumerate as being wanting in American society, "we have simply the whole of human life left," you beg (to my sense) the question. I should say we had just so much less of it as these same "paraphernalia" represent, and I think they represent an enormous quantity of it. I shall feel refuted only when we have produced (setting the present high company—yourself and me—for obvious reasons apart) a gentleman who strikes me as a novelist—as belonging to the company of Balzac and Thackeray. Of course, in the absence of this godsend, it is but a harmless amusement that we should reason about it, and maintain that if right were right he should already be here. I will freely admit that such a genius will get on *only* by agreeing with your view of the case—to do something great he must feel as you feel about it. But then I doubt whether such a genius—a man of the faculty of Balzac and Thackeray—*could* agree with you! When he does I will lie flat on my stomach and do him homage—in the very centre of the contributor's club, or on the threshold of the magazine, or in any public place you may appoint!—But I didn't mean to wrangle with you—I meant only to thank you and to express my sense of how happily you turn those things.—I am greatly amused at your picture of the contributing blood-hounds whom you are holding in check. I wish immensely that you would let them fly at me—though there is no reason, certainly, that the decent public should be bespattered, periodically, with my gore. However my tender (or rather my very tough) flesh is prescient already of the Higginsonian fangs. Happy man, to be going, like that, to see your plays acted. It is a sensation I am dying (though not as yet trying) to cultivate. What a tremendous quantity of work you must get through in these years! I am impatient for the next *Atlantic*. What is your *Cornhill* novel about? I am to precede it with a poorish story in three numbers—a tale purely American, the writing of which made me feel acutely the want of the "paraphernalia." I *must* add, however (to return for a moment to this), that I applaud and esteem you highly for not feeling it; i.e. the want. You are certainly right—magnificently and heroically right—to do so, and on the day you make your readers—I mean the readers who know and appreciate the paraphernalia—do the same, you will be the American Balzac. That's a great mission—go in for it! Wherever you go, receive, and distribute among your wife and children, the blessing of yours ever,

H. James jr.

HENRY JAMES

From His Notebooks†

["*. . . the old world—my choice, my need, my life . . .*"]‡

In the late fall of 1881, Henry James began to keep a notebook recording his "impressions" and *données* for fiction and drama. The following extract was written in 1881 but constitutes a retrospective of his decision to settle in Europe and offers an account of his year in Paris during which *The American* was written.

Brunswick Hotel, Boston, November 25th, 1881.

If I should write here all that I might write, I should speedily fill this as yet unspotted blank-book, bought in London six months ago, but hitherto unopened. It is so long since I have kept any notes, taken any memoranda, written down my current reflections, taken a sheet of paper, as it were, into my confidence. Meanwhile so much has come and gone, so much that it is now too late to

† From *The Notebooks of Henry James*, eds. F. O. Matthiessen and Kenneth B. Murdock (New York: Oxford University Press, 1947). Numbered footnotes are from the Matthiessen-Murdock edition. Ellipsis points represent deletions by Matthiessen and Murdock, asterisks deletions by the editor of the present edition.

‡ *Notebooks*, pp. 23–27.

catch, to reproduce, to preserve. I have lost too much by losing, or rather by not having acquired, the note-taking habit. It might be of great profit to me; and now that I am older, that I have more time, that the labour of writing is less onerous to me, and I can work more at my leisure, I ought to endeavour to keep, to a certain extent, a record of passing impressions, of all that comes, that goes, that I see, and feel, and observe. To catch and keep something of life—that's what I mean. Here I am back in America, for instance, after six years of absence, and likely while here to see and learn a great deal that ought not to become mere waste material. Here I am, *da vero*, and here I am likely to be for the next five months. I am glad I have come—it was a wise thing to do. I needed to see again *les miens*, to revive my relations with them, and my sense of the consequences that these relations entail. Such relations, such consequences, are a part of one's life, and the best life, the most complete, is the one that takes full account of such things. One can only do this by seeing one's people from time to time, by being with them, by entering into their lives. Apart from this I hold it was not necessary I should come to this country. I am 37[3] years old, I have made my choice, and God knows that I have now no time to waste. My choice is the old world—my choice, my need, my life. There is no need for me today to argue about this; it is an inestimable blessing to me, and a rare good fortune, that the problem was settled long ago, and that I have now nothing to do but to act on the settlement.—My impressions here are exactly what I expected they would be, and I scarcely see the place, and feel the manners, the race, the tone of things, now that I am on the spot, more vividly than I did while I was still in Europe. My work lies there—and with this vast new world, *je n'ai que faire*. One can't do both—one must choose. No European writer is called upon to assume that terrible burden, and it seems hard that I should be. The burden is necessarily greater for an American—for he *must* deal, more or less, even if only by implication, with Europe; whereas no European is obliged to deal in the least with America. No one dreams of calling him less complete for not doing so. (I speak of course of people who do the sort of work that I do; not of economists, of social science people.) The painter of manners who neglects America is not thereby incomplete as yet; but a hundred years hence—fifty years hence perhaps—he will doubtless be accounted so. My impressions of America, however, I shall, after all, not write here. I don't need to write them (at least not *à propos* of Boston); I know too well what they are. In many ways they are extremely pleasant; but, Heaven forgive me! I feel as if my time were terribly wasted here! . . .

3. He was actually thirty-eight.

It is too late to recover all those lost impressions—those of the last six years—that I spoke of in beginning; besides, they are not lost altogether, they are buried deep in my mind, they have become part of my life, of my nature. At the same time, if I had nothing better to do, I might indulge in a retrospect that would be interesting and even fruitful—look back over all that has befallen me since last I left my native shores. I could remember vividly, and I have little doubt I could express happily enough, if I made the effort. I could remember without effort with what an irresistible longing I turned to Europe, with what ardent yet timid hopes, with what indefinite yet inspiring intentions, I took leave of *les miens*. I recall perfectly the maturing of my little plan to get abroad again and remain for years, during the summer of 1875; the summer the latter part of which I spent in Cambridge. It came to me there on my return from New York where I had been spending a bright, cold, unremunerative, uninteresting winter, finishing *Roderick Hudson* and writing for the *Nation*. (It was these two tasks that kept me alive.) I had returned from Europe the year before that, the beginning of September, '74, sailing for Boston with Wendell Holmes and his wife as my fellow passengers. I had come back then to 'try New York,' thinking it my duty to attempt to live at home before I should grow older, and not take for granted too much that Europe alone was possible; especially as Europe for me then meant simply Italy, where I had had some very discouraged hours, and which, lovely and desirable though it was, didn't seem as a permanent residence, to lead to anything. I wanted something more active, and I came back and sought it in New York. I came back with a certain amount of scepticism, but with very loyal intentions, and extremely eager to be 'interested.' As I say, I was interested but imperfectly, and I very soon decided what was the real issue of my experiment. It was by no means equally soon, however, that I perceived how I should be able to cross the Atlantic again. But the opportunity came to me at last—it loomed before me one summer's day, in Quincy St. The best thing I could imagine then was to go and take up my abode in Paris. I went (sailing about October 20th, 1875) and I settled myself in Paris with the idea that I should spend several years there. This was not really what I wanted; what I wanted was London—and Paris was only a stopgap. But London appeared to me then impossible. I believed that I might arrive there in the fulness of years, but there were all sorts of obstacles to my attempting to live there then. I wonder greatly now, in the light of my present knowledge of England, that these obstacles should have seemed so large, so overwhelming and depressing as they did at that time. When a year later I came really to look them in the face, they absolutely melted away. But that year in Paris was not a lost year—on the contrary. On my way thither I spent something like a fortnight in London; lodging at Story's Hotel, in Dover St. It was November—dark, foggy, muddy, rainy—and I knew scarcely a creature in the place. I don't remember calling on anyone but Lady Rose and H. J. W. Coulson, with whom I went out to lunch at Petersham, near Richmond. And yet the great city seemed to me enchanting, and I would have given my little finger to remain there rather than go to Paris. But I went to Paris, and lived for a year at 29 Rue de Luxembourg (now Rue Cambon). I shall not attempt to write the history of that year—further than to say that it was time by no means misspent. I learned to know Paris and French affairs much better than before—I got a certain familiarity with Paris (added to what I had acquired before) which I shall never lose. I wrote letters to the *New York Tribune*, of which, though they were poor stuff, I may say that they were too good for the purpose (of course they didn't succeed). I saw a good deal of Charles Peirce that winter—as to whom his being a man of genius reconciled me to much that was intolerable in him.[4] In the spring, at Madame Turgenieff's, I made the acquaintance of Paul Joukowsky. *Non ragioniam di lui—ma guarda e passa.* I don't speak of Ivan Turgenieff, most delightful and lovable of men, nor of Gustave Flaubert, whom I shall always be so glad to have known; a powerful, serious, melancholy, manly, deeply corrupted, yet not corrupting, nature. There was something I greatly liked in him, and he was very kind to me. He was a head and shoulders above the others, the men I saw at his house on Sunday afternoons—Zola, Goncourt, Daudet, etc. (I mean as a man—not as a talker, etc.) I remember in especial one afternoon (a weekday) that I went to see him and found him alone. I sat with him a long time; something led him to repeat to me a little poem of Th. Gautier's—*Les Vieux Portraits* (what led him to repeat it was that we had been talking of French poets, and he had been expressing his preference for Théophile Gautier over Alfred de Musset—*il était plus français,* etc.). I went that winter a great deal to the Comédie Française—though not so much as when I was in Paris in '72. Then I went every night—or almost. And I have been a great deal since. I may say that I know the Comédie Française. Of course

4. James's reaction to Peirce was summed up in a letter home at the time: 'He is a very good fellow—when he is not in ill-humour; then he is intolerable. But, as William says, he is a man of genius . . .' Peirce wrote to William: 'Your brother is looking pretty well, but looks a little serious. . . . He is a splendid fellow. I admire him greatly and have only discovered two faults in him. One is that his digestion isn't quite that of an ostrich and the other is that he isn't as fond of turning over questions as I am, but likes to settle them and have done with them. A manly trait too, but not a philosophic one.'

I saw a great deal of the little American 'set'—the American village encamped *en plein Paris*. They were all very kind, very friendly, hospitable, etc; they knew up to a certain point their Paris. But ineffably tiresome and unprofitable. Their society had become a kind of obligation, and it had much to do with my suddenly deciding to abandon my plans of indefinite residence, take flight to London and settle there as best I could. I remember well what a crime Mrs. S. made of my doing so; and one or two other persons as to whom I was perfectly unconscious of having given them the right to judge my movements so intimately. Nothing is more characteristic of certain American women than the extraordinary promptitude with which they assume such a right. I remember how Paris had, in a hundred ways, come to weary and displease me; I couldn't get out of the detestable *American* Paris. Then I hated the Boulevards, the horrible monotony of the new quarters. I saw, moreover, that I should be an eternal outsider. I went to London in November, 1876. I should say that I had spent that summer chiefly in three places: at Étretat, at Varennes (with the Lee Childes), and at Biarritz—or rather at Bayonne, where I took refuge being unable to find quarters at Biarritz. Then late in September I spent a short time at St. Germain, at the Pavillon Louis XIV. I was finishing *The American*. The pleasantest episode (by far) of that summer was my visit to the Childes; to whom I had been introduced by dear Jane Norton; who had been very kind to me during the winter; and who have remained my very good friends. Varennes is a little moated *castel* of the most picturesque character, a few miles from Montargis, *au coeur de l'ancienne France*. I well recall the impression of my arrival—driving over from Montargis with Edward Childe—in the warm August evening and reaching the place in the vague twilight, which made it look precisely like a *décor d'opéra*. I have been back there since—and it was still delightful; but at that time I had not had my now very considerable experience of country visits in England; I had not seen all those other wonderful things. Varennes therefore was an exquisite sensation—a memory I shall never lose. I settled myself again in Paris—or attempted to do so (I like to linger over these details, and to recall them one by one); I had no intention of giving it up. But there were difficulties in the Rue de Luxembourg—I couldn't get back my old apartment, which I had given up during the Summer. I don't remember what suddenly brought me to the point of saying—'Go to; I will try London.' I think a letter from William had a good deal to do with it, in which he said, 'Why don't you?—That must be the place.' A single word from outside often moves one (moves *me* at least) more than the same word infinitely multiplied as a simple voice from within. I *did* try it, and it has succeeded beyond my most ardent hopes. * * *

["*. . . the most cherished of all my projects . . .*"]†

From time to time during his early career, James's interest in the drama was stirred to fresh enthusiasm. Attending the Théâtre Français and the London stage, reading and reviewing plays and performances, James eventually committed himself to playwriting between 1889–94. The following excerpts from his notebooks trace the gradual development of an interest that led to the writing of the play version of *The American,* which was produced by Edward Compton, who played the title character, at Southport in January of 1891. A moderate success in the provinces, *The American* was taken to London in September 1891 for presentation at the Opera Comique. It played for two months, failed, and eventually closed in the late fall. James rewrote the last act, in order to provide it with a happy ending, but the play never caught on, although Compton's repertory company occasionally played it thereafter in the provinces.

[*Winter, 1881–82*] * * * Now and here I have only one feeling—the desire to get at work again. It is nearly six months that I have been resting on my oars—letting the weeks go, with nothing to show for them but these famous 'impressions'! Prolonged idleness exasperates and depresses me, and though now that I am here, it is a pity not to move about and (if the chance presents itself) see the country, the prospect of producing nothing for the rest of the winter is absolutely intolerable to me. If it comes to my having to choose between remaining stationary somewhere and getting at work, or making a journey during which I shall be able to do no work, I shall certainly elect for the former. But probably I shall be able to compromise: to see something of the country and yet work a little. My mind is full of plans, of ambitions; they crowd upon me, for these are the productive years of life. I have taken aboard by this time a tremendous quantity of material; I really have never taken stock of my cargo. After long years of waiting, of obstruction, I find myself able to put into execution the most cherished of all my projects—that of beginning to work for the stage. It was one of my earliest—I had it from the first. None has given me brighter hopes—none has given me sweeter emotions. It is strange nevertheless that I should never have done anything—and to a certain extent it is ominous. I wonder at times that the dream should not have faded away. It comes back to me now, however, and I ache with longing to settle down at last to a sustained attempt in this direction. I think there is really reason enough for my not having

† From *The Notebooks of Henry James,* ed. F. O. Matthiessen and Kenneth B. Murdock (New York: Oxford University Press, 1947), pp. 37–39, 44–45, 99–100, 111.

done so before: the little work at any time that I could do, the uninterrupted need of making money on the spot, the inability to do two things at once, the absence of opportunities, of openings. I may add to this the feeling that I could afford to wait, that, looked at as I look at it, the drama is the ripest of all the arts, the one to which one must bring most of the acquired as well as most of the natural, and that while I was waiting I was studying the art, and clearing off my field. I think I may now claim to have studied the art as well as it can be studied in the contemplative way. The French stage I have mastered; I say that without hesitation. I have it in my pocket, and it seems to me clear that this is the light by which one must work today. I have laid up treasures of wisdom about all that. What interesting hours it has given me—what endless consideration it has led to! Sometimes, as I say, it seems to me simply deplorable that I should not have got at work before. *But it was impossible at the time,* and I knew that my chance would come. Here it is; let me guard it sacredly now. Let nothing divert me from it; but now the loss of time, which has simply been a maturing process, will become an injurious one. *Je me résume,* as George Sand's heroes say. I remember certain occasions; several acute visitations of the purpose of which I write come back to me vividly. Some of them, the earliest, were brought on merely by visits to the theatre—by seeing great actors, etc.—at fortunate hours; or by reading a new piece of Alex. Dumas, of Sardou, of Augier. No, my dear friend, nothing of all that is lost. *Ces emotions-là ne se perdent pas; elles rentrent dans le fonds même de notre nature; elles font partie de notre volonté.* The *volonté* has not expired; it is only perfect today. Two or three of the later occasions of which I speak have been among the things that *count* in the formation of a purpose; they are worth making a note of here. What has always counted, of course, has been the Comédie Française; it is on that, as regards this long day-dream, that I have lived. But there was an evening there that I shall long remember; it was in September, 1877. I had come over from London; I was lodging in the Avenue d'Antin—the house with a *tir* behind it. I went to see *Jean Dacier,* with Coquelin as the hero; I shall certain<ly not> forget that impression. The piece is, on the whole, I suppose, bad; but it contains some very effective scenes, and the two principal parts gave Coquelin and Favart a magnificent chance. It is Coquelin's *great* chance, and he told me afterwards in London that it is the part he values most. He is everything in it by turns, and I don't think I ever followed an actor's creation more intently. It threw me into a great state of excitement; I thought seriously of writing to Coquelin, telling him I had been his school-mate, etc.[5] It held up a glowing light to me—seemed to point to my own path. If I could have sat down to work then I probably should not have stopped soon. But I didn't; I couldn't; I was writing things for which I needed to be paid from month to month. (I like to remind myself of these facts—to justify my innumerable postponements.) I remember how, on leaving the theatre—it was a lovely evening—I walked about a long time under the influence not so much of the piece as of Coquelin's acting of it, which had made the thing so human, so brilliant, so valuable. I was agitated with what it said to me that I might do—what I ought to attempt; I walked about the Place de la Concorde, along the Seine, up the Champs Elysées. That was nothing, however, to the state I was thrown into by meeting Coquelin at breakfast at Andrew Lang's, when the Comédie Française came to London. The occasion, for obvious reasons, was unpropitious, but I had some talk with him which rekindled and revived all my latent ambitions. At that time, too, my hands were tied; I could do nothing, and the feeling passed away in smoke. But it stirred me to the depths. Coquelin's personality, his talk, the way the *artist* overflowed in him—all this was tremendously suggestive. I could say little to him there—not a tittle of what I wished; I could only listen, and translate to him what *they* said—an awkward task! But I listened to some purpose, and I have never lost what I gained. It excited me powerfully; I shall not forget my walk, afterwards, down from South Kensington to Westminster. I met Jack Gardner, and he walked with me to leave a card at the Speaker's House. All day, and for days afterward, I remained under the impression. It faded away in time, and I had to give myself to other things. But this brings it back to me; and I may say that those two little moments were landmarks. There was a smaller incident, later, which it gives me pleasure to recall, as it gave me extreme pleasure at the time. John Hare asked me (I met him at dinner at the Comyns Carrs')—urged me, I may say—to write a a play, and offered me his services in the event of my doing so. I shall take him at his word. When I came back from Scotland in October last I was

5. James had been for a time Coquelin's schoolmate at the Collège Communal in Boulogne, as he tells us in *A Small Boy and Others* (1913). When he wrote that book he looked back on Coquelin as 'the most interesting and many-sided comedian, or at least the most unsurpassed dramatic *diseur* of the time.' As early as 1877, in his essay on *The Théâtre Français* in the *Galaxy* for April, he devoted several appreciative paragraphs to Coquelin, but it was the performance of Lomon's *Jean Dacier* in September that brought his enthusiasm to its peak. The experience proved indeed unforgettable, and ten years later, in his essay on Coquelin in the *Century* for January 1887, James described just as he does here in the notebook his emotional excitement and his late evening walk after leaving the theater. The play, a four-act tragedy in verse, he called Coquelin's 'highest flight in the line of rhymed parts.'

full of this work; my hands were free; my pocket lined; I would have given a £100 for the liberty to sit down and hammer away. I imagined such a capital winter of work. But I had to come hither instead. If that however involves a loss of part of my time, it needn't involve the loss of all!

* * *

[*Late fall, 1882*] * * * It was a simple, serious, wholesome time. Mother's death appeared to have left behind it a soft beneficent hush in which we lived for weeks, for months, and which was full of rest and sweetness. I thought of her, constantly, as I walked to Boston at night along those dark vacant roads, where, in the winter air, one met nothing but the coloured lamps and the far-heard jingle of the Cambridge horse-cars. My work at this time interested me, too, and I look back upon the whole three months with a kind of religious veneration. My work interested me even more than the importance of it would explain—or than the success of it has justified. I tried to write a little play (*D<aisy> M<iller>*) and I wrote it; but my poor little play has not been an encouragement. I needn't enter into the tiresome history of my ridiculous negotiations with the people of the Madison Square Theatre, of which the Proprietors behaved like asses and sharpers combined; this episode, by itself, would make a brilliant chapter in a realistic novel. It interested me immensely to write the piece, and the work confirmed all my convictions as to the fascination of this sort of composition. But what it has brought <me> to know, both in New York and in London, about the manners and ideas of managers and actors and about the conditions of production on our unhappy English stage, is almost fatally disgusting and discouraging. I have learned, very vividly, that if one attempts to work for it one must be prepared for *disgust*, deep and unspeakable disgust. But though I am disgusted, I do not think I am discouraged. The reason of this latter is that I simply can't afford to be. I have determined to take a year—even two years, if need be—more, in experiments, in studies, in attempts. The dramatic form seems to me the most beautiful thing possible; the misery of the thing is that the baseness of the English-speaking stage affords no setting for it. How I am to reconcile this with the constant solicitation that presses upon me, both from within and from without, to get at work upon another novel, is more than I can say. It is surely the part of wisdom, however, not to begin another novel at once—not to commit myself to a work of *longue haleine*. I must do *short* things, in such measure as I need, which will leave me intervals for dramatic work. I say this rather glibly—and yet I sometimes feel a woeful hunger to sit down to another novel. If I can only *concentrate* myself: this is the great lesson of life. I have hours of unspeakable reaction against my smallness of production; my wretched habits of work—or of un-work; my levity, my vagueness of mind, my perpetual failure to focus my attention, to absorb myself, to look things in the face, to invent, to produce, in a word. I shall be 40 years old in April next: it's a horrible fact! I believe however that I have learned how to work and that it is in moments of forced idleness, almost alone, that these melancholy reflections seize me. When I am really at work, I'm happy, I feel strong, I see many opportunities ahead. It is the only thing that makes life endurable. I must make some great efforts during the next few years, however, if I wish not to have been on the whole a failure. I shall have been a failure unless I do something *great!*

* * *

De Vere Gardens, May 12, 1889.

I interrupt some other work this moist still Sunday morning to make a few notes on the subject of the play I have engaged to write for Edward Compton. I needn't go over the little history of this engagement and the reasons—they are familiar enough—which led me to respond to the proposal coming to me from him while I was in Paris last December. I had practically given up my old, valued, long cherished dream of doing something for the stage, for fame's sake, and art's, and fortune's: overcome by the vulgarity, the brutality, the baseness of the condition of the English-speaking theatre today. But after an interval, a long one, the vision has revived, on a new and a very much humbler basis, and especially under the lash of necessity. Of art or fame *il est maintenant fort peu question*: I simply *must* try, and try seriously, to produce half a dozen—a dozen, five dozen—plays for the sake of my pocket, my material future. Of how little money the novel makes for me I needn't discourse here. The theatre has sought me out—in the person of the good, the yet unseen, Compton. I have listened and considered and reflected, and the matter is transposed to a minor key. To accept the circumstances, in their extreme humility, and do the best I can *in* them: this is the moral of my present situation. They are the reverse of ideal—but there is this great fact that for myself at least I may make them better. To take what there *is*, and use it, without waiting forever in vain for the preconceived—to dig deep into the actual and get something out of *that*—this doubtless is the right way to live. If I succeed a little I can easily—I think—succeed more; I can make my own conditions more as I go on. The field is common, but it is wide and free—in a manner—and <amusing?>. And if there is money in it that will greatly help: for all the profit that may come to me in this way will mean real freedom for one's general artistic life: it all hangs together (time, leisure, independence for 'real literature,' and, in addition, a great deal of experience of *tout un côté de la vie*). Therefore my plan is to try with a settled resolution—that is, with a full determination to return repeatedly to the charge, overriding, annihilating, despising the boundless discouragements, disgusts, *écœurements*. One should *use* such things—grind them to powder. . . .

His proposal is that I shall make a play of the *American*, and there is no doubt a play in it. I must extract the simplest, strongest, baldest, most rudimentary, at once most humorous and most touching one, in a form whose main *souci* shall be pure situation and pure point combined with pure brevity. Oh, how it must not be too good and how very bad it must be! *À moi*, Scribe; *à moi*, Sardou, *à moi*, Dennery!—Reduced to its simplest expression, and that reduction must be my play, *The American* is the history of a plain man who is at the same time a fine fellow, who becomes engaged to the daughter of a patrician house, being accepted by her people on acct. of his wealth, and is then thrown over (by *them*) for a better match: after which he turns upon them to recover his betrothed (they have bullied her out of it), through the possession of a family secret which is disgraceful to them, dangerous to them, and which he holds over them as an instrument of compulsion and vengeance. They are frightened—they feel the screw: they dread exposure; but in the novel the daughter is already lost to the hero—she is swept away by the tragedy, takes refuge in a convent, breaks off her other threatened match, renounces the world, disappears. The hero, injured, outraged, resentful, feels the strong temptation to *punish* the Bellegardes, and for a day almost yields to it. Then he does the characteristically magnanimous thing—the characteristically good-natured thing—throws away his opportunity—lets them 'off'—lets them go. In the play he must do this—*but* get his wife.

[With the composition of *The American*, which he thought for a while of calling *The Californian*, James hoped to begin the realization of his dream of writing successfully for the theater. He worked out a four-act structure, but by providing a happy ending he produced a piece less substantial and less moving than his novel. His letters at the time are filled with excitement and expectation over this new venture, as is the journal of Alice James, who in an English sanitarium at this juncture was her brother's close confidante.

The American, with Edward Compton in the role of Christopher Newman, and his wife, Virginia Bateman, in that of Claire de

Cintré, went through a promising tour in the provinces. It came to London in the autumn of 1891 for only a moderate success—a two months' run—with Elizabeth Robins as Claire. Leon Edel has discussed this production and all other aspects of James' theatrical career in *Henry James: Les Années Dramatiques* (1931).

By the time of the production James had also completed four other plays, *Tenants, Disengaged, The Album,* and *The Reprobate,* though none of these reached the stage. But he was still full of hopes, and wrote to William James: 'I feel at last as if I had found my *real* form, which I am capable of carrying far.' But as Granville-Barker has remarked, it was too bad that James knew as his model the French theater at one of its worst periods.]

* * *

October 22d, 1891, 34 De Vere Gdns. I finished yesterday my difficult paper on J<ames> R<ussell> L<owell> for the January *Atlantic* and I must immediately get into the work promised to Kinloch-Cooke. I am emerging a little from all the *Déboires* and distresses consequent on the production of *The American* by Edward Compton, and I needn't note them here to remind myself what the episode has been, and still, in a measure, *is*; nor to feel how much it gives me something to live for in the future. I shall live, I trust, for several things; but a very prominent one, surely, shall be the firm—the exquisitely still and deep-rooted resolution—to compass, in the theatre, the solid, the honourable (so far as anything can be honourable there!), the absolute and interesting success. Meanwhile the soothing, the healing, the sacred and salutary refuge from all these vulgarities and pains is simply to lose myself in this quiet, this blessed and uninvaded workroom in the inestimable effort and refreshment of art, in resolute and beneficent production. I come back to it with a treasure of experience, of wisdom, of acquired material, of (it seems to me) seasoned fortitude and augmented capacity. Purchased by disgusts enough, it is at any rate a boon that now that I hold it, I feel I wouldn't, I oughtn't, to have missed. Ah, the terrible law of the artist—the law of fructification, of fertilization, the law by which everything is grist to his mill—the law, in short, of the acceptance of all experience, of all suffering, of *all* life, of *all* suggestion and sensation and illumination. To keep at it—to strive toward the perfect, the ripe, the only best; to go on, by one's own clear light, with patience, courage and continuity, to live with the high vision and effort, to justify one's self—and oh, so greatly!—all in time: this and this alone can be my only lesson from *anything*. Vague and weak are these words, but the experience and the purpose are of wedded gold and adamant. The consolation, the dignity, the joy of life are that discouragements and lapses, depressions and darknesses come to one only as one stands *without*—I mean without the luminous paradise of art. As soon as I really re-enter it—cross the loved threshold—stand in the high chamber, and the gardens divine—the whole realm widens out again before me and around me—the air of life fills my lungs—the light of achievement flushes over all the place, and I believe, I see, I *do*.

Henry James to Alice James, June 6, 1890†

["... *These castles in Spain* ..."]

Palazzo Barbaro, Venice.
June 6th [1890].

Dearest Sister,

I am ravished by your letter after reading the play (keep it locked up, safe and secret, though there are three or four copies in existence) which makes me feel as if there had been a triumphant première and I had received overtures from every managerial quarter and had only to count my gold. At any rate I am delighted that you have been struck with it exactly as I have tried to strike, and that the pure practical character of the effort has worked its calculated spell upon you. For what encourages me in the whole business is that, as the piece stands, there is not, in its felicitous form, the ghost of a "fluke" or a mere chance: it is all "art" and an absolute address of means to the end—the end, viz., of meeting exactly the immediate, actual, intense British conditions, both subjective and objective, and of acting in (to a minute, including entr'actes) 2 hours and ¾. Ergo, I can do a dozen more infinitely better; and I am excited to think how much, since the writing of this one piece has been an education to me, a little further experience will do for me. Also I am sustained by the sense, on the whole, that though really superior acting would help it immensely, yet mediocrity of handling (which is all, at the best, I am pretty sure, that it will get) won't and can't kill it, and that there may be even something sufficiently general and human about it, to make it (given its eminent actability) "keep the stage," even after any first vogue it may have had has passed away. That fate—in the poverty-stricken condition of the English repertory—would mean profit indeed, and an income to my descendants. But one mustn't talk of this kind of thing yet. However, since you have been already so deeply initiated, I think I will enclose (keep it sacredly for me) an admirable letter I have just received from the precious Balestier in

† From *The Letters of Henry James*, ed. Percy Lubbock (New York: Scribner's, 1920), I, 166–70.

whose hands, as I wrote you, I placed the settlement of the money-question, the terms of the writing agreement with Compton. Compton saw him on Monday last—and I send the letter mainly to illustrate the capital intelligence and competence of Balestier and show you in what good hands I am. He will probably strike you, as he strikes me, as the perfection of an "agent"—especially when you consider that he has undertaken this particular job out of pure friendship. Everything, evidently, will be well settled—on the basis, of course, which can't be helped, of production in London only about the middle of next year. But by that time I hope to have done a good bit more work—and I shall be beguiled by beginning to follow, in the autumn, the rehearsals for the country production. Keep Balestier's letter till I come back—I shall get another one from him in a day or two with the agreement to sign. . . . These castles in Spain are at least exhilarating: in a certain sense I should like you very much to communicate to William your good impression of the drama—but on the whole I think you had better not, for the simple reason that it is very important it shouldn't be talked about (especially so long) in advance—and it wouldn't be safe, inasmuch as every whisper gets into the papers—and in some fearfully vulgarized and perverted form. You might hint to William that you have read the piece under seal of secresy to me and think so-and-so of it—but are so bound (to me) not to give a sign that he must bury what you tell him in tenfold mystery. But I doubt if even this would be secure—it would be in the *Transcript* the next week.

* * *

Ever your Henry.

Henry James to Edmund Gosse, January 3, 1891†

["*. . . the vulgar ordeal of to-night . . .*"]

Prince of Wales Hotel,
Southport.
Jan. 3rd [1891].

My dear Gosse,

I am touched by your *petit mot*. De gros mots seem to me to be so much more applicable to my fallen state. The only thing that can be said for it is that it is not so low as it may perhaps be to-

† From *The Letters of Henry James,* ed. Percy Lubbock (New York: Scribner's, 1920), I, 172. Sir Edmund Gosse (1849–1928), was an author and critic. Librarian of the House of Lords, he was a close friend of James. His *petit mot* was a short note of encouragement on the opening of the play. The phrase *petit mot* is translatable idiomatically as "kind words" and *gros mots* as "rough language."

morrow—after the vulgar ordeal of to-night.[6] Let me therefore profit by the few remaining hours of a recognizable *status* to pretend to an affectionate reciprocity. I am yours and your wife's while yet I *may* be. After 11 o'clock to-night I *may* be the world's —you know—and I may be the undertaker's. I count upon you both to spend this evening in fasting, silence and supplication. I will send you a word in the morning—wire you if I can—if there is anything at all to boast of. My hopes rest solely on intrinsic charms —the adventitious graces of art are not "in it." I am so nervous that I miswrite and misspell. Pity your infatuated but not presumptuous friend,

Henry James.

P.S. It would have been delightful—and terrible—if you had been able to come. I believe Archer is to come.

P.P.S. I don't return straight to London—don't get there till Tuesday or Wednesday. I shall have to wait and telegraph you which evening I can come in.

Henry James to Mrs. Hugh Bell, January 8, 1891†

["... 'is it going?' ... —'Rather!' ..."]

34 De Vere Gardens, W.
Jan. 8th [1891].

Dear Mrs. Bell,

Your most kind gratulatory note deserved an answer more gratefully prompt than this. But I extended my absence from town to a short visit at Cheltenham, and the whole thing was virtually, till yesterday, a complete extinction of leisure. Delightful of you to want "details." I think, if I were to inflict them on you, they would all be illustrative of the cheering and rewarding side of our feverish profession. The passage from knock-kneed nervousness (the night of the *première*, as one clings, in the wing, to the curtain rod, as to the *pied des autels*) to a simmering serenity is especially life-saving in its effect. I flung myself upon Compton after the 1st act: "In heaven's name, is it *going?*" "Going?—Rather! You could hear a pin drop!" Then, after that, one felt it—one *heard* it—one blessed it—and, at the end of all, one (after a decent and discreet delay) simpered and gave oneself up to *courbettes* before the curtain, while the applausive house emitted agreeable sounds from a kind of gas-flaring indistinguishable dimness and the gratified Compton

6. Opening night of the play version of *The American*. [*Editor.*]

† From *The Letters of Henry James*, ed. Percy Lubbock (New York: Scribner's, 1920), I, 173–74. Florence Bell (later Lady Bell) was a London friend of Henry James.

publicly pressed one's hand and one felt that, really, as far as Southport could testify to the circumstance, the stake was won. Of course it's only Southport—but I have larger hopes, inasmuch as it was just the meagre provincial conditions and the limited provincial interpretation that deprived the performance of all adventitious aid. And when my hero and heroine and another friend supped with me at the inn after the battle, I felt that they were really as radiant as if we were carousing among the slain. They *seem* indeed wondrous content. The great feature of the evening was the way Compton "came out" beyond what he had done or promised at rehearsal, and acted really most interestingly and admirably—if not a "revelation" at any rate a very jolly surprise. His part is one in which I surmise he really counts upon making a large success—and though I say it who shouldn't, it is one of incontestable opportunities. However, all this is to come—and we stumble in judgment. Amen. Voilà, ma chère amie. You have been through all this, and more, and will tolerate my ingenuities. . . .

All merriment to *your* "full house."

Yours most truly,
Henry James.

Henry James to Robert Louis Stevenson, January 12, 1891†

[". . . *my tribute to the vulgarest of the muses* . . ."]

34 De Vere Gardens, W.
January 12th, 1891.

My dear Louis,

* * * In the provinces I had the other night, at Southport, Lancashire, with the dramatization of an early novel—*The American*—a success dont je rougis encore. This thing is to be played in London only after several months—and to make the tour of the British Islands first. Don't be hard on me—simplifying and chastening necessity has laid its brutal hand on me and I have had to try to make somehow or other the money I don't make by literature. My books don't sell, and it looks as if my plays might. Therefore I am going with a brazen front to write half a dozen. I have, in fact, already written two others than the one just performed; and the success of the latter pronounced—really *pronounced*—will probably precipitate them. I am glad for all this that you are not here.

† From *The Letters of Henry James*, ed. Percy Lubbock (New York: Scribner's, 1920), I, 174–79. Stevenson (1850–1894), poet, essayist and novelist, was a close friend of James. The phrase "dont je rougis encore" means "about which I am still blushing."

* * *

January 19th.—I stopped this more than a week ago, and since then I have lacked time to go on with it—having been out of town for several days on a base theatrical errand—to see my tribute to the vulgarest of the muses a little further on its way over the provincial circuit and re-rehearse two or three portions of it that want more effective playing. Thank heaven I shall have now no more direct contact with it till it is produced in London next October. * * *

Henry James.

Henry James to William James, February 6, 1891†

["... *in the fever of dramatic production* ..."]

34 De Vere Gardens, W.
Feb. 6th, 1891.

My dear William,

Bear with me that I haven't written to you, since my last, in which I promised you a better immediate sequel, till the receipt of your note of the 21st, this a.m., recalls me to decency. Bear with me indeed, in this and other ways, so long as I am in the fever of dramatic production with which I am, very sanely and practically, trying to make up for my late start and all the years during which I have *not* dramatically produced, and, further, to get well ahead with the "demand" which I—and others for me—judge (still very sanely and sensibly) to be *certain* to be made upon me from the moment I have a *London*, as distinguished from a provincial success. (You can form no idea—outside—of how a provincial success is confined to the provinces.) Now that I have tasted blood, c'est une rage (of determination to *do*, and triumph, on my part,) for I feel at last as if I had found my *real* form, which I am capable of carrying far, and for which the pale little art of fiction, as I have practised it, has been, for me, but a limited and restricted substitute. The strange thing is that I always, universally, knew *this* was my more characteristic form—but was kept away from it by a half-modest, half-exaggerated sense of the difficulty (that is, I mean the practical odiousness) of the conditions. But now that I have accepted them and met them, I see that one isn't at all, needfully, their victim, but is, from the moment one *is* anything, one's self, worth speaking of, their *master*; and may use them, command them, squeeze them, lift them up and better them. As for the form *itself*, its honour and inspiration are (à défaut d'autres) in its

† From *The Letters of Henry James*, ed. Percy Lubbock (New York: Scribner's, 1920), I, 179–81.

difficulty. If it were easy to write a good play I couldn't and wouldn't think of it; but it is in fact damnably hard (to this truth the paucity of the article—in the English-speaking world—testifies,) and that constitutes a solid respectability—guarantees one's *intellectual* self-respect. At any rate I am working hard and constantly—and am just attacking my 4th! . . .

* * *

Farewell, dear William, and bear with my sawdust and orange-peel phase till the returns begin to flow in. The only hitch in the prospect is that it takes so long to "realise." *The American,* in the country, played only on Friday nights, with the very low country prices, gives me nothing as yet to speak of—my royalty making only about £5–0–0 for each performance. Later all this may be thoroughly counted upon to be different.

Ever your
Henry.

Henry James to Robert Louis Stevenson, February 18, 1891†

["*. . . I feel as if I had at last* found *my form . . .*"]

34 De Vere Gardens, W.
Feb. 18th, 1891

My dear Louis,

* * * In writing the other day I told you more or less what I was doing—*am* doing—in these elderly days; and the same general description will serve. I am doing what I can to launch myself in the dramatic direction—and the strange part of the matter is that I am doing it more or less seriously, as if we *had* the Scène Anglaise which we haven't. And I secretly dream of supplying the vile want? Pas même—and my zeal in the affair is only matched by my indifference. What is serious in it is that having begun to work in this sense some months ago, to give my little ones bread—I find the *form* opens out before me as if there were a kingdom to conquer—a kingdom forsooth of ignorant brutes of managers and dense cabotins of actors. All the same, I feel as if I had at last *found* my form—my real one—that for which pale fiction is an ineffectual substitute. God grant this unholy truth may not abide with me more than two or three years—time to dig out eight or ten rounded masterpieces and make withal enough money to enable me to retire in peace and plenty for the unmolested business of a *little* supreme

† From *The Letters of Henry James,* ed. Percy Lubbock (New York: Scribner's, 1920), I, 181–83.

writing, as distinguished from gouging—which is the Form above-mentioned. * * * I enfold you all in my sympathy and am ever your faithfullest

Henry James.

Henry James to Robert Herrick, August 7, 1907†

[". . . *on the matter of my revisions* . . ."]

Rye, August 7th. 1907

Dear Robert Herrick,

* * * All thanks, at any rate, for your so curious and urgent remarks on the matter of my revisions,[7] in respect to some of the old stuff I spoke of to you in connection with the plan of an édition définitive. I am greatly touched by your having felt and thought strongly enough on the matter to take the trouble to remonstrate at the idea of my re-touching. The re-touching with any insistence will *in fact* bear but on one book (*The American*—on *R. Hudson* and the *P. of a Lady* very much less) but in essence I shouldn't have planned the edition at all unless I had felt close revision—wherever seeming called for—to be an indispensable part of it. I do every justice to your contention, but don't think me reckless or purblind if I say that I hold myself really right and you really wrong. The *raison d'être* (the edition's) is in its being selective as well as collective, and by the mere fact of leaving out certain things (I have tried to read over *Washington Square* and I *can't*, and I fear it must go!) I exercise a control, a discrimination, I treat certain portions of my work as unhappy accidents. (Many portions of many—of all—men's work are.) From that it is but a step further —but it is 1 o'clock a.m. and I've written seven letters and I won't attempt to finish that sentence or expand my meaning. Forgive my blatant confidence in my own lucid literary sense! If I had planned not to re-touch—that is revise closely—I would have reprinted *all* my stuff and that idea is horrific. You also will be ravished! Trust me and I shall be justified. But good night, and pardon my untidy scrawl and my belated incoherence. Recall me kindly to your wife and believe me,

Your always,
Henry James

† From *Selected Letters of Henry James*, ed. Leon Edel (London: Rupert Hart-Davis, 1956), pp. 189–91. Herrick (1868–1938), a Chicago novelist and teacher, had complained of James's extensive revision of *The American* for the Scribner "New York Edition." This letter was written from James's residence at Lamb House, Rye, Sussex.

7. For the selective New York Edition of his novels and tales Henry James revised many of his early works. The edition was first issued in twenty-four volumes between 1907 and 1909. [*Editor.*]

Henry James to Mrs. G. W. Prothero, September 14, 1913†

[". . . *when you have eaten your beef and potatoes* . . ."]

Rye. Sept. 14*th*, 1913

This, please, for the delightful young man from Texas,[8] who shews such excellent dispositions. I only want to meet him half way, and I hope very much he won't think I don't when I tell him that the following indications as to five of my productions (splendid number—I glory in the tribute of his appetite!) are all on the basis of the Scribner's (or Macmillan's) collective and revised and prefaced edition of my things, and that if he is not minded somehow to obtain access to *that* form of them, ignoring any others, he forfeits half, or much more than half, my confidence. So I thus amicably beseech him—! I suggest to give him as alternatives these two slightly different lists:

1. Roderick Hudson.
2. The Portrait of a Lady.
3. The Princess Casamassima.
4. The Wings of the Dove.
5. The Golden Bowl.

---

1. The American.
2. The Tragic Muse.
3. The Wings of the Dove.
4. The Ambassadors.
5. The Golden Bowl.

The second list is, as it were, the more "advanced." And when it comes to the shorter Tales the question is more difficult (for characteristic selection) and demands separate treatment. Come to me about that, dear young man from Texas, later on—you shall have your little tarts when you have eaten your beef and potatoes. Meanwhile receive this from your admirable friend Mrs. Prothero.

Henry James

† From *Selected Letters of Henry James*, ed. Leon Edel (London: Rupert Hart-Davis, 1956), pp. 136–37. Mrs. Prothero was the wife of George W. Prothero (1848–1922), distinguished historian and editor; the Protheros were friends of James for many years.

8. The young man from Texas was Stark Young, later a distinguished American drama critic, who had appealed to Mrs. Prothero for guidance in reading James. Mrs. Prothero in turn conveyed the appeal to the author himself, and received this reply.

Criticism

Contemporary Reception

In the following section I have sought to provide extracts of all the known contemporary reviews of *The American* which appeared in American and British magazines. In general, only plot summaries have been deleted. The reviews are arranged chronologically under "American Reviews" and "British Reviews" in order to accent the national differences between the two groups of reviewers.

American Reviews

From *The Nation*, January 11, 1877†

The *Atlantic* for January contains a number of good things and some poor ones. Mr. James's story, "The American," which has now reached its eighteenth chapter, has gradually become the familiar feature of the magazine, for which most of its readers from month to month grow impatient, and it is a story which certainly gets more interesting as it goes on. We confess to having had at first a feeling of irritation at being called upon to take an interest in a specimen of a type which, as a type, is, to say the least, not aesthetically attractive. The self-made American, who has suddenly grown rich by "operations" of one kind or another, and has taken himself and his wealth to Europe, is a familiar enough character in literature, but usually the character has been made a comic one, and we have been called upon to laugh at the ridiculous figure cut by our compatriot in the gilded saloons of the effete but critical Europeans, or at his shocking display of ignorance and barbarism as he wanders through "specimen ruins" and "specimen galleries." Mr. James, however, has placed before himself a very different task. He has undertaken to make use of this same type as a serious character in a love story. Newman, as we understand him, is a man who by means of a God-given talent for making money has, while still a young man, accumulated a great fortune (we confess to a sneaking curiosity as to which side of the market he operated upon), and while being in externals an entirely untrained and unsophisticated person, is possessed of that tact and adaptability to

† From *The Nation* 14, (January 11, 1877), 29.

circumstances and refinement of mind which have always been set down as distinguishingly American traits by such unbiassed observers as the English. This man is now taken to France, made to fall in love with a charming French widow, of a family as old and blue-blooded as any in France, filled with and living on the pride of ancestry, ignorant of any world but their own, and looking down with sovereign contempt upon all persons "in trade." It is in this atmosphere of perfectly cold politeness and perfect inanity that our American barbarian lover has to appear to advantage, and to interest the reader. That he does so at all is a striking proof of Mr. James's power as a novelist, and he unquestionably does so a great deal. Of the story as a whole it would be rash to express an opinion till it is completed; but it is safe to say that it is by far the most important contribution to American fiction made for a long time.

From *The Atlantic Monthly*, March 1877†

* * * In reading lately, in The Nation, some remote praise of Mr. James's story of The American by a critic who "confessed to having had at first a feeling of irritation at being called upon to take an interest in a specimen of a type which, as a type, was to say the least not aesthetically attractive," I felt a concern which I wish to express for the condition of a mind so febrile in its sensitiveness as to be shocked at the bare thought of a type like Newman being introduced into a novel, as hero. I at once perceived how greatly this select being must have to limit his reading of fiction, in order to retain any nervous system whatever. Such a story as Le Père Goriot, or César Birotteau, for example, would not simply subject him to "nervous irritation" at the start, but must prostrate him for days. Freytag's Soll und Haben would be very damaging to him. Adam Bede, Silas Marner, and Alton Locke should be kept under lock and key wherever there is danger of this gentleman's accidentally getting hold of them. I do not quite like to think of the consequences of his coming in contact with Thackeray's Hoggarty Diamond; and there are people so common in Shakespeare's plays that I am sure those dramas cannot be pleasant reading to The Nation's critic. How does he manage with Sancho Panza, or Gil Blas? So superior a critic is cut off from the great variety of fiction in which ruder readers delight. For instance, in a case like Reade's Love Me Little, Love Me Long, the lover, Dodd, is not a whit more aesthetic than the lover, Newman, in Mr. James's American. A devout admirer of The Nation, however, tells me we should be glad that a person of such nice discrimination has not long before this

† "The Contributors' Club," *The Atlantic Monthly* 39, (March 1877), 359–68.

perished through suffering from vulgar types in literature. I should like to believe that the case is not so bad as it seems, and that this critic appears more precariously situated than he is, simply because he has allowed himself to talk rubbish.

From *The Independent*, May 17, 1877†

In Mr. Henry James, Jr., we have narrowly missed having a writer of the first rank. But the miss in his case is as good as a mile, for it is of an absolutely ruinous character. It is not in art, but in spirit that Mr. James fails. As a writer he uses quite faultless English, and as an observer of character he is possessed of great keenness and wisdom. His various books have been eminently readable, in the highest sense of the adjective, and some of his short stories have been almost without a flaw in their glittering beauty. * * * *The American*, his new novel, has been appearing in *The Atlantic Monthly*, and is now published in book form by James R. Osgood & Co. It is a better novel than "Roderick Hudson," but it is in the same style. It is a polished, philosophical, and absolutely cold-blooded story. The only indication of artistic failure is a sort of letting-down in the last chapter or two, as though the fastidious writer had wearied even of his art. But supercilious culture and haughty accuracy are not equipment enough for a good novel. Theodore Winthrop, or even Miss Braddon, is preferable. Mr. James ought to undergo a literary change of heart. A good novel ought to be a painting, not a mirror. Soul is better than shimmer.

From *The Nation*, May 31, 1877‡

* * * It is very natural that novelists should grow tired of ending their stories with a fine wedding and the imaginative statement that the newly-married couple always lived happy afterwards. But it is also to be remembered that if readers ask that a love-story should end with a marriage or a definite statement of some satisfactory reason why the marriage did not occur, it is because they know that a real passion leads to marriage unless there is some insuperable obstacle in the way, and that this is a law which does not admit of exceptions. It may very well happen that a slight matter may turn off a half-hearted man who has deluded himself with an unfounded notion that he is in love, when he is only interested; but if he is ever in earnest he is earnest then unless he has deceived himself in some way. Now, it is impossible to suppose that Newman had not his

† From "Two New Novels," *The Independent* 29 (May 17, 1877), 9.

‡ From "James's *American*," by T. S. Perry, *The Nation* 14 (May 31, 1877), 325–26.

whole heart in this matter. It was the one love of his life, and all the mothers and brothers in Christendom would have been no more guard for Madame de Cintré than half a dozen cobwebs. * * *

Now, either the reader has been all along mistaken about Newman's real feeling for Madame de Cintré, or this hero is totally unworthy of the sympathy that is surely given him. A man of his sort cannot sacrifice his life's happiness, and, what is more, that of the woman he loves, who had never known what happiness was, for a mere whim. It was very well for him to let the sixty thousand dollars go which he mentions early in the book, but there is no analogy between that renunciation and the final one, for he had plenty of money besides, whatever became of those thousands, while there was no woman who could replace Madame de Cintré. It is here that the element of passion is wanting, and it is not satisfactorily replaced by the drawing of Newman's extreme good-nature. Its absence is the more noticeable because in the account of Newman's wooing there is a beautiful passage, where Madame de Cintré accepts him, which promises real ardor in the energetic American.

But, apart from this, how much there is to admire in the novel! The different threads are managed with rare skill. The episodical story of Valentin and his doings is told most admirably, and it serves the purpose of bringing out more clearly the excellence of Newman's character. There is great completeness and symmetry in these chapters. But the best thing of all, in our opinion, is the delicacy with which Madame de Cintré is drawn, with her shyness and gracious delicacy. The success here, attained as it is by that apparent simplicity which is the height of art, gives the novel a place among the best modern studies of society, and makes it an honorable example of Mr. James's serious endeavor to attain excellence only by careful choice of methods.

From *The Atlantic Monthly*, July 1877†

It is perfectly manifest that The American takes a place in advance of Roderick Hudson; it has the same sort of merits and the same sort of faults, yet on the whole it must be rated as more successful than Mr. James's former effort. Precisely why it deserves this distinction may not be a thing fully explainable; but there are at least three points that support the claim: the characters are better chosen, the hero and heroine and Madame de Bellegarde having far more intrinsic interest than any corresponding persons in Roderick Hudson; the movement, the grouping, and final disposition of all the persons contain more of that symbolic quality essen-

† From "Recent Literature," by George Parsons Lathrop, *The Atlantic Monthly* 40 (July 1877), 108–9.

tial to the best artistic successes; and lastly, the author's treatment has gained perceptibly in approaching nearer to an air of simple human fellowship. It would be hard, among recent novels, at least, to find a more acute or vigorous full-length portrait than that of Christopher Newman, in the first pages of this book. * * * This is one out of a hundred similar bits of vivid picturing woven into Mr. James's pages with a lavish hand. It is a little too long for the point involved; and in general Mr. James begins to show as a distinct trait of style a fluency which tends at times to the verbose; but we cite it as recalling the perfect clearness, combined with ease, which the author commands at will. This "touch" of his stands him in good stead for familiarizing the reader with a situation and a scenery rather unusual. * * * Yet we are bound to take some serious exceptions. The episode of young Babcock, the feebly aesthetic Unitarian, is expanded beyond all proportion. We cannot at all countenance Mr. James's optimistic estimate of young Valentin, whom he expressly calls "the best fellow in the world," and otherwise gilds beyond his deserving; and the fate which overtakes the persons whose side the reader is compelled to favor is to our thinking not a fair reward for one's sympathy. A more mature consideration might very possibly have shown Mr. James that Madame de Cintré, Newman, and their pathetic auxiliary, Mrs. Bread, were by no means forced by their circumstances to the wretched condition he assigns them. Merely as a question of artistic obligation, it seems to us that having introduced the element of intrigue, in Newman's discovery of the paper criminating old Madame de Bellegarde, Mr. James should have treated this element more consistently. One may disdain incident of that sort, but the appetite which it excites for some striking and dramatic result is a perfectly lawful one. The plot having been turned into the channel of intrigue, therefore, our aesthetic sense is not satisfied by the event here led up to. Mr. James pleads indirectly for a judgment that this issue was made inevitable by the character of Newman. It was his "fundamental good-nature," we are told, which caused him to refrain from publishing the Bellegarde secret to the *beau monde*; and on this good-nature the Bellegardes relied. Perhaps we ought to accept this reasoning, but it seems to us that good-nature is a meagre excuse for a man so profoundly in love as Newman with Madame de Cintré. So insufficient is it that the course which he takes in destroying his paper makes his passion appear suddenly and totally to evaporate, notwithstanding Mr. James's careful portrayal of his despondent and blighted after-years. We may admit that Newman could not have disgraced the family and then married Madame de Cintré as a daughter of that family; the attitude of triumph would have been too petty, even if practicable. But is it any more dignified for him to exult in having at least given Madame de Bellegarde a terrible scare? Another defect is that this French noble family are far from likely to have had the faintest conception of that American good-nature on which Mr. James hints that they relied. The logic of fiction is not that of philosophy, and this story might have had a different ending without defeating consistency. Nevertheless it is good as it stands. It is an impressive composition, and will repay a second reading. That it so naturally raises the question just discussed is a fact in proof of its force; and even if one should be seriously dissatisfied with the termination, it is worth considering whether the catastrophe was not essential in order to show how venomous and fatal is the power belonging to aristocracy when it has been warped by age, avarice, and falsehood.

From *The Galaxy*, July 1877†

Mr. Henry James, who needs no other passport than his name to the favor of the readers of "The Galaxy," has just published another novel, which is so good that we regret very much that it is not better. For, as it seems, it so easily might have been made better, that we feel as if defrauded of a perfect enjoyment which, in the nature of things, we ought to have. Mr. James's purely literary work is always good, neat, finished, with an air of elegance about it which is too rare in the writing of American authors. In this respect "The American" is better than its predecessor, "Roderick Hudson." The writer's hand is steadier, and the work is of more even excellence. But we are not sure that in the former book there are not isolated passages of greater vivacity and stronger imaginative power than can be found in this one.

The plot of "The American" has the great merit of originality, and it is well constructed. * * *

It must be confessed that, with such possibilities in the story, this is rather a lame and impotent conclusion. A story ought to have a manifest and impressive end, just as much as a house ought to have a manifest and characteristic entrance. * * * Instead of this, the close of the American's career, the retirement of Mme. de Cintré from the world, the bringing to light of a deed of darkness that would have ruined the ancient house of Bellegarde, all are frittered away, and the end of the story "peters out" just as some tropical rivers which are deep and strong soak away in the sand and really flow no whither. * * *

We have another fault to find with Mr. James, which is with the title of his book, and the inferences which it measurably warrants

† From "Current Literature," *The Galaxy* 24 (July 1877), 135–38.

abroad. Mr. Christopher Newman is certainly a fair representative of a certain sort, and a very respectable sort, of American; but he is not such a man that Mr. James, himself an American living in Europe, is warranted in setting him up before the world as "*The* American." Men like Newman are already too commonly regarded as the best product, if not the only product, of two hundred and fifty years of American life, and a hundred of republican institutions. But let us argue a little *ad hominem,* and ask Mr. James if Christopher Newman fairly represents the larger number of his associates when he is at home. We fancy not. Why then put him forth thus set up on the pedestal of the definite article? If Mr. James had chosen to write his novel with Newman for hero, and to call it by his name, or Mme. de Cintré's, or any other, and to let Newman go as a representative of a certain kind of American who gets rich in California, very well; but to have an American hold this man up to the world as *the* American is not highly satisfactory.

And this objection has to do with another of more importance, which is that Mr. James's hero is entirely insufficient for the part which he is called upon to play. The motive of the book is the bringing of a representative, supposed to be admirable, of a democratic and trading community into contact with persons of the oldest and highest aristocratic family connections and traditions of Europe, and the presentation of the former in such a light that he carries with him the sympathies of the reader. Other than this the book can have no conceivable motive at all. Now to produce such an effect, Mr. James's hero should have been a man of some mark, clever, if not brilliant, a man who by the force of his own personality might be likely to break down the social prejudices at least of the woman who consents that he may make love to her. Whereas, Newman, although an honorable and respectable man, intelligent in his way, and well-behaved enough, is so entirely lacking in attractive personal qualities, and, although not exactly uncouth, so raw in his manner, that no one wonders why the Bellegardes, being at heart dishonorable people, seize the first opportunity of getting rid of him. He is after all only just what Mr. James makes them call him, "a commercial person," which he might be, and yet be all the rest that he is not. Our only wonder is how a woman like Mme. de Cintré can be brought to look upon him with eyes of personal favor. We are speaking of a woman such as the figure of Mme. de Cintré stands for. For as to the heroine herself, her personality is of the vaguest. She leaves no impression of individuality upon us; we are told certain things about her, indeed, but she is almost a lay figure. Again, as to Newman, there are certain gross inconsistencies which prevent us from accepting him as a real living personage. We see that he is in mind and body rather strong; he is also in mind and body rather *gauche*. Nevertheless Mr. James from time to time puts words into his mouth and thoughts into his mind which only belong to a person of social and intellectual culture and of delicate apprehension. The old Marquise de Bellegarde, who does not conceal her haughtiness or her family pride from him, says to him one day frankly, "I would rather favor you on the whole than suffer you. It will be easier." To which Newman at once replies, "I am thankful for any term. But for the present *you have suffered me long enough*. Good night." And he takes his leave. Again, in reply to a cynical remark by Valentin as to the virtue of old Mr. Nioche, Newman says, "It seems to me that you [he and Mlle. Noémie] are very well matched. You are both hard cases, and M. Nioche and I, I believe, *are the only virtuous men to be found in Paris*." Now the delicate retort of the first of these speeches, and the irony of the second, are not in keeping with the rest that we see of Newman, nor are they consistent with the natural character of a man who left school at ten, and who drifted round the far West in his youth, and in early manhood grew rich in California.

It is only with his hero and his heroine, however, that Mr. James has been unsuccessful. His French people and his French-Americans are admirable. They have the air, all of them, of careful studies from the life, and more. For that they might be and yet lack life themselves; but on the contrary, they live. The old Marquise de Bellegarde is clearly strongly imagined. How truthful the delineation may be as the type of a *grande dame* of the legitimist society of France can only be told by those who have had the opportunity of entering that society, but it has the air of truth about it, as certain portraits have of which we have not seen the originals. So it is with the brothers Bellegarde, the elder of whom, although he is a weak creature, kept erect only by family pride, still impresses us with his individuality, even when he "walks up and down the drawing-room in silence like a sentinel at the door of some smooth-fronted citadel of the proprieties," while poor Valentin lives and breathes and wins us to love him and to mourn his death, his behavior as to the cause of which is thoroughly and exquisitely French. But perhaps the most vivid portraiture in the book is that of Mlle. Noémie. She is at least the Marquise's rival in this respect; and how the crime-blackened old *grande dame* would have drawn herself up at the thought of even the mention of Noémie's name and hers together! Mr. James has very deftly made this thoroughly Parisian young person reveal herself to us, instead of describing her himself. He has had the skill to show us what she is by the impression that she makes on others, and by acts and words of her own that rather suggest than tell plainly what is passing in her mind. And her father, poor old broken down reprobate, trying to cover up his consent to her life from his own eyes—he too is admirable and pitiable. Mr. James's book, for the sake of those personages, although somewhat disappointing at the end, will richly repay reading.

From *The Literary World*, July 1877†

The American is a very modern novel; with no flavor of the past and no prophecy of the future, but on the exact level of the present. Mr. James's forte consists in placing Americans in a European setting—always a difficult task, as the writer is apt to fail either in the environment or the character. Mr. James fails in neither; he knows his own countrymen, and he knows Europe. His delineation of French character here is as thorough and accurate as that of the American. * * * The story in itself is too slight to interest, the *dénouement* being evident at the outset; half the characters are utterly detestable, and the other half without attraction. No gentle reader will shed a tear or heave a sigh over the most tragic of its pages. The characters are not presented for sympathy but for inspection, and in truth they stand out very clearly, but we do not care to prolong the acquaintance. What then is the charm of the book? One less dull was never written, and it has enough weight to hold the attention of the most exacting reader. Its power consists in the brilliancy of its literary execution, and in the accurate delineation of character. It is a clear-cut book. The characters are more than photographed; they walk through the pages. There is none of the mistiness that enveloped our recent friend, Mr. Deronda. Every person and scene are thoroughly eliminated from their surroundings, and brought before us clear and precise. We can say nothing better of its literary quality than that it affects us like good painting. That one art should carry the effect of another is skill indeed. We trust Mr. James will not take it amiss if we suggest that his book has too much of these fine qualities to accompany its tone; they are not in the "concatenation accordingly," as Tony Lumpkin says in the play. It is not agreeable to witness Pegasus ploughing. Nearly the finest thing in the book is the keen sarcasm of the morbid moral sensitiveness of the young Unitarian clergyman, but we incline to think that as between the author and the preacher, the latter has the best of it, and that the former could not do a better thing than to place himself under the ministrations of the Rev. Mr. Babcock before beginning his next book. Or, if that be impossible, let him ponder the maxim "art for art" till he thoroughly feels its

† From "Recent Fiction," *The Literary World* 9 (July 1877), 29–30.

hollowness. Seriously, we think Mr. James's admirable talent demands a better field and atmosphere than he here allows himself, and a nobler set of characters to be used for the illustration of some higher purpose. The author evidently has a dread of the serious; it is his weakness. We must object also to the company into which he introduces us. This bright American book comes perilously near being a French novel, from which may the good Lord long deliver us!

From *Scribner's*, July 1877†

Those who have faith in the growth of literature according to seed and soil, have long cherished the hope—deferred from season to season—that the "great"-ness which characterizes so many American things would soon develop itself in fiction. A great American novel has seemed to many a confident and hopeful patriot to be heralded with the incoming of each new writer. Mr. James early showed qualities which justified the turning of expectant gaze in his direction. The "Passionate Pilgrim," "A Modern Madonna," and "The Last of the Valerii," showed some qualities which might well grow to greatness. It is true that in "Madame De Mauves" and in "Roderick Hudson," expectation received a warning; but Mr. James had given such unmistakable evidence of originality and delicacy, and of skillful *technique*, that when the first chapters of "The American" made their appearance we were justified in looking for a novel thoroughly American in character and sufficiently good to satisfy our national literary longing. It was evident that the movement of the story was to be on foreign soil,—where its author is so much at home,—and that but one of its important characters was to be of our own people, but this one character was so thoroughly of the best typical American sort as to afford a safe basis for the highest hopes that might be built upon it. Big, rich, frank, simple-hearted, straightforward, and triumphantly successful, he satisfied us entirely by his genuine and hearty manliness, and he seemed to carry in his very blood a genius for success in any direction toward which his modest strength might be turned.

* * *

The process by which Mr. James created in the minds of his readers an ideal so different from that which he himself had conceived, is not easy to explain, unless by the suggestion that he set forth external evidences which had fallen uncomprehended under

† From "Culture and Progress: 'The American,'" *Scribner's* 14 (July 1877), 406–7.

his notice, and which meant far more to us than they did to him. Traits in which he found only material for artistic delineation, indicate to those who really know the type of American to whom they belong, a nobility and heroism which it seems never to have been his good fortune to detect. Certain it is that while in drawing this character he furnishes food for admiring contemplation, he was himself quite ignorant of its significance.

* * *

In palliation of the conspicuous failure of this attempt at novel-writing, reviewers have been profuse in praise of Mr. James's excellent "style,"—a style where delicate and skillful diction are seconded by that trick of suggestive "under-statement" toward which modern fashion so greatly tends. With occasional awkward lapses, Mr. James's style is very good indeed, and a good style is essential to a good novel; so is good dress essential to the completeness of a well mannered and charming person. But the most easy and graceful writing, unsustained by a living subject, hangs tame and unsatisfying, like fine raiment on a clotheshorse. It may be suggested that Mr. James aimed at some other ending of his story than the conventional marriage. To this we answer that a marriage with Madame de Cintré need not have ended the story; it might have been used only as a means for placing Newman in a position to show the value of his rare good qualities. Also, a marriage was by no means necessary to the success of the story. Madame de Cintré might have taken the black veil and Newman's career might have ended in sadness and desolation. But it was an imperative condition that he should have *tried* to marry the woman he loved, and if he must fail, that his failure should be in no wise weak and spiritless. Any man with the force of character needed to make the manufacture of washtubs a stepping stone to a great fortune, whether he were an American or not, would have had that in him which would have driven him even to a desperate effort to reclaim a promised wife, whose selfish relations were stealing her away from him, and whom they were dooming to a life of hard seclusion.

It is the best compliment we can pay to Mr. James's writing to say that he gave us such a living interest in his hero, that we are made angry by his own failure to comprehend the character he had created. Can it be that we owe such a fiasco in some degree to the fact that the author has been unconsciously twisted out of his own individuality by the strong influence of Tourguéneff's example? Tourguéneff, however, would justify so miserable an ending; he is remorseless, but he does not shock or disappoint.

From *Appleton's Journal*, August 1877†

The position of an American, fresh from the comparative crudity of the New World and confronted with the maturer social forms, the stereotyped ideas, and the artistic riches of the Old, seems to have an inexhaustible interest for Mr. Henry James, Jr. It furnishes the motive for most of his short stories, it was the dominant feature of "Roderick Hudson," and is almost the sole theme of his latest work, "The American." For this reason there is a certain sameness in his work which, but for his fertility of invention, would detract seriously from its interest; and yet, in spite of identity of situation and similarity of externals, there is an almost complete contrast between "Roderick Hudson" and "The American." In the former, the interest is almost exclusively personal and individual—the characters are more important than, and substantially independent of, their surroundings; in the latter, the individual is subordinated to the social type, and beneath and around the persons whose little drama nominally occupies the stage we are made to see and feel the warring forces of two opposing civilizations. The situation certainly is one of deep and many-sided interest. * * *

* * *

Without going more deeply into the plot, and thus impairing the pleasure of those readers who have not yet perused the book, we could not do justice to the many admirable and delightful qualities of the story. It teems in every part with the overflowings of a rich and full mind; and an indefinable atmosphere of culture, and refinement, and high thought, imparts a charm over and above the more special attractions. The descriptive portions are as delightful as in all Mr. James's work, the social perspective is admirably harmonious and sustained, and the characters pique curiosity where they do not inspire a more genuine interest. Newman himself is hardly so impressive a personage as Roderick Hudson, but Mr. James has never hitherto produced anything equal to the portrait of Madame de Cintré, whose presence pervades the book like a delicate and exquisite perfume. The minor characters, too, are exceptionally well defined and vividly delineated, and throughout there is a sense both of power and of power well applied. If one pronounced opinion upon it after reading two-thirds, we could understand how it should be considered not only a good novel but a great one; but it must be confessed, as a serious qualification of our praise, that the story breaks down sadly toward its close. It is not merely that the end is painful and disappointing—the most unobservant reader must know that in real life love does not always

† From "Books of the Day," *Appleton's Journal* (new series) 3 (August 1877), 189–90.

result in wedding-bells; but in the great crisis of their lives even Madame de Cintré fails to fulfill our ideal of her, and Newman conducts himself so that we almost resent the affectionate interest that we have allowed ourselves to feel for him. Our minds are diverted from the great pity we would otherwise feel for his unhappy fortune by the doubt whether, after all, he really knew what love was, and by the suspicion that we have from the beginning overrated both his moral fibre and his intellectual capacity. This is a sad flaw, indeed, but it is the only drawback upon such work as we seldom have the opportunity of enjoying, and is by no means sufficient to deter the intelligent reader from participating in the feast. "The American" is a book to be read slowly and reflectively, and read thus it will leave a flavor upon the palate as of rich Falernian.

From *The Eclectic*, August 1877†

The first thought that occurs to one after reading "The American" is that the opulence of power displayed in it ought to have made it a novel of the first rank, and precisely why it fails of being such it is somewhat difficult to say. * * * But we fear that it was the very effectiveness of this situation—its wide-reaching suggestiveness and interest—that spoiled Mr. James's book as a novel. In his anxiety to point the contrast and essential antagonism between two such alien civilizations as those of Republican America and Bourbon France, he has subordinated his characters to the machinery of his story, so to speak, and thus deprived them of that personal individuality and self-determining force without which neither real nor fictitious persons can establish any strong claim upon our sympathies or interest. * * * Hence, the reader is dissatisfied with the manner in which "The American" ends, not because it is painful, but because it mars the conception which he has been led to form of the two principal characters in the story; because it seems incongruous with what has gone before; and because it is manifestly the result, not of spontaneously-acting natural causes, but of a preexistent social theory in the author's mind.

In order to reach cause for fault-finding, however, it is necessary to go very deep into the structure of the novel; for its salient qualities, taken separately, we have nothing but heartiest praise. The portrait of Madame de Cintré would be sufficient by itself to lift the book altogether above the level of current fiction; yet there are half a dozen other characters whose natures are laid bare to us with scarcely less delicacy and precision of touch. The incidents are plausible and sufficiently varied, the accessories partake of the mul-

† From "Literary Notices," *Eclectic* 26 (August 1877), 249–50.

tifarious splendors of Paris, and the affluence of resource exhibited in every direction renders the story at once a stimulus and an enjoyment.

From *The Library Table,* August 30, 1877†

We have sometimes questioned within ourselves whether the gift of criticism does not in a measure preclude the art of romancing—whether one mind can possess analytic and synthetic qualities which would fit it, however unequally, to assume the antagonistic characters of critic and criticised.

Mr. James seems to us pre-eminently the critic; a peculiar distinctive nicety of expression, a cultivated taste, and keen analytic ability create in him at once a severe but just and impartial judge. Equally true is it that he possesses rare abilities as a novelist; but always here and there the mantle of the romancer parts to discover the severer garb of the critic beneath;—he lays as it were a finger of one hand upon the pulse of human nature, while in the other he holds, but half concealed, the keen knife of the surgeon. * * * Through all these chapters runs the undertone of sarcasm that betrays the *critic*: it is only later in the volume that the *author* warms to his work. * * *

This self-confidence of Newman is, rightly taken, a key to the unexpected *dénouement* of his *affaire* with Madame de Cintré. The Bellegardes he treats according to his knowledge of human nature; but his knowledge is from an American stand-point and experience only. The Bellegardes model their behavior toward Newman according to their experience from the narrow stand-point of the French *haute noblesse.* They consent to the alliance of a daughter of their house with a man repulsive to every instinct of their petty natures, but in truth it is "for value received." Another and a better match presents itself, and an excuse is found for breaking the first. Understanding at last, natures too foreign at first for his comprehension, and with a love born of republican principles and fostered by a stern self-reliance and self-respect, Newman finds means, rough, but sufficiently powerful, to bend them to his wishes. He omits, however, to take into consideration the gentle conscience or strong sense of honor in the breast of Madame de Cintré. Gently she eludes the grasp of either party by donning the garb of the *religieuse.* Religious fanaticism is the strongest breastplate a timid heart can wear; so Christopher Newman is left with "nothing to be thankful for and nothing to ask."

The work is throughout excellent in conception; it only lacks

† From "New Novels," *The Library Table* 3 (August 30, 1877), 154–55.

here and there sufficient warmth, a greater depth of coloring to give it tone.

From *The North American Review,* September 1877†

Mr. Henry James's latest book has had, as it deserved to have, a somewhat exceptional reception. Not only has it been the subject of more careful and excellent criticism than has fallen to the lot of any other American novel of recent years, but it has called forth, both in print and elsewhere, much of that earnest discussion which is the best evidence of the impression made by uncommonly strong work; and in this instance the discussion has been of more than ordinary value in itself.

There has been no question—as, indeed, we think there can be none—with regard to Mr. James's novel, looked at from one point of view. The perfection of his literary skill is almost beyond cavil. His style has rare, strong qualities in admirable combination. It is delicate without weakness; there is a peculiar refinement in it, without a touch of pedantry or a moment's sacrifice of idiomatic force; it is rich without being fantastic, and individual without mannerisms. In this Mr. James compels the tribute of a hearty admiration; and we join willingly with those who give it without reservation. Whatever may be in dispute about him, he is, before all things, a master of the technical portion of his art, and so easily first among the men around him that we should look in vain, perhaps, for a comparison. What Mr. Howells wrote of his first book is true of all he has produced; it is "a marvel of delightful workmanship."

But the discussion with regard to "The American" has been upon another point; and one which concerns not only Mr. James's own prospective place in literature, but incidentally involves, in some degree, the dangerously broad question what a great novel really is.

Mr. James has given us a book appealing almost entirely—we are tempted to say wholly—to the reader's intellectual side. The enjoyment we derive from it is purely intellectual enjoyment. It is obvious to the warmest of his admirers (we do not count ourselves the least among the number), that imagination is not the impelling force with him; that he does not write under the pressure of a strong creative power. On the contrary, he is the representative of a class of men to whom, ordinarily, expression does not seem worth while; of Emerson's "great silent crowd" of highly cultured lookers-on, who feel no impulse toward speech. * * * It is a rare strength that enables Mr. James to be in this class and yet not of it. But it

† From "New American Novels," by E. L. Burlingame, *North American Review* 125 (September 1877), 309–15.

has not been quite great enough to enable him to shake off the habit of one who is altogether a *spectator ab extra*; the critic and the analyst, rather than the sharer, of strong feeling.

Not that he is not immeasurably far away from that class of writers who make the reader feel as though he were attending merely on a series of experiments,—a kind of psychological clinic; the quality of his art alone would keep him from any error such as this. With him what Leslie Stephen calls "the cool, hard, and steady hand necessary for psychological dissection" is gentle and kindly in its touch. You do not notice it; you are not conscious of its passage, or of the work that it is doing. Only, he is contented with the mere exhibition of his skill and accuracy; consciously he seems to stop there, as though there were no need of going further. It is not necessary that you should feel when the persons of his story feel,—only that you should see that *they* are feeling. It is not needful that you should be in *rapport* with them,—that when a bundle of nerves is laid bare you should feel each one tingle, and when a glimpse of a passion is discovered you should be put in keen enough sympathy with it to know the rest. The delicate and subtile analysis is followed throughout with all a student's interest; but it is an interest that attaches almost altogether to the process, very little to its suggestions or results, and least of all to the characters that may have been its subjects.

We do not ask for better bread than can be made with wheat, however; nor appreciate "The American" the less because it seems to us rather an almost perfect study, than a piece of completed or in any sense creative work. It is only because Mr. James stands so near the very head of the school in which he has enrolled himself, that what he writes inevitably raises a question as to the limitations of that school. We doubt whether he and his companions are not confined, by the very conditions of their method, to the production of admirable specimens of skilful workmanship instead of real creations, we do not listen the less hopefully to those of his critics who believe that he will prove the doubt a groundless one. In the reaction which is strong just now against all crudity and carelessness there is danger that they may expect of his rare skill some things which skill alone cannot supply; yet he has shown himself so thoroughly a master in all that he has undertaken, that the one step higher may also be within his power. Nationality and surroundings are the only things "The American" of Mr. James's present story has in common with the heroes of "Roderick Hudson" and the shorter sketches that made up its author's earlier volume. Christopher Newman is a new type with him; a more strongly marked and finished one than any he has touched before, and one so carefully studied that it is impossible to give a fair idea of it without the fine lights and shades of his own admirable picture. There is nothing of its kind in fiction better than the paragraph in which this hero first appears,—a man who "fills out the national mould with an almost ideal completeness." * * *

This unsurpassed bit of description is so absolutely necessary to any comment on the story in which Newman plays a part, that we make no apology for the length of the quotation. With it, the general conception of the novel is half told. Newman had lived the vigorous, quickly successful life of such a man; among other things he had made himself an early fortune. "Life had been for him an open game, and he had played for high stakes. He had won at last and carried off his winnings; and now, what was he to do with them?" The first suggestions of this question had led him to give up business at thirty-six,—not formally, as men do ordinarily, but suddenly, from a momentary, overmastering impulse. He became suddenly aware that there was another life whose possibilities he had not tested. "I seemed," he says to his friend Tristram, "to feel a new man inside my old skin, and I longed for a new world. . . . As soon as I could get out of the game I sailed for Europe." This was how "The American" came to be in Paris. Knowing the man, how fresh a type he represents in fiction, how familiar a one, in fact,—catching immediately the full spirit of Mr. James's purpose in putting him suddenly in high relief against a background so opposite in color, we follow the story from these first few pages with an interest which is never suffered to flag, through a succession of character studies that are most perfect exhibitions of literary skill.

Madame de Cintré, who, with her surroundings, makes up that sharp contrast to his leading character without which Mr. James is never quite content, is to our mind the least successful figure in the book. We can well understand that a certain vagueness and haziness about his delineation of her should be a part of Mr. James's plan, for the sharp, decisive lines of Newman are thus most effectively brought out; but we are not prepared to find her so colorless as to seem somewhat inconsistent with the part she has to play. Beside the women of "Roderick Hudson" she is certainly not a successful piece of drawing; and the ability that Mr. James there showed in the depicting of his heroines leads to a little disappointment that Madame de Cintré should be left so mere an outline.

To atone for this, however, Mr. James has devoted more attention to his minor characters than is his habit; in this case possibly because each one of them adds such a vivid touch of color to the contrasted ground against which his leading figure stands, as we have said, in high relief. Madame de Cintré's mother, Madame de Bellegarde, the central stone of that hard wall against which poor Newman strikes, is a masterpiece of skilful drawing. * * * Her son,

Urbain de Bellegarde, the head of the house, is scarce behind this picture. * * * Best of all, however, is a less serious figure than Mr. James is wont to draw, Madame de Cintré's younger brother Valentin. A thorough Frenchman, a thorough light-heart through and through,—the only appearance in Mr. James's books of a type that Thackeray himself might have created,—Valentin is as living a personage as Newman himself. * * *

The ending of the novel will disappoint many beside those who look for a conventional *dénouement*. Its inconsistency with all the probabilities of Newman's character has been the chief objection brought against it by the critics; and it is a sound one. But to us there seems to be another fault as well. The close is somewhat blurred and ineffective; the point that Mr. James seeks to make in his last pages is lost in a vagueness which leaves the reader not unsatisfied, as much strong work will do inevitably,—but positively discontented, and searching dimly for some reason why such sharp and tangible purposes and figures should pass so quickly into smoke.

From *The Catholic World*, December 1878†

* * *

It will be hotly urged by Mr. James's friends, who are more numerous than his critics, that in *The American* we have just the countertype to *St. Elmo*; that the essence of the story is natural, the style vivacious and simple, the action rapid but not turgid and confusing, the situations probable, the effects logical, the outcome rational. Perhaps the harshest thing which can be said of this book is simply that it is not interesting; the publishers' ledger undoubtedly confirms this more than suspicion. We take it as an illustration of the better class of American novels; not as a popular novel, for it lacks that vitalization of interest which is essential to popular success. That Mr. James has talent for writing fiction is apparent from others of his efforts as well as from this; and it is criticism which he needs to spur him into a more artistic use of his gifts. Matthew Arnold insists that the rule of true and fruitful English criticism may be summed up in a word—disinterestedness. The treatment which *The American* received from our home critics displayed so little of this quality that we trust we shall not be accused of endeavoring to make up the deficiency. Mr. James' novel, judged by the standard set up at the outset—that "morality of effect shall follow from truth of representation"—must be ranked low. That it contains much accuracy or representation is true; that much of it is

† From "The American Novel—With Samples," *Catholic World* 28 (December 1878), 331–34.

vague, sketchy work, as dim in the author's comprehension as to the reader's perception, is also true; and the clearest truth of all is that its effect is wholly aside from morality. It would be unfair to say that its effect is immoral; but a book without a positive effect one way or the other must be weak as a work of art, inefficient, and without an aim. What is the aim of *The American*? It is impossible to say. Not to inculcate any lesson of morals. To improve the manners of Americans abroad? That were worthy of an American novelist; but the average reader is either so little disposed to analysis that he (or she, more often) will see nothing in the language, the attitudes, the ambition, the motives of Mr. Christopher Newman to censure and avoid; or the intended effect will be lost upon those keen enough to be amused by Mr. Newman's "pertinacious audacity," for such readers are too keen to read the book through, except in a flippant and careless way. It has not plot enough to hold an habitual novel-reader. Newman ceased attending school at twelve years of age; he served through the war and came out of it a general, of course; he had no money, no friends, and conveniently for the author, no relatives. He went to San Francisco penniless, and amassed a fortune with great speed. He goes to Paris to "be amused" and to buy a wife—a "great woman." This is scarcely according to life. The American, no matter how quickly he makes his money, never thinks of going away from his own country to get a wife. * * *

Does anybody know now what Madame looked like? Is there any evidence in this description to justify anybody, even Newman, in falling in love with her? Madame was the daughter of the Marquise de Bellegarde, who had two sons, one of whom, Valentin, is killed in a duel, after partly revealing to Newman that his mother and brother killed his father in order to compel his sister to marry De Cintré, who died in a couple of years. The Bellegardes, despising Newman, but anxious to sell the widow to him, at first consented to the marriage, then changed their minds. She was wholly under their control, and went into a Carmelite convent—a serious step much easier to take in fiction than in fact. He obtained from an old English servant of the family a dying declaration by the marquis that madame had killed him, and with this Newman attempted what in fact would be called blackmail. He threatened the De Bellegardes that he would show the paper to their acquaintances if they did not restore Mme. de Cintré to him. In the management of this part of his plot, "if plot it may be called," Mr. James shows nothing but feebleness. If Newman believed Mme. de Bellegarde guilty of the heinous offence charged, it was his duty to place the facts in the hands of the police. Morality would have demanded that. If he did not believe her guilty, what a brutal coward was he not to taunt an old woman with so atrocious an accusation, and threaten to blacken her among her friends! But the author intends that we shall believe madame guilty, and that we shall understand that Newman so considered her. Yet he used her crime only as a threat for the furtherance of his personal ends, and when he found that this could do him no good he destroyed the murdered man's statement. Thus there was neither Christian morality nor what the unchristian world calls "honor" in Newman's conduct. This man is represented as uneducated, clownish, given to profanity and "slang" and to stretching out of his legs; but manly, independent, generous, chivalrous. Some of the blame might be removable from his conduct could the plea be made that, although he held madame guilty, he had too much affection for her daughter to expose a crime whose disgrace would extend over the entire family. He did not keep the secret. He told a gossipy woman that the paper which he burned in her presence contained something which would "damn them if it were known." * * *

How much reputation the Bellegardes had left after Mrs. Tristram had finished retailing the story of Newman's burnt paper and grievous innuendo the author does not tarry to tell, for at this point the story ends. There is nothing in *The American* to improve anybody's morals or manners; and the style, as an illustration of American progress in literary art, is not likely to bring us credit. The conception of the story is wanting in breadth, clearness, vigor, life; there is not a gentleman or lady between its covers; and foreigners, reading it as a representative American novel, would be sorely puzzled to know if Newman, whom Mr. James characterizes as not only "a fine American" but also "a fine man," is a good specimen of our national manhood. He is asked if this is his "first time in Europe," and answers, "Yes, very much so"; he describes a hack in which he had been riding as "having a greasy line along the top of the drab cushions, as if it had been used for a great many Irish funerals"; and when asked whether he desired a wife of a particular nationality, the "fine American" answers, "No Irish need apply." To make his success in life "perfect" he wants to see "a beautiful woman perched on the pile"; he is sure that if people "notice my wife and admire her" "I shall be mightily tickled"; and his figures of speech are drawn from the prize-ring and other equally refined associations. Mr. James does not intend to use for himself the careless language which he habitually sputters out of the mouth of his fine American. He says that Newman in the presence of women was neither shy nor awkward: "Grave, attentive, submissive, often silent, he was *simply swimming in a sort of rapture of respect*."

We have given this book more space than it is entitled to; yet it has been proclaimed as one of the very best American novels ever written. To be sure this is saying little; but before laying it aside is it not pardonable to inquire whether the bad types of our men and women are not caricatured enough by foreigners; whether it is commendable in American authors not merely to lampoon the national foibles which ought to be lampooned, but to paint an illiterate and audacious gawk in a pretendedly fine frame and label him a representative American? A good specimen of the sturdy, honest, and peculiar American is "Robert Pagebrook" in Mr. George Cary Eggleston's *A Man of Honor.*

English Reviews

From *The Athenaeum,* July 7, 1877†

Mr. James's 'American' will interest English readers greatly, as a clever presentment of a characteristic type of his countrymen, in search of adventures in the paradise to which good Americans go. * * * The sombre termination of the book is, perhaps, a necessity, where there is so hopless an antagonism between inclination and supposed duty as in Madame de Cintré's case; but the general impression left is humorous. Whether lightly discussing the situation with Valentin, his gay young friend, a fine type of a French aristocrat of a modern kind, or fencing with the authorities of the house of De Bellegarde, the Marquis and her son, who are as impenetrable in their pride and as satisfied of the excellence of their motives as if the ordinary rules of morality were set aside in their favour, there is an incisiveness mingled with *naiveté* about the American which makes the dialogue unusually spirited. Withal he is a thoroughly good fellow, and the reader's sympathies follow him throughout his hopeless struggle with the polished wickedness of his opponents. Madame de Cintré's character is also very happily drawn. The want of backbone which causes her to fail in her engagement to Newman, under the pressure of what she has been taught to regard as her primary duty to her family, is only what might be expected from a virtuous young Frenchwoman brought up in the aristocratic *faubourg.* Her faithfulness to her attachment, which drives her to the convent for escape, is only another side of the same loving and submissive nature. Mlle. Noémie and her miserable father, who does *not* play the part of Virginius, are amusing

† From "Novels of the Week," *The Athenaeum* (London) 2593 (July 7, 1877), 14–15.

in their wretched way. On the whole, Mr. James's story breaks fresh ground, and will be read with interest.

From *The Academy*, July 14, 1877†

We have but one thing against Mr. James, and we wish we could say as much for most of the novelists whose work comes before us. He has read Balzac, if it be possible, just a little too much; has read him until he has fallen into the one sin of his great master, the tendency to bestow refined dissection and analysis on characters which are not of sufficient intrinsic interest to deserve such treatment. No doubt this is a fault which savours of virtue; but still it is a fault, and a fault which renders it extremely difficult to fix one's attention on *The American* until the excellence of Mr. James's manipulation fairly forces one for very shame to interest oneself in his story. The hero and heroine are the chief stumbling-blocks. * * * There are several minor characters who are decidedly better than the principals. Such are the old Marquise, who bears, however, a rather perilous likeness to Lady Kew; her younger son, a capital fellow and a partisan of the ill-treated Yankee; a matchmaking and platonically flirtatious American matron, and others. Also we have a ghastly family secret, a fatal duel, and a retirement to a convent; so that Mr. James has been by no means stingy of what some people will regard as the solids of his feast. But we wish we could like his chief figures. The portrait of his countryman must of course be taken as accurate, and is evidently sympathetic. But if not only the *naïf* consciousness and avowal of being as good as anybody else, but also the inability to understand how the anybody else may possibly differ from him on this point, be taken from life, the defect of repulsion strikes us as a serious one. There is, moreover, something exceedingly jarring to our possibly effete nerves in the idea of a man who seriously entertains the idea of revenging himself for a personal slight by making use of a family secret which he has surreptitiously got hold of. It is true he does not do it, but he threatens to do so, and tries to make profit of the threat. After this we cannot help feeling on the side of his enemies, scoundrels as they are. And the lady, though her temperament and French ideas of duty explain her conduct not insufficiently, is far too shadowy and colourless. The book is an odd one, for, though we cannot call it a good book, there is no doubt whatever that it is worth a score of the books which we are wont truly enough in a sense to call good.

† From "*The American*," by George Saintsbury, *The Academy* 12 (July 14, 1877), 33.

From *The Spectator*, July 21, 1877†

An American who has made his fortune in the States goes to spend it, after the manner of his race, in Paris. * * * The story, if such it can be called, ends with showing us beauty and virtue in a convent, and vice triumphant in Hyde Park. There is much cleverness in the pictures of Parisian life, but except the "American" himself, there is no one for whom it is possible to feel any kind of regard. Madame de Cintré herself, whom the hero loves, we have to take, so to speak, on trust, for we see little reason for his thinking her so admirable. It may easily be concluded, therefore, that the effect of the whole book is scarcely agreeable.

From *The Saturday Review*, August 18, 1877‡

It is our pleasant duty, almost for the first time within the last few years, to give considerable praise to an American novel. Mr. Henry James, junior, has produced a work which has hit something like orginality without falling into eccentricity, and reaches excitement without descending to what is technically called "sensation." Mr. James's method is, if internal evidence goes for anything, founded on that of M. Mérimée and his disciple M. Tourguenef. That is, he is not afraid of devoting much study to characters whose connexion with the plot of his story is of the slightest kind. It is, indeed, in character-drawing of this sort that the author's merit lies. His talent for construction does not seem to be very great. It is probable that some of his readers will be irritated when they arrive at the revelation, the promise of which has allured them.

One can, however, forgive faults of this kind for the sake of the author's happy turn of expression, which is brought out in the description of his hero's state in the first pages of his novel. * * *

* * *

Just before he dies, Valentin, after making a set apology for his relations' conduct, gives Newman a clue to a family mystery, the knowledge of which he may use to redress his wrong. It is here, as has been before hinted, that the author's execution fails him. The means by which Newman finally discovers the scent are utterly impossible; and there is little merit in his making no use of his discovery, because the evidence which he could bring forward is practically not worth a straw. Our wonder is, not that Mme. de

† From "Current Literature," *The Spectator* 50 (July 21, 1877), 925.

‡ From "The American," by Walter Pollock, *The Saturday Review* 44 (August 18, 1877), 214–15.

Bellegarde should defy him, but that she should quail even for a moment. It must, we think, be admitted that Mr. James's management of the relations between his characters on which his plot depends is not happy. But against this may be set the unusual merits displayed in his treatment of many of the personages considered as separate persons.

From *The Graphic*, September 8, 1877†

"The American," by Henry James, Junior (Boston: Osgood and Co.: Trübner).—Christopher Newman * * * wins the lady's heart, and gains the consent—reluctantly given, it is true—of her mother and elder brother to her marriage with him, in spite of his having been defiled by trade. Then—on grounds which we imperfectly understand—this consent is revoked; and—on grounds which we understand a great deal less—Madame de Cintré holds herself bound to submit to the decision of her family; takes a broken-hearted farewell of her lover; and goes into a Carmelite Convent. Such is the story, which, as a story, cannot be pronounced very attractive. But the sketches of Parisian life are clever and well-executed, and Mr. James talks well and with insight about his characters, though he hardly makes us believe in them as real. Perhaps, artistically speaking, the best among them is the astute Mademoiselle Noémie Nioche, detestable little adventuress as she is. Madame de Cintré, we incline to think, might have been a fine conception had she been worked out, but as here shown to us she is hardly more than a shadow. Still, the book is not without power of a kind.

From *The Academy*, May 10, 1879‡

We noticed Mr. James's *American* at the time of its appearance across the Atlantic. Since that time its author has been industrious, and has made not infrequent appearances before an English audience. *The American*, however, continues to be if not exactly his best or most finished piece of work, at any rate that in which his powers are most clearly shown, and in which they have best grappled with a subject on the great scale. It is also, perhaps, the work which most clearly exhibits Mr. James's great defect, the defect of expending immense pains on characters which are not worth the trouble. It is unfortunately impossible to like Mr. James's characters: it is also impossible to get up a good healthy dislike of them;

† From *The Graphic* 16 (September 8, 1877), 230.

‡ From "New Novels," by George Saintsbury, *The Academy* 15 (May 10, 1879), 408.

and, at the same time, his art, though by no means small, is not sufficient to put liking or disliking out of the question, as is the art of Flaubert or Thackeray. Notwithstanding which, all persons who have not yet read *The American* may be recommended to read it now.

From *The British Quarterly Review*, July 1879†

* * * Mr. James writes with an individuality and a strength that must give him amongst novelists a rank of a high order. It is not easy to say in what his distinctive qualities consist. The plot of his stories is subordinate to his character-drawing, and his delineations of character are subordinate to the keen penetration, originality and suggestiveness of his remarks on men and things. His stories have sequence and purpose, but he does not care much for the unities, and still less for poetical justice; they come to no completed development. Like the experiences of life, they have no end at which we can rest; things do not get wound up, his heroes and heroines are not 'happy ever afterwards,' the end that there is is generally the reverse. His strong relentless realism leaves a large amount of failure and continuing happiness; life is left going on with many unravelled threads in its warp and woof; the story that is, is a mere vehicle for sentiment. * * * We are no great sticklers for conventionality in novel writing, but a novel is an ideal work of art, and we cannot help thinking that the art is defective in construction which leaves issues so loose and destinies so vague. A chronicle has essential differences from a story. The great excellences of Mr. James would be not less, but more, if an artistic plot were more completely wrought out. The character-drawing is more effective than the story-telling, but somehow it does not come up to our ideal. * * * Mr. James, that is, does not win our full sympathies for any of his characters; they are too remote from us; we feel no strong enthusiasm for any of them. Perhaps Valentin takes closer hold of us than anyone else. Newman's love-making, for instance, never clarifies itself from the practical purpose of a sensible, high-toned, honourable business man. The higher domain of imagination and passion is never entered. He is a novel fellow, and Claire would have been happy as his wife, but the tone through all is prosaic and realistic. The strength of the writer, and it is very great, lies in the kind of keen, sententious remark of which Thackeray is the great English master. Every page is full of pregnant sentences, laying bare the motives and processes of life; not however, as with Thackeray, blended with touches of imagination, pathos, and passion so

† From "Contemporary Literature," *British Quarterly Review* 70 (July 1879), 141–42.

as to excite strong sympathy as well as admiration. Mr. James works in a medium of satire, not fierce but subtle, which interposes as a thin mist between his characters and the reader. * * * Nevertheless, in virtue of the qualities we have indicated, the story is a remarkable one, full of sensible remark and intellectual power, the cynical element being, however, predominant. Mr. James does not, as one of his critics has strangely said, present us with ideals, only with types somewhat exaggerated. The word clever is perhaps the most fitting epithet of characterisation. The book is stimulating in the sense in which olives stimulate the palate. We are interested and absorbed from first to last. Every paragraph is weighted with social wisdom, and is clear cut and incisive as a Dutch picture. His characters are by no means ideals, as with a strange misconception they have been designated; they are types, with a certain exaggeration, necessary for impression. To jaded novel-readers the story is a fine tonic.

From *The Westminster Review*, January 1880†

Perhaps the best of the novels this quarter is not only a reprint, but not even written by an Englishman. What is the particular excellence of Mr. James's novels? * * * The first thing which strikes us is the care which he takes to make everything quite plain for the reader. He fills up all details. He spares no pains to bring out his characters into full relief. There is nothing slovenly about his writing. Many of our ablest novelists, especially women, seem to write with a sort of sympathetic ink, which requires holding to some fire before the words become plain. Not so Mr. James. * * * This is Mr. James's secret—he gets upon good terms with his reader. But to do this, as Thackeray did it, and Mr. James still does it, requires not only a great deal of humour, but also a great deal of art.

† From "Belles Lettres," *Westminster Review* 57 (January 1880), 285–86.

Twentieth-Century Criticism

LEON EDEL

[A Portrait Rich in National Ambiguities]†

Henry James's financial situation on reaching the French capital had been as follows: he had drawn upon his father's letter of credit in London to pay for new clothes and for his installation in the Rue de Luxembourg; he had certain miscellaneous sums outstanding from the *Nation* and the *Galaxy*, and had arranged to have them paid directly to him, instead of to Quincy Street; royalties from the book publication of *Roderick* (it was published in Boston on November 20, 1875) were to be sent to his father to reimburse him for the sums owing him. He was committed to start another novel for Howells, but a certain lapse of time was necessary following the serialization of *Roderick*, just ending. He was, therefore, short of funds. His fortnightly letters to the *Tribune* did not even cover his rent; his fugitive reviewing and other writings would barely feed him. He needed about $150 a month; and the only practical course open to him was to start a new serial, as quickly as possible, in some other magazine. He would have to explain to Howells that he could not afford to wait. Having already had tentative talks with the editors of the *Galaxy*, he wrote to them from Paris on December 1, 1875 that he proposed "to take for granted, as soon as I can, that you will be ready to publish, on receipt of them, the opening chapters of a novel." It was then that he announced he had begun *The American* sooner than expected. He planned to complete it in nine months and his price would be $150 an instalment. He would thus earn in three-quarters of a year more than *Roderick* had brought in during a twelve-month.

He learned presently that *Transatlantic Sketches* had yielded a royalty balance of $200 at the end of the year and this money had gone directly to Quincy Street. On January 24 he received a letter from his mother accusing him of extravagance, and informing him that his autumn draft on his father had been "excessive and inconvenient." Henry replied at once. Her words had given him "a

† "*The American*," in *Henry James: The Conquest of London, 1870–1881*, by Leon Edel (Philadelphia: J. B. Lippincott Company, 1962), pp. 245–60.

wretched hour." It was true, he said, that he had drawn more largely, and at shorter intervals, "than could be at all agreeable to you." Nevertheless this had been a necessity of his situation. "I have hardly had my expenses off my mind an hour since I have been abroad, and I had arranged my life here, in Paris, well within my means." Paris was not cheap; but it was not as dear as New York and "once under way, as I am now, I am in for nothing that I cannot face." He had not known, he said, that his father's resources were curtailed, or he would have been "doubly and triply careful." He said he was certain that by the end of the year he would have a balance in his favor "and I shall be able to refund and compensate inconveniences." He added: "Banish from your mind your visions of my extravagance. I am living simply as well as physical well-being, and decent mental cheerfulness seem, in a lonely life, to demand."

The effect of his mother's letter was, for the moment, to undermine Henry's sense of security. He could draw no further on his father; and he had to find ways to keep his pen busy. This may explain his suddenly developing a ten-day headache, not as violent or feverish as the one he had had in Florence when William was with him, but sufficiently uncomfortable to keep him at home. He had to cancel his plans to attend a fancy-dress party at the Viardots', and Turgenev came the morning after to comfort Henry and describe to him the fun he had missed.

The *Galaxy* did not reply, and Henry stopped writing *The American.* Instead he hastily wrote two tales—"Crawford's Consistency" and "The Ghostly Rental"—in his old, pre–*Roderick Hudson* vein. He deemed them inferior and sold them to *Scribner's* for $300. Meanwhile Howells wrote to say he would take Henry's serial whenever he was ready to let him have it. Henry ruefully replied: "I took for granted that the *Atlantic* would begin nothing till June or July, and it was the money question solely that had to determine me." *The American,* he said, was the only subject "mature enough in my mind to use immediately. It has in fact been used somewhat prematurely; and I hope you find enough faults in it to console you for not having it in the *Atlantic.*" He said, however, that if the *Galaxy* continued to ignore him, or if its editors were not satisfied, he would ask them to forward the first instalment to Howells. His price remained $150 a month for nine instalments.

Howells was determined to keep Henry in the *Atlantic*, and he lost no time in offering to take *The American* if the *Galaxy* did not want it. Henry, on his side, laid down an ultimatum: "If you are unable to begin *The American* at the latest in the May *Galaxy*, I must forego the pleasure of having the story appear in the magazine. I decided it should be plain that this and the price I fixed per number ($150) were the only terms on which I offered it." He repeated: "These then are my terms—$150 a number—to commence in May—and failing this to send the copy instantly to Cambridge." The editors of the *Galaxy* obliged. Howells scheduled the serial to begin in the *Atlantic*'s June issue.

I

The American was a firm, rapid stride on the part of Henry James into full literary maturity. The endless debate of *Roderick Hudson* gave way now to determination and action. Henry had found it necessary in his first large novel to create two characters to express his full intention; he was able now to make of these one substantial individual who embodied both the active-creative part of himself as well as the still-lingering Cambridge cautionary elements. It took Rowland Mallet, playing god, to complete Roderick; Christopher Newman also wants to play god—to the whole world—but in the process he stands aggressively planted on his own two feet. The novelist's divided and conflicting selves had come together: unified, he could launch them in the Old World, in Paris, where he himself was now launched.

He had told Howells he was writing the novel "prematurely." What he meant by this was that he was uncomfortably close to his materials; there was an almost excessive flow of daily incident from life into his book without proper assimilation of it. The consequence was that this novel, of all of James's works, is written, as might be said, "off the top of his head." Yet he had long nourished the image of Christopher Newman. He had thought of him one day, while riding in an American horse-car, as the figure of a robust American confronting an aristocratic society. The point of his story would be that this American should suffer at the hands of persons "pretending to represent the highest possible civilization and be of an order in every way superior to his own." The old idea could now be brought together with Henry's new environment. He would write a novel about an American businessman and his siege of Paris, of that Faubourg St. Germain about which Henry had read in Balzac, and of which he himself was having only a passing glimpse. He speaks in the novel of "those grey and silent streets of the Faubourg whose houses present to the outer world a face as impassive and as suggestive of the concentration of privacy as the blank walls of Eastern seraglios." The streets he had in mind were the Rue de l'Université, where much of the novel's action takes place, the Rue de Lille and the Rue de Bellechasse, where in later years he was to call often on the Daudets. There was also the Rue du Faubourg St. Germain, and the short Rues Monsieur and Madame. Other streets a little farther out of the "*old* residential and noble parts of the city" were the Rue St. Dominique, the Rue de

Grenelle and the Rue de Varenne, where long after he was to join the group of "sarabandists," as he called them, frequenting the home of Edith Wharton. In Henry's time there were a great many fine old *hôtels* in these streets, with their wide gates and coachyards such as may still be seen in some quarters of Paris. Henry had hoped that some of these gates would swing open for him; he would have liked to visit the Balzacian scenes. His American, Christopher Newman, however, has a much higher hope—that of marrying into one of the Faubourg's old aristocratic families. He reflects, in a measure, some of Henry's frustration at not achieving entrance into this world which Eugène de Rastignac had conquered and in which, through his saturated reading of French novels, Henry felt himself, in his imagination, to be initiate. The result is that the Faubourg which Henry creates is in part the Faubourg of literature, rather than that of life; on which he superimposes the few shreds of fact and the glimpses he himself had had during the reception at the Duc d'Aumale's and his meeting with the Orleanist princess. These episodes would be converted into the great party in the house of the Bellegardes.

Newman is thus an image of Henry's Parisian life of action, while at the same time being a mordant portrait of an American—a portrait indeed so rich in national ambiguities that several generations of readers have seen him largely as an expansive, generous, warm-hearted hero without sufficiently noticing that he embodies also everything that Henry disliked in the United States. Newman's qualities show the American character in all its forthrightness and innocence as well as in its predatory aspects. Books written in recent years about "the quiet American," "the nice American" and "the ugly American" represent facets of James's hero. The Californian was in some respects "quiet," and his author even claimed for him a certain "shyness," which is nowhere present in the book. He was "nice" in many ways. But there was in him a strong and vulgar streak of materialistic self-satisfaction which Henry had understood from the first and to which many American readers preferred to close their eyes. Constance Rourke, in a brilliant essay on the humor in the book, long ago pointed to the way in which James achieved a remarkable synthesis of an American "type": his naïveté, his boastfulness, his impatience with cant; but there is also his total failure to grasp deeper human values. Americans reading this book are often apt to overlook that side of Newman which Charles Dudley Warner noticed, when *The American* was still appearing in the *Atlantic Monthly,* and about which he wrote to Julian Hawthorne: "It seems to me the cleverest thing James ever did; perhaps it is too clever. He actually makes us believe it possible to marry a Californian boor to a Bellegarde, and then he cruelly breaks the match."

"Boor" may be too strong a word, but the boorishness in Newman resides not in his pretensions—decidedly superficial—to cultivating art or architecture; it is the side of him which is at once pride in being a "self-made" man and in his crass unawareness that there are things in this world which cannot be bought. Little phrases and occasional sentences throughout the book tell us these things: Henry James however has handled his character so adroitly and placed him so distinctly in the position of an individual wronged and thwarted that they are not sufficiently noticed. The very description of his protagonist reveals this. Newman has "an eye in which innocence and experience were singularly blended." It is "frigid and yet friendly, frank yet cautious, shrewd yet credulous, positive yet skeptical, confident yet shy, extremely intelligent and extremely good-humored." There is also "something vaguely defiant in its concessions, and something profoundly reassuring in its reserve." Newman would seem to be that future paradox in the civilized world: the American who is hospitable to life's chances, but who is "committed to nothing in particular" save his own incredible self-assurance.

Christopher Newman begins with the belief that "Europe was made for him, and not he for Europe." He has for his standard "the ideal of one's own good-humored prosperity." His "specialty" has been "to make the largest possible fortune in the shortest possible time." When the Marquise de Bellegarde says that she is a "proud and meddlesome old woman" his only answer can be, "Well, I am very rich." He has made his pile of money, and what he dreams of is a wife, "there must be a beautiful woman perched on the pile, like a statue on a monument." She has, indeed, to be "the best article on the market." Newman is not often embarrassed, for "his unconscious *sang-froid* was boundless." He has "not only a dislike, but a sort of moral mistrust, of uncomfortable thoughts." If he avoids mental discomfort, however, he has no real sense of physical comfort. He may have "a relish for luxury and splendor," yet he "scarcely knew a hard chair from a soft." He has as a prime conviction "that a man's life should be easy" and it is the ease of one who has had a continent to conquer, who has lost and made fortunes in leather, washtubs, copper. At the same time he possesses that morbid fear of idleness which had colored Henry's days in Cambridge. "Elegant leisure comes hard," he says. He confesses also to never having had "time to feel things."

He does not wave the Stars and Stripes belligerently. However, with his wealth he carries the solid belief that his homeland is "the greatest country in the world" and that Americans "could put all Europe in their breeches pocket." Americans, Newman remarks (and it is one of Henry's slyest digs at his erstwhile home), who speak ill of their country "ought to be carried home in irons and compelled to live in Boston." And he adds that "this, for Newman, was putting it very vindictively." When he is told that he has "a sort of air" of being thoroughly at home in the world, he ascribes this to the privilege of being an American citizen. "That sets a man up." And what lets a man down, he comes to discover, is being thwarted. Even though he is an American, he cannot arrange life entirely on his terms, or according to his values. "He had a burning, tingling sense of personal outrage. He had never in his life received so absolute a check"—this when the aristocratic family changes its mind. It cannot swallow a commercial American as a son-in-law. Newman finds the sensation of defeat intolerable.

He is never more American than in his belief that "energy and ingenuity can arrange everything," and that a willing American can learn anything. When Newman remarks that the Bellegarde house in the Faubourg is "curious," Valentin asks him whether he is interested in architecture. He replies, with a typical statistic, that he had visited four hundred and seventy churches during his summer's travel. "Perhaps," Valentin responds, "you are interested in theology."

"You are the great Western Barbarian," he is told, "stepping forth in his innocence and might, gazing a while at this poor effete Old World and then swooping down on it." This is one side of Newman, a side thoroughly dissimulated, however, behind the energy, geniality and "drive" with which he moves through the book, impervious to all save his own anchored dollars and the sense they give him that he can do as he pleases. The novel is a story of an American who discovers in the end that he simply can't.

II

This was the thin ice on which James skated—the thin ice of American national sensitivity—and his performance in the novel, in spite of all the fustian and melodrama, is brilliant. Even though he sketched an innocent Western Barbarian, he shows us also the candor of his innocence and the courage of his ignorance. The central irony of the book is that Newman has not been corrupted by his gold; he is still one of "nature's noblemen" and he can, in the end, be as moral and therefore as noble as the old corrupt Europeans. The truth is that in her own way the Marquise de Bellegarde is simply a European Christopher Newman; she sits upon her aristocratic sanctity with the same tough possessiveness and assurance as that with which Newman sits on his pile of dollars. In the struggle between the two, it is Newman who emerges the good

Christian. The woman he loves, or rather prizes, and wishes to take possession of as if she were a railroad or a mine, has immured herself in a convent in a street named the Rue d'Enfer. In this street Newman once again stands before a wall that bars his way, a wall "pale, dead, discolored." He goes to Notre Dame; and sitting there, he hears "far-away bells chiming off, at long intervals, to the rest of the world,"[1] and decides that revenge isn't "his game." Critics have spoken of this splendid scene as an act of "renunciation." Newman merely recognizes the realities before him. He could take his revenge, but he will not regain Claire de Cintré. And because the Bellegardes have been cruel to him is no reason for him now to be cruel to them. A good American, a shrewd businessman, does not indulge in waste effort.

It is a good ending to the story and it does impart to Newman an aura of nobility. The original readers of the novel did not experience this. They felt as frustrated as Newman; they had hoped for a happy ending; they had read the *Atlantic* instalments from month to month, in the fond belief that their author would give Newman the prize. Howells pleaded with him to do so; Lizzie Boott, on behalf of herself and Alice Bartlett, asked for the happiness of seeing Newman married. On the other hand, Fanny Kemble, in the serenity of her old age, and speaking out of her trans-Atlantic experience, expressed a fear that he should put the marriage through. "*Voyons*," Henry wrote to Howells, "they would have been an impossible couple." And he went on to argue that they would have had no place to live: Claire de Cintré would have hated New York, and Newman could not dwell in France. Leaving out Asia and Africa, there would be "nothing left but a farm out West." Newman was confronted by an insuperable difficulty from which the only issue, as far as Henry could see, was forfeiture. The image he chose was singularly apropos: it described the barriers of the Faubourg and the Rue d'Enfer: "We are each the product of circumstances and there are tall stone walls which fatally divide us. I have written the story from Newman's side of the wall, and I understand so well how Madame de Cintré couldn't really scramble over from *her* side! If I had represented her as doing so, I should have made a prettier ending, certainly; but I should have felt as if I were throwing a rather vulgar sop to readers who don't really know the world and who don't measure the merit of a novel by its correspondence to the same." In replying to Lizzie Boott he also argued that Claire wasn't really in love with Newman and "that in putting it into Newman's power to forgive and contemptuously 'let

1. Into his revision of this passage many years later Henry infused more poetry, speaking of "far-away bells chiming off into space at long intervals, the big bronze syllables of the Word."

off' the haughty Bellegardes, I was doing quite the most dramatic and inspiring thing." He reminded Lizzie: "I am a realist."

This is the fundamental point. In telling Howells that his unhappy ending corresponded to life and in insisting that he was a realist, Henry James overlooked the essential fact that he had written a romantic novel. His persons were real enough; their backgrounds were real; but the story of what happened to them moved across the borderland of the actual and the imaginary which Hawthorne liked to celebrate—although Hawthorne's "imaginary" often went as far as the supernatural. Henry's resided simply in the melodrama of his plot, that element of the arbitrary in his situation which he endowed with plausibility, but which, on the whole, was quite as impossible as any melodrama can be when it is closely scrutinized. Having aroused the reader's sympathies on Newman's behalf, and having made the reader endure the death of the charming Valentin, Henry continued to turn the bright sunshine of the book into depressing gloom by locking up Claire in a convent and crushing Newman in an unhappy ending no more "real" than would have been a happy one. It was not so much a question of throwing a sop to his readers as making the book true to itself; given the book's initial character, its ending was false. Henry was to recognize this; he did substitute a happy ending when he dramatized the novel; and in his late preface he made the romanticism of the book his greatest plea for the reader's acceptance of its improbabilities. He recognized that the Bellegardes "would positively have jumped at my rich and easy American" and not have minded any drawbacks; moreover there were "few drawbacks to mind."

This being the case, why did Henry insist on breaking off the marriage instead of seeking means to unite his lovers—as lovers usually are united in romantic novels? This was always to be one of his problems; and we may speculate that having ruled out marriage for himself he found it genuinely difficult to offer it to those of his heroes with whom he was in some way identified. The marriage tie, to Henry's vision, was a tie which enslaved: and women represented a threat to man's sovereignty. They were lovely creatures to be admired, to meet in drawing rooms and have a *tête-à-tête* with in some quiet corner; one could ride with them in the Campagna—all this was possible, and nothing more. To accept them as mates was to court the disaster symbolized by Roderick's fate. Henry's tales of the artist-life invariably contain the admonition that marriage could only be a burden to the creator, a distraction, a form of servitude fatal to art. Identified with Newman as an active and independent individual, Henry shut up Claire de Cintré in the convent as he shut women away from himself. And in endowing Claire with weakness and inconstancy he underlined his sense of women's fickleness as well as his own fear of them. One of the pot-boilers written for *Scribner's* during the period when he was waiting for an answer from the *Galaxy*, shows the extent to which Henry was pondering this question. In this tale, "Crawford's Consistency," the genial hero, Crawford, like Newman, falls in love with a young American girl, strongly in the clutches of her family, who at first accept him and then turn him down. The action in this instance is perhaps genuinely irrational and inconsistent: the Bellegardes, after all, offered good reasons for their repudiation of the match. Crawford, on the rebound, marries a common woman who ends by ruining his life and ill-treats him to the point of pushing him down some steps and crippling him. This crude story, based on an anecdote told Henry by his father, reflected an old and tried theme in his tales—from the very first one, written when he was turning twenty. It embodies his two visions of woman: the young and the unattainable or the cruel and the destructive; who reverses roles with the husband, and wields her strength to the point of physical violence.

Bernard Shaw was to say to Henry years later that an author can give victory to one side as easily as to another; this was a truth in Shaw's didactic theory of art, which hardly fitted the aesthetic world of Henry James. Certainly it did not apply to tragedy, where the inexorable course of events admits of only one solution. In the case of *The American*, Henry James decidedly did have the choice: and in his strong feeling that such a choice did not exist, he revealed his commitment to the only solution he could then envisage.

III

It is clear that Henry realized only in retrospect that *The American*, for all its attention to the real, was a form of the romantic. Nor, apparently, was he aware that, for all his seriousness, he was writing a high comedy. "I suspect it is the tragedies in life that arrest my attention more than the other things and say more to my imagination," he told Howells even while he was writing his monthly instalment of the comic chapters of *The American*. To be sure, anyone reading the earlier tales of James, in which he dealt with American adventures in Europe and their impassioned brooding, as they proclaimed their disinherited state, would hardly have discerned in them the writer of comedy. For one who felt himself to have this penchant for the tragedies of life, Henry managed to write an amazing number of successful high comedies during the next few years: upon them, indeed, he built his greatest fame. In *The American*, Henry for the first time revealed to the full the two genuinely original elements in his work that were to constitute his claim to renown during the first half of his writing life: his grasp of the contrasts in manners between America and Europe and his subtle vein of humor, as original as any in the nineteenth century.

Certain critics recognized this as soon as they read his new novel. "Among American story-writers," said the reviewer of the *Globe*, a newspaper published in the city to which Newman would have confined recalcitrant Americans, "Henry James stands alone—imitating no one, and, as yet, having no imitators." This was completely true. Earlier writers had barely sketched his American-European theme; and none had seen the humor in it. Indeed Henry himself was not yet fully aware of all that he carried of it in his head. What was discernible in *The American* was the sureness and lightness of his touch, and to grasp the vividness and humor, one must read the unrevised version of the novel, that version which readers of the *Atlantic* had from month to month and which, with very little change, was issued in volume form in 1877. The later version, systematically and exhaustively revised in 1905 for the New York Edition, is almost another book—perhaps a better one, in terms of structure and style; but it lacks the pristine qualities, the visual sharpness, and the intensity with which Henry, feeling himself as good as the Europeans, wrote this tale in a Paris that kept him at arm's length.

The touch of comedy is present on almost every page—save those which James gives over to unutterable melodramatic gloom. Even when he is describing the death of Valentin, however, he is unable to resist the comic delineation of the aristocrats round the deathbed: and there is even buried humor, for one of them hands Newman a volume of Faublas, which we may be certain was known to few of the *Atlantic* readers— *Les Amours du Chevalier de Faublas*, an ancient frivolous novel of seductions and *amours* that would have made the strait-laced American shudder. James himself felt the allusion recondite; in his revised version he substituted Choderlos de Laclos' *Les Liaisons Dangereuses*, which served the purpose equally well.

Henry's scenes between Newman and the aristocrats are nearly always on a double plane of comedy: the exchange of wit is constant, and quite often it contains also an element of mockery of which Newman is unaware. Thus when Newman offers a recital of his life to the Bellegardes and tells them of his sisters' early marriages, he mentions that one of them had made a match with the owner of the largest India rubber house in the West. "Ah," observes the Marquise, "you make houses also of India rubber." And young Madame de Bellegarde takes up the cue: "You can stretch them as your family increases." Newman finds this hilarious, wholly unaware that between the lines they are laughing at him. This is the kind of wit Oscar Wilde was to put successfully on the stage. The fat duchess asks Newman whether it isn't true that he has founded an American city and would be richer still "if you didn't grant lands and houses free of rent to all newcomers who'll pledge themselves never to smoke cigars." This concept of the marriage of feudalism with puritanism is but one of the ironic ways in which James keeps the play of comedy constant. Or simply the casual remark of the Marquise de Bellegarde, when she first meets Newman: "You're an American. I've seen several Americans." To which Newman archly replies, "There are several in Paris." And not least, the charming touch of old M. Rochefidèle, who has seen his American long ago: "Almost the first person I ever saw—to notice him—was an American." Newman learns it was "the great Dr. Franklin."

This is the comedy which flows easily from the characters and from the situation in which Henry placed them. The dialogue throughout the book is vivid and lively. If Newman himself proves he can indulge in give and take, it is only to make himself more pleasing to the grand and the mighty of the Faubourg. The Marquise does concede he is polite; the Duchess finds him very amusing. He is guilty of one serious error and it is his undoing—when at his engagement party he asks the Marquise to parade with him among the guests, as if to give him the *cachet* he lacks. She does up to a point, but she reaches a moment when she has to say to him, "This is enough, sir." His failure in tact has been complete. Advertising and salesmanship, so to speak, have overcome shrewdness and caution. From this point on, Newman's good fortune goes into decline.

IV

Roderick Hudson had represented Henry's final dialogue with Quincy Street, a last tug at the silver cord. He had made his choice, and his story of Christopher Newman was symbolic of his own stepping-forth into the world—as a new man. But the vivid personalities of Quincy Street, the conflict of its strong egos, remained. The rivalry with William emerges in *The American* no longer in the complaining terms of the Cambridge time, but simply as a hard fact of life. The unpleasant Marquis de Bellegarde, who is fifteen years senior to his brother, Valentin (as William was fifteen months older than Henry), represents one extreme of old feeling; the other is the portrait of the American clergyman Newman encounters during his travels. And here, at last, William recognized himself. "Your second instalment of *The American* is prime," he wrote. "The morbid little clergyman is worthy of Ivan Sergeyevich. I was not a little amused to find some of my own attributes in him—I think you found my 'moral reaction' excessive when I was abroad."

By the same token, the second son, Valentin, in this version of Henry's familial experience, is charming, ineffectual and doomed. Dominating the book is the matriarchal old Marquise, the archetypal mother-figure of all Henry's work, in whose hands husbands are crushed or robbed of their manhood, or—as in this instance—actually murdered. The melodrama harks back to James's blood-and-thunder tales.

The book's reception in America was mixed. It was, however, read more attentively, and aroused more discussion, than anything James had ever done before. The character of Newman was generally liked, although some reviewers felt Henry might have found a nicer American to oppose to the aristocrats; and Henry's friend T. S. Perry was not even sure that Newman had made an honest fortune; he wondered "which side of the market he operated upon." The style, the technique, the narration were universally praised. The strongest fire of the critics was reserved for the plot: the failure to provide a happy ending, they argued, was inconsistent with what the story had prepared them for: and certain critics again significantly saw Henry's detached and "cold-blooded" attitude toward his personages. This might be "realism," yet it revealed a critic, an analyst, "rather than the sharer of strong feeling." The originality of James's international theme was recognized, and nearly all the critics were prepared to consider the novel an important contribution to American literature. They were not yet prepared however—and this they said—to place Henry beside Hawthorne, or Trollope, or Dickens—or for that matter George Eliot.

OSCAR CARGILL

[A Surge of Patriotic Indignation]†

It was in an "American horse-car," according to James's recollection, that the germinal idea for *The American* came to him. ". . . I found myself, of a sudden, considering with enthusiasm, as the theme of a 'story,' the situation in another country and an aristocratic society, of some robust, but . . . cruelly wronged, compatriot: the point being in especial that he should suffer at the hands of persons pretending to represent the highest possible civilization. . . . He would arrive at his just vindication and he would fail of . . . vulgarly enjoying it. . . . All he would have at the end would be

† "*The American*," in *The Novels of Henry James*, by Oscar Cargill (New York: Macmillan, 1961), pp. 41–61.

therefore just the moral convenience, indeed the moral necessity, of his practical, but quite unappreciated, magnanimity . . ."[1] If this is a true account, and there is no reason to suppose that it is not, James consciously began *The American* with the idea that his hero's native traits should be thrown into sharp and functional contrast with those of another society; he deliberately dedicated himself to the defense of the salient virtues of his countrymen.

James amplified his initial idea, however, by suggestions from many sources, the first being Turgenev:

> . . . *The American* (1877) is based largely on Turgenev's *A Nest of Gentlefolk* (1858). The home of the Bellegardes, in *The American*, is evidently also a "nest of gentlefolk." In each novel the hero does not "belong"—Lavretski's family background, half-peasant and half-landlord, is incongruous; Newman is American middleclass. Perversely, each falls in love with the rarest bird in the nest. In each novel one of the lovers has been married. . . . In Turgenev's novel Lavretski has been unhappily married and the problem derives from Lisa's religion, which will not permit her to love a married man. In James's novel, however, it is the heroine who has been unhappily married. There the past marriage becomes only a small factor in the "conflict," which consists mainly in the opposition of the aristocratic Bellegarde family to their daughter's projected marriage to the bourgeois-democratic American. . . .
>
> Another reason for shifting the past marriage to the heroine was James's desire to locate the dramatic conflict even more centrally in her consciousness. For in both novels . . . the determining "crisis" takes place *within* the heroine. It is, in James's phrase, "the dusky, antique consciousness of sin in this tender, virginal soul" [*re* Lisa] that carries the day. In each novel the conflict is resolved by the heroine's decision to enter a convent. James was fascinated by the final scene of *A Nest of Gentlefolk*, in which the hero gains admission to the heroine's convent: "She knows of his presence, but she does not even look at him; the trembling of her downcast lids alone betrays her sense of it. 'What must they both have thought, have felt,' asks the author. . . . With an unanswered question his story characteristic-

1. *The Art of the Novel: Critical Prefaces by Henry James*, ed. Richard P. Blackmur (New York, 1934), pp. 21–22. James's recollection of the homely origin of his tale possibly led Constance Rourke to surmise a connection with one of the most popular farces of the day, Tom Taylor's *Our American Cousin* (1858), which "achieved its first great success when James was a lad of fifteen; the play created an immense volume of talk, and was continued for many years." "The American," *The Question of Henry James*, ed. F. W. Dupee (New York, 1945), p. 140. I can see very little in this conjecture. *The American* ran in the *Atlantic* from June, 1876, to May, 1877. It was published in book form in the latter month in Boston; the first authorized edition appeared in England in Mar., 1879. Leon Edel and Dan H. Laurence, *A Bibliography of Henry James* (London, 1957), pp. 31–33, 307; A4a, c; D259. I quote from the first authorized edition.

ally closes." In *The American* James reproduced both the scene and the unanswered question at the end.[2]

James began work on *The American* shortly after reaching Paris at the end of 1875.[3] Going constantly to the theater and devouring printed plays[4] while he was developing his novel from Turgenev's *A Nest of Gentlefolk*, Henry James must have been struck by the parallel afforded to the situation in Turgenev's novel in a device being exploited with great effectiveness by Emile Augier upon the French stage—the "intrusion-plot." As many as twenty-two of Augier's twenty-five plays, according to Professor Girdler B. Fitch, utilize this device as their principal plot mechanism:

> To state this theme in its simplest form, suspending qualifications for the moment, the basic action of a typical Augier play is this: *Into a group there comes an intruder whose presence is resisted by one or more persons and accepted by one or more, with resulting conflict, until someone's eyes are opened to the true situation, to the danger, or to a possible solution.* Different outcomes are possible, but the most frequent is the elimination of the intruder.[5]

Remembering that the group "is usually the family,"[6] one is struck instantly by the completeness with which this formula covers *The American*. The "intruder" is Christopher Newman and the "group" the Bellegardes; the Marquis and Marquise resist his "intrusion," but Valentin, the young Marquise, and Mme de Cintré (she, only for a time) accept it. At the end of the conflict, Newman is eliminated as a suitor for Claire de Cintré's hand. James must

2. Daniel Lerner, "The Influence of Turgenev on Henry James," *The Slavonic and East European Review*, XX (Dec., 1941), 43–44; Cornelia Kelley, *The Early Development of Henry James* (Urbana, 1930), p. 241, also cites *A Nest of Gentlefolk* as a source, but does not develop the idea. She also cites "Crawford's Consistency" as a source, but while it does have a situation like that in the novel, the relationship would appear to be the other way around.

3. Alan Wade, *The Scenic Art* (New Brunswick, N.J., 1948), p. 42, says in December, 1875. H.J. to W. D. Howells, Feb. 3rd [1876]: "Shortly after coming to Paris, finding it a matter of prime necessity to get a novel on the stocks immediately, I wrote to F. P. Church, offering him one for the *Galaxy* to begin in March, and was sending off my first instalment of MS. when your letter arrived." *The Selected Letters of Henry James*, ed. Leon Edel (New York, 1955), p. 65. H.J. to William, Dec. 3, [1875]: "I shall speedily begin in the *Galaxy* another novel. . . ." Ralph Barton Perry, *The Thought and Character of William James* (2 vols., Boston, 1935), I, 362.

4. "I know the Théâtre Français by heart." H.J. to William, July 29, 1876. F. O. Matthiessen, *The James Family* (New York, 1948), p. 343.

5. "Emile Augier and the Intrusion-Plot," *PMLA*, LXIII (Mar., 1948), 274–280. We know certainly that Henry James saw the following plays by Augier: *Post Scriptum*, *L'Aventurière*, *Paul Forestier*, *Lions et renards*, *Gendre de M. Poirier*, *Les Fourchambault*, *Le Mariage d'Olympe*, *Les Lionnes pauvres*, and *Maître Guérin*. *Wade*, pp. 7, 81, 83, 85, 89, 116–117, 198, 204.

6. "M. Emile Augier, on his social side, is preoccupied with the sanctity of the family, as they say in France; he 'goes in,' as they say in England, for the importance of the domestic affections." Henry James, "M. Augier," *The Scenic Art*, pp. 116–117. This essay appeared under "Notes" in the *Nation* on July 27, 1878.

have rejoiced in his seized parallel, for he had few intimate acquaintances in Paris in 1876 and almost no entrée into French domestic circles.[7] His knowledge of the Bellegardes was derived largely, it would appear, from his reading of French novels and from the presentation of French nobility on the Parisian stage. If there are elements of melodrama in the depiction of the Bellegardes, they are faithfully copied from the current drama. After all, James's Marquise had merely withheld medicine from her husband and allowed him to die, but the Marquis de Puygiron, in the most famous of all Augier's plays, to protect his family name when he discovers that his defiant daughter-in-law had been a courtesan, executes her as she stands in the doorway about to depart.[8] Many traits of the Puygirons suggest those of the hostile Bellegardes. Not only *Olympe's Marriage* but other plays have a compromising "scrap of paper" in them which falls into the hands of the intruder, as does Mrs. Bread's letter, to the embarrassment of the resistants. And most plays have duels, as has "the American.[9]

But while James was working at *The American* there was put on at the Théâtre Français a play by Alexandre Dumas, *fils*, on February 14, 1876, entitled *L'Étrangère*, which boldly infused internationalism into the intrusion-plot. James was not only drawn to this play by the extended advance notice of it in *Figaro*, which filled most of the issue,[1] but because of his special interest in the work of Dumas, *fils*, which had provided him, as Viola Dunbar has convincingly shown,[2] with the main features of the plot of *Roderick Hudson*. James reacted violently and at length to this play:

> . . . *L'Étrangère* strikes me as a rather desperate piece of floundering in the dramatic sea. . . . The "Foreigner" who gives

7. ". . . The slender thread of my few personal relations hangs on, without snapping, but it doesn't grow very stout." H.J. to his father, Paris, Apr. 11, [1876]. *The Letters of Henry James*, ed. Percy Lubbock (2 vols., New York, 1920), I, 45. Mervyn Jones-Evans exaggerates James's Parisian reception in 1875–1876. "Henry James's Year in France," *Horizon*, XIV (July, 1946), 52–60.

8. *Olympe's Marriage* in *Camille and Other Plays*, ed. Stephen S. Stanton (New York, 1957), p. 226. James says, "the modern theatre has few stronger pieces than *L'Aventurière* and *Le Mariage d'Olympe*. . . ." Wade, p. 116. In "The Siege of London," the following exchange occurs between Mrs. Headway and one of her companions at a presentation of *L'Aventurière:*

"I'm rather disappointed," Mrs. Headway went on. "But I want to see what becomes of that woman."

"Donna Clorinde? Oh, I suppose they'll shoot her; they generally shoot the women, in French plays," Littlemore said.

The reference would seem to be to the Augier play in which this occurs. See *The Great Short Novels of Henry James*, ed. Philip Rahv (New York, 1944), p. 234.

9. *Théâtre complet d'Emile Augier* (7 vols., Paris, 1895).

1. See "Paris Revisited," Wade, pp. 39–40. This was the first of James's articles to appear in the New York *Tribune*. It was published on Dec. 11, 1875, but dated "November 22nd, 1875."

2. "A Source for *Roderick Hudson*," *Modern Language Notes*, LXIII (May, 1948), 303–310. The source is *L'Affaire Clemenceau* which James had reviewed in the *Nation* on Oct. 11, 1866. See *Roderick Hudson*, p. 21.

its title to the piece, and who is played by that very interesting actress, Mme Sarah Bernhardt, is a daughter of our own democracy, Mrs. Clarkson by name. She explains in the second act, by a mortal harangue—the longest, by the watch, I have ever listened to—that she is the daughter of a mulatto slave girl by a Carolinian planter. As she expresses it herself, "My mother was pretty: he remarked her; I was born of the remark." Mrs. Clarkson, however, has next to nothing to do with the play, and she is the least successful figure the author has ever drawn. Why she should be an American, why she should have Negro blood, why she should be the implacable demon she is represented, why she should deliver the melodramatic and interminable *tirade* I have mentioned, why she should come in, why she should go out, why, in short, she should exist—all this is the perfection of mystery. She is like the heroine of an old-fashioned drama of the Boulevard du Crime who has strayed unwittingly into a literary work, in which she is out of time with all her companions. She is, on Dumas' part, an incredible error of taste. It must be confessed, however, that her entrance into the play has masterly effectiveness. . . .[3]

L'Étrangère is a hodgepodge of theatrical motifs of the sensational kind, yet Francisque Sarcey, the best critic of the Parisian stage of the nineteenth century, while noting its limitations, praises the very American elements Henry James most objects to:

> Such is this curious play which savors both of high comedy and cheap melodrama, an unbelievable mixture of extravagant fantasies, of strange boldnesses, of shocking vulgarities, and of incomparable passages; where two masterly scenes, that of the introduction of Mrs. Clarkson in the first act and that of the discussion with the Yankee in the fifth, stand out against a background of pure inventions which remind one of Ponson du Terrail and of d'Ennery. . . .[4]

Henry James's reaction to the play appears, from this comparison, to be the result of a jealous Americanism. "To be a cosmopolite is not, I think, an ideal," James wrote after *The American* had appeared; "the ideal should be to be a concentrated patriot."[5] It is possible that this conviction was formed in him by seeing

3. Wade, pp. 57–58; under the heading "Parisian Affairs," this was James's ninth letter to the N.Y. *Tribune*. Published on Mar. 25, 1876, it is dated Feb. 28, 1876; hence James saw *L'Étrangère* early in its run. Of course he may have got some details from the *Figaro* account, which, however, he says was lacking in particulars.

4. *Quarante ans de théâtre* (8 vols., Paris, 1901–1902), V, 300. For a summary of the play and commentary, see Henry S. Schwartz, *Alexandre Dumas, fils, Dramatist* (New York, 1927), pp. 71–74. Schwartz mentions, however, very few of the points which I enumerate in the next paragraph, to be got only from the play itself.

5. *Portraits of Places* (London, 1883), p. 75. "Occasional Paris," in which this statement appears, was dated "1877" by James.

L'Étrangère upon the boards. Like Lowell, who introduced him to the French theater, James could be very critical of his countrymen,[6] but let an outsider assail them and he was up in arms.[7] A surge of patriotic indignation prompted his assault on the play in his letter to the *Tribune*, but it carried him beyond this report to make his work in hand an almost retaliatory response upon the French.

For, although he scoffed at Dumas's play, James was strongly influenced by it. Mistress Clarkson, who is divorced by her husband, has formed a working arrangement with the latter, through which he conducts all their affairs in America and sees her only occasionally; Dumas's satire of the loose domestic arrangements of some Americans probably prompted James's satire of the almost casual relationship of the elderly Touchetts in *The Portrait of a Lady*. Mistress Clarkson's unusual given name, "Noémie" (Mr. Clarkson has named a town for her in Utah), gave Mlle Nioche her alliterative first name in *The American*. The mistake of M. Mariceau in giving his daughter Catherine in marriage to the Duke may have suggested to James Claire de Cintré's first marriage. Because Mr. Clarkson is responsible for the return of the compromising letter to the Duchesse de Septmonts, James has his hero refrain from exhibiting to the Bellegardes' Parisian circle the character-destroying and incriminating letter which comes into his possession. Of course, Clarkson does merely a gallant thing; he is not beset, in this connection, by a torturing moral dilemma, as Newman is. James's conception of his hero, aggrandized by patriotism and constant reference to Turgenev's Lavretski, confers on him values beyond Clarkson's reach; the simple action of the latter, however, is the germ of his own.

But in the main, as I have said, the effect of *L'Étrangère* upon James was to create a desire to refute the play; in *The American* everything goes by opposites: Clarkson is restive to get back to the West to make more money in gold mining; Newman is a Californian who has made his money quietly in manufacturing and has no desire to return to business. Both Clarksons pointedly mention large sums of money in casual conversation; Newman scarcely alludes to his wealth. Mistress Clarkson pays 25,000 francs to be

6. An odd conjunction of elements, quite in line with my thought, appears in a letter to William, July 29th [1876]: ". . . My life there [Paris—he was at Étretat] makes a much more succulent figure in your letters, my mention of its thin ingredients as it comes back to me, than in my own consciousness. A good deal of Boulevard and Third-rate Americanism: few retributive relations otherwise. I know the Théâtre Français by heart!" *Letters*, I, 51.

7. He rejoiced in the prospect of disaster coming to Dumas: "I went for an hour to Flaubert's. . . . they were talking about the great theatrical event, Alexandre Dumas's *L'Étrangère*. . . . They all detest Dumas—very properly, and predict for him a great fiasco before long." H.J. to Alice James, Feb. 22 [1876], *Parisian Sketches*, ed. Leon Edel and Ilse Lind (New York, 1957), p. 242.

received by the Duchesse and to drink a cup of tea (her hostess smashes the cup afterwards); whereas Newman is indifferent to society and wishes only the hand of Claire. While Clarkson is free in gunplay—he not only defeats three robbers in the West but as a substitute duelist kills the villain of the play, the corrupt Duc Maximin de Septmonts, Newman abjures all violence and looks upon dueling as barbarous. Indeed, the whole torturing sequence which leads to Count Valentin's foolish duel and death may be thought of as an eloquent refutation to the supposition, which might have arisen from Clarkson's stage behavior, that Americans took human lives lightly and found gunplay a sport. Clarkson declines to view the Septmont picture gallery, declaring he has other things to do; James locates Newman in the Salon Carré of the Louvre in the first episode of his novel, not to demonstrate his cultivated taste in pictures, but to show that, unlike Clarkson, he had a yearning to know something about art, even if his country was not so rich in galleries as Europe. Further, there is apposite allusion to art and music throughout James's novel. Mistress Clarkson has long been animated to revenge her mother upon all males; in his struggle Newman finally rejects the revenge motive.[8] Look upon *The American* as a reply to *L'Étrangère* and James's reasons for choice of episode and motivation, in instance after instance, become transparent. He is justifying American ways against a European caricature of them.

In reacting against Dumas's play, James not only made the intruder morally victorious, but by emphasizing all the antitheses between the play and his novel, and between Newman and the hostile Bellegardes, brought about a true clash of character based upon *mores*—and created what is really the first international novel.[9] In "A Passionate Pilgrim" (1871), "The Madonna of the Future" (1873), and "Madame de Mauves" (1874), James had been unconsciously yet instinctively moving toward the creation of the international tale,[1] yet it took precisely the combination of circumstances described here to produce the authentic thing; the catalyst like *L'Étrangère* was needed to precipitate *The American*, for the international novel is not one in which a foreign setting gives merely a romantic interest, as in the tales of F. Marion

8. Alexandre Dumas, *fils, L'Étrangère: Comédie in cinq actes* (Paris, n.d. [1908], 148 pp.

9. "*The American* (1877) was an almost scientific study of internationalism. . . ." Ernest A. Baker, *The History of the English Novel* (10 vols., London, 1938), IX, 248.

1. James in his Preface to *The Reverberator* describes these tales as "sops *instinctively* thrown to the international Cerberus formidably posted *where I doubtless then didn't quite make him out*, yet from whose capacity to loom larger and larger with the years there must already have sprung some chilling portent." *The Art of the Novel*, p. 194. (Italics mine.)

Crawford or Ernest Hemingway. An international novel is one in which a character, usually guided in his actions by the *mores* of one environment, is set down in another, where he must employ all his individual resources to meet successive situations, and where he must intelligently accommodate himself to the new *mores*, or, in one way or another, be destroyed. It is the novelist's equivalent of providing a special medium in a laboratory for studying the behavior of an organism, only here it is a device for the revelation of character. James appears to have been the first to realize the potentialities of the type and to bring it to full development.[2]

The author of an international novel assumes responsibilities that localized fiction does not impose. He must avoid distortion in the opposition of characters and, while generalizing on national traits, keep a sense of the uniqueness, in every instance, of the representatives of those traits. Yet the form does of itself provide a refuge for the novelist—if all can be seen from the protagonist's point of view, his obtuseness or blindness may conceal the author's limitations in reporting the milieu and behavior of the protagonist's opposition. Reflecting on *The American* some thirty years later, James remembers his "infatuation" with making Newman "consistent," with giving the effect through him to the novel of a "*centre*." "He supremely matters; all the rest matters only as he feels it, treats it, meets it." Admitting one lapse in the treatment of his protagonist when he permits Newman to neglect Mme de Cintré after he has been introduced to the Bellegarde circle as her fiancé but at the same time indicating that attention to Claire which evoked response from her must "add to her eventual shame," James is still content to let the novel "stand or fall by his more or less convincing image."[3]

James managed the externals and patent indicatives of his representative American with ease. Newman's appearance and his speech[4] avoid the caricature and burlesque of current stage presentations of the Yankee, but nevertheless suggest his limitations in

2. Oscar Cargill, "The First International Novel," *PMLA*, LXIV (Dec., 1958), 418–425, in which the claim made for the Baroness Tautphoeus by Howells [*Heroines of Fiction* (2 vols., New York, 1901), II, 139] is examined, along with those which might be made for Turgenev and even Howells himself, and all are seen as less valid than one which might be made for Henry James.

3. *The Art of the Novel*, pp. 37–39. The fault is really deeper than the neglect which the novelist acknowledges. Though chiefly concerned with textual improvements, Isadore Traschen has brilliantly demonstrated James's lack of knowledge of passion in this novel. James is interested "in the ethical problems love created rather than in love itself." "James's Revisions of the Love Affair in *The American*," *New England Quarterly*, XXIX (Mar., 1956), 43–62.

4. Particularly a kind of unconscious brag in his talk. See especially the speech in which he tells the Tristrams he wants "the best article in the market" for a wife. "Newman could only have been drawn by a countryman who had studied . . . his admirable and truly national characteristics," M.L.H., "Mr. Henry James, Jr., and His Critics," *The Literary World*, XIII (Jan. 14, 1882), 11.

dress and address. On the score of his psychology James endowed Newman with the most salient trait of his countrymen—a self-confidence and easy assurance, which is not egotism, carries him unruffled through most situations. "You've got something it worries me to have missed," said Valentin. "It's not money, it's not even brains, though evidently yours have been excellent for your purpose. It's not your superfluous stature. . . . It's a sort of air you have of being imperturbably, being irremovably and indestructibly (that's the thing) at home in the world. . . ." Newman explains his assurance by saying it's his consciousness "of honest toil, of having produced something . . . somebody has been willing to pay for," but when Valentin objects that he has known successful manufacturers of soap who have left him "perfectly cold," Newman settles for "just the regular treat of being an American citizen. . . . That sets a man right up." In Walt Whitman's perfect phrase, Christopher Newman "stands aplomb in the midst of things."

Newman's assurance is responsible for some of his lesser traits, for example, his utter candor. It contains an admixture of naïveté, when it is a handicap to him, but it is also tinged with shrewdness, and may be dry and winey. "It's a great pity you have made me your enemy," he tells Mme de Bellegarde, after complimenting her on her "pluck." "I should have been one of your greatest admirers." Another by-product of the hero's confidence is his magnanimity. Newman is consistently tolerant. Before he goes abroad, he abandons an advantage over an unscrupulous opponent, sacrificing with it sixty thousand dollars, just as he fails later to press his advantage over the Bellegardes. "Newman's revenge was to forego his revenge," writes Ernest A. Baker; "he, at any rate, could afford to be generous."[5] But this is ever so slightly the wrong emphasis; it treats his action as an advantageous tactic rather than as the product of "one of the large and easy impulses generally characteristic of his type."[6] Secure and unassailable in his manliness, if not in his

5. *The History of the English Novel,* IX, 249. Messrs. R. B. West, Jr., and R. W. Stallman have an interesting suggestion in regard to Newman's destruction of the letter: "He could not use his own weapon (the letter) to fulfill the merely formal purpose of upholding his honor; although Valentin felt obliged to use his (pistols) in an affair involving a woman for whom he no longer cared. . . ." *The Art of Modern Fiction* (New York, 1949), p. 585.

6. *The Art of the Novel,* p. 22. Note Newman's response to Valentin's surmise that they will "get on," being so very different, "like fish and fowl," as not to quarrel: " 'Oh, I never quarrel,' said Newman rather shortly." p. 122. Joseph Wood Krutch (*The Modern Temper,* New York, 1929, pp. 155–160) appears to read too much into Newman's conclusion that "revenge was not his game" when he makes it an effect of James's aestheticism—"he realized that an act of revenge was inappropriate to that style." Mme de Talyas gallantly throws her lover's letters into the flames when she sees no purpose any longer in using them to keep the lover from her rival in Octave Feuillet's *The Amours of Phillippe,* tr. Mary N. Sherwood (Philadelphia, 1860). But see Floyd C. Watkins, "Christopher Newman's Final Instinct," *Nineteenth-Century Fiction,* XII (June, 1957), 85–88, which reveals a final weakness in Newman.

manners, Newman's silent commentary on the conduct of the Bellegardes, his judgment, is the hardest thing they have to bear.

Newman is so exemplary of the American type that he lacks something as an individual. It is in an effort to individualize him, probably, that Babcock, the young Unitarian minister from Dorchester, Massachusetts, is introduced into the story. Newman's easy acceptance of Europe and "want of moral reaction" readily mark him off from this dutiful seeker of "impressions," with his guidebook knowledge of pictures and churches but with his secret detestation of Europe; the points of difference between the two men, however, seem relatively inconsequential in the action of the story. We are hardly shown those personal traits of the hero which have a particular appeal for Claire de Cintré, who surely was not prepared to fall in love with just the pure American type, whatever his material possessions. As a matter of fact, the grounds for affection between Newman and Valentin are much more clearly exposed than those for deep attachment between Newman and Valentin's sister.

However satisfactory Newman may be judged to be as a type, he is ever so much less satisfactory as a "*centre*." It is true that James keeps him in focus admirably, but it is not true that he endows him with much perceptivity, despite his final illumination. Constance Rourke has cited the supreme example of his obtuseness: "He should have known that to ask the old Marquise to parade through her own rooms on his arm the evening of the ball would be almost an affront. When the journey was accomplished and she said, 'This is enough, sir,' he might have seen the gulf widening before his eyes."[7] That Newman grows cannot be controverted—but he puts a distance between himself and Tom Tristram, which is not a measure of tremendous enlargement, although it awakens admiration in Tristram's wife. If he transcends the Bellegardes—and he does—it takes the tremendous wrench to land him there. "A story in which the main actor is so uninitiated can bear no very close resemblance to the story of Isabel Archer or Lambert Strether," writes Joseph Warren Beach. "There is no revelation of anything through Newman's consciousness—nothing depends upon his *understanding*. There is in fact no spiritual dilemma. That is why the book is not among the greatest of its author's. . . ."[8] Identification with Christopher Newman on the reader's part, because of his

7. Rourke, p. 151.

8. *The Method of Henry James* (New Haven, 1918), pp. 204–205. Baker agrees with this (IX, 249), but Michael Swan, in his introduction to the Chiltern Library edition (London, 1949, p. 3), sees Newman as "an embryo Strether, the hero of *The Ambassadors*." Swan even imagines "James, had all the circumstances of his life been different, growing into a Newman." This is extravagant.

imperceptivity, presents considerable difficulty, save perhaps to a most ardent American reader.[9]

James failed to avail himself thoroughly of the most obvious advantage in making Newman imperceptive, namely, of ascribing to Newman's ignorance whatever James himself did not know about the Bourbon faction in the old aristocracy of France. Yet the Bellegardes, in the main, are permitted to reveal themselves too directly. Overestimating the consequence of Dumas's *L'Étrangère,* he replied to it in kind (for which he might be forgiven), but at some hazard to the accuracy of his portraiture. It is not to be wondered at that, unaware of his provocation, Marie-Reine Garnier has charged James with "slander." James's conception of the deportment of Valentin (who, on Newman's first visit to the Rue de l'Université, for his diversion offers to show him over the house, "like the guardian of a museum") and that of Urbain's wife (who chatters like a magpie before a stranger) is held grossly untrue to their breeding. James's representation of the aristocratic milieu is held to be nothing less than "night in the realism of the description of manners."[1] In a generally favorable study of James, Marie-Anne de Bovet challenges the verisimilitude of *The American* on the same score. It is incredible to her that Madame de Cintré should have been prevented by her mother from marrying the man she loved, and she concludes that James's Faubourg Saint-Germain is wholly legendary.[2]

It might be noted, however, that the Bovet and Garnier critiques were written, respectively, twenty-three and fifty-nine years after the time represented in the novel, and that the one farthest removed is the more severe. This raises the question if James's recent French critics are in a better position than he was to know what the *ancien régime* was like. Cornelia Kelley expressed just such a doubt in regard to the Garnier critique and cited a more nearly contemporary French review by Thérèse Bentzon,[3] who is not surprised to

9. Yet James returns to the defense of Newman as a "*centre*" in the Preface to *The Princess Casamassima* where he lists him as one of his "mirrors." *The Art of the Novel,* p. 70.

1. *Henry James et la France* (Paris, 1927), pp. 35–36. See also Cyrille Arnavon, *Histoire littéraire des Etats-Unis* (Paris, 1953), p. 293. One cannot help wondering if there is not also in the French criticism of James on this score a bit of tart retaliation. He had criticized Balzac for exactly what he is now criticized for: "He [Balzac] began very early to write about countesses and duchesses; . . . the manner in which he usually portrays the denizens of the Faubourg St. Germain obliges us to believe that the place they occupy in his books is larger than they occupied in his experience." *French Poets and Novelists* (London, 1878), p. 93.

2. "Un Ecrivain cosmopolite, Henry James," *La Nouvelle Revue* (Feb. 1, 1891), pp. 532–556. Cornelia Kelley, however, cites the obedience of French girls to their mothers that James noted in "A French Watering Place," New York *Tribune,* August 12, 1876. *The Early Development of Henry James* (Urbana, 1930), p. 241, note 15.

3. Not "M. Bentzon" as given by Miss Kelley, p. 241; "Bentzon" is the pseudonym of Marie Thérèse Blanc. *Revue des Deux Mondes* (May 1, 1883), pp. 126–127. See also T. Bentzon, *Les Nouveaux romanciers américains* (Paris, 1885), pp. 71–92.

find Newman "so living, so real" but is "amazed" at the fidelity of the drawing of Valentin de Bellegarde, "one of the last specimens of gallant, expansive, spiritual French gentlemen," and that of the young Marquise de Bellegarde, and especially that of Mlle Nioche. Though, as we have seen, James relied almost wholly on the current French drama for his portraits of the aristocracy and seems as faithful in his representations as those on the contemporary stage (which appears itself to have been hostile, if not limited), he perhaps had some small, special knowledge of the characters signalized by Mlle Bentzon. For Noémie Nioche, James may well have drawn upon his memory of one of his French governesses, Mlle Augustine Danse, whom he terms an "adventuress" and compares with Becky Sharpe:

> The daughter of a political proscript who had but just escaped . . . and who wrote her micawberish letters from Gallipolis, Ohio, she subsequently figured to my imagination . . . as the most brilliant and most genial of irregular characters, exhibiting the Parisian "mentality" at its highest, or perhaps rather at its deepest, and more remarkable for nothing than for the consummate little art and grace with which she had for a whole year draped herself in the mantle of our innocent air.[4]

For the young Marquise, James may have drawn on a long-remembered vision of a titled young lady whom he saw on one of his journeys, boldly supplemented by his acquaintance with the central figure in Octave Feuillet's *La petite comtesse* (1857).[5] And is it not possible that Count Valentin was created in much the same way, from a remembered person and supplementary reading?[6] Valentin indeed might have been concocted from the genial John La Farge[7] and anyone of the numerous young counts who appear in the plays of Augier, Dumas, Marivaux, and Scribe. None of these persons is conventional or representative, and James safely risked their portraiture.

For readers partisan to Newman, his implacable opponents, Urbain and his mother, are drawn with convincing skill. Yet neither such a reader's satisfaction nor their proximity to their prototypes on the French stage is a wholly valid argument for their authenticity. In their exchanges with Newman they are perhaps

4. *A Small Boy and Others* (New York, 1913), pp. 307, 308, 328–330.
5. *Notes of a Son and Brother* (New York, 1914), pp. 55–57.
6. James recalls being in his youth at Homburg and Baden-Baden in those "September days in which French society, so far as it was of the Empire, at least, moved more or less up [those places]; and we met it in expressive samples. . . ." *Notes of a Son and Brother*, p. 54. Did James recall a "sample" in Valentin? I think the impressions were very general and less than his reading.
7. Ibid., pp. 63, 84–96.

more convincing than in their behavior. The Marquis is given the greatest line in the book when, in response to Newman's revelation that Valentin had apologized for his family, Urbain murmurs but two words, "*Le misérable!*" Though James presents her as without scruple, the elderly Marquise in all her encounters with the hero carries her high role successfully, allowing Newman only an instant of penetration into her fear. Adopting the rather shoddy device of making Mme de Bellegarde French only by marriage, James covered himself against minor implausibilities, but his skill in legitimizing her growing coldness toward Newman because of his unwitting gaucheries compensates for the evasive tactic.

James's greatest failure in the book is not to acquaint his reader thoroughly with his heroine; he withheld a great deal about Claire de Cintré in the mistaken notion that any development other than fragmentary of her character would detract from the presentation of his hero;[8] actually Newman's values would have been increased by a clearer definition of what he valued. Least of all did James properly prepare us for Claire's decision to seek refuge in a convent. With the example of Turgenev's Lisa before him, James should have early given us intimation of Claire's spiritual dedication, of her propensity toward asceticism, which leads her in her final scene with Newman to declare, in response to his entreaties, "I'm as cold as that flowing river!"[9] It is as though James saw her final act as wholly a check upon her family—they could no longer use her as a pawn—and as though the novelist lacked a sense of the convent as refuge and the religious life as a vocation. Newman, who had not been deeply disturbed at the prospect of marrying a Catholic—which would have been a very momentous issue with

8. With this protected type of eligible young Frenchwoman James plainly had no acquaintance at all. His autobiographical volumes and letters (as far as published) confirm this.

9. The limitation of Claire de Cintré is her coldness, her perfection. Tom Tristram calls her "a great white doll of a woman who cultivates quiet haughtiness." Like Mrs. Tristram, who says of Claire, "She is perfect!" her own brother Valentin declares, "I have never seen a woman half so perfect or so complete"; but he also says, "She looks like a statue which had failed as stone, resigned itself to its grave defects, and come to life as flesh and blood, to wear white capes and long trains." Even Newman cannot tell with her where urbanity ends and sincerity begins. Ray B. West, Jr., and R. W. Stallman (*The Art of Modern Fiction*, New York, 1949, p. 857) write, "Her name suggests a halo; Claire de Cintré—an arch of light—a lighted window, the bright window through which the reader peers towards perfection." One wonders, however, if James (sometime resident of New England) did not have the colder lunar rainbow in mind. So deeply introverted a type was beyond the powers, not only of James, but of any fictionist in the seventies to describe. Further, had James shown Claire before the end in all her complexity, he would have made his hero a more deluded man than he now appears to be. But what else could have been his sense of his heroine when he told Howells that marriage between his central pair was "impossible"? Claire occupies a position between Mme de Mauves and Mrs. Abient.

most of his Protestant contemporaries in 1868, reacts from her announcement that she will become "A nun—a Carmelite nun. . . . For life, with God's leave" with characteristic Protestant horror, not unshared, seemingly, by his creator:[1]

> The idea struck Newman as too dark and horrible for belief, and made him feel as he would have done if she had told him she was going to mutilate her beautiful face or drink some potion that would make her mad. . . .

The horror is protracted in later scenes as Newman views and visits the convent in the Rue d'Enfer; then the reflective reader recalls Newman's tolerant indifference to the perturbations of the Reverend Mr. Babcock earlier in the novel. It becomes apparent that James has substituted a general anticlericism, inadequate for his crisis, for Turgenev's careful development of Lisa's religious convictions. *The American* devotes as much attention to religion as does *A Nest of Gentlefolk*, but the emphases are wrong, and as a consequence, Claire is far beneath Lisa as a source of interest.[2]

If, with the important exception of Claire de Cintré, the French characters of *The American* are passably accurate in a static way, the action in which James involves them is not so persuasively plausible. "I was so possessed of my idea that Newman should be ill-used," James acknowledges, ". . . that I attached too scant an importance to its fashion of coming about." The Bellegardes "would positively have jumped" at Newman, according to James's later judgment; that they did not, gives them a "queer falsity."[3] One wonders also at Mme de Bellegarde's dark crime; though she is made utterly capable of it, as capable of Regina Giddens in *The Little Foxes* (who duplicates her act), it does not seem wholly plausible that she could not have accomplished her purpose of marrying Claire to M. de Cintré without the death of her husband.

1. One should note, of course, a totally different attitude toward the Church in "The Altar of the Dead." I have wondered if, in Newman's reaction to the Church at this time, there is not a sly reference to the "Newman controversy." Newman became a Cardinal in 1879.

2. ". . . with this lady, altogether, I recognize a light plank, too light a plank, is laid for the reader over a 'dark' psychological abyss. The delicate clue to her character is never definitely placed in his hand." *The Art of the Novel*, p. 39. The reader is not alone if he has failed to understand Claire. Her own brother Valentin, and obviously her family, misunderstands her. Valentin assures Newman, "But in proportion as Claire seems charming, you may fold your arms and let yourself float with the current; you are safe. She is so good!" But the reader should see beyond the Bellegardes.

3. Ibid., p. 35. Pelham Edgar, *Henry James: Man and Author* (London, 1927), p. 243, gives another example of too facile plotting: ". . . the first difficulty was evidently to establish relations for Newman in the great world. To this end the out-at-the-elbows device of a convent friendship had to be adopted. . . . Claire de Cintré refused to let her childish intimacy with the present Mrs. Tristram die. . . ."

In the New York edition of the novel Claire speaks of the "curse" upon her house, and James adds a phrase to the deathbed note of M. de Bellegarde, explaining the reasons for his wife's action: "It's in order to marry my beloved daughter to M. de Cintré *and then go on herself all the same*." Royall Gettmann thinks that this is a hint that Mme de Bellegarde herself was carrying on an adulterous affair with M. de Cintré and intended to continue it after her daughter's marriage.[4] This idea is fully developed in the stage version of *The American*;[5] hence the interesting question arises: Did James restore an original feature of the crime or add an implication after dramatization had revealed the weakness of Mme de Bellegarde's motivation? We know that a difference of opinion developed between Howells, the editor of the *Atlantic* in which *The American* was serialized, and Henry James over the ending of the novel, but the only surviving letter would seem to indicate that Howells had protested merely because the ending was "unhappy," for James points out that Claire and Newman would have made "an impossible couple."[6] Perhaps, as a concession to Howells, James toned down the Marquise's crime, but I do not incline much to that view.

Even with the original serial ending, James's invention rarely led him so far astray as in this novel, and his later defense of it as a romance validated by the convincing quality of its hero[7] only

4. "Henry James's Revision of *The American*," *American Literature*, XVI (Jan., 1945), 292. Mr. Gettmann remarks that this adds "a stronger motive for the murder." It also makes *The American* more like the plays James was seeing on the Parisian stage, with their inevitable adultery. John A. Claire (in "*The American:* A Reinterpretation," *PMLA*, LXXIV [Dec., 1959], 613–618) suggests "that Mrs. Bread, the true mother of Claire de Cintre, was a blackmailer claiming both Newman and the Marquise de Bellegarde as victims; that Newman, by dint of his characteristic American naïveté and his opacity as a judge of character, was completely 'taken in' by her ruse; and that Claire's refusal to accept Newman in marriage came as a direct result of her having been informed by the Bellegardes of her true parents—the old Marquis and his 'meanest of mistresses,' Catherine Bread." I am not prepared to accept this suggestion, for (1) it would too closely duplicate the forcing device used with Christina in *Roderick Hudson*, (2) it would ennoble Mme de Bellgarde beyond any intention James would have appeared to have at this time, (3) with Newman's intention to take Claire to America, it would make strange their opposition to the marriage, (4) it calls for giving credence to the Marquise's invention that Catherine Bread had been her husband's mistress, and (5) the idea of Mrs. Bread's blackmailing the Marquise is untenable on the basis of their characters.

5. Robert P. Falk, "Henry James and the 'Age of Innocence,'" *Nineteenth-Century Fiction*, VII (Dec., 1952), 184–185.

6. *The Selected Letters of Henry James*, ed. Leon Edel (New York, 1955), pp. 68–69: "I quite understand that as an editor you should go in for 'cheerful endings'; but I am sorry that as a private reader you are not struck with the inevitability of the *American* dénouement. I fancied that most folks would feel that Mme. de Cintré *couldn't*, when the finish came, marry Mr. N[ewman]; . . . they would have been an impossible couple. . . ."

7. "I had been plotting arch romance without knowing it. . . ." *The Art of the Novel*, p. 25. But note also (Preface to *The Golden Bowl*): ". . . the many sorry businesses of *The American*" (p. 344). This does not indicate that the complacency of the earlier Preface was lasting.

underlines its limitations. "By the time *The American* was written, Pelham Edgar ventures, "he had already achieved his emancipation from romantic extravagance. Christopher Newman has no impulse to scale the walls of the Convent of the Rue d'Enfer, but paces the streets like an ordinary disappointed man."[8] The extravagances of the plot, in all deference to Mr. Edgar, conflict with the substantial realism of the materials of the story and produce a disharmony that is limiting in its effect. In correcting Dumas, James fell into the ways of the sensational dramatist, with the result that *The American* is a weaker novel than *Roderick Hudson*,[9] which preceded it, and *The Portrait of a Lady*, which came after. A portion of that weakness may be assigned to the fact that it was a pioneer experiment with the international novel and the further fact that James wrote as an emotionally aroused American.[1]

8. Edgar, p. 242. Contrast: "La fin du récit est rempli d'invraisemblances, non pas dans les sentiments, mais dans les situations; on l'attribuerait volontiers à Miss Braddon, aux romanciers à sensation, plutôt qu'à un raffiné tel que Henry James." Bentzon, *Les Nouveaux romanciers américains*, p. 82.

9. Henry Popkin shrewdly observes that *The American* "is a particular favorite of those readers who do not generally care for James." "The Two Theatres of Henry James," *New England Quarterly*, XXIV. (Mar., 1951), 70. "In spite of the morbid plot and the final futility of the principal character as well as of the book itself, Mr. James in many ways is very nearly at his best in *The American*." John Curtis Underwood, *Literature and Insurgency* (New York, 1915), p. 76. William Lyon Phelps calls it "a work of genius . . . this masterpiece . . . this great work of art." *The Advance of the English Novel* (New York, 1919), pp. 315–316. "Christopher Newman remains for all time the wistful American business man who spends his life hankering after the fine things he has missed." Van Wyck Brooks, *The Pilgrimage of Henry James* (New York, 1925), p. 102. A notable exception, however, occurs to me: John Macy, who described Henry James as "like a great scientific mind imprisoned with a few bugs," attacks *The American* for lack of realism: "If Mr. Newman . . . had been an Englishman, the story would have gone just as well. . . . What Newman says is not distinctly American in substance, in tone, in turn of phrase." *The Spirit of American Literature* (New York, 1911), pp. 328–330.

1. There are two good articles on the revisions which James made in *The American* for the New York edition. Isadore Traschen devotes his paper largely to the way in which James emphasized and elaborated on certain aspects of Newman's "innocence" and "barbarism," which are one and the same. "An American in Paris," *American Literature*, XXVI (Mar., 1954), 67–77. Max F. Schulz, in a more elaborate essay, extends the treatment of Newman, showing how the added details are frequently to aspects more offensive to the Bellegardes, while their characters are made more intolerant, passionate, and intemperate. Metaphors involving castles and wines are extended throughout the text. Newman's operations are inflated: instead of making soap, he now makes "mountains of soap," and a five-figure income becomes a six-figure one. "The Bellegardes' Feud with Christopher Newman: A Study of H.J.'s Revision of *The American*," *American Literature*, XXVII (Mar., 1955), 42–55. James's chief problem in revision, I would suggest, was to make a novel, which was essentially a reply to a satire that had been completely missed in America, completely plausible just as fiction. It was an almost insuperable task.

"Americans in Europe are *outsiders*; that is the great point thrown into relief by all zealous efforts to controvert it. . . . We are not only out of the European circle politically and geographically; we are out of it socially, and for excellent reasons. We are the only great people of the civilized world that is a pure democracy, and we are the only great people that is exclusively commercial." Henry James, "Americans Abroad," *The Nation*, XXVII (Oct. 3, 1878), 208–209. The whole article, pertinent to Newman, was brought to my attention by Dan Laurence.

IRVING HOWE

Henry James and the Millionaire†

"I was seated in an American 'horsecar,' " Henry James was later to recall, "when I found myself, of a sudden, considering with enthusiasm as the theme of a 'story,' the situation, in another country and an aristocratic society, of some robust but insidiously beguiled and betrayed, some cruelly wronged, compatriot; the point being in especial that he should suffer at the hands of persons pretending to represent the highest possible civilization. . . . What would he 'do' in that predicament, how would he right himself, or how, failing a remedy, would he conduct himself under his wrong?"

This succinctly put, is the situation of Henry James' *The American.* * * * An American is "cruelly wronged" by a family of proud aristocrats, he finds evidence that its maternal head once committed "an abomination not otherwise known," and then in a moment of fine renunciation refrains from publicizing his secret. *The American* is the first full-scale expression of James' view of the conflict between European and American civilization, a view later rendered more complex and ambiguous but not abandoned; it is one of the earliest efforts by an American novelist to represent *the* American who, because of the country's geographical and cultural isolation, is taken to be radically different from Europeans; and in itself it is an arresting though imperfect work of art, done in James' swift and light-toned early manner, but already marked by that preoccupation with disaster which is to scar his later work.

The notion that there is a "national character" is impossible to defend as an abstract proposition; it is obnoxious when it becomes a spur to chauvinism, yet it is lent a quasi-respectable aura by the frequency with which we turn to it in our spontaneous social intercourse. James did not, we may safely assume, think of "national character" in terms so generalized when he wrote *The American,* but it is nonetheless significant that his leading figure is Christopher Newman who, as critics have been quick to notice, is to be taken as that new man arising from the aftermath of Christopher Columbus' blundering voyage. Whole aspects of American experience were closed to James, most conspicuously that aspect associated with the name of Mark Twain; but then James' ignorance of the pioneer west was matched by Twain's ignorance of "international society." Yet James did know enough about America to realize that

† From *Tomorrow* 9 (January 1950), 53–55.

the American, if he were to be summoned to fictional reality, would have to be located in the west. Though the immediate view one gains of Christopher Newman is an American millionaire in Europe seeking culture and marriage (presumably only the latter can be conveniently had in the United States), James is careful to inform us that Newman made his money in San Francisco.

Here, however, James succumbs to a major inconsistency in the scheme of his novel. The notion of "national character" is relevant only to a country with a homogeneous culture; it might, for example, be meaningful to speak of "New England character" with regard to that period when New England was ribbed by Puritanism. But how is one to speak of "national character" in a country fractured into sharply varying regions, northeast, south and west, each formed by a different topography, economy and tradition? Plainly, that is impossible—unless one assumes that the dominant national personality is the result of one of these regional influences or a blend of them. In effect, that is what most writers about American "national character" have assumed. The American type, usually taken to be a self-reliant, industrious individualist, is conceived as a cross-breeding between two sectional types; the western farm-pioneer and the northeastern businessman. Of course, with each step in this process of abstraction we move further away from the actualities of experience, and consequently such types must be viewed as usable assumptions rather than literal descriptions.

Now in trying to depict *the* American at a time when American life was no longer homogeneous, James unwittingly formed Newman from a confusing pastiche of standardized sectional traits. Physically and socially Newman is a westerner; once, James assures us, he even swapped tales with cowboys; and he has the westerner's expected easy ways with money, his democratic expansiveness of manner, and his eagerness, fortune assured, to pry open the temples of culture. Thus far Newman is consistently drawn—not yet an individualized character, but a recognizable and serviceable type. But James, being above all a novelist of individual relations, must try to render Newman as unique, and to the extent that he does so Newman emerges not as a westerner but as a New Englander, a descendant of Hawthorne's men of conscience and a forerunner of James' own Lambert Strether in *The Ambassadors*. Unlike Strether, Newman is capable of quick action, but the refinements of sensibility James so generously pours into him are difficult to reconcile with what James says *about* him: namely, that he is a western magnate. In more abstract novelistic terms we might say that Newman as a type conflicts with Newman as a character, and that while each is independently credible they are not lifelike when joined together. But though we are more likely to be drawn to the sensitive character than the expansive type, it is upon the latter that James' fable of the American victimized in Europe must necessarily rest. (Of course, it might be objected that a westerner *could* have the sensibility credited to Newman; which is true. But in a novel, particularly one aspiring to display cultural contrasts, we must be concerned with the likely probability rather than the unlikely possibility.)

The valuable English critic, F. R. Leavis, writes that James chooses "as the representative of American decency and genuineness, a type of which he knows virtually nothing—the businessman—and offers us quite incredible idealization. Christopher Newman, having started from nothing, emerges from making his pile in the post–Civil War decade, crude (in the sense of being socially innocent) but unworldly, and finely sensitive to moral values; and because of this is at a disadvantage in dealing with the corrupt and subtle French aristocrats who victimize him. It is romantic, unreal and ridiculous."

And so it is—if one thinks of Newman merely as the businessman James says he is. But as an American influenced by the Emerson-Thoreau milieu of moral earnestness, which is what for many pages Newman actually is, he seems, if still romantic, quite real and credible. If one sees the difficulties of the novel as due less to James' romantic idealization than to his confusion and ignorance about certain aspects of American experience, one is in a position to locate the book's weaknesses in terms of James' own intellectual history. And at the same time we are also in a position to appreciate the novel's very considerable strengths: its firm sense of the cultural difference between America and Europe, a sense to be improved upon but never made obsolete; its witty portrait of Newman, a quite perfect vehicle for James' blend of affection and criticism *vis-à-vis* his native country; and its ultimate ascent to the pathos of Newman's renunciation, an act incredible in Newman the western type but highly credible in Newman the American individual.

* * *

At least in its latter part, this story is highly spiced with romantic melodrama. But there are moments of very great power and pathos in its execution, Newman's final desolation being rendered with particular vividness. * * *

This is prose of the deepest gravity and magnificence, but it can hardly hide the structural weakness of the action it carries. In James' preface to *The American*, written some thirty-four years after the novel, he noted several faults himself. One of them, his belief that a family like the Bellegardes "would positively have jumped at my rich and easy American," is open to question; tradition does not always bow to money. A far more serious fault is that Claire's readiness to renounce Newman, though vaguely explicable in terms of the French family tradition, is unsatisfactory. "The delicate clue to her conduct," James admitted, "is never definitely placed in [the reader's] hand . . ." Time has aggravated this weakness, for it is harder for us to appreciate a woman's renunciation of love in the name of family loyalty than it was for the readers of *The American* when it appeared in 1876.

There are thus several layers of disharmony in the novel—within Newman's character itself; between the book's early bantering tone and its melodramatic climax; between the romantic quality of James' feeling for his hero and the subject-matter which requires the most sober realistic treatment; between the decisive action of several of the characters, particularly Claire, and the dim view we have of their motives. In the history of James' art, *The American* is a transitional novel in which his characteristic subject-matter is developed but the means for its full dramatic realization are not yet fully at hand or controlled. James is still too much the obtrusive "writer" telling about rather than representing, exercising his charm on the reader rather than granting his characters the full free stage.

In his later novels the idealized American (so inexplicable, by the way, to those critics who think of James as a mere snobbish expatriate) is repeatedly presented, though not in as self-contradictory a person as Newman. In James' last and unfinished novel, *The Ivory Tower*, there is a penitent millionaire, Frank Betterman, who hopes that his wealth may yet be used for purposes finer than his own. But there is also Abel Gaw, another millionaire, unrepentant to the last. And guiltily flanking these old men are Gaw's niece and Betterman's nephew, appalled by "the black and merciless things that are behind the great possessions." The black and merciless things—these words reflect the final balancing of James' vision, the end of his long hope that some beneficence might result from the enlightenment of the American millionaire.

JAMES W. TUTTLETON

Henry James: The Superstitious Valuation of Europe†

James's ambivalent feelings about America led him to crisscross the Atlantic in the early 1870s, testing his impressions of the viabil-

† From *The Novel of Manners in America*, by James W. Tuttleton (New York: W. W. Norton & Co., 1974), pp. 48–50, 59–70.

ity of the Old World and the New as subject and setting of his art. Yielding to "the importunate presence of tradition of *every* kind—the influence of an atmosphere electrically charged with historic intimations and whisperings,"[1] young James suffered from "the great American disease"—"the appetite, morbid and monstrous, for colour and form, for the picturesque and romantic at any price."[2] In Europe, where life seemed "raised to a higher power, because more richly charged, more significantly composed, and more completely informed,"[3] James, like Cooper before him, embarked on a passionate pilgrimage to escape the bland homogeneity of life in America; the passion for money-making and the indifference to culture, social grace, and intellectual refinement here; the absence of a genuine variety of social types, and, as a consequence, the superficial American literary culture crippling to the aspiring artist. Summing up, he observed of Howells's A *Foregone Conclusion* that "our native-grown imaginative effort" had to make "small things do great service. Civilization with us is monotonous, and in the way of contrasts, of salient points, of chiaroscuro, we have to take what we can get."[4]

Troubled, at the same time, by the feeling that America ought to be a rich enough ground for the writer, he debated with himself the value of complete expatriation. His inner dialogue or this vexing point lasted more than forty years; it constitutes, in its way, an extensive catalogue of counterstatements, a rich commentary on the relation of the artist to his regional and moral environs. At times he felt that the American writer "*must* be tethered in native pastures."[5] Even Hawthorne, he occasionally felt, "forfeited a precious advantage in ceasing to tread his native soil"; and he envied Turgenev that "like those of all great novelists" his works "savour strongly of his native soil."[6] His intermittent doubt of the value of expatriation even led him to urge his brother William to insure that his sons contracted "local saturations and attachments in respect to their *own* great and glorious country, to learn, and strike roots into, its infinite beauty . . . and variety." He felt that if his nephews did sink themselves in America, "they won't, as I do now, have to assimilate, but half-heartedly, the alien splendours." He urged William to make the boys "stick fast and sink up to their necks in everything their *own* countries and climates can give," since "its

1. Henry James to Elizabeth Boott, 10 December 1873, quoted in Nathalia Wright, *American Novelists in Italy* (Philadelphia, 1965), p. 201.
2. Henry James, "Four Meetings," in *The Portable Henry James*, ed. Morton D. Zabel (New York, 1951), p. 47.
3. Herbert Croly, "Henry James and His Countrymen," in *The Question of Henry James*, ed. F. W. Dupee (New York, 1945), p. 29.
4. Henry James, "Howells's 'Foregone Conclusion,' " *Nation*, 7 January 1875, pp. 12–13.
5. Henry James, *The Letters of Henry James*, ed. Percy Lubbock, 2 vols. (New York, 1920), I: 396.
6. Henry James, *French Poets and Novelists* (London, 1919), p. 220.

being that 'own' will double their *use* of it."[7] James is said to have complained to Hamlin Garland that "the mixture" of the Old World and the New in him "proved disastrous" because it "made of me a man who is neither American nor European."[8]

But these counterstatements, usually provoked by homesickness, were at best generally valid for the would-be expatriate, not ultimately true for James himself. Brooks and Parrington felt that James's expatriation ruined his writing because it deprived him of the subjects and situations, the social order and the moral orientation, that might have generated great art.[9] But for James, as William Troy has argued, "residence in England, rather than being a source of sterility and corruption, was an indispensable condition of fulfillment."[1] As James ultimately decided: "My choice is the Old World—my choice, my need, my life."[2]

At the time of his departure in 1875, James was known chiefly as a reviewer, essayist, and short story writer. His first novel, *Watch and Ward* (1871), had not brought him recognition. "Conceived as a study of Boston manners," the novel dealt, as Leon Edel has rightly observed, "rather with the moeurs of Quincy Street."[3] James consistently disclaimed it in later years and spoke of *Roderick Hudson* as his first novel, and critics have generally been pleased to do the same. But the early stories, reviews, and travel essays constituted a gathering in of the preparations for what was to be his great theme as a novelist of manners—"The Americano-European legend." In "A Bundle of Letters" (1879) Louis Leverett spoke his author's mind in saying, "I am much interested in the study of national types; in comparing, contrasting, seizing the strong points, the weak points, the point of view of each."[4] The decade from 1872 until 1882 most interests the student of James's international novels—and I limit myself, arbitrarily, to this period—for it is the chief period "of his studies in comparative national psychology and manners," the period when "he spent part of his time on one side of the water and part on the other, and the people in his stories followed in his footsteps."[5]

* * *

James's decision to settle in Paris was an unwise one. Although he was boasting to Howells in May of 1876 that he was "turning

7. James, *Letters*, I: 316.
8. Quoted in Simon Nowell-Smith's *The Legend of the Master* (New York, 1948), p. 104.
9. Vernon L. Parrington, *The Beginnings of Critical Realism in America, 1860–1920* (New York, 1930); Van Wyck Brooks, *The Pilgrimage of Henry James* (New York, 1925).
1. William Troy, "The New Generation," in *Henry James: A Collection of Critical Essays*, ed. Leon Edel (Englewood Cliffs, N.J., 1963), p. 84.
2. Henry James, *The Notebooks of Henry James*, eds. F. O. Matthiessen and Kenneth B. Murdock (New York, 1961), p. 23.
3. Leon Edel, *Henry James*, vol. 2. *The Conquest of London: 1870–1881* (Philadelphia, 1962), p. 44.
4. Henry James, "A Bundle of Letters," *Tales* (London, 1962), 4:442.
5. Croly, "Henry James and His Countrymen," p. 30.

into an old, and very contented, Parisian" who felt as if he had "struck roots into the Parisian soil, and were likely to let them grow tangled and tenacious there,"[6] before long he was complaining that he really saw nothing of Parisian society. No one introduced him; he had no entrée into the exclusive drawing rooms of the Faubourg St. Germain. He felt cut off from the aristocracy which gave *ton* to the civilization he wished to portray. His situation was not much better than it had been earlier when he complained that "the waiters at the *restaurants* are as yet my chief society." By July he was confiding to William "a long-encroaching weariness and satiety with the French mind and its utterance," a desire "only to feed on English life and the contact of English minds." All he could claim for the experience of Paris was having learned the Théâtre Français by heart, "a good deal of Boulevard and third rate Americanism."[7] "The longer I live in France, the better I like the French personality," he observed to William, "but the more convinced I am of their bottomless superficiality."[8] These feelings underlay his move to London in December of 1876.

It is not surprising that James's response to Paris colored the novel he was then writing and that the exclusiveness of French society and the "bottomless superficiality" of the French mind found satiric expression in his new novel, *The American.* For one thing, his choice of a French setting discharged one obligation James felt to be incumbent on the American novelist of manners, the "terrible burden" of having to deal with Europe: "The burden is necessarily greater for an American—for he *must* deal, more or less, even if only by implication, with Europe; whereas no European is obliged to deal in the least with America. No one dreams of calling him less complete for not doing so. . . . The painter of manners who neglects America is not thereby incomplete as yet; but a hundred years hence—fifty years hence perhaps—he will doubtless be accounted so."[9]

The most direct stimulus to his new novel seems to have been the insult to the American character in the *L'Étrangère* (1876) of Alexandre Dumas *fils,* then playing at the Théâtre Français. Both James's letters of the period and his review of the play in the *New York Tribune* suggest that "surge of patriotic indignation" which aroused his "desire to refute the play."[1] In defending the American character, James took hints from Turgenev's *A Nest of Gentlefolk* (1858) and employed a dramatic device, borrowed from Augier, called the "intrusion plot." In its simplest form, this term describes

6. James, *Letters,* I: 48.
7. *The Selected Letters of Henry James,* ed. Leon Edel (New York, 1955), pp. 41, 50, 51.
8. Quoted in Edel's *Henry James: The Conquest of London,* p. 263.
9. *The Notebooks of Henry James,* p. 24.
1. Oscar Cargill, *The Novels of Henry James* (New York, 1961), p. 45.

the arrangement of dramatic actions which constitutes for James the structure of his formal themes: "Into a group there comes an intruder whose presence is resisted by one or more persons and accepted by one or more, with resulting conflict, until someone's eyes are opened to the true situation, to the danger, or to a possible solution. Different outcomes are possible, but the most frequent is the elimination of the intruder."[2]

The intruder, in this case, is a young American millionaire who goes to Paris to cultivate himself and falls in love with the daughter of an aristocratic family who first permit Newman's attentions, then reject him as a possible son-in-law because he is a "commercial person." In the quality of his response to the de Bellegardes and of theirs to him, James reveals the character of Newman and his antagonists and tests the values expressed in the manners of the two cultures they represent.

Christopher Newman, as his name suggests, is meant to represent the new man of the New World—a kind of Christopher Columbus in reverse—confronting the complexity and mystery of the Old World, where the qualities that have elevated him in America are of little social significance. A casual optimist with few principles but an extraordinary "unconscious *sang-froid*," a San Franciscan who is "horribly Western" and who knows nothing about culture, a democrat innocent of the knowledge of hierarchical class arrangements and ignorant of social forms, Newman is a young self-made man of action and enterprise, a pragmatist who has made his way up from a battlefield commission in the Civil War to the zenith of American commerical success: he is a millionaire manufacturer of leather goods and washtubs. The novel opens in the Salon Carré of the Louvre, where, with an "aesthetic headache," Newman sits on an ottoman, his long legs casually extended, lounging "in profound enjoyment of his posture." To the interested observer, Newman is a comic example of the American "national mould." His expression has that typically American "vagueness which is not vacuity, that blankness which is not simplicity, that look of being committed to nothing in particular, of standing in an attitude of general hospitality to the chances of life, of being very much at one's own disposal, so characteristic of many American faces. It was our friend's eye that chiefly told his story; an eye in which innocence and experience were singularly blended."[3]

The experience which his appearance suggests is that of a man who has "sat with Western humorists in knots, round cast-iron stoves, and seen 'tall' tales grow taller without toppling over," whose "sole aim in life had been to make money," but who has rejected

2. G. B. Fitch, "Emile Augier and the Intrusion-Plot," *PMLA*, 63 (1948), 274–280.

3. Henry James, *The American* (New York, 1960), p. 19.

the Darwinian business ethic of the Gilded Age, renounced revenge on his competitors, and given up business itself. The innocence which his glance suggests is that of a man who has only recently discovered in Europe "a very rich and beautiful world" which had "not all been made by sharp railroad men and stock-brokers." If Culture had once seemed to him "a proceeding properly confined to women, foreigners, and other unpractical persons," Raphael and Titian and Rubens had "inspired our friend, for the first time in his life, with a vague self-mistrust." In order to improve his mind, he takes in Europe, for his world is "a great bazaar, where one might stroll about and purchase handsome things." Europe he regards as made for him. He wishes to cultivate art and sees 470 churches; he wishes to cultivate society and becomes the familiar of M. Nioche and his daughter, a coquette. Above all, he wishes to marry "a magnificent woman," a "great woman," a beautiful woman—"I mean beautiful in mind and in manners, as well as in person. It is a thing every man has an equal right to. . . ." In wanting to possess "the best article in the market," Newman is, as Mrs. Tristram puts it so precisely, "the great Western Barbarian, stepping forth in his innocence and might, gazing a while at this poor effete Old World, and then swooping down on it."

In Claire de Cintré he almost manages to make off with its best prize. But not quite. If she suggested to Newman "the sense of an elaborate education," she had passed "through mysterious ceremonies and processes of culture in her youth"; she had been "fashioned and made flexible to certain exalted social needs." A woman of "goodness, beauty, intelligence, a fine education, personal elegance," and noble birth, she is, in fine, exactly what Newman has been looking for. As he says to her younger brother Valentin, adumbrating Gatsby's conception of Daisy, "She is my dream realized."

The family, however, is another affair, and it is in Christopher Newman's confrontation with the de Bellegardes that some of James's finest comedy emerges. They are a family with an eight-hundred-year-old name; their secluded hotel is in the exclusive Faubourg St. Germain; they constitute "the skim of the milk of the old noblesse." They are exclusive, associating only with their peers, among whom are some of "the best-preserved specimens" of "the Legitimists and the Ultramontanes." They admit of no changes, no intrusions of the modern. The Marquis has but a "single political conviction": "He believed in the divine right of Henry of Bourbon, Fifth of his name, to the throne of France." The gentlemen in their drawing rooms perpetuate the wig and carry on the "profuse white neck cloth of the fashion of 1820." They do not go out; they do not know Paris. Few of them have ever seen an American, although the city is crawling with them; and only a few remember having seen the great Dr. Franklin. To the American Mrs. Tristram, they are "mounted upon stilts a mile high, and with pedigrees long in proportion."

The dowager Marquise de Bellegarde is described as a "feudal countess of a mother" who "rules the family with an iron hand" and who allows Claire to "have no friends but of her own choosing, and to visit only in a certain sacred circle." She is preeminently "a woman of conventions and proprieties" whose "word is the world of things immutably decreed." If Newman is rich, she is proud, and in her world her power over her children counts for more than his money. Her son, the Marquis, is, as his name indicates, urbane. Valentin remarks, "He is a very remarkable man; he has the best manners in France. He is extremely clever; indeed he is very learned. He is writing a history of The Princesses of France Who Never Married." Opposed to Newman's suit, Urbain is capable of a fine "transcendent patronage" in dealing with an American who in all tranquillity does not suspect "the relativity of his own place in the social scale." It is principally through Urbain de Bellegarde and Newman that James dramatizes the conflict between the manners of the American democrat and the French aristocrat. The Marquis's deportment is always mechanically polite, correct, polished, aristocratic, and impersonal: "His manners seemed to indicate a fine, nervous dread that something disagreeable might happen if the atmosphere were not purified by allusions of a thoroughly superior cast." To Newman he is "a man of forms and phrases and postures; a man full of possible impertinences and treacheries." "What under the sun is the man afraid of?" Newman asks himself. "Does he think I am going to offer to swap jack knives with him?" In a Paris filled with American tourists demanding fried ham and cornbread for breakfast, who could be sure?

What the Marquis fears is, simply, Newman as a brother-in-law. Newman is unprepared to feel the social delicacy of his candidacy for marriage to Claire. After all, the de Bellegarde women had always married well; none had ever married into even the *petite noblesse*; there has never been a case, as Valentin tells Newman, of "a misalliance among the women." But it is characteristic of Newman that he believes that anything is possible—with a strong will, good intentions, and enough cash. That there should be anything more powerful than his will seemed to him impossible, and it is a mark of his comic optimism that he is never in doubt about his final goal (to win Claire) but only about the precise means of achieving it (the "everlasting proprieties" that have a hand in everything that she does).

The title of the novel suggests that Newman is intended to be representative of the American character. And in one sense he is. For Newman synthesizes some of the most salient characteristics of the American people. Although James thoroughly deplored some of these characteristics, it is those personal, individualizing traits of his large, generous, easy nature which distinguish him from the other Americans in the novel—particularly Tom Tristram and Mr. Babcock—and which justify James's sympathy with him. Tristram is an idle expatriate who judges a country by the quality of its cigars, who has lived amidst the beauty of Paris for years but who has never been inside the Louvre, and who cannot allude to America without superciliousness: "He irritated our friend by the tone of his allusions to their native country, and Newman was at a loss to understand why the United States were not good enough for Mr. Tristram. He had never been a very conscious patriot, but it vexed him to see them treated as little better than a vulgar smell in his friend's nostrils, and he finally broke out and swore that they were the greatest country in the world, that they could put all Europe into their breeches' pockets, and that an American who spoke ill of them ought to be carried home in irons and compelled to live in Boston." Tristram's attitudes illustrate what James called "the baleful spirit of the cosmopolite," the "uncomfortable consequence of seeing many lands and feeling at home in none." If the passionate pilgrimage produced only Tom Tristrams, it were better not taken. As James was later to observe, no doubt apropos of the many Tristrams in Europe, "To be a cosmopolite is not, I think, an ideal; the ideal should be to be a concentrated patriot."[4]

Mr. Babcock illustrates the opposite danger. If Newman is the Westerner, Babcock is the New Englander, a minister from Dorchester travelling in Europe on funds supplied by his congregation in order to improve his mind and culture. But for all his reverence before the treasures of Europe, "European life seemed to him unscrupulous and impure." He wished to give himself up to its beauty, but like Mary Garland he had a too highly developed set of moral prejudices. Art and Life are Extremely Serious Things to Babcock, but, deprived of spontaneity, he responds to Europe in terms of how he thinks he ought to feel about what he sees.

Newman falls between these two types. He is neither the deracinated expatriate, at home nowhere, nor the American ascetic moralist-patriot, at home only in "safe" Dorchester. James's inclusion of these other Americans indicates his perception, as Irving Howe has suggested, that "the notion that there is a 'national character' is impossible to defend as an abstract proposition."[5] Yet few writers, in fact, were more "obsessed, and to some extent en-

4. Henry James, *Portraits of Places* (Boston, 1884), p. 75.

5. Irving Howe, "Henry James and the Millionaire," *Tomorrow* 9 (1950): 53.

thralled, by the manifold paradox of our American self-consciousness"[6] than James, and few writers have understood more perceptively how the institutionalization of our social experience gives shape and form to the American "identity." Writing to Thomas Sergeant Perry, James defined his sense of the relationship between the developing American identity, coming to consciousness in the New World, and the fixed condition of national types in the Old: "We are Americans born—*il faut en prendre son parti.* I look upon it as a great blessing; and I think that to be an American is an excellent preparation for culture. We have exquisite qualitites as a race, and it seems to me that we are ahead of European races in the fact that more than either of them we can deal freely with forms of civilization not our own, can pick and choose and assimilate and in short (aesthetically &c) claim our property wherever we find it. To have no national stamp has hitherto been a regret and a drawback, but I think it not unlikely that American writers may yet indicate a vast intellectual fusion and synthesis of the various National tendencies of the world is the condition of more important achievements than any we have seen."[7] James's objection to the provincialism of America lay precisely in our failure to realize the possibility of choice in creating a new, unique, national body of manners. As Frederick Hoffman has observed, this relationship between freedom and consciously chosen forms links James to the central American situation: "The American self is free to choose; no premium is put upon his adherence to traditional form or manners."[8] Isabel Archer in *The Portrait of a Lady* appeals to us because, having come to Europe to observe the formal order of social experience, she uses her knowledge—as she tells Mrs. Touchett—to *choose* whether or not she will assimilate any of its conventions. Newman, though far richer, has paradoxically less freedom than she. Although Osmond respects "a magnificent form" as much as the Bellegardes, she can disobey him without serious consequences for their already estranged relationship. Newman, however, must accommodate himself to arbitrary European customs—vexing and irrational as they seem to the pragmatic American mind—in order to win Claire and to show the European aristocracy that "we aren't barbarians."

Though Newman cares little for the proprieties of the Faubourg St. Germain, he loves Claire deeply enough to want to learn "to do what is required over here," to comply with all the proper usages, to establish his claim to equality with the de Bellegardes—on their terms. He therefore pleads for instruction, begs to be tutored in the

6. John Kinnaird, "The Paradox of an American 'Identity,'" *Partisan Review* 25 (1958): 381.

7. James, *Selected Letters*, pp. 22–23.

8. Frederick J. Hoffman, "Freedom and Conscious Form: Henry James and the American Self," *Virginia Quarterly Review* 37 (1961): 275.

forms. This tourist attitude led James to observe in a review of Albert Rhodes's *The French at Home* that "the American demand for information about Parisian manners and customs seems to amount to what is commercially called a 'steady run.' . . ."[9] Thus Newman demands of Valentin: "If there is any thing particular to be done, let me know and I will do it. I wouldn't for the world approach Madame de Cintré without all the proper forms. If I ought to go and tell your mother, why I will go and tell her. I will go and tell your brother, even. I will go and tell any one you please. As I don't know any one else, I begin by telling you."

Newman's ignorance of polite manners, however, his ignorance of even what constitutes a social obligation, in view of his ambition, cannot help producing a broad comedy of manners. He at first mistakes Urbain for the butler; he is on terms of easy familiarity with cicerones, guides, couriers, and the coquette Noémie Nioche. He telegraphs his engagement to America before it is formally announced and then brandishes the congratulatory replies in the face of Mme de Bellegarde. He threatens to stage an engagement party at his hotel, unaware that the "everlasting proprieties" require that Mme de Bellegarde give it. He parades the old marquise around the room on the evening of the party, mortally embarrassing her in the presence of her guests. And the result of these violations of decorum is a comedy which—from the viewpoint of the complicated artifice of European social forms—shows that Newman is indeed the barbarian. As one critic in the *Nation* observed in 1878: "America is not a good training-school of manners for the multitude. Not that Americans wish to be offensive—on the contrary, they are very good-natured; but they seem not to know the kind of treatment or attention (*égard* is the French word) a civilized being has the right to expect from a stranger."[1]

Despite his vulgarity, the real source of Newman's appeal is that he can perceive the distinction between "natural" and "artificial" behavior, between "the special intention" and "the habit of good manners," between urbanity and sincerity. Newman insists, on the ground of nature and sincerity, that he is both civilized and noble. His is precisely the claim Cooper's Eve makes in *Home As Found*, that the American gentleman enjoys the highest social station among civilized nations. To be sure, Mr. Effingham would very probably never have admitted Newman to the character of a gentleman, but the democrat Newman cannot understand why he is not as good as anybody. As Laboulaye observed, "*Tout Américaine à Paris se croît gentilhomme.*" When Valentin is horrified at New-

9. Henry James, review of *The French at Home* by Albert Rhodes (New York, 1875), in the *Nation*, 5 August 1875, p. 92.

1. I. M. (Frederick Sheldon), "The American Colony in France," *Nation*, 18 April 1878, p. 258.

man's ambition to marry Claire because he is not noble, Newman exclaims: "The devil I am not!"

> "Oh," said Bellegarde a little more seriously, "I did not know you had a title."
>
> "A title? What do you mean by a title?" asked Newman. "A count, a duke, a marquis? I don't know anything about that. I don't know who is and who is not. But I say I am noble. I don't exactly know what you mean by it, but it's a fine word and a fine idea: I put in a claim to it."
>
> "But what have you to show, my dear fellow, what proofs?"
>
> "Anything you please! But you don't suppose I am going to undertake to prove that I am noble. It is for you to prove the contrary."
>
> "That's easily done. You have manufactured wash-tubs."
>
> Newman stared a moment. "Therefore I am not noble? I don't see it. Tell me something I have *not* done—something I cannot do."
>
> "You cannot marry a woman like Madame de Cintré for the asking."
>
> "I believe you mean," said Newman slowly, "that I am not good enough."
>
> "Brutally speaking—yes!"

Newman is defeated because he wages his campaign in the arena of European manners and customs. He seeks to appropriate for himself proprieties and amenities which are totally foreign and too complex for him to grasp. As an American he has not developed a social style that is both expressive of the national character and distinguished and beautiful enough to oppose to the European. Instead he has sought to ape the European, and, repeatedly caught in the postures of imitation, Newman appears all the more grotesque. "Am I stepping about like a terrier on his hind legs?" Much of the time, unfortunately, he is. As one observer of Americans in Paris argued in 1878, "it is much better form to be American and to have a national individuality of one's own than to offer to foreign eyes a pale imitation of European models."[2]

Newman is, from the democratic viewpoint, admirable enough—although we cannot help seeing the ridiculous in his playing the wrong kind of game with the wrong kind of people. What one of Howells's characters says in *Through the Eye of the Needle* is perfectly apropos, that "we haven't socially evolved from ourselves; we've evolved from the Europeans, from the English. I don't think you'll find a single society rite with us now that had its origin in our peculiar national life, if we have a peculiar national life."[3] Instead

2. Ibid., p. 259.
3. William Dean Howells, *Through the Eye of the Needle* (New York, 1907), p. 63.

of exploiting the freedom of a unique social experience to create beautiful, new, and distinctive social forms, Americans sought both to impose on the democratic New World an aristocratic social pattern developed in the Old World and, returning to the Old, to beat the Europeans on their own ground. Much later, when James toured the United States after the turn of the century, he took little comfort in the uses to which Americans had put their freedom in the intervening quarter century. Virtually, he discovered, Americans had no manners or forms: "The ugliness—one pounced, indeed, on this as on a talisman for the future—was the so complete abolition of *forms;* if, with so little reference to their past, present or future possibility, they could be said to have been even so much honoured as to be abolished."[4]

This passage of time also put in clearer perspective the social character of the exclusive houses of the Faubourg St. Germain. And in the preface to *The American* he later argued that if he had properly gauged the depths of their cynicism, the de Bellegardes "would positively have jumped . . . at my rich and easy American, and not have 'minded' in the least any drawback. . . ."[5] Virtually isolated from the society he had tried to examine, his portrait failed of verisimilitude. Leon Edel has observed that "the Faubourg which Henry creates is in part the Faubourg of literature, rather than that of life. . . ."[6] But to have permitted the marriage of Claire and Newman would have been to pander to the sentimentality of an audience brought up on Maria Cummins, Mrs. Southworth, and Augusta Jane Evans Wilson, to throw, as James put it, "a rather vulgar sop to readers who don't really know the world and who don't measure the merit of a novel by its correspondence to the same." In defense of his conclusion, James observed to Howells that the marriage of Claire and Newman "would have been impossible: they would have been an impossible couple, with an impossible problem before them. For instance—to speak very materially—where would they have lived? It was all very well for Newman to talk of giving her the whole world to choose from: but Asia and Africa being counted out, what would Europe and America have offered? Mme. de C. couldn't have lived in New York; depend upon it; and Newman, after his marriage (or rather *she*, after it) couldn't have dwelt in France. There would have been nothing left," he added facetiously, "but a farm out West."[7] It would be a mistake to underrate James's objection here, for the question of where such an exotic couple might have lived was a real one, as Howells had discovered in *A Chance Acquaintance* and *The Rise of Silas*

4. Henry James, *The American Scene* (New York, 1907), p. 24.

5. James, *The Art of the Novel*, pp. 35–36.

6. Edel, *Henry James: The Conquest of London*, p. 249.

7. James, *Selected Letters*, pp. 68–69.

Lapham, where the socially mismatched couples must settle in California and Mexico. James tackled the paradox of the aristocratic woman married to an American living in New York in "Lady Barberina." In this tale the social impasse comes right down to the practical question of "Who in New York society is possibly distinguished enough to lead Lady Barberina in to dinner?"

* * *

RICHARD POIRIER

[The Comedy of Fixed and Free Characters]†

James began *The American* in Paris, the scene of the novel, in the winter of 1875, during the months when *Roderick Hudson* was ending its run in the *Atlantic Monthly.* These circumstances are important to an understanding of the similarities and differences between the two novels. It is not surprising that both, coming so close to one another in time, reveal in their comedy essentially the same biases about established society and individual aspiration. In *The American,* as in *Roderick Hudson,* comedy results, for the most part, from the dramatization of the conflict between what have been called in the previous chapter the 'free' and the 'fixed' characters. Those who are 'free,' in this case Newman, Valentin, Claire, and, to an extent, Mrs. Tristram, are people who are still exploring the possibilities of their own characters and whose perceptions are not warped by social allegiances or blighted by self-absorption. The 'fixed' characters, though they may be relatively genial, like Tom Tristram, or intelligent and sophisticated, like Madame de Bellegarde and her son Urbain, are contented with what they have, taking particular satisfaction, in the case of the Bellegardes, from a place in a conventionally constituted society. They do not endanger their self-satisfaction by any 'fine intensification or wide enlargement'[1] of consciousness such as James describes in the Preface to *The Princess Casamassima.* This sharp contrast in types of character is modified by the minor plot of the novel, but only to make the satire on Parisian society the more devastating and general. Noémie is presented as a corrupt version of a 'free' spirit—she escapes the limitations of her social and economic status by becoming a lorette—and her father is an ironic

† "*The American,*" in Richard Poirier, *The Comic Sense of Henry James: A Study of the Early Novels* (New York: Oxford University Press, 1960), pp. 44–50.

1. *The Art of the Novel,* p. 67. [Henry James, *The Art of the Novel* (New York: Scribner's, 1934)—*Editor.*]

version of a 'fixed' one—he pretends to restrict his daughter's activity at the same time that he accepts a living from it.

Both *Roderick Hudson* and *The American* are about ambition and futility, and in each case the ultimate frustration of an ambitious ideal is mysterious and melodramatic. Roderick cannot understand why he loses Christina any more than Newman can understand why Claire must refuse to marry him. Each woman submits to the will of her mother, while in both cases the force of maternal coercion is assisted by something intimidating out of the past. This includes the irregularity of Christina's birth as well as Claire's sense not only that she is obliged to obey her mother but also that she is fated by the history of her family to accept a lifetime of unhappiness. James allows for the inference in both cases that the factors which cause the failure of hope and ambition are distinctly European—they are associated with the mysteries of tradition or, in Christina's case, with the polite form of the oldest profession. At the same time the ambition of the 'free' characters is made peculiarly American—it is a matter of securing the future by possessing the 'ideal' in some palpable form, so that Christina is the human embodiment of that 'ideal beauty' which Roderick tries to represent in his sculpture, and Claire is the necessary evidence that Newman's life has been a success. 'To make it perfect, as I see it,' he remarks with a minimum of jocularity, 'there must be a beautiful woman perched on the pile, like a statue on a monument.'[2]

The two novels are alike, finally, in the kinds of literary expression which result from the contrasts which I have briefly described. Comedy exposes and evaluates the difference between 'free' and 'fixed' characters, while melodrama results from the self-assertions of would-be 'free' characters whose ambitions are being thwarted or 'fixed' by forces over which they have no control. But here we come to an important difference between the two novels. The melodrama in *The American* is not satirized at any point, as it continually is in *Roderick Hudson*. This is but one reason why the two novels, despite their many similarities, are quite different in the *kinds* of comedy they include and in the particular emphasis which it is allowed to give to experience.

The comedy in *The American* has very little to do with melodrama, conceived as any theatrically stylized and self-indulgent expression. A character and his way of expressing himself are treated comically because of some representative social characteristic. Even when melodrama does occur in the novel it is treated in

2. *The American* (Boston, 1877), p. 48. Hereafter, the novel will be designated *Am.* James revised Newman's remark only to make it even more extravagant: 'There must be a lovely being perched on the pile like some shining statue crowning some high monument,' in *The American* (London, 1921), p. 43. Subsequent references to this edition will be to *Am.* rev.

the sympathetic way that is reserved in *Roderick Hudson* only for the melodrama of Roderick's death at the end. There, and in *The American* as a whole, melodrama is accepted as a legitimate response to the reality of mystery and evil. In the chapter in which Newman has his final interview with Claire, for example, he gives 'a powerful thump with his clenched fist on his knee,'[3] delivers a 'great rap on the floor with his stick, and a long, grim laugh,'[4] sits 'looking at her with a long inarticulate murmur,' which in the revision becomes a 'wail,'[5] and strikes his heart, declaring that 'what I feel here is a glowing fire!'[6] Such conduct on Roderick's part over the loss of Christina was the object of some of James's and Rowland's wittiest irony, while in *The American* the laughter comes not from the reader or the observer, but from the very character who is being melodramatic. He is laughing 'grimly' at the discovery that reality itself is apparently melodramatic in its ultimate expressions. There is nothing approaching satiric comedy in the presentation of Newman's intensity of feeling.

This deference on the part of James to his hero is, we shall see, fully justified by the dramatic movement of the novel. But it is also a symptom of the most obvious fact about the uses of comedy in *The American*. Whenever we find it, even when it affectionately makes fun of Newman in the early scenes, it is always used to enhance the hero's character or to abuse those who fail to recognize his value. Their failure to do so, however, is made more important as a revelation of the way a fixed social position, rather than personal incapacity, has limited their sensibilities. Individuals as such are not grotesques in this novel. Society, as it is represented by Parisian aristocracy or the demi-monde of Noémie, is the grotesque image in the reflected light of which James sees certain individuals as more or less comic.

Comedy, in *The American* is almost entirely social satire. Unlike *Roderick Hudson*, where the emphasis is explicitly not upon a social or national type but upon an individual personality, *The American* is concerned with the public identity of its characters, their nationality, and their relationship to an historically observable and hierarchical Parisian society. The failure of hope and ambition in *Roderick Hudson* have nothing to do with social status or with one's being an American. Roderick's failure is a failure of character. Newman has no failings, or at least none which accumulate to determine his fate. His defeat is ascribed to the sinister workings of social cultism, not to the limitations of his intelligence. Rather than innocent or unaware, he is, to use James's terms in the Preface,

3. *Am.*, p. 358.
4. *Am.*, p. 361.
5. *Am.*, p. 366. Cf. *Am.* rev., p. 367.
6. *Am.*, p. 363.

'beguiled' and 'betrayed.'[7] It cannot be called a failure of awareness that he refuses to accept the pretensions of the Bellegardes, since in James's comedy there is the evidence that we, too, are to doubt the reality of their superiority. Even his one deficiency is a part of his virtue. Because of the healthiness of his own mind he has none of the imagination which would let him see in the foreground of social manners the decadence and evil which lurks, to his ultimate undoing, in the background. He possesses the high principles of Rowland, but because, as Mr. Dupee observes,[8] he also has the animal spirits of Roderick, along with considerably more strength and confidence of will, he feels, as Rowland never does, an absolute optimism in the effectiveness of his own ambitions.

Newman, therefore, cannot reflect for us, as Rowland could, the subtleties of other people's actions and the complicated moral possibilities behind their manners. As a result, James himself is a very active character in the novel, his satiric voice being in evidence whenever his hero is treated shabbily. It thunders to his defence through the niceties of Parisian social decorum, never more characteristically than during the party given by Madame de Bellegarde to signify Newman's engagement to her daughter:

> M. de Bellegarde then presented his prospective brother-in-law to some twenty other persons of both sexes, selected apparently for their typically august character. In some cases this character was written in a good round hand upon the countenance of the wearer; in others Newman was thankful for such help as his companion's impressively brief intimations contributed to the discovery of it. There were large, majestic men, and small demonstrative men; there were ugly ladies in yellow lace and quaint jewels, and pretty ladies with white shoulders from which jewels and everything else were absent. Every one gave Newman extreme attention, every one smiled, every one was charmed to make his acquaintance, every one looked at him with that soft hardness of good society which puts out its hand but keeps its fingers closed over the coin. If the marquis was going about as a bear-leader, if the fiction of Beauty and the Beast was supposed to have found its companion-piece, the general impression appeared to be that the bear was a very fair imitation of humanity. Newman found his reception among the marquis's friends very 'pleasant'; he could not have said more for it. It was pleasant to be treated with so much explicit politeness; it was pleasant to hear neatly turned civilities, with a flavor of wit, uttered from beneath carefully-shaped mustaches; it was pleasant to see clever Frenchwomen—they all seemed clever—turn their backs to their partners to get a good look at the strange American whom Claire

7. *The Art of the Novel*, p. 22.
8. Dupee, *Henry James*, p. 98. [F. N. Dupee, *Henry James* (New York: William Sloane Associates, 1951)—*Editor*.]

de Cintré was to marry, and reward the object of the exhibition with a charming smile.[9]

Although Newman is himself aware that he is possibly 'behaving like a d——d fool,' he cannot reflect in any way adequate to James's purposes either the insidiousness of manner in this social occasion or the resentments which, from the style of the passage, James himself seems to feel. The word 'pleasant,' as Newman uses it, has none of the sneering bitterness that it accumulates as James repeatedly applies it to subtly inappropriate objects. The tone is strident largely because of the pattern of repetitions, not only of words but of grammatical structure. Thus, in the style itself there is a mocking exaggeration of the way in which the patronizing manners of these people depend upon the reiteration of customary form. James's tone in this brings to mind one of Dr. Sloper's reactions to Lavinia's irony: 'My dear Lavinia, do you call that irony? I call it pugilism.[1] No one in this novel is consistently deputized, as Rowland is in *Roderick Hudson* and Ralph in *The Portrait of a Lady*, to provide a standard in the presence of which obtuseness and oddity are *rendered* comically absurd without our being told about it. As a result, James enters the fray himself, and temporarily sacrifices that detachment and superior uninvolvement which customarily distinguishes his point of view. In comparison with the comedy we find in the other early novels, even when it is openly satiric, the comedy at this point and at others in *The American* is exceptionally crude. James seems to be personally involved, even personally vengeful, and, hovering as he does in this passage on the edge of diatribe, he reveals a conspicuous though momentary failure of the emotional security which Mr. R. G. Soderberg[2] aptly describes as a defining quality of his humour. This leads to the speculation, for which there is considerable evidence, that there is a large element of self-identification in James's treatment of Newman and of his experience in Parisian society.

This is to contradict Miss Cornelia Kelley's remark, which fairly represents the views of critics before and after her, that *The American* 'is not at all autobiographic.'[3] Her notion of the relevance of autobiography to the novel is limited, however, to the verifiable facts about James's life as compared with the fictional facts of Newman's. In such a comparison it is perfectly obvious that Newman is as unlike James as it is possible for him to be. He has made his own fortune in wash-tubs and leather, he has been close to vagrancy, he is not an artist, he is not from a well-to-do family, and

9. *Am.*, pp. 280–1.
1. *Washington Square* (London, 1921), p. 174.
2. R. G. Soderberg, *The Comic Element in Henry James*, unpublished dissertation (Leeds University, England), p. 2.
3. Cornelia Kelley, *The Early Development of Henry James*, p. 238. [(Urbana: University of Illinois Press, 1930)—*Editor*.]

he is very untutored. No one would deny, however, that writers, like other men, often choose to see themselves precisely in those people whose personal histories are most unlike their own. It is part of a commendable human vanity which leads one to feel that people very different from oneself probably suffer from the same hurts or take delight in the same pleasures. So it is that Newman's obvious differences from his creator could make James the more anxious to associate himself with his particular social difficulties in Paris. What is known of James's life in that city before and during the composition of *The American* helps us to understand why his comedy is so actively and personally expended on the side of his hero. In fact, it is possible to observe in James's account of Paris and of French writers some of the explanations not only for the tone of his satire but also for the metaphors which help to characterize the victims and the benefactors of it.

ROYAL A. GETTMANN

Henry James's Revision of *The American*†

The present study aims to compare the first and final editions of *The American* with respect to prose style, characters, and plot and to deduce from the differences and from the Prefaces James's general theory of revision. Since James said that, of all his works, *The American* most needed and most deserved revision,[1] the texts of this novel should provide the best illustration of his practice in revising.[2]

Turning to a comparison of the two texts of *The American:* the notion that the later James was unable or unwilling to ask a plain

† From *American Literature*, 16 (1945), 279–95.

1. Robert Herrick, "A Visit to Henry James," *Yale Review*, XII, 735 (July, 1923). See also the Preface to *The Golden Bowl* in Henry James, *The Art of the Novel* (New York, 1934), p. 344.

I submitted this article before I had seen F. O. Matthiessen's interesting essay on James's revision of *The Portrait of a Lady*. His study, "The Painter's Sponge and Varnish Bottle," *American Bookman*, I, 49–68 (Winter, 1944) is reprinted in his *Henry James: The Major Phase* (New York, 1944).

2. Critical opinion on the nature and the value of James's revisions is divided. Robert Herrick, op. cit., and Miss Hélène Harvitt, *PMLA*, XXXIX, 203–227 (March, 1924), believe that the revised texts are labored, ambiguous, and excessively analytical. But Professor Raymond Havens, *PMLA*, XL, 433 (March, 1925), and Miss Theodora Bosanquet, *Henry James at Work* (2d ed., London, 1927), p. 17, and Pelham Edgar, *Henry James: Man and Author* (London, 1927), pp. 237–241, find that James revised in the interest of clarity and expressiveness. Herrick contends that the changes in *The American* are so radical that the hero has been transmogrified from an ingenuous young man into an old, self-conscious, sophisticated egotist, whereas Miss Bosanquet affirms that James "allowed himself new freedoms" beyond matters of diction and sentence structure.

question or give a direct answer[3] is not borne out by the changes he made in the novel. The alterations in diction constantly move in the direction of the specific, the concrete, and the explicit. James's search for the exact word is illustrated in the following emendation: "Well, I suppose I am happy," said Newman, meditatively" > ". . . said Newman, almost pensively."[4] The overtone of melancholy in *pensively* is precisely calculated to bring out Newman's sense of what he has missed in life. Another example occurs in the description of Newman's state of mind four months after his introduction to Mme de Cintré. He is still under the spell of that lady's eyes, and he wishes to see more of them. James had written: "Throughout these rather formless meditations he sometimes thought of his past life," but he revised to: "But there came to him sometimes too, through this vague rich forecast, the thought of his past life. . . ."[5] The emendation is sound, for Newman was not simply meditating but meditating on the future. In this same passage there is another typical alteration. Originally James wrote of Newman's past years in business: "They seemed far away now, for his present attitude was more than a holiday, it was almost a rupture." In 1907 James changed *rupture* to *repudiation* because he now saw that Newman was not merely breaking with his past but was wilfully renouncing it. On every page there are such emendations as these: "standing in an attitude of general hospitality" > "posture of general hospitality"; "domicile" > "rooms"; "odor of democracy" > "strong smell of democracy": "forgetfulness" > "detachment." Taken in their contexts, these changes show that one of James's intentions in revising was to replace the general word with the exact word.

James also sought to intensify concreteness in the revised *American*—that is, to thicken the sensuous texture of his writing. Sometimes he achieved this by changing nouns, as in the following examples:

1877	1907
. . . innumerable young women in irreproachable toilets . . . (6)	. . . innumerable young women in long aprons, on high stools. . . . (2)
I don't care for pictures. (24)	I don't care for inanimate canvas or for cold marble beauty. . . . (22)

3. See, for example, Edith Wharton's amusing story of how, on an automobile trip, James asked a direction of an old pedestrian and completely befuddled him. Mrs. Wharton came to the rescue with the simple words, "Where is King's Road?" (*A Backward Glance*, New York, 1934, pp. 242–243).

4. 1877, p. 43; 1907, p. 44. [In this note and others "1877" refers to the Boston Osgood edition of 1877 and "1907" to the Scribner "New York Edition" of 1907—*Editor*.]

5. 1877, p. 94; 1907, p. 101.

. . . he had no more wish to hurry her, any more than he would have had the wish to hurry a golden sunrise. (238)	he had no more wish to hurry her than he would have had to hurry the slow flushing of the east at dawn. (271)
I have seen nothing objectionable except my husband leaning against the wall. . . . (283)	. . . except my husband leaning against that adorably faded strawberry damask of the other room. . . . (325)

As the last example indicates, James frequently added modifiers in order to secure concreteness. He constantly pointed up his nouns by inserting adjectives and prepositional phrases, as in the following passages:

1877	1907
. . . a cerulean cravat. . . . (8)	. . . a blue satin necktie of too light a shade. . . . (4)
. . . he is some vulgar wretch. . . . (303)	. . . a big hard breathing red-faced animal (348)
"A duel—that will give me a push!" cried Mademoiselle Noémie, clapping her little hands. (305)	"A meeting and a big noise—that will give me a push!" said Noémie, clapping with a soft thud her little pearl-coloured hands. (350)

Even more noticeable is James's heavy use of adverbial modifiers. Although he was careful in his choice of verbs and adjectives, James felt the need of making each one more precise and concrete, as the following passages show:

1877	1907
His voice, always very mild and interrogative, gradually became as soft and as tenderly argumentative as if he had been talking to a much-loved child. (157)	His voice, always very mild, almost flatly soft and candidly interrogative for such a full organ, had become as edgeless and as tenderly argumentative as if he had been talking to a much-loved child. (171)
. . . while Newman executed his obeisance. (278)	. . . while Newman performed with all his length his liberal obeisance. He always made his bow, as he wrote his name, very distinctly. (319)
"You killed your husband." (429)	"You cruelly killed your helpless husband." (490)

To the same effect there are hundreds of changes such as these: "happier > "distinctly happier"; "oh, we will discuss it, and let you know!" > "Oh, we'll discuss it thoroughly, and we'll promptly let you know"; "turning her face towards him" > "vaguely, rather indirectly, turning her face to him."

James took special pains with the verbs and adverbs in the stage directions of the dialogue. In the original version he had been rather overliberal with such labels as "Newman asked" and "said Mrs. Tristram," even when the words of the dialogue made clear the name of the speaker. Another novelist, say Jane Austen or Hemingway, would have deleted some of these, but James chose to develop them so that the reader is aware of the tone and mood of the speaker. Some typical changes are these: "said Newman" > "his friend soothingly returned"; "observed Newman" > "he calmly pleaded"; "Newman demanded" > "he demanded with an insistence that came easily to him now. At times these changes sink to the level of novelty-hunting. To cite an extreme case: in the first version the villain "asked very softly," whereas in the revision he "inordinately fluted." And the following directions do not label the speaker so much as they call attention to themselves: "she said" > "she sweetly shrilled"; "Newman declared" > "Newman roundly returned"; "said Madame de Cintré" >"she safely enough risked."

The dialogue in the revision is at times more idiomatic than it is in the original. In 1877 James had avoided contractions and colloquialisms, but in 1907 he was more tolerant of them. This is especially true of Newman's speeches, as the following examples will show: "I have been my own master all my life" > "I've skipped about in my shirt all my life"; "Oh, horrors!" >"Oh, shucks!"; "Yes" > "Yes—I'll be hanged if I ain't sure!"; "You are sad, eh?" > "You've got a sentimental stomach-ache, eh?" Such changes hardly bear out the view that James changed Newman from a simple American to a sophisticate, at least so far as his speech is concerned.

The greatest stylistic difference between the two versions of *The American* is the marked increase in figures of speech. It is obvious that in rereading the novel James translated plain statements into metaphors. Many of the figures simply make concrete an abstract noun or a generalized statement. This kind of figure is illustrated in the following passages:

1877	1907
Yes, this seeing of the world was very pleasant, and he would willingly do a little more of it. (93)	Yes, these waters of the free curiosity were very soothing, and he would splash in them till they ran dry. (100)

. . . and it was both uncomfortable and slightly contemptible to feel obliged to square one's self with a standard. (82)	. . . one shouldn't hunt about for a standard as a lost dog hunts for a master. (87)
The old lady greeted Newman with majestic formality, and, looking round her, called several of the persons who were standing near. They were elderly gentlemen, of what Valentin de Bellegarde had designated as the high-nosed category; two or three of them wore cordons and stars. (273)	His hostess greeted him with a fine hard urbanity and, looking round, called to several of the persons standing at hand. They were elderly gentlemen with faces as marked and featured and filled-in, for some science of social topography, as, to Newman's whimsical sense, any of the little towered and battered old towns, on high eminences, that his tour of several countries during the previous summer had shown him; they were adorned with strange insignia, cordons and ribbons and orders, as if the old cities were flying flags and streamers and hanging out shields for a celebration. . . . (313)

Some of the figures are essentially witty. In them James is playing with words and ideas or invoking surprise through the swift incongruity between the two elements in the figure. Of the many instances the following are typical:

1877	1907
. . . he was too short, as he said, to afford a belly. (118)	. . . he was too short a story as he said, to afford an important digression. (129)
The truth is that circumstances had done much to cultivate in Mrs. Tristram a marked tendency to irony. Her taste on many points differed from that of her husband, and though she made frequent concessions it must be confessed that her concessions were not always graceful. They were founded upon a vague project she had of some day doing something	The truth is that cirucumstances had done much to cultivate in Mrs. Tristran the need for any little intellectual luxury she could pick up by the way. Her taste on many points differed from that of her husband; and though she made frequent concessions to the dull small fact that he had married her it must be confessed that her reserves were not always muffled in pink gauze. They were founded upon

very positive, something a trifle passionate. What she meant to do she could by no means have told you; but meanwhile, nevertheless, she was buying a good conscience, by installments. (35)	the vague project of her some day affirming herself in her totality; to which end she was in advance getting herself together, building herself high, enquiring, in short, into her dimensions. (35–36)
The marquis appeared to have decided that the fine arts offered a safe subject of conversation, as not leading to startling personal revelations. . . . His manners seemed to indicate a fine, nervous dread that something disagreeable might happen if the atmosphere were not purified by allusions of a thoroughly superior cast. "What under the sun is the man afraid of?" Newman asked himself. "Does he think I am going to offer to swap jack-knives with him?" It was useless to shut his eyes to the fact that the marquis was profoundly disagreeable to him. (198–199)	The Marquis appeared to have decided that the fine arts offered a safe subject of conversation, as not leading to uncouth personal revelations. . . . his manner seemed to indicate a fine nervous dread that something disagreeable might happen if the atmosphere were not kept clear of stray currents from windows opened at hazard. "What under the sun is he afraid of?" Newman asked himself. "Does he think I'm going to offer to swap jack-knives with him?" It was useless to shut his eyes to the fact that the Marquis was as disagreeable to him as some queer, rare, possibly dangerous biped, perturbingly akin to humanity, in one of the cages of a "show." (219)

Some of the figures in the revision have the qualities of a seventeenth-century conceit: they are compounded of incongruous elements; they are spun out at great length; they create the thought rather than merely illustrate it. They are tools and materials rather than ornaments. In such figures the revised text differs markedly from the original, and the thought is altered, refined, and expanded, as in the following:

1877	1907
He had little of the small change of conversation, and his stock of ready-made formulas and phrases was the scantiest. (217)	He had little of the small change of conversation and rarely rose to reach down one of those ready-made forms and phrases that drape, whether fresh or frayed, the hooks and pegs of the general wardrobe of talk—that repository in which alone so many persons qualify

for the discipline of society, as supernumerary actors prepare, amid a like provision, for the ordeal of the footlights. He was able on the other hand, at need, to make from where he sat one of the long arms that stretch quite out of place—to the effect, as might mostly be felt, of coming back with some proposition as odd as a single shoe. (242)

The foregoing kind of figure will not be approved by all readers and writers. If it is assumed that a figure of speech in narrative prose should lend itself to illustration by way of pencil or brush, the example just quoted will fail the test. But it cannot be said that James was laboriously contriving this figure for the sake of gratuitously decorating an idea that was more clearly and simply expressed in the text of 1877, for the two passages are not identical in meaning. The original makes the simplest kind of statement about Newman as a conversationalist; the revision makes the generalization, then adds a qualification, expands this into a comment upon society and conversation, and concludes with a new note on Newman as a talker.

To summarize: in revising *The American* James freely added modifiers, substituted exact, concrete words for general terms, reworked conventionalized figures of speech, and recast direct statements as figures. Although these changes result in sentences which are longer and more involved than those in the first edition, they do not fundamentally change the meanings: they refine and expand and comment upon the original ideas.

* * *

In revising *The American* James made no essential changes in the characters. Although he underscored a line here and lightened one there, he did not add or erase. In saying this I have in mind the following test question: Do the alterations justify or demand a change in the words one would use to describe a character or his motives or his actions? In every instance I find that no change is required, that at most I merely add the qualification "more" or "less." To cite a simple example: in the original version Newman is thirty-six years old, whereas in the revision he is forty-two and a half. But this difference does not change Newman from a young man to an old one. In both texts James's point is that Newman, after long experience in the workaday world of money-making, had reached the age of reflection. In the 1877 version he began to ask questions at age thirty-five, in the 1907 version at age forty.

James's practice in revising is well illustrated in his treatment of Newman's ingenuous declaration that he will make a great marriage. Early in the novel the American avers:

> "I want to make a great hit. I want to take my pick. My wife must be a magnificent woman. . . . I want a great woman. . . . What else have I toiled and struggled for, all these years? . . . now what am I to do with my success? To make it perfect, as I see it, there must be a beautiful woman perched on the pile, like a statue on a monument. . . . I want to possess, in a word, the best article in the market."[6]

Taken at face value, this declaration is very like what Newman would have called a commercial proposition. It comes dangerously near alienating the sympathy of the reader and jarring his credulity. James, on rereading the novel, was fully aware of the risk involved in Newman's speech, but he decided: "I had to take that over with the rest of him and fit it in."[7] To have changed Newman's attitude or to have canceled this episode would have been something more than revision: it would have called for rewriting. And so James retained Newman's words.

He did, however, make a few changes which slightly reduce Newman's rashness and his confidence in money. For example, he deleted a passage in which the American declares that he will make the lucky woman

> "a very handsome offer. . . . Everything she wishes. If I get hold of a woman that comes up to my standard, I shall think nothing too good for her. . . . To combine the qualities I require seems to be difficult, but when the difficulty is vanquished it deserves a reward."[8]

To the same effect James left off the second clause in the following sentence: "I know the best can't be had for mere money, but I rather think money will do a good deal."[9] James dulled the edge of Newman's self-assurance, which was rather excessive in a character whom the reader was to admire and pity. Thus he deleted a page which ran as follows:

> "I have never thought much about the reasons that make it proper for people to turn up their noses, and so I can only decide the question offhand. Looking at it in that way I can't see anything in it. I simply think, if you want to know, that I'm as good as the best. . . . To tell the truth, I have always had a rather good opinion of myself; a man who is successful can't help it."[1]

6. 1877, pp. 47–48; 1907, p. 49.
7. *The Art of the Novel,* p. 39.
8. 1877, p. 145.
9. 1877, p. 34; 1907, p. 33.
1. 1877, pp. 146–147.

In Newman's proposal of marriage James also moderated the American's strictures on the class system of Europe, but in that same speech Newman still declares: "I can assure you there's quite enough of me to last. . . ."[2]

In Herrick's opinion James distorted Newman by changing him from a blunt, simple American to an old egotist, too self-conscious and sophisticated to be attractive. As a matter of fact, the original Newman was by no means obtuse. Although he was short on information and had little capacity for systematic, abstract thinking, he was a man of imagination. In 1907 James made slight changes in two of Newman's remarks about himself:

1877	1907
"I am not intellectual." (43)	"I don't come up to my own standard of culture." (45)
"I am a highly civilized man." (44)	"I have the instincts—have them deeply—if I haven't the forms of a high civilization." (45)

The revised statements, it seems to me, do justice to Newman as James originally conceived him.

James, then, did not make his hero more intelligent and sensitive;[3] he only rendered more clearly the intelligence and sensibility which were implicit in the deeds and words of Newman in the 1877 version. This kind of change is illustrated in the following passage, which gives Newman's response to Valentin's question whether he was interested in religion:

1877	1907
"Not particularly. Are you a Roman Catholic, madam?" And her turned to Madame de Cintré. (108)	Newman thought. "Not actively." He found himself speaking as if it were a railroad or a mine; so that the next moment, to correct this, "Are you a Roman Catholic, madam?" he inquired of Madame de Cintré. (117–118)

Again, when the Marquis too coolly and politely asks Newman whether he is traveling for pleasure, the American's state of mind is made clear in the revision:

2. 1907, p. 169.
3. The only change in this direction is that Newman now takes with him on his tour of the Continent six volumes of Ruskin (1907, p. 103).

1877	1907
"Oh, I am knocking about to pick up one thing and another. Of course I get a good deal of pleasure out of it." (174)	"Well, I'm visiting your country sir," Newman replied with a certain conscious patience—a patience he felt he on his side too could push, should need be, to stiffness; "and I confess I'm having a good time in it. Of course I get a good deal of pleasure out of it." (189)

There are many passages in the revision in which Newman exhibits an awareness of the attitudes and motives of others. For example, he asks Mme de Cintré whether she has been worried by the fear of annoying her mother and brother. In the original James merely gave Mme de Cintré's answer, whereas in the revision he supplies Newman's response to her words:

1877	1907
"I had undertaken more than I could carry out. I have very little courage; I am not a heroine." (197)	"I had undertaken more than I could carry out. I've very little courage; I'm not a heroine." She said this, he could feel, to be very true with him; and it touched him as if she had pressed into his hand, for reminder, some note she had scrawled or some ribbon or ring she had worn. (218)

And James goes one step further: he makes Newman aware of others' awareness of his attitudes and motives. This interplay of consciousness is typically illustrated in the following passages:

1877	1907
She was a woman for the light, not for the shade; and her natural line was not picturesque reserve and mysterious melancholy, but frank, joyous, brilliant action, with just so much meditation as was necessary, and not a grain more. To this, apparently, he had succeeded in bringing her back. He felt, himself, that he was an antidote to oppressive secrets; what he offered her	She was a creature for the sun and the air, for no sort of hereditary shade or equivocal gloom; and her natural line was neither imposed reserve nor mysterious melancholy, but positive life, the life of the great world—his great world—not the *grand monde* as there understood if he wasn't mistaken, which seemed squeezable into a couple of rooms of that inconvenient and ill-warmed house: all with

was, in fact, above all things a vast, sunny immunity from the need of having any.

(218)

nothing worse to brood about, when necessary, than the mystery perhaps of the happiness that would so queerly have come to her. To some perception of his view and his judgement, and of the patience with which he was prepared to insist on them, he fondly believed himself to be day by day bringing her round. She mightn't, she couldn't yet, no doubt, wholly fall in with them, but she saw, he made out, that he had built a bridge which would bear the very greatest weight she should throw on it, and it was for him often, all charmingly, as if she were admiring from this side and that the bold span of arch and the high line of the parapet—as if indeed on occasion she stood straight there at the spring, just watching him at *his* extremity and with nothing, when the hour should strike, to prevent her crossing with a rush.

(244–245)

These passages, which might be multiplied many times over,[4] show the extensive alterations that James made in the expository and narrative parts of *The American*. The revisions do not, however, change the character of Newman. At most they emphasize a motive or mood already present in the first version or supply the state of mind for the actions and speeches. And the crucial dramatic passages—e.g., Newman's pronouncement about a great marriage, his proposal, his interviews with the de Bellegardes—all these remain essentially unchanged. Here we find, I think, the key to James's theory of revision. He looked upon Newman as a conscientious biographer looks upon his subject: he had no right to change in 1907 what Newman said and did in 1877, but he could speculate about the states of mind back of those deeds and words. This is what James must have meant when, after freely acknowledging the weaknesses in *The American*, he concluded ". . . clinging to my hero as to a tall, protective, good-natured elder brother in

4. See, for example, the interview between Newman and Mrs. Bread (1877, pp. 224–226; 1907, pp. 254–256) and the love scene (1877, p. 239; 1907, p. 272).

a rough place, I leave the record to stand or fall by his more or less convincing image."[5]

The same thing is true of the other characters in the novel. Rereading in 1907, James saw that the most serious defect in *The American* was the conduct of the Marquise and her older son. He now felt that in actual life the "house of de Bellegarde . . . would . . . have comported itself in a manner as different as possible from the manner to which my narrative commits it."[6] Instead of holding aristocratically aloof from Newman, they would have squeezed him for every possible dollar. James also saw that the Marquise's murder of her husband was insufficiently accounted for. The whole conduct of the de Bellegardes, he admitted, was "much more showy . . . than sound."[7] Yet they remain the same in the 1907 version. If there is a shift, it is to make them even more heartless and corrupt. Thus in the original, when Newman first met the Marquise, he "walked up to the old lady by the fire and shook hands with her," but in the revision he "came sufficiently near to the old lady by the fire to take in that she would offer him no handshake."[8] In the revised scene in which the de Bellegardes break with Newman, the latter speaks and thinks of the mother in such terms as *hag, odious,* and *offensive,* stronger words than he used in 1877.[9]

The motive behind the de Bellegardes' rejection of Newman is the same in both versions—namely, they cannot reconcile themselves to "a commercial person." But the motivation of the murder is perhaps changed. The circumstances of the crime are as follows: the Marquis and his wife did not get on well, and he "admired pretty women." When the daughter, Claire, reached eighteen, the mother insisted upon her marrying de Cintré, an odious man of fifty-five. The father objected, violently quarreled with his wife, and took to bed, never to rise again. The mother's reasons for making the match were de Cintré's willingness to take a small settlement and his high social position. But in the revised version James may have added another and a darker motive. I say *may* because I am uncertain as to the meaning of an inserted statement, which I italicize, in the paper which the old Marquis wrote on his deathbed:

> My wife has tried to kill me and has done it; I'm horribly, helplessly dying. It's in order to marry my beloved daughter to M. de Cintré *and then go on herself all the same*. With all my soul I protest—I forbid it. I'm not insane—ask the doctors, ask Mrs. B. It was alone with me here to-night; she attacked me and put me to death. It's murder if murder ever was. Ask the doctors, tell everyone, show everyone this.[1]

5. *The Art of the Novel,* p. 39.
6. Ibid., p. 35.
7. Ibid.
8. 1977, p. 167; 1907, p. 181.
9. 1877, pp. 323–327; 1907, pp. 372–376.
1. 1877, p. 406; 1907, p. 464.

If *go on herself all the same* means that the Marquise was involved in an adulterous relation with de Cintré, then James has added a stronger motive for the murder. This interpretation finds some support in one other emendation which James made in Mrs. Bread's review of the murder:

1877	1907
"My lady had long ago got over her jealousy, and she had taken to indifference." (392)	"My lady had long ago got over 'minding'—minding, I mean, the worst; for she had had plenty of assistance for throwing things off." (447)

The phrase, *plenty of assistance*, may mean that the Marquise sought consolation in extramarital relations. But even if we accept this reading, it motivates only the murder; it does not affect the de Bellegardes' rejection of Newman. In short, James left the de Bellegardes just about as they were in 1877 even though he saw that their conduct was an "affront to verisimilitude." He might have changed them, but then, he explained, the situation and subject "wouldn't have been the theme of *The American* as the book stands, the theme to which I was from so early pledged."[2]

James did, however, slightly change the younger son, Valentin—to be more exact, he emphasized the warmth and intimacy of the attachment between Valentin and Newman. In the original version the two men immediately responded to each other, but James, by many small strokes, strengthened the relation to one of deep affection. Thus, Valentin addresses the American not "with almost impudent frankness" but with "confidence and candour."[3] Instead of merely liking something about the young Frenchman, Newman now suddenly yearns to know him. The heightened sympathy between the two men is also shown in the following passage, in which Valentin responds to Newman's statement that he never quarrels:

1877	1907
"Never? Sometimes it's a duty—or at least it's a pleasure." (122)	"You mean you just shoot? Well, I notify you that *till* I'm shot, I shall have had a greater sense of safety with you than I have perhaps ever known in any relation of life." (133)

In the scene in which Newman informs Valentin of his intention to court Claire de Cintré, James modifies the Frenchman's amusement

2. *The Art of the Novel*, p. 36.

3. 1877, p. 118; 1907, p. 128.

by leaving out a half page, one of the longer deletions in the revision.[4] And one of Newman's speeches at Valentin's deathbed is changed so that it comes more from the heart.[5]

One important character remains to be considered—Mme de Cintré. She is untouched by the revision despite James's recognition in 1907 that she was too sketchily treated to win the belief of the reader, that in her case he had laid "too light a plank . . . over a 'dark' psychological abyss."[6] But to have thrown more light upon her would have blurred the focus on Newman; and this was a price that James did not wish to pay.

The changes which James made in *The American* square exactly with his general statements on the subject of revision. Looking back on his preparation of the New York edition, James said that before he began work he had mistakenly identified revision with rewriting, whereas in the actual event they had "almost nothing in common."[7] He soon distinguished between them, for to a correspondent who objected to his revising *Roderick Hudson* he replied: ". . . to attempt to retouch the *substance* of the thing would be as foolish as it would be (in a *done* and impenetrable structure) impracticable. What I have tried for is a mere revision of surface and expression. . . ."[8] Revision, then, might be ever so thorough, but it was fundamentally different from rewriting.

James did not clearly define the latter. Even in his last word on the subject he said: "What re-writing might be was to remain—it has remained for me to this hour—a mystery."[9] But one may suppose that it involved such things as these: compressing or extending the time covered in a novel; omitting, adding, or redisposing episodes; altering the situation which sets the plot in motion; changing the forces which bring about the resolution; omitting or adding characters or changing their traits and motives. As we have seen, James did none of these in what he said was his most thorough revision, that of *The American*.

But this does not mean that James regarded revision as a superficial matter. On the contrary, he thought it required the fullest use of the imagination. In his first Preface he declared that to revise was "to live back into a forgotten state, into convictions . . . credulities . . . reasons of things . . . old motives."[1] And in his final Preface he repeatedly stressed "renewal of vision," retracing of footsteps, the "process of re-dreaming," and the thrill of discovering that "the 'old' matter is there, re-accepted, re-tasted, exquisitely re-assimilated and re-enjoyed, believed in, to be brief, with the same

4. 1877, p. 148; 1907, p. 162.
5. 1877, pp. 343–344; 1907, p. 394.
6. *The Art of the Novel*, p. 39.
7. Ibid., p. 339.
8. *The Letters of Henry James* (New York, 1920), II, 55.
9. *The Art of the Novel*, p. 339.
1. Ibid., p. 11.

'old' grateful faith. . . ."[2] When James was unable to rekindle the original, creative glow of a novel, he simply excluded it from the New York edition. Thus he said that he was unable "to read over *Washington Square*. . . . it must go."[3] He could not revise the book, and he did not believe in rewriting.

But if James could reread an early work, if the "germ" was still swollen with values, if the "predicament" raised moral problems and rendered human sensibilities, if the central character had an inner validity—then James could revise. In the Preface to *Roderick Hudson* he compared himself to a painter who places one of his old works on an easel. With a moist sponge he cleans up the picture. If the "canvas does obscurely flush," the painter at once uses his brush and varnish bottle. The sponge reveals the old subject matter only if the artist is able to "live back . . . the old relation," and the varnish brings out more clearly and makes more durable the original values. Revision was active, sympathetic rereading in the light of a quarter-century of study of and practice in the art of fiction. During that time James had experienced the growth of an "immense array of terms, perceptional and expressional";[4] and as he reread in 1906–07, these terms "simply looked over the heads" of those he had set down on his page in 1877. Revision consisted of accepting those terms, of redirecting the original values in a "myriad more adequate channels." The alterations were not determined by any set theory. James was unable to "forecast these chances and changes and proportions,"[5] nor was he, after the event, able to draw up a general rule. "The term that superlatively, that finally 'renders,' is a flower that blooms by a beautiful law of its own (the fiftieth part of a second often so sufficing it) . . . it is *there* already, at any moment, almost before one can either miss or suspect it."[6]

It is wrong, then, to assume that James the Reviser mercilessly manhandled the works of James the First. As a matter of fact, he regarded his novels as independent creations, as having an existence of their own. He respected them just as a scrupulous biographer or historian respects actual people and historical events. Newman did not come to James's mind as a list of analyzed, excogitated motives and qualities; he appeared spontaneously as a self-contained, independent person who had to be treated as a unity. He could not be revised by simply adding or subtracting a trait or reversing an action. To have made such changes would, in James's view, have been the equivalent of a biographer's staying the execution of Louis XVI or a historian's tampering with the Battle of Waterloo.

2. Ibid., pp. 339–340.
3. Herrick, op. cit., p. 736.
4. *The Art of the Novel*, p. 339.
5. Ibid., p. 342.
6. Ibid.

With respect to revision James took a position midway between that of, say Charles Reade and that of George Moore. Reade was indignant about *Blackwood's* editorial pressure on *The Woman Hater* when it appeared as a serial, but when he issued the novel in book form he used the serial text with only four inconsequential changes in phrasing. James would have called that irresponsible republication. Moore, on the other hand, completely rewrote *A Modern Lover*. James would have called that irresponsible re-writing.

LEON EDEL

[The Revised Ending of the Play] †

The "honorable" run of *The American* was not of sufficient duration to establish Edward Compton as a London manager. He gave up the Opera Comique and returned to the provinces, and for two decades he continued to be a part of the British tributary theatre, keeping alive a repertory of half a hundred plays and presenting them in all corners of the United Kingdom. He retained *The American* in this repertory but complained to James that the last act, one of unmitigated gloom—Valentin dead, Claire bound for a convent—was out of harmony with the rest of the play. "He has now played it every Friday for several months and had time to feel country audiences," Henry James wrote to William almost a year after the end of the London run. The audiences were "*very* friendly indeed up to the end of the 3rd" but they drooped over the fourth.

During the autumn of 1892 James wrote a new fourth act "in a comedy-sense—heaven forgive me" and took it to Bath on November 14, where the Compton Comedy Company was playing. "So the 4th is now *another* 4th," he announced to William, "which will basely gratify their artless instincts and British thick-wittedness and thanks to it the poor old play will completely save one's honor (which is all I care for) as a permanent and regular thing. It will be much for it to 'keep the stage.' The Comptons are delighted with the new Act (a feat of unspeakable difficulty) and it is played for the first time at Bristol next week (without of course the smallest reference to any change. Please never *make* any.)"

Apparently the Comptons were not as secretive. The *Bristol Times and Mirror* for November 26, 1892 announced that the new

† From *The Complete Plays of Henry James*, ed. Leon Edel (Philadelphia: J. B. Lippincott, 1949), pp. 241–52.

act had won a "distinctly favorable" verdict of a large and enthusiastic audience." The review went on:

> . . . the curtain falls on a fine climax in the third act and Mr. James is to be congratulated on a decided hit. In the fourth act, which he has entirely rewritten, he has strengthened his play considerably. He makes the pretty flirt, Noémie bring about a reconciliation between Lord Deepmere and his antagonist Comte Valentin; and this in the most natural way possible. Though why on earth he should introduce Mrs. Bread to tell again the story of the skeleton in the Bellegarde cupboard it is difficult to imagine. Everyone knows all about it, and a valuable ten minutes of theatrical lifetime might be well spared both to actors and audience.

One advantage of the new act not noted in the press was that there was no scenic change now for Act III to Act IV—a considerable aid to production on the road.

A typescript of the new fourth act—here printed for the first time—with some of the pages missing, was found among James's papers. It is impossible to say whether this was the definitive form of the act or a draft for the version James gave to Compton.

Fragment of New Fourth Act for The American

Same scene as Act Third. On the rise of the Curtain enter rapidly, busily, the DOCTOR, *centre. Feeling in his pocket for a pencil, and looking about for paper, he goes, right, to the table, on which he sees a portfolio and on which his hat has already been placed. He takes a bit of paper from the portfolio and, standing and bending over, hastily writes. Enter* NOÉMIE, *in her hat and jacket, left, with several unopened letters in her hand.*

DOCTOR [*folding the small paper and giving it to* NOÉMIE] Something to be *sent* for—for the *nurse*.

NOÉMIE [*who has laid down her letters, anxious*] Isn't the Count *better?*

DOCTOR [*taking his hat*] I can't *say!*

NOÉMIE [*disappointed*] But I thought this morning was to *show!*

DOCTOR. I promised nothing, Mademoiselle. It was a necessary experiment.

NOÉMIE. But surely it has *succeeded!*

DOCTOR. It *may* succeed. It's too soon to *judge*.

NOÉMIE [*at right, persistent*] When *can* you judge?

DOCTOR [*at left, hesitating, looking at his watch*] He's quiet—I shall come back at *one*. [Exit DOCTOR, *left*.]

NOÉMIE [*at centre, unfolding the small paper he has given her;*

with, while she looks at it, uplighted eyebrows and a slight grimace of anxiety] I must *send.* [*Then gathering up the letters she has laid down and reading from the postmarks on the envelopes.*] New York, Boston, Chicago, London, Rome, Bombay! [*While she speaks the last word enter* NEWMAN, *centre: perceptibly altered, paler, worn and worried. She turns eagerly as she hears him.*] Is he *quiet?*

NEWMAN [*with a manner different from hitherto—rather curt, preoccupied and impatient*] As quiet as if he'd *money* on it. Are those my *letters?*

NOÉMIE [*giving him the letters*] I just brought them *in.*

NEWMAN [*looking rapidly at the successive envelopes, then, with impatient disappointment, chucking them toward the table, so that they fall and lie scattered on the floor*] You might as well have brought a row of pins!—They ain't what I *want!*

NOÉMIE [*after an instant, reassuringly*] What you want will *come,* Mr. Newman. [*Then with intenser decision*] I *know* it will come!

NEWMAN. You talk, Miss Noémie, as if you had a private *wire!*

NOÉMIE [*precipitately*] Well, I *have!* [*Then catching herself up*] I know more than you *think.*

NEWMAN [*turning away, on* his *side, restlessly, with irritation, an eclipse of his old geniality*] "Think"?—I've ceased to think. I've ceased to almost to *feel.*

NOÉMIE [*taking the risk, as he goes nervously, vaguely up, as if wandering and looking about him for something that hasn't come to pass, that still doesn't appear*] You may be sure that *she* hasn't! She'll take pity on you *yet!*

NEWMAN [*struck, then facing her abruptly*] Whom are you *talking* about?

NOÉMIE [*slightly disconcerted by his manner and explaining*] I thought you alluded—to a certain lady!

NEWMAN [*with strong emphasis*] I *never* allude—to a certain lady!

NOÉMIE [*apologetic*] I was misled by your eagerness for [*vague*] some communication.

NEWMAN. The communication I'm eager for is a communication—"answer paid"!

NOÉMIE. There's a quarter, no doubt, from which you're *not* expecting news. But [*after an instant*] I daresay you'll have some, all the *same!*

NEWMAN. I won't have any if I can *help* it! I've had about enough to *last* me!

NOÉMIE. Of course I'm thinking of some *better* news!

NEWMAN [*with a certain irritation*] You think too much, Miss Noémie. [*Knocking over, with his restless motion, and with some violence, a jar, or some object on the table.*] You had better imitate my *repose!*

NOÉMIE [*laughing*] Your repose is bad for the furniture.

NEWMAN. Oh, if I should *really* lie down I guess you'd have to *renew* it! [*Then with a quick revulsion, penitent, with his hand out*] Forgive my cussedness! There are moments when I don't know what to *do* with myself!

NOÉMIE [*with sympathy, taking his hand*] You're awfully *worried!*

NEWMAN [*admitting, explaining*] About the results of the Count's operation. We hoped for an unmistakeable effect.

NOÉMIE. Which doesn't take *place?*

NEWMAN. It's a bad moment to *pass.* I can see the surgeon's *uneasy.*

NOÉMIE. And the *others*—who were *present?*

NEWMAN. If we're not reassured by this afternoon, they're to meet *again.*

NOÉMIE. And if the operation's a *failure*—

NEWMAN [*interrupting, sombre, raising his arms and letting them fall*] The *worst* may happen!

NOÉMIE [*with feeling, with resolution*] The worst shan't happen! His natural strength's immense!

NEWMAN [*considering, agreeing*] Yes, greater, even now, than *mine! I can't* recuperate!

NOÉMIE [*smiling at him, soothingly*] You want a *nurse!*

NEWMAN. I want about *fifty!*

NOÉMIE If the effect you speak of, for the Count, *does* take place—

NEWMAN [*interrupting*] He'll come up in an hour!

NOÉMIE [*with surprise*] In an *hour?*

NEWMAN [*confident*] In a *minute*—in a *day,* in a *week!* [*With a bitter smile.*] Oh, faster than *I!*

NOÉMIE [*with recurring intention and significance*] Oh, *you,* Mr. Newman—!

NEWMAN [*impatient, weary, interrupting*] Don't speak of *me*—I ain't sure I'm *alive!*

NOÉMIE [*with spirit*] Well, some other people are, thank heaven, and *while* there's life, in any quarter, I've always heard there's *hope!* [*Then, as* NEWMAN, *fidgetty, moves away again with a gesture of nervous pessimism*] We must *pray* for the Count!

NEWMAN. You *can't* pray. [*Then, in a more explanatory tone, as he turns back to* NOÉMIE *again*] I've a *double* anxiety, and a deadly *impatience.* The letter I'm looking for is a letter from *Mrs. Bread.*

NOÉMIE [*struck*] Their English housekeeper?

NEWMAN. The plain Wiltshire woman! I wrote to her three days ago—I begged her to *come* to me.

NOÉMIE [*thinking, suggesting*] Perhaps your letter never *reached* her.

NEWMAN. To their country home. That's where they've *gone.*

NOÉMIE [*wondering again*] You asked her to come up to Paris?

NEWMAN. To render me a service.

NOÉMIE [*after an instant*] What service can *she* render you?

NEWMAN [*at the centre door*] That's just what I want to *see!* [*Exit* NEWMAN, *centre.*]

NOÉMIE [*alone, picking up the fallen letters and putting them into her pocket while she repeats his words*] "A double anxiety—a deadly impatience"? And what are *mine*, I should like to know? [*Eagerly, seeing* NIOCHE *at the left. Enter* NIOCHE, *left.*] Who *is* it?

NIOCHE [*announcing*] *Milord Deepmere!* [*Enter* LORD DEEPMERE, *with his arm in a sling, left.*]

NOÉMIE [*with relief, as he takes her hand and raises it respectfully to his lips.*] At *last!*

NIOCHE [*to* NOÉMIE] Shall I inform Mr. Newman?

NOÉMIE [*giving him the little folded paper left by the* DOCTOR *and which she has kept in her hand during the scene with* NEWMAN] No—you'll go out for *this*. [*Exit* NIOCHE, *who has taken the paper obediently, left; on which* NOÉMIE *goes on, warningly, to* DEEPMERE] Be very *quiet*—we've reached the *crisis*.

DEEPMERE [*disappointed, anxious*] Isn't he *better?*

NOÉMIE. We shall know at noon. [*Then pressingly*] Have you been to the *Convent?*

DEEPMERE. I've just *left* it. She'll *come!*

NOÉMIE. *A la bonne heure!* You followed my *instructions?*

DEEPMERE. To the *letter!* I left your note yesterday, with my own card, on which I wrote a few words. This morning I had a gracious line from her asking to see me at an early hour.

NOÉMIE. And she *did* see you?

DEEPMERE. In the parlour, for five minutes. She's free, a *pensionnaire*, she can receive.

NOÉMIE. She has taken no vow?

DEEPMERE. Not so *soon*—in three *weeks!* She has only taken *refuge*—she has only been *waiting*.

NOÉMIE. For Mr. Newman to try *again?*

DEEPMERE. For her brother to come back to *life!* She has a passionate desire to *see* him.

NOÉMIE. Then why hasn't she come before?

DEEPMERE. How could she enter the house of the man she feels she has terribly *injured?*

NOÉMIE. I hope that if she's coming now it isn't because she has *ceased* to feel it.

DEEPMERE. It's because you've appealed to her for poor Bellegarde, from whom it's only her dread of *meeting* Mr. Newman that has separated her.

NOÉMIE [*thinking*] Does she count on me, by chance, to arrange that she shall *not* meet Mr. Newman?

DEEPMERE. She didn't tell me so, but she rather let me see it.

NOÉMIE [*with decision*] Then she let you see a great piece of *nonsense!* I've a perfect little plan that the poor things *shall* meet!

DEEPMERE. Your little plans are no business of mine. I performed your errand to render you the service you required, and you may imagine the *courage*—you must do justice to the *heroism*, I needed, to present myself before her while [*with an expression of strong feeling, of repentant bitterness, and a significant nod toward the other room*] her brother lies there in such a state!

NOÉMIE. I rendered *you* a service, rather, by putting it in your power to entreat her to *forgive* you!

DEEPMERE. How *will* she forgive me—if Bellegarde doesn't pull through?

NOÉMIE [*after an instant*] I don't know how *she* will, Milord—but I know very well that *I* won't!

DEEPMERE [*nervously, gloomily*] I worry myself half to *death,* I'm sick and sore with *suspense!*

NOÉMIE. You have your *alleviations,* Milord—your frequent visits to this house.

DEEPMERE. I come to *ask*—I come to *watch*; but it's *not* an alleviation—for you only torment me *more!*

NOÉMIE. Mr. Newman makes it *up* to you—he makes everything up to *everyone!*

DEEPMERE. He's as kind as he's *queer*—I never did him justice. But what comfort is there in a man who's in still worse spirits than myself?

NOÉMIE. He *is,* to-day, I admit. Therefore you had better not *see* him.

DEEPMERE. I don't *want* to see him. When there's a bad report of Bellegarde I don't want to look any one in the *face!*

NOÉMIE [*minimising*] There isn't exactly a *bad* report.

DEEPMERE [*objecting*] But if there isn't exactly a *good* one—? The only good one will be to see him standing *there!*

NOÉMIE [*after another instant*] Well, Milord—you *shall* see him!

DEEPMERE [*incredulous, with a backward nod of his head*] If you could only have a little plan for *that!*

NOÉMIE. I *have* a little plan! I'm wiser than the doctors. *Leave* it to me!

DEEPMERE. I don't know what you mean, but I'm ready to say *this* to you—that if he gets *well*— [*pausing, hesitating.*]

NOÉMIE. [*waiting*] If he gets well?

DEEPMERE [*continuing*] By any intervention of *yours,* there's nothing on *earth* you may ask of me that I won't gladly *give* you!

NOÉMIE. Thank you, Milord. As a general thing I don't *have* to "ask"!

DEEPMERE. Don't you sometimes have to *choose?*

NOÉMIE [*after a moment*] Do I understand that in the event you speak of I *may?*

DEEPMERE [*emphatically*] *Anything* that's mine!

NOÉMIE [*after another instant, looking at him*] I'll *choose!*—Now leave me to receive the Countess! [*Seeing* NIOCHE, *left*] My father will show you out.

Re-enter NIOCHE, *left with a small packet.*

NIOCHE [*with the packet, to* NOÉMIE] I give it to the nurse?

DEEPMERE [*to* NIOCHE, *on a motion of assent from* NOÉMIE] Don't mind me! [NIOCHE *bows and exits with packet at centre, and*

DEEPMERE *goes up, to* NOÉMIE.] You must really let me come *back!*

NOÉMIE [*looking at him an instant*] Did you *mean* what you said just now?

DEEPMERE. Did you mean what *you* said?

NOÉMIE [*with a nod of decision*] I *meant* it!

DEEPMERE. Well—*I* meant it!

NOÉMIE. Then shake hands—*à l'anglaise!* [*He gives her his hand and she gives it a vigorous "British" shake, up and down.*] Come back at *one*.

DEEPMERE. At one! [*Exit* LORD DEEPMERE, *left. Re-enter* NIOCHE, *centre.*]

NOÉMIE. What does she say?

NIOCHE [*with his finger to his lips*] Shshsh!

NOÉMIE [*imitating him*] "Shshsh" indeed! We've got hold of the *Countess!*

NIOCHE [*astonished*] Got *hold* of her?

NOÉMIE. She's coming at any moment.

NIOCHE [*bewildered*] Then what shall we do with Mr. Newman!

NOÉMIE. Get hold of *him!*

NIOCHE [*alarmed*] But think of the possible consequences of their meeting!

NOÉMIE. They're just what I *have* thought of! I shall bring them together, and you must *help* me.

NIOCHE. What shall I *do?*

NOÉMIE. See that she comes straight in *here*.

NIOCHE [*troubled, incredulous*] If he knows she's in here he'll go *out!*

NOÉMIE. I'll keep him at home! [*Seeing* NEWMAN, *centre.*] Here he *is*—watch for *her!*

Re-enter NEWMAN, *centre. Exit* NIOCHE, *left.*

[Four pages of the manuscript are missing at this point.]

. . . *his hand into* NEWMAN'S *arm—exeunt* NEWMAN *and* DOCTOR, *centre. Re-enter* NIOCHE, left.]

NIOCHE [*announcing*] Madame la Comtesse de Cintré.

NOÉMIE [*to herself, with happy emotion*] Ah!

Enter, left, MADAME DE CINTRÉ. *Exit* NIOCHE, *discreetly, left.*]

NOÉMIE [*curtseying very respectfully*] *Madame!*

CLAIRE [*graciously, but very gravely*] Mademoiselle.—Let me acknowledge instantly my great obligation to you; but let me also say that I have presumed to find in your intervention a pledge that the step I am taking in response to it shall be attended with inconvenience—to *no* one.—May I see my brother *instantly?*

NOÉMIE. You must allow me to prepare him for your visit.

CLAIRE [*surprised*] He doesn't *expect* me?

NOÉMIE [*smiling*] We don't let him *expect!*

CLAIRE [*anxious*] He's very *weak*, then—he's *worse?*

NOÉMIE. He'll be better when he has seen you!

CLAIRE [*nervous*] I shall be very brief.

NOÉMIE. So shall I, Madame. [*Then, indicating a chair.*] Be so good, meanwhile, as to be seated.

CLAIRE [*uneasy, standing, looking round the room and recognising it*] Is there no place in the house in which my intrusion will be less apparent than *here?*

NOÉMIE [*smiling*] Trust me, Madame, to have measured your risk and to have your interests at *heart!*

CLAIRE. It's only because I trust you that I'm here. Shall I see you again before I leave the house?

NOÉMIE. That will depend, Madame, on your own inclination.

CLAIRE. Let me make sure, at any rate, of this opportunity of thanking you for the kindness Lord Deepmere informs me you have shown my brother. [*Hesitating, then with suppressed emotion, a kind of painful effort.*] And if there have been *other* ministrations—and *other* charities—[*Hesitating again with her emotion, pausing.*]

NOÉMIE [*at right, seeing* NEWMAN, *centre*] I've done what I *could*, Madame!

Re-enter NEWMAN, *centre.*

CLAIRE [*at left, violently struck, to herself*] Ah! [*Exit* NOÉMIE, *rapidly, discreetly, by the staircase. Arrested, at centre, violently, on his side, a moment, by the sight of* MADAME DE CINTRÉ, *then controlling himself with a strong effort,* NEWMAN *comes down on right. They stand an instant on opposite sides of the stage, not looking at each other. At last, sadly, coldly, but without anger,* CLAIRE *exclaims*] The work of that young lady!

NEWMAN [*after an instant, looking straight before him*] That young lady *means* well!

CLAIRE. I hesitated half the night—but I've *come!*

NEWMAN. I know what it's for. It must have seemed to you hard you *shouldn't!*

CLAIRE. It seemed *impossible!* But I never *dreamed*—of disturbing you. [NEWMAN *looks at her, at this, and there is another silence between them while she stands, motionless and expressionless, with her eyes on the ground*] Mayn't I go to him?

NEWMAN. I must say a word to him *first.*

CLAIRE [*after an instant, as* NEWMAN *doesn't move*] I hoped he might *know.*

NEWMAN. I haven't told him.

CLAIRE [*struck, vague*] You *knew* then I was coming?

NEWMAN. I learned it five minutes ago. If I had done so sooner I would have kept out of your way.

CLAIRE [*as impersonally as possible*] Let me get out of yours. [*Then, after another instant, as he still doesn't move.*] But before I do so, let me express in one word—[*Pausing, faltering in her effort to efface all emotion, to be utterly passionless.*]

NEWMAN [*with a sudden faint hope*] In one word?

CLAIRE [*as if to say all she means, but at the same time to check him by her manner—to make any outbreak impossible*] The intensity of my gratitude.

NEWMAN [*after standing an instant with his eyes on the ground suddenly shaken by irresistible feeling and breaking out into a single abrupt cry of passionate appeal*] Claire!

CLAIRE [*straightening herself and speaking with rapid and colourless formality*] Be so very good as to *tell* him! [NEWMAN, *who has instantly, at the sight of her manner, controlled himself again, stands one instant more and gives her one long, fixed and intensely searching look. Then, as if satisfied afresh that he has indeed lost her forever and that nothing more can pass between them, he decides, gives a gesture in which he seems to dash away the last shadow of his hope, and goes out rapidly at centre.* MME. DE CINTRÉ, *left alone, sinks slowly, and as if with the sense of momentary liberation from the worst distress, into the nearest chair, where she sits an instant staring, with infinite sadness, before her. Then slowly, dolorously, hopelessly.*] Ah, miserable *me!*

Re-enter, left, NIOCHE, *at the sound of whose entrance* MME. DE CINTRÉ *quickly springs up.*

NIOCHE [*announcing*] Mrs. Bread!

Enter MRS. BREAD, *while* NIOCHE, *always on tiptoe, retires. Exit* NIOCHE, *left.*

CLAIRE [*startled at the sight of* MRS. BREAD] *You?*

MRS. BREAD [*equally startled on her own side*] Have you come *back* to him?

CLAIRE [*with a sharp, clear gesture of negation, then, as if to explain everything*] Valentin's very *ill!*

MRS. BREAD [*surprised*] He told me he was *better!*

CLAIRE [*vague*] *Who* told you?

MRS. BREAD. Mr. Newman—he *wrote* to me.

CLAIRE [*still more surprised, wondering*] To come to Valentin?

MRS. BREAD. To come to *him.*

CLAIRE [*struck, wondering*] To *him?* For what purpose?

MRS. BREAD. To answer some questions.

CLAIRE [*after an instant, mystified, with dawning anxiety*] *What* questions?

MRS. BREAD. That's what I came up to find out. [MME. DE CINTRÉ *stands looking at her an instant, then, as if with an idea, an alarm, goes up nervously to centre, where, as if listening, she remains another instant.* MRS. BREAD, *who has passed to right, goes on.*] Is the Count *worse?*

CLAIRE [*coming quickly and abruptly down to her*] Catty—what does Mr. Newman *want* of you?

MRS. BREAD [*impenetrable*] Have you *seen* Mr. Newman?

CLAIRE. For a moment. He's coming back!

MRS. BREAD. Then can't you take pity on him?

CLAIRE [*alarmed, listening*] Hush!

MRS. BREAD [*persisting, pleading*] *Everything's* not over?

CLAIRE. Everything! [*Then, with abrupt decision.*] Catty—you must leave the house with me.

MRS. BREAD [*reluctant, vague*] *Now?*

CLAIRE. When I've seen my brother.

MRS. BREAD. And before I've seen Mr. Newman?

CLAIRE [*with the climax of her uneasiness and her appeal, repeating her question of a moment before*] Catty—what does he *want* of you?

MRS. BREAD [*seeing* NEWMAN, *centre*] *Ask* him!

Re-enter NEWMAN, *centre.*

NEWMAN [*after stopping an instant, moved, at the sight of* MRS. BREAD, *says to her formally*] You shall *see* him [*Then to* CLAIRE.] Please go in *first.*

CLAIRE [*who has given him a long, fixed, searching look, exactly like the one he has given her before his last exit, and who has then transferred her eyes to* MRS. BREAD *with the same effect until* MRS. BREAD *uneasily turns away and* NEWMAN *passes up to hold back the drapery of the door at centre*] With the understanding, please, that her visit terminates with *mine.*

NEWMAN [*surprised*] That you take her *away?*

CLAIRE [*down at the left, after looking again from* NEWMAN *at centre to* MRS. BREAD *at right.*] In a very few minutes. [*Exit* CLAIRE *rapidly, centre.*]

NEWMAN [*sombre, still holding the curtain and looking after her*] She's lost—she's *lost!* [*Then dropping the curtain, almost dashing it from him with a gesture of sudden anguish; coming down to* MRS. BREAD *and speaking in a different tone.*] Are you going *away* with her?

MRS. BREAD. She told me she *wishes* it!

NEWMAN [*struck, thinking*] *Why* does she wish it?

MRS. BREAD. My arrival upsets her.

NEWMAN [*catching at every ray of hope*] Upsets her?

MRS. BREAD. Just as my departure upsets her mother.

NEWMAN [*struck, cheered*] The Marquise tried to prevent it!

MRS. BREAD [*smiling*] Almost by force!

NEWMAN [*smiling*] That's just what I want to *see!*

MRS. BREAD [*more gravely*] It has cost me my *home.*

NEWMAN. I'll give you another. You've made a great sacrifice for me.

MRS. BREAD. Wasn't that what you *asked* for?

NEWMAN. It was *indeed,* Mrs. Bread! But no one knows better than I that we don't always *get* what we ask for!

MRS. BREAD. Sometimes we get more! [*After an instant*] The *Marquis* has also come.

NEWMAN [*struck*] He's *here?*

MRS. BREAD He's in *Paris.* He must have arrived last night.

NEWMAN [*greatly interested*] Will he come to this *house?*

MRS. BREAD [*after an instant*] He never was particularly *shy!*

NEWMAN [*encouraged, considering*] Well, I think that's *good*.

MRS. BREAD. What do you think it's good *for?*

NEWMAN. I'll tell you in a moment, but there's something I want you to tell me first. [*She gives a sign of willingness, and he goes on.*] From what you know of the state of my account should you suppose I had about *one cent* in the bank?

MRS. BREAD [*vague*] In the bank?

NEWMAN. The *Countess*, Mrs. Bread, is the bank—a splendid but deadly institution. Should you say she had been touched for one *instant* by the miserable spectacle I present?

MRS. BREAD. I was struck just now by the way she *looked* at you.

NEWMAN. The way she looked at me [*thinking, piecing it together*] seemed to me to show that she's *afraid* of something; and if she's afraid of anything—she ain't indifferent.

MRS. BREAD. I owe you the truth, Mr. Newman. Whatever she may be afraid of she's not afraid of relenting!

NEWMAN. How can you answer for *that?*

MRS. BREAD. I *begged* her, before you came *in*, to relent.

NEWMAN. And what did she say?

MRS. BREAD. She says it's too *late*.

NEWMAN [*struck, smitten, with his last hope dashed, and giving a gesture of despair which definitely indicates this*] Well then—if it's too late for *her*, it's not too late for *me!* I stand before you, Mrs. Bread, as a man with a damnable grievance, and I call upon you to help me to prove that I can give back blow for blow.

MRS. BREAD [*after an instant, impressed, very gravely*] *Now* I understand, sir, why you've *sent* for me.

NEWMAN. I can't bow my head, and I can't break my spirit! It may be very rude, it may be a trifle barbarous of him, but the injured man, the *natural* man, in me, cries *out*. He cries to you, Mrs. Bread, and I'm glad you've guessed the *reason!*

MRS. BREAD. You'll make a tremendous *demand* of me.

NEWMAN [*anxious*] You don't mean to say you'll *reject* it?

MRS. BREAD. I can't help thinking a little of the consequences.

NEWMAN. They're just what I want to *see!*

MRS. BREAD. But if I satisfy you—too *late* [*hesitating*]—where's the use—

NEWMAN [*interrupting*] It's never too late to feel better, and there's *always* some use in being satisfied!

MRS. BREAD [*after considering an instant and composing herself*] Permit me then to ask what it is you already *know*.

NEWMAN. I already know that in that abominable hour, ten years ago, when two French gentlemen lost their lives— [*Pausing.*]

MRS. BREAD. Yes, Mr. Newman.

NEWMAN. The late Marquis, instructed by his daughter, *did* find on the spot a person—suspected, individually or *un*suspected—who was keeping an appointment with his son-in-law.

MRS. BREAD. And that person—?

NEWMAN. That person, Mrs. Bread—that person, I have been able to ascertain, was M. de Bellegarde's own wife, the mother of his children, the mother of her *lover's* wife! [MRS. BREAD *sinks into a chair and sits an instant with her face covered with her hands, while* NEWMAN, *pausing with the effect of his words, stands looking at her.*] So that in the miracle of her successful disappearance and the consequent security of her abominable secret, her audacious reproach to her daughter of having, without justice and without mercy, sent a father and a husband to their death—

MRS. BREAD [*interrupting, rising, completing, with a different manner*] Has made the darkness of that daughter's life, has made her seeming ignorance a ground on which the Marquis has always triumphantly appealed.

NEWMAN. Therefore if such an ignorance is turned to knowledge and such a ground is knocked away—

MRS. BREAD [*interrupting again, with decision*] The Countess will only plunge deeper into her convent!

NEWMAN [*struck with the painful and plausible force of this, but resolutely throwing it off*] Then I shan't be worse off than I *am!*

MRS. BREAD. But if you know the truth what more do you *want?*

NEWMAN. I want the evidence.

MRS. BREAD [*thinking, with a sad and ominous but affirmative nod*] Ah, the evidence—!

NEWMAN. The evidence *exists?*

MRS. BREAD. It exists.

NEWMAN. And in your *hands!*

MRS. BREAD. In my hands.

NEWMAN. Then *give* it to me.

MRS. BREAD. I'll give it to you. But you must give me my *time.*

NEWMAN. Certainly—that's why I want you to *stay* with me.

MRS. BREAD. If I stay with you I can't go with the Countess.

NEWMAN [*with decision*] Of *course* you can't go with the Countess!

MRS. BREAD [*after another instant*] I'll *stay* with you!—But [*looking round her*] *where* shall I stay?

NEWMAN [*seeing* NOÉMIE *at the foot of the stairs, and with a gesture that indicates and introduces her to* MRS. BREAD] This young lady'll *show you.*

Re-enter, at the moment MRS. BREAD *speaks and so as to encounter* NEWMAN'S *presentation,* NOÉMIE *from the staircase. She inclines herself graciously to* MRS. BREAD, *but before she can speak the* DOCTOR *breaks joyously in from the centre. Re-enter the* DOCTOR, *centre.*

DOCTOR [*coming down, in high jubilation*] Great news—great news! He's *better!*

THE THREE OTHERS [*eagerly at once*] *Better!*

[One page of the manuscript is missing at this point.]

. . . *instant; then, uncontrollably, she breaks out*] Mr. Newman, what do you *want* of her?

NEWMAN [*after an instant*] I want her to talk about *you!*

CLAIRE [*passionately*] *Don't* talk about *me!* I can't *leave* her to you.

NEWMAN [*bitterly*] It's little enough indeed you *leave* to me!

CLAIRE [*after an instant during which she has stood with her eyes on the ground and then raised them, speaking gently, pleadingly*] Don't I leave you *my brother?*

NEWMAN [*with a slow headshake*] He's *my* brother, *now*.

CLAIRE. Then act as if you were *his!* He'll take *care* of you—as you have taken care of *him*.

NEWMAN [*struck, thinking*] He'll take *care* of me!

CLAIRE [*pressingly*] Then *call* her to me!

NEWMAN [*after an instant*] What you ask of me is a terrible *sacrifice*.

CLAIRE. I ask it because you're loyal—because you're generous.

NEWMAN. I want to be generous—but [*after an instant, struggling*] —don't put my generosity on the *rack!*

CLAIRE. Don't put my terrors and my sorrows, and don't refuse the only service I ever *asked* you!

NEWMAN [*passing up and round, struggling, thinking, stops short, arrested, close to* VALENTIN's *door; then suddenly, after listening a moment, breaks out to* MME. DE CINTRÉ, *with irresistible cheer and from where he stands*] I hear his old *laugh!*

CLAIRE. God be praised!

NEWMAN [*coming down*] God be praised!

CLAIRE [*at right, suppliant*] *Call* her to me!

NEWMAN [*at left, after a moment of intense inward struggle, culminating in a victory, while he again, for an instant, stands looking at her*] Hanged then if I *care!* [*With a snap of his fingers and a tone of high decision, giving up, as it were all his own cause*] I'll *call* her to you! [*Exit* NEWMAN, *rapidly, with all the energy of his renunciation, centre.*]

CLAIRE [*alone an instant at right, with the strong emotion of her relief*] He *is* loyal—he *is* generous!

Re-enter NIOCHE, *left.*

NIOCHE [*announcing*] Milord Deepmere!

Re-enter DEEPMERE, *left. Exit* NIOCHE, *left.*

DEEPMERE [*eagerly, anxiously, to* CLAIRE] Is your brother *better?*

CLAIRE. He's *better!* [*Then checking a happy demonstration on* DEEPMERE's *part, as if she too just hears the laugh that has been heard by* NEWMAN] Shshsh—you can *hear* him!

Re-enter NIOCHE, *left.*

NIOCHE [*announcing*] Monsieur le Marquis de Bellegarde!

Enter, left, the MARQUIS DE BELLEGARDE. NIOCHE *remains.*

DEEPMERE [*grave, formal, to the* MARQUIS] You're brother's *better*.

MARQUIS [*more formal still and very superior*] It was in the hope of hearing so that I took this unconventional step! [*Then to* MME. DE CINTRÉ, *whom he has made some demonstration of surprise at finding, and with whom he has exchanged a fixed, firm look*]

We were under the impression, Madam, that you had retired to a convent.

CLAIRE [*with a touch of intensely refined and exquisite comedy*] Your impression, my dear brother, was an impression I've *hitherto* shared!

DEEPMERE [*struck by this, eager, appealing to her*] Ah, you've come *back—?*

CLAIRE [*troubled, struggling with herself and turning away from him*] Don't *ask* me!

Re-enter, rapidly, MRS. BREAD, *centre.*

MRS. BREAD [*coming down, excited, joyous*] The Count's on his *feet*—the Count's coming *in!*

NIOCHE [*catching up the good news, jubilant also*] Perhaps we shall see him at luncheon—which I've just been requested to *announce!*

MARQUIS. Luncheon? I've scarcely come to a *meal!*

MRS. BREAD [*to* MME. DE CINTRÉ] I'm at your ladyship's service—I'm ready to go.

CLAIRE [*after an instant, abruptly*] Then *I'm* not!

MRS. BREAD [*astonished*] You're *not?*

CLAIRE [*still with her agitation, abruptly again*] Stay *with* me! [*Then seeing* VALENTIN, *between* NEWMAN *and* NOÉMIE, *at the door*] Here he *is!*

Enter, centre, VALENTIN, *supported on either side by* NEWMAN *and* NOÉMIE. *In a short silk dressing-jacket and light trousers and slippers, with a bright silk handkerchief round his neck, he is pale and weak but smiling and happy; he has an arm in the arm of each of his companions. They stop with him half way down, and he pauses an instant, looking at the others; then he sinks, gently and with relief into the chair which* NIOCHE *has gone quickly round to place in a position to receive him.*

VALENTIN [*to* CLAIRE] My sister—you've worked a *miracle.*

NEWMAN [*who has looked, surprised, at the* MARQUIS] A miracle!

NOÉMIE. A miracle!

VALENTIN [*to* DEEPMERE] My poor friend, give me your hand. [*He holds out his hand to* DEEPMERE, *who rushes forward and grasps it.* DEEPMERE *then comes down again, following* NOÉMIE, *who when* VALENTIN *sinks into the chair, behind which* NIOCHE *remains standing, has passed to the extreme right.*]

NEWMAN [*still at* VALENTIN'*s left, after a continued fixed look at the* MARQUIS] Marquis, I guess you had better give him *yours.*

The MARQUIS *comes forward, more majestically, for this purpose, and he and* MRS. BREAD *address themselves together to* VALENTIN *while* NIOCHE *continues behind his chair and* NEWMAN *moves further to left.* CLAIRE, *on the right, after her brother's words to her, has dropped into the chair at the table and sits there, with her eyes on the ground, in intense concentration.*

NOÉMIE [*triumphant, down in front, to* DEEPMERE] *Don't* you see him there before you?

DEEPMERE [*grateful, ardent*] Exquisite woman—how did you *do* it?

NOÉMIE [*radiant with the success of her machination, and indicating with a nod* MME. DE CINTRÉ, *behind them and at their left*] I made *her* do it!

DEEPMERE [*pressing*] Couldn't you make her do something *else?*

NOÉMIE [*after a glance back at her*] She *will* do it!

DEEPMERE [*looking too, embracing the situation and thoroughly satisfied with it*] Well—what shall I *give* you?

NIOCHE [*behind* VALENTIN'S *chair, before* NOÉMIE *can answer, to* NEWMAN] I ought to mention, sir, that I've been requested to announce your *luncheon.*

NEWMAN [*speaking gaily to* VALENTIN *and quitting the position from which he has been watching* MME. DE CINTRÉ, *to change places with* NIOCHE, *who passes to the left*] My dear fellow, what do you say to *luncheon?*

VALENTIN [*leaning back in his chair*] I am afraid I must have it *here* and that I must ask you to *join* me.

NEWMAN [*behind* VALENTIN'S *chair, while the* MARQUIS, *quitting* VALENTIN, *comes down on left and* MRS. BREAD *comes down on right, below* MME. DE CINTRÉ *and above* NOÉMIE *and* DEEPMERE] With pleasure, Valentin. Marquis, won't *you* join him?—Lord Deepmere, won't *you?*—Miss Noémie, won't *you?*

NOÉMIE [*to* NEWMAN, *while the* MARQUIS, *down at the left, considering, hesitating, solemnly smooths his hat and* NEWMAN *and* VALENTIN *wait and watch for his answer*] Thank you very much —I must go!

DEEPMERE [*eagerly, to* NOÉMIE, *while* VALENTIN *and* NEWMAN *continue to watch the* MARQUIS, *and* MRS. BREAD, *on the right, rests her eyes expectantly on* MME. DE CINTRÉ *who, at her table, sits motionless, detached, immersed in repressed agitation*] Before you go—what shall I *give* you?

NOÉMIE. Give me [*hesitating*]—give me—[*pausing, smiling.*]

DEEPMERE [*in the liveliest suspense*] *What,* Mademoiselle?

NOÉMIE [*aloud, so that the others hear her and* NEWMAN'S *invitation to* DEEPMERE *is practically answered*] Give me your arm! [*She takes it while* DEEPMERE, *breathing again, offers it with extravagant alacrity, and they stand together at right.*]

MRS. BREAD [*to* CLAIRE] I *am* at your ladyship's service to leave the *house.*

NEWMAN [*looking at* CLAIRE, *who, still seated in her agitation, has made no answer*] Perhaps *you,* Madame de Cintré, will give us the honour of your company?

MARQUIS [*down at left, majestically, during the silence that follows on* CLAIRE'S *part*] I regret, Mr. Newman, that I am unable to accept your invitation. [*After an instant*] I must carry to my mother, without delay, this remarkable news of her son.

CLAIRE [*rising rapidly, checking him as he is in the act of going, while, as she moves,* NEWMAN, *quitting* VALENTIN, *comes nearer to her, and* MRS. BREAD, *passing to centre, occupies* NEWMAN'S *place behind* VALENTIN'S *chair*] Urbain! [*The* MARQUIS *stops, surprised, as with a challenge, and* CLAIRE *goes on speaking out loud and clear*] You can carry our mother as well some remarkable news that I've determined—and [*looking about to the others*] I'm glad you should all *hear* it!—to become Mr. Newman's *wife!*

NEWMAN [*springing to her, and as he folds her in his arms*] That's *just* what I wanted to *see!*

Selected Bibliography

I. HENRY JAMES: WRITINGS

BIBLIOGRAPHIES

Beebe, Maurice, and Stafford, William T. "Criticism of Henry James: A Selected Checklist." *Modern Fiction Studies,* 12 (1966), 117–77.

Edel, Leon, and Laurence, Dan H. *A Bibliography of Henry James.* 2nd ed., rev. London: Rupert Hart-Davis, 1961.

Foley, Richard Nicholas. *Criticism in American Periodicals of the Works of Henry James.* Washington, D.C.: Catholic University of America Press, 1944.

Gale, Robert L. "Henry James," in *Eight American Authors: A Review of Research and Criticism,* ed. James Woodress. Rev. ed. New York: W. W. Norton & Co., 1971.

Holman, C. Hugh, compiler. *The American Novel Through Henry James.* New York: Appleton-Century-Crofts, 1966. "Goldentree Bibliography" Series.

TEXTS

The American. Manuscript Revision, 1908. Facsimile. London: The Scolar Press and Oxford University Press, 1975.

The Novels and Tales of Henry James. 26 vols. New York: Scribner's, 1907–17. "The New York Edition."

The Novels and Tales of Henry James. 35 vols. London: Macmillan, 1921–23.

The Art of the Novel, ed. R. P. Blackmur. New York: Scribner's, 1934. Includes prefaces to "The New York Edition."

The Complete Tales of Henry James, ed. Leon Edel. 12 vols. Philadelphia: Lippincott, 1962–65.

The Notebooks of Henry James, ed. F. O. Matthiessen and Kenneth Murdock. New York: Oxford University Press, 1947.

Henry James: Autobiography, ed. F. W. Dupee. New York: Criterion Books, 1955. A one-volume reprint of *A Small Boy and Others, Notes of a Son and Brother,* and *The Middle Years.*

Henry James: Letters, ed. Leon Edel. Cambridge, Mass.: Harvard University Press. Vol I, 1974; Vol. II, 1975.

The Complete Plays of Henry James, ed. Leon Edel. Philadelphia: Lippincott, 1949.

The Letters of Henry James, ed. Percy Lubbock. 2 vols. New York: Scribner's, 1920.

Selected Letters of Henry James, ed. Leon Edel. London: Rupert Hart-Davis, 1956.

II. HENRY JAMES: GENERAL CRITICISM

Anderson, Quentin. *The American Henry James.* New Brunswick: Rutgers University Press, 1957.

Andreas, Osborn. *Henry James and the Expanding Horizon: A Study of the Meaning and Basic Themes of James's Fiction.* Seattle: University of Washington Press, 1948.

Auchincloss, Louis. *Reading Henry James.* Minneapolis: University of Minnesota Press, 1975.

———. *Reflections of a Jacobite.* Boston: Houghton Mifflin, 1961.

Beach, Joseph Warren. *The Method of Henry James.* Rev. ed. Philadelphia: Alfred Saifer, 1954.

Bell, Millicent. *Edith Wharton and Henry James. The Story of Their Friendship.* New York: Braziller, 1965.

Bowden, Edwin T. *The Themes of Henry James: A System of Observation Through the Visual Arts.* New Haven: Yale University Press, 1956.

Brooks, Van Wyck. *The Pilgrimage of Henry James.* New York: E. P. Dutton, 1925.

Buitenhuis, Peter. *The Grasping Imagination: The American Writings of Henry James*. Toronto: University of Toronto Press, 1970.

Canby, Henry Seidel. *Turn East, Turn West*. Boston: Houghton Mifflin, 1951.

Cargill, Oscar. *The Novels of Henry James*. New York: Macmillan, 1961.

Cary, Elisabeth L. *The Novels of Henry James*. New York: G. P. Putnam's, 1905.

Crews, Frederick C. *The Tragedy of Manners: Moral Drama in the Later Novels of Henry James*. New Haven: Yale University Press, 1957.

Delbaere-Garant, Jeanne. *Henry James: The Vision of France*. Paris: Société d'Editions, 1970.

Dupee, F. W. *Henry James*. New York: William Sloane Associates, 1951. Rev. ed. 1956.

———, ed. *The Question of Henry James*. New York: Holt, 1945.

Edel, Leon. "The Americano-European Legend," *University of Toronto Quarterly*, 36 (1967), 321–334.

Edel, Leon. *Henry James*. 5 vols. Philadelphia: Lippincott, 1953–1972.

———. *Henry James*. University of Minnesota Pamphlets on American Writers. Minneapolis: University of Minnesota Press, 1960.

———, ed. *Henry James: A Collection of Critical Essays*. Englewood Cliffs, N.J.: Prentice-Hall, 1963.

Edgar, Pelham. *Henry James: Man and Author*. Boston: Houghton Mifflin, 1927.

Fabris, Alberta. *Henry James e la Francia*. Roma: Edizioni di Storia e Letteratura, 1969.

Falk, Robert. *The Victorian Mode in American Fiction, 1865–1885*. East Lansing: Michigan State University Press, 1965.

Gale, Robert L. *The Caught Image: Figurative Language in the Fiction of Henry James*. Chapel Hill: University of North Carolina Press, 1964.

Garnier, M. R. *Henry James et la France*. Paris: Librairie Ancienne Honoré Champion, 1927.

Geismar, Maxwell. *Henry James and the Jacobites*. Boston: Houghton Mifflin, 1963.

Harlow, Virginia. *Thomas Sergeant Perry: A Biography and Letters to Perry from William, Henry, and Garth Wilkinson James*. Durham, N.C.: Duke University Press, 1950.

Herrick, Robert. "A Visit to Henry James," *The Yale Review*, 12 (1923), 724–41.

Hoffmann, Charles G. *The Short Novels of Henry James*. New York: Bookman Associates, 1957.

Holder, Alan. *Three Voyagers in Search of Europe: A Study of Henry James, Ezra Pound, and T. S. Eliot*. Philadelphia: University of Pennsylvania Press, 1966.

Holder-Barrell, Alexander. *The Development of Imagery and Its Functional Significance in Henry James's Novels*. Bern: Francke Verlag, 1959.

Jefferson, D. W. *Henry James*. Edinburgh: Oliver and Boyd, 1964.

———. *Henry James and the Modern Reader*. Edinburgh: Oliver and Boyd, 1964.

Jones-Evans, Mervyn. "Henry James's Year in France," *Horizon*, 14 (1946), 52–60.

Kelley, Cornelia Pulsifer. *The Early Development of Henry James*. Urbana: University of Illinois Press, 1930.

Krook, Dorothea. *The Ordeal of Consciousness in Henry James*. New York: Cambridge University Press, 1962.

Krutch, Joseph Wood. *The Modern Temper*. New York: Harcourt, 1929.

Leavis, F. R. *The Great Tradition*. New York: George Stewart, 1949.

Lebowitz, Naomi. *The Imagination of Loving: Henry James's Legacy to the Novel*. Detroit: Wayne State University Press, 1965.

Lebowitz, Naomi, ed. *Discussions of Henry James*. Boston: D. C. Heath, 1962.

Levy, Leo B. *Versions of Melodrama: A Study of the Fiction and Drama of Henry James, 1865–1897*. Berkeley: University of California Press, 1957.

Liljegren, Sten Bodvar. *American and European in the Works of Henry James*. Lund: Lund Universitets Arsskrift, 1920.

Mackenzie, Manfred. "Henry James: Serialist Early and Late," *Philological Quarterly* 41 (1962), 492–99.

McElderry, Bruce R. Jr. *Henry James*. New York: Twayne Publishers, 1965.

Matthiessen, F. O. *Henry James: The Major Phase*. New York: Oxford University Press, 1944.

—. *The James Family*. New York: Knopf, 1947.

Nowell-Smith, Simon, ed. *The Legend of the Master: Henry James.* New York: Scribner's, 1948.

Poirier, Richard. *The Comic Sense of Henry James.* New York: Oxford University Press, 1960.

Popkin, Henry. "The Two Theatres of Henry James," *New England Quarterly* 24 (1951), 69–83.

Powers, Lyall H. *Henry James: An Introduction and Interpretation.* New York: Holt, Rinehart, and Winston, 1970.

———. *Henry James and the Naturalist Movement.* East Lansing: Michigan State University Press, 1971.

Samuels, Charles T. *The Ambiguity of Henry James.* Urbana: University of Illinois Press, 1971.

Sanford, Charles L. *The Quest for Paradise: Europe and the American Moral Imagination.* Urbana: University of Illinois Press, 1961.

Sears, Sallie. *The Negative Imagination: Form and Perspective in the Novels of Henry James.* Ithaca, N.Y.: Cornell University Press, 1968.

Sharp, Sister M. Corona. *The "Confidante" in Henry James.* Notre Dame, Ind.: University of Notre Dame Press, 1963.

Spender, Stephen. *The Destructive Element.* London: Jonathan Cape, 1935.

Stafford, William T. "Henry James the American: Some Views of his Contemporaries," *Twentieth Century Literature* 1 (1955), 69–76.

Stevenson, Elizabeth. *The Crooked Corridor: A Study of Henry James.* New York: Macmillan, 1949.

Stewart, J.I.M. *Eight Modern Writers.* New York: Oxford University Press, 1963.

Stone, Edward. *The Battle and the Books: Some Aspects of Henry James.* Athens, Ohio: Ohio University Press, 1964.

Swan, Michael. *Henry James.* London: Arthur Barker, 1952.

Tanner, Tony, ed. *Henry James: Modern Judgments.* London: Macmillan, 1969.

Vaid, Krishna Baldev. *Technique in the Tales of Henry James.* Cambridge: Harvard University Press, 1964.

Ward, J. A. *The Imagination of Disaster: Evil in the Fiction of Henry James.* Lincoln: University of Nebraska Press, 1961.

Ward, J. A. *The Search for Form: Studies in the Structure of James's Fiction.* Chapel Hill: University of North Carolina Press, 1967.

Wegelin, Christof. *The Image of Europe in Henry James.* Dallas: Southern Methodist University Press, 1958.

Weinstein, Philip M. *Henry James and the Requirements of the Imagination.* Cambridge: Harvard University Press, 1971.

Weisenfarth, Joseph. *Henry James and the Dramatic Analogy.* New York: Fordham University Press, 1963.

West, Ray B., and Stallman, R. W. *The Art of Modern Fiction.* New York: Rinehart, 1959.

Winner, Viola H. *Henry James and the Visual Arts.* Charlottesville: University of Virginia Press, 1970.

Winters, Yvor. *In Defense of Reason.* Denver: Alan Swallow, 1947.

Wright, Walter F. *The Madness of Art: A Study of Henry James.* Lincoln: University of Nebraska Press, 1962.

III. HENRY JAMES: CRITICISM OF *THE AMERICAN*

Antush, John V. "The 'Much Finer Complexity' of History in *The American*," *Journal of American Studies* 6 (1972), 85–95.

Backus, Joseph M. " 'Poor Valentin' or 'Monsieur le Comte': Variation in Character Designation as Matter for Critical Consideration in Henry James's *The American*," *Names* 20 (1972), 47–55.

Bhatnagar, O. P. "*The American:* A Revaluation," *Indian Journal of American Studies* 1 (1971), 51–61.

Bernard, F. V. "James's Florabella and the 'Land of the Pink Sky,' " *Notes and Queries* 13 (1966), 70.

Blasing, Mutlu. "Double Focus in *The American*," *Nineteenth-Century Fiction* 28 (1973), 74–84.

Brooks, Cleanth. "The American Innocence" *Shenandoah* 16 (1964), 21–37.

Butterfield, R. W. "*The American*" in *The Air of Reality: New Essays on Henry James*, ed. John Goode. London: Methuen and Co., Ltd., 1972.

Cargill, Oscar. "The First International Novel," *PMLA* 73 (1958), 418–25.

Cestre, Charles. "La France dans l'oeuvre de Henry James," *Revue Anglo-Américaine* 10 (October 1932), 1–13, 112–22.

Clair, John A. "*The American:* A Reinterpretation," *PMLA* 74 (1959), 613–618.

Cook, G. A. "Names in *The American,*" *CEA Critic* 28 (1966), 5.

Creeth, Edmund. "Moonshine and Bloodshed: A Note on *The American,*" *Notes and Queries* (new series) 9 (1962), 105–6.

Gargano, James W. "Foreshadowing in *The American,*" *Modern Language Notes* 74 (1959), 600–1.

Goldsmith, Arnold L. "Henry James's Reconciliation of Free Will and Fatalism," *Nineteenth-Century Fiction* 13 (1958), 109–26.

Hays, H. R. "The Limitations of Christopher Newman," in *Henry James: The American,* ed. Gerald Willen. New York: T. Y. Crowell Co., 1972.

Hoftun, Sigmund. "The Point of View in Henry James's *The American,*" *Edda* 61 (1961), 169–76.

Hoffman, Frederick J. "Freedom and Conscious Form: Henry James and the American Self," *Virginia Quarterly Review* 37 (1961), 269–85.

Horowitz, Floyd R. "The Christian Time Sequence in Henry James's *The American,*" *CLA Journal* 9 (1966), 234–45.

Knox, George. "Romance and Fable in James's *The American,*" *Anglia* 83 (1965), 308–23.

Lerner, Daniel. "The Influence of Turgenev on Henry James," *Slavonic Review* 20 (1941), 28–54.

Lombardo, Agostino. "Henry James, *The American* e il mito di Otello," in *Friendship's Garland: Essays Presented to Mario Praz on His Seventieth Birthday.* 2 vols. Roma: Edizioni di Storia e Letteratura, 1966.

Moore, John R. "An Imperfection in the Art of Henry James," *Nineteenth-Century Fiction* 13 (1959), 351–56.

Noda, Hisashi. "A Note on Mrs. Tristram and the Education of Christopher Newman," *Kyushu American Literature* (Fukuoka, Japan) 10 (1967), 50–60.

Parker, Hershel. "An Error in the Text of Henry James's *The American,*" *American Literature* 38 (1965), 316–18.

Pritchett, V. S. "Babcockism," *New Statesmen and Nation* 59 (1960), 863–64.

Reynolds, Larry. "Henry James's New Christopher Newman," *Studies in the Novel* 5 (Winter 1973), 457–68.

Rosenbaum, S. P. "Two Henry James Letters on *The American* and *Watch and Ward,*" *American Literature* 30 (1959), 533–37.

Rourke, Constance. *American Humor: A Study of the National Character.* New York: Harcourt Brace, 1931.

Scholes, James Bert. *Henry James's The American: A Study Guide.* Bound Brook, N.J.: Shelley Publishing Co., 1963.

Schulz, Max F. "The Bellegardes' Feud with Christopher Newman: A Study of Henry James's Revision of *The American,*" *American Literature* 27 (1955), 42–55.

Secor, Robert. "Christopher Newman: How Innocent is James's American?" *Studies in American Fiction* 1 (1973), 141–53.

Stafford, William T. "The Ending of Henry James's *The American:* A Defense of the Early Version," *Nineteenth-Century Fiction* 18 (1963), 86–89.

———, ed. *Studies in "The American."* Columbus, Ohio: Charles E. Merrill, 1971.

Szala, Alina. "Henry James's *The American* Simplified," *Kwartalnik Neofilologiczny* (Warsaw) 16 (1969), 61–64.

Tick, Stanley. "Henry James's *The American:* Voyons," *Studies in the Novel* (North Texas State University) 2 (1970), 276–91.

Traschen, Isadore. "An American in Paris," *American Literature* 26 (1954), 67–77.

———. "Henry James and the Art of Revision." *Philological Quarterly* 35 (1956), 39–57.

———. "James's Revisions of the Love Affair in *The American,*" *New England Quarterly* 29 (1956), 43–62.

Van Der Beets, Richard. "A Note on Henry James's Western Barbarian," *Western Humanities Review* 17 (1963), 175–78.

Vanderbilt, Kermit. "James, Fitzgerald, and the American Self-Image," *Massachusetts Review* 6 (1965), 289–304.

Watkins, Floyd C. "Christopher Newman's Final Instinct," *Nineteenth-Century Fiction* 12 (1957), 85–88.

Willen, Gerald, ed. *Henry James: The American.* New York: T. Y. Crowell, 1972.

Zeitlow, Edward R. "A Flaw in *The American,*" *CLA Journal* 9 (1966), 246–54.

NORTON CRITICAL EDITIONS

AUSTEN *Emma* edited by Stephen M. Parrish
AUSTEN *Pride and Prejudice* edited by Donald J. Gray
Beowulf (the Donaldson translation) edited by Joseph M. Tuso
Blake's Poetry and Designs selected and edited by Mary Lynn Johnson and John E. Grant
BOCCACCIO *The Decameron* selected, translated, and edited by Mark Musa and Peter E. Bondanella
BRONTË, CHARLOTTE *Jane Eyre* edited by Richard J. Dunn
BRONTË, EMILY *Wuthering Heights* edited by William M. Sale, Jr. *Second Edition*
Robert Browning's Poetry selected and edited by James F. Loucks
Byron's Poetry selected and edited by Frank D. McConnell
CARROLL *Alice in Wonderland* selected and edited by Donald J. Gray
CERVANTES *Don Quixote* (the Ormsby translation, substantially revised) edited by Joseph R. Jones and Kenneth Douglas
Anton Chekhov's Plays translated and edited by Eugene K. Bristow
Anton Chekhov's Short Stories selected and edited by Ralph E. Matlaw
CHOPIN *The Awakening* edited by Margaret Culley
CLEMENS *Adventures of Huckleberry Finn* edited by Sculley Bradley, Richmond Croom Beatty, E. Hudson Long, and Thomas Cooley *Second Edition*
CLEMENS *A Connecticut Yankee in King Arthur's Court* edited by Allison R. Ensor
CLEMENS *Pudd'nhead Wilson* and *Those Extraordinary Twins* edited by Sidney E. Berger
CONRAD *Heart of Darkness* edited by Robert Kimbrough *Second Edition*
CONRAD *Lord Jim* edited by Thomas Moser
CONRAD *The Nigger of the "Narcissus"* edited by Robert Kimbrough
CRANE *Maggie: A Girl of the Streets* edited by Thomas A. Gullason
CRANE *The Red Badge of Courage* edited by Sculley Bradley, Richmond Croom Beatty, E. Hudson Long, and Donald Pizer *Second Edition*
Darwin edited by Philip Appleman *Second Edition*
DEFOE *Moll Flanders* edited by Edward Kelly
DEFOE *Robinson Crusoe* edited by Michael Shinagel
DICKENS *Bleak House* edited by George Ford and Sylvère Monod
DICKENS *Hard Times* edited by George Ford and Sylvère Monod
John Donne's Poetry selected and edited by A. L. Clements
DOSTOEVSKY *Crime and Punishment* (the Coulson translation) edited by George Gibian *Second Edition*
DOSTOEVSKY *The Brothers Karamazov* (the Garnett translation revised by Ralph E. Matlaw) edited by Ralph E. Matlaw
DREISER *Sister Carrie* edited by Donald Pizer
ELIOT *Middlemarch* edited by Bert G. Hornback
FIELDING *Tom Jones* edited by Sheridan Baker
FLAUBERT *Madame Bovary* edited with a substantially new translation by Paul de Man
GOETHE *Faust* translated by Walter Arndt and edited by Cyrus Hamlin
HARDY *Jude the Obscure* edited by Norman Page
HARDY *The Mayor of Casterbridge* edited by James K. Robinson
HARDY *The Return of the Native* edited by James Gindin
HARDY *Tess of the d'Urbervilles* edited by Scott Elledge *Second Edition*
HAWTHORNE *The Blithedale Romance* edited by Seymour Gross and Rosalie Murphy
HAWTHORNE *The House of the Seven Gables* edited by Seymour Gross
HAWTHORNE *The Scarlet Letter* edited by Sculley Bradley, Richmond Croom Beatty, E. Hudson Long, and Seymour Gross *Second Edition*
George Herbert and the Seventeenth-Century Religious Poets selected and edited by Mario A. Di Cesare

HOMER *The Odyssey* translated and edited by Albert Cook
HOWELLS *The Rise of Silas Lapham* edited by Don L. Cook
IBSEN *The Wild Duck* translated and edited by Dounia B. Christiani
JAMES *The Ambassadors* edited by S. P. Rosenbaum
JAMES *The American* edited by James A. Tuttleton
JAMES *The Portrait of a Lady* edited by Robert D. Bamberg
JAMES *The Turn of the Screw* edited by Robert Kimbrough
JAMES *The Wings of the Dove* edited by J. Donald Crowley and Richard A. Hocks
Ben Jonson and the Cavalier Poets selected and edited by Hugh Maclean
Ben Jonson's Plays and Masques selected and edited by Robert M. Adams
MACHIAVELLI *The Prince* translated and edited by Robert M. Adams
MALTHUS *An Essay on the Principle of Population* edited by Philip Appleman
MELVILLE *The Confidence-Man* edited by Hershel Parker
MELVILLE *Moby-Dick* edited by Harrison Hayford and Hershel Parker
MEREDITH *The Egoist* edited by Robert M. Adams
MILL *On Liberty* edited by David Spitz
MILTON *Paradise Lost* edited by Scott Elledge
MORE *Utopia* translated and edited by Robert M. Adams
NEWMAN *Apologia Pro Vita Sua* edited by David J. DeLaura
NORRIS *McTeague* edited by Donald Pizer
Adrienne Rich's Poetry selected and edited by Barbara Charlesworth Gelpi and Albert Gelpi
The Writings of St. Paul edited by Wayne A. Meeks
SHAKESPEARE *Hamlet* edited by Cyrus Hoy
SHAKESPEARE *Henry IV, Part I* edited by James J. Sanderson *Second Edition*
Bernard Shaw's Plays selected and edited by Warren Sylvester Smith
Shelley's Poetry and Prose edited by Donald H. Reiman and Sharon B. Powers
SMOLLETT *Humphry Clinker* Edited by James L. Thorson
SOPHOCLES *Oedipus Tyrannus* translated and edited by Luci Berkowitz and Theodore F. Brunner
SPENSER *Edmund Spenser's Poetry* selected and edited by Hugh Maclean *Second Edition*
STENDHAL *Red and Black* translated and edited by Robert M. Adams
STERNE *Tristram Shandy* edited by Howard Anderson
SWIFT *Gulliver's Travels* edited by Robert A. Greenberg *Revised Edition*
The Writings of Jonathan Swift edited by Robert A. Greenberg and William B. Piper
TENNYSON *In Memoriam* edited by Robert Ross
Tennyson's Poetry selected and edited by Robert W. Hill, Jr.
THOREAU *Walden and Civil Disobedience* edited by Owen Thomas
TOLSTOY *Anna Karenina* (the Maude translation) edited by George Gibian
TOLSTOY *War and Peace* (the Maude translation) edited by George Gibian
TURGENEV *Fathers and Sons* edited with a substantially new translation by Ralph E. Matlaw
VOLTAIRE *Candide* translated and edited by Robert M. Adams
WATSON *The Double Helix* edited by Gunther S. Stent
WHITMAN *Leaves of Grass* edited by Sculley Bradley and Harold W. Blodgett
WOLLSTONECRAFT *A Vindication of the Rights of Woman* edited by Carol H. Poston
WORDSWORTH *The Prelude: 1799, 1805, 1850* edited by Jonathan Wordsworth, M. H. Abrams, and Stephen Gill
Middle English Lyrics selected and edited by Maxwell S. Luria and Richard L. Hoffman
Modern Drama edited by Anthony Caputi
Restoration and Eighteenth-Century Comedy edited by Scott McMillin

persiflage (42)
verdancy (63)
capon (93)
intaglio (175)